Vold's Theoretical Criminology

Vold's Theoretical Criminology

EIGHTH EDITION

JEFFREY B. SNIPES
San Francisco State University

THOMAS J. BERNARD
The Pennsylvania State University

ALEXANDER L. GEROULD
De Anza College

New York   Oxford
OXFORD UNIVERSITY PRESS

Oxford University Press is a department of the University of Oxford.
It furthers the University's objective of excellence in research,
scholarship, and education by publishing worldwide. Oxford is a registered
trade mark of Oxford University Press in the UK and certain other countries.

Published in the United States of America by Oxford University Press
198 Madison Avenue, New York, NY 10016, United States of America.

For titles covered by Section 112 of the US Higher Education
Opportunity Act, please visit www.oup.com/us/he for the latest
information about pricing and alternate formats.

Library of Congress Cataloging-in-Publication Data

Names: Bernard, Thomas J., author. | Snipes, Jeffrey B., author. | Gerould,
    Alexander L., author.
Title: Vold's theoretical criminology / Thomas J. Bernard, The Pennsylvania
    State University, Jeffrey B. Snipes, San Francisco State University,
    Alexander L. Gerould, San Francisco State University.
Description: Eighth edition. | New York : Oxford University Press, [2019] |
    Includes bibliographical references and index. | Summary: "The standard
    text in the field, Vold's Theoretical Criminology is universally known
    by scholars in the discipline. Taking a largely historical approach, it
    discusses both classic and contemporary theories, presenting historical
    context and empirical research for each one. The book concludes with a
    chapter on assessing theories and their policy implications"—Provided by publisher.
Identifiers: LCCN 2019033690 (print) | LCCN 2019033691 (ebook) | ISBN
    9780190940515 (hardback) | ISBN 9780190084417 (ebk) | ISBN 9780190940522 (ebk)
Subjects: LCSH: Criminal anthropology. | Criminology. | Deviant behavior. |
    Social conflict.
Classification: LCC HV6035 .V6 2019 (print) | LCC HV6035 (ebook) | DDC
    364.2—dc23
LC record available at https://lccn.loc.gov/2019033690

LC ebook record available at https://lccn.loc.gov/2019033691

Printing number: 9 8 7 6 5
Printed by LSC Communications, Inc., United States of America.

DEDICATION

This book is dedicated to Shawn Snipes,
for all his love and support.

We would like to thank everyone at Oxford University Press
who has worked on this book alongside us, especially
Steve Helba and Kora Fillet.

CONTENTS

PREFACE

It is our great pleasure to carry on the tradition of building upon George Vold's original *Theoretical Criminology*. *Vold's Theoretical Criminology* is one of the longest-running texts in the field, with its first edition published in 1958. This span of sixty years has seen a total of eight editions, with the following authors and coauthors, in sequence: George Vold, Thomas Bernard, Jeffrey Snipes, and Alexander Gerould.

As we determined which materials to update, sections to add, and reorganizations to make, we were informed by the rigorous and highly specific reviews of the previous edition by fifteen anonymous reviewers; we are greatly appreciative of their contributions.

The former Chapter 16, on assessing criminology theories, has been merged with Chapter 1, the introduction to theory and crime. Chapter 2, on theory and policy in context, now has more information about how crime data is collected, and a discussion and analysis of trends in crime over the past five years (covering the period since the seventh edition). Chapter 3 now includes a section on the neoclassical school, has a revamped and updated section on deterrence theory, and an expansion of routine activities that includes L-RAT (lifestyle routine activities theory). To Chapter 4 we added a new section on epigenetics, a promising new area in line with the biosocial movement in criminology. We include a section on Freud and psychoanalysis in Chapter 5, and we expanded the section on research that uses personality tests. Chapter 6 includes a discussion of the modern applicability of Durkheim.

Chapters 7 and 8 are now reversed in order from the previous edition. Chapter 7 is now strain theories, and Chapter 8 is on neighborhoods and crime. Chapter 7 has undergone considerable reorganization, and it contains a significantly expanded section on Agnew's general strain theory and research evaluating it. In Chapter 8, we now discuss micro-places, and we added a section on social disorganization and crime in rural areas. Chapter 9 now has a new section on Tarde's laws of imitation and Bandura's social learning theory. It also contains a new section on assessing Akers's social learning theory, as well as an expansion of Athens's theory of violentization, which includes policy implications he recently put forth. Zimbardo's Lucifer effect is no longer included in this chapter, and labeling theory has been moved here from the chapter on conflict theory. In Chapter 10 we added a significant amount of new research that assesses Gottfredson and Hirschi's general theory of crime, which is based on self-control. Chapter 11 is now solely dedicated to conflict theory, as we moved labeling theory to Chapter 9. This chapter has a new section on minority threat theory.

Chapter 12 now covers Marxist, postmodern, and green criminology. Approximately a quarter of the chapter is devoted to green criminology, which is a new addition to this volume. Chapter 13 includes a new section on the narrowing of the gender gap in violence, as well as some discussion of the backlash to feminist criminology. Chapter 14 is renamed "Developmental and Life-Course Theories." In this chapter we discuss the influence of the developmental theorist Glen Elder Jr. on later developmental and life-course theories of crime; include some discussion of Laub and Sampson's follow-up book to Sampson and Laub's age-graded theory; and we have a new section on future directions in developmental and life-course theory, which is largely spent discussing desistance from criminal behavior. Chapter 15 has updated several integrated theories with recent research evaluating their hypotheses. A new, brief conclusion examines the proliferation of theory in criminology, and assesses the policy relevance of the multitude of criminological theories.

New to this edition is a supplement, which includes a bank of test questions useful for all instructors, especially for those who use this volume in undergraduate courses.

Vold's Theoretical
Criminology

CHAPTER 1

───

Theory and Crime

Criminology as a field of study has been well documented by a long line of excellent and distinguished textbooks going back many decades.[1] Most of these texts concentrate on presenting facts that are known about the subject of crime. For example, they discuss the extent and distribution of criminal behaviors in society; the characteristics of criminal law and procedure; the characteristics of criminals; and the history, structure, and functioning of the criminal justice system. The theoretical material presented in these texts is usually somewhat limited. Almost all texts review the major theories about the causes of criminal behavior, and some texts present other theoretical material such as sociology of law, philosophy of punishment, or theories of correctional treatment.

As a text in theoretical criminology, this book does not concentrate on presenting the facts known about crime, although at least some of these facts are presented in the various chapters. Instead, it concentrates on the theories that are used to explain the facts. The theories themselves, rather than the facts about criminality, are the focus of this book.[2]

Basically, a theory is part of an explanation.[3] It is a sensible way of understanding something, of relating it to the whole world of information, beliefs, and attitudes that make up the intellectual atmosphere of a people at a particular time or place. In the broad scope of history, there are two basic types of theories of crime. One relies on spiritual, or other-world, explanations, while the other relies on natural, or this-world, explanations. Both types of theories are ancient as well as modern.

SPIRITUAL EXPLANATIONS

Spiritual explanations of crime are part of a general view of life in which many events are believed to result from the influence of otherworldly powers. For example, primitive people regarded natural disasters, such as famines,

1

floods, and plagues, as punishments for wrongs they had done to the spiritual powers.[4] They responded by performing sacred rites and rituals to appease these powers.

A spiritual view of the world was closely tied to the origin and development of the modern criminal justice system.[5] In the Middle Ages in Europe, crime was a largely private affair in which the victim or the victim's family obtained revenge by inflicting a similar or greater harm on the offender or the offender's family. But private vengeance had a tendency to start blood feuds as each side inflicted greater harms on the other side. These feuds could continue for many years until one or the other family was completely wiped out. The feudal lords therefore instituted methods by which God could indicate who was innocent and who was guilty. The first such method was trial by battle. Both parties would swear to the truth of their claims in the dispute. Then they, or their designated representatives, would fight each other. God would give victory to the righteous person, defeating the one who had just sworn a false oath. Thus the family of the loser would have no grounds for exacting vengeance on the winner, and the blood feuds were ended.

The problem with trial by battle was that great warriors (and those who could afford to hire them as designated representatives) could commit as many crimes as they wanted because God would always give them victory. Therefore somewhat later in history, trial by ordeal was instituted. In this method the accused was subjected to difficult and painful tests, from which an innocent person (protected by God) would emerge unharmed while a guilty person would die a painful death. For example, a common method of determining whether a woman was a witch was to tie her up and throw her into water that had just been blessed.[6] Generally, if the accused sank, she was considered innocent, but if she floated, she was guilty. Other forms of ordeal included running the gauntlet and walking on fire. Trial by ordeal was condemned by the pope in 1215 and was replaced by compurgation, in which the accused gathered together a group of twelve reputable people who would swear that he or she was innocent. The idea was that no one would lie under oath for fear of being punished by God. Compurgation ultimately evolved into testimony under oath and trial by jury.

Spiritual explanations of crime appeared in the New World in the Puritan colony on Massachusetts Bay. During the first sixty years of its existence, this colony experienced three serious crime waves that were thought to be caused by the devil. The most serious of these crime waves occurred in 1692, when the community was thought to have been invaded by a large number of witches.[7]

Our modern prison system also originated in association with a spiritual explanation of crime. Around 1790, a group of Quakers in Philadelphia conceived the idea of isolating criminals in cells and giving them only the Bible to read and some manual labor to perform. The Quakers thought that criminals would then reflect on their past wrongdoings and repent.[8] They used the term *penitentiary* to describe their invention, a place for penitents who were sorry for their sins.

Today, many religious individuals and groups explain crime in spiritual terms. For example, Charles Colson was special counsel to President Richard M. Nixon and served seven months in prison for his part in the Watergate affair. As a result of his prison experience, he underwent a religious conversion and founded Prison Fellowship International, which now operates in more than one hundred countries to reform criminal justice and to bring the Christian message to prisoners.[9] Colson attributes crime to sinful human nature and argues that religious conversion is the only "cure" for crime.[10]

NATURAL EXPLANATIONS

Spiritual explanations make use of otherworldly powers to account for what happens; natural explanations make use of objects and events in the material world to explain the same things. Like the spiritual approach, the natural approach to explanation is ancient as well as modern.

The early Greeks developed naturalistic, this-world explanations far back in their history. For example, Hippocrates (460 B.C.) provided a physiological explanation of thinking by arguing that the brain is the organ of the mind. Democritus (420 B.C.) proposed the idea of an indestructible unit of matter, called the atom, as central to his explanation of the world around him. With Socrates, Plato, and Aristotle the ideas of unity and continuity came to the fore, but the essential factors in all the explanations remained physical and material.

By the first century B.C., Roman thought had become thoroughly infused with naturalism. For example, Roman law combined the spiritualism of the Hebrew tradition with the naturalism of the Greek tradition to provide a natural basis for penalties as well as for rights. The Hebrew doctrine of divine sanction for law and order merged with Greek naturalism and appeared in Roman law as a justification based on the "nature of things." Later, the rule of kings by divine right became a natural law that looked to the nature of things for its principal justification.

In the sixteenth and seventeenth centuries, writers such as Hobbes, Spinoza, Descartes, and Leibniz studied human affairs as physicists study matter, impersonally and quantitatively. Modern social science continues this naturalistic emphasis. The disagreements among social scientists are well known, but at least they have in common that they seek their explanations within observable phenomena that are found in the physical and material world.

SCIENTIFIC THEORIES

Scientific theories are one kind of natural explanation. In general, they make statements about the relationships between observable phenomena.[11] For example, some scientific theories in criminology make statements about the relationship between the certainty or severity of criminal punishments and the volume of criminal behaviors in society. Others make statements about the relationship between the biological, psychological, or social characteristics of individuals and the likelihood that these individuals will engage in criminal behaviors. Still others make statements about the relationship between the social characteristics of individuals and the likelihood that these individuals will be defined and processed as criminals by the criminal justice system. All these characteristics can be observed, and so all these theories are scientific.

Because they make statements about the relationships among observable phenomena, a key characteristic of scientific theories is that they can be falsified.[12] The process of attempting to falsify a scientific theory involves systematically observing the relationships described in the theory and then comparing the observations to arguments of the theory itself. This process is called research: that is, the assertions of the theory are tested against the observed world of the facts.[13] If the observations are inconsistent with the assertions of the theory, then the theory is falsified. If the observations are consistent with the assertions of the theory, then the theory becomes more credible, but it is not proved; there are always alternative theories that may also explain the same observed relationships.

A theory can gain a great deal of credibility if all the reasonable alternative theories are shown to be inconsistent with the observed world of facts. At that point, the theory may simply be accepted as true. However, it is always possible that some new facts will be discovered in the future that are inconsistent with the theory, so that a new theory will be required. For example, Newton's laws of physics were accepted as true for two hundred years, but they were replaced by Einstein's theory of relativity at the beginning of the twentieth century because of the discovery of some new facts.[14]

Six criteria may be used to evaluate a scientific theory: comprehensiveness (is broad in scope); precision and testability (defines constructs well, is open to measurement through falsifiable hypotheses); parsimony (is presented in a simple fashion); empirical validity (accounts for evidence that disconfirms it, in addition to confirming evidence); heuristic value (generates intellectual stimulation in other fields); and applied value (offers solutions to problems).[15] When reading the theories presented in this volume, the reader may wish to consider them along these dimensions.

CAUSATION IN SCIENTIFIC THEORIES

Causation is one type of relationship among observable variables, and all scientific theories in criminology make causal arguments of one type or another. Generally speaking, causation in scientific theories means three things: correlation, time sequence, and the absence of spuriousness. However, to be meaningful scientific theories should also have a theoretical rationale—in this discussion, we also consider the need for theories to propose mechanisms by which variables may influence each other.

Correlation means that things tend to vary systematically in relation to each other. For example, height and weight are correlated: people who are taller generally weigh more, and people who are shorter generally weigh less. The relation is not perfect—some short people weigh more, and some tall people weigh less. But the tendency still exists for more height to go with more weight and less height to go with less weight. This is called a "positive" correlation.

A "negative" correlation is when more of one thing tends to be associated with less of the other. For example, the more miles you have on your car, the less money it generally is worth. As with height and weight, the relation is not perfect because some old cars are worth a lot and some new cars are not worth much. But for cars in general, mileage and price are negatively correlated.

Correlation, whether positive or negative, is necessary for causation. If two things do not vary together in some systematic way, such as height and IQ, then the one cannot cause the other. But correlation alone is not sufficient for causation. You also need a good reason to believe that a causal relation exists. This is the theoretical rationale, the second element of scientific causation.

For example, some criminologists argue that harsh erratic discipline by parents increases the likelihood of delinquency in their children.[16] There must be a correlation: parents who use such techniques must be more likely to have children who are delinquent than parents who use moderate consistent discipline. But there also must be a theoretical rationale—a coherent explanation of why these techniques by the parents may cause delinquency in the children.

A theoretical rationale would be that harsh discipline conveys anger, rather than love, and increases the chance that the child will rebel and engage in delinquency to get back at the parents. In addition, erratic discipline means that most of the time there is no punishment for misbehavior anyway. So in this example, a theoretical rationale exists that, if coupled with evidence of a correlation, would support a conclusion that harsh erratic discipline causes delinquency.

But correlation and theoretical rationale are not enough to infer causation. Imagine, for example, two loving parents who have a delinquent child. Moderate consistent discipline just does not work, and eventually when the child gets into trouble, the parents either do nothing (because nothing works anyway) or use harsh discipline (because they are angry and frustrated).[17] In this scenario, the child's delinquency causes the parents' harsh erratic disciplinary techniques.

The problem is the *direction* of causation: Does the discipline cause the delinquency, or does the delinquency cause the discipline? The solution can be found by determining time sequence, the third element of scientific causation. If the discipline comes first and the delinquency comes later, then we would conclude that the discipline causes the delinquency. But if the delinquency comes first and the discipline comes later, we would conclude that the delinquency causes the discipline.

The fourth and final element of meaningful scientific causation is called the absence of spuriousness. Suppose that parents in high-crime neighborhoods are more likely, for social and cultural reasons, to use harsh erratic discipline even when their children are not delinquent. And suppose that for the same reasons, children in high-crime neighborhoods are more likely to engage in delinquency, regardless of the parents' disciplinary techniques. It may look like there is a causal relationship between harsh erratic discipline and delinquency, but in fact both the discipline and the delinquency could be caused, in one way or another, by the high-crime neighborhood.

In this example, the relationship between delinquent behavior and parental disciplinary techniques would be spurious. But suppose the researchers control for the neighborhood—that is, suppose they compare parents in the neighborhoods who use harsh erratic discipline with other parents in the same neighborhoods who use moderate consistent discipline. Then if they find that delinquency is associated with harsh erratic discipline, it cannot be because of the neighborhood. In this case, it is reasonable to conclude that a causal relation exists.

The conclusion that a causal relation exists, however, is always a statement about probability, never an assertion of certainty. To say that harsh erratic discipline causes delinquency is like saying that smoking causes cancer. Most people who smoke do not get cancer. Rather, smokers have a greater probability of getting cancer than do nonsmokers. Similarly, if our causal theory is correct, then children who are raised with harsh erratic discipline are more likely to become delinquent than are children who are raised with moderate consistent discipline, but there is no absolute guarantee about this outcome.[18]

The whole point of causal theories is to gain power and control over the world in which we live. When we want less of something (such as crime and delinquency) or more of something (such as law-abiding behavior), we try to find out the causes of what we desire. Then we try to influence those causes to get what we want.

Even though causal theories in social science deal only with probabilities, knowing about the probabilities can be useful for policy purposes. For example, if harsh erratic discipline actually does increase the probability of delinquency, even if by a small amount, then it may be useful to try to affect parenting styles. Special classes could teach effective disciplinary techniques to parents whose children are otherwise at risk of becoming delinquent (e.g., because they live in a high-crime neighborhood). If these classes succeeded in changing the disciplinary techniques used by parents, then we should end up with less delinquency in the future. In fact, such classes appear to reduce delinquency by significant amounts over the long run.[19]

All scientific theories in criminology make causal arguments, but there are different categories in which we can classify them. One such categorization divides criminological theories into those based on individual differences, structure/process, or the behavior of law.

THREE CATEGORIES OF CRIMINOLOGICAL THEORIES

Some theories focus on characteristics of individuals that are thought to increase or decrease the probabilities that an individual will engage in crime. In reviewing these characteristics, it is important to keep two points in mind. First, none of these characteristics absolutely determines that the person will engage in crime. Most people with these characteristics do not engage in crime at all—it is just that people with these characteristics are somewhat more likely than are other people to engage in crimes.[20] Second, while these characteristics may increase the probability that a particular individual will engage in crime, they may have no effect on overall crime rates. The following is a list of individual differences characteristics that are associated with increases in the probability of committing criminal behavior:

1. A history of early childhood problem behaviors and of being subjected to poor parental child-rearing techniques, such as harsh and inconsistent discipline; school failure; and the failure to learn higher cognitive skills, such as moral reasoning, empathy, and problem solving.
2. Certain neurotransmitter imbalances, such as low serotonin; certain hormone imbalances, such as high testosterone; central nervous system deficiencies, such as frontal or temporal lobe dysfunction; and autonomic nervous system variations, such as unusual reactions to anxiety.
3. Ingesting alcohol, a variety of illegal drugs, and some toxins like lead; head injuries; and complications during a subject's pregnancy or birth.
4. Personality characteristics, such as impulsivity, insensitivity, a physical and nonverbal orientation, and a tendency to take risks.
5. Thinking patterns that focus on trouble, toughness, smartness, excitement, fate, and autonomy and a tendency to think in terms of short-term rather than long-term consequences.
6. Association with others who engage in and approve of criminal behavior.
7. Weak attachments to other people, less involvement in conventional activities, having less to lose from committing crime, and weak beliefs in the moral validity of the law.
8. A perception that there is less risk of punishment for engaging in criminal behavior.
9. Masculinity as a gender role.

All these factors somewhat differently affect individuals at different ages. In addition, the following set of differences seems to increase the probability that a person will be a victim of crime:

10. Frequently being away from home, especially at night; engaging in public activities while away from home; and associating with people who are likely to commit crime.

In contrast to individual difference theories, we will also discuss a wide range of structure/process theories, especially in the later chapters of this book. These theories assume that some situations are associated with higher crime rates, regardless of the characteristics of the individuals within them. The theories therefore attempt to identify variables in the situation itself that are associated with higher crime rates.

In discussing these theories, it is important to keep several points in mind. First, these theories tend to be complex and descriptive, and it is sometimes hard to determine the proposed causes of crime. To the extent that this is true, the policy recommendations of the theory will be vague. Second, these theories have often been interpreted and tested at the individual level. Such testing necessarily involves some variation of the "ecological fallacy,"[21] and it has led to considerable confusion about the theories themselves. Third, situations with high crime rates often have a large number of variables, all of which are correlated with each other and all of which are correlated with crime—for example, poverty, inequality, high residential mobility, single-parent families, unemployment, poor and dense housing, the presence of gangs and illegal criminal opportunities, inadequate schools, and the lack of social services. It can be extremely difficult to determine which (if any) of these variables is causally related to high crime rates and which have no causal impact on crime at all.[22] In each theory in this category, there will be some structural characteristic that is associated with some rate or distribution of crime. This is the "structure" portion of a structure/process theory. There will also be a description of the supposed reasons why normal people in this structural situation may demonstrate a greater probability of engaging in crime than people in other situations. This is the "process" portion of a structure/process theory. The following structural arguments describe societal characteristics that seem to be associated with higher crime rates.

1. Economic modernization and development is associated with a rise in property crime rates. Property crime tends to increase until the society is highly developed and then to hold steady at a high level. The processes that result in this pattern of crime involve changes in routine activities and in criminal opportunities, which eventually are balanced by the increasing effectiveness of countermeasures.

2. Cultures that emphasize the goal of material success at the expense of adherence to legitimate means are associated with high rates of

utilitarian crime; an unequal distribution of legitimate means to achieve material success is associated with an inverse distribution of utilitarian crime; and in situations without legitimate means to economic success, the development of illegitimate means is associated with increased utilitarian crime, while the lack of such development is associated with increased violent crime. In these situations, the inability to achieve status by conventional criteria is associated with status inversion and higher rates of nonutilitarian criminal behavior. The processes involved in these structural patterns involve either frustration or the simple tendency to engage in self-interested behavior.

3. Neighborhoods with high unemployment, frequent residential mobility, and family disruption tend to have high crime rates. The processes involve neighborhood anonymity that results in social disorganization.

4. Media dissemination of techniques and rationalizations that are favorable to law violation are associated with increased rates of law violation. The process involves direct learning of techniques and rationalizations and indirect learning of the consequences that criminal behaviors have for others.

5. Joblessness and racism can generate an inner-city code of the street that promulgates normative violence in a variety of situations. The process includes feelings of hopelessness and alienation among inner-city residents and the generation of an oppositional subculture as a means of maintaining self-respect.

6. Increases in the objective certainty of punishments are associated with reductions in crime rates, but increases in the objective severity of punishments seem to be associated either with no changes or with increases in crime rates. In addition, crackdowns on certain types of crimes are associated with short-term reductions in the rates of those crimes that may extend beyond the life of the crackdown policy itself.

7. Societies that stigmatize deviants have higher crime rates than do those that reintegrate deviants. The process involves blocked legitimate opportunities and the formation of subcultures.

8. Societies in which some people control others have higher crime rates than do societies in which people control and are controlled by others in approximately equal amounts. The process involves people's natural tendency to expand their control.

There is no contradiction between structure/process theories and individual difference theories. Nothing in the structure/process theories contradicts the assertion that there are some people who are more likely to engage in crime regardless of their situation. Similarly, nothing in the individual difference theories contradicts the assertion that there are some situations in which people, regardless of their individual characteristics, are more likely to engage in crime. These are separate assertions, and both types of theories can be integrated into a larger theory of criminal behavior.

ᴵ Theories of the behavior of criminal law suggest that the volume of crime and the characteristics of criminals are determined primarily by the enactment and enforcement of laws. Most people who are convicted of crimes are poor, but not because poverty causes crime. Rather, the actions typical of poor people are more likely to be legally defined as crimes, and the laws that apply to such crimes are more likely to be strictly enforced. Consider the death penalty as an example. Criminologists who hold this view argue that there are differences in the enforcement of laws: wealthy and powerful people who kill are less likely to be arrested, tried, or convicted or are convicted of a less serious offense and given a more lenient sentence. These criminologists also argue that there are differences in the enactment of laws. Under felony murder laws, an offender is liable for first-degree murder if a death results from the commission of certain dangerous felonies, such as robbery or burglary. No intent to kill is required, because the intent to commit the lesser offense is transferred to the greater one.[23] In contrast, many serious injuries and deaths that are associated with corporate decision-making occur where there is the intent to commit a lesser offense (for example, to violate health or safety laws), combined with the full knowledge that the decision may result in serious injury and death to a number of innocent people. If a law similar to felony murder were applied to white-collar crime, then death row might be filled with corporate executives.

The following are some assertions about the behavior of criminal law.

1. When the social solidarity of a society is threatened, criminal punishment increases independent of whether crime increases.
2. The enactment and enforcement of criminal laws reflect the values and interests of individuals and groups in proportion to their political and economic power.
3. In addition to stratification, the quantity of law that is applied in particular cases is influenced by morphology, culture, organization, and the extent of other forms of social control.
4. Regardless of what other interests are served by the criminal law, it must serve the economic interests of the owners of the means of economic production.
5. Actions that involve simple and immediate gratification of desires but few long-term benefits are exciting and risky but require little skill or planning and generally produce few benefits for the offender while causing pain and suffering to the victim are more likely to be defined and processed as criminal than are other actions.

Theories of the behavior of criminal law do not contradict theories of criminal behavior. More than anything else, they ask a different question: Why are some behaviors and people, but not others, defined and processed as criminal?

The chapters in this volume have been organized primarily for the sake of convenience and clarity; no necessary separateness or mutual exclusiveness should be inferred. In general, the chapters are organized in the historical sequence in which the theories originated, so that the earliest theories are presented first. This organization is intended to provide the reader with a sense of how the field of criminology has evolved over time. One exception to this general rule is Chapter 2, which explores the intersections of theory and policy by examining the recent crime drop in the United States.

Chapter 3 focuses on the classical and neoclassical schools of criminology, since this was the origin of criminology itself. It begins with historical materials on how classical criminology emerged as a field of study during the eighteenth and nineteenth centuries and then brings that discussion up to date by presenting theory and research on deterrence and routine activities. Chapters 4 and 5 examine biological and psychological theories, since these were the first types of positivist theory to emerge. Because later theories and research in criminology focused more strongly on social factors, they are presented in later chapters. Critical theories (such as those of the behavior of law) are also included among the later chapters. Most chapters contain modern as well as historical materials, beginning with the work of the early theorists and then presenting more recent theories and research that take the same general point of view. After all the different types of theories are presented, Chapter 15 discusses attempts to integrate the different theories into broader approaches. A brief conclusion offers thoughts on the current state of theorizing in criminology and its relevance to policy.

KEY TERMS

theory	theoretical rationale
spiritual explanations	direction of causation
trial by battle	time sequence
trial by ordeal	absence of spuriousness
compurgation	control
penitentiary	probability
natural explanations	individual difference theories
scientific theories	structure/process theories
falsification	theories of the behavior of
causation	criminal law
correlation	

DISCUSSION QUESTIONS

1. In what ways do spiritual, sometimes called demonological, explanations of crime still enter into the criminal justice system today?
2. Provide examples of how a correlation, but not causation, can be found between a given situation and criminality.
3. Using a multifactor approach, create a hypothetical individual with various biological, psychological, and sociological backgrounds. Alter the individual's attributes and, as you do so, assess how you think the changes would affect the individual's probability (risk level) of offending.

NOTES

1. A large number of. textbooks focus on general criminology, including Larry J. Seigel, *Criminology*, 13th ed. (Boston: Cengage, 2018); Frank Schmalleger, *Criminology Today*, 8th ed. (New York: Pearson, 2016); John E. Conklin, *Criminology*, 11th ed. (New York: Pearson, 2012); and Freda A. Adler, Gerhard O. W. Mueller, and William S. Laufer, *Criminology*, 9th ed. (New York: McGraw-Hill, 2017).
2. Some recent texts that focus on criminology theory include J. Mitchell Miller, Christopher J. Schreck, and Richard Tewkesbury, *Criminology Theory*, 4th ed. (New York: Pearson, 2014); Mark M. Lanier and Stuart Henry, *Essential Criminology*, 4th ed. (New York: Avalon Publishing, 2014); Ronald Akers, Christine S. Sellers, and Wesley G. Jennings, *Criminological Theories: Introduction, Application, and Evaluation*, 7th ed. (New York: Oxford University Press, 2016); and Franklin P. Williams III and Marilyn D. McShane, *Criminological Theory*, 7th ed. (New York: Pearson, 2017). Several books of readings also focus on criminology theories, including Lanier and Henry, eds., *The Essential Criminology Reader* (Boulder, CO: Westview Press, 2004); Francis T. Cullen, Robert S. Agnew, and Pamela Wilcox, *Criminological Theories*, 6th ed. (New York: Oxford University Press, 2017); Eugene McLaughlin and John Muncie, eds., *Criminological Perspectives*, 3rd edition (London: Sage, 2013); and Suzette Cote, *Criminological Theories* (Thousand Oaks, CA: Sage, 2002).
3. Arthur L. Stinchcombe, *Constructing Social Theories* (New York: Harcourt, Brace & World, 1968), pp. 3–5.
4. Graeme Newman, *The Punishment Response* (Philadelphia: Lippincott, 1978), pp. 13–25.
5. Harry Elmer Barnes, *The Story of Punishment*, 2nd ed. rev. (Montclair, NJ: Patterson Smith, 1972), pp. 7–10.
6. Newman, *The Punishment Response*, p. 97.
7. Kai T. Erikson, *Wayward Puritans* (New York: John Wiley, 1966).
8. Harry Elmer Barnes and Negley K. Teeters, *New Horizons in Criminology* (New York: Prentice Hall, 1945); and Negley K. Teeters, *The Cradle of the Penitentiary: The Walnut Street Jail at Philadelphia, 1773–1835* (Philadelphia: Temple University Press, 1955).

9. Charles Colson, *Life Sentence* (Grand Rapids, MI: Baker, 1999).

10. Charles Colson, "Toward an Understanding of the Origins of Crime," in *Crime and the Responsible Community*, ed. John Stott and Nick Miller (London: Hodder and Stoughton, 1980).

11. Stinchcombe, *Constructing Social Theories*, pp. 15–17.

12. Ibid., pp. 5–6; Thomas J. Bernard, "Twenty Years of Testing Theories: What Have We Learned and Why," *Journal of Research in Crime and Delinquency* 27 (1990): 325–347.

13. Thomas J. Bernard and R. Richard Ritti, "The Role of Theory in Scientific Research," in *Measurement Issues in Criminology*, ed. Kimberly L. Kempf (New York: Springer-Verlag, 1990), pp. 1–20.

14. Thomas S. Kuhn, *The Structure of Scientific Revolutions* (Chicago: University of Chicago Press, 1969).

15. See, e.g., the descriptions of each criteria discussed in Kenneth M. Cramer, "Six Criteria of a Viable Theory: Putting Reversal Theory to the Test," *Journal of Motivation, Emotion, and Personality* 1 (2013): 9–16.

16. Robert J. Sampson and John H. Laub, *Crime in the Making* (Cambridge, MA: Harvard University Press, 1993).

17. For example, Eric A. Stewart, Ronald L Simons, Rand D. Conger, and Laura V. Scaramella, "Beyond the Interactional Relationship Between Delinquency and Parenting Practices," *Journal of Research in Crime and Delinquency* 39 (2002): 36–59, argued that the child's involvement in the legal system increases ineffective parenting.

18. For example, see David P. Farrington, "Early Predictors of Adolescent Aggression and Adult Violence," *Violence and Victims* 4 (1989): 79–100. This article reports the percentage of juveniles who engage in delinquency for each of a large number of characteristics. Thus, it gives a good sense of how much (or how little) a particular characteristic affects the probability of engaging in delinquency.

19. See, for example, Peter W. Greenwood, Karyn E. Model, C. Peter Rydell, and James Chiesa, "Diverting Children from a Life of Crime" (Santa Monica, CA: RAND Corporation, 1996).

20. See, for example, David P. Farrington, "Early Predictors of Adolescent Aggression and Adult Violence," *Violence and Victims* 4 (1989): 79–100. This article gives percentages for a large number of characteristics of those who engage in adolescent aggression, teenage violence, and adult violence and who have been convicted of a violent crime.

21. W. S. Robinson, "Ecological Correlations and the Behavior of Individuals," *American Sociological Review* 15 (June 1950): 351–357.

22. This is because these variables are all highly correlated, leading to the statistical condition of multicollinearity, which causes model estimations to be inaccurate.

23. Hazel B. Kerper, *Introduction to the Criminal Justice System* (St. Paul, MN: West, 1972), pp. 111–112.

CHAPTER 2

—

Theory and Policy in Context
The Great American Crime Decline

This is a text on theoretical criminology, and Chapter 1 emphasized the importance of theory in the field and that, by and large, this book will focus on theories rather than facts about crime. However, there is increasing pressure on criminologists to show how theory relates to trends in crime and how theory and policy are connected. It is well to have criminological theories that vary in their perspective, tradition, and formative processes, but how do the myriad theories connect to our current crime landscape? While the remaining chapters in the book address the types of theories, this chapter will discuss how some of the theories (and their associated policies) may or may not help explain one of the most monumental criminological occurrences in modern history: the Great American Crime Decline,[1] taking place from the early 1990s to the present day. Exploring this crime decline will help us see how criminologists are in a constant struggle to explain real-world phenomena with the theories they proclaim are the most relevant and predictive.

After providing some basic data on crime trends over the past few decades, this chapter contrasts two approaches to explaining why the United States had such high levels of violence by the early 1990s. One takes the position that the increase in crime was related to very real sociological root causes—poverty, to name one. The other takes the position that the increase in crime was related not to economic poverty but to moral poverty—children not learning right from wrong and associated ills such as drug abuse. The former is a liberal argument; the latter is a more conservative approach.

Following the publication of these works, crime—especially violent crime—began its incredible descent across the United States. Within a few years of this decline, around the turn of the twenty-first century, as it appeared it may have teeth and not be a temporary downtick, hoards of scholars began to proffer explanations for it; this chapter examines several of the more prominent reasons given. A decade later the crime decline kept on

14

path, and in one city in particular—New York—violent crime declined at a rate much greater than the nation's overall rate. The chapter concludes by discussing what may have been different in New York to warrant such a spectacular change for the better.

CRIME IN THE UNITED STATES: THE PAST HALF-CENTURY

Figures 2-1 and 2-2 display the crime trends for violent crime and property crime rates from 1960 to 2017. Violent crime indexes are comprised of murders, rapes, robberies, and aggravated assaults. Property crime consists of burglaries, larceny thefts, and vehicle thefts. Both indexes are calculated using data from the FBI, which gathers reported crime counts across categories from police departments voluntarily participating. Crime rates are calculated by adjusting raw numbers per capita, such as crime per 100,000 citizens. Crime rates allow for meaningful comparisons across jurisdictions and over time.

These Uniform Crime Report (UCR) data published by the FBI has some significant problems.[2] It underreports actual crime, because many victims fail to report crime; further, underreporting varies across crime categories. Crime committed in areas where the police do not participate in reporting (about 4%) is not included. Police may misclassify or falsify reported crime statistics. Certain crime types, such as tax evasion, hazardous waste dumping, and white-collar crimes, are not included. Finally,

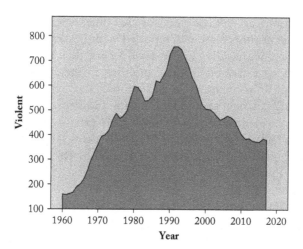

FIGURE 2-1 Violent Crime in the United States (index rates per 100,000) 1960–2017.
(Configured using Uniform Crime Reports Data, FBI, Crime in the United States.)

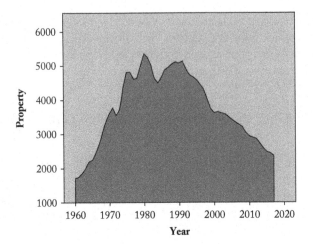

FIGURE 2-2 Property Crime in the United States (index rates per 100,000) 1960–2017.
(Configured using Uniform Crime Reports Data, FBI, Crime in the United States.)

police might only report the most serious offense in a multiple-offense incident to the FBI.

Crime victimization surveys such as the National Crime Victimization Survey (NCVS), which interviews a sample of individuals twice a year, asking them for information about offenses they may or may not have reported to the police, could help address the "shadow figure," or degree of underreporting, but these surveys suffer flaws as well—for example, "victimless" crimes are not counted, nor are crimes against businesses; there is no independent confirmation of reported victimizations; and interviewees may have difficulties recalling information accurately.[3] As an effort to collect more sophisticated data on criminal offenses, in the 1980s officials began designing and implementing the National Incident-Based Reporting System (NIBRS), which should account for all offenses, not just the most serious in any incident, and contain much more extensive information about the offenders and the victims than the UCR does. However, a very small proportion of police departments in the United States currently participate in NIBRS.[4] Thus data from this chapter are from the Uniform Crime Report, despite its flaws.

As the 1960s progressed, there was an explosion of both violent and property crime. In the 1980s violent crime continued its climb, while property crime began to level off. In 1960 there was a violent crime rate (per 100,000 inhabitants) of 161 and a property crime rate of 1,726. By 1991 these rates had skyrocketed to 758 and 5,140, representing increases of 371 percent in violent crime and 198 percent in property crime. Beginning in the early 1990s, both violent and property crime began their famous declines. In 2017 the rates were 383 and 2,362, respectively. This represents a decrease in violent crime of 49 percent and a decrease in property crime of 54 percent (from 1991 to 2017).

TWO OPPOSING NARRATIVES OF THE CRIME WAVE

In 1996 and 1998 two influential works were published addressing the question of why crime was so high by the early 1990s. Both relied on data from the early to mid-1990s, and while crime had just begun its descent, none of the authors could foresee that it would plummet over the next twenty years; instead, they focused on what was wrong in the United States—what factors were responsible for the miserable state of affairs, especially with regard to violent crime. These works were considerably different in their explanations, and a brief tour of them will demonstrate how divided conservative and liberal ideologies were on the crime problem in the United States. The first work was *Body Count: Moral Poverty . . . And How to Win America's Work Against Crime and Drugs*,[5] by conservative authors William Bennett, John DiIulio, and John Walters. The second was *Crime and Punishment in America: Why the Solutions to America's Most Stubborn Social Crisis Have Not Worked—And What Will*,[6] by liberal author Elliott Currie.

Body Count was named for the escalating homicide numbers as well as for the eponymous Blood gang member who got his name because "When da shootin's ova', das what I do, coun' da bodies."[7] The book began by shocking its readers with stories and statistics about how violent the United States had become by the early 1990s. In the course of a single business trip, one of *Body Count*'s authors (in each city as he arrived) read of teenagers killing foreign tourists in Florida, the murder of Michael Jordan's father by teenagers, an abduction of a little girl by a convicted sex offender, the murder of a woman waiting to pick up her daughter from a Bible study class, the homicide of a seventeen-year-old boy at a high school football game, and a murder-for-hire of a businessman ordered by his former father-in-law.[8] The authors pointed out that the country's murder rate was 5.1 per 100,000 in 1965 and had risen to 9.5 by 1993.[9] From 1985 to 1994 the *adult* homicide rate *dropped* by 25 percent, whereas the homicide rate for eighteen- to twenty-four-year-olds *jumped* by 61 percent.[10] Black males aged fourteen to twenty-four represented about 1 percent of the population, and this had remained stable over the past decade (mid-1980s to mid-1990s) yet this demographic now accounted for 17 (instead of 9) percent of homicide victims and 30 (instead of 17) percent of perpetrators.[11]

Body Count's authors predicted that as of the mid-1990s crime was going to soar further, due to a combination of an increasing proportion of juveniles in the population and a new generation of "superpredators," offenders who are the "youngest, biggest, and baddest generation any society has ever known."[12] This group of juveniles was "radically impulsive, brutally remorseless youngsters, including ever more preteenage boys, who murder, assault, rape, rob, burglarize, deal deadly drugs, join gun-toting gangs, and create serious communal disorders. They do not fear the stigma of arrest, imprisonment, or the pangs of conscience."[13] Superpredators would act out in extreme violence at the slightest sense of being disrespected. They placed no value whatsoever on their victims' lives. These superpredators, according to *Body Count*, were an entirely different sort of entity than youth criminals in the middle of the twentieth century. So what accounted for their emergence?

Before answering this question, *Body Count* dismissed the overall influence on crime of several explanatory factors put forth by both liberals and conservatives. For liberals, they addressed the variables of poverty and racism. Poverty will be discussed at more length later in this chapter, but to these authors, poverty did not matter much because during periods of increased government spending on social programs (creating more opportunities), as well as overall improved economic prosperity (such as the 1960s), crime still soared. *Body Count's* straightforward argument against the liberal notion that racism and racial disproportionality in the justice system is a source of crime was that different races simply commit different levels of crime.[14]

The authors also discounted the impact of several conservative theories: that crime would be mitigated with "tougher" prisons, greater use of the death penalty, wider availability of guns to law abiders, and closing legal loopholes such as *Miranda* constraints. Making prisons less "coddling" and "no-frills" will not work, because most criminals do not expect to end up in prison. (See Chapter 3 of this book for a discussion of deterrence theory.) Utilizing the death penalty as a crime control method was futile, because the legal system is set up to protect most murderers from execution. Putting either more guns out there (following the theory that guns in good citizens' hands are a deterrent) or fewer guns (following the notion that we need to keep them out of the hands of the bad guys) has not been shown to reverse crime trends; highly specific gun-related policies that can reduce crime need to be explored, but currently, gun policies have little impact on crime. Finally, legal protections afforded suspects during the Warren Court, such as *Miranda*, may work to the advantage of a small percentage of offenders, but they have a very small effect on the total crime rate.[15]

So what did account for high violence and drug use rates among young men? Not *economic* poverty, to *Body Count*, but *moral* poverty. Moral poverty is

> the poverty of being without loving, capable, responsible adults who teach you right from wrong; the poverty of being without parents and other authorities who habituate you to feel joy at others' joy, pain at others' pain, satisfaction when you do right, remorse when you do wrong; the poverty of growing up in the virtual absence of people who teach

morality by their own everyday example and who insist that you follow suit. In the extreme, moral poverty is the poverty of growing up severely abused and neglected at the hands of deviant, delinquent, or criminal adults.[16]

Those youth living with moral poverty experience an inability to control their impulses and a lack of empathy. Early drug use, to these authors, was a huge player in the crime-causing formula, so deeply entangled with criminal acts that the two together were a virtual cocktail for a career in crime. Those living in moral poverty were contrasted with those raised in moral health—the latter were raised by loving parents or guardians and grow up with a network of caring adults who afford them both encouragement and discipline and who teach by example. *Body Count*'s authors were careful to indicate that the presence of moral poverty or moral health was the driving force of crime no matter what the child's race, socioeconomic status, or any other demographic.[17]As evidence in support of their thesis that moral poverty causes crime, the authors pointed to a number of studies that have explored the effect of family and other contextual factors on crime and delinquency, such as parental criminality, parental absence, child maltreatment, and neighborhood criminogenic characteristics—such as the prevalence of felons, ex-felons, and drug addicts.[18]

Body Count concluded with some prescriptions that could presumably help avoid "get-tough" strategies for addressing the problems of the drug-crime connection and moral poverty, including stigmatizing drug use; boosting the potency of the institutions of families, churches, schools, and the media; eliminating needless barriers to adoption; and, to them, most important, restoring bonds of affection, devotion, and love between adults and children, and "remembering God."[19] Simultaneously, though, the authors put forth an extensive defense of get-tough approaches to street criminals—especially chronic offenders—involving both punishment (doing a better job of implementing incapacitation policies especially with the most serious and frequent offenders), supervision (reforming probation and parole practices to allow for more effective monitoring), and policing (adopting zero-tolerance approaches to law enforcement).[20] It is the latter set of policies that *Body Count* is best known for: a conservative punishment-oriented approach to crime and justice. Its authors believed that the nation's government had been failing its citizens egregiously by being too lenient on criminals. To them, social policies had failed, and it was up to law enforcement and the correctional system to protect the people.

Writing in response to *Body Count*, Elliott Currie, a left-of-center criminologist, attempted to dismantle the notion that stricter punishment was the answer, argued that an economic form of poverty was behind the crime increase, and offered social policy–based solutions, in his 1998 book *Crime and Punishment in America*. Currie had a couple years more data than did

Bennett et al., so he had bare evidence of the beginning of the great crime decline. Of that, he wrote, "While guarded optimism may be in order, complacency is not. And there is no guarantee that the respite we are now enjoying will last."[21] Thus, like *Body Count*, in *Crime and Punishment in America*, Currie was operating under the assumption that crime was near its all-time high and there was no solid evidence that it would ameliorate.

Currie began by highlighting that the state and federal prison population rose dramatically from 1971 (200,000) to 1996 (1.2 million).[22] Even accounting for population, this was a near quadrupling of the incarceration rate. The increase in incarceration particularly affected black men. For example, in California, Currie observed that "four times as many black men are 'enrolled' in state prison as are enrolled in public colleges and universities."[23] This was caused predominantly by the war on drugs, as in the decade from 1985 black state prison inmates there for drug offenses swelled in numbers by over 700 percent.[24] In concluding his remarks on the growth of prisons, Currie stated, "Short of major wars, mass incarceration has been the most thoroughly implemented government social program of our time."[25] Given the magnitude of the investment in incarceration, it would seem that a large return would be in order; not the case, said Currie. Violent crime rose considerably over the same twenty-five-year period that the prison population did, especially among the young and impoverished.

Whereas *Body Count* blamed the crime escalation on moral poverty and an overly lenient prison system, Currie assigned fault to the rise of poverty and income inequality and lack of social services spending.

> An American child under eighteen was half again as likely to be poor in 1994 as twenty years earlier, and more and more poor children were spending a long stretch of their childhood, or all of it, below the poverty line. The poor, moreover, became increasingly isolated, spatially and economically, during these years—trapped in ever more impoverished and often chaotic neighborhoods, without the support of kin or friends, and successive administrations cut many of the public supports—from income benefits to child protective services—that could have cushioned the impact of worsening economic deprivation and community fragmentation.[26]

To Currie, the increased dollars spent on prison were taken from public services such as education and housing, especially services for poor children.

Currie went head to head with Bennett et al. in attempting to debunk the notion that "prison works," addressing three "myths": leniency, efficacy, and costlessness. With respect to leniency, he took issue with *Body Count*'s authors' famous saying that was published in news outlets nationwide that "only 1 in 100 violent crimes results in a prison sentence."[27] Though correct factually, Currie said it was wrong to use this statistic as fodder for putting violent and recidivist criminals behind bars for longer periods of time; instead, the statistic was a direct result of a poor rate of *arrest* and a poor rate of *convictions* for those arrested. Currie also said that lengthy incarceration is not efficacious, as *Body Count* argued. He pointed, for example, to jurisdictions where less punitive sentencing policies were accompanied by declines in homicide and, by contrast, to jurisdictions where more punitive sentencing correlated to more violent crime.[28] Regarding the costlessness myth, Currie dismissed DiIulio's argument that "for every dollar we spend to keep a serious criminal behind bars, we save ourselves at least two or three. The $16,000 to $25,000 a year it takes to incarcerate a felon is in fact a bargain, when balanced against the social costs of the crimes he would commit if free."[29] Because the money spent on incarceration *in aggregate* did not reduce crime, it was disingenuous to base costlessness on an analysis of that unique subset of career violent offenders for whom incarceration does have a payout.

Currie's proposed solutions were not further expanding incarceration, nor "remembering God," but attacking the crime problem through prevention, social action, and reforming the justice system with a kind-handed approach. First, he assailed the notion that the first round of preventative methods (largely from the 1960s) was attempted and failed.[30] Those programs, for the most part, were too small both in scope and in funding, and naturally never had the potential to transform communities and individuals prone to criminal behavior. To Currie, much had been learned since the 1960s, and that there were four areas of emphasis that had a basis in evidence and that could work if properly implemented: "preventing child abuse and neglect, enhancing children's intellectual and social development, providing support and guidance to vulnerable adolescents, and working intensively with juvenile offenders."[31] Currie's solutions included home visiting by outsiders; working with families at high risk for abuse; enhancing school performance; providing jobs for vulnerable adolescents; and implementing "multisystemic therapy," which viewed youth as placed within a nest of interconnected systems, including family, peers, school, communities, and the job market.[32] As for social action, Currie argued that broader measures must be taken to ensure noncriminogenic environments, including reducing poverty with higher wages and an improved social security system.[33] With respect to the justice system, Currie concluded that rather than using get-tough approaches, such as extreme incarceration, boot camps, or punitive probation, Americans should identify those rehabilitation programs that *do* work and implement them on a large scale.[34]

Crime and Punishment in America and *Body Count* did have one key intersection: both believed in the importance of focusing on changing adolescents' environments, and both highlighted family health. However, the former pushed for interventions based on rehabilitation and fighting poverty and argued against punitive measures, whereas the latter wanted to bolster institutions such as the church, combat moral poverty, and use the penal system more fully and efficiently. Regarding the future, both works envisioned a future where crime would remain high (unless their proposed set of interventions was implemented). Instead, as their respective printing presses were cooling off, the United States' great crime decline was in full force and would sustain to the present day.

EXPLAINING THE 1990s DECLINE

From 1991 to 2001 homicide rates decreased by 43 percent, violent crime indexes by 34 percent, and property by 29 percent. Furthermore, this decline occurred among all geographic areas and all demographic groups.[35] Researchers scrambled to unearth the causes, especially since conventional wisdom, such as that voiced by Currie and Bennett et al., was that crime would continue to explode. Two of the most prominent works analyzing the decline were economist Steven Levitt's 2004 article, "Understanding Why Crime Fell in the 1990s," and Berkeley professor Franklin Zimring's 2007 book *The Great American Crime Decline*.[36] This section discusses some of the more prominent explanations, organized into two categories. The first is comprised of factors that are constantly shifting over time: economic measures, population demographics, police strength, and imprisonment rates. The second pertains to time-specific accounts of phenomena that occurred sometime prior to the drop: the emergence of the crack epidemic, the legalization of abortion, and unleaded gasoline. The following section will address in detail what some have come to believe is a powerful explanation: changes in policing *quality*.

One of the most natural responses for average citizens when asked to account for changes in crime rates is to suggest the economy is responsible—downturns for increases in crime and upturns for decreases. Yet the relationship between economic factors and crime is complex, and decades of research have shown very few consistent findings (and many nonintuitive).[37] From 1991 to 2001 the real GDP per capita increased by about 30 percent, and the annual unemployment rate fell from 6.8 to 4.8 percent.[38] However, as Levitt argues, much of the impact of the economy on crime may be mediated through government budgets (e.g., increased monies available for police may result in an increase in police strength that in turn reduces crime). In fact, as the economy was swelling in the 1990s, President Clinton's initiative to hire 100,000 new police officers was well underway.[39] According to Zimring, in his analysis of a number of studies on the effect of economy on crime during this time period, "the range . . . estimates, from one-quarter to 40% of the total property crime decline, is a substantial part of the 1990s story."[40] If this were true, that would still leave 60 to 75 percent of the decline in property crime unaccounted for. Finally remains the question of what happened to income inequality during this time period. By all accounts, the share of wealth captured by those at the top (e.g., 1%) continued to increase throughout the 1990s.[41] Moreover, income inequality continued to expand through the 2000s, as crime's great decline persevered. By 2012, after the Great Recession of 2007–2008, the US Census Bureau had declared that the income gap between the rich and the poor was the widest since 1967. The Gini index measures income distribution: a zero represents perfectly even distribution, whereas a one represents complete concentration. Its low was in 1968, at .351. Since then it has been rising, and by 2012, it was .456.[42] The general conclusion that income inequality is associated with violence *across* societies has not seemed to apply to the effect of inequality on crime *within* the United States during the period of the decline. What is not forecastable is whether if inequality continues its ascent, it will reach a tipping point past which it will impact crime rates.

Another explanation offered to account for the crime decline pertained to changing demographics, in particular the aging of the baby boomers. People age out of crime with a fairly dramatic trajectory. After World War II there was an explosion of babies. Following the Great Depression, when family growth was impractical, and the war, when family growth was often impossible, young couples gave birth at record rates. The boomer era lasted for about fifteen to twenty years (the most common period cited is 1946–1964), after which boomer mothers had reached the end of their fertility, the birth control pill emerged, and Americans became more material, with less money to spend on large families. Because most crime is caused by those in their late teens and early twenties, one would expect a large baby explosion in the 1940s and 1950s to result in crime increases in the 1960s and 1970s, which indeed did occur. From 1980 to 2000, the fifteen- to twenty-four-year-old population dropped by 26 percent. If you divide that twenty-year period into four periods of five years, crime rates declined in all except for 1985–1990, when youth offending rates increased beyond their normally high rate.[43]

On the surface, the baby-boomer argument seems a strong candidate for explaining the crime drop. However, if one takes what Zimring referred to as a predictive versus a retrospective approach to analyzing age structures and crime, the strength of the relationship is questionable. Retrospectively, Levitt estimated that changes in the age distribution "may have reduced homicide and violent crime by a few percent and property crime by as much as 5–6 percent."[44] Zimring noted that even an age-based 6 percent decrease in larceny during this period would account for 26 percent of the total decline in larceny.[45] Levitt referred to all property crime rather than just larceny and concluded that "demographic shifts may account for a little more than one-sixth of the observed decline in property crime in the 1990s, but are not an important factor in the drop in violent crime."[46] Predictively, though, age structure's impact in more recent years was not impressive. The percent of the US population of fifteen- to twenty-four-year-olds in

1980, 1990, 2000, and 2010 was 18.7, 14.9, 13.9, and 14.1.[47] While the youth population leveled off by the late 1990s, crime continued its decline.

Two law-and-order lines of reasoning were also put forth to explain the decline. The first was that the *amount* of law enforcement (measured by number of police officers) was increased and that the more cops, the less crime.[48] Levitt included this variable as one of his "four factors that explain the decline in crime" and not as one of his "six factors that played little or no role in the crime decline."[49] He pointed to a number of econometric works (including his own) which showed that increasing the number of police can reduce crime: from 1991 to 2001 the effect of an increase in overall police numbers on crime, he argued, was about 5 to 6 percent.[50] Zimring noted that Levitt was selective in what studies he chose to include in his examination of the effect of police size and that "the moderate growth in policing certainly had no more than a 5% impact on crime rates and probably much less than that."[51]

The second enforcement-oriented argument was—in line with conservative thinkers—that prison expansion through the 1990s helped explain the crime drop. Imprisonment is theorized to reduce crime through its incapacitation effect (physically removing offenders from society) and general deterrent effect (demonstrating to the general population what happens when one commits crime). Levitt noted that of the prison growth between the mid-1970s and 2000, more than half occurred during the 1990s. Over two million people were incarcerated (at some point) in 2000, four times as many as in 1972.[52] According to him, the increase in incarcerated individuals during the 1990s was associated with about a 12 percent drop in homicides and violent crime, an 8 percent drop in property crime, and accounted for one-third of the total decline in crime.[53] Zimring's analysis of the effect of imprisonment distinguished between the deterrent and incapacitation effects. With deterrence, the best measure of incarceration would be the proportional increase in prison population (representing the increased threat of imprisonment), whereas with incapacitation, the best measure would be the aggregate number of incarcerated individuals (representing the number of crimes prevented by the physical barrier between offenders and the public).

While crime in the United States from the mid-1970s until 2000 followed what Zimring referred to as a "roller-coaster pattern," the increase in incarceration was "uninterrupted."[54] For both types of incarceration effects, Zimring noted that trends in neither of their measures could reliably predict crime shifts since 1975.[55] After discussing a number of issues that confuse the process of determining the effect of one on the other—such as diminishing returns once incarceration reaches sky-high levels, elasticity (an economic concept usually referring to supply and demand dynamics), the difficulty with measuring marginal general deterrence, and a focus on the cumulative effect of imprisonment (which could explain why the crime decline was the greatest toward the end of the period studied, 1995–2000)—Zimring concluded by pointing to contrasting estimates. At the low end, incarceration explained 10 percent of the 1990s crime decline, and at the upper end it explained 27 percent of the drop.[56]

All of the explanations mentioned so far are of factors that constantly shift over time. The next three are of events that occurred sometime prior to the 1990s but had an effect that may have kicked in during that decade. The first is the emergence and recession of the crack cocaine epidemic, oft-studied by Alfred Blumstein.[57] Crack is a form of cocaine—produced by mixing powder cocaine with sodium bicarbonate and heating it—which is extremely concentrated and produces a much stronger high than powder and lasts for a much shorter time. Because of its high-to-price ratio, among other characteristics, it became extremely popular, especially in inner cities. It burst on the scene in the early to mid-1980s and immediately inspired gangs to control the crack market, with territoriality becoming key, and heavy, intergang handgun violence resulting. Levitt pointed out that the most compelling evidence in favor of a crack effect on crime is that homicide rates among black males fourteen to twenty-four years old soared in 1985 for a decade and then began a rapid descent from the mid-1990s to 2000. It is this demographic that would have been most likely to be affected if crack markets did affect homicide rates.[58]

Levitt nonetheless was moderate in his estimation of the total effect of crack on the crime decline. He noted that there was a dearth of adequate empirical studies on the causality question, but said he believed that crack did play some role for homicide rates. He estimated that the decline of crack led to about a 6 percent reduction in overall homicides in the 1990s, which would account for 15 percent of the total decline in homicide.[59] Zimring began his analysis by asserting that the rise and fall of crack, relative to the rise and fall of crime, could be summed up by the saying, "the nice thing about hitting your head against a stone wall is that it feels so good when you stop."[60] Nonetheless, while he gave credence to the rise of crack affecting the increase in crime, he was more skeptical about the rebound effect—that the decline in crack was responsible for the crime drop. First, he posed an alternative theory for the decline: that after such a dramatic increase among the young black demographic, a drop was sure to eventually occur. This is a phenomenon known as "regression to the mean," which means that when any variable departs dramatically from its historical average, it may naturally return toward the average, often times just as rapidly. Second, he asked why crime would have continued its decline after the crack markets had quieted in the early to mid-1990s.

The continuation, according to Zimring, would not be explained by either crack markets or regression to the mean.[61] Zimring attacked the crack–crime connection in another fashion as well: the crime drop in the 1990s was extremely broad, occurring across all crime types, whereas crack markets only should have affected certain types of crime (why would they have reduced auto thefts or rapes, for example?). Additionally, homicides did not drop faster than the other crimes, a fact which made it difficult for one to argue that the effect of crack markets contributed substantially to at least one portion (homicides) of the drop.

A phenomenon with even a more delayed hypothesized effect on crime than the rise and fall of the crack cocaine was the decision to legalize abortion in 1973, in the Supreme Court decision *Roe v. Wade*. Although its impact on crime may have been suggested as early as 1990, it was not until Levitt, with his colleague John Donohue, published an article in the *Quarterly Journal of Economics* in 2001 that this proposed effect became commonly discussed within scholarly circles, media, and laypersons.[62] The role of the legalization of abortion impacting crime can be summarized simply: abortion reduces the number of unwanted children, who are at a greater risk for crime. Children who were birthed (and kept) because abortion was not legal may have grown up in negative home environments with feelings of parental resentment and, according to a body of research, were more likely to become involved in crime.[63] In support of the abortion–crime link Donohue and Levitt pointed to several pieces of evidence, including that the states which legalized abortion three years prior to *Roe v. Wade* had crime declines occurring earlier than the rest of the nation and that data over time show a strong inverse relationship between abortion legalization and crime, if one lags the effect of abortion.[64] There is approximately a twenty-year gap between the legalization of abortion and the beginning of the crime drop—this is consistent with the tendency for criminals to become active in their late teens and early twenties. The magnitude of the abortion–crime relationship was significant, according to Levitt: "Extrapolating the conservative estimates of [Donohue and Levitt's study] to cover the period 1991–2000, legalized abortion is associated with a 10 percent reduction in homicide, violent crime, and property crime rates, which would account for 25–30 percent of the observed crime decline in the 1990s."[65]

Donohue and Levitt's article sparked much controversy, both in terms of public outcry over its substance and implications by liberals and conservatives on both sides of the abortion divide, but as well in criticisms of its methodology by other economists.[66] In his book Zimring spent considerable time analyzing the abortion effect[67] (while he did not rule it out as a factor, he did not believe it had near the effect Donohue and Levitt postulated). Two conclusions of Zimring's analysis are worth pointing to. First, Zimring argued that while Donahue and Levitt's theory was based on the idea that those aborted would have been more likely to be at-risk for criminal activity (teenage single moms, economically disadvantaged), demographic trends following *Roe v. Wade* in fact showed that both the raw numbers and relative percentage of births with risk markers *increased*, rather than decreased.[68]

Second, to Zimring, a problem with the type of analysis engaged in by Donohue and Levitt is that it was specific to the United States and was driven by a decline in need of a theory. In other words, after the decline oc-curred, it was easy to look for explanations that were *consistent* with it:

> There is a special danger in testing the magnitude of an impact in a time period where the decline in crime is one reason for establishing the theory of the decline. The big drop in crime in the 1990s was one original basis for the abortion dividend theory. Any theory that fit well with the actual crime declines of the 1990s might get credit for crime drops that were in fact unexplained.[69]

Zimring's preferred method of analysis would be that when testing the mag-nitude of something such as abortion policy on crime, examine effects trans-nationally, such that the single-country decline is not what is driving the explanation.

The final explanation for the 1990s crime drop discussed in this section is similar to abortion policy in that it required about a twenty-year lagged effect, but it is different in that tests of it have been carried out across nations, within nations, and even within cities, and it is purported to explain not only the crime drop of the 1990s but the crime rise in the 1960s and 1970s. This was not a commonly discussed explanation at the time Levitt and Zimring were evaluating the alternatives, its most exciting findings had not been published yet. In 2013 Kevin Drum wrote an article in the popular *Mother Jones* magazine titled "America's Real Criminal Element: Lead."[70] Drum had spent countless hours poring through works on all the explana-tions for the crime drop discussed so far in this chapter, and they concluded the problem was that it was impossible to disentangle the factors; they all happened at the same time. Going a different route, he considered crime as an epidemic:

> Experts often suggest that crime resembles an epidemic. But what kind? Karl Smith . . . has a good rule of thumb for categorizing epidemics: If it spreads along lines of communication, he says, the cause is information. Think Bieber Fever. If it travels along major transportation routes, the cause is microbial. Think influenza. If it spreads out like a fan, the cause is an insect. Think malaria. But if it's everywhere, all at once—as both the rise of crime in the '60s and '70s and the fall of crime in the '90s seemed to be—the cause is a molecule.[71]

The molecule responsible for the crime epidemic and crime decline, accord-ing to some researchers, was tetraethyl lead, introduced in the 1920s by General Motors and exploding in use with the post–World War II auto frenzy. Drum reviewed twenty years of studies of the effect of crime on lead, from 1994 to 2013, conducted by researchers Rick Nevin, Jessica Wolpaw Reyes, Howard Mielke, and Sammy Zahran. The mechanisms by which lead exposure affects children's development and future criminal proclivity are discussed in Chapter 4 of this book; they are neurological, affect boys more than girls, and bring about increased aggression, impulsiveness, ADHD, and lower IQ.

Nevin's research began in the mid-1990s and was premised on the notion that there is a direct relationship between atmospheric lead (caused by leaded gasoline consumption) and crime: as lead emissions from cars rose from the postwar period until the early 1970s, violent crime followed (but lagged by twenty-three years).[72] As lead was removed from gasoline during the 1970s, violent crime declined (with a similar lag). A later study of his found that the lead-crime curve fit applied not only in the United States but in Canada, Great Britain, Finland, France, Italy, New Zealand, and West Germany.[73] Reyes analyzed the effects of lead emissions on crime at the state level. The rate of reduction of lead in gas during the 1970s and 1980s varied significantly by state, and she found that the lead-crime curve matched state by state.[74] Most recently, Mielke and Zahran found that among six US cities with good lead emissions and crime data going back to the 1950s—Minneapolis, Chicago, Indianapolis, Atlanta, San Diego, and New Orleans—the lead-crime curves fit in all six cases, with a lag of twenty-two years. Additionally, within a single city, New Orleans, they found that crime rates by neighborhood were associated with lead-based paint in homes and lead-dust-contaminated communities.[75]

After reviewing these findings, Drum wondered why the lead explanation for crime has been all but ignored by criminologists, with the exception of James Q. Wilson (a well-known conservative criminologist who cointroduced broken windows theory), who had acknowledged it in 2011, shortly before his death.[76] One reason was that criminologists tend to look for sociological explanations for crime, rather than medical reasons. Another looked to the impact of interest groups:

> Political Conservatives want to blame the social upheaval of the '60s for the rise in crime that followed. Police Unions have reasons for crediting its decline to an increase in the number of cops. Prison guards like the idea that increased incarceration is the answer. Drug warriors want the story to be about drug policy. If the actual answer turns out to be lead poisoning, they all lost a big pillar of support for their pet issue. And while lead abatement could be big business for contractors and builders, for some reason their trade groups have never taken it seriously.[77]

The lead explanation for crime trends, thus, is an argument by a small number of researchers who are not predominantly criminologists. If it does hold up to empirical scrutiny, it may explain a portion of long-term crime trends but is unlikely to account for the many roller-coaster oscillations in crime.[78]

There remained one last explanation for at least some portion of the great crime decline that is discussed in the next section: quality of policing. Proponents of this explanation typically look to New York City, since it is well known to be on the forefront of modern policing strategies (as of the early

1990s) and the crime drop there was extreme. Levitt concluded that policing strategies did not have much overall impact on the crime decline in New York because (1) New York's drop occurred three years before Commissioner William Bratton took over; (2) policing strategies occurred at the same time as the number of police grew; (3) other major cities such as Los Angles and Washington, DC, with problematic policing, nonetheless had great crime drops; and (4) New York had some of the highest abortion rates in the nation, beginning three years before *Roe v. Wade*.[79] Proponents of the notion that better policing fueled the decline could counter his first argument by saying he misunderstood New York policing during that era, that in fact Bratton (and Jack Maple, one of his lieutenants), as chief of the New York City Transit Unit prior to becoming commissioner, positively influenced crime in New York City. Subway crime—especially robberies—accounted for a significant amount of New York's safety problems, and so innovations in the Transit Unit were of major import in the early stages of the policing transformation. As for Levitt's other arguments, Zimring would take them on, armed with another decade of data, in his 2012 book *The City That Became Safe*.

THE CITY THAT BECAME SAFE

While the nation's crime dropped substantially through the 1990s, Zimring's latest book was devoted to understanding why New York's crime drop was larger than the nation's overall and continued to decline dramatically throughout the 2000s, distinguishing it from the country's other large cities. On a combination of three dimensions, New York was a special case, based on the size, length, and breadth of its drop. In two of the most reliably measured crimes, homicides and auto thefts, other cities' statistics paled to New York's from 1990 to 2009. The Big Apple's rates plummeted by 82 percent (homicides) and 94 percent (auto thefts), compared to 71 and 68 percent for Los Angeles, 47 and 69 percent for Chicago, 64 and 74 percent for Houston, and 38 and 72 percent for Philadelphia.[80] Looking at the seven index crime rates—homicide, rape, robbery, assault, burglary, auto theft, and larceny—New York's decline placed first in all categories over Los Angeles, Houston, San Diego, San Jose, and Boston (with one exception: assaults dropped 67% in New York compared to 78% in L.A.).[81] In terms of length, Zimring noted that while New York's decline was smaller in 2000 to 2009 than in 1990 to 2000, in all of the index crimes, there was a singular, uninterrupted downward trajectory from 1990 to 2009.[82] New York also experienced great breadth in its drop both by crime type (all major crimes declined in a parallel fashion) and geography (the four most populated boroughs, each the size of a major city itself, all experienced similar declines for all index crimes).[83]

Zimring asked why the New York crime decline was twice as long and twice as large as the national trend. "What pushed this city into the unprecedented condition of 80% drops in most street crime? There were no obvious changes in population, economy, education, or criminal justice sanctions that seem likely candidates to explain the double dose of crime decline . . . . There were large changes in policing, and some combination of new cops, new tactics, and new management appears a likely cause of much of New York's advantage over other cities."[84] While admitting that it is impossible to disentangle the various policing variables from each other to isolate their independent effects explaining the "New York effect" (the additional decline in New York not explained by the national crime drop), Zimring's analysis speculated that there were five policing measures that made a difference, two of them proven and three of them probable.

The two tactics NYPD employed that Zimring believed "almost certainly" reduced crime were hotspots policing and the targeting of drug markets. Hotspots policing involves aggressive patrol, surveillance, and enforcement in those areas that are most criminogenic and have repetitive patterns of violent crime. The positive effects of hotspots policing are well documented.[85] In New York "open-air" drug markets have historically been associated with extreme violence. The New York strategy was to target these areas and drive the dealing inside, since the violence occurs as part of the open-air nature of these markets. Thus, drug use did not decline in New York over this time period (e.g., as measured by overdoses), but the violence associated with street-level dealing and territoriality disputes did.

Three variables that probably made a difference, according to Zimring, were Compstat, getting drugs off the street, and more manpower. Compstat is a managerial concept and involves the gathering of crime information in a timely manner, mapping crimes, and having regular meetings with top brass, holding leaders of geographical divisions accountable for crime activity in their areas. New York's targeting of gun reduction (accomplished through aggressive stop-and-frisks and other investigational strategies) may have made a difference, as evidenced by gun homicides dropping more quickly than non–gun homicides.[86] Finally, the size of the overall police force in New York grew during the 1990s and may have influenced the drop during that time period, but it was unlikely to have made much of a difference in the ongoing drop during the 2000s.[87]

Some of Zimring's statistical analysis in *The City That Became Safe* could be challenged by more rigorous scientific methods, but the overall message the books sent was strong. Crime in New York declined more dramatically than crime anywhere else, and no one has found any more plausible explanations for the New York effect than policing quality. To the extent this was true, other cities could learn from New York.

One need only to look at crime statistics across different cities over time to realize that tremendous disparities exist. To demonstrate this, we used UCR data to calculate violent crime rates (per 100,000 people) from 2014 to

2017 in five large- and medium-sized cities that are the source of frequent attention by crime researchers: New York, Los Angeles, Chicago, Baltimore, and St. Louis. In 2017 these rates were 539 (New York), 761 (Los Angeles), 1,099 (Chicago), 2,027 (Baltimore), and 2,082.3 (St. Louis). So for example, Chicago had a violent crime rate approximately twice that of New York. Disparities are also large in changes in crime over recent years. From 2014 to 2017 New York's violent crime rate *decreased* by 9.7 percent, while rates *increased* in other cities by 24 percent (Chicago, St. Louis), 51 percent (Baltimore), and 55 percent (Los Angeles). These are dramatic fluctuations, especially considering that the overall national violent crime rate changed from 362 in 2014 to 383 in 2017 (an increase of only 5.8%).

It is logical, then, that understanding crime trends requires analysis of events and conditions experienced in different jurisdictions. In Los Angeles, for example, information emerged showing that the city had been significantly underreporting violent crime from at least 2005 to 2012 (during that period 14,000 violent assaults were reported as minor, thereby not showing up in the violent crime rate).[88] Still, this resulted in about a 7 percent undercount of actual violent crime, which is not overly helpful in explaining the 55 percent increase in the years following.

In other cities, some have tried to explain rapid increase by local and nationwide narratives relating to police behavior. In 2014 police shot and killed Michael Brown, a black man, in Ferguson Missouri (near St. Louis), a controversial use-of-force incident which ignited activists across the nation, many of whom were already building the Black Lives Matter movement in response to the death of Trayvon Martin in Florida. In Chicago, also in 2014, police fatally shot a seventeen-year-old African American, Laquan McDonald, as he walked away from them, carrying a knife. In Baltimore the next year, Freddie Gray, also African American, died after the Baltimore Police Department failed to properly secure him in a transport van. After these incidents an anti-law enforcement wave developed around the nation, and especially in the particular affected cities.

Heather MacDonald, author of books such as *The War on Cops*,[89] has been especially vocal in arguing that violent crime in urban areas across the country increased in 2015 because law enforcement began "de-policing" (what she refers to as the "Ferguson Effect") as a result of anger against police for these highly volatile and well publicized incidents.[90] Police, the argument goes, were less likely to make arrests and get involved in anything but the most serious crimes, after Ferguson (in the social media age), apprehensive of street-level outrage, negative community response, and fear of personal civil and criminal liability.[91] The single study systematically assessing the Ferguson effect, looking at crime data in the year preceding and following the incident, found no systematic changes in overall nationwide violent or property trends, but did find that robbery rates increased, and some cities such as Baltimore and St. Louis experienced large increases in homicide rates post-Ferguson.[92] However, New York experienced a nationally publicized incident similar to the others—Eric Garner died after being put in a chokehold during an arrest for selling black-market cigarettes in 2014—and yet the city's violent crime rate did not increase in 2015 as it did in the other cities. And Los Angeles's massive increase in violent crime between 2014 and 2017 cannot be explained by any specific city-specific incident involving police use of force. In a way, each city, and even each neighborhood within a city, is its own laboratory when it comes to understanding crime.

CONCLUSIONS

This chapter began by exhorting criminological theoreticians to think how various criminological frameworks apply to the real-world landscape and how some theories may be more policy relevant than others during certain time frames. It discussed the magnitude of the crime drop that occurred in the United States from the early 1990s to the present day. It contrasted two sets of researchers' explanations, one of the crime wave occurring from the 1960s to the 1990s, and one from the 1990s on. Currie and Bennett et al. took different approaches to explaining the wave, whereas Levitt and Zimring had their share of disagreements over what accounted for the great decline. It ended with a discussion of crime in New York and policing tactics.

Many variables were discussed as part of the various thinkers' views on the reasons for crime trends. Some of these were poverty, income inequality, racism, incarceration, moral poverty, parent–child bonds, drug use, the war on drugs, religion, child abuse and neglect, age, law enforcement size, the crack epidemic, gangs, abortion, lead, and police quality. These variables will all be discussed in some way or another as part of the many theories of crime examined in the remainder of the book. They will appear in, for example, control theories and psychological theories (parent–child bonds), biological theories (drug use, lead), conflict theories (the war on drugs, income inequality, racism), classical/deterrence theories (incarceration, police size, police quality), strain theories (gangs), and neighborhood and developmental theories (age, lead, abortion). Policy implications will sometimes arise naturally; at other times, they will be tenuous at best. If lead is a major influencing factor on crime, for example, communities with lead hazards ought to be cleaned up. If police size matters, resources should be spent building police force. If police quality matters, best practices in policing should be a priority for government funding. By contrast, if abortion legalization did in fact have something to do with the crime drop, what would be any current policy implications? If poverty affects crime, how do we eliminate poverty?

Some criminologists believe that only by addressing what they view as the root causes of crime, such as social structure and economic measures, can crime be reduced. Others take a pragmatic view that deeply entrenched societal factors are immovable in the short or mid-run, and that crime can be reduced quickly and efficaciously based on such theories as opportunity, deterrence, and routine activities, and that is where resources should be allocated. The contrasting approaches play out particularly poignantly in the case of poverty and violence. Whereas root causes theorists have traditionally argued that poverty must be dealt with prior to seeing violence wane, an emerging movement has grown arguing just the opposite. In the bestselling 2014 book *The Locust Effect: Why the End of Poverty Requires the End of Violence*, Gary Haugen and Victor Boutros make this point:

> At this critical inflection point in the fight against global poverty, we must clearly elevate an aspect of poverty in our world that is both under-appreciated and very distinct . . .
>
> That aspect of poverty is *violence*—common, everyday, predatory violence. The way our world works, poor people—*by virtue of their poverty*—are not only vulnerable to hunger, disease, homelessness, illiteracy, and a lack of opportunity; they are also vulnerable to violence. Violence is as much a part of what it means to be poor as being hungry, sick, homeless, or jobless. In fact . . . violence is frequently the problem that poor people are most concerned about. It is one of the core reasons they are poor in the first place, and one of the primary reasons they stay poor. Indeed, we will simply never be able to win the battle against extreme poverty unless we address it.[93]

This volume's intention is, and always has been, to provide a history and analysis of the major theories of crime. At the same time, theoretical criminologists are in an era where it is increasingly important for them to be relevant, for their theories to have direct, tangible policy implications, for their analyses to better society. In this spirit, the reader is encouraged to reflect upon the various theories in the text, as to which are most relevant in the modern era.

KEY TERMS

Great American Crime
  Decline
Uniform Crime Reports
National Crime Victimization
  Survey
superpredator
moral poverty
criminogenic

income inequality
Gini index
baby boomer
incapacitation
lagged effect
tetraethyl lead
New York effect
Ferguson effect

DISCUSSION QUESTIONS

1. How did the explanations for the 1990s crime drop put forth in *Crime and Punishment in America* and *Body Count* reflect to some extent the political nature of their authors?
2. What is the importance of figuring out what was behind the crime decline to the field of criminology as a whole?
3. Which explanations for the crime decline required the use of a lagged effect, and why?
4. In what ways were the New York experience the same as and different from the national experience, in terms of the crime decline?
5. What is the overall plausibility of the lead explanation for crime trends?
6. What are some of the ways in which the abortion explanation may cause public and policy-related controversies?
7. Considering the question of whether a Ferguson effect exists, in what ways is it important to understand both enforcers' motivations and behavior as well as that of law violators?

NOTES

1. Named after Franklin E. Zimring, *The Great American Crime Decline* (New York: Oxford University Press, 2007).
2. See, for example, chapter 2 in Anthony Walsh, *Criminology: The Essentials* (Thousand Oaks, CA: Sage, 2015).
3. Ibid., p. 30.
4. Arguments toward furthering the use of NIBRS are put forth by Kevin J. Strom and Erica L. Smith, "The Future of Crime Data: The Case for the National Incident-Based Reporting System (NIBRS) as a Primary Data Source for Policy Evaluation and Crime Analysis," *Criminology and Public Policy* 16 (2017): 1027–1048.
5. William J. Bennett, John J. DiIulio Jr., and John P. Walters, *Body Count: Moral Poverty . . . And How to Win America's War Against Crime and Drugs* (New York: Simon & Schuster, 1996).
6. Elliott Currie, *Crime and Punishment in America: Why the Solutions to America's Most Stubborn Social Crisis Have Not Worked—and What Will* (New York: Henry Holt and Company, 1998). Currie also published a second edition of this work in 2013, including an afterword, but the discussion of the book in this chapter pertains to the 1998 edition.
7. Bennett et al., *Body Count*, p. 31, quoting interview from Mark S. Fleisher, *Beggars and Thieves: Lives of Urban Street Criminals* (Madison: University of Wisconsin Press, 1995), p. 143.
8. Bennett, *Body Count*, pp. 11–12.

9. Ibid., p. 19, citing *Murder in America* (International Association of Chiefs of Police, May 1995), p. 13.

10. Bennett, *Body Count*, p. 21, citing James Alan Fox, *Trends in Juvenile Violence* (Bureau of Justice Statistics, December 1994), p. 2.

11. Bennett, *Body Count*, p. 22, citing Fox, *Trends in Juvenile Violence*, p. 2.

12. Bennett, *Body Count*, p. 26.

13. Ibid., p. 27.

14. Ibid., pp. 41–47.

15. Ibid., pp. 47–55.

16. Ibid., p. 56.

17. Ibid., p. 57.

18. Ibid., pp. 60–63.

19. Ibid., pp. 187–208.

20. Bennett et al., *Body Count*, pp. 83–136.

21. Currie, *Crime and Punishment in America*, p. 4.

22. Ibid., pp. 12–13.

23. Ibid., p. 13.

24. Ibid.

25. Ibid., p. 21.

26. Ibid., p. 31.

27. Ibid., p. 40.

28. Ibid., pp. 57–63.

29. Ibid., p. 67.

30. Robert Martinson, "What Works? Questions and Answers About Prison Reform," *The Public Interest* (1974): 22–54.

31. Currie, *Crime and Punishment in America*, p. 81.

32. Ibid., pp. 80–109.

33. Ibid., pp. 110–161.

34. Ibid., pp. 162–184.

35. See, e.g., Steven D. Levitt, "Understanding Why Crime Fell in the 1990s: Four Factors That Explain the Decline and Six That Do Not," *Journal of Economic Perspectives* 18 (2004): 163–190, at pp. 167–168.

36. Zimring, *The Great American Crime Decline*; Levitt, "Understanding Why Crime Fell in the 1990s." For diverse perspectives on the crime decline, see also Alfred Blumstein and Joel Wallman, eds., *The Crime Drop in America* (Cambridge: Cambridge University Press, 2000).

37. Thomas J. Bernard, Jeffrey B. Snipes, and Alexander L. Gerould, *Vold's Theoretical Criminology*, 6th ed. (New York: Oxford University Press, 2010), pp. 93–114.

38. Levitt, "Understanding Why Crime Fell in the 1990s," p. 170.

39. Violent Crime Control and Law Enforcement Act of 1994. Established US Department of Justice, Office of Community Oriented Policing Services.

40. Zimring, *The Great American Crime Decline*, p. 68.

41. See, e.g., Thomas Piketty and Emmanuel Saez, "Income Inequality in the United States 1913–1998," *Quarterly Journal of Economics* 1 (2003): 1–39.

42. Carmen DeNavas-Walt, Bernadette D. Proctor, and Jessica C. Smith, *Income, Poverty, and Health Insurance Coverage in the United States: 2011* (Washington, DC: US Department of Commerce, US Census Bureau, 2012).

43. Zimring, *The Great American Crime Decline*, p. 62.

44. Levitt, "Understanding Why Crime Fell in the 1990s," p. 172.

45. Zimring, *The Great American Crime Decline*, p. 62.

46. Levitt, "Understanding Why Crime Fell in the 1990s," p. 172.

47. US Census Bureau, *Age and Sex Composition in the United States*.

48. Much controversy surrounds the various explanations for why more police would decrease crime. After the Kansas City Preventive Patrol Experiment concluded that police patrol presence accomplished very little in terms of a variety of criminal justice outcomes, the search began for why and how the overall number of police could impact crime rates and other community health outcomes (see George L. Kelling, Tony Pate, Duane Dieckman, and Charles E. Brown, *The Kansas City Preventive Patrol Experiment Summary Report* [Washington, DC: The Police Foundation, 1974]).

49. See Levitt, "Understanding Why Crime Fell in the 1990s." His "Six Factors That Played Little or No Role in the Crime Decline" were "The Strong Economy of the 1990s," "Changing Demographics," "Better Policing Strategies," "Gun Control Laws," "Laws Allowing the Carrying of Concealed Weapons," and "Increased Use of Capital Punishment." His "Four Factors That Explain the Decline in Crime" were "Increases in the Number of Police," "The Rising Prison Population," "The Receding Crack Epidemic," and "The Legislation of Abortion."

50. Ibid., p. 177.

51. Zimring, *The Great American Crime Decline*, p. 79.

52. Levitt, "Understanding Why Crime Fell in the 1990s," p. 177.

53. Ibid., pp. 178–179.

54. Zimring, *The Great American Crime Decline*, p. 49.

55. Ibid., p. 50.

56. Ibid., p. 55.

57. Blumstein was the principal proponent of the argument that changes in crack cocaine markets were at least partially responsible for the crime drop. See, for example, Blumstein and Wallman, *The Crime Drop in America*.

58. Levitt, "Understanding Why Crime Fell in the 1990s," pp. 179–180.

59. Ibid., p. 181.

60. Zimring, *The Great American Crime Decline*, p. 82.

61. Ibid., p. 83.

62. John Donahue and Steven Levitt, "Legalized Abortion and Crime," *Quarterly Journal of Economics* 116 (2001): 379–420. Their argument became the topic of widespread public discussion especially with the publication of Steven D. Levitt and Stephen J. Dubner, *Freakonomics: A Rogue Economist Explores the Hidden Side of Everything* (New York: William Morrow, 2005).

63. Levitt, "Understanding Why Crime Fell in the 1990s," p. 182.

64. Ibid., p. 182.

65. Ibid., p. 183.
66. See, e.g., Theodore Joyce, "Did Legalized Abortion Lower Crime?" *Journal of Human Resources* 39 (2004): 1–28; John J. Donahue and Steven D. Levitt, "Further Evidence That Legalized Abortion Lowered Crime: A Reply to Joyce," *Journal of Human Resources* 39 (2004): 29–49.
67. Zimring, *The Great American Crime Decline*, pp. 85–103.
68. Ibid., pp. 94–95.
69. Ibid., p. 103.
70. Kevin Drum, "America's Real Criminal Element: Lead," *Mother Jones*, Jan./Feb. 2013, pp. 29–62.
71. Ibid., pp. 30–31.
72. Rick Nevin, "How Lead Exposure Relates to Temporal Changes in IQ, Violent Crime, and Unwed Pregnancy," *Environmental Research* 83 (2000): 1–22.
73. Rick Nevin, "Understanding International Crime Trends: The Legacy of Preschool Lead Exposure," *Environmental Research* 104 (2007): 315–336.
74. Jessica W. Reyes, "Environmental Policy as Social Policy? The Impact of Childhood Lead Exposure on Crime." Working paper no. 130097. Cambridge, MA: National Bureau of Economic Research.
75. Howard W. Mielke and Sammy Zahran, "The Urban Rise and Fall of Air Lead (Pb) and the Latent Surge and Retreat of Societal Violence," *Environment International* 43 (2012): 48–55.
76. James Q. Wilson, "U.S. News: Hard Times, Fewer Crimes—The Economic Downturn Has Not Led to More Crime—Contrary to the Experts' Predictions; So What Explains the Disconnect? Big Changes in American Culture, Says James Q. Wilson," *Wall Street Journal, Europe*, May 31, 2011.
77. Drum, "America's Real Criminal Element," p. 34.
78. Some unpublished research has countered the lead-crime relationship. See Wayne Hall, "Did the Elimination of Lead from Petrol Reduce Crime in the USA in the 1990s?" [version 2; referees: 2 approved, 1 approved with reservations], *F1000Research* 2013:156 (https://doi.org/10.12688/f1000research.2-156.v2).
79. Levitt, "Understanding Why Crime Fell in the 1990s," pp. 172–173.
80. Franklin E. Zimring, *The City That Became Safe: New York's Lessons for Urban Crime and Its Control* (New York: Oxford University Press, 2011), p. 4 (for New York); p. 16 (for the other cities).
81. Ibid., p. 18.
82. Ibid., p. 6.
83. Ibid., pp. 8–14.
84. Ibid., p. 151.
85. See, e.g., Anthony Braga and David Weisburd, *Policing Problem Places: Crime Hot Spots and Effective Prevention* (New York: Oxford University Press, 2010).
86. Zimring *The City That Became Safe*, p. 144; Jeffrey Fagan, Franklin E. Zimring, and J. Kim, "Declining Homicide in New York: A Tale of Two Trends," *Journal of Criminal Law and Criminology* 88 (1998): 1277–1324.
87. Zimring, *The City That Became Safe*, pp. 138–140.

88. Ben Poston, Joel Rubin, and Anthony Pesce, "LAPD Underreported Serious Assaults, Skewing Crime Stats for 8 Years," *Los Angeles Times*, October 15, 2015.
89. Heather MacDonald, *The War on Cops* (New York: Encounter Books, 2016).
90. Heather MacDonald, "The Ferguson Effect Lives On," *City Journal*, December 23, 2016.
91. David C. Pyrooz, Scott H. Decker, Scott E. Wolfe, and John A. Shjarback, "Was There a Ferguson Effect on Crime Rates in Large U.S. Cities?" *Journal of Criminal Justice* 46 (2016): 1–8.
92. Ibid. Other studies examined whether the Ferguson incident affected killing of citizens by police and murders of police officers, concluding no such effects. Edward R. Maguire, Justin Nix, and Bradley A. Campbell, "A War on Cops? The Effects of Ferguson on the Number of U.S. Police Officers Murdered in the Line of Duty," *Justice Quarterly* 34 (2017): 739–758; Bradley A. Campbell, Justin Nix, and Edward Maguire, "Is the Number of Citizens Fatally Shot by Police Increasing in the Post-Ferguson Era?" *Crime & Delinquency* 64 (2018): 398–420.
93. Gary A. Haugen and Victor Boutros, *The Locust Effect: Why the End of Poverty Requires the End of Violence* (New York: Oxford University Press, 2014), p. 43.

CHAPTER 3

—

Classical Criminology

"Classical" criminology is most often associated with the name of the Italian Cesare Bonesana, marchese de Beccaria (1738–1794). Beccaria's work was based on a kind of free-will rationalistic hedonism, a philosophical tradition going back many centuries. Beccaria proposed a simple model of human choice that was based on the rational calculation of costs and benefits. On the basis of this model, he argued that punishments should be proportional to the seriousness of offenses so that the cost of crime always exceeds its reward. Potential offenders then would be deterred—that is, rational calculation would lead them to avoid committing crime. This approach became the basis for all modern criminal justice systems.

Today, classicism includes three different but related strands of theory and research, all of which are strongly related to practical policy recommendations to reduce crime. The first focuses on theory and research about the deterrent effect of criminal justice policies. The "rational choice" perspective develops a more complex view of how offenders in particular situations calculate their costs and benefits. This approach leads to policy recommendations that focus on changing situations in order to influence a potential offender's calculations. The final approach argues that rationally calculating potential offenders respond to opportunities to commit crimes and that these opportunities are systematically related to the routine activities by which people live their lives. The policy recommendations focus on limiting criminal opportunities, rather than increasing the deterrent effect of criminal justice policies.

THE SOCIAL AND INTELLECTUAL BACKGROUND
OF CLASSICAL CRIMINOLOGY

Classical criminology emerged at a time when the naturalistic approach of the social contract thinkers was challenging the spiritualistic approach that had dominated European thinking for more than a thousand years. This spiritualistic approach formed the basis for criminal justice policies in most of Europe. Classical criminology was a protest against those criminal justice policies and against the spiritual explanations of crime on which they were based.

One of the most important sources for these spiritual explanations of crime was found in the theology of St. Thomas Aquinas (1225–1274), who lived five hundred years before Beccaria.[1] Aquinas argued that there was a God-given "natural law" that was revealed by observing, through the eyes of faith, people's natural tendency to do good rather than evil. The criminal law was based on and reflected this natural law. People who commit crime (i.e., violate the criminal law) therefore also commit sin (i.e., violate the natural law).

This spiritual explanation of crime, and others like it, formed the basis for the criminal justice policies in Europe at the time. Because crime was identified with sin, the state claimed the moral authority to use many horrible and gruesome tortures on criminals. It did so because the state claimed that it was acting in the place of God when it inflicted these horrible punishments on criminals.[2]

Beginning with Thomas Hobbes (1588–1678), "social contract" thinkers substituted naturalistic arguments for the spiritualistic arguments of people like Aquinas.[3] While Aquinas argued that people naturally do good rather than evil, Hobbes argued that people naturally pursue their own interests without caring about whether they hurt anyone else. This situation leads to a "war of each against all" in which no one is safe because all people look out only for themselves.

Hobbes then argued that people are rational enough to realize that this situation is not good for anyone. So people agree to give up their own selfish behavior as long as everyone else does the same thing at the same time. This is what Hobbes called the "social contract"—something like a peace treaty that everyone agrees to because they are all exhausted from the war of each against all. But the social contract needs an enforcement mechanism in case some people cheat and begin to pursue their own interests without regard to whether other people get hurt. This is the job of the state. According to Hobbes, everyone who agrees to the social contract also agrees to grant the state the right to use force to maintain the contract.

Other social contract philosophers, such as Locke (1632–1704), Montesquieu (1689–1755), Voltaire (1694–1778), and Rousseau (1712–1778) followed Hobbes in constructing philosophies that included a natural and rational basis for explaining crime and the state's response to it. These theories differed from each other in many ways, but all were rational and naturalistic approaches to explaining crime and punishment, as opposed to the dominant spiritualistic approach. By the middle of the 1700s, just before Beccaria wrote his book, these naturalistic ideas were well known and widely accepted by the intellectuals of the day, but they did not represent the thinking of the politically powerful groups that ruled the various states in Europe. Those ruling groups still held to the spiritual explanations of crime, so that crime was seen as manifesting the work of the devil. Consequently, the criminal justice systems of the time tended to impose excessive and cruel punishments on criminals.

Beccaria was a protest writer who sought to change these excessive and cruel punishments by applying the rationalist, social contract ideas to crime and criminal justice. His book was well received by intellectuals and some reform-minded rulers who had already accepted the general framework of social contract thinking.[4] Even more important for the book's acceptance, however, was the fact that the American Revolution of 1776 and the French Revolution of 1789 occurred soon after its publication in 1764.[5] These two revolutions were both guided by naturalistic ideas of the social contract philosophers. To these revolutionaries, Beccaria's book represented the latest and best thinking on the subject of crime and criminal justice. They therefore used his ideas as the basis for their new criminal justice systems. From America and France, Beccaria's ideas spread to the rest of the industrialized world.

BECCARIA AND THE CLASSICAL SCHOOL

Cesare Bonesana, marchese de Beccaria, was an indifferent student who had some interest in mathematics.[6] After completing his formal education, he joined a group of young men who met regularly to discuss literary and philosophical topics. Beccaria was given an assignment in March 1763 to write an essay on penology, a subject about which he knew nothing. The essay was completed in January 1764 and was published under the title "Dei deliti e delle pene" ("On Crimes and Punishments") in the small town of Livorno in July of that year, when Beccaria was twenty-six years old.[7]

In common with his contemporary intellectuals, Beccaria proposed various reforms to make criminal justice practice more logical and rational. He objected especially to the capricious and purely personal justice that the judges were dispensing and to the severe and barbaric punishments of the time. The following principles summarize Beccaria's ideas about how to make the criminal justice system both just and effective:

1. The role of the legislatures, according to Beccaria, should be to define crimes and to define specific punishments for each crime.[8] This view contrasted with the practice of Beccaria's time, when legislatures passed general laws and left the implementation up to the discretion of the judges.

2. The role of judges should be to determine guilt—that is, whether the defendant had committed a crime. Once that determination was made, then the judge should follow the law in determining the punishment. Instead of vast discretion, Beccaria argued that judges

should have no discretion whatsoever: "Nothing is more dangerous than the popular axiom that it is necessary to consult the spirit of the laws. It is a dam that has given way to a torrent of opinions."[9]

3. The seriousness of a crime is determined by the extent of harm that it inflicts on society. Beccaria argued that other factors were irrelevant in determining seriousness, including the intent of the offender: "Sometimes, with the best intentions, men do the greatest injury to society; at other times, intending the worst for it, they do the greatest good."[10]

4. The purpose of punishment is to deter crime. Therefore, punishments should be proportionate to the seriousness of the crime: "It is to the common interest not only that crimes not be committed, but also that they be less frequent in proportion to the harm they cause society. Therefore, the obstacles that deter man from committing crime should be stronger in proportion as they are contrary to the public good, and as the inducements to commit them are stronger."[11] This argument contrasted with the view that criminal punishments should convey religious symbolism, with the state acting in the place of God.

5. Punishments are unjust when their severity exceeds what is necessary to achieve deterrence: "For punishment to attain its end, the evil which it inflicts has only to exceed the advantage derivable from the crime; in this excess of evil one should include the certainty of punishment and the loss of the good which the crime might have produced. All beyond this is superfluous and for that reason tyrannical."[12]

6. Excessive severity not only fails to deter crime but actually increases it: "The severity of punishment of itself emboldens men to commit the very wrongs it is supposed to prevent; they are driven to commit additional crimes to avoid the punishment for a single one. The countries and times most notorious for severity of penalties have always been those in which the bloodiest and most inhumane of deeds were committed, for the same spirit of ferocity that guided the hand of the legislators also ruled that of the parricide and assassin."[13]

7. Punishments should be prompt: "The more promptly and the more closely punishment follows upon the commission of a crime, the more just and useful will it be. I say more just, because the criminal is thereby spared the useless and cruel torments of uncertainty. . . . I have said that the promptness of punishment is more useful because when the length of time that passes between the punishment and the misdeed is less, so much the stronger and more lasting in the human mind is the association of these two ideas, crime and punishment."[14]

8. Punishments should be certain: "The certainty of a punishment, even if it be moderate, will always make a stronger impression than the fear of another which is more terrible but combined with the hope of impunity; even the least evils, when they are certain, always terrify men's minds."[15]

Beccaria also emphasized that the laws should be published so that the public may know what they are and support their intent and purpose, that torture and secret accusations should be abolished, that capital punishment should be abolished and replaced by imprisonment, that jails be more humane, and that the law should not distinguish between the rich and the poor. Beccaria summarized his ideas in a brief conclusion to his book:[16]

> In order for punishment not to be, in every instance, an act of violence of one or of many against a private citizen, it must be essentially public, prompt, necessary, the least possible in the given circumstances, proportionate to the crimes, dictated by the laws.

Beccaria's ideas were quite radical for his time, so he published his book anonymously and defended himself in the introduction against charges that he was an unbeliever or a revolutionary. But the Roman Catholic Church condemned the book in 1766 because of its rationalistic ideas, and the book was placed on the church's Index of Forbidden Books, where it remained for more than two hundred years. Despite the opposition of the church, Beccaria's ideas were extremely well received by his contemporaries.

Following the French Revolution of 1789 Beccaria's principles were used as the basis for the French Code of 1791.[17] The great advantage of this code was that it set up a procedure that was easy to administer. It made the judge only an instrument to apply the law, and the law undertook to prescribe an exact penalty for every crime and every degree thereof. Puzzling questions about the reasons for or cause of behavior, the uncertainties of motive and intent, and the unequal consequences of an arbitrary rule were all deliberately ignored for the sake of administrative uniformity. This was the classical conception of justice—an exact scale of punishments for equal acts without reference to the individual involved or the circumstances in which the crime was committed.

As a practical matter, however, the Code of 1791 was impossible to enforce in everyday situations, and modifications were introduced. These modifications, all in the interest of greater ease of administration, are the essence of the so-called neoclassical school.

THE NEOCLASSICAL SCHOOL

The greatest practical difficulty in applying the Code of 1791 came from ignoring differences in the circumstances of particular situations.[18] The Code treated everyone exactly alike, in accordance with Beccaria's argument that only the act, and not the intent, should be considered in determining the punishment. Thus first offenders were treated the same as repeaters, minors were treated the same as adults, insane the same as sane, and so on. No society, of course, will permit its children and other helpless incompetents to be treated in the same manner as its professional criminals. The French were no exception. Modifications in practice began, and soon there were revisions of the Code itself.

The Code of 1810[19] tipped the lid just a little in permitting some discretion on the part of the judges. In the Revised French Code of 1819 there is definite provision for the exercise of discretion on the part of the judges in view of certain objective circumstances, but still no room for consideration of subjective intent. The set, impersonal features of even this revised Code Napoléon then became the point of attachment for a new school of reformers whose cry was against the injustice of a rigorous code and for the need of individualization and for discriminating judgment to fit individual circumstances. These efforts at revision and refinement in application of the classical theory of free will and complete responsibility—consideration involving age, mental condition, and extenuating circumstances—constitute what is often called the neoclassical school.

Thus, the neoclassical school represented no particular break with the basic doctrine of human nature that made up the common tradition throughout Europe at the time. The doctrine continued to be that humans are creatures guided by reason who have free will, and who therefore are responsible for their acts and can be controlled by fear of punishment. Hence, the pain from punishment must exceed the pleasure obtained from the criminal act; their free will determines the desirability of noncriminal conduct. The neoclassical school therefore represented primarily the modifications necessary for the administration of the criminal law based on classical theory that resulted from practical experience.

The neoclassical view is, with minor variations, "the major model of human behavior held to by agencies of social control in all advanced industrial societies (whether in the West or the East)."[20] Its widespread acceptance in contemporary legal systems is probably a result of the fact that this view provides support for the most fundamental assumption on which those systems are based. Classical criminology provides a general justification for the use of punishment in the control of crime. Since punishment for that purpose has always been used in the legal system, it should not be surprising that this is the theory to which legal authorities adhere.

In addition, classical theory was attractive to legal authorities for a more general reason. It is based on social contract theory, which holds that all people have a stake in the continued existence of the authority structure, since without it society would degenerate into a "war of each against all." Since crime contributes to this degeneration, it was ultimately in the best interests of all people, even criminals, to obey the law. Social contract theorists saw crime as a fundamentally irrational act, committed by people who, because of their shortsighted greed and passion, were incapable of recognizing their own long-term best interests.[21] The fact that crime was concentrated in the lower classes was taken to be a symptom of the fact that these classes were filled with irrational, dangerous people.[22]

The ease with which the classical system of justice could be administered rested largely on this view. It supported the uniform enforcement of laws without questioning whether those laws were fair or just. Specifically, social contract theorists did not take into account the fact that some societies are unfair. For some groups, the costs of adhering to the social contract may be few and the benefits great; for other groups, the costs may be great and the benefits few. The latter group will probably have less allegiance to the social contract, and this may be expressed in the form of a higher crime rate.

That is a far different perspective than the view that high-crime groups are filled with irrational and dangerous people. Rather than relying solely on punishments, it would imply that an additional way to reduce crime is to increase the benefits of adhering to the social contract among the high-crime groups in society.[23] This option was not attractive to the social contract theorists, who were themselves members of the propertied class. Thus, they addressed the problem in such a way as to justify the existence of inequalities. Hobbes, for example, argued that lower-class persons could adhere to the social contract if taught to believe that the status quo was inevitable.[24] Locke maintained that all persons were obligated to obey the laws of society, since all gave their "tacit consent" to the social contract. But he also argued that only persons with property were capable of making the laws, since only they were capable of the fully rational life and only they would defend the "natural right" of the unlimited accumulation of property.[25]

Beccaria's position on defending the status quo was somewhat confusing. He argued that it was natural for all to seek their own advantage, even at the expense of the common good, and that this was the source of crime. Thus he did not share the view of the social contract that the laws (which he said "have always favored the few and outraged the many") could impose massive injustices on the poor.[26] Thus, Beccaria was not solely concerned with the establishment of a system of punishment. He recognized the problem of inequality in society, and implied that it was wrong to punish lawbreakers when the laws themselves were unjust. This aspect of Beccaria's writing is sometimes ignored, so that classical criminology is identified with the social contract position that crime is essentially irrational.[27] Beccaria seems to have implied that there are broader social causes behind the crime problem, but he did not make these arguments specific. One of the effects of the neoclassical adaptation of Beccaria theory was to prune carefully all of these radical elements from his work, leaving only the easily administered system of punishment as the response to crime.[28]

FROM CLASSICAL THEORY TO DETERRENCE RESEARCH

During the 1800s the naturalistic approach of classical criminology became the basis for virtually all criminal justice systems in the world, replacing the spiritualistic philosophy that had been dominant up to that time. Beccaria's theory, however, was not subjected to empirical tests until 1968, when Gibbs published the first study that actually attempted to test the deterrence hypothesis.[29] Gibbs defined the certainty of punishment as the ratio between the number of admissions to state prisons for a given crime and the number of those crimes known to the police in the prior year. He defined severity as the mean number of months served by all persons convicted of a given crime who were in prison in that year. Gibbs found that greater certainty and severity of imprisonments was associated with fewer homicides in the fifty states for the 1960s (the effect of certainty was about twice as great as the effect of severity). Gibbs concluded that homicide may be deterred by both the certainty and severity of imprisonment.

The following year, Tittle computed similar statistics on certainty and severity for all seven "index offenses" in the FBI Uniform Crime Reports.[30] His results indicated that more certainty was associated with less crime for all seven offenses. However, with the exception of homicide, more severity (i.e., more time in prison) was associated with more crime, not less. Tittle concluded that the certainty of imprisonment deters crime, but that severity only deters crime when certainty is high.

In 1970, Chiricos and Waldo argued that Tittle's results on certainty could be explained by variations in police record-keeping.[31] If police in a particular jurisdiction handle many offenses informally without making an official record, then that jurisdiction will have lower official crime rates (because fewer criminal events are officially recorded) and greater certainty of imprisonment (because the more serious offenses are recorded, and those offenses are more likely to result in imprisonment). But if police meticulously make official records for every single criminal event, then that jurisdiction will have higher official crime rates (because more criminal events are officially recorded) but less certainty (because many of these criminal events will not be serious and therefore will not result in imprisonment).

Similarly, in 1974, Glaser and Zeigler challenged Gibbs's conclusion that increased imprisonment deters homicide.[32] They pointed out that death penalty states have substantially higher murder rates than do non–death penalty states, but murderers in death penalty states who are not executed serve shorter prison sentences than do murderers in non–death penalty states. This is the pattern that both Gibbs and Tittle had found: shorter prison sentences and higher murder rates (in death penalty states) and longer prison sentences and lower murder rates (in non–death penalty states). Glaser and Zeigler argued that it is unlikely that longer prison sentences deter homicide while the death penalty does not deter it. Instead, they attributed all three of these statistics (higher murder rates, use of the death penalty, and shorter prison sentences for murderers who are not executed) to a lower valuation of human life in states that use the death penalty.

This brief review of a few early studies gives a sense of the complexity of the issues involved in what otherwise would seem like a simple assertion about the effectiveness of criminal punishment. In 1975 this complexity was more fully revealed in a book by Gibbs, who presented a lengthy and sophisticated theoretical analysis of the issue along with an extensive review of relevant empirical research.[33] This book was followed in 1978 by a report from the National Academy of Sciences that focused directly on the research and reached the cautious conclusion that the evidence favoring a deterrent effect was greater than the evidence against it.[34]

NAGIN'S REVIEW OF DETERRENCE RESEARCH

In 1998 and again in 2013, Daniel Nagin conducted a comprehensive review of the evidence on deterrence. In this section, we summarize key findings from the latter review.[35] In the previous section, we discussed two key elements of deterrence: certainty of arrest and conviction and severity of punishment upon conviction. A third element is celerity, or swiftness of punishment. For example, the legal handling of white-collar offenders, who are likely out on bail, may drag on for years before resolution—this lack of celerity may weaken the deterrent effect of punishment for this type of offender. Deterrence may also be specific or general. Specific deterrence operates when one's punishment for a prior wrongdoing reduces the likelihood of subsequent offenses, whereas general deterrence relates to the threat of punishment (for example, seeing others punished prevents a potential law violator from engaging in criminal behavior). Nagin's review covers four categories of deterrent effects: imprisonment, policing, capital punishment, and perceptual deterrence.

Studies of the deterrent effect of imprisonment employ two general methodologies: cross-sectional (are levels of imprisonment in different jurisdictions causally associated with different levels of criminal behavior?) and longitudinal (do changes in imprisonment over time result in a changes in criminal behavior?). Both types of studies may have methodological and theoretical shortcomings.[36] Nonetheless, according to Nagin, several studies have demonstrated "convincing evidence of the deterrent effect of imprisonment on incarceration."[37] For example, the immediate threat of imprisonment, even short-term, for failing to pay court-ordered fines has been shown to be an effective deterrent—in this instance certainty is high, as is celerity, and while severity is only short-term incarceration, it seems draconian when compared to the option of paying a fine and staying out of jail.[38] Project HOPE in Hawaii, an intervention designed to reduce positive drug tests, arrests, and imprisonment, accomplished this by administering short-but-certain periods of lockup for failed drug tests and other probation violations by offenders enrolled in the program.[39] And California's "Three Strikes and You're Out" approach was shown to have a reduction in arrests for offenders who had already been convicted of two strikes (compared to those whose trial for a second strike resulted in a conviction of a nonstrikeable offense).[40] Laws such as California's Three Strikes can bring about a lengthy prison sentence (e.g., twenty-five years) for a conviction that otherwise would have resulted in only a few years. In terms of simply increasing already-long sentences, Nagin says there may be a "concave relationship between the magnitude of deterrent effects and sentence length, which implies decreasing marginal deterrence returns to increases in sentence length."[41]

Policing may deter would-be offenders from criminal behavior in two primary ways—overall size of police staffing levels, and policing strategies such as hotspots policing, problem-oriented policing, and Operation Ceasefire.[42] Police strength (manpower) has been shown to deter crime to some extent, as have strategies, at times with controversial results. See Chapter 2 of this volume pertaining to size, hotspots policing, and other general strategies, and see the section later in the current chapter for a discussion of ceasefire programs.

One of the most contentious areas of study within deterrence theory is whether capital punishment deters homicide. In 1975, Isaac Ehrlich published a study arguing that every execution prevents seven to eight homicides; a subsequent report by the National Research Council criticized the analysis and concluded there was no convincing evidence of this.[43] Over the next thirty-some years researchers continued to address the question, but an updated report by the National Research Council in 2012 (coauthored by Nagin) formed the same conclusion: "Research to date on the effect of capital punishment on homicide is not informative about whether capital punishment decreases, increases, or has no effect on homicide rates."[44] Three primary factors affecting the ability of these studies to accurately determine whether there is a deterrent effect are that a small portion of homicides are eligible for the death penalty, and of these few result in a death sentence, and even fewer result in an execution; studies are not able to demonstrate that would-be murderers perceive that they may be caught, sentenced to death, and executed; and that certain assumptions of many statistical models employed by this research are not defendable.[45]

The final type of deterrence in Nagin's review examines the extent to which people perceive risks of sanctions and how they respond to those perceptions. Dated general population surveys showed that only a small proportion of the public (but the majority of incarcerated offenders) was able to correctly identify maximum penalties for various offense types, such as robbery, but were generally able to rank order severity of punishment across offenses (e.g., robbery is punished more severely than larceny). General population surveys on more prevalently committed offenses such as marijuana use and drunk driving showed a respectable level of identification of risks of apprehension for these offenses and knowledge of policies.[46] *Accuracy* of perceptions of arrest, celerity, and severity is important in determining deterrent effects of such perceptions.

Perceptions of risk may be impacted by one's prior experience in the criminal justice system. For example, Pogarsky and Piquero argue that there is a "resetting effect" in which offenders lower their perceived certainty of punishment after they are actually are punished, on the basis of the (seemingly illogical) reasoning that once you have been caught, you are less likely to be caught again.[47] They found that this resetting effect occurs with low-rate offenders but not with high-rate offenders. They suggested that this effect occurs because chronic, experienced offenders do not consider the certainty of punishment in their decision-making. If offenders alter their perceptions (whether logically or not) as they gain experience in offending and in getting caught, then this presents a problem of causality in perceptual research. Other research has shown that being arrested increases subjective probabilities of apprehension, but mostly for less experienced offenders, who base perceptions of risk more on their current arrest ratios (arrests per law violations) than their prior subjective probabilities (more experienced offenders place more weight on prior perceptions).[48]

Nagin states that is important to understand two other things about deterrence. First, the punishment itself (such as experiences within prison) may actually *increase* one's criminal behavior. Second, it can be difficult to separate incapacitation effects from deterrent effects. Incapacitation means that incarcerated individuals cannot themselves carry out crimes while locked up (unless they order them done by others), whereas deterrence relates to their decisions made by the threat of apprehension and punishment.[49]

RATIONAL CHOICE AND OFFENDING

The classical model of human choice assumes that offenders rationally calculate the costs and benefits of committing a crime. Proponents of several theories have examined the situations and circumstances in which potential offenders engage in such rational calculations and find that they have the opportunity to commit a crime.[50] These theories do not explain the motivation to commit crime; rather, they assume that there are always people around who will commit a crime if given a chance.

For example, looting often accompanies large-scale disasters such as floods, earthquakes, violent storms, wars, and riots. Homeowners and storeowners flee the disaster, leaving their property unprotected. The police are often busy with more pressing matters, such as saving human lives. People who would not normally commit crime may take advantage of the opportunities in the disaster situation and steal whatever they think they can get away with. Because these theories focus on situations that offer opportunities for rational, calculating potential offenders to commit crime, they are sometimes called "opportunity theories."

The forgoing example of looting involves "situational selection," which describes the types of situations that motivated offenders select to commit their crimes.[51] In general, motivated offenders consider the ease of access to the target, the likelihood of being observed or caught, and the expected reward. This perspective assumes that offenders are largely rational in their decision-making processes, so the process is associated with rational choice theories of crime.[52]

Rational choice theories develop, at a much greater length, Beccaria's original simple model of human choice, as described earlier in this chapter. Their goal, however, is to consider how potential offenders may weigh the costs and benefits in particular situations and then to determine how those situations may be changed so that potential offenders will decide not to commit crime. Thus, rational choice theories are associated with "situational crime prevention,"[53] rather than with the deterrent effects of the certainty and severity of punishments.

These theories assume that all crime is purposeful, committed with the intention to benefit the offenders. The cardinal rule of rational choice theories is never to dismiss a criminal act as wanton or senseless or irrational, but rather to seek to understand the purposes of the offender.[54] Such theories also assume that the rationality of criminals is always limited—that is, "in seeking to benefit themselves, offenders do not always succeed in making the best decisions because of the risks and uncertainty involved."[55] Finally, the theories assume that offenders' decision-making is quite different for different types of crimes.[56] For example, the same offenders may commit both robbery and rape, but these offenses are committed against different victims, in different settings, with different weapons, and with different purposes. Thus, situational crime prevention must have a crime-specific focus. On the basis of these principles, rational choice theories recommend that situations be changed to increase the perceived effort and risks, reduce the perceived benefits, and thus alter the offender's decision-making process and subsequent behavior.[57] This approach has been applied in many different situations, including airport baggage screening (which has virtually eliminated airplane hijackings); target hardening in post offices, convenience stores, and banks (which has achieved reductions in robberies); and the prevention of gatherings of drunken youths at bar-closing time (which has reduced alcohol-induced violence).[58] In a related use of the rational choice approach, crime prevention through environmental design (CPTED) seeks to alter human behavior by changing the physical landscape; such efforts include the use of improved lighting, enhanced natural surveillance, and the reallocation of gathering areas.[59] Rational choice–based crime prevention measures have also targeted corporate offenders, who typically consider future consequences and choose their crimes after considering the risks and benefits.[60]

Critics of situational crime prevention have questioned its ultimate benefits, claiming that crime is merely "displaced," moved in time or space in response to concentrated prevention efforts.[61] Research, however, has found that displacement is "seldom total and often inconsequential" and that surrounding locals often experience a "diffusion" of benefits from the specifically targeted areas.[62] Another criticism of the rational choice approach, more broadly, relates to the role that substances or certain emotional states (such as anger) may play in criminal behavior. For example, alcohol is involved in many instances of violent crime. Some question whether people who are under the influence of alcohol rely on logical assessments of costs and benefits when deciding whether to engage in crime. If the rational choice model deteriorates under conditions of intoxication, this significantly affects the model's usefulness to the extent that intoxicants are prevalent among criminal offenders. As one example of research on this issue, Exum randomly assigned subjects to varying degrees of alcohol intoxication (drinking vodka) and anger (being falsely told they were a half-hour late to their appointment), and tested the aggressiveness of their reaction to a conflict scenario.[63] Although alcohol and anger did not increase the perceived benefits of aggression or decrease the perceived costs, when the subjects were angry and intoxicated, their risk-benefit calculus played a far weaker role in predicting their level of aggression, compared to subjects who were not angry or drunk. In other words, these people may be able to perform cost-benefit analysis, but ultimately their behavior may occur independently of such analysis.[64]

ROUTINE ACTIVITIES AND VICTIMIZATION

An approach similar to rational choice theories of crime has been used to explain differences in the rates at which groups are victimized.[65] Hindelang and his colleagues argued that the differences in risks of victimization are associated with differences in lifestyles, which they described in terms of "routine daily activities," both vocational activities (work, school, keeping house, etc.) and leisure activities.[66] In general, they argued that people who are younger, male, unmarried, poor, and African American have higher risks of victimization than do people who are older, female, married, wealthy, and European American because the former group has an increased tendency to be away from home, especially at night; to engage in public activities while away from home; and to associate with people who are likely to be offenders.[67] These habits lead to an increased risk of property and personal victimization.

Cohen and Felson argued that certain changes in the modern world have provided motivated offenders with a greatly increased range of opportunities to commit crime.[68] They pointed out that most violent and property crimes involve direct contact between the offender and the "target"—that is, the person or property of the victim.[69] These crimes therefore require the convergence in time and space of a motivated offender, a suitable target, and the absence of a capable guardian (police) to prevent the crime. Most criminology theories assume that changes in crime rates reflect changes in the number of motivated offenders or changes in the strength of their motivation. But Cohen and Felson argued that changes in crime rates may instead be explained in terms of changes in the availability of targets and the absence of capable guardians. This is exactly what happens when looting follows a disaster—there is no increase in criminal motivation, but suddenly there are many available targets and few capable guardians.

Cohen and Felson argued that there has been a great increase in the availability of targets and in the absence of capable guardians in the modern world as a result of changes in routine activities—that is, how normal people live their lives in terms of work, home life, child-rearing, education, and leisure. When people are home, they function as guardians for their own property. But the routine activities of modern life have led to the "dispersion of activities away from family and household," which means that many households no longer have capable guardians for extended and fairly predictable periods. In addition, there has been a large increase in goods that are portable and therefore suitable as targets for thieves. For example, Cohen and Felson calculated that in 1975, $26.44 in motor vehicles and parts was stolen for each $100 of these goods that were consumed. In comparison, $6.82 worth of electronic appliances, and 12 cents worth of furniture and nonelectronic household durables, were stolen for every $100 that were consumed. The vast differences in the worth of goods that are stolen are due to the suitability of the goods as targets for theft. Cohen and Felson then demonstrated that changes in crime rates in the United States from 1947 to 1974 can be explained largely by these trends. In 1947, people were home more of the time and more of what they owned was similar to furniture; by 1974, people were away from home more of the time and more of what they owned was similar to cars and electronic appliances. So despite large increases in crime during that period, there may have been no changes in the number of motivated offenders or in the reasons for the offenders' motivations.

The related research of environmental criminologists has sought to explain the spatial and temporal aspects of offenders' behavior, asserting that offenders typically commit their crimes in bounded areas that are consistent with their routine activities and do not travel far from such sites in search of criminal opportunities.[70] As McNeely says in her review of lifestyle-routine activities (L-RAT), it "explains crime events as the products of day-to-day activities that influence the extent to which opportunities for crime exist."[71] Whereas earlier theories of routine activities were primarily at the macro level, most recent applications are at the micro level. She discusses three categories of these: individual victimization, individual offending, and crime and place.

Five factors mediate the relationship between victim characteristics (such as race, age, gender) and victimization: exposure, proximity, attractiveness, guardianship, and crime properties, as proposed by Cohen and colleagues.[72] More visible people or objects are likelier to be victimized. This means that victims more similar demographically to potential offenders are more likely to experience victimization by them, as their lifestyles result in greater physical intersection based on the sorts of activities they engage in. Physical proximity is also a key predictor of victimization; motivated offenders are more likely to take advantage of people nearby, rather than travel long distances. Individuals who are more attractive (financially or symbolically) are more prone to victimization. The greater guardianship one has, the less likely one is to be victimized. This may include physical guardianship (locking windows), self-protection (carrying mace), or social guardianship (having neighbors watch their backs). Lastly, crime specificity can influence victimization, because exposure, proximity, attractiveness, and guardianship are more likely to play a role for instrumental type of crimes, such as theft, robbery, or burglary, rather than expressive crimes such as assault or rape. Even across instrumental crimes, different factors are more important when predicting victimization of different crime types; for example, burglaries may require more advance planning (and knowledge of victim behavior) than spur-of-the moment street robberies ("snatch-and-grabs").[73] In addition to these five mediators, recent research has also shown that individuals with low self-control (see Chapter 10 in this book for an explanation of this term) are more likely to be victimized, given their propensity toward riskier behavior.[74]

Just as lifestyle can regulate individuals' probability of victimization, it can also affect the motivation and opportunities of offenders. These include such activities as unstructured socializing with delinquent friends, time spent in center-city areas, use of alcohol, and time spent driving.[75] Additionally, "handlers" may reduce opportunities for people to offend. These include parents, significant others, teachers, and probation officers, through their informal social control and perhaps formal supervision.[76] Handlers' success in preventing crime is influenced by their social connection to offenders, their willingness and opportunities to intervene, and understanding of situations that lend themselves to higher offense propensities.[77]

L-RAT has also been extended to the study of crime at micro-places,[78] such as blocks, plazas, residential addresses, bars, liquor stores, and other hotspots. A well-known study in Minneapolis showed that about half of all calls for service came from a mere three percent of addresses.[79] At public micro-places, potential offenders may hang out there frequently and have great familiarity with their geographic and guardianship features, as well as with the patterns of potential victims in the area. Empirical analysis of interactions at micro-places has become more sophisticated. For example, Olaghere and Lum recently published a study of interactions of drug dealers in Baltimore, using systematic social observation (SSO), analyzing closed-circuit television (CCTV) footage of illegal transactions before, during, and after the transactions took place.[80] They explore the micro-routines used by drug dealers in managing their environment—selecting the buyers, monitoring potential threats, handling the transactions, and so forth. Applications of routine activities theory have also transcended physical interactions to the world of cybercrime, analyzing, for example, how different types of online guardianship are associated with varying probabilities of victimization through identity theft.[81]

FOCUSED DETERRENCE: OPERATION CEASEFIRE

The past two decades have witnessed a different sort of deterrence strategy that has its theoretical underpinnings in both rational choice and routine activity theories, and has produced some very encouraging evaluations of its effects on crime. In discussing the heavily studied relationship between imprisonment and crime, Durlauf and Nagin explored the question of whether both could be reduced (rather than, for example, increased imprisonment being necessary for reduced crime).[82] After reviewing a number of focused deterrence studies, they concluded that rather than using imprisonment wholesale to deter crime, it may be much more strategic to rely on modern police interventions that target high-risk individuals and groups and may have not only a specific deterrence value but also a general deterrence toward other similarly situated individuals and groups. Both routine activities and rational choice theories lead police to systematically alter the opportunities available to offenders. A shift in cost-benefit analysis can make it less desirable for offenders to engage in crime. Interventions that target the most dangerous people and groups may be the most impactful. This was the strategy adopted by one of the earliest and best known of these focused deterrence programs, Boston's Operation Ceasefire, the brainchild of David Kennedy, assisted by Anne Piehl and Anthony Braga in its design, implementation, and evaluation.[83]

The backdrop to Operation Ceasefire was the explosion of homicides in Boston committed by youth. From 1984 to 1994 handgun homicide victimizations committed by those younger than eighteen went up by 418 percent, and those with other types of guns increased by 125 percent.[84] In 1995 the Boston Gun Project began as a problem-oriented policing program aimed at reducing youth homicides in Boston (defining youth as under twenty-one). This project would implement Ceasefire in 1996. Ceasefire had two primary strategies: attack the supply of guns to youth and generate strong deterrence to gang violence. The first was a supply-side strategy and incorporated traditional enforcement strategies, identifying firearm sources by gun tracing and shutting down traffickers.[85] The second strategy—referred commonly to as "pulling levers"—was Ceasefire's unique, innovative approach to deterrence.

The Gun Project's analysis found that 1,300 gang members, fewer than 1 percent of the same age group in the city, accounted for at least 60 percent of all youth homicide in Boston. Of the 125 offenders associated with 155 youth homicides over a five-year period, 77 percent (96) had had an average of 9.7 arraignments on criminal charges. In other words, a small body of gang youth were high-rate offenders and responsible for a great amount of homicide.[86] The "few account for many" concept is pervasive in criminal justice and is evidenced by such findings as that of Wolfgang, Figlio, and Sellin in Philadelphia (6% of a youth cohort were responsible for more than half of all its offenses)[87] and Lawrence Sherman's in Minneapolis (3% of the city's street addresses were linked to 50% of calls for police service).[88]

Ceasefire researchers noted that gang members' high rates of criminal offending made them vulnerable targets for enforcement because they were committing so many different types of offenses, often openly; were often on restrictions due to parole, probation, or being out on bail; and even if they couldn't be easily convicted of a given serious crime, their daily lives could become quite unpleasant if they were the subject of heavy, focused enforcement efforts. While traditional enforcement efforts also have taken advantage of these vulnerabilities, Ceasefire's unique approach, rather than attempt to wipe out gangs altogether, was to focus entirely on eliminating *violence*.[89] This could be accomplished by "pulling every lever" available on the gang or gangs in question: shutting down drug markets, serving warrants, enforcing probation restrictions, making disorder arrests, dealing more strictly with any resulting cases as they made their way through prosecution and adjudication, deploying federal enforcement powers, and the like.[90]

Knowing that deterrent operations can only have success if their targets know about them, Ceasefire engaged a number of unique "advertising" tactics to ensure this. These included formal sit-downs with selected gangs; talking with inmates in juvenile correctional facilities; attending school assemblies; one-on-one conversations between police gang officers, probation, and parole officers, with gang members and at times their families; and employing Boston gang outreach workers to communicate Ceasefire's existence and message to gang members.[91] The message was, in essence, to quit the violence or face the mammoth wrath of the criminal justice system coming at all angles.

An evaluation of Ceasefire examined Boston youth homicides (age twenty-four and under) prior to (January 1991 to May 1996) and after (June 1996 to June 1998) the intervention was put into effect.[92] During the preintervention period, these homicides averaged forty-four per year. The intervention was put into place in May 1996. Homicides fell to twenty-six in 1996 and to fifteen in 1997 (which was the smallest number of youth homicides in Boston since 1976). Overall, the Ceasefire intervention was associated with a 63 percent decrease in youth homicides. Other measures of gang violence were also examined, and the evaluation showed that Ceasefire was associated with a 32 percent drop in monthly calls of shots fired, and a 25 percent decrease in youth gun assaults. The evaluation controlled for other Boston-specific factors that may correlate with youth homicide (such as employment rate and changes in youth population). Additionally, it examined changes in youth homicide rates in other cities during the same time period to make sure the dramatic drop in Boston was not experienced in cities without the intervention.

Although this evaluation produced encouraging results, some researchers pointed to its weak quasi-experimental design.[93] The outcome measure was overall youth homicides (and shootings) in Boston and did not test whether the intervention affected the behavior of the particular gangs being targeted. Additionally, there were no control groups in the design (no examination of the behavior of gangs not being targeted). A later evaluation (2014) of Boston Ceasefire was published by Braga and colleagues, incorporating a stronger research design.[94] Ceasefire was discontinued in 2000, despite only five gang-motivated homicides in 1999; this increased to thirty-seven by 2006. In January 2007 a new commissioner reinstated Ceasefire, and nineteen gangs were targeted from this time through December 2010. This evaluation was able to match comparison gangs to sixteen of the nineteen Ceasefire gangs (based on a number of similarities), thus determining whether the behavior of Ceasefire-targeted gangs varied from the behavior of the comparison gangs. It "estimated that the reconstituted Boston Ceasefire intervention generated a 31.3 [percent] reduction in total shootings for treated gangs relative to total shootings for matched comparison gangs."[95]

Operation Ceasefire has been replicated in one form or another in many cities other than Boston, including Los Angeles, Indianapolis, Chicago, Baltimore, Minneapolis, Lowell (Massachusetts), and Cincinnati, with mostly positive results in the cities in which efforts were evaluated. Some focused deterrence strategies address not just groups but also problematic (e.g., repeat) offenders, such as Chicago's CeaseFire (Project Safe Neighborhoods), targeting parolees tied to guns and gangs who were returning to dangerous neighborhoods,[96] and HOPE (Hawaii Opportunity with Probation Enforcement), targeting substance-abusing probationers.[97]

The tide of focused deterrence interventions such as Ceasefire-type programs is swelling across the United States, and as Papachristos (from the Chicago version) has stated, "In a sense, CeaseFire has become a *social movement*, not simply an intervention program."[98] Some have argued that the politics and political careers intertwined with programs like CeaseFire have interfered with the process of neutral and objective scientific evaluation.[99] As these programs continue to expand, pressure has mounted to ensure quality evaluations measure their impact. Braga and Weisburd—after a comprehensive search of over two thousand potentially relevant studies—identified eleven that met their criteria "whether the interventions involved focused deterrence strategies and whether the studies used randomized controlled trial designs or nonrandomized quasi-experimental designs."[100] Ten of the eleven studies, they found, demonstrated strong reductions in criminal behavior resulting from the strategies; still, Braga and Weisburd pointed to the need for the greater use of randomized experimental designs when evaluating these programs.[101]

While focused deterrence interventions use primarily punitive measures, many involve a carrot-and-stick approach, which combines pulling levers with providing an array of social services such as social work consultations, job opportunities, and counseling. The message is, "If you cause harm, we will come down on you, but if you conform, we will help you integrate (or reintegrate) into law-abiding society." In fact, in Ceasefire programs, during "call-ins," gang members with criminal evidence against them are called to forums where they meet not only an array of law enforcement personnel but also providers of social services. The carrot-and-stick approach is especially compatible with the rational choice perspective, because it addresses both sides of the calculus: rather than just deterring through punitive sanctions, it offers special benefits to not offend—it makes the cost-benefit analysis more complex and can result in changing the overall motivation of offenders in a fashion beyond the simple desire not to get caught or punished. Tillyer, Engel, and Lovins argue that in fact, in the long run, the sustainability of focused deterrence strategies will depend on their ability to consistently offer offenders a meaningful package of social services.[102]

CONCLUSIONS

This chapter has reviewed criminological theory and research focusing on deterrence, rational choice, and routine activities. All three approaches are based on the relatively simple classical model of human choice, as originally proposed by Beccaria. In general, none of this research has directly attempted to test that model. Rather, each approach has developed policies that should reduce crime if its model is correct. Research has then tested the effectiveness of these policies, and the results are taken as evidence about the validity of the underlying classical model of human choice.

In general, support for the deterrence hypothesis is much greater today than it was twenty years ago. Nevertheless, the research seems to indicate that current policies place too much emphasis on the severity of punishments and not enough on their certainty. These research findings are consistent with Beccaria's argument that too much severity in punishments actually is a cause of crime. In addition, the massive explosion in imprisonment in the United States since 1970 appears to have had some impact on crime, but not as much impact as other factors that are unrelated to deterrence. The overall conclusion at this point, while tentative, seems to be that further increases in the severity of punishments will probably have no impact on crime reduction and, for various reasons, may actually increase crime. Increases in the certainty of apprehension, conviction, and punishment, on the other hand, will probably result in further reductions in crime. Some argue that punishment or simulated punishment may actually have the opposite effect of deterrence. For example, Scared Straight, a once-popular program that takes delinquents and at-risk juveniles into prisons to observe prison life and interact with adult inmates, may actually increase the future criminality of these adolescents.[103] While the process by which this happens is only speculative, one possibility is that Scared Straight glorifies prison life instead of deterring at-risk juveniles who frequently emphasize toughness and masculinity when around peers. And with the death penalty, some researchers, when explaining higher rates of homicide in jurisdictions that utilize capital punishment, hypothesize there may be a brutalization effect that tends to devalue human life, thereby increasing homicide.[104]

A greater potential for crime reduction is probably found in the rational choice and routine activities approaches, which base their policy recommendations on altering the situations and circumstances in which potential offenders rationally calculate the costs and benefits of crime. Although these approaches are relatively new, they have already been credited by some analysts with playing a role in the drop in crime of the 1990s. And, while rational choice–based crime control policies have considerable long-range potential for achieving continued crime reduction, concern has been raised as to whether such efforts that are reliant upon increased security, surveillance, and policing can be implemented in a manner that protects community interests without threatening civil liberties and creating a fortress society or a culture of control.[105] Focused deterrence policies such as Operation Ceasefire, which combine deterrence with incentives, have had great initial success in reducing crime among targeted offenders or would-be offenders; it is unclear at this point to what extent civil liberties may be affected by these interventions.

KEY TERMS

deterrence
rational calculation/choice
routine activities
criminal opportunities
natural law
classical and neoclassical schools
social contract thinkers
discretion
spirit of the laws
promptness/swiftness of
    punishment (celerity)
certainty of punishment
severity of punishment
Project HOPE
published laws

empirical tests
perception of risks
perceptual deterrence
scenario research
deterrable offenders
resetting effect
brutalization effect
routine activities
L-RAT (lifestyle routine
    activities theory)
situational crime prevention
pulling levers
focused deterrence strategies
Operation Ceasefire
Scared Straight

DISCUSSION QUESTIONS

1. In what ways are Cesare Beccaria's ideas embodied in modern penal codes and sentencing schemes?
2. What findings has deterrence research made regarding the certainty and severity of punishment? How would you explain these findings?
3. What is the difference between specific deterrence and general deterrence? What sorts of crimes are more likely to be deterred by each of these types of deterrence?
4. What type of offenders would be termed deterrable offenders? Specifically, what makes these types of offenders more deterrable?
5. As a policymaker, how would you make the objective risks of getting caught known to potential offenders?
6. What happened to US crime rates in the 1990s? Using a multifactor approach, how would you explain this trend?
7. How do routine activities theorists explain the rises and declines of national crime rates?
8. Can you think of any hotspots or micro-places near your residence where criminal activity is abundant? What features of those areas may contribute to increased criminality?
9. How might L-RAT be used to educate people how to avoid being a crime victim?
10. How are focused deterrence strategies different from other types of deterrence?
11. Why is advertising an important feature of deterrence?
12. How does a carrot-and-stick approach work when addressing chronic violence?

NOTES

1. A brief review of Aquinas's ideas can be found in Thomas J. Bernard, *The Consensus-Conflict Debate* (New York: Columbia University Press, 1983), chap. 3.
2. Piers Beirne, *Inventing Criminology* (Albany: State University of New York Press, 1993), pp. 11–12. A widely quoted example from this period was the execution of Damiens, who had stabbed the king of France in 1757. See Michel Foucault, *Discipline and Punish* (New York: Pantheon, 1977), pp. 3–5.
3. A discussion of Hobbes and his relation to Aquinas can be found in Bernard, *The Consensus-Conflict Debate*, chap. 4.
4. Graeme Newman and Pietro Marongiu, "Penological Reform and the Myth of Beccaria," *Criminology* 28 (1990): 325–346.
5. Beccaria's work was extensively quoted by Thomas Jefferson, John Adams, and other American revolutionaries. See David A. Jones, *History of Criminology* (New York: Greenwood Press, 1986), pp. 43–46.

6. An account of the life and work of Beccaria may be found in Beirne, *Inventing Criminology*, chap. 2. See also Randy Martin, Robert J. Mutchnick, and W. Timothy Austin, *Criminological Thought: Pioneers Past and Present* (New York: Macmillan, 1990); and Elio D. Monachesi, "Pioneers in Criminology: Cesare Beccaria (1738–1794)," *Journal of Criminal Law, Criminology and Police Science* 46 (1955): 439–449, reprinted in Hermann Mannheim, *Pioneers in Criminology* (Montclair, NJ: Patterson Smith, 1972), pp. 36–50.

7. Cesare Beccaria, *On Crimes and Punishments*, translated by Henry Paolucci (Indianapolis: Bobbs-Merrill, 1963).

8. Ibid., pp. 13–14.

9. Ibid., pp. 14–15.

10. Ibid., pp. 64–65.

11. Ibid., p. 62.

12. Ibid.

13. Ibid., pp. 43–44.

14. Ibid., pp. 55–56.

15. Ibid., pp. 58–59.

16. Ibid., p. 99.

17. John L. Gillin, *Criminology and Penology*, 3d ed. (New York: Appleton-Century-Crofts, 1945), p. 229.

18. This section, as well as the two paragraphs immediately preceding it, are taken largely from the 4th edition of this volume (Vold, Bernard, and Snipes, 1998). Several anonymous reviewers of the 7th edition strongly suggested an expansion of Beccaria's work and the neoclassical school be included in the current (8th) edition, and we agreed it was appropriate to do so.

19. In addition to the Revolutionary Code of 1791, other Napoleonic codes of the period often mentioned are Code de procédure civile, 1806; Code de commerce, 1807; Code d'instruction criminelle, 1980; the Code pénal, 1810; and the revised Code pénal, 1819.

20. Ian Taylor, Paul Walton, and Jock Young, *The New Criminology* (New York: Harper and Row, 1973), pp. 9–10.

21. Ibid., p. 3.

22. See, for example, the discussion of Locke's view of the irrationality of the lower classes in C. B. MacPherson, *The Political Theory of Possessive Individualism* (New York: Oxford University Press, 1962), pp. 232–238.

23. E.g., James Q. Wilson, *Thinking about Crime* (New York: Vintage, 1983), pp. 117–144.

24. MacPherson, *The Political Theory of Possessive Individualism*, p. 98.

25. Ibid., pp. 247–251.

26. Beccaria, *On Crimes and Punishments*, p. 43.

27. Taylor, Walton, and Young, *The New Criminology*, pp. 1–10.

28. For a radical interpretation of Beccaria's theory, see Lynn Mcdonald, *The Sociology of Law and Order* (London: Faber and Faber, 1976), pp. 40–42. McDonald argues that Beccaria is a "complete and recognizable conflict theory."

29. Jack P. Gibbs, "Crime, Punishment and Deterrence," *Southwestern Social Science Quarterly* 48 (1968): 515–530. In the same year, the economist Gary S. Becker ("Crime and Punishment: An Economic Approach," *Journal of Political Economy* 76 [1968]: 169–217) published a largely theoretical argument

that both crime and criminal justice could be explained as choices resulting from cost-benefit analyses.

30. Charles R. Tittle, "Crime Rates and Legal Sanctions," *Social Problems* 16 (1969): 409–423. Index offenses include murder and nonnegligent manslaughter, forcible rape, robbery, aggravated assault, burglary, larceny-theft, and motor vehicle theft.

31. Theodore G. Chiricos and Gordon P. Waldo, "Punishment and Crime: An Examination of Some Empirical Evidence," *Social Problems* 18 (1970): 200–217. Chiricos and Waldo, in turn, were challenged by Charles H. Logan, "General Deterrent Effects of Imprisonment," *Social Forces* 51 (1972): 64–73.

32. Daniel Glaser and Max S. Zeigler, "Use of the Death Penalty v. Outrage at Murder," *Crime and Delinquency* 20 (1974): 333–338. See also Glaser, "A Response to Bailey," *Crime and Delinquency* 22 (1976): 40–43.

33. Jack P. Gibbs, *Crime, Punishment and Deterrence* (New York: Elsevier, 1975). Two other largely theoretical analyses were published just prior to Gibbs's work: Franklin E. Zimring and Gordon J. Hawkins, *Deterrence: The Legal Threat in Crime Control* (Chicago: University of Chicago Press, 1973); and Johannes Andenaes, *Punishment and Deterrence* (Ann Arbor: University of Michigan Press, 1974). However, Gibbs was the first author to extensively review empirical research on the matter.

34. Alfred Blumstein, Jacqueline Cohen, and Daniel Nagin, eds., *Deterrence and Incapacitation: Estimating the Effects of Criminal Sanctions on Crime Rates* (Washington, DC: National Academy of Sciences, 1978), p. 7. See also Philip Cook, "Research in Criminal Deterrence: Laying the Groundwork for the Second Decade," in *Crime and Justice: A Review of Research*, vol. 2, ed. Norval Morris and Michael Tonry (Chicago: University of Chicago Press, 1980), pp. 211–268. Cook's article also focused on the research but reached the more optimistic conclusion that "the criminal justice system, ineffective as it may seem in many areas, has an overall crime deterrent effect of great magnitude" (p. 213).

35. Daniel S. Nagin, "Deterrence in the Twenty-First Century," *Crime and Justice: A Review of Research* 42 (2013): 199–263; Nagin, "Deterrence: A Review of the Evidence by a Criminologist for Economists," *American Review of Economics* 5 (2013): 83–105. These articles both cover the same topics, for the most part, but the review for economists is more compact; page numbers in citations to Nagin's review in this section will refer to this work.

36. Nagin, "Deterrence,", p. 86. For a comprehensive treatment of these flaws, see Daniel S. Nagin and Steven N. Durlauf, "Imprisonment and Crime: Can Both be Reduced?," *Criminology and Public Policy* 10 (2011): 9–54.

37. Nagin, "Deterrence," p. 86.

38. Ibid., p. 87, referring to David Weisburd, Tomer Einat, and Matt Kowalski, "The Miracle of the Cells: An Experimental Study of Interventions to Increase Payment of Court-Ordered Financial Obligations," *Criminology and Public Policy* 7 (2008): 9–36.

39. Nagin, "Deterrence," p. 87, citing Angela Hawken and Mark Kleinman, *Managing Drug-Involved Probationers with Swift and Certain Sanctions: Evaluating Hawaii's Project HOPE. rep 230444* (Washington, DC: National Institute of Justice, 2009).

40. Nagin, "Deterrence," p.87, discussing Erik Helland and Alexander Tabarrok, "Does Three Strikes Deter? A Nonparametric Estimation," *Journal of Human Resources* 42 (2007): 309–330. However, this research was conducted before California voters reformed the Three Strikes law in 2012, requiring the third strike to be for a serious felony, rather than any felony.

41. Nagin, "Deterrence," p. 101.

42. Ibid., pp. 88–91.

43. Ibid., p. 91. See Isaac Ehrlich, "The Deterrent Effect of Capital Punishment: A Question of Life and Death," *American Economic Review* 65 (1975): 397–417, and National Research Council, *Deterrence and Incapacitation: Estimating the Effects of Criminal Sanctions on Crime Rates* (Washington, DC: National Academy, 1978).

44. Nagin, "Deterrence," p. 91. See National Research Council, *Deterrence and the Death Penalty*, ed. Daniel S. Nagin and John V. Pepper (Washington, DC: National Academy, 2012).

45. Ibid., pp. 91–93.

46. Ibid., pp. 93–94. See also Robert Apel, "Sanctions, Perceptions, and Crime: Implications for Criminal Deterrence," *Journal of Quantitative Criminology* 29 (2013): 67–101.

47. Greg Pogarsky and Alex R. Piquero, "Can Punishment Encourage Offending? Investigating the 'Resetting' Effect," *Journal of Research in Crime and Delinquency* 40 (2003): 95–120.

48. Nagin, "Deterrence," p. 94, citing Edward P. Mulvey, *Highlights from Pathways to Desistance: A Longitudinal Study of Serious Adolescent Offenders. Juvenile Justice Fact Sheet*. (Washington, DC: US Department of Justice, 2011).

49. Nagin, "Deterrence," p. 84. Regarding the former, Nagin refers us to Daniel S. Nagin, Francis T. Cullen, and Cheryl L. Jonson, "Imprisonment and Reoffending," in *Crime and Justice: A Review of Research* 38, ed. Michael Tonry (Chicago: University of Chicago Press, 2009).

50. For a review, see Christopher Birkbeck and Gary LaFree, "The Situational Analysis of Crime and Deviance," *Annual Review of Sociology* 19 (1993): 113–137.

51. Ibid., pp. 124–126.

52. Derek B. Cornish and Ronald V. Clarke, eds., *The Reasoning Criminal* (New York: Springer-Verlag, 1986).

53. See Graeme Newman, Ronald V. Clarke, and S. Giora Shoham, eds., *Rational Choice and Situational Crime Prevention: Theoretical Foundations* (Dartmouth, UK: Ashgate, 1997).

54. Ronald V. Clarke and Derek B. Cornish, "Rational Choice," in *Explaining Criminals and Crime*, ed. Raymond Paternoster and Ronet Bachman (Los Angeles: Roxbury, 2001), p. 25.

55. Ibid., p. 24.

56. For an analysis of offenders' decision-making in general, see Vokan Topalli, "Criminal Expertise and Offender Decision-Making: An Experimental Analysis of How Offenders and Non-Offenders Differentially Perceive Social Stimuli," *British Journal of Criminology* 45 (2005): 269–295. On decision-making

specifically by burglars, see Claire Nee and Amy Meenaghan, "Expert Decision Making in Burglars," *British Journal of Criminology* 46 (2006): 935–949.

57. See Ronald V. Clarke, ed., *Situational Crime Prevention: Successful Case Studies*, 2nd ed. (Albany, NY: Harrow and Heston, 1997).

58. Ibid., p. 5.

59. Timothy Crowe, *Crime Prevention Through Environmental Design*, 2nd ed. (Woburn, MA: Butterworth-Heinemann, 2000); and Ian Colquhoun, *Design Out Crime: Creating Safe and Sustainable Communities* (Burlington, MA: Elsevier, 2004).

60. For an analysis of how rational choice–based deterrence is well suited to corporate offenders, see Neal Shover and Andy Hochstetler, *Choosing White-Collar Crime* (New York: Cambridge University Press, 2006). See also Anne Alvesalo, Steve Tombs, Erja Virta, and Dave Whyte, "Re-imagining Crime Prevention: Controlling Corporate Crime?" *Crime, Law & Social Change* 45 (2006): 1–25; Nicole Leeper Piquero, M. Lyn Exum, and Sally S. Simpson, "Integrating the Desire-for-Control and Rational Choice in a Corporate Crime Context," *Justice Quarterly* 22 (2005): 252–280.

61. For the original analysis of displacement, see Thomas A. Repetto, "Crime Prevention and the Displacement Phenomenon," *Crime and Delinquency* 22 (1976): 166–167.

62. For studies finding the displacement effect to be insignificant and suggesting a diffusion of benefits, see David Weisburd, Laura A. Wycoff, Justin Ready, John E. Eck, Joshua C. Hinkle, and Frank Gajewski, "Does Crime Just Move Around the Corner? A Controlled Study of Spatial Displacement and Diffusion of Crime Control Benefits," *Criminology* 44 (2006): 549–592; and Ronald Clarke, ed., *Situational Crime Prevention: Successful Case Studies*, 2nd ed. (Guilderland, NY: Harrow and Heston, 1997), pp. 28–33.

63. M. Lyn Exum, "The Application and Robustness of the Rational Choice Perspective in the Study of Intoxicated and Angry Intentions to Aggress," *Criminology* 40 (2002): 933–966.

64. For a general argument on the "over-rationalized conception of man in the rational choice perspective," see Willem De Haan and Jaco Vos, "A Crying Shame," *Theoretical Criminology* 7 (2003): 29–54.

65. Michael J. Hindelang, Michael R. Gottfredson, and James Garofalo, *Victims of Personal Crime* (Cambridge, MA: Ballinger, 1978). James Garofalo, "Reassessing the Lifestyle Model of Criminal Victimization," in *Positive Criminology: Essays in Honor of Michael J. Hindelang*, ed. Michael Gottfredson and Travis Hirschi (Beverly Hills, CA: Sage, 1987), updates the theory and argues that there is no substantive difference between the lifestyle and the routine activities approaches. See also Michael G. Maxfield, "Lifestyle and Routine Activity Theories of Crime," *Journal of Quantitative Criminology* 3 (1987): 275–282.

66. Hindelang et al., *Victims of Personal Crime*, p. 241.

67. For a good summary, see Robert F. Meier and Terance D. Miethe, "Understanding Theories of Criminal Victimization," in Michael Tonry, ed., *Crime and Justice: An Annual Review of Research* 17 (1993): 459–499. See also Birkbeck and LaFree, "The Situational Analysis of Crime and Deviance."

68. Lawrence E. Cohen and Marcus Felson, "Social Change and Crime Rate Trends: A Routine Activity Approach," *American Sociological Review* 44 (1979): 588–608. Where Cohen and Felson focus on crime-rate trends of predatory crimes, Felson himself extended this approach to a broader range of crimes and examined the implications of routine activities for individual offending. See Marcus Felson, "Linking Criminal Choices, Routine Activities, Informal Control, and Criminal Outcomes," in *The Reasoning Criminal*, ed. Cornish and Clarke, pp. 119–128; *Marcus Felson, Crime and Everyday Life* (Thousand Oaks, CA: Pine Forge Press, 1994); and Felson and Michael R. Gottfredson, "Social Indicators of Adolescent Activities Near Peers and Parents," *Journal of Marriage and the Family* 46 (1984): 709–714.

69. Some crimes—for example, many white-collar crimes—do not involve direct contact. Cohen and Felson addressed such crimes in *Crime and Everyday Life*, 3rd ed. (Thousand Oaks, CA: Sage, 2002), pp. 93–104, in which they applied a routine activities, opportunity-based approach and called for the abandonment of the "poorly named" white-collar crime in favor of the term "crimes of specialized access."

70. Jerry H. Ratcliffe, "A Temporal Constraint Theory to Explain Opportunity-Based Spatial Offending Patterns," *Journal of Research in Crime and Delinquency* 43 (2006): 261–291; Derek J. Paulsen and Matthew B. Robinson, *Spatial Aspects of Crime: Theory and Practice* (Boston: Pearson Education, 2004). For an introduction to crime pattern theory, which states that "nodes" or anchor points in offenders' daily lives dictate their travel patterns and influence their spatial crime commission opportunities, see Patricia Brantingham and Paul Brantingham, *Environmental Criminology* (London: Waveland Press, 1981), pp. 7–26. For a work that analyzed criminal activities in a larger social and ecological framework, see Marcus Felson, *Crime and Nature* (Thousand Oaks, CA: Sage, 2006).

71. Susan McNeeley, "Lifestyle-Routine Activities and Crime Events," *Journal of Research in Crime and Delinquency* 31 (2015): 30–52.

72. Ibid., p. 32, citing Lawrence E. Cohen, James R. Kluegel, and Kenneth C. Land, "Social Inequality and Predatory Criminal Victimization: An Exposition and Test of a Formal Theory," *American Sociological Review* 46 (1981): 505–524.

73. McNeeley, "Lifestyle-Routine Activities and Crime Events," pp. 33–35.

74. Ibid., p. 35, citing among others Travis C. Platt, Jillian J. Turanovic, Kathleen A. Fox, and Kevin A. Wright, "Self-Control and Victimization: A Meta-Analysis," *Criminology* 52 (2014): 87–116.

75. McNeeley, "Lifestyle-Routine Activities and Crime Events," p. 36. See D. Wayne Osgood and Amy L. Anderson, "Unstructured Socializing and Rates of Delinquency," *Criminology* 42 (2004): 519–549; Lieven J.R. Pauwels and Robert Swensson, "Exploring the Relationship between Offending and Victimization: What Is the Role of Risky Lifestyles and Low Self-Control? A Test in Two Urban Samples," *European Journal on Criminal Policy and Research* 17 (2011): 163–177.

76. McNeeley, "Lifestyle-Routine Activities and Crime Events," p. 36. See Marcus Felson, "Linking Criminal Choices, Routine Activities, Informal Control, and Criminal Outcomes," in *The Reasoning Criminal*, ed. Cornish and Clarke, pp. 119–128.

77. McNeeley, "Lifestyle-Routine Activities and Crime Events," p. 36, citing Marie S. Tillyer and John E. Eck, "Getting a Handle on Crime: A Further Extension of Routine Activities Theory," *Security Journal* 24 (2011): 179–193.

78. McNeeley, "Lifestyle-Routine Activities and Crime Events," p. 37.

79. Lawrence W. Sherman, Patrick R. Gartin, and Michael E. Buerger, "Hot Spots of Predatory Crime: Routine Activities and the Criminology of Place," *Criminology* 27 (1989): 27–55.

80. Ajima Olaghere and Cynthia Lum, "Classifying 'Micro' Routine Activities of Street-Level Drug Transactions," *Journal of Research in Crime and Delinquency* 55 (2018): 466–492.

81. E.g., Matthew L. Williams, "Guardians Upon High: An Application of Routine Activities Theory to Online Identity Theft in Europe at the Country and Individual Level," *British Journal of Criminology* 56 (2016): 21–48.

82. Steven N. Durlauf and Daniel S. Nagin, "Imprisonment and Crime: Can Both Be Reduced?," *Criminology and Public Policy* 10 (2011): 13–54.

83. For a history of Operation Ceasefire in Boston and elsewhere, see David M. Kennedy, *Don't Shoot: One Man, a Street Fellowship, and the End of Violence in Inner-City America* (New York: Bloomsbury, 2011).

84. James A. Fox, *Trends in Juvenile Justice* (Washington, DC: US Department of Justice, Bureau of Justice Statistics, 1996).

85. David M. Kennedy, Anne M. Piehl, and Anthony A. Braga, "Youth Violence in Boston: Gun Markets, Serious Youth Offenders, and a Use-Reduction Strategy," *Law and Contemporary Problems* 59 (1996): 147–196.

86. David M. Kennedy, "Pulling Levers: Chronic Offenders, High-Crime Settings, and a Theory of Prevention," *Valparaiso University Law Review* 31 (1997): 449–484, at p. 452.

87. Marvin E. Wolfgang, Robert M. Figlio, and Thorsten D. Sellin, *Delinquency in a Birth Cohort* (Chicago: University of Chicago Press, 1972).

88. Lawrence W. Sherman, Patrick R. Gartin, and Michael E. Buerger, "Hot Spots of Predatory Crime: Routine Activities and the Criminology of Place," *Criminology* 27 (1989): 27–56.

89. Kennedy, "Pulling Levers," pp. 461–462.

90. Ibid., p. 462.

91. Ibid., p. 463.

92. Anthony A. Braga, David M. Kennedy, Elin J. Waring, and Anne Morrison Piehl, "Problem-Oriented Policing, Deterrence, and Youth Violence: An Evaluation of Boston's Operation Ceasefire," *Journal of Research in Crime and Delinquency* 38 (2001): 195–225.

93. See, e.g., Jeffrey Fagan, "Policing Guns and Youth Violence," *Future Child* 12 (2002): 133–151; Richard Rosenfeld, Robert Fornango, and Eric Baumer, "Did Ceasefire, Compstat, and Exile Reduce Homicide?," *Criminology and Public Policy* 4 (2005): 419–450.

94. Anthony A. Braga, David M. Hureau, and Andrew V. Papachristos, "Deterring Gang-Involved Violence: Measuring the Impact of Boston's Operation Ceasefire on Street Gang Behavior," *Journal of Quantitative Criminology* 30 (2014): 113–139.

95. Ibid., p. 134.

96. Andrew V. Papachristos, Tracey L. Meares, and Jeffrey Fagan, "Attention Felons: Evaluating Project Safe Neighborhoods in Chicago," *Journal of Empirical Legal Studies* 4 (2007): 223–272.

97. Angela Hawken and Mark Kleiman, *Managing Drug Involved Probationers with Swift and Certain Sanctions: Evaluating Hawaii's HOPE.* Final report submitted to the National Institute of Justice (Washington, DC: US Department of Justice, 2009).

98. Andrew V. Papachristos, "Too Big to Fail: The Science and Politics of Violence Prevention," *Criminology and Public Policy* 10 (2011): 1053–1061, at 1056.

99. Ibid.

100. Anthony A. Braga and David L. Weisburd, "The Effects of Focused Deterrence Strategies on Crime: A Systematic Review and Meta-Analysis of the Empirical Evidence," *Journal of Research in Crime and Deliquency* 49 (2012): 323–358.

101. Ibid., p. 347.

102. Marie Skubak Tillyer, Robin S. Engel, and Brian Lovins, "Beyond Boston: Applying Theory to Understand and Address Sustainability Issues in Focused Deterrence Initiatives for Violence Reduction," *Crime and Delinquency* 58 (2012): 973–997.

103. Anthony Petrosino, Carolyn P. Petrosino, and John Buehler. *"Scared Straight" and Other Juvenile Awareness Programs for Preventing Juvenile Delinquency.* Campbell Systematic Reviews (2004). DOI: 10.4073/csr2004.2.

104. See, for example, William C. Bailey, "Deterrence, Brutalization, and the Death Penalty," *Criminology* 36 (1998): 711–733, which examined homicide in Oklahoma following its return to capital punishment in 1990. The study found consistent support for a brutalization effect for a variety of killings involving both strangers and nonstrangers.

105. For works critical of such crime control methods and their links to governmental policies, see David Garland, *The Culture of Control: Crime and Social Order in Contemporary Society* (Chicago: University of Chicago Press, 2001); Jonathan Simon, *Governing Through Crime: How the War on Crime Transformed American Democracy and Created a Culture of Fear* (New York: Oxford University Press, 2007); Katherine Beckett and Steve Herbert, "Dealing with Disorder: Social Control in the Post-Industrial City," *Theoretical Criminology* 12 (2008): 5–30; and Mike Davis, *City of Quartz: Excavating the Future in Los Angeles* (New York: Vintage Books, 1992). For accounts suggesting that such crime control measures can be consistent with notions of social justice, see Ian Loader and Neil Walker, *Civilizing Security* (New York: Cambridge University Press, 2007); K. M. Lersch, *Space, Time and Crime* (Durham, NC: Carolina Academic Press, 2004); and Clarke, *Situational Crime Prevention.*

—

CHAPTER 4

Biological Factors
and Criminal Behavior

This chapter focuses on biological characteristics that are said to be associated with an increased risk of engaging in criminal behavior. Modern biological theories in criminology do not argue for biological determinism. Rather, these theories argue that certain biological characteristics increase the probability that individuals will engage in behaviors, such as violent or antisocial behaviors, that are legally defined as criminal or delinquent.[1] Only an increased probability is asserted, not an absolute prediction that everyone with these characteristics will commit crimes. In addition, many of these theories focus on the interaction between biological characteristics and the social environment.[2] Certain biological characteristics may have little impact on crime in some situations but a large impact in other situations. Thus, these are best described as "biosocial" theories.

In this chapter, we review some of the dominant research on biology and crime. First, we examine the historical origins of this point of view in theories that focused on the physical appearance of the criminal. Second, we examine biological factors that are hereditary, which result from the genes that individuals receive from their parents at the time of conception. Third, we examine biological factors that originally may be hereditary but may change during the life course in response to environmental conditions. Fourth, we examine biological factors that originate in the environment. Finally, we review and discuss the biosocial approach to criminology.

BACKGROUND: PHYSICAL APPEARANCE
AND DEFECTIVENESS

The earliest biological theories in criminology emphasized physical appearance as the distinguishing mark of the criminal. Criminals were thought to be somehow different, abnormal, defective, and therefore inferior biologically.

This biological inferiority was thought to produce certain physical characteristics that made the appearance of criminals different from that of noncriminals. The real explanation of criminal behavior, however, was biological defectiveness and inferiority—physical and other characteristics were only symptoms of that inferiority.

The belief that criminals have an unusual physical appearance goes back to ancient times. For example, Socrates was examined by a Greek physiognomist who found that his face revealed him as brutal, sensuous, and inclined to drunkenness. Socrates admitted that such was his natural disposition but said he had learned to overcome these tendencies.[3] In 1775, Johan Caspar Lavater (1741–1801), a Swiss scholar and theologian, published a four-volume work on physiognomy that received nearly as much favorable attention as Beccaria's work had only eleven years earlier. In this work, Lavater systematized many popular observations and made many extravagant claims about the alleged relationship between facial features and human conduct.

Where physiognomy studied the face, phrenology studied the external shape of the skull. Phrenologists assumed that the shape of the skull revealed the shape of the brain inside and that different parts of the brain were associated with different faculties or functions of the mind. Therefore, the shape of the skull would indicate how the mind functioned. In 1791, the eminent European anatomist Franz Joseph Gall (1758–1828) started publishing material on the relationships between head conformations and the personal characteristics of individuals. His student and onetime collaborator, John Gaspar Spurzheim (1776–1832), carried their doctrines to England and America, lecturing before scientific meetings and stimulating interest in their ideas.[4]

LOMBROSO, THE BORN CRIMINAL, AND POSITIVIST CRIMINOLOGY

Cesare Lombroso (1835–1909) extended the tradition of physiognomy and phrenology by studying all anatomical features of the human body, not merely the features of the face or the shape of the skull.[5] Lombroso relied on Darwin's theory of evolution to argue that criminals were biological throwbacks to an earlier evolutionary stage, people more primitive and less highly evolved than their noncriminal counterparts. He used the term *atavistic* to describe such people.

Darwin first proposed the theory of evolution in his 1859 book *On the Origin of Species*, which argued that natural selection through survival of the fittest explained diversity in the animal kingdom. In his 1871 book *Descent of Man*, Darwin applied evolutionary theory to human beings. As a relatively minor point in this book, he stated that some individuals may be reversions to an earlier evolutionary stage: "With mankind some of the worst dispositions which occasionally without any assignable cause make their appearance in families, may perhaps be reversions to a savage state, from which we are not removed by many generations."[6] Five years later, Lombroso published his theory of the atavistic criminal, which was based on and further developed this idea of Darwin's.

Lombroso was a doctor in the Italian army who was concerned about the problems, including crime, of soldiers who came from Southern Italy.[7] The theory of atavism originated when Lombroso had a flash of insight while performing an autopsy on a thief:[8]

> On laying open the skull I found on the occipital part, exactly on the spot where a spine is found in the normal skull, a distinct depression which I named median occipital fossa, because of its situation precisely in the middle of the occiput as in inferior animals, especially rodents. . . . At the sight of that skull, I seemed to see all of a sudden, lighted up as a vast plain under a flaming sky, the problem of the nature of the criminal—an atavistic being who reproduces in his person the ferocious instincts of primitive humanity and the inferior animals.

Lombroso later performed sixty-six additional autopsies on criminals and examined the physical characteristics of a fairly large number of living people, including both criminals and noncriminals. His findings were presented in his book *L'uomo delinquente* (*The Criminal Man*), which appeared in 1876. Lombroso argued that various physical characteristics were linked to crime, including deviations in head size and shape, asymmetry of the face, large jaws and cheekbones, unusually large or small ears or ears that stand out from the head, fleshy lips, abnormal teeth, receding chin, abundant hair or wrinkles, long arms, extra fingers or toes, or an asymmetry of the brain.[9] These characteristics were said to resemble the characteristics of lower animals, such as monkeys and chimpanzees.

In later editions of his book, Lombroso broadened his theory considerably. In those editions, he argued that there are three major classes of criminals: (1) "born criminals," which he understood as atavistic reversions to a lower or more primitive evolutionary form of development and were thought to constitute about one-third of the total number of offenders; (2) "insane criminals," in which he grouped idiots, imbeciles, paranoiacs, sufferers from melancholia, and those afflicted with general paralysis, dementia, alcoholism, epilepsy, or hysteria (strange bedfellows, to be sure); and (3) "criminaloids," who did not have any special physical or mental characteristics but whose mental and emotional makeup were such that under certain circumstances they engage in criminal behavior. Criminaloids were said to be a majority of all criminals, while born and insane criminals were relatively rare.

Where his original theory focused solely on physical features, Lombroso's later thinking looked more and more to social and environmental factors, rather than to biological and psychological ones. Lombroso's last book, *Crime, Its Causes and Remedies*, was a summary of his life work specially prepared for American readers. Published in 1911, two years after Lombroso's death, it included discussions of many factors that are related to crime causation, of which by far the largest number were environmental rather than biological. These factors included such things as climate, rainfall, the price of grain, sex and marriage customs, criminal laws, banking practices, national tariff policies, the structure of government, church organization, and the state of religious belief.[10]

Today, Lombroso is known primarily for his original idea of the atavistic criminal, but his real contribution to criminology was his work related to criminaloids. With this group, Lombroso took an approach that was based on the concept of multiple-factor causation, where some of the factors are biological, others are psychological, and still others are social. All these factors were used in an effort to explain increases or decreases in the probability that a given individual would engage in criminal behavior. This basic approach came to be known as positivist criminology, as described in Chapter 1, and is utilized by a wide range of criminologists today.

GORING'S REFUTATION OF THE BORN CRIMINAL

Lombroso's theory of the born criminal generated strong reactions, both favorable and unfavorable, among his contemporaries. In response to criticisms of his theory, Lombroso offered to have an impartial committee study one hundred born criminals, one hundred criminaloids, and one hundred normal persons. He also offered to retract his theories if the physical, mental, and psychological characteristics of the three groups were found to be identical. This challenge was never really met, since Lombroso's opponents said it was impossible to distinguish among the three groups accurately.

However, a study by Charles Goring, begun in England in 1901 and published in 1913, was to some extent a response to Lombroso's challenge.[11] Lombroso had asserted that criminals, compared with the general population, would show anomalies (i.e., differences or defects) of head height, head width, and degree of receding forehead, as well as differences in head circumference, head symmetry, and so on. In comparing prisoners with the officers and men of the Royal Engineers, Goring found no such anomalies. He also compared other characteristics, such as nasal contours, color of eyes, color of hair, and left-handedness, but found only insignificant differences. Finally, Goring compared groups of different kinds of criminals (burglars, forgers, thieves, and so forth) on the basis of thirty-seven specific physical characteristics and concluded that there were no significant differences between one kind of criminal and another that were not more properly related to the selective effects of environmental factors.[12]

The only difference that Goring found was that the criminals were one to two inches shorter than the noncriminals of the same occupational groups and weighed from three to seven pounds less.[13] Goring was satisfied that these differences were real and significant and interpreted them as indicating a general inferiority of a hereditary nature.[14] Goring's theory of hereditary inferiority is discussed later in the section on family studies.

Later assessments of Goring's work generally found more support for Lombroso's theories than Goring admitted.[15] Even today, some researchers have examined whether "minor physical anomalies," including some of the characteristics discussed by Lombroso, may have a relationship to violence.[16] But the weight of expert opinion was against the proposition that criminals are somehow physically different from noncriminals, and the general conclusion of Goring on the matter came to be accepted by most criminologists:[17]

> Both with regard to measurements and the presence of physical anomalies in criminals, our statistics present a startling conformity with similar statistics of the law-abiding class. Our inevitable conclusion must be that there is no such thing as a physical criminal type.

BODY TYPE THEORIES

Some of the more interesting attempts to relate criminal behavior to physical appearance are the so-called body type theories. The body type theorists argue that there is a high degree of correspondence between the physical appearance of the body and the temperament of the mind.

The work of William Sheldon,[18] especially his book on delinquent youths, is a good example of a body type theory. Sheldon took his underlying ideas from the fact that a human begins life as an embryo that is essentially a tube made up of three different tissue layers, namely an inner layer (or endoderm), a middle layer (or mesoderm), and an outer layer (or ectoderm). Sheldon then constructed a corresponding physical and mental typology that was consistent with the known facts from embryology and the physiology of development. The endoderm gives rise to the digestive viscera; the mesoderm, to bone, muscle, and tendons of the motor-organ system; the ectoderm, to connecting tissue of the nervous system, skin, and related appendages. Sheldon's basic type characteristics of physique and temperament are briefly summarized in the following scheme:[19]

Physique	Temperament
1. Endomorphic: relatively great development of digestive viscera; tendency to put on fat; soft roundness through various regions of the body; short tapering limbs; small bones; soft, smooth, velvety skin.	1. Viscerotonic: general relaxation of body; a comfortable person; loves soft luxury; a "softie" but still essentially an extrovert.

(Continued)

Physique	Temperament
2. Mesomorphic: relative predominance of muscles, bone, and the motor organs of the body; large trunk; heavy chest; large wrists and hands; if "lean," a hard rectangularity of outline; if "not lean," they fill out heavily.	2. Somotonic: active, dynamic person; walks, talks, gestures assertively; behaves aggressively.
3. Ectomorphic: relative predominance of skin and its appendages, which includes the nervous system; lean, fragile, delicate body; small, delicate bones; droopy shoulders; small face, sharp nose, fine hair; relatively little body mass and relatively great surface area.	3. Cerebrotonic: an introvert; full of functional complaints, allergies, skin troubles, chronic fatigue, insomnia; sensitive to noise and distractions; shrinks from crowds.

Each person possesses the characteristics of the three types to a greater or lesser degree. Sheldon therefore used three numbers, each between 1 and 7, to indicate the extent to which the characteristics of the three types were present in a given individual. For example, a person whose somatotype is 7-1-4 would possess many endomorphic characteristics, few mesomorphic characteristics, and an average number of ectomorphic characteristics.

Sheldon presented individual case histories, uniformly written according to a rigorous case outline, of two hundred young males who had had a period of contact, during the decade 1939–1949, with the Hayden Goodwill Inn, a small, somewhat specialized, rehabilitation home for boys in Boston. He found that these youths were decidedly high in mesomorphy and low in ectomorphy, with the average somatotype being 3.5-4.6-2.7. Sheldon had earlier studied two hundred college students who were apparently nondelinquents and had found that the average somatotype was 3.2-3.8-3.4. The difference between these two groups with respect to mesomorphy and ectomorphy is significant (p, .001).[20]

The association between mesomorphy and delinquency was also found in a study by the Gluecks, who compared five hundred persistent delinquents with five hundred proved nondelinquents.[21] The two groups were matched in terms of age, general intelligence, ethnic-racial derivation, and residence in underprivileged areas. Photographs of the boys were mixed together and then visually assessed for the predominant body type. By this method, 60.1 percent of the delinquents, but only 30.7 percent of the nondelinquents, were found to be mesomorphs.[22] The analysis included a study of sixty-seven personality traits and forty-two sociocultural factors to determine which of these were associated with delinquency.[23] The Gluecks found that mesomorphs, in general, were "more highly characterized by traits particularly suitable to the commission of acts of aggression (physical strength, energy, insensitivity, the tendency to express tensions and frustrations in action), together with a relative freedom from such inhibitions to antisocial adventures as feelings of inadequacy, marked submissiveness to authority, emotional instability, and the like."[24] They also found that those mesomorphs who became delinquent were characterized by a number of personality traits that are not normally found in mesomorphs, including susceptibility to contagious diseases of childhood, destructiveness, feelings of inadequacy, emotional instability, and emotional conflicts.[25] In addition, three sociocultural factors—careless household routine, lack of family-group recreations, and meagerness of recreational facilities in the home—were strongly associated with delinquency in mesomorphs.[26]

Such studies indicating a relationship between body type and criminal behavior have been criticized on several grounds, significantly, that they had a small sample size and that they were not repeatable.[27] Sheldon's methodology specifically was criticized for failing to begin with a random sample, using "a priori reasoning and subjective ratings," mismeasuring and manipulating photographs, "computational errors," and a failure to use "appropriate statistics."[28] Furthermore, the relationship between body build and behavior may be indirect. As Anderson noted, a physically large child may find that physical force is an effective way to end a conflict, while a physically smaller child may realize the need to resolve disputes in an alternative manner.[29]

FAMILY STUDIES

Explanations of human behavior in terms of heredity go far back in antiquity and are based on the commonsense observation that children tend to resemble their parents in appearance, mannerisms, and disposition. Scientific theories of heredity originated about 1850 and were more extensively worked out over the next fifty or seventy-five years. In connection with the development of the theory of heredity, new statistical methods were devised by Francis Galton and his students (notably Karl Pearson) to measure degrees of resemblance or correlation.[30] Charles Goring used these new statistical techniques in his study of English convicts, in which he refuted Lombroso's theory of the born criminal.

Goring assumed that the seriousness of criminality could be measured by the frequency and length of imprisonments.[31] He therefore attempted to find out what physical, mental, and moral factors were correlated with that measure. Goring found that those with frequent and lengthy imprisonments were physically smaller than other people and were mentally inferior. Although there could be an environmental component to these factors, Goring believed that they both were primarily inherited characteristics.

Goring also found that there were high correlations between the frequency and length of imprisonment of one parent and that of the other, between the imprisonment of parents and that of their children, and between the imprisonment of brothers. Goring argued that these findings could not be explained by the effect of social and environmental conditions, since he found little or no relationship between the frequency and length of imprisonment and such factors as poverty, nationality, education, birth order, and broken homes. Goring therefore concluded that criminality (i.e., frequent or lengthy imprisonment) was associated with inherited, but not with environmental, characteristics and recommended that to reduce crime, people with those inherited characteristics not be allowed to reproduce.[32]

There are serious problems with Goring's argument.[33] The most important problem concerns the fact that Goring attempted to establish the effect of heredity by controlling for and eliminating the effect of environment. To accomplish that goal, it is necessary to have accurate measurements of all the environmental factors involved, but he obviously did not have these measures. The failure to measure environmental influence adequately resulted in an overemphasis on the influence of heredity.

Later studies of the families of criminals encountered a similar problem. In general, there are many similarities among family members in their tendencies to commit crime.[34] The problem is that it is extremely difficult to control for the effects of a similar environment within the family itself. If family members resemble each other in their tendency to commit crime, it may be because they all live in the same environment and the similar environment causes the similar tendency to commit crime, rather than because they share a similar heredity. Because this problem is so difficult, criminologists for the most part no longer attempt to establish the role of heredity in crime by studying families.

EARLY TWIN AND ADOPTION STUDIES

Goring faced the problem of adequately controlling the effects of the environment so that the role of heredity in the origin of crime could be established. This proved to be extremely difficult, and other researchers have come up with an alternate strategy for achieving the same goal. This strategy essentially controls the effects of heredity by studying the criminality of twins and adoptees.

In genetics, there is a clear-cut distinction between identical and fraternal twins. Identical twins (monozygotic) are the product of a single fertilized egg and have identical heredity; fraternal twins (dizygotic) are the product of two eggs simultaneously fertilized by two sperms and therefore have the same relation as ordinary siblings.[35] Thus, differences in the behavior of fraternal twins can be explained by differences in heredity, but differences in the behavior of identical twins cannot. Any greater similarity of behavior in identical twins, compared to that of fraternal twins, is therefore taken as a measure of the influence of heredity on behavior.

A number of studies have used this approach in trying to determine the role of heredity in crime. All have tended to show a greater similarity of criminal behavior among identical than among fraternal twins.[36] For example, Christiansen used the official Twins Register of Denmark to study all twins born in the Danish Islands between 1881 and 1910 when both twins lived at least until age fifteen, a total of about 6,000 pairs.[37] He then used the official Penal Register to determine whether either twin, or both, had been found criminal or delinquent. Christiansen found 67 cases in which at least one of a pair of male identical twins was registered as a criminal, and in 24 of these cases (35.8%), the other twin was also registered. For male fraternal twins, he found this to be true in only 14 out of 114 cases (12.3%). For females, he found "criminal concordance" in 3 out of 14 cases of identical twins (21.4%) and in 1 out of 23 cases of fraternal twins (4.3%). Christiansen later demonstrated that concordance was higher for more serious than for less serious criminality.[38]

The principal difficulty with this method is that the greater similarity of behavior of identical twins may be due to a greater similarity in their environmental experiences because identical twins are physically more similar than are fraternal twins.[39] One way to control for the possibility that identical twins share a more common environment than do fraternal twins would be to study twins who were reared apart. Grove and his colleagues looked at thirty-two sets of identical twins who were separated shortly after birth,[40] and Christiansen looked at eight pairs of identical twins who were raised apart.[41] Although these studies were based on a small sample of twins, they both found evidence that antisocial behavior can be inherited.

In 1992, Walters performed a meta-analysis of fourteen twin studies published from 1930 to 1984, attempting to assess whether these studies on the whole found evidence of a gene–crime relationship.[42] He took into account such factors as the sample sizes of the studies, the quality of the research designs, the gender and nationality of the twins, and the year of the studies. Walters concluded that on the average, these studies showed evidence of a hereditary basis of criminality.

An updated review of the research on twins, however, argued that its results must be interpreted in the context of other recent knowledge about the origin and development of delinquency. In this context, the authors argued that the greater "criminal concordance" of identical versus fraternal twins is best interpreted as the result of "behavioral contagion," an approach that emphasizes similar environments and the performance of behaviors that occur among those who are socially related, rather than of a similar heredity.[43] So the issue is by no means settled, and research on twins continues in the attempt to separate out the effects of heredity and environment.[44]

Another method for determining the effects of heredity on criminality is to study the records of adoptees. For example, Hutchings and Mednick examined the records of all nonfamily male adoptions in Copenhagen in which the adoptees had been born between 1927 and 1941.[45] First, they grouped the boys according to whether they had criminal records and then looked at the criminal records of the biological fathers. A total of 31.1 percent of the boys who had no criminal record had biological fathers with criminal records, but 37.7 percent of the boys who had committed only minor offenses and 48.8 percent of the boys who themselves had criminal records had biological fathers with criminal records.[46] These figures indicate that adopted boys are more likely to commit crimes when their biological fathers have a criminal record.

Next, the researchers grouped the biological and adoptive fathers according to whether they had criminal records and then looked at the criminal records of the boys. They found an interactive effect between the criminality of the biological and the adoptive fathers.[47] When only one was criminal, the effect was not as great as when both were criminal. In addition, the magnitude of the effect of the criminality of the adoptive father was weaker than the effect of criminality of the biological father.

Hutchings and Mednick then selected all the criminal adoptees whose fathers (both biological and adoptive) had been born after 1889 to maximize the reliability of police records. The 143 adoptees who met this criterion were matched with 143 noncriminal adoptees on the basis of the age and occupational status of the adoptive fathers. The criminal adoptees were found to have a higher percentage of criminal adoptive fathers (23% versus 9.8%), of criminal biological fathers (49% versus 28%), and of criminal biological mothers (18% versus 7%).[48]

This sample of Danish adoptees was expanded to females and the entire country of Denmark and reanalyzed by Mednick and his colleagues.[49] These researchers found that the probability of the adoptees being convicted of a crime was influenced by the number of court convictions of their biological parents, but not of their adoptive parents. This was true for property offenses but not for violent offenses. Later reanalyses of the same data found that the socioeconomic status of the adoptive and biological parents, the personality disorders of the biological parents, and the number of placements before the final adoption all influenced adoptees' convictions.[50] Again, these relationships held mostly for property offenses but not for violent offenses.

Walters performed a meta-analysis of thirteen adoption studies published between 1972 and 1989, finding significant evidence of the heritability of crime and antisocial behavior.[51] However, two limitations of adoption studies may be mentioned. First, in several of the studies, the adoptive parents engaged in criminal behavior at much lower rates than the normal population.[52] This finding makes it difficult to generalize about the effects of family environment and to examine the interaction between environment and genetics in its potential joint influence on behavior. Second, several studies found hereditary effects for petty and property offenses, but not for more serious and violent offenses. But this result may reflect the fact that petty and property offenders are more likely to be frequent offenders. Thus, hereditary effects would be much easier to find with those offenders than with serious and violent offenders, who commit crimes infrequently.

MAOA: THE WARRIOR GENE

Neurotransmitters are chemicals that allow for the transmission of electrical impulses within the brain and are the basis for the brain's processing of information. As such, they underlie all types of behaviors, including antisocial behavior.[53] A variety of studies have suggested that the levels of three different neurotransmitters may be associated with antisocial behavior: serotonin, dopamine, and norepinephrine. Most of the focus on neurotransmitters' influence on antisocial and aggressive behavior, however, has been on serotonin and dopamine. Raine's discussion of neurotransmitters in his 2013 book *The Anatomy of Violence* acknowledged that "we have a long way to go in understanding the neurochemistry of violence,"[54] but generally documents that low serotonin or increased dopamine, especially when combined with certain contextual situations, are linked to violence.

Neurotransmitters are metabolized in the brain by a genetically encoded enzyme called monoamine oxidase (MAOA). Responsible for the breakdown of the neurotransmitters, MAOA may influence behavior if its level of activity is exceedingly low or high. Low MAOA activity in the brain, for example, results in significantly high levels of dopamine and norepinephrine, which may bring about low self-control and heighten aggression.[55]

The relevance of MAOA to violence and aggression can be traced to Hans Brunner's work in the Netherlands. Brunner researched four generations of an extended family who had exhibited a bizarre range of behavioral issues that included violence and aggression in many of the males. A genotype of the families showed a mutant form of the MAOA gene; this mutant form had near-zero functional MAOA. His investigation of this family began in 1978 and fifteen years later, in 1993, was published in *Science*.[56] Two years later a research team discovered that deleting the MAOA gene in mice caused them to become extremely aggressive and vicious toward other mice.[57]

Next up was one of the most impactful studies ever of the role genetics play in behavior, published in *Science* in 2002. Moffitt and Caspi and colleagues measured MAOA activity as part of the Dunedin Multidisciplinary Health and Development Study.[58] The 1,037 members of the Dunedin cohort were assessed approximately every two years from ages three to twenty-six. During early childhood (ages three to eleven), 8 percent of the children experienced "severe" maltreatment and 28 percent experienced "probable" maltreatment. This finding, along with MAOA activity, was used to predict antisocial behavior, which was comprised of adolescent conduct disorder, convictions for violent crimes, personality dispositions toward violence, and symptoms of antisocial personality disorder.

The researchers first found that early maltreatment strongly predicted future antisocial behavior, but that MAOA activity did not. However, they then found that the interaction between MAOA and maltreatment significantly affected antisocial behavior, both as a composite measure and for all four individual measures. That is, maltreated children were more likely to engage in antisocial behavior if they also had low MAOA activity levels in their brains. The study concluded that a person's genetic heritage moderates the effect that environment has on that person's behavior.[59] Subsequent meta-analyses of this effect (studies that average the effects of many studies) from 2006 and 2014 have confirmed this finding.[60]

Now commonly referred to as the "warrior gene," MAOA was found to exist in low levels among the Maori (the indigenous Polynesians of New Zealand); this was contrasted to the finding that New Zealand Caucasians had only one-half the level of genotype resulting in low levels of MAOA.[61] The expansion of research on MAOA to groups beyond whites has generated much controversy, much in the same fashion that research on race and IQ has (see Chapter 5). While the original controversy had to do with the implications of how the Maori would be treated given these findings, it extended to racial differences in the United States with the discovery that a rare variation of the gene (MAOA-2R), which is linked even more to violence than MAOA, is found more often in African Americans than in whites.[62] The question of the overall impact of genes such as MAOA on violence will continue to be explored; one very recent study of Finnish prisoners estimated that MAOA and another gene, CDH13, could explain 5–10 percent of all severe violent crime in that country.[63]

Although neurotransmitter levels initially are determined by genetics, it is possible to manipulate them with drugs, such as lithium carbonate (for serotonin), reserpine (for norepinephrine), and various antipsychotic drugs (for dopamine). The research on whether these manipulations can actually reduce antisocial behavior is mixed, but it includes some encouraging results.[64] Neurotransmitter levels can also be affected by changes in the environment. For example, changes in diet can significantly increase the levels of serotonin, dopamine, and norepinephrine, which could possibly reduce the tendency to engage in violent or antisocial behavior. In addition, living in stressful conditions (such as inner-city areas) can dramatically lower serotonin levels and increase the tendency to engage in these behaviors.[65]

HORMONES

In addition to neurotransmitter levels, much research has been generated on the effect of hormone levels on human behavior, including aggressive or criminal behavior. Interest in hormones dates back to the mid-1800s, when biochemists were first able to isolate and identify some of the physiological and psychological effects of the secretions of the endocrine glands (hormones). Most recent attention that has been paid to hormone levels and aggressive or criminal behavior has related to either testosterone or female premenstrual cycles.[66]

The role of testosterone in the aggressiveness of many animal species has been well documented,[67] but a question remains as to whether testosterone plays a significant role in human aggressive and violent behavior. Raine reviewed some of this literature, finding mixed results.[68] Studies have demonstrated that castration of sexual offenders has greatly reduced recidivism for sex crimes specifically, but not nonsexual crimes or other antisocial or violent behavior.[69]

A major problem with this research is that there are several possible causal paths between testosterone and aggressive behavior.[70] In general, researchers want to know whether high testosterone levels cause increased aggression. But it is possible that the causal path is in the opposite direction—that certain types of aggressive behavior may cause an increase in testosterone production.[71] A third possibility is that some individuals may generally have normal levels of testosterone but may respond to certain types of situations with large increases in testosterone. These people may have an increased tendency to engage in aggressive behavior because of their high testosterone levels, even though their testosterone levels measure as normal most of the time. Finally, social variables may intervene in the relationship between testosterone and antisocial behavior. For example, high testosterone may result in a person being poorly integrated into social networks, and then the reduced social integration may cause higher levels of crime and deviance.[72] In addition, the interaction between testosterone and violence may be moderated by other biological variables. For example, research has suggested that the relationship between testosterone and aggression may be indirect, since high testosterone levels have been correlated with low serotonin levels. Thus, it may be that the combination of high hormonal and low neurotransmitter levels explains why some men react impulsively and aggressively when frustrated.[73] These various possible causal links highlight the need for additional biosocial research on the causes of criminal behavior.

Although most research on hormones and crime has focused on males, some work has examined the role that hormones play in crime by females, especially in connection with the menstrual cycle. Biological changes after ovulation have been linked to irritability and aggression.[74] Research has been mixed on the strength of this linkage, but at least a small percentage of women are susceptible to cyclical hormone changes that result in a patterned increase in hostility.[75] This patterned increase is associated with fluctuations in female hormones and a rise in testosterone, to which some women appear to be quite sensitive.

THE CENTRAL NERVOUS SYSTEM

The central nervous system contains neurons and systems that exist within the brain and spinal cord. Of particular importance in research on aggression and violence is the outer portion of the brain, the cerebral cortex, which consists of two hemispheres divided into four lobes: frontal, temporal, parietal, and occipital. Most attention paid by investigators who have studied antisocial behavior has been to the frontal and temporal lobes, since these lobes are involved with goal-directed behavior, impulses, and emotions. Disturbances or irregularities within the frontal lobe generally influence neuropsychological performance, while the temporal lobe in general appears to involve behaviors that are more directly emotional in expression.[76]

One common way of measuring brain abnormalities is through the use of the electroencephalograph (EEG). The EEG measures electrical brain activity and can detect abnormalities in brain wave patterns. Hundreds of studies have examined EEG activity in various types of criminals.[77] Most reviewers have agreed that repeat violent offenders are characterized by EEG abnormalities, but the relationship between psychopathy and EEG indicators is more uncertain.[78] Raine pointed out that most of this research is too broad in focus, and while it may point to some general relationship between dysfunctional behavior and EEG abnormalities, much more specific information is needed about the processes by which brain wave activity may affect behavior.[79]

More direct measures of the central nervous system have become available: brain-imaging techniques. These techniques include computerized tomography (CT), magnetic resonance imaging (MRI), positron emission tomography (PET), and single photon emission tomography (SPECT). These new brain-imaging procedures have been used to detect structural and functional abnormalities in both the frontal and temporal lobes.[80] After a comprehensive review of brain-imaging studies, Raine concluded:[81]

> An integration of findings from these studies gives rise to the hypothesis that frontal dysfunction may characterize violent offenders while temporal lobe dysfunction may characterize sexual offending; offenders with conjoint violent and sexual behavior are hypothesized to be characterized by both frontal and temporal lobe dysfunction.

THE AUTONOMIC NERVOUS SYSTEM

In addition to the central nervous system, there is a relatively separate part of the nervous system, called the autonomic nervous system (ANS), which controls many of the body's involuntary functions, such as blood pressure, heart and intestinal activity, and hormone levels. The ANS is especially active in a "fight-or-flight" situation, when it prepares the body for maximum efficiency by increasing the heart rate, rerouting the blood from the stomach to the muscles, dilating the pupils, increasing the respiratory rate, and stimulating the sweat glands. Lie detectors measure these functions and use them to determine whether a subject is telling the truth. The theory is that as children, most people have been conditioned to anticipate punishment when they tell a lie. The anticipation of punishment produces the involuntary fight-or-flight response, which results in a number of measurable changes in heart, pulse, and breathing rate and, because sweat itself conducts electricity, in the electric conductivity of the skin.

The anxiety reaction in anticipation of punishment has been described by some researchers as the primary socializing agent for children.[82] Children are conditioned by their parents to anticipate punishment in certain types of situations, and the anxiety they then feel (usually called conscience or guilt) often leads them to avoid these situations. Because the anxiety reaction in anticipation of punishment is essentially an autonomic nervous system function related to the fight-or-flight response, the level of socialization in children may depend, at least in part, on the functioning of that system. Specifically, if the fight-or-flight response is activated slowly or at low levels in situations in which punishment is anticipated or fails to deactivate quickly when the situation changes, then the child will be difficult to socialize.

A number of studies of autonomic nervous system functioning have measured the same peripheral functions that are measured by a lie detector. For example, Mednick[83] maintained that the rate of skin conductance response (SCR) recovery—the time between when the skin conducts the most electrical current and when that conductance returns to normal levels—can be taken to measure the general rate of recovery in the autonomic nervous system. If so, SCR recovery would measure the rate at which fear is reduced following the removal of the threatening situation. Mednick pointed out that the reduction in fear is the most powerful reinforcer known to psychology. When fear is reduced quickly, the individual receives a large reinforcement for avoiding the punishment, and conditioning is more likely to occur.

The results of research on this whole line of reasoning, however, have been mixed. In general, research has found that antisocial individuals have lower levels of skin conductance, as well as lower heart rates, when they are in resting situations.[84] These physiological measures may indicate that antisocial people have lower levels of ANS functioning. But Mednick argued that a crucial indicator of this lower ANS functioning is skin conductance response recovery—that is, its return to normal levels after the person is presented with an aversive stimulus, such as punishment. Earlier studies generally supported Mednick's argument that antisocial individuals would show slow recovery of skin conductance response after presentation with punishment; however, later research has generally failed to support this finding.[85]

However, the point of Mednick's argument is that antisocial people may be physiologically more difficult to condition than other people. Some studies have directly attempted to compare conditioning in antisocial and normal people. These studies have been similar to Pavlov's famous experiments with dogs: Pavlov would ring a bell just before he gave the dogs food, and conditioning was said to occur when the dogs salivated at the sound of the bell. Raine reviewed six similar studies that generally supported the notion that antisocial people are harder to condition than are regular people.[86] On the other hand, this finding applied only to people from poor social backgrounds.[87] It would suggest that even if low ANS functioning can explain some crime, it cannot explain lower-class crime. Overall, there is some evidence that ANS functioning may be related to criminal behavior, but it is difficult to draw firm conclusions at this point.

ENVIRONMENTALLY INDUCED BIOLOGICAL COMPONENTS OF BEHAVIOR

Up to this point we have discussed research on hereditary factors that influence antisocial and criminal behavior (such as the family, twins, and adoption studies) and research that has addressed factors that may be hereditary but may also change over time owing to environmental influences (such as hormones, neurotransmitter levels, and skin conductance responses to stimuli). Now we examine research on several biological factors that may influence criminal behavior but are clearly environmental. These factors include drug and alcohol abuse, diet and toxin intake, head injury, and complications of pregnancy and delivery.

There are many possible relationships between drug and alcohol abuse and violent behavior: biological, psychosocial, social, cultural, and economic. For example, violence and crime may result from an addict's need to get money to buy drugs or from wars between rival drug gangs over the right to sell drugs in certain areas. Because the range of literature is so broad in these areas, we do not summarize it here.[88] Instead, we present a few brief comments on the strictly biological links between violence and alcohol or drug use.

Alcohol is known to increase aggressive behavior temporarily in lower doses (when people get nasty) and temporarily decrease aggressive behavior in higher doses (when people pass out).[89] Many people believe that the increased aggressiveness at lower doses occurs because alcohol tends to release people from their inhibitions, but there is little evidence for this belief. An alternative explanation is that alcohol increases the production of the endocrine system, especially testosterone, but again, there is little evidence for this explanation.

Serotonin is a possible mediating factor between alcohol and violence. Because alcohol is known to decrease serotonin, and low serotonin is known to increase aggression, it seems logical to infer that low serotonin is one reason why alcohol increases aggression. Research has found physiological evidence both for and against this mediating role for serotonin in the relationship between alcohol and aggression, but "a relatively much larger body of evidence exists in support of such a role."[90] Other researchers believe that there may be a genetic basis for the relationship between alcohol and violence, but there has been no confirmation of this belief to date. So while the relationship between alcohol and violence is probably the strongest of any drug, especially for males, the reason for this relationship remains unclear.[91]

Other drugs that may have a biological association with violence are opiates, amphetamines, cocaine, hallucinogens, and steroids. Opiates are known to reduce aggressive and violent behavior temporarily, although chronic use may increase the possibility of violent behavior. Withdrawal from opiates is related to aggressive behavior as well.[92] There is still no direct evidence of a biological effect of cocaine use on violent behavior,[93] although the association between crack cocaine and violence in inner cities is well established.[94] Marijuana use most likely decreases or does not affect violent human behavior, while PCP, when used over a long term, may increase aggressive behavior. Chronic use of amphetamines may provoke violent outbursts in humans, but usually only when the individuals are already prone to violent behavior.[95] Similarly, the use of LSD and steroids may intensify violent behavior in those who are already prone to violence.[96]

Various studies have found correlations between nutrition or toxin intake and antisocial or aggressive behavior, but the methodological shortcomings of these studies make it difficult to conclude that causal relationships exist. Most commonly studied are sugar and cholesterol consumption and lead toxicity.[97]

Research in the 1980s showed hypoglycemia (low blood sugar), which is caused, in part, by excess sugar intake, to be common in habitually violent criminals. Numerous methodological problems with these studies were cited by Kanarek[98] and cast significant doubt on whether sugar intake causes antisocial behavior. Sugar has also been associated with hyperactivity in children, but again, there is reason to doubt the validity of most of the research that has supported the association.[99] More research on the potential negative consequences of sugar that is methodologically solid is needed before any conclusions should be drawn on the sugar–violence link. Research has also examined a possible link between blood cholesterol and violent behavior, but these studies have suffered from the same sorts of problems as the research on sugar and violent behavior.[100] Finally, exposure to lead in diet and environment has been shown to affect brain functioning negatively, bringing about learning disabilities and hyperactive attention-deficit disorder in children, and it may increase the risk for antisocial behavior.[101] A recent study by Jessica Wolpaw Reyes (see Chapter 2's discussion of lead and the crime drop) has demonstrated the negative effects of early childhood exposure to lead on childhood behavior problems, teen aggression, and young adult criminality.[102]

Several studies have found a correlation between head injury and criminal and antisocial behavior; whether the relationship is causal is another matter.[103] Such head injury can be detected by medical tests, such as X-rays, CAT scans, and spinal taps. A variety of studies have found that prisoners and violent patients have reported a large number of head injuries that involved the loss of consciousness. Mednick and colleagues found some support for a relationship between brain damage and violent behavior among juveniles in a study of children who were born at a hospital in Copenhagen between 1959 and 1961.[104] Those who later became violent delinquents had generally good medical, physical, and neurological reports during pregnancy and delivery, despite relatively poor social conditions. However, they had significantly worse physical and neurological status at one year of age. Similar findings were reported by Dorothy Lewis and her colleagues.[105] Lewis also found a strong association between parental criminality and the presence of serious medical problems in their children. She suggested that delinquency among children with criminal parents may reflect the combined physical and psychological effects of parental neglect and battering, rather than any genetic factors.[106]

Raine discussed some possible scenarios that would account for the association between head injury and criminal behavior. For example, in abusive homes children are more likely to incur head injuries, and these homes may also be more conducive to criminal behavior among offspring who are raised in them.[107] Still, Raine cited evidence that the link between head injury and criminal behavior may be at least partially causal.[108] Some processes by which head injury may influence negative behaviors are (1) a greater sensitivity to the effects of alcohol; (2) decreasing cognitive and social skills; (3) headaches and irritability that increase the possibility of violent outbursts; and (4) damage to the frontal and temporal lobes of the brain that increases anxiety, anger, and hostility.[109]

Another possible source of CNS deficits (which have been linked to aggressive behavior) is complications of pregnancy and delivery.[110] A study by Kandel and Mednick examined data on 216 children who were born between 1959 and 1961 in Copenhagen.[111] The group of 216 was selected from an original cohort of 9,125 children because their parents were schizophrenic, psychopathic, or character disordered; the children were therefore considered to be at a high risk of becoming delinquent. The research examined pregnancy complications (such as infections, chemotherapy, and jaundice) and delivery complications (such as a ruptured perineum, weak secondary labor, and a ruptured uterus) and measured criminal behavior with arrest records for property and violent offenses when the subjects were twenty to twenty-two years old. Pregnancy complications were not significantly related to offending rates, but delivery complications were related to violent offending: 80 percent of violent offenders had greater than average delivery complications, compared to 30 percent of property offenders and

47 percent of nonoffenders.[112] A subsequent study found that violent offending occurs most often among individuals with both a high number of delivery complications and parents with psychiatric problems.[113] Another study found that delivery complications, combined with rejection by the mother before one year of age, were associated with serious violent crime at age eighteen.[114]

EPIGENETICS AND THE ROLE OF HERITABILITY STUDIES IN BIOSOCIAL CRIMINOLOGY

Over the past decade, heritability studies such as those reported earlier in this chapter "have been published at a rapid and seemingly increasing pace."[115] These studies compare observed characteristics of individuals (phenotypes) within and between families varying in genetic relationships, and attempt to partition the percentage of given human characteristics that can be assigned to genes (G) or the environment (E). Overall, these studies have shown large heritability (from 30 to 90%) across a range of criminal behaviors, such as delinquency, arrests, and gang membership,[116] and sometimes conclude that family environment has little influence on these behaviors.

In this section we summarize a work of Callie Burt and Ronald Simons, who argue that these heritability studies should be discontinued in light of recent advances in what is referred to as the "postgenomic era."[117] Burt and Simons challenge heritability studies methodologically as well as conceptually, argue that it is pointless to partition influences into environmental or biological ones, and state that biosocial criminologists should "move beyond heritability toward research grounded in the reality that genetic effects on human behavior are meaningful only when considered in combination with environmental influences."[118]

In critiquing the methodological problems with heritability studies, Burt and Simons argue that major assumptions required by twin and adoption studies are often not mentioned, and are often violated, rendering these studies' conclusions suspect, and leading to the overestimation of the effects of genetic contributions to behavior. In the section of heritability studies earlier in this chapter, we discussed that a problem with studies of twins raised apart is that monozygotic (MZ), or identical twins (who share all their DNA), in fact experience more similar environments than dizygotic (DZ), or fraternal twins (who share only about half of their DNA). These studies rely on nine assumptions, one being the "equal environment assumption" (EEA). Burt and Simons point to a large body of research challenging this assumption: MZ twins are more likely to receive similar treatment by their parents, to share the same friends and classroom, to spend time together and identify with one another, and so forth.[119] Later in this book we discuss sociological theories that relate to the powerful influence parenting and peers can have on one's behavior; if MZ twins vary significantly compared to DZ twins with respect to parenting and peers, this is especially problematic for the accuracy of conclusions made by studies relying on the EEA assumption, and probably results in the inflation of their estimates of heritability.[120]

Adoption studies have methodological limitations as well. Burt and Simons discuss four of these: late separation, nonrepresentativeness and range restriction, selective placement, and prenatal influences. First, while some adoptees are separated at birth, others are adopted after spending considerable time with their biological parent. If a parent–child bond has formed it is difficult to separate out environmental from genetic influences, as early childhood plays a prominent role in a child's development.[121] Second, adoptive parents are not very representative of the general population, as they are more likely to be affluent, better educated, and live in better communities.[122] This range restriction can result in downplaying environmental effects and inflating genetic ones.[123] Third, the assumption that there is no association between characteristics of the adoptive family and biological parents may be violated due to selective placement—the fitting of the child to the home, which can result in children seen as less desirable being placed in families viewed as less desirable.[124] Finally, birth mothers may influence their children through prenatal conditions, such as toxins, poor nutrition, and poor medical care, all of which may increase risk of crime,[125] and are shared environmental factors that would nonetheless be placed in the genetic category by studies partitioning the variance.[126]

Although some researchers point to studies of Twins Reared Apart (TRA) to defend heritability of crime and antisocial behavior, Burt and Simons note that these studies too have methodological limitations, but more importantly, there are very few of them, and only one that directly examines antisocial behavior.[127]

According to Burt and Simons, beyond methodological problems with twin and adoption studies, they also are conceptually problematic, because genetic and environmental influences simply cannot be additively partitioned; this is due in part to genetic–environment covariance and genetic–environment interaction.[128]

> *Genetic–environmental covariance* occurs when certain genotypes are associated with particular environments. . . . Scholars have used the example of children's genetically influenced behavioral problems evoking harsh parental discipline, which in turn, could increase behavior problems. It is an ongoing matter of debate as to how to classify this covariance in the calculus of heritability; certainly many, if not most, scholars would agree it fits neatly in neither G nor the E category.[129]

Another example of covariance pertains to skin pigmentation. Those with darker skin, which is genetically coded, are more likely to be raised in criminogenic environments (greater racial discrimination, lower socioeconomic status, higher disadvantage). "Surely, most scientists believe that classifying offending that results from racial discrimination because of skin pigmentation as purely 'genetic' is preposterous."[130] The ability to partition effects into genetic and environmental categories also relies on the assumption that there are not significant *interactions* between the two. Yet accumulative research suggests "rather than the rare exception, gene-environment (G x E) interactions seem to be the rule."[131] For an example of such an interaction, refer back to the study discussed earlier in this chapter, addressing MAOA and childhood maltreatment.

Aside from gene-environment covariance and interaction, the field of molecular genetics has shown that the human genome itself (an individual's entire DNA sequence) is dynamic and responds to the environment. According to the "postgenomic" view, genes are intrinsically part of the human developmental system; that is to say, environment regulates our genetic activity. DNA only produces RNA and proteins when it is activated by the epigenome, which is a complex regulatory system, allowing expression of a gene, and the epigenome is influenced by the environment. So while the existence of a particular gene is inherited, its activation may be a product of environmental conditions.[132] "Epigenetics focuses on the mechanisms of gene regulation in gene expression and phenotype, which can last for months, years, or across the life span and can even be transmitted onto future generations."[133] This phenomenon is referred to as the *neogenome*, and challenges the view that genes and the environment can be considered independently.[134] Based on these modern developments as well as their methodological critique of heritability studies, Burt and Simons call for an end to heritability studies in criminology, recommending instead that biosocial criminologists proceed with research that recognizes the interplay between genes and the environment, when examining influences on behavior.[135] One of the contributions of "the postgenomic paradigm" is new development in social neuroscience, which traditionally assumed the adult brain is generally fixed in size and inability to create new neurons. Now "evidence suggests not only that neuroplasticity takes place in childhood and is influenced by environmental variables identified as important in traditional criminology theory and research but also that it continues in adulthood."[136] Burt and Simons conclude:

> Importantly, new environments and experiences can change gene expression and alter biological systems. In other words, systems can be recalibrated and the brain can be resculpted. As such, the new paradigm is a biosocial life perspective. Under this paradigm, the challenge for biosocial criminologists entails (1) identifying how adverse environments sculpt an individual's physiology, especially the brain, to respond to environmental events with aggression, coercion, or violence; and (2) ascertaining how environments or experiences (whether naturally occurring changes or interventions) can change the person's biological systems and, in turn, their response to situations. Importantly, we believe that not only

are such integrative efforts potentially valuable for understanding the biological processes through which the environment influences development and behavior, but also such knowledge has the potential to inform social interventions to prevent crime and humanely reform offenders (e.g., meditation, CBT, exercise, and nutrition).[137]

Others feel that epigenetics is too new a field to command conclusions as strong as Burt and Simons's.[138] Burt and Simons's article also provoked a strong, negative response by scientists who engage in heritability studies, prompting a back-and-forth argument. Their challengers point to a number of problems with the article and resist any call to ending twin research, arguing that it is very much integral to biosocial criminology.[139] Wright et al., for example, say that Burt and Simons "cherry-picked the studies they cited in support of their position regarding the biasing impact of the equal environments assumption (EEA),"[140] "misquoted and characterized scholars,"[141] got the math wrong in their analysis of the effects of violations of model assumptions, and "made the claim that an entire class of statistical models, as well as the finding generated from thousands of studies based on these models, is 'fatally flawed,'"[142] without meeting the burden of proof that is required for such a bold claim. This will be likely be an ongoing debate with stakes of considerable magnitude. As Wright et al. note, if Burt and Simons's call is heeded, research based on twins will no longer be published in criminology, but will in almost every other discipline.[143]

Despite the contentiousness of this debate, many will likely take a middle ground, such as Rocque and Posick, who see epigenetics as nascent but promising, and also do not believe in abandoning heritability studies.[144] They also do not see biosocial criminology as any kind of paradigm shift in criminology, viewing it instead as the normal development of a maturing field, and that disputes over biosocial criminology are not productive to criminology as a whole. More important than these debates, to them, is how biosocial criminologists can advance public policy: "The value of biosocial criminology will ultimately lie in how well it can advance our understanding of how and why antisocial behavior happens and how it can be prevented."[145]

CONCLUSIONS

To the extent that most modern criminologists are trained in sociology, there has been a longstanding skepticism about biological explanations of criminal behavior. However, biosocial approaches to the study of crime are founded on the idea that the environment and biological makeup interact in significant ways to influence behavior.[146]

These theories are necessarily part of a multiple-factor approach to criminal behavior. The presence of certain biological factors is said to increase the likelihood, but not to determine absolutely, that an individual will engage in criminal behaviors. In addition, biological factors are said to increase the likelihood that an individual will engage in criminal behaviors when these factors interact with psychological or social factors.

Several examples of these interactions have been discussed in this chapter. One of the most notable examples was found in the study by Moffitt, Caspi, and colleagues on the interaction between MAOA activity and maltreatment, as described in the section on neurotransmitters.[147] In the past, biologically oriented and sociologically oriented criminologists have often been at odds with each other. Both sides have overstated their own positions and refused to acknowledge the partial validity of their opponents' views. This situation is changing as criminologists on both sides are recognizing the need for biosocial theories that examine not only the separate contribution of sociological and biological phenomena to criminal behavior but the interaction of these perspectives as well. This emerging synthesis of perspectives will probably benefit biological criminology, since extreme biological views often raise images of determinism among some audiences, who subsequently react negatively to the furthering of such research and to any policies that are based on it. For example, Lombroso's theories were used to fuel the eugenics movement in the early 1900s, helping influence the persecution of the Jewish. And as Raine has pointed out, society already is engaged in "passive eugenics" by not allowing those serving life in prison to reproduce.[148]

KEY TERMS

biological determinism
increased probability
interaction
biosocial theories
physiognomy
phrenology
atavistic
born criminals
insane criminals
criminaloids
multiple-factor causation
anomalies
physical criminal type
somatotypes
endomorphic
mesomorphic
ectomorphic
inherited characteristics
    (heritability of crime)
twin studies
adoption studies

neurotransmitters
the warrior gene/Monoamine
    oxidase (MAOA)
hormones
testosterone
central nervous system
cerebral cortex
frontal lobes
temporal lobes
electroencephalograph (EEG)
brain-imaging techniques
autonomic nervous system
anxiety reaction
socialization
skin conductance response
drug and alcohol abuse
nutrition or toxin intake
head injury
epigenetics
Equal Environment
    Assumption (EEA)

DISCUSSION QUESTIONS

1. What body types have been found to be more associated with criminality? What developmental factors may explain such a correlation?
2. Provide examples of ways in which the failure to control for environmental variables may have contaminated the twin studies and their findings of hereditary criminality.
3. What are neurotransmitters? To what extent have their levels been correlated with criminality? How may environmental factors affect neurotransmitter levels?
4. Why was the reporting of the findings regarding monoamine oxidase in the journal *Science* considered so important?
5. What directionality problems have testosterone studies brought to light?
6. What would be examples of biological conditions that would increase an individual's probability (risk) of offending? What are the policy implications of biological risk factors—that is, what should be done?
7. Biological theories often meet with great resistance in the social sciences. Why? Can you think of past historical examples of where biological theories were misused? What dangers could you foresee regarding such misuse?

NOTES

1. Gail S. Anderson, *Biological Influences on Criminal Behavior* (Boca Raton, FL: Simon Fraser University Publications, 2007); and Diana Fishbein, *Biobehavioral Perspectives in Criminology* (Belmont, CA: Wadsworth, 2001), pp. 9–12.
2. For a brief overview of the biosocial approach, including evolutionary, behavior genetic, and neurophysiological approaches, see Anthony Walsh, "Introduction to the Biosocial Perspective," in *Biosocial Criminology: Challenging Environmentalism's Supremacy*, ed. Anthony Walsh and Lee Ellis (New York: Nova Science, 2003), pp. 3–12. For a review of biosocial studies, see Adrain Raine, "Biosocial Studies of Antisocial and Violent Behavior in Children and Adults: A Review," *Journal of Abnormal Child Psychology* 30 (2002): 311–326. For a broader presentation of the area, see Anthony Walsh, *Biosocial Criminology* (Cincinnati, OH: Anderson, 2002).
3. Havelock Ellis, *The Criminal*, 2nd ed. (New York: Scribner, 1900), p. 27. A popular discussion of the symbolic meanings of physical appearance, including the tendency to link beauty to goodness and ugliness to evil, can be found in Robin Tolmach Lakoff and Raquel L. Scherr, *Face Value: The Politics of Beauty* (Boston: Routledge & Kegan Paul, 1984).
4. See Nicole Rafter, "The Murderous Dutch Fiddler: Criminology, History, and the Problem of Phrenology," *Theoretical Criminology* 9 (2005): 65–96. See also Leonard Savitz, Stanley H. Turner, and Toby Dickman, "The Origin of Scientific Criminology: Franz Joseph Gall as the First Criminologist," in *Theory in Criminology*, ed. Robert F. Meier (Beverly Hills, CA: Sage, 1977), pp. 41–56.

5. Information about Lombroso's life and work can be found in Randy Martin, Robert J. Mutchnick, and W. Timothy Austin, *Criminological Thought: Pioneers Past and Present* (New York: Macmillan, 1990), chap. 2; and Marvin E. Wolfgang, "Cesare Lombroso," in *Pioneers in Criminology*, 2nd ed., ed. Hermann Mannheim (Montclair, NJ: Patterson Smith, 1972), pp. 232–291. For a more critical view, see Stephen Jay Gould, *The Mismeasure of Man* (New York: Norton, 1981), chap. 4, in which Lombroso's theory of atavism was presented in its historical and scientific context. Gould argued that scientists of the time, desiring to prove their own superiority and the inferiority of other racial and ethnic groups, cloaked their prejudices in the veil of objective science.

6. Charles Darwin, *Descent of Man* (London: John Murray, 1871), p. 137. For a review of applications of evolutionary psychology to the problem of crime, see Walsh, *Biosocial Criminology*, chap. 3. While this model provides an organizing framework for understanding events, it seems impossible to prove or disprove. See J. S. Adler, "On the Border of Snakeland: Evolutionary Psychology and Plebeian Violence in Industrial Chicago, 1875–1920," *Journal of Social History* 36 (2003): 541–560.

7. At that time, the "Southern question" was a popular concern, with allegations in the press and among politicians that "the Southerners are inferior beings . . . lazy, incapable, criminal, and barbaric." See Antonio Gramsci, "Some Aspects of the Southern Question," in *Gramsci: Selections from Political Writings*, ed. Quintin Hoare (New York: International Publishers, 1978), p. 444.

8. Cesare Lombroso, *L'uomo delinquente (The Criminal Man)*, 4th ed. (Torino: Bocca, 1889), p. 273, as quoted by Enrico Ferri, *Criminal Sociology* (New York: D. Appleton, 1900), p. 12.

9. This is a partial listing adapted from the basic work by Gina Lombroso Ferrero, *Criminal Man According to the Classification of Cesare Lombroso* (New York: Putnam, 1911), pp. 10–24, 1911 edition reprinted by Patterson Smith, Montclair, NJ, 1972.

10. Cesare Lombroso, *Crime: Its Causes and Remedies*, 1912 edition reprinted by Patterson Smith, Montclair, NJ, 1972.

11. Edwin D. Driver, "Introductory Essay," in Charles Goring, *The English Convict: A Statistical Study*, 1913 edition reprinted by Patterson Smith, Montclair, NJ, 1972, p. vii.

12. Goring, *The English Convict*, pp. 196–214.

13. Ibid., p. 200.

14. Ibid., p. 287, esp. Table 119.

15. Driver, "Introductory Essay," p. v.

16. See Raine, "Biosocial Studies of Antisocial and Violent Behavior in Children and Adults," 311–326; see also Fishbein, *Biobehavioral Perspectives in Criminology*, pp. 65–66. These are said to result from prenatal influences, rather than from evolutionary atavism.

17. Goring, *The English Convict*, p. 173 (italics in the original).

18. William H. Sheldon (with various associates), *Psychology and the Promethean Will*, 1936; *Varieties of Human Physique*, 1940; *The Varieties of Temperament*, 1942; *Varieties of Delinquent Youth*, 1949; and *Atlas of Man*, 1954. All

published by Harper, New York and London. Information about the life and work of Sheldon can be found in Martin et al., *Criminological Thought*, chap. 2. A thirty-year follow-up on Sheldon's work can be found in Emil Hartl, *Physique and Delinquent Behavior* (New York: Academic Press, 1982).

19. The schematic arrangement of basic types has been constructed from the discussion in Sheldon, *Varieties of Delinquent Youth*, pp. 14–30.

20. Juan B. Cortés, *Delinquency and Crime* (New York: Seminar Press, 1972), p. 14. A significance level of .001 indicates that there is less than one in a thousand probability that the differences were due to chance.

21. Sheldon Glueck and Eleanor Glueck, *Physique and Delinquency* (New York: Harper, 1956).

22. Ibid., p. 9.

23. For a complete list of these traits and factors, see ibid., pp. 27–31.

24. Ibid., p. 226.

25. Ibid., p. 221.

26. Ibid., p. 224.

27. Anderson, *Biological Influences on Criminal Behavior*, pp. 21, 144.

28. Nicole Rafter, "Somatotyping, Antimodernism, and the Production of Criminological Knowledge," *Criminology* 45 (2007): 805–833 at pp. 815–816.

29. Anderson, *Biological Influences on Criminal Behavior*, p. 21.

30. See Jeffrey M. Stanton, "Galton, Pearson, and the Peas: A Brief History of Linear Regression for Statistics Instructors," *Journal of Statistics Education* 9:3 (2001).

31. Goring treated crime as a strictly legal category and thus preferred the term *convict* to the term *criminal*. See Driver, "Charles Buckman Goring," in Charles Goring, *The English Convict*, pp. 431–433, and "Introductory Essay," pp. ix–x.

32. Driver, "Charles Buckman Goring," pp. 439–440.

33. See Edwin H. Sutherland and Donald R. Cressey, *Criminology*, 10th ed. (Philadelphia: Lippincott, 1978), p. 120.

34. For example, see David C. Rowe and David P. Farrington, "The Familial Transmission of Criminal Convictions," *Criminology* 35 (1997): 177–201. See also Walsh, *Biosocial Criminology*, chap. 2. Glenn D. Walters and W. White Thomas, "Heredity and Crime: Bad Genes or Bad Research?" *Criminology* 27 (1989): 455–485, discussed methodological flaws in this type of research and concluded that there is evidence of heritability of crime and violence. They provided a variety of suggestions for improving the research.

35. Humans share 99 percent of their genes with other humans. Dizygotic twins share 50 percent of the remaining 1 percent whereas monozygotic twins share all the remaining 1 percent. See Adrian Raine, *The Psychopathology of Crime* (San Diego, CA: Academic Press, 1993), p. 54.

36. See a summary of such studies in Fishbein, *Biobehavioral Perspectives in Criminology*, pp. 27–29.

37. Karl O. Christiansen, "Threshold of Tolerance in Various Population Groups Illustrated by Results from the Danish Criminologic Twin Study," in *The Mentally Abnormal Offender*, ed. Anthony Vivian Smith de Reuck and Ruth Porter (Boston: Little, Brown, 1968), pp. 107–116.

38. Karl O. Christiansen, "Seriousness of Criminality and Concordance among Danish Twins," in *Crime, Criminology, and Public Policy*, ed. Roger Hood (New York: Free Press, 1974), pp. 63–77.

39. Referring to his own study, Christiansen ("Seriousness of Criminality and Concordance among Danish Twins," p. 77) stated: "Nothing in these results, however, can be interpreted as indicating that a higher twin coefficient in [identical] than in [fraternal] twins, or in pairs with more serious than in pairs with less serious forms of criminality, is due to the ... predominant part played by heredity in the causation of crime." See also Steffen Odd Dalgaard and Einar Kringlen, "A Norwegian Twin Study of Criminality," *British Journal of Criminology* 16 (1976): 213–232. They found that when twins were grouped according to their mutual closeness, all differences between identical and fraternal twins disappeared. They concluded that "the significance of hereditary factors in registered crime is non-existent." For a criticism of this study, see R. A. Forde, "Twin Studies, Inheritance and Criminality," *British Journal of Criminology* 18 (1978): 71–74. In addition, Raine (*The Psychopathology of Crime*, p. 58) pointed out that there are problems in the accuracy of labeling twins as monozygotic or dizygotic. The most accurate method is DNA fingerprinting, which is not usually employed. Other methods have various degrees of reliability.

40. W. M. Grove, E. D. Eckert, L. Heston, T. J. Bouchard, N. Segal, and D. T. Lyken, "Heritability of Substance Abuse and Antisocial Behavior: A Study of Monozygotic Twins Reared Apart," *Biological Psychiatry* 27 (1990): 1293–1304.

41. Christiansen, "A Review of Criminality Among Twins," in *Biosocial Bases of Criminal Behavior*, ed. S. A. Mednick and K. O. Christiansen (New York: Gardner Press, 1977), pp. 89–108.

42. Glenn D. Walters, "A Meta-Analysis of the Gene-Crime Relationship," *Criminology* 30 (1992): 595–613.

43. Marshall B. Jones and R. Jones Donald, "The Contagious Nature of Antisocial Behavior," *Criminology* 38 (2000): 25–46.

44. Research has used longitudinal data involving both identical and fraternal twins, rather than focusing on the much smaller number of twins raised apart. See, for example, Thalia C. Eley, Paul Lichtenstein, and Terrie E. Moffitt, "A Longitudinal Behavioral Genetic Analysis of the Etiology of Aggressive and Nonaggressive Antisocial Behavior," *Development and Psychopathology* 15 (2003): 383–402; J. Taylor, M. McGue et al., "Sex Differences, Assortative Mating, and Cultural Transmission Effects on Adolescent Delinquency: A Twin Family Study," *Journal of Child Psychology and Psychiatry* 41 (2000): 433–440; and Jeanette Taylor, Matt McGue, William G. Iacono, and David T. Lykken, "A Behavioral Genetic Analysis of the Relationship Between the Socialization Scale and Self-Reported Delinquency," *Journal of Personality* 68 (2000): 29–50.

45. Barry Hutchings and Sarnoff A. Mednick, "Criminality in Adoptees and Their Adoptive and Biological Parents: A Pilot Study," in *Biosocial Bases of Criminal Behavior*, ed. Mednick and Christiansen, pp. 127–141.

46. Ibid., p. 131, Table 4.
47. Ibid., p. 132, Table 6. See also ibid., p. 137, Table 8.
48. Ibid., p. 134.
49. Sarnoff A. Mednick, W. H. Gabrielli, and Barry Hutchings, "Genetic Influences in Criminal Convictions: Evidence from an Adoption Cohort," *Science* 224: 891–894 (1984). For a review of all adoption analyses see Gregory Carey, "Genetics and Violence," in *Understanding and Preventing Violence*, vol. 2, ed. Albert Reiss, Klaus Miczek, and Jeffrey Roth (Washington, DC: National Academy Press, 1994), pp. 34–39.
50. K. T. VanDusen, Mednick, Gabrielli, and Hutchings, "Social Class and Crime in an Adoption Cohort," *Journal of Criminal Law and Criminology* 74 (1983): 249–269; L. A. Baker, "Estimating Genetic Correlations Among Disconcordant Phenotypes: An Analysis of Criminal Convictions and Psychiatric Hospital Diagnoses in Danish Adoptees," *Behavior Genetics* 16 (1986): 127–142; Baker, W. Mack, T. E. Moffitt, and S. A. Mednick, "Etiology of Sex Differences in Criminal Convictions in a Danish Adoption Cohort," *Behavioral Genetics* 19 (1989): 355–370; Moffitt, "Parental Mental Disorder and Offspring Criminal Behavior: An Adoption Study," *Psychiatry: Interpersonal and Biological Processes* 50 (1987): 346–360.
51. Walters, "A Meta-Analysis of the Gene-Crime Relationship," pp. 604–605. The overall effect in the adoption studies was somewhat stronger than that in the twin studies, but this is probably because the adoption studies had larger samples than the twin studies, making it easier to achieve statistical significance.
52. Carey, "Genetics and Violence," p. 43.
53. P. A. Brennan, S. A. Mednick, and J. Volavka, "Biomedical Factors in Crime," in *Crime*, ed. James Q. Wilson and Joan Petersilia (San Francisco: ICS Press, 1995), p. 82. For an introduction to neurotransmitters see Walsh, *Biosocial Criminology*, chap. 4; Raine, *The Psychopathology of Crime*, pp. 83–84; and Fishbein, *Biobehavioral Perspectives in Criminology*, pp. 35–41.
54. Adrian Raine, *The Anatomy of Violence: The Biological Roots of Crime* (New York: Pantheon Books, 2013), p. 58.
55. Fishbein, *Biobehavioral Perspectives in Criminology*, pp. 40–41.
56. H. G. Brunner, M. Nelen, X. O. Breakfield, H. H. Ropers, and B. A. van Oost, "Abnormal Behavior Associated with a Point Mutation in the Structural Gene for Monoamine oxidase A," *Science* 262 (1993): 578–580.
57. O. Cases, I. Seif, J. Grimsby, P. Gaspar, and K. Chen, "Aggressive Behavior and Altered Amounts of Brain Serotonin and Norepinephrine in Mice Lacking MAOA," *Science* 268 (1995): 1763–1766.
58. Avshalom Caspi, Joseph McClay, Terrie E. Moffitt, Jonathan Mill, Judy Martin, Ian W. Craig, Alan Taylo, and Richie Poulton, "Role of Genotype in the Cycle of Violence in Maltreated Children," *Science* 297 (2002): 851–854. Only boys were examined for MAO activity for complex reasons related to the fact that the MAO gene is located on the X chromosome, of which females have two, whereas males have only one.

59. For a summary of studies replicating Caspi et al., as well as for a discussion of issues regarding gene/environment interaction and their implications regarding free will, rational choice and legal responsibility, see William Bernet, Cindy L. Vnencak-Jones, Nita Farahany, and Stephen A. Montgomery, "Bad Nature, Bad Nurture, and Testimony Regarding MAOA and SLC6A4 Genotyping at Murder Trials," *Journal of Forensic Science* 52 (2007): 1362–1371; Kelly Burns and Antoine Bechara, "Decision Making and Free Will: A Neuroscience Perspective," *Behavioral Sciences and the Law* 25 (2007): 263–280; Hans-Ludwig Kroeber, "The Historical Debate on Brain and Legal Responsibility—Revisited," *Behavioral Sciences and the Law* 25 (2007): 251–261.

60. J. Kim-Cohen, A. Caspi, A. Taylor, B. Williams, R. Newcombe, I. W. Craig, and T. E. Moffitt, "MAOA, Maltreatment, and Gene-Environment Interaction Predicting Children's Mental Health: New Evidence and a Meta-Analysis," *Molecular Psychiatry* 11 (2006): 903–913; Amy L. Byrd and Stephen B. Manuck, "MAOA, Childhood Maltreatment, and Antisocial Behavior: Meta-Analysis of a Gene-Environment Interaction," *Biological Psychiatry* 75 (2014): 9–17.

61. See Raine *The Anatomy of Violence*, pp. 53–55, for a discussion of research on the Maori.

62. Kevin M. Beaver, John Paul Wright, Brian B. Boutwell, J. C. Barnes, Matt DeLisi, and Michael G. Vaughn, "Exploring the Association Between the 2-Repeat Allele of the MAOA Gene Promoter Polymorphism and Psychopathic Personality Traits, Arrests, Incarceration, and Lifetime Antisocial Behavior," *Personality and Individual Differences* 54 (2013): 164–168.

63. J. Tihonen, M-R Rautianen, H. M. Ollila, E. Repo-Tilhonen, M. Virkkunen, A. Palotie, O. Pietlainen, K. Kristiansson, M. Joukamaa, H. Lauerma, J. Saarela, S. Tyni, H. Vartiainen, J. Paananen, D. Goldman, and T. Paunio, "Genetic Background of Extreme Violent Behavior," *Molecular Psychiatry* (2014): 1–7.

64. For a review, see D. A. Brizer, "Psychopharmacology and the Management of Violent Patients," *Psychiatric Clinics of North America* 11 (1988): 551–568.

65. Fishbein, *Biobehavioral Perspectives in Criminology*, p. 15.

66. Ibid., pp. 41–45.

67. For an excellent overview, see Paul Brain, "Hormonal Aspects of Aggression and Violence," in *Understanding and Preventing Violence*, vol. 2, ed. Reiss, Miczek, and Roth, pp. 173–244.

68. Raine, *The Psychopathology of Crime*. For another review of research on testosterone and aggression, see David Benton, "Hormones and Human Aggression," in *Of Mice and Women: Aspects of Female Aggression*, ed. Kaj Björkqvist and Pirkko Niemelä (San Diego, CA: Academic Press, 1992), pp. 37–48.

69. See Anderson, *Biological Influences on Criminal Behavior*, pp. 136–139, for a summary of studies regarding castration and recidivism.

70. See Julie Aitken Harris, "Review and Methodological Considerations in Research on Testosterone and Aggression," *Aggression and Violent Behavior* 4 (1999): 273–291. See also Robert M. Sapolsky, *The Trouble with Testosterone* (New York: Touchstone, 1998), pp. 147–159.

71. Brain, "Hormonal Aspects of Aggression and Violence," p. 221. See also Albert J. Reiss and Jeffrey Roth eds., *Understanding and Preventing Violence*, vol. 1 (Washington, DC: National Academy Press, 1993), p. 119.

72. See, e.g., Alan Booth and D. Wayne Osgood, "The Influence of Testosterone on Deviance in Adulthood: Assessing and Explaining the Relationship," *Criminology* 31 (1993): 93–117.

73. For a review of this research, see Anderson, *Biological Influences on Criminal Behavior*, pp. 133–134.

74. See R. F. Haskett, "Premenstrual Dysphoric Disorder: Evaluation, Pathophysiology and Treatment," *Progress in Neuro-Psychopharmacology and Biological Psychiatry* 11 (1987): 129–135; and E. P. Trunell and C. W. Turner, "A Comparison of the Psychological and Hormonal Factors in Women with and Without Premenstrual Syndrome," *Journal of Abnormal Psychology* 97 (1988): 429–436.

75. Diana Fishbein, "The Psychobiology of Female Aggression," *Criminal Justice and Behavior* 19 (1992): 99–126.

76. For a review of neuropsychological indicators of brain dysfunction and abnormal behavior, see Raine, *The Psychopathology of Crime*, pp. 103–127.

77. Ibid., p. 175.

78. Ibid., pp. 175–176.

79. Ibid., pp. 177–180. EEG abnormalities and EP (evoked potential) responses may be indicative of several possible problems, including CNS instability, underarousal, or subcortical epilepsy. Lumping all EEG abnormalities together is a mistake, since they may refer to different problems that may have different effects on behavior.

80. Ibid., p. 130.

81. Ibid., p. 155.

82. Hans J. Eysenck, *Crime and Personality* (Boston: Houghton Mifflin, 1964), pp. 100–119; Gordon Trassler, "Criminal Behavior," in *Handbook of Abnormal Psychology*, ed. Hans J. Eysenck (London: Putnam, 1972); and Sarnoff A. Mednick, "A Biosocial Theory of the Learning of Law-Abiding Behavior," in *Biosocial Bases of Criminal Behavior*, ed. Mednick and Christiansen, pp. 1–8.

83. Mednick, "A Biosocial Theory of the Learning of Law-Abiding Behavior," pp. 2–4.

84. Pauline S. Yaralian and Adrian Raine, "Biological Approaches to Crime," in *Explaining Criminals and Crime*, ed. Raymond Paternoster and Ronet Bachman (Los Angeles: Roxbury, 2001), pp. 57–72.

85. Ibid., p. 59.

86. Ibid., pp. 59–60.

87. Ibid., p. 60.

88. For a broad review of the drug and violence literature, see Alfred S. Friedman, "Substance Use/Abuse as a Predictor to Illegal and Violent Behavior: A Review of the Relevant Literature," *Aggression and Violent Behavior* 3 (1998): 339–355. See also Diana H. Fishbein and Susan E. Pease, *The Dynamics of Drug Abuse* (Boston: Allyn & Bacon, 1996); and Reiss and Roth, *Understanding and Preventing Violence*, vol. 1, chap. 4.

89. The discussion of alcohol and violence is summarized from Reiss and Roth, *Understanding and Preventing Violence*, pp. 189–191.

90. Abdulla A.-B. Badawy, "Alcohol and Violence and the Possible Role of Serotonin," *Criminal Behaviour and Mental Health* 13 (2003): 31–44, p. 32.

91. Friedman, "Substance Use/Abuse as a Predictor to Illegal and Violent Behavior," but see Helene Raskin White and Stephen Hansell, "The Moderating Effects of Gender and Hostility on the Alcohol-Aggression Relationship," *Journal of Research in Crime and Delinquency* 33 (1996): 450–470. See also M. Lyn Exum, "Alcohol and Aggression: An Integration of Findings from Experimental Studies," *Journal of Criminal Justice* 34 (2006): 131–145.

92. Reiss and Roth, *Understanding and Preventing Violence*, p. 192.

93. Ibid., p. 194.

94. Friedman, "Substance Use/Abuse as a Predictor to Illegal and Violent Behavior."

95. Ibid.

96. Reiss and Roth, *Understanding and Preventing Violence*, p. 195; and Ingemar Thiblin, Marianne Kristiansson, and Jovan Rajs, "Anabolic Androgenic Steriods and Behavioural Patterns Among Violent Offenders," *Journal of Forensic Psychiatry* 8 (1997): 299–310.

97. This discussion is taken primarily from Robin B. Kanarek, "Nutrition and Violent Behavior," in *Understanding and Preventing Violence*, vol. 2, ed. Reiss, Miczek, and Roth, pp. 515–539.

98. Ibid., pp. 523–526.

99. Ibid., pp. 530–531.

100. Ibid., pp. 533–534.

101. Diana H. Fishbein, "Biological Perspectives in Criminology," *Criminology* 28 (1990): 27–72.

102. Jessica Wolpaw Reyes, "Lead Exposure and Behavior: Effects on Antisocial and Risky Behavior among Children and Adolescents," *Economic Inquiry* 53 (2015): 1580-1605.

103. S. Mednick, V. Pollock, J. Volavka, and W. Gabrielli, "Biology and Violence" in *Criminal Violence*, ed. M. Wolfgand and N. Weiner (Beverly Hills, CA: Sage, 1982), pp. pp. 52–58.

104. Ibid., p. 55.

105. Dorothy Otnow Lewis, Shelley S.Shanok, and David A. Balla, "Perinatal Difficulties, Head and Face Trauma, and Child Abuse in the Medical Histories of Seriously Delinquent Children," *American Journal of Psychiatry* 136 (1979): 419–423. See also Dorothy Otnow Lewis, Shelley S. Shanok, Jonathan H. Pincus, and Gilbert H. Glaser, "Violent Juvenile Delinquents: Psychiatric, Neurological, Psychological, and Abuse Factors," *Journal of the American Academy of Child Psychiatry* 18 (1979): 307–319; and Dorothy Otnow Lewis, *Vulnerabilities to Delinquency* (New York: Spectrum, 1981).

106. Dorothy O. Lewis, Shelley S. Shanok, and David A. Balla, "Parental Criminality and Medical Histories of Delinquent Children," *American Journal of Psychiatry* 136 (1979): 288–292.

107. Raine, *The Psychopathology of Violence*, p. 193.

108. Ibid., pp. 193–194.
109. Ibid., pp. 194–195.
110. For reviews, see Fishbein, *Biobehavioral Perspectives in Criminology*, pp. 65–70; and Yaralian and Raine, "Biological Approaches to Crime," pp. 67–68.
111. Elizabeth Kandel and Sarnoff A. Mednick, "Perinatal Complications Predict Violent Offending," *Criminology* 29 (1991): 519–529.
112. Ibid., p. 523.
113. P. Brennan, S. A. Mednick, and E. Kandel, "Congenital Determinants of Violent and Property Offending," in *The Development and Treatment of Childhood Aggression*, ed. D. J. Pepler and K. H. Rubin (Hillsdale, NJ: Lawrence Erlbaum, 1993), pp. 81–92.
114. Adrian Raine, Patricia Brennan, and Sarnoff A. Mednick, "Interaction Between Birth Complications and Early Maternal Rejection in Predisposing Individuals to Adult Violence," *American Journal of Psychiatry* 154 (1997): 1265–1271.
115. Callie H. Burt and Ronald L. Simons, "Pulling Back the Curtain on Heritability Studies: Biosocial Criminology in the Postgenomic Era," *Criminology* 52 (2014): 223–262, at 224.
116. Ibid., citing among others Danielle Boisvert, John Paul Wright, Valerie Knopik, and Jamie Vaske, "Genetic and Environmental Overlap between Low Self-Control and Delinquency," *Journal of Quantitative Criminology* 28 (2012): 477–507; John Wright, Kevin Beaver, Matt DeLisi, and Michael Vaughn, "Evidence of Negligible Parenting Influences on Self-Control, Delinquent Peers, and Delinquency in a Sample of Twins," *Justice Quarterly* 25 (2008): 544–569; Beaver et al., "Exploring the Association between the 2-Repeat Allele of the MAOA Gene Promoter Polymorphism and Psychopathic Personality Traits, Arrests, Incarceration, and Lifetime Antisocial Behavior"; J. C. Barnes, Brian Boutwell, and Kathleen A. Fox, "The Effect of Gang Membership on Victimization: A Behavioral Genetic Explanation," *Journal of Criminal Justice* 40 (2012): 94–102.
117. Burt and Simons, "Pulling Back the Curtain on Heritability Studies," p. 224.
118. Ibid., p. 226.
119. Ibid., pp. 232–232, referring to studies such as David M. Evans and Nicholas G. Martin, "The Validity of Twin Studies," *GeneScreen* 1 (2000): 77–79; Allan V. Horowitz, Tami M. Videon, Mark F. Schmitz, and Diane Davis, "Rethinking Twins and Environments: Possible Sources for Assumed Genetic Influences in Twin Research," *Journal of Health and Social Behavior* 44 (2003): 111–129; Nikole J. Cronk, Wendy S. Slutske, Pamela A. F. Madden, Kathleen K. Bucholz, Wendy Reich, and Andrew C. Heath, "Emotional and Behavioral Problems Among Female Twins: An Evaluation of the Equal Environments Assumption," *Journal of the American Academy of Child and Adolescent Psychiatry* 41 (2002): 829–837.
120. Burt and Simons, "Pulling Back the Curtain on Heritability Studies", pp. 232–236.
121. Ibid., p. 238.

122. See, e.g., Mike Stoolmiller, "Implications of the Restricted Range of Family Environments for Estimates of Heritability and Nonshared Environment in Behavior-Genetic Adoption Studies," *Psychological Bulletin* 125 (1999): 392–409.

123. Burt and Simons, "Pulling Back the Curtain on Heritability Studies," p. 239.

124. Ibid., pp. 239–240. See, e.g., Jay Joseph, "Genetic Research in Psychiatry and Psychology: A Critical Overview," in *Handbook of Developmental Science, Behavior, and Genetics*, ed. Kathryn E. Hood, Carolyn T. Halpern, Gary Greenberg, and Richard M. Learner (Malden, MA: Wiley-Blackwell, 2010).

125. Burt and Simons, "Pulling Back the Curtain on Heritability Studies," p. 240, citing Raine, "Biosocial Studies of Antisocial Behavior in Children and Adults: A Review."

126. Burt and Simons, "Pulling Back the Curtain on Heritability Studies," citing Dalton Conley, "Commentary; Reading Plomin and Daniels in the Post-Genomic Age," *International Journal of Epidemiology* 40 (2011): 596–598.

127. Burt and Simons, "Pulling Back the Curtain on Heritability Studies," p. 242.

128. Ibid., pp. 242–243.

129. Ibid., p. 243, citing Robert Plomin, Valerie S. Knopik, and Jenae M. Neiderhiser, *Behavioral Genetics*, 3rd ed. (New York: Worth, 2012).

130. Burt and Simons, "Pulling Back the Curtain on Heritability Studies," p. 243.

131. Ibid.

132. Ibid., p. 244, citing among others Evan Charney, "Genes and Ideologies," *Perspectives on Politics* 6 (2012): 299–319.

133. Burt and Simons, "Pulling Back the Curtain on Heritability Studies," p. 244.

134. Charney, "Genes and Ideologies."

135. Burt and Simons, "Pulling Back the Curtain on Heritability Studies," pp. 246–247, noting that biosocial criminologists are already doing this (citing Anthony Walsh and Kevin M. Beaver, *Biosocial Criminology: New Directions in Theory and Research* [New York: Routledge, 2009]).

136. Burt and Simons, "Pulling Back the Curtain on Heritability Studies," p. 249, citing Erik B. Bloss, William G. Janssen, Bruce S. McEwen, and John H. Morrison, "Interactive Effects of Stress and Aging on Structural Plasticity in the Prefrontal Cortex," *Journal of Neuroscience* 30 (2010): 6726–6731; Richard J. Davidson and Bruce McEwen, "Social Influences on Neuroplasticity: Stress and Interventions to Promote Well-Being," *Nature Neuroscience* 15 (2012): 689–695.

137. Burt and Simons, "Pulling Back the Curtain on Heritability Studies," p. 250.

138. Terrie E. Moffitt and Amber Beckley, "Abandon Twin Research? Embrace Epigenetic Research/Premature Advice for Criminologists," *Criminology* 53 (2015): 121–126.

139. See John Paul Wright, J. C. Barnes, Brian B. Boutwell, Joseph A. Schwartz, Eric J. Connolly, Joseph L. Nedelec, and Kevin M. Beaver, "Mathematical Proof Is Not Minutiae and Irreducible Complexity Is Not a Theory; A Final Response to Burt and Simons and a Call to Criminologists," *Criminology* 53 (2015): 113–120.

140. Ibid., p. 113.

141. Ibid., p. 114.
142. Ibid., p. 117.
143. Ibid., p. 118.
144. Michael Rocque and Chad Posick, "Paradigm Shift or Normal Science? The Future of (Biosocial) Criminology," *Theoretical Criminology* 21 (2017): 288–303.
145. Ibid., p. 296.
146. See Walsh, "Introduction to the Biosocial Perspective"; Raine, "Biosocial Studies of Antisocial and Violent Behavior in Children and Adults"; and Walsh, *Biosocial Criminology*.
147. Caspi et al., "Role of Genotype in the Cycle of Violence in Maltreated Children."
148. Raine, *The Anatomy of Violence*, p. 365. Also, more generally see his discussion of the ethical and policy implications of neurocriminology, pp. 329–373.

CHAPTER 5

Psychological Factors
and Criminal Behavior

This chapter examines theories that explain criminal behavior primarily in terms of the psychological characteristics of the individual. There are two main types of psychological theories: those that focus on intelligence and those that focus on personality.

Low intelligence has probably been the psychological characteristic that has most often used to explain criminal and delinquent behavior. It was an important type of theory in the early years of the twentieth century, but it fell out of favor when research using IQ tests showed little or no difference in intelligence between criminals and noncriminals. Since the 1970s, however, there has been renewed support for this hypothesis, particularly with respect to juvenile delinquents.

The term *personality* refers to the emotional and behavioral attributes that tend to remain stable as the individual moves from situation to situation. Sigmund Freud's psychoanalytic theory may relate to some forms of criminal behavior, but is difficult to test. Some researchers use personality tests to attempt to measure different aspects of the personality, much as IQ tests attempt to measure intelligence. Other researchers focus on specific personality characteristics that are thought to be associated with crime and delinquency, such as the antisocial personality and impulsivity.

Psychological theories also consider biological and situational factors in their explanations of criminal behavior. Much of the biological research reviewed in Chapter 4 has been conducted by psychologists and psychiatrists and can be considered part of psychological or psychiatric theories of crime. These theories also consider the impact of the situation on the individual and explain behavior by relating the situation with the individual's biological and psychological characteristics. Situational factors, however, will be discussed in the chapters on sociological theories of criminal behavior. Psychological theories that argue that criminal behavior is the result of normal learning processes are discussed in Chapter 9.

INTELLIGENCE AND CRIME: BACKGROUND
IDEAS AND CONCEPTS

The language and literature of all peoples have words to describe and stories to illustrate the conduct of "dull-witted" or "slow" individuals whose intelligence is no more than that of a young child. From a spiritualistic point of view, such people were sometimes thought to be possessed by the devil and forced into exile and almost certain death. With the transition from spiritual explanations to naturalistic ones, ideas about this affliction were modified. Instead of being explained as curses of God, they were explained as curses of nature. Inheritance and family line of descent, as described in Darwin's theory of evolution, became the naturalistic way of accounting for such misfortunes.[1]

Richard Dugdale used this basic idea to explain the history of a family he called the "Jukes."[2] As part of his work for the Prison Association of New York, Dugdale found six members of this family in a county jail in 1874. He traced the genealogy of the family back over two hundred years and found a history of "pauperism, prostitution, exhaustion, disease, fornication, and illegitimacy." He attributed this melancholy history to the "degenerate" nature of the family. His study had a striking impact on the thinking at the time, despite the fact that it was based on unreliable, incomplete, and obscure information and was filled with value judgments and unsupported conclusions. For example, Henderson, writing in 1899, cited the Jukes as typical of families of degenerates and argued that private charitable work to alleviate the suffering of these people was actually allowing them to reproduce in great numbers, resulting in "the rising tide of pauperism, insanity, and crime which threatens to overwhelm and engulf our civilization."[3] He argued that this "deterioration of the common stock" must be resisted by segregating such inferior people in institutions and not allowing them to reproduce. US public and legal policy often reflected this principle. For example, in 1927 the Supreme Court upheld a Virginia law that forced the sterilization of mentally disabled people, stating that "three generations of imbeciles are enough."[4]

These studies of degenerate families supported the popular opinion that criminals are what they are because they do not understand the hazardous nature of criminality or the satisfying rewards of a law-abiding life.[5] But accurate comparisons call for exact measurements, and therefore the critical investigation of the relationship between crime and mental ability could come only after the development of intelligence tests and their applications to this problem.

IQ TESTS AND CRIMINAL BEHAVIOR

Intelligence tests as we know them today originated with the work of the distinguished French psychologist Alfred Binet (1857–1911), who was the director of the psychological laboratory at the Sorbonne.[6] In 1904 Binet became a member of a commission to formulate policy for the administration of special classes for students who were doing poorly in the Paris public schools. As part of that role, he devised a practical test to measure the mental functioning of students. Collaborating with Theodore Simon, who was the medical officer of the Paris schools, Binet assembled a large number of small tasks related to everyday life that involved the basic reasoning processes. These tasks were then arranged in ascending difficulty so that the first tasks could be performed by very young children, while the last could be performed only by adults. Their first scale of tasks appeared in 1905 and was called the Binet-Simon Scale of Intelligence.

This scale was revised in 1908, at which time the concept of "mental age" was added to the scale.[7] Each task was assigned a mental age—for example, a task that could be performed by an average nine-year-old but not by an average child who was eight or younger would be assigned a mental age of nine. Each child who took the test then could be assigned a mental age—that is, the mental age of the last tasks the child could perform. Then the child's mental age could be compared with his or her chronological age.

In 1912, the psychologist William Stern suggested that mental age should be divided by chronological age and the results multiplied by 100. The result of this calculation would be called the intelligence quotient, or IQ (a quotient being the answer in a division problem). Children whose mental ages were greater than their chronological ages would have IQs above 100, while those whose mental ages were less than their chronological ages would have IQs below 100.

This test was revised again shortly before Binet's death in 1911. At that time, Binet expressed reservations about the ways in which his test was being used. The test had been designed to identify children who were doing poorly in school so that they could receive special help. Binet argued that the test should not be used to identify children of superior intelligence, since it was not designed for that purpose. He also warned against using the test to label slower students as unteachable so that instead of being helped, they would be ejected from the schools. Binet was strongly committed to the view that slower students could improve their performance if properly helped, and he set up special classes in the Paris schools for the children who did poorly on his tests. He wrote with pleasure of the success of these classes, arguing that the pupils increased not only their knowledge but their intelligence as well: "It is in this practical sense, the only one accessible to us, that we say that the intelligence of these children has been increased. We have increased the intelligence of a pupil: the capacity to learn and to assimilate instruction."[8] Thus, Binet rejected the idea that intelligence is a fixed and inborn quantity that cannot be changed.

With the success of the Binet-Simon scale in Paris, numerous revisions, extensions, and adaptations were made in many lands. In the United States, Binet's tests and articles were translated into English and popularized by

H. H. Goddard of the New Jersey Training School for the Feeble Minded at Vineland. Goddard gave intelligence tests to all the inmates at his institution at Vineland and to all new inmates on admission. This testing program disclosed no inmate with a mental age over thirteen. Goddard therefore concluded that mental age twelve (IQ 75 on the then commonly held assumption that full mental ability is reached at chronological age sixteen) marked the upper limit of feeblemindedness.

With that standard as the basis for comparison, Goddard and many other psychologists gave intelligence tests to the inmates of prisons, jails, hospitals, and various other public institutions. Goddard examined a large number of such studies on the intelligence of criminals.[9] The proportion of criminals who were diagnosed as feebleminded in these studies ranged from 28 percent to 89 percent, with the median study finding that 70 percent of criminals were feebleminded. Goddard therefore concluded that most criminals were feebleminded.

Goddard also discovered a large group of "defectives" who were living in the pine barrens of New Jersey and traced their heritage back to a man who had had an illegitimate child by a "feebleminded" barmaid.[10] Of 480 descendants of this union, Goddard claimed that 143 were feebleminded, 36 were illegitimate, 33 were sexually immoral, 24 were confirmed alcoholics, 3 were epileptics, 3 were criminals, and 8 were keepers of houses of prostitution. The man later married a righteous Quaker woman, a union ultimately resulting in 496 "normal" descendants who "married into the best families of their state."

Goddard mourned the "havoc that was wrought by one thoughtless act"[11] and concluded that criminality and feeblemindedness were two aspects of the same degenerate state, so that all feebleminded people were potential criminals. Feeblemindedness was said to be caused by a recessive gene that obeyed the normal rules of inheritance that were originally formulated by Gregor Mendel.[12] Thus, Goddard argued that feeblemindedness could be eliminated through selective breeding. This conclusion led to his recommendation that the feebleminded be institutionalized and not allowed to reproduce.[13]

These ideas dominated the thinking of mental testers for a time but were directly challenged by the results of intelligence tests that were administered to draftees during World War I. Following Goddard, the Army Psychological Corps at first made the conventional assumption that those of mental age twelve or below were feebleminded and therefore not fit for military service. This procedure led to a diagnosis of feeblemindedness for nearly half the draftees,[14] which was generally recognized as false. Thus, Goddard wrote in 1921, a few years after the war ended, "The most extreme limit that anyone has dared to suggest is that one percent of the population is feebleminded."[15] By 1928, Goddard had concluded that feeblemindedness might be remedied by education and that it was not necessary to segregate the feebleminded in institutions and to prevent them from reproducing. Goddard was frank about his own change of mind: "As for myself, I think I have gone over to the enemy."[16]

Publication of the results of World War I testing also provided a new perspective on the relationship between intelligence and crime. A number of studies were done comparing the performance of prisoners with that of draftees on intelligence tests. These studies generally found insignificant differences between the two groups, and several studies found that prisoners actually scored higher than draftees.[17] As a result of such studies, feeble-mindedness largely disappeared as a basis for explaining criminal behavior.

DELINQUENCY, RACE, AND IQ

Although it is no longer believed that a large number of criminals are feeble-minded, the IQs of criminals and delinquents became embroiled in a controversy concerning the relationship between intelligence and race. African Americans, on average, score about 15 points lower than European Americans on IQ tests. Some scholars have used the difference in IQ scores to explain the difference in crime and delinquency rates between the races.

This controversy originated in a lengthy article by Arthur Jensen, published in the *Harvard Educational Review* in 1969.[18] Jensen argued that IQ tests measure a factor that is important for performance in Western industrialized societies and that about 80 percent of the individual differences in this score is determined by genetic rather than environmental differences. He concluded that remedial education programs had failed for precisely this reason.

Jensen's article reverberated in many fields. In criminology, it was used in 1976 by Gordon to argue that variations in delinquency rates are best explained by variations in IQ.[19] Gordon cited Jensen to the effect that IQ is largely a biological factor and quoted several studies that supported the hypothesis that delinquency is related to the biology of the individual. He pointed to the similarity between the distribution of IQ scores and the distribution of delinquency and demonstrated that data from court records from Philadelphia and national rates for commitment to training schools could be duplicated merely by assuming that all youths (both African American and European American) with IQs below a certain level, and no youths above it, became delinquent. This coincidence "virtually necessitate(s) that there be some more reasonable functional relationship within sex between IQ and delinquency that is common or nearly common to both races."[20]

The following year, Hirschi and Hindelang reviewed a number of studies that were related to IQ and delinquency.[21] They argued that low IQ was at least as important as class or race in predicting delinquency, that delinquency is consistently related to low IQ within race and within class (e.g., lower-class delinquents are more likely to have low IQs than are lower-class nondelinquents) and that the principal sociological theories of delinquency "have been saying for some time that IQ should be related to delinquency for the same reason social class is, or should be, related to it." Although decreasing proportions of criminals and delinquents were classified as feebleminded because of the repeated lowering of the "normal" mental age, Hirschi and Hindelang pointed out that the differences between delinquents and nondelinquents never entirely disappeared and seemed to stabilize at about 8 IQ points.[22]

Studies since Hirschi and Hindelang's article have continued to find IQ differences between delinquents and nondelinquents that do not seem to be caused by problems in administering the tests.[23] In addition, more serious delinquent offenders have even lower IQ scores than do minor offenders,[24] and low IQ scores among young children are associated with later offending when these children become adolescents and adults.[25] Finally, IQ differences have been found between adult offenders and nonoffenders—for example, Moffitt found a 17-point IQ difference between adult nonoffenders and adult "life-course persistent" offenders.[26]

More recently, attention has focused on the verbal abilities of delinquents, as measured by IQ tests, and on the difference between the "verbal IQ" and the so-called performance IQ. The verbal IQ measures the person's comprehension of language, while the performance IQ measures the degree of nonverbal contact with environment and the capacity to work in concrete situations. For most people, the verbal and performance IQ scores are close to each other. But delinquents consistently show a large gap between the two scores, with lower verbal IQ scores but basically normal performance IQ scores.[27]

Quay suggested several reasons why low verbal IQ may be associated with delinquency.[28] First, low verbal ability may lead to school problems, and the school problems may then lead to delinquency. Second, low verbal abilities may be associated with a variety of other psychosocial problems, and these other problems may then lead to delinquency. Finally, low verbal abilities may lead to a failure to develop higher-order cognitive processing, such as moral reasoning, empathy, and problem solving. The lack of these cognitive processes may then lead to delinquency.

Others, however, have pointed out that verbal IQ is affected by educational achievement, while performance IQ is not.[29] They have suggested that the pattern of low verbal but normal performance IQ among delinquents simply reflects the fact that delinquents tend to underachieve in schools, particularly if they are from the lower socioeconomic class.

INTERPRETING THE ASSOCIATION BETWEEN DELINQUENCY AND IQ

It seems clear that whatever it measures, low IQ scores are associated with crime and delinquency. But it is still necessary to explain why people with low scores on IQ tests are more likely to commit crimes than are those with high scores. The explanation one accepts will depend to a large degree on one's view of what IQ measures.

The first approach is to assume that IQ measures some form of abstract reasoning or problem-solving ability and that this ability is largely inherited.[30] Gordon, for example, assumed this perspective and suggested that ineffective child-rearing practices by low-IQ parents may be the cause of delinquency among their low-IQ children.[31] Hirschi and Hindelang also believed that IQ measures innate ability, but they argued that IQ influences delinquency through its effect on school performance: low-IQ youths do poorly in school, which leads to anger at the school and to truancy, which then leads to delinquency.[32] Gottfredson and Hirschi suggested that youths with low intelligence tend to seek short-term immediate gratifications, and that these actions often turn out to be criminal.[33] A similar argument was made by Wilson and Herrnstein, who suggested that those with low IQs are inclined to commit "impulsive crimes with immediate rewards."[34] All these interpretations assume that IQ measures some form of innate ability.

A second approach argues that IQ does not measure innate ability but instead measures qualities that are related to the dominant culture. Jane Mercer illustrated the meaning of cultural bias by constructing a test of simple behavioral tasks related to intelligence, such as being able to tie one's own shoes by age seven.[35] The test was given to samples of lower-class African Americans and Mexican Americans and middle-class European Americans, all of whom had IQs below 70. Ninety-one percent of the African Americans passed the test, along with 61 percent of the Mexican Americans, but none of the European Americans. This finding would indicate that many African Americans and Mexican Americans are more intelligent than would appear from their IQ scores. Critics of this argument point out that children from nondominant cultures do not improve their performance on IQ tests that have been designed specifically to eliminate cultural biases and that children from some nondominant cultures, particularly Asian ones, have superior scores on IQ tests.[36]

A third approach argues that IQ measures general abilities, but that these abilities are largely determined by a person's environment. For example, Simons cited a number of studies that reported IQ gains averaging about 15 points when low-IQ, lower-class children were placed in special classes, where most of the gains were produced in about one year's time.[37] Simons concluded that IQ is best viewed as "a broad set of verbal and problem-solving skills which are better labeled academic aptitude or scholastic readiness." He pointed out that the questions on verbal intelligence tests are virtually indistinguishable from those on reading comprehension tests and that the score distributions from the two types of tests are virtually identical. He also cited a study that showed that children in the early grades of lower-class African American schools and of middle-class African American schools had similar scores on reading comprehension tests, but by the eighth grade, there were large differences between the two groups. This finding suggests that lower-class children stagnate in schools for some reason and that they are not mentally inferior to begin with. Finally, Simons pointed out that delinquents are almost always described as unmotivated students and asked why anyone would think that these students would be motivated to perform to the best of their ability on the day the IQ tests are administered when they are not motivated to do so on any other school day.

The third approach has received impressive support from research on what is known as the "Flynn effect." In the 1980s, James Flynn demonstrated that average IQ has been rising for at least sixty years in all countries for which data are available (about twenty countries).[38] This finding has been widely replicated by other researchers and is generally estimated between 9 and 15 points per generation. Such changes in IQ cannot be explained by changes in genetics. Flynn himself hypothesized that IQ measures abstract problem-solving ability, rather than intelligence, and that increases in this ability are explained by changes in the environment.[39] These changes may include such things as better nutrition and better schooling, but experimental data in support of any particular factors are weak at present.

PERSONALITY AND CRIMINAL BEHAVIOR—SIGMUND FREUD AND PSYCHOANALYSIS

The term *personality* refers to the complex set of emotional and behavioral attributes that tend to remain relatively constant as the individual moves from situation to situation.[40] Words like *aggressive, belligerent, suspicious, timid, withdrawn, friendly, cooperative, likable, argumentative,* and *agreeable* have long been used to describe or express impressions of some of these qualities. Our discussion of personality and its relationship to delinquency and criminal behavior covers (1) psychoanalytical theory, (2) research that focuses on personality tests to attempt to measure different aspects of the personality, and (3) research that focuses on specific personality characteristics.

Freud's work grew from the field of psychiatry, which encapsulated the experience of medical doctors in dealing with the basic problem of mental disease. Control of the dangerous and often outrageous behavior of the mentally and emotionally disturbed has been a problem in society from the earliest times. Historically, it has often been indistinguishable from the control of the dangerous and often outrageous behavior of the criminal. By the time of Sigmund Freud (1856-1939), all of the basic concepts of abnormal psychology had been developed out of experience in dealing with disturbed persons.[41] Sigmund Freud lived most of his life in Vienna and published most of his important ideas during the first forty years of the twentieth century.[42] Freud first adopted the idea of the unconscious, as used by earlier psychiatrists, arguing that the behaviors could be explained by traumatic experiences in early childhood that left their mark on the individual despite the fact that the individual was not consciously aware of those experiences.

As a way to treat these problems, Freud invented a technique he called "psychoanalysis." The central idea of psychoanalysis was free association: the patient relaxed completely and talked about whatever came to mind. By exploring these associations, the individual was able to reconstruct the earlier events and bring them to consciousness. Once the patient was conscious of these events, Freud argued that the events would lose their unconscious power and the patient would gain conscious control and freedom in his or her life.

Freud later revised his conceptions of the conscious into the id and the superego. *Id* was a term used to describe the great reservoir of biological and psychological drives, the urges and impulses that underlie all behavior. That includes the libido, the full force of sexual energy in the individual, as diffuse as the "will to live" found in all animals. The id is permanently unconscious, and responds only to what Freud called "the pleasure principle"—if it feels good, do it. The *superego*, in contrast, is the force of self-criticism and conscience and reflects requirements that stem from the individual's social experience in a particular cultural milieu. The superego may contain conscious elements in the form of moral and ethical codes, but it is primarily unconscious in its operation. The superego arises out of the first great love attachment the child experiences, with her or her parents. The child experiences them as judgmental, and ultimately internalizes their values as an *ego-ideal*— that is, as an ideal conception of what he or she should be. Finally, what Freud called the *ego* is the conscious personality. It is oriented toward the real world in which the person lives (termed by Freud the "reality principle"), and attempts to mediate between the demands of the id and the prohibitions of the superego.[43]

Given this basic organization of the personality, Freud explored how the ego handles the conflicts between the superego and the id. The basic problem is one of guilt: the individual experiences all sorts of drives and urges coming from the id, and feels guilty about them because of the prohibitions of the superego. There is a variety of ways in which the individual may handle the situation. In *sublimation* the drives of the id are diverted to activities approved of by the superego. For example, aggressive and destructive urges may be diverted to athletic activity. Sublimation is the normal and healthy way the ego handles the conflicts between the drives of the id and the prohibitions of the superego. In *repression*, in contrast, those drives are stuffed back into the unconscious and the individual denies they exist. This may result in a variety of strange effects on behavior. One possible result is a *reaction formation*, such as when a person with repressed sexual desires becomes very prudish about all sexual matters. Another result might be *projection*, in which, for example, a person with repressed homosexual urges frequently sees homosexual tendencies in others.

Freud believed that these basic conflicts were played out in different ways at different points in the life cycle. Of particular interest to him were the experiences of early childhood. He argued that each infant goes through a series of phases in which the basic drives were oriented around, first, oral drives, then anal drives, and finally genital drives. During the genital stage (around the ages of 3 and 4) the child is sexually attracted to the parent of the opposite sex and views the same-sex parent as competition. This is the famous Oedipus complex in boys, and the comparable Electra complex in girls. If the guilt produced by these urges is not handled adequately by the ego, it leaves a lasting imprint of the personality that affects later behavior.

Within the psychoanalytic perspective, criminal and delinquent behaviors are attributed to disturbances or malfunctions in the ego or superego. The id, by contrast, is viewed as a constant and inborn biologically based source of drives and urges; it does not vary substantially among individuals. Freud himself did not discuss criminal behavior to any great extent. He did, however, suggest that at least some individuals performed criminal acts because they possessed an overdeveloped superego, which led to constant feelings of guilty and anxiety.[44] There is a consequent desire for punishment to remove the guilt feelings and restore a proper balance of good against evil. Unconsciously motivated errors (i.e. careless or imprudent ways of committing the crime) leave clues so that the authorities may more readily apprehend and convict the guilty party, and thus administer suitably cleansing punishment. This idea was extensively developed by later Freudians.[45] Criminality of this type is said to be appropriate for treatment through psychoanalysis, since it can uncover the unconscious sources of guilt and free the person from the compulsive need for punishment.

While excessive guilty from an *overdeveloped* superego is one source of criminal behavior within the psychoanalytic framework, August Aichhorn, a psychoanalytically oriented psychologist, suggested alternate sources for crime and delinquency based on his years of experience running an institution for delinquents.[46] He found that many children in his institution had *underdeveloped* superegos, so that their delinquency and criminality were primarily expressions of an unregulated id. Aichhorn treated these children by providing a happy and pleasurable environment, so as to promote the type of identification with adults that the child failed to experience earlier. He commented that most training schools "attempted through force, through fear of punishment, and without rewards of love to make the delinquent socially acceptable. Since most of their charges belong to the type just described, they only exaggerated what the parents had already begun and consequently they were doomed to failure."[47] Freud approved of these techniques in his foreword to Aichhorn's book, and concluded that they, rather than psychoanalysis per se, were appropriate in the case of young children and of adult criminals dominated by their instincts.[48]

Aichhorn also suggested that other types of delinquents existed, including those who from an abundance of love, were permitted to do anything they wanted by overprotective and overindulgent parents.[49] He did not find that there were many of these, but they required different treatment techniques than the delinquents created by the absent or excessively severe parents described earlier. Finally, there were a few delinquents who had well-developed superegos but who identified with criminal parents.[50] Again, these required very different treatment techniques.

Much of later psychoanalytic theorizing with respect to criminal behavior is consistent with these three types of delinquents first suggested by Aichhorn.[51] Healy and Brommer, for example, examined 105 pairs of brothers, in which one brother was a persistent delinquent and the other was a nondelinquent.[52] They concluded that the delinquent brother had failed to develop normal affectional ties with his parents due to a variety of situational factors. Delinquency, they argued, was essentially a form of sublimation in which delinquents attempt to meet basic needs that are not being met by their families. Bowlby focused on early maternal deprivation as the origin of delinquency, arguing similarly that the basic affectional ties had failed to form.[53] Redl and Wineman found that "children who hate" lacked factors leading to identification with adults, such as feelings of being wanted, loved, encouraged, and secure.[54] They said that these children not only lacked adequate superegos, but their egos had been organized to defend the unregulated expression of their id desires. Redl and Wineman called this the "delinquent ego." Like Aichhorn, they recommended that these children be treated with unconditional love, to promote the identification with adults they lacked in earlier childhood.

The most common criticism of psychoanalytic theory as a whole is that it is untestable. Against this criticism, several authors have argued that Freud's ideas can be expressed in testable hypotheses, that these hypotheses have been tested in a great deal of empirical research, and that the results of the research have generally supported the theory.[55] A more specific criticism is that the psychoanalytic explanation of a particular individual's behavior often seems subjective and out of reach of objective measuring devices. These explanations are formulated after the behavior has occurred and rely heavily on interpretations of unconscious motivations. They may make a great deal of sense, but there is no way to determine the accuracy of the analyst's interpretation of an individual case within the framework of accepted scientific methodology.[56] In addition to these criticisms of psychoanalytic theory in general, several criticisms also have been made about psychoanalytic explanations of crime. The central assertion of this explanation is that at least some crime is caused by "unconscious conflicts arising from disturbed family relationships at different stages of development, particularly the oedipal stage."[57] This argument may apply to some crimes that would appear irrational, but many crimes seem quite conscious and rational and therefore not caused by unconscious conflicts. In addition, as a treatment technique, psychoanalysis requires a lengthy and usually quite expensive process that simply is not available to ordinary criminals. To date, psychoanalysis has not been particularly useful in either understanding crime or responding to it.

RESEARCH USING PERSONALITY TESTS

Psychological tests to measure personality differences have been developed more or less parallel to intelligence tests. Inevitably, delinquents and criminals have been tested with these "personality inventories" to discover how their personalities differ from those of nondelinquents and noncriminals.

In 1950, the Gluecks published an intensive study that compared five hundred delinquent and nondelinquent boys.[58] They argued that "the delinquent personality" is not so much a matter of the presence or absence of certain characteristics but is more a matter of the interrelatedness of these characteristics. The Gluecks summarized their impression of this interrelationship of characteristics as follows:[59]

> On the whole, delinquents are more extroverted, vivacious, impulsive, and less self-controlled than the non-delinquents. They are more hostile, resentful, defiant, suspicious, and destructive. They are less fearful of failure or defeat than the non-delinquents. They are less concerned about meeting conventional expectations, and are more ambivalent toward or far less submissive to authority. They are, as a group, more socially assertive. To a greater extent than the control group, they express feelings of not being recognized or appreciated.

Besides clinical examination, personality can also be assessed with a "personality inventory," a psychological test that is somewhat similar to an IQ test. The most widely known is the Minnesota Multiphasic Personality Inventory (MMPI), which is a list of 550 statements that were developed to aid in psychiatric diagnosis.[60] Also utilized prevalently is the California Psychological Inventory (CPI), which words questions in a less clinical fashion.[61] Waldo and Dinitz examined ninety-four personality studies that were conducted between 1950 and 1965 and found that about 80 percent of these studies reported statistically significant differences between criminals and noncriminals.[62] Their work was replicated by Tennenbaum for studies between 1966 and 1975.[63] The most impressive results were found with Scale 4 of the MMPI, previously called the "psychopathic deviate" scale, which consistently produced significant results. However, this scale was constructed to distinguish between offenders and nonoffenders and even contains questions about past offending. Thus, higher scores on this type of scale contain little information about basic personality dimensions, especially as related to antisocial behavior.[64]

Miller and Lynam examined the relationship between four different multidimensional personality models and antisocial behavior (ASB).[65] These models are all newer than the MMPI, and they all propose comprehensive constructs that measure personality broadly, rather than focusing on "pathological" elements. Each model has been extensively tested by personality researchers, with supportive results.[66] Miller and Lynam conducted a meta-analysis of empirical research from 1963 to 2000 on the relationship between these dimensions and antisocial behavior. On the basis of this research, they concluded that the personality characteristics that characterize individuals who commit crimes are best understood in terms of two distinct and separate dimensions: agreeableness and conscientiousness.[67] Offenders tend to be low in agreeableness—that is, they tend to be hostile, self-centered, spiteful, jealous, and indifferent to others. They also tend to be low in conscientiousness—that is, they tend to lack ambition, motivation, and perseverance; have difficulty controlling their impulses; and hold nontraditional and unconventional values and beliefs. Miller and Lynam added two qualifications to this description. First, they stated that these personality characteristics may not cause crime; rather, both the crime and the personality may be caused by some third variable, such as early childhood experiences or parenting style. Second, they added that the effects of such personality characteristics on antisocial behavior may be moderated by the environment, such as school or neighborhood conditions.[68]

Jones, Miller, and Lynam, noting the abundance of research on the effects of personality on antisocial behavior and aggression in the twenty-first century, meta-analyzed these studies published from 2000 to 2010, based on the Five Factor Model (FFM) of personality.[69] This model

> posits five primary personality domains: Neuroticism (i.e., tendency to experience negative emotions such as depression, shame, stress), Extraversion (i.e. tendency to seek the company of others, experience positive emotions, and interact with others and the world in an approach-oriented manner), Openness to experience (i.e., openness to different ideas, emotions, values, and experiences), Agreeableness (i.e., interpersonal strategies and reactions), and Conscientiousness (i.e., ability to delay gratification, persevere in the face of difficulty, and consider the consequences of one's behavior prior to acting).[70]

These five factors are broad traits (higher-order), and Jones et al. speak to the need to examine the role played by lower-order traits (facets) within each broad trait in explaining ASB and aggression. Each of the five traits is comprised of six facets. It is important to go narrower, they say, because while a broad trait may have an insignificant effect on one of these outcomes, facets within the trait may be significantly associated with them. Their meta-analysis therefore resulted in sixty coefficients (5 factors X six facets X two outcome measures). Approximately two-thirds of these were statistically significant.[71] For Neuroticism, anxiety was negatively associated with ASB; angry hostility, depression, and impulsiveness were positively associated with both outcomes; and vulnerability was positively associated with aggression. With respect to Extraversion, warmth was negatively associated with both outcomes, assertiveness was positively associated with aggression, and excitement seeking was positively associated with ASB. Several facets of Openness were significantly associated with the outcomes: feelings (negative with both outcomes), actions and ideas (positive with ASB). All facets of Agreeableness were negatively associated with both ASB and aggression (trust, straightforwardness, altruism, compliance, modesty, and tender-mindedness). Similarly, all facets of Conscientiousness were negatively associated with both outcomes (competence, order, dutifulness, achievement striving, self-discipline, and deliberation). A very recent (2019) meta-analysis by Vise et al., which updated the Jones et al. study, incorporating seventy-three new studies and using sophisticated Bayesian procedures, confirmed the major findings with a higher level of statistical precision.[72]

Jones et al. recognize that mainstream criminology theories have largely ignored the role of personality, and believe that there would be benefits to rectifying this. Although there are changes in the average level of personality traits across one's development, personality is relatively stable over time. Because both personality and ASB are partly inherited, one may help explain the other. Personality may also moderate the effects of constructs from major criminology theories and ASB, as well. For example, in general strain theory (see Chapter 7 of this volume), stress may result in either externalizing behaviors (such as drug use) or internalizing behavior (such as anxiety). Personality traits may help us to understand why some individuals externalize whereas others internalize behavior in throes of stress.[73]

PSYCHOPATHY AND ANTISOCIAL PERSONALITY DISORDER

The fifth edition of the official *Diagnostic and Statistical Manual of Mental Disorders, fifth edition* (*DSM-V*) of the American Psychiatric Association states that "the essential feature of Antisocial Personality Disorder is a pervasive pattern of disregard for, and violation of, the rights of others that begins in childhood or early adolescence and comes into adulthood."[74] The diagnosis may be made when there are at least three of the following six characteristics: (1) repeated violations of the law that are grounds for arrest; (2) repeated lying, use of aliases, or conning others for personal profit or pleasure; (3) impulsivity or failure to plan ahead; (4) repeated physical fights or assaults; (5) reckless disregard for safety of self or others; (6) repeated failure to sustain consistent work behavior or honor financial obligations; and (7) lack of remorse.

The *DSM-V* distinguishes "antisocial personality disorder" from "adult antisocial behavior," which is criminal behavior that occurs without the presence of any personality disorder. A person should be diagnosed as having an antisocial personality when these characteristics are "inflexible, maladaptive, and persistent, and cause significant functional impairment or subjective distress." This disorder is said to have "a chronic course but may become less evident or remit as the individual grows older, particularly by the fourth decade of life."

The *DSM-V* does not distinguish *antisocial personality disorder* (APD) from the older terms *sociopath* and *psychopath* but considers these three terms to be synonymous. In contrast, Hare argued that psychopaths are a much smaller and much more difficult group. These individuals are characterized by egocentricity, grandiosity, impulsivity, recklessness, contentment with the self, and a total lack of conscience.[75] Because of their egocentricity and self-satisfaction, they have extremely poor prospects for successful treatment. But Hare contended that many individuals who meet the *DSM* criteria for APD are not psychopaths and do not share the same pessimistic prognosis. In agreement with Hare that the psychopath is an extreme subset of those with APD, Blair, Mitchell, and Blair argued that the "crucial aspect of psychopathy" is the emotional impairment, which is biologically based. These authors further asserted that the 5 percent of criminals who are responsible for the disproportionate amount of crime are primarily psychopaths.[76]

Despite the fact that Hare considers psychopaths to be a very small group, Cleckley pointed out that in practice, "the term psychopath (or antisocial personality) as it is applied by various psychiatrists and hospital staffs sometimes becomes so broad that it can be applied to almost any criminal."[77] Cleckly argued that the majority of psychopaths are not criminals, and the majority of criminals are not psychopaths. Psychopaths may be found in any profession, including business, science, medicine, and psychiatry.[78] Typical psychopaths differ from typical criminals in that their actions seem less purposeful, they cause themselves needless sorrow and shame, and they usually do not commit major crimes or crimes of violence.[79]

Hare recommended that treatment of psychopathic individuals can be successful if it utilizes their own focus on their self-interest. Basically, the idea is to teach psychopathic individuals basic pro-social life skills to help them avoid the needless troubles that their behaviors cause.[80] Other psychiatrists, however, have recommended that these people be locked up until they reach middle age, or even that they be executed.[81] These psychiatrists have assumed that these persons will continue to commit antisocial actions if they are allowed to remain free. However, this assumption was not supported by a study by William McCord, who did extensive work on psychopaths and crime.[82] McCord found that delinquents who had been diagnosed as psychopathic at two juvenile institutions had only slightly worse recidivism rates than other delinquents at the same institutions, and that several years after their release, the recidivism rates were identical.

Walters reviewed research on what he called the "violence-prone personality," including the extent to which such a personality might be inherited and the extent to which it is stable across time and across situations.[83] For a whole variety of reasons, he rejected this concept and argued that it should be replaced with eight more specific concepts. Walters later severely criticized psychopathy as a general theory of crime, arguing that it is afflicted with a whole host of severe problems.[84]

CLINICAL PREDICTION OF FUTURE DANGEROUSNESS

Psychiatric attempts to predict the future dangerous and violent behavior of offenders have had little success in the past.[85] For example, a ten-year study in Massachusetts by Kozol and associates involved the use of extensive psychiatric and social casework services in an attempt to predict the future likely dangerousness of a group of high-risk offenders prior to their release from prison.[86] As it turned out, the researchers were unable to predict nearly two-thirds of the violent crime that ultimately occurred (thirty-one crimes out of forty-eight), and nearly two-thirds of the persons whom they predicted would be violent (thirty-two persons out of forty-nine) were not. Because of the probable occurrence of such errors, Morris argued that it is fundamentally unjust to detain anyone on the basis of a prediction of his or her future behavior.[87] In addition, the idea that a person can be punished for what he or she might do, rather than for what he or she has actually done, seriously threatens the basic notions of freedom of the individual from unwarranted governmental control.[88]

Monahan extensively reviewed the clinical techniques for predicting violent behavior and concluded that it can only be done within restricted circumstances.[89] Specifically, he concluded that it is possible to estimate the probability of a violent act in the immediate future when the person is going to remain in a situation that is essentially similar to ones in which he or she had committed violent acts in the past. Monahan presented a complex procedure for estimating this probability, which included (1) a comparison of the circumstances that the offender was likely to encounter in the near future with the circumstances in which the offender had committed violent acts in the past; (2) the recency, severity, and frequency of violent acts the individual had committed in the past; and (3) general statistics on the probability of violence for individuals who are similar in age, sex, race, class, history of drug abuse, residential and employment stability, and educational attainment. Monahan stated that it is not possible to predict violence over a long period or to predict it when a person was moving from one situation to a different one (e.g., on being released from prison). He also maintained that this type of prediction is entirely separate from the diagnosis of mental disease and that if mental disease is also of interest, a separate examination must be undertaken. Finally, Monahan argued that psychologists should confine themselves to estimating the probability of a violent act and should not recommend whether any official action should be taken in a given case. According to Monahan, criminal justice officials are responsible for deciding whether or not to take official actions, while the role of psychologists and psychiatrists is to provide accurate information on which to base these decisions. Mills elaborates on this point:

> The field of risk assessment simply needs more research in the area of criminal justice risk perception and communication. In a broader sense, we need to understand how a decision-maker understands and incorporates risk information within the decision-making process. It simply does not matter how good we are, or think we are, at assessing risk for future violence; if the decision-maker hears (perceives) something different than what we are saying, then the risk assessment could be for naught, society made no safer, and the offender disadvantaged.[90]

ACTUARIAL PREDICTION OF LATER CRIME AND DELINQUENCY

Psychological and psychiatric researchers have now turned away from the question of trying to predict whether particular individuals will commit acts of violence in the future.[91] Instead, researchers are now attempting to identify factors that are associated with an increased or decreased likelihood that an individual will commit a crime in the future. With respect to particular individuals, then, the prediction becomes probabilistic: this individual has many factors and so has a high risk of committing a crime in the future, while that individual has few factors and so has a low risk. This type of prediction is called "actuarial prediction," as opposed to the "clinical prediction" described in the previous section.

Some of this research has focused on delinquency, rather than on adult criminality, and on less serious crime, rather than on more serious violence, since these are easier to predict. The strongest predictor of later delinquent and criminal behavior is earlier childhood problem behaviors, such as disruptive classroom conduct, aggressiveness, lying, and dishonesty.[92] This means that the same individuals who caused the most problems when they were young children will also cause the most problems when they are adolescents and adults. Other factors in early childhood that are associated with later delinquency and crime include poor parental child management techniques, offending by parents and siblings, low intelligence and educational attainment, and separation from parents.[93] These findings suggest that the later crime and delinquency may be associated with or caused by early childhood experiences.

Research on the predictors of future delinquency has generally led to an optimistic view about the ability to influence those factors. For example, Loeber and Farrington argued that it is "never too early" and also "never too late" to intervene successfully even with the most serious and violent juvenile offenders.[94] This optimism is in stark contrast to the earlier pessimism about the ability of psychiatrists and psychologists to treat psychopathy and antisocial personality disorder.

DEPRESSION AND DELINQUENCY

Some researchers have studied the relationship between depressed mood and delinquency in childhood and adolescence. There is evidence that these two phenomena are correlated, but there is considerable disagreement about what causes what.

Some have argued that depression causes delinquency. For example, Eisenberg contended that depressed children experience shame and tend to lack empathy for other people, and both of these characteristics have been found to be directly associated with delinquency and aggression.[95] Others have argued that delinquency causes depression. For example, Capaldi noted that delinquent behaviors are associated with antisocial styles of interaction that lead to rejection in an adolescent's relationships with peers, parents, and teachers, among others. This social rejection, in turn, results in depressive symptoms.[96]

The association between delinquency and depression may also be spurious, which would mean that some other factor is causing both to occur. Carron and Rutter provided one possible mechanism that could do this: parents' depression.[97] Depression in the parents may be transmitted to the child directly, while marital discord that results from parents' depression may environmentally influence the child toward conduct disorders and delinquency. Consistent with this view was a study by Marcotte and colleagues that found that lower levels of family support are related to both depression and delinquency in children.[98] Depressed and maritally conflicted parents may be unable to provide necessary emotional support to children who then become at risk for both delinquency and depression.

Earlier studies of the depression-delinquency link have been mostly cross-sectional, but longitudinal studies are necessary to establish time sequence—whether the delinquency or the depression comes first and therefore is the cause. Beyers and Loeber studied 506 Pittsburgh adolescent males aged thirteen to seventeen.[99] Adjusting for other risk factors, they found that these two phenomena were strongly correlated: depressed youths tend to commit delinquent acts, and delinquent youths tend to report being depressed. Over time, each factor influenced the other but in different ways. Delinquency during childhood was associated with higher levels of depression later on. But depression in adolescence was associated with a slower-than-usual "exit" from delinquency as the person made the transition to adulthood.[100]

It seems clear that there is a strong association between depression and delinquency and that there may be causal effects that operate in both directions. Future longitudinal research will need to focus on the magnitude and nature of the causal relationship between the two. One recent study, employing data from the National Longitudinal Study of Adolescent Health, provided support for the possibility that the link between depression and delinquency may be mediated by a third variable. Remster found that the relationship between depression and delinquency disappears once self-control is controlled for; that depression lowers self-control, which in turn increases delinquency.[101] Self-control is discussed in Chapter 10. Depression may also itself serve as a mediator between other variables and delinquency. For example, parental abuse has been found to affect delinquency by increasing an adolescent's level of depression, resulting in his or her associating with delinquent peers and engaging in nonviolent delinquent activities.[102]

IMPULSIVITY AND CRIME

A rather diverse group of researchers have suggested that impulsivity is the key personality feature associated with antisocial behavior.[103] In general, these researchers have assumed that impulsivity is manifested in high levels of activity (especially when the person acts without thinking), a tendency to become impatient and to seek immediate gratification, and a tendency to become distracted.[104]

One theory that focused on this characteristic was by Wilson and Herrnstein.[105] Farrington described this as a "typical psychological explanation of crime, incorporating propositions seen in several other psychological theories."[106] In general, these propositions include the assumption that crime is inherently rewarding, so that we all would commit it unless we were restrained by internal inhibitions. These internal inhibitions are associated with what is normally called "conscience" and are developed primarily in early childhood by parents through their child-rearing practices. While criminal behavior may be directly learned through modeling by parents, peers, or the media, most crime is assumed to be the result of the failure to learn internal inhibitions against it.

Within the context of these general assumptions, Wilson and Herrnstein proposed that the key individual-level factor associated with criminality is the tendency to think in terms of short-term, rather than long-term, consequences. The rewards from not committing a crime almost always are in the future, while the rewards from committing it almost always are in the present. The tendency to think in terms of short-term consequences is associated with a variety of factors, including impulsivity and low intelligence. Wilson and Herrnstein also argued that the tendency to engage in criminal actions is associated with five other types of factors: (1) certain features of family life, such as poor child-rearing techniques, can produce weak internalized inhibitions; (2) membership in subcultures, such as street gangs, can increase the value that is placed on crime; (3) the mass media can directly affect aggressiveness through modeling and can indirectly affect it by convincing people they are being treated unfairly; (4) the economic system can influence the ability to achieve rewards through legitimate activity; and (5) schools can influence whether children believe they can achieve rewards through legitimate activity. Wilson and Herrnstein reviewed a massive amount of data to support their theory, but the extent to which these data support the theory has been questioned by several reviewers.[107]

Glenn Walters also proposed a theory with a strong focus on impulsivity as an enduring personality characteristic.[108] Walters defined "lifestyle criminals" as those who are characterized by "a global sense of irresponsibility, self-indulgent interests, an intrusive approach to interpersonal relationships, and chronic violation of societal rules, laws, and mores." He argued that these criminals have eight specific thinking patterns that allow them to perpetuate this pattern of actions. With mollification, these criminals point out the inequities and unfairnesses of life and blame others for their own choices. The cutoff is some visual image or verbal cue (e.g., "f ____ it"), which has the effect of terminating all thought in the moment and simply allows the criminals to act without worrying about the consequences. A sense of entitlement means that any actions are considered justifiable to achieve what is desired. Power orientation means that these criminals believe it is a dog-eat-dog world, and those who are strong can do whatever they can get away with. Sentimentality is the tendency for these criminals to look back at all the good things they have done in their lives and to claim that they therefore should not be held responsible for the bad things. Superoptimism is the tendency to believe that nothing bad will ever happen to them, including being punished for the crimes they commit. Cognitive indolence means that they do not pay attention to the details in life. Discontinuity means that they fail to follow through on commitments, to carry out intentions, and to remain focused on goals over time.

MOFFITT'S LIFE-COURSE-PERSISTENT OFFENDERS

A theory with a strong focus on impulsivity is Moffitt's theory of "life-course-persistent" offenders.[109] Moffitt described these offenders as a small group of people who engage "in antisocial behavior of one sort or another at every stage of life." Examples of such behavior would be biting and hitting at age four, shoplifting and truancy at age ten, drug dealing and car theft at age sixteen, robbery and rape at age twenty-two, and fraud and child abuse at age thirty.[110]

Moffitt argued that these behaviors begin with early neuropsychological problems that are caused by such factors as drug use or poor nutrition by the mother while she is pregnant, complications at birth resulting in minor brain damage, or deprivation of affection or child abuse and neglect after birth. These neuropsychological problems then tend to generate a cycle that results in an impulsive personality style. Parents of children who have these problems often have psychological deficiencies themselves, and their attempts to discipline and socialize their children tend to intensify the children's problem behaviors.[111] As the children age, these problems can directly cause problems by interfering with their ability to control their behavior and to think of the future consequences of their actions. In addition, these problems can disrupt the children's success in school, which can reduce their ability to acquire rewards in legitimate activities and increase the likelihood that they will turn to illegitimate, antisocial actions for rewards. A number of studies have produced supportive results.[112]

Moffitt contrasted life-course-persistent offenders with what she called "adolescent-limited" offenders who desist from delinquency as they mature to adults.[113] Nagan and Land were able to separate a group of life-course-persistent offenders from adolescent-limited offenders.[114] They also found that the life-course-persistent group could be separated into low- and high-level chronic offenders. Nagan, Land, and Moffitt then found that adolescent-limited offenders do not completely desist from antisocial behavior after adolescence, but still engage in behaviors, such as heavy drinking, drug use, fighting, and minor criminal acts.[115] Finally, Moffitt and her colleagues found that poor neuropsychological status predicts delinquency that begins in early childhood but not that which begins in adolescence.[116] However, in an analysis of the Cambridge Study in Delinquent Development (discussed in Chapter 14 on developmental theories), Piquero, Farrington, and Blumstein found that life-course-persistent offenders could not be identified prospectively using childhood and adolescent risk factors.[117]

In another study on impulsivity and crime, Caspi, Moffitt, and their colleagues examined personality traits in two different groups: about one thousand youths who were born in Dunedin, New Zealand, in 1972–1973 and about five hundred ethnically diverse twelve- and thirteen-year-old boys from Pittsburgh.[118] They found that crime proneness was associated with a combination of impulsivity and "negative emotionality," which they described as "a tendency to experience aversive affective states such as anger, anxiety, and irritability." Youths with "negative emotionality," they suggested, perceive more threats and dangers than do other people in the normal affairs of daily life. When these youths also have "great difficulty in modulating impulses," they tend to turn these negative emotions quickly into actions. Using an analogy from the Wild West, they described these youths as "quick on the draw."

POLICY IMPLICATIONS OF PERSONALITY RESEARCH

Researchers may be close to identifying personality characteristics that are associated with an increased risk of crime and delinquency. Research on modern personality scales has found that offenders tend to be low in agreeableness (i.e., hostile, self-centered, spiteful, jealous, and indifferent to others) and low in conscientiousness (i.e., they lack ambition, motivation, and perseverance; have difficulty controlling their impulses; and hold nontraditional and unconventional values and beliefs). This view is relatively similar to Moffitt's conclusion that crime proneness is associated with a combination of impulsivity and "negative emotionality."

To say that these personality characteristics cause crime and delinquency, however, is not useful unless there is some way to deal with the characteristics themselves. This is a problem with theories like Wilson and Herrnstein's, which describe impulsivity as a stable personality characteristic but have few indications for how to change it.

Walters's theory, in contrast, connects impulsivity to eight thinking patterns. The policy implications therefore focus on changing these thinking patterns through cognitive restructuring techniques. The question for this theory is the extent to which these techniques can successfully change the thinking patterns and therefore reduce future crime and delinquency. If these techniques produce real results, then Walters's theory will gain credibility.[119] But if they cannot, then the theory will probably fade into obscurity.

Moffitt's theory is the most promising from a policy point of view because it explains the causes of the impulsivity itself—the early neuropsychological problems, the cyclical interactions with parents that tend to intensify the children's problem behaviors, and the later problems in school that are caused by impulsivity and then result in crime and delinquency. If scientists can fully understand the origins of impulsivity, then we may be able to intervene early in children's lives in ways that reduce crime and delinquency when they become teenagers and adults.

Much as with impulsivity studies, psychologists have concluded that a variety of factors in early childhood are useful for predicting later criminal and delinquent behavior. Depression may be one such factor, although the chicken-and-egg relationship between depression and delinquency still must be worked out. Other factors include problem behaviors in young children, early school failure, and poor child-management techniques by parents. Early interventions with high-risk children can address these problems. For example, special classes can teach parenting skills to parents of high-risk children, and the high-risk children themselves can get extra help in school that can reduce the risk of school failure. In fact, such polices seem to produce significant reductions in later crime and delinquency in high-risk children. In addition, they cost much less than locking up the offenders after their crimes have already been committed.[120] Thus, these policies appear to have great potential for reducing future crime and delinquency by intervening early in the lives of young and troubled children.

CONCLUSIONS

There is a widespread perception that people with low intelligence and/or certain personality characteristics are more likely to commit crime and delinquency. There may be truth to this perception, but the research to date has been insufficient to support any strong conclusions.

At present, it seems best to conclude that low intelligence has no direct causal impact on crime and delinquency. The differences in IQ scores between delinquents and nondelinquents probably result from environmental rather than genetic factors. In particular, these differences probably reflect the underachievement of delinquents in schools. In addition, if there is any causal link at all between low intelligence and crime, it is probably mediated by some other factor, such as school failure. To the extent that this is the case, then policies to reduce crime and delinquency should deal with the actual cause (e.g., the school failure), rather than with the low intelligence.

The research linking personality to crime has been beset with a whole host of methodological problems.[121] These problems have led many criminologists, even those who are largely favorable to this approach, to discard the research as meaningless.[122] Research, such as that focused on impulsivity, seems to be addressing these methodological problems, so that researchers may be closing in on personality characteristics that are actually associated with crime.

On the other hand, even if psychological characteristics play a role in the causes of crime, it is not yet clear that the role is a large one. For example, Sampson and his colleagues analyzed data on three thousand individuals aged eight to twenty-five.[123] They found that 60 percent of the variation in violent crime was explained by neighborhood characteristics, parents' marital status, and immigrant status. In contrast, only about 6 percent of the variation was explained by IQ and impulsivity. This finding suggests that even if there is a role for psychological factors in explaining crime, that role may be small.

Psychological theories assume that some individuals are more likely to commit crime, regardless of the situation they are in. But it is also true that some situations are more likely to be associated with crime, regardless of the people who are in them. To understand the behavior of most criminals and delinquents, it may be more profitable to start by analyzing the situations that people find themselves in, rather than their psychological characteristics.

KEY TERMS

IQ tests
verbal IQ
performance IQ
personality
Jukes and Kallikaks
selective breeding
innate ability
general abilities
Flynn effect
psychoanalysis
id
superego
ego
personality inventory
agreeableness

conscientiousness
five factor model
antisocial personality disorder
actuarial prediction
clinical prediction
depression
delinquency
impulsivity
intelligence
internal inhibitions
lifestyle criminals and life-
   course-persistent offenders
neuropsychological problems
adolescent-limited offenders
negative emotionality

DISCUSSION QUESTIONS

1. What are the policy implications of assessing intelligence according to an IQ test?
2. Is intelligence a fixed inborn quantity or something malleable and plastic?
3. What reasons would account for the difference between IQ rates between delinquent and nondelinquents?
4. What may explain the Flynn effect?
5. Despite the difficulty in testing Freud's theories, does psychoanalytic theory have any relevant implications for the study of deviant behavior?
6. What factors have criminologists used to explain the development of an antisocial personality?
7. Give examples of traits that one would expect to see in someone who has antisocial personality disorder.

NOTES

1. Charles R. Darwin, *On the Origin of Species* (New York Penguin, 1968 [1859].
2. Richard L. Dugdale, *The Jukes: A Study in Crime, Pauperism and Heredity* (New York: Putnam, 1877); reprinted by Arno, New York, 1977.
3. C. R. Henderson, "The Relation of Philanthropy to Social Order and Progress," *Proceedings of the National Conference of Charities and Correction* 26 (1899): 1–15; partially reprinted in Frederic L. Faust and Paul J. Brantingham, eds., *Juvenile Justice Philosophy*, 2nd ed. (St. Paul, MN: West, 1979), pp. 48–57.
4. *Buck v. Bell*, 274 U.S. 200, 208 (1927).

5. Another popular early idea was "moral insanity," which was a precursor of psychiatric concepts like antisocial personality. Like degeneracy, it was a naturalistic approach that generated considerable opposition from the dominant spiritualistic explanation of this phenomenon. It eventually more or less merged with degeneracy and feeblemindedness into a single explanation. See Nicole Hahn Rafter, "The Unrepentant Horse-Slasher: Moral Insanity and the Origins of Criminological Thought," *Criminology* 42 (2004): 979–1008.

6. The following account is derived from Stephen Jay Gould, *The Mismeasure of Man* (New York: Norton, 1981), pp. 146–158.

7. This method of determining IQ has now been discarded in favor of one employing means and standard deviations. For a discussion of the present method, as well as a discussion of the problems of the mental age method, see Lee J. Cronbach, *Essentials of Psychological Testing*, 3rd ed. (New York: Harper & Row, 1970), pp. 215–218.

8. Quoted in Gould, *The Mismeasure of Man*, p. 154.

9. H. H. Goddard, *Feeblemindedness: Its Causes and Consequences* (New York: Macmillan, 1914); reprinted by Arno, New York, 1972.

10. H. H. Goddard, *The Kallikak Family, A Study in the Heredity of Feeble-Mindedness* (New York: Macmillan, 1912). Goddard called this family the "Kallikaks" because the name combined the Greek words for "beauty" (*kallos*) and "bad" (*kakos*). Gould, *The Mismeasure of Man*, pp. 168–171, pointed out that Goddard had diagnosed feeblemindedness among this family by sight and did not administer any intelligence tests to them. Goddard also included pictures of them in his book that had been retouched to make them appear evil and retarded.

11. Goddard, *The Kallikaks*, p. 103.

12. Goddard, *Feeblemindedness*, p. 539. See the discussion in Gould, *The Mismeasure of Man*, pp. 158–164.

13. For current reflections on this era, see John Doris, "Social Science and Advocacy: A Case Study," *American Behavioral Scientist* 26 (1982): 199–234. See also Hamilton Cravens, *The Triumph of Evolution: American Scientists and the Heredity-Environment Controversy, 1900–1941* (Philadelphia: University of Pennsylvania Press, 1978); and Michael M. Sokal, ed., *Psychological Testing and American Society: 1890–1930* (New Brunswick, NJ: Rutgers University Press, 1987). For a discussion of intelligence tests at this time with an emphasis on its ideological underpinnings, see Russell Marks, *The Idea of IQ* (Washington, DC: University Press of America, 1981).

14. Robert M. Yerkes, ed., "Psychological Examining in the United States Army," in *Memoirs of the National Academy of Sciences*, vol. 15 (Washington, DC: US Government Printing Office, 1921), p. 791. See also John Carson, "Army Alpha, Army Brass, and the Search for Army Intelligence," *Isis* 84 (1993): 278–309.

15. H. H. Goddard, "Feeblemindedness and Delinquency," *Journal of Psycho-Asthenics* 25 (1921): 173.

16. H. H. Goddard, "Feeblemindedness: A Question of Definition," *Journal of Psycho-Asthenics* 33 (1928): 224–225.

17. See, for example, Simon H. Tulchin, *Intelligence and Crime* (Chicago: University of Chicago Press, 1939), reprinted 1974; and Carl Murchison, *Criminal Intelligence* (Worcester, MA: Clark University Press, 1926), chap. 4.

18. Arthur R. Jensen, "How Much Can We Boost IQ and Scholastic Achievement?" *Harvard Educational Review* 39 (1969): 1–123. For a popularized and favorable discussion of Jensen's argument, see Daniel Seligman, *A Question of Intelligence: The IQ Debate in America* (New York: Carol Publishing Group, 1992). A brief review of the controversy can be found in R. A. Weinberg, "Intelligence and IQ: Landmark Issues and Great Debates," *American Psychologist* 44 (1989): 98–104. A broader overview can be found in Raymond E. Fancher, *The Intelligence Men: Makers of the IQ Controversy* (New York: Norton, 1985).

19. Robert Gordon, "Prevalence: The Rare Datum in Delinquency Measurement and Its Implications for the Theory of Delinquency," in *The Juvenile Justice System*, ed. Malcolm W. Klein (Beverly Hills, CA: Sage, 1976), pp. 201–284.

20. In a later article ("SES versus IQ in the Race-IQ-Delinquency Model," *International Journal of Sociology and Social Policy* 7, no. 3 [1987]: 30–96), Gordon responded to the criticism that his results reflected differences in social class, not in intelligence. If that were the case, Gordon reasoned, then more direct measures of class would predict delinquency better than IQ. Gordon then demonstrated that several more direct measures of class, including male income, family income, educational attainment, and occupational status, could not do what the IQ data had done: duplicate the data from the Philadelphia juvenile court records and the national training school commitment rates merely by assuming that all youths below a certain level, and no youths above it, became delinquent.

21. Travis Hirschi and Michael J. Hindelang, "Intelligence and Delinquency: A Revisionist Review," *American Sociological Review* 42 (1977): 572–587.

22. Hirschi and Hindelang (ibid., p. 580) argued that IQ as an explanation of crime and delinquency had been ignored in criminology because a bias arose against it in the 1920s. At that time, IQ as an explanation of crime and delinquency was associated with the physicians (such as Goring and Goddard) who had dominated the field of criminology since the time of Lombroso. Sociologists were beginning to take over the field, and they were eager to focus attention on the effects of social conditions and away from the characteristics of the individual. Hirschi and Hindelang referred specifically to Edwin H. Sutherland, "Mental Deficiency and Crime," in *Social Attitudes*, ed. Kimball Young (New York: Henry Holt, 1931), pp. 357–375; partially reprinted in Stephen Schafer and Richard D. Knudten, eds., *Criminological Theory* (Lexington, MA: D. C. Heath, 1977), pp. 157–160.

23. Ronald Blackburn, *The Psychology of Criminal Conduct* (Chichester, UK: John Wiley, 1993), pp. 186–189.

24. Alfred Blumstein, David P. Farrington, and Soumyo Moitra, "Delinquency Careers," in *Crime and Justice: A Review of Research*, ed. Michael H. Tonry and Norval Morris (Chicago: University of Chicago Press, 1985), pp. 187–219; and Deborah W. Denno, *Biology and Violence* (New York: Cambridge University Press, 1990).

25. Paul D. Lipsitt, Stephen L. Buka, and Lewis P. Lipsitt, "Early Intelligence Scores and Subsequent Delinquency," *American Journal of Family Therapy* 18 (1990): 197–208.

26. Terrie E. Moffitt, "Life-Course-Persistent and Adolescent-Limited Antisocial Behavior," *Psychological Review* 100 (1993): 674–701.

27. R. J. Herrnstein, "Criminogenic Traits," in *Crime*, ed. James Q. Wilson and Joan Petersilia (San Francisco: Institute for Contemporary Studies Press, 1995), pp. 49–53.

28. Herbert C. Quay, "Intelligence," in *Handbook of Juvenile Delinquency*, ed. Quay (New York: John Wiley, 1987), pp. 106–117.

29. Gary Groth-Marnat, *Handbook of Psychological Assessment* (New York: Van Nostrand Reinhold, 1984), p. 76.

30. Genetics experts have estimated that about 60% of the variation in IQ is accounted for by genes. For reviews, see R. J. Herrnstein and Charles Murray, *The Bell Curve* (New York: Free Press, 1994); and Anthony Walsh, "Intelligence and Antisocial Behavior," in *Biosocial Criminology: Challenging Environmentalisms' Supremacy*, ed. Anthony Walsh and Lee Ellis (New York: Nova Science, 2003). Therefore, at the present time, a variety of research is exploring the mechanisms by which IQ may be inherited. For example, neurophysiological research is examining whether intelligence is associated with "gray matter" in the brain (e.g., Paul M. Thompson, Tyrone D. Cannon, Katherine L. Narr, Theo van Erp, Veli-Pekka Poutanen, Matti Huttunen, Jouko Lönnqvist, Carl-Gustaf Standertskjöld-Nordenstam, Jaakko Kaprio, Mohammad Khaledy, Rajneesh Dail, Chris I. Zoumalan, and Arthur W. Toga, "Genetic Influences on Brain Structure," *Nature Neuroscience* 4 [2001]: 1–6), while genetic research is examining whether certain chromosomal loci, or "DNA markers," can distinguish between those with low and high IQ (e.g., Robert Plomin, Gerald E. McClearn, Deborah L. Smith, Sylvia Vignetti, Michael J. Chorney, Karen Chorney, Charles P. Venditti, Steven Kasarda, Lee A. Thompson, Douglas K. Detterman, Johanna Daniels, Michael Owen, and Peter McGuffin, "DNA Markers Associated with High Versus Low IQ: The IQ Quantitative Trait Lock (QTL) Project," *Behavior Genetics* 24 [1994]: 107–118). However, the 60% estimate is generally based on comparisons of the IQ scores of identical and fraternal twin pairs and requires the assumption that all twins, regardless of type, experience equally similar environments in terms of the influence on IQ. Other researchers have disputed this assumption, arguing that identical twins experience more similar environments than do fraternal twins. See the discussion of twins in chapter 4, especially note 39. For a scathing attack on the genetics-IQ link, including the 60% estimate, see Leonard Leibman, "Herrnstein and Murray, Inc.," *American Behavioral Scientist* 39 (1995): 25–34.

31. Gordon, "Prevalence," p. 269.

32. Hirschi and Hindelang, "Intelligence and Delinquency." This argument is consistent with research that has shown that the school characteristics that are associated with educational failure are the same as the school characteristics that are associated with delinquency: high student-teacher ratios, low

student attendance, high student turnover, and poor academic quality. See D. A. Hellman and S. Beaton, "The Pattern of Violence in Urban Public Schools," *Journal of Research in Crime and Delinquency* 23 (1986): 102–127; Kenneth Polk, "The New Marginal Youth," *Crime and Delinquency* 30 (1984): 648–659; and W. T. Pink, "Schools, Youth, and Justice," *Crime and Delinquency* 30 (1984): 439–461.

33. Michael R. Gottfredson and Travis Hirschi, *A General Theory of Crime* (Stanford, CA: Stanford University Press, 1990).

34. James Q. Wilson and Richard J. Herrnstein, *Crime and Human Nature* (New York: Simon & Schuster, 1985).

35. Jane Mercer, "IQ: The Lethal Label," *Psychology Today*, September 1972, pp. 44–47ff. For a critique of Mercer, see Robert A. Gordon, "Examining Labelling Theory: The Case of Mental Retardation," in *The Labelling of Deviance: Evaluating a Perspective*, ed. Walter R. Gove (New York: Halsted-Wiley, 1975), pp. 35–81.

36. See J. Loehlin, "Group Differences in Intelligence," in *Handbook of Intelligence*, ed. R. Sternberg (Cambridge: Cambridge University Press, 2000), pp. 176–193. On the superior scores of Asian groups on these tests, see Seligman, *A Question of Intelligence*; and J. Rushton, "Race and Crime: A Reply to Roberts and Gabor," *Canadian Journal of Criminology* 32 (1990): 315–334.

37. Ronald L. Simons, "The Meaning of the IQ-Delinquency Relationship," *American Sociological Review* 43 (1978): 268–270. See also Scott Menard and Barbara J. Morse, "A Structuralist Critique of the IQ-Delinquency Hypothesis: Theory and Evidence," *American Journal of Sociology* 89 (1984): 1347–1378. They argued that IQ exerts no causal influence on delinquent behavior but is a criterion used for differential treatment in certain institutional settings.

38. James R. Flynn, "The Mean IQ of Americans: Massive Gains, 1932 to 1978," *Psychological Bulletin* 95 (1984): 29–51; "Massive IQ Gains in 14 Nations: What IQ Tests Really Measure," *Psychological Bulletin* 101 (1987): 171–191; "IQ Gains over Time," in *Encyclopedia of Human Intelligence*, ed. R. J. Sternberg (New York: Macmillan, 1994), pp. 617–623; "Searching for Justice: The Discovery of IQ Gains over Time," *American Psychologist* 54 (1999): 5–20. The countries were Australia, Austria, Belgium, Brazil, Britain, Canada, China, Denmark, East Germany, France, Israel, Japan, the Netherlands, New Zealand, Northern Ireland, Norway, Sweden, Switzerland, the United States, and West Germany.

39. Flynn, "IQ Gains over Time" and "Searching for Justice."

40. This section is adapted from the 4th edition of this volume (Vold, Bernard, and Snipes, 1998). Several anonymous reviewers of the 7th edition strongly suggested including psychoanalytic theory in the current (8th) edition, and we agreed it was appropriate to do so.

41. The concept of the *unconscious* was developed by von Hartman (1842–1906) and further developed by Morton Prince (1854–1929). See N. D. C. Lewis, *A Short History of Psychiatric Achievement* (New York: Norton, 1941).

42. A very readable account of Freud's life, interwoven with accounts of his theories and those of his companions, can be found in Peter Gay, *Freud: A Life for Our Time* (New York: Norton, 1988).

43. Fritz Redl and Hans Toch, "The Psychoanalytic Explanation of Crime," in *Psychology of Crime and Criminal Justice*, ed. Hans Toch (New York: Holt, Rinehart, and Winston, 1979).

44. Sigmund Freud, "Criminals from a Sense of Guilt," in *The Standard Edition of the Complete Psychological Works of Sigmund Freud*, ed. Sigmund Freud, James Strachey, and Anna Freud (London: Hogarth Press, 1955).

45. This idea is elaborated in such works as Walter Bromberg, *Crime and the Mind: A Psychiatric Analysis of Crime and Punishment* (New York: Macmillan, 1965); Seymour L. Halleck, *Psychiatry and the Dilemmas of Crime* (New York: Harper and Row, 1967); David Abrahamsen, *The Psychology of Crime* (New York: Columbia University Press, 1960); Erich Fromm, *Escape from Freedom* (New York: Farrar & Rinehart, 1941); William A. White, *Crimes and Criminals* (New York: Farrar & Rinehart, 1933); and Theodor Reik, *The Compulsion to Confess* (New York: Farrar, Straus, and Cudahy, 1945).

46. August Aichhorn, *Wayward Youth* (New York: Viking, 1963).

47. Ibid., p. 209.

48. Sigmund Freud, "Introduction," in Aichhorn, *Wayward Youth*.

49. Aichhorn, *Wayward Youth*, pp. 200–202.

50. Ibid., pp. 224–225.

51. Blackburn, *The Psychology of Criminal Conduct*, pp. 113–115.

52. William Healy and Augusta Bronner, *New Light on Delinquency and Its Treatment* (New Haven, CT: Yale University Press, 1931).

53. John Bowlby, Child Care and the Growth of Love (Baltimore: Penguin, 1953). A review of research about his theory is presented in J. E. Hall-Williams, *Criminology and Criminal Justice* (London: Butterworths, 1982), pp. 59–68.

54. Fritz Redl and David Wineman, *Children Who Hate* (New York: The Free Press, 1951).

55. Seymour Fisher and Roger P. Greenberg, *The Scientific Credibility of Freud's Theories and Therapy* (New York: Basic Books, 1977); Paul Kline, *Fact and Fantasy in Freudian Theory*, 2nd ed. (New York: Methuen, 1981).

56. See, e.g, Hervey Cleckley, *The Mask of Sanity* (St. Louis, MO: Mosby, 1976).

57. Blackburn, *The Psychology of Criminal Conduct*, pp. 115–116.

58. Sheldon Glueck and Eleanor Glueck, *Unraveling Juvenile Delinquency* (New York: Commonwealth Fund, 1950). These data were used in later studies by Robert J. Sampson and John H. Laub, *Crime in the Making,* 1993, and Laub and Sampson, *Shared Beginnings: Divergent Lives,* 2003, both published by Harvard University Press, Cambridge, MA. See the discussion of these studies in chapter 14.

59. Glueck and Glueck, *Unraveling Juvenile Delinquency*, p. 275.

60. For general information about the MMPI, see W. Grant Dahlstrom, George Welsh, and Leona Dahlstrom, *An MMPI Handbook* (Minneapolis: University of Minnesota Press, 1972).

61. Lewis Aiken, *Psychological Testing and Assessment* (New York: Allyn Bacon, 2005).
62. Gordon P. Waldo and Simon Dinitz, "Personality Attributes of the Criminal: An Analysis of Research Studies, 1950–1965," *Journal of Research in Crime and Delinquency* 4 (1967): 185–202.
63. David J. Tennenbaum, "Personality and Criminality: A Summary and Implications of the Literature," *Journal of Criminal Justice* 5 (1977): 225–235.
64. Joshua D. Miller and Donald Lynam, "Structural Models of Personality and Their Relation to Antisocial Behavior: A Meta-Analytic Review," *Criminology* 39 (2001): 765–798.
65. Ibid.
66. The four models propose a total of eighteen different personality dimensions. Eight of the dimensions had at least a moderate effect on antisocial behavior, while six others had no effect whatsoever. Miller and Lyman argued that there is considerable overlap among all these dimensions, particularly those that are related to antisocial behavior. This explains why all the models could be well supported by research despite their differences. It also explains why Miller and Lynam were able to collapse the results into two basic personality dimensions.
67. Miller and Lynam, "Structural Models of Personality and Their Relation to Antisocial Behavior," p. 780.
68. Ibid., p. 781–782. These two qualifications, together with the fact that there are two distinct personality dimensions, distinguish Miller and Lynam's argument from the "low self-control" argument of Gottfredson and Hirschi, *A General Theory of Crime*. See the discussion in chapter 10.
69. Shayne E. Jones, Joshua D. Miller, and Donald R. Lynam, "Personality, Antisocial Behavior, and Aggression," *Journal of Criminal Justice* 39 (2011): 329–337.
70. Ibid., p. 330.
71. Ibid., p. 332, Table 3.
72. Colin E. Vize, Katherine L. Collison, Joshua D. Miller, and Donald R. Lynam, "Using Bayesian Methods to Update and Expand the Meta-Analytic Evident of the Five-Factor Model's Relation to Antisocial Behavior," *Clinical Psychology Review* 67 (2019): 61–77.
73. Jones et al., "Personality, Antisocial Behavior, and Aggression," p 329.
74. *Diagnostic and Statistical Manual of Mental Disorders*, 5th ed. (Washington, DC: American Psychiatric Association, 2013), pp. 659–663.
75. Robert D. Hare, *Without Conscience: The Disturbing World of the Psychopaths Among Us* (New York: Guilford Press, 1999). For a popularized book that used the term *sociopath*, see Martha Stout, *The Sociopath Next Door* (New York: Random House, 2006). Stout claimed that 4 percent of people are sociopathic. She said that these people are charming and spontaneous, but they cannot love and have no conscience.
76. James Blair, Derek Mitchell, and Karina Blair, *The Psychopath: Emotion and the Brain* (Malden, MA: Blackwell, 2006), pp. 14, 154. For an article linking psychopathy with chronic offending, see Michael G. Vaughn and Matt

DeLisi, "Were Wolfgang's Chronic Offenders Psychopaths? On the Convergent Validity Between Psychopathy and Career Criminality," *Journal of Criminal Justice* 36 (2007): 33–42.

77. Hervey Cleckley, *The Mask of Sanity* (St. Louis, MO: Mosby, 1976), p. 263.

78. Ibid., pp. 188–221.

79. Ibid., pp. 261–263.

80. Hare, *Without Conscience*.

81. For a critical discussion of such recommendations, see Charles Patrick Ewing, "Preventive Detention and Execution: The Constitutionality of Punishing Future Crimes," *Law and Human Behavior* 15 (1991): 139–163.

82. William McCord, *The Psychopath and Milieu Therapy* (New York: Academic Press, 1982). See also William McCord and Jose Sanchez, "The Treatment of Deviant Children: A Twenty-Five-Year Follow-Up Study," *Crime and Delinquency* 29 (1983): 238–253.

83. Glenn D. Walters, "Disposed to Aggress? In Search of the Violence-Prone Personality," *Aggression and Violent Behavior* 5 (2000): 177–190.

84. Glenn D. Walters, "The Trouble with Psychopathy as a General Theory of Crime," *International Journal of Offender Therapy and Comparative Criminology* 48 (2004): 133–148.

85. For a review, see Blackburn, *The Psychology of Criminal Conduct*, pp. 328–335.

86. Harry L. Kozol, Richard J. Boucher, and Ralph F. Garofalo, "The Diagnosis and Treatment of Dangerousness," *Crime and Delinquency* 18 (1972): 371–392.

87. Norval Morris, *The Future of Imprisonment* (Chicago: University of Chicago Press, 1974), pp. 71–73.

88. Ibid., pp. 83–84.

89. John Monahan, *Predicting Violent Behavior* (Beverly Hills, CA: Sage, 1981).

90. Jeremy F. Mills, "Violence Risk Assessment: A Brief Review, Current Issues, and Future Directions," *Canadian Psychology* 58 (2017): 40–49.

91. E.g., Jeremy F. Miller ("Advances in the Assessment and Prediction of Interpersonal Violence," *Journal of Interpersonal Violence* 20 [2005]: 236–241) stated: "Perhaps the most important lesson learned in the past 20 years is that clinical judgment is a poor and inconsistent method by which to make estimates about the likelihood for violence in the future."

92. See, e.g., Mark W. Lipsey and James H. Derzon, "Predictors of Violent of Serious Delinquency in Adolescence and Early Adulthood," in *Serious and Violent Juvenile Offenders: Risk Factors and Successful Interventions*, ed. Rolf Loeber and David P. Farrington (Thousand Oaks, CA: Sage, 1998), pp. 86–105; and Lynn Kartzer and Sheilagh Hodgins, "Adult Outcomes of Child Conduct Problems," *Journal of Abnormal Child Psychology* 25 (1997): 65–81.

93. For overviews, see Terrence P. Thornberry, David Huizinga, and Rolf Loeber, "The Causes and Correlates Studies: Findings and Policy Implications," *Juvenile Justice* 9 (Washington, DC: Office of Juvenile Justice and Delinquency Prevention, September 2004); J. David Hawkins, Todd I. Herrenkohl, David P. Farrington, Devon Brewer, Richard F. Catalano, Tracy W. Harachi, and Lynn Cothern , "Predictors of Youth Violence," *Juvenile Justice Bulletin*

(Washington, DC: Office of Juvenile Justice and Delinquency Prevention, April 2000); and David P. Farrington, "Predictors, Causes, and Correlates of Male Youth Violence," in *Youth Violence*, ed. Michael Tonry and Mark H. Moore (vol. 24 of *Crime and Justice: A Review of Research*) (Chicago: University of Chicago Press, 1998), pp. 421–475.

94. Rolf Loeber and David P. Farrington, "Never Too Early, Never Too Late: Risk Factors and Successful Interventions for Serious and Violent Juvenile Offenders," *Studies on Crime and Crime Prevention* 7 (1998): 7–30. See also James Garbarino, *Lost Boys: Why Our Sons Turn Violent and How We Can Save Them* (New York: Free Press, 1999).

95. N. Eisenberg, "Emotion, Regulation, and Moral Development," *Annual Review of Psychology* 51 (2000): 665–697. For an argument that links shame and lack of empathy to aggression, see June P. Tangney, Patricia E. Wagner, D Hill-Barlow, Daniel Marschall, and Richard A. Gramzow, "Relation of Shame and Guilt to Constructive Versus Destructive Responses Across the Lifespan," *Journal of Personality and Social Psychology* 70 (1996): 797–809.

96. D. Capaldi, "Co-occurrence of Conduct Problems and Depressive Symptoms in Early Adolescent Boys: I. Familial Factors and General Adjustment at Grade 6," *Development and Psychopathology* 3 (1991): 277–300; and Capaldi, "Co-occurrence of Problems and Depressive Symptoms in Early Adolescent Boys: II. A 2-Year Follow-Up at Grade 8," *Development and Psychopathology* 4 (1992): 125–144. See also Gerald Patterson, J. Reid, and T. Dishion, *A Social Interactional Approach: Antisocial Boys* (vol. 4) (Eugene, OR: Castalia, 1992), which argues that childhood antisocial behavior leads to rejection and low self-esteem, resulting in association with delinquent peers, antisocial attitudes, and depression.

97. C. Caron and M. Rutter, "Co-morbidity in Child Psychopathology: Concepts, Issues, and Research Strategies," *Journal of Child Psychology and Psychiatry* 132 (1991): 1063–1080.

98. Genevieve Marcotte, Diane Marcotte, and Therese Bouffard, "The Influence of Familial Support and Dysfunctional Attitudes on Depression and Delinquency in an Adolescent Population," *European Journal of Psychology of Education* 17 (2002): 363–376. See also Inga-Dora Sigfusdottir, George Farkas, and Eric Silver, "The Role of Depressed Mood and Anger in the Relationship between Family Conflict and Delinquent Behavior," *Journal of Youth and Adolescence* 33 (2004): 509–522.

99. Jennifer M. Beyers and Rolf Loeber, "Untangling Developmental Relations Between Depressed Mood and Delinquency in Male Adolescents," *Journal of Abnormal Child Psychology* 31 (2003): 247–266.

100. Ibid., p. 259. See also Margit Wiesner, "A Longitudinal Latent Variable Analysis of Reciprocal Relations Between Depressive Symptoms and Delinquency Across Adolescence," *Journal of Abnormal Psychology* 112 (2003): 633–645, which found different effects by gender. For boys, Wiesner speculated that delinquency jeopardizes future career prospects, but that the depression does not kick in until later in high school when the reality of the situation becomes clear. Thus, for boys, delinquency comes first and depression comes

later. Wiesner speculated that girls who engage in delinquency are heavily sanctioned, which results in depression at the time. However, these girls then refrain from delinquency to eliminate the sanctions. They therefore improve their overall well-being and stop being depressed.

101. Brianna Remster, "Self-Control and the Depression-Delinquency Debate," *Deviant Behavior* 35 (2014): 66–84.

102. Sukkyung You and Sun Ahlim, "Development Pathways from Abusive Parenting to Delinquency: The Mediating Role of Depression and Aggression," *Child Abuse & Neglect* 46 (2015): 152–162, citing Y. Jang and J. Song, "Influence of the Experience of the Childhood Abuse on the Self-Esteem and Suicidal Thought in the Adolescence Period," *Korean Research for Policy Sciences* 20 (2011): 80–104; J. Kim, "Influence of Depression and Aggression of Adolescents on Cyber and Real-World Delinquency Mediated by Type of Internet Use," *Journal of School Social Work* 24 (2013): 31–59.

103. See, for example, the collection of articles in Alan R. Felthous, ed., "Impulsive Aggression," *Behavioral Sciences & the Law* 16 (1998): 281–389; David P. Farrington, "Have Any Individual, Family, or Neighbourhood Influences on Offending Been Demonstrated Conclusively?" in *Integrating Individual and Ecological Aspects of Crime*, ed. Farringson, Robert J. Sampson, and P. O. Wikstrom (Stockholm, Sweden: Swedish National Council for Crime Prevention, 1993), pp. 3–37; E. E. Gorenstein and J. P. Newman, "Disinhibitory Psychopathology," *Psychological Review* 87 (1980): 301–315; Jennifer L. White, Terrie E. Moffitt, Avshalom Caspi, Dawn Jeglum Bartusch, Douglas J. Needles, and Magda Stouthamer-Loeber, "Measuring Impulsivity and Examining Its Relationship to Delinquency," *Journal of Abnormal Psychology* 103 (1994): 192–205; Marvin Zuckerman, "Personality in the Third Dimension," *Personality and Individual Differences* 10 (1989): 391–418; and Jeffrey A. Gray, "Drug Effects on Fear and Frustration," in *Handbook of Psychopharmacology: Drugs, Neurotransmitters, and Behavior*, vol. 8, ed. Leslie L. Iversen, Susan D. Iversen, and Solomon H. Snyder (New York: Plenum, 1977).

104. White et al., "Measuring Impulsivity and Examining Its Relationship to Delinquency."

105. Wilson and Hernnstein, *Crime and Human Nature*, esp. chap. 7.

106. Farrington, "Introduction," Crime and Human Nature, pp. xix–xx.

107. See book reviews by Lawrence E. Cohen, *Contemporary Sociology* 16 (1987): 202–205; and Jack P. Gibbs, *Criminology* 23 (1985): 381–388. In addition, Gottfredson and Hirschi, *A General Theory of Crime*, criticized the theory as being theoretically contradictory.

108. Glenn D. Walters, *The Criminal Lifestyle: Patterns of Serious Criminal Conduct* (Newbury Park, CA: Sage, 1990). Walters's work is based, in part, on the earlier description of fifty-two "thinking errors" by Samuel Yochelson and Stanton E. Samenow, *The Criminal Personality*, vols. 1 and 2 (New York: Jason Aronson, 1976, 1977).

109. Moffitt, "Life-Course-Persistent and Adolescent-Limited Antisocial Behavior."

110. Ibid., p. 679.

111. Ibid., p. 682.
112. For a review, see Terrie E. Moffitt and Anthony Walsh, "The Adolescence-Limited/Life-Course Persistent Theory of Antisocial Behavior: What Have We Learned?" in *Biosocial Criminology: Challenging Environmentalism's Supremacy*, ed. Anthony Walsh and Lee Ellis (New York: Nova Science, 2003), pp. 125–144. These authors pointed particularly to a study by Avshalom Caspi, Terrie E. Moffitt, Phil A. Silva, Magda Stouthamer-Loeber, Robert F. Krueger, and Pamela S. Schmutte, "Are Some People Crime-Prone?" *Criminology* 32 (1994): 163–195, which showed a significant gene-environment interaction between the maltreatment of children and a specific genotype that interacts with maltreatment. This study was discussed in chapter 3.
113. Moffitt, "Life-Course-Persistent and Adolescent-Limited Antisocial Behavior."
114. Daniel Nagan and Kenneth Land, "Age, Criminal Careers, and Population Heterogeneity," *Criminology* 31 (1993): 327–362.
115. Daniel Nagan, Kenneth Land, and Terrie E. Moffitt, "Life-Course Trajectories of Different Types of Offenders," *Criminology* 33 (1995): 111–139.
116. Terrie E. Moffit, Donald Lynam, and Phil Silva, "Neuropsychological Tests Predicting Persistent Male Delinquency," *Criminology* 32 (1994): 277–300.
117. Alex R. Piquero, David P. Farrington, and Alfred Blumstein, *Key Issues in Criminal Career Research: New Analyses of the Cambridge Study in Delinquent Development* (New York: Cambridge University Press, 2007), p. 205, citing John H. Laub and Robert J. Sampson, *Shared Beginnings, Divergent Lives: Delinquent Boys to Age 70* (Cambridge, MA: Harvard University Press, 2003).
118. Caspi et al., "Are Some People Crime-Prone?"
119. See Glenn D. Walters, "Recidivism in Released Lifestyle Change Program Participants Short-Term Outcome of Inmates Participating in the Lifestyle Change Program," *Criminal Justice and Behavior* 32 (2005): 50–68. This article reported that 291 inmates who completed Walter's program were significantly less likely to be arrested or reincarcerated than were 89 released inmates who had not completed the program.
120. See, for example, Peter W. Greenwood, Karyn E. Model, C. Peter Rydell, and James Chiesa, *Diverting Children from a Life of Crime* (Santa Monica, CA: RAND Corporation, 1996).
121. These are reviewed in Robert F. Krueger, Pamela S. Schmutte, Avshalom Caspi, Terrie E. Moffitt, Kathleen Campbell, and Phil A. Silva, "Personality Traits Are Linked to Crime Among Men and Women: Evidence from a Birth Cohort," *Journal of Abnormal Psychology* 103 (1995): 328–338. See also Moffitt, "Life-Course-Persistent and Adolescent-Limited Antisocial Behavior." For a brief defense of trait-based personality theories, see Caspi et al., "Are Some People Crime-Prone?," pp. 164–165.
122. See, e.g., Gottfredson and Hirschi, *A General Theory of Crime*, p. 209. Their theory of crime is close to a personality theory and is presented in chapter 10.
123. Robert J. Sampson, Jeffrey D. Morenoff, and Stephen Raudenbush, "Social Anatomy of Racial and Ethnic Disparities in Violence," *American Journal of Public Health* 95 (2005): 224–232.

CHAPTER 6

———

Durkheim, Anomie, and Modernization

Whereas the preceding two chapters examined the role of biology and psychology in explaining behavior, Emile Durkheim's focus was on the impact of social forces. He argued that economic inequality is a natural and inevitable human condition that is not associated with social maladies, such as crime, unless there is also a breakdown of social norms or rules. Durkheim called such a breakdown "anomie" and argued that it had occurred in his own society as a result of the rapid social changes accompanying the modernization process. Like Lombroso's theories, written approximately twenty years earlier, Durkheim's theories were, in part, a reaction to the classical assumptions that humans were free and rational in a contractual society. But where Lombroso had focused on the determinants of human behavior within the individual, Durkheim focused on society and its organization and development.

Durkheim's theories are complex, but his influence on criminology has been great. This chapter examines his theories and discusses them in the context of later research on the relationship between crime and modernization. But Durkheim's ideas also appear in several later chapters. In 1938, Robert K. Merton revised Durkheim's conception of anomie and applied it directly to American society. This and other similar theories are now known as strain theories of crime and delinquency and are presented in Chapter 7. In the 1920s, a group of Chicago sociologists used his theories, among others, as the basis of an extensive research project linking juvenile delinquency to rapid social changes in urban areas. These studies now focus on the impact of neighborhoods on crime and are presented in Chapter 8. In 1969, Travis Hirschi returned to Durkheim's original conception of anomie and used it as the basis for his control theory of delinquency. Control theories are discussed in Chapter 10. Finally, Durkheim's view of "crime as normal" is the basis for social reaction views of the law-enactment process, which are discussed in Chapter 11.

EMILE DURKHEIM

Emile Durkheim (1858–1917) has been called "one of the best known and one of the least understood major social thinkers."[1] Presenting his thought is no easy task, since "the controversies which surround this thought bear upon essential points, not details."[2] For this reason, it is best to approach his work by first considering the political and intellectual climate in which it evolved.

The nineteenth century in France was an age of great turmoil generated by the wake of the French Revolution of 1789 and by the rapid industrialization of French society. Speaking of these two revolutions, Nisbet pointed out that "in terms of immediacy and massiveness of impact on human thought and values, it is impossible to find revolutions of comparable magnitude anywhere in human history."[3] The writings of the day were filled with a "burning sense of society's sudden, convulsive turn from a path it had followed for millennia" and a "profound intuition of the disappearance of historic values— and with them, age-old securities, as well as age-old tyrannies and inequalities—and the coming of new powers, new insecurities, and new tyrannies that would be worse than anything previously known unless drastic measures were taken."[4]

Sociology had been developed by Auguste Comte in the first half of the nineteenth century largely in response to the effects of these two revolutions; it was part of a more general effort to construct a rational society out of the ruins of the traditional one.[5] Sociologists saw themselves providing a rational, scientific analysis of the monumental social changes that were occurring, in order to "mastermind the political course of 'social regeneration.'"[6] This regeneration would consist primarily of the reestablishment of social solidarity, which appeared to have substantially disintegrated in French society.

Emile Durkheim was born in a small French town on the German border one year after the death of Comte. After completing his studies, he spent several years teaching philosophy in secondary schools in the French provinces near Paris. He then spent a year in Germany, where he studied social science and its relation to ethics. Durkheim's publication of two articles as a result of these studies led to the creation of a special position for him at the University of Bordeaux, where, in 1887, he taught the first French university course in sociology. In 1892, Durkheim received the first doctor's degree in sociology awarded by the University of Paris, and ten years later, he returned to a position at the university, where he dominated sociology until his death in 1917.

Durkheim's analysis of the processes of social change involved in industrialization is presented in his first major work, *De la division du travail social (The Division of Labor in Society)*,[7] written as his doctoral thesis and published in 1893. In it, he described these processes as part of the development from the more primitive "mechanical" form of society into the more advanced "organic" form. In the mechanical form, each social group in society is relatively isolated from all other social groups and is basically self-sufficient.[8] Within these social groups, individuals live largely under identical circumstances, do identical work, and hold identical values. There is little division of labor, with only a few persons in the clan or village having specialized functions. Thus, there is little need for individual talents, and the solidarity of the society is based on the uniformity of its members.

Contrasted with the mechanical society is the organic society, in which the different segments of society depend on each other in a highly organized division of labor. Social solidarity is no longer based on the uniformity of the individuals but on the diversity of the functions of the parts of the society. Durkheim argued that all societies were at some stage between the mechanical and the organic, with no society being totally one or the other. Even the most primitive societies could be seen to have some forms of division of labor, and even the most advanced societies would require some degree of uniformity of its members.[9]

Law plays an essential role in maintaining the social solidarity of each of these two types of societies, but in different ways. In the mechanical society, law enforces the uniformity of the members of the social group and thus is oriented toward repressing any deviation from the norms of the time. In the organic society, on the other hand, law regulates the interactions of the various parts of society and provides restitution in cases of wrongful transactions.

Because law plays such different roles in the two types of societies, crime appears in different forms. Durkheim argued that to the extent that a society remains mechanical, crime is "normal" in the sense that a society without crime would be pathologically overcontrolled. As the society develops toward the organic form, it is possible for a pathological state, which he called anomie, to occur, and such a state would produce a variety of social maladies, including crime. Durkheim developed his concept of "crime as normal" in his second major work, *The Rules of the Sociological Method*,[10] published in 1895, only two years after *The Division of Labor*; he went on to develop anomie in his most famous work, *Suicide*,[11] published in 1897. These concepts are explored in the following sections.

CRIME AS NORMAL IN MECHANICAL SOCIETIES

Mechanical societies are characterized by the uniformity of the lives, work, and beliefs of their members. All the uniformity that exists in a society, that is, the "totality of social likenesses," Durkheim called the "collective conscience."[12] Since all societies demand at least some degree of uniformity from their members (in that none are totally organic), the collective conscience may be found in every culture. In every society, however, there will always be a degree of diversity in that there will be many individual differences among its members. As Durkheim said, "There cannot be a society in which the individuals do not differ more or less from the collective type."[13]

To the extent that a particular society is mechanical, its solidarity will come from the pressure for uniformity exerted against this diversity. Such pressure is exerted in various degrees and in various forms. Its strongest form consists of criminal sanctions, while weaker forms may consist of designating certain behaviors or beliefs as morally reprehensible or merely in bad taste. As Durkheim noted:

> If I do not submit to the conventions of society, if in my dress I do not conform to the customs observed in my country and my class, the ridicule I provoke, the social isolation in which I am kept, produce, although in attenuated form, the same effects as a punishment in the strict sense of the word. The constraint is nonetheless efficacious for being indirect.[14]

Durkheim argued that "society cannot be formed without our being required to make perpetual and costly sacrifices."[15] These sacrifices, embodied in the demands of the collective conscience, are the price of membership in society, and fulfilling the demands gives the individual members a sense of collective identity, which is an important source of social solidarity.

More important, however, is the fact that these demands are constructed so that it is inevitable that a certain number of people will not fulfill them. The number must be large enough to constitute an identifiable group, but not so large as to include a substantial portion of the society. This enables the large mass of the people, all of whom fulfill the demands of the collective conscience, to feel a sense of moral superiority, identifying themselves as good and righteous, and opposing themselves to the morally inferior transgressors who fail to fulfill these demands. It is this sense of superiority, of goodness and righteousness, that Durkheim saw as the primary source of social solidarity. Thus, criminals play an important role in maintaining social solidarity, since they are among the group of those identified by society as inferior, which allows the rest of society to feel superior.

The punishment of criminals also plays a role in the maintenance of social solidarity. When the dictates of the collective conscience are violated, society responds with repressive sanctions not so much for retribution or deterrence, but because without them, those who are making the "perpetual and costly sacrifices" would become severely demoralized.[16] For example, when a person who has committed a serious crime is released with only a slap on the wrist, the average, law-abiding citizens may become terribly upset. They may feel they are playing the game by the rules, so everyone else should, too. The punishment of the criminal is necessary to maintain the allegiance of average citizens to the social structure. Without it, average citizens may lose their overall commitment to the society and their willingness to make the sacrifices necessary for it. But beyond this, the punishment of criminals also acts as a visible, societal expression of the inferiority and blameworthiness of the criminal group. It reinforces the sense of superiority and righteousness found in the mass of the people and thus strengthens the solidarity of the society.

Crime itself is normal in society because there is no clearly marked dividing line between behaviors that are considered criminal and those that are considered morally reprehensible or merely in bad taste. If there is a decrease in behaviors that are designated as criminal, then there may be a tendency to move behaviors that were previously designated as morally reprehensible into the criminal category. For example, not every type of unfair transfer of property is considered stealing. But if there is a decrease in the traditional forms of burglary and robbery, there then may be an associated increase in the tendency to define various forms of white-collar deception as crime. These behaviors may always have been considered morally reprehensible, and in that sense they violated the collective conscience. They were not, however, considered crimes. Society moves them into the crime category because criminal sanctions are the strongest tool available to maintain social solidarity.

Since the institution of punishment serves an essential function, it will be necessary in any society. As Durkheim stated:

> Imagine a society of saints, a perfect cloister of exemplary individuals. Crimes, properly so called, will there be unknown; but faults which appear venial to the layman will create there the same scandal that the ordinary offense does in ordinary consciousnesses. If, then, this society has the power to judge and punish, it will define these acts as criminal and will treat them as such. For the same reason, the perfect and upright man judges his smallest failings with a severity that the majority reserve for acts more truly in the nature of an offense.[17]

Thus, a society without crime is impossible. If all the behaviors that are presently defined as criminal no longer occurred, new behaviors would be placed in the crime category.[18] Crime, then, is inevitable because there is an inevitable diversity of behavior in society. The solidarity of the society is generated by exerting pressure for conformity against this diversity, and some of this pressure will inevitably take the form of criminal sanctions. As Durkheim said:

> Let us make no mistake. To classify crime among the phenomena of normal sociology is not merely to say that it is an inevitable, although regrettable, phenomenon, due to the incorrigible wickedness of men; it is to affirm that it is a factor in public health, an integral part of all societies.[19]

The abnormal or pathological state of society would be one in which there was no crime. A society that had no crime would be one in which the constraints of the collective conscience were so rigid that no one could oppose them. In this type of situation, crime would be eliminated, but so would the possibility of progressive social change. Social change is usually introduced by opposing the constraints of the collective conscience, and those who do so are frequently declared to be criminals. Thus, Socrates and Jesus were declared criminals, as were Mahatma Gandhi and George Washington. The leaders of the union movement in the 1920s and 1930s were criminalized, as were the leaders of the civil rights movement of the 1960s. If the demands of the collective conscience had been so rigidly enforced that no crime could exist, then these movements would have been impossible also. Thus, crime is the price that society pays for the possibility of progress. As Durkheim wrote:[20]

> To make progress, individual originality must be able to express itself. In order that the originality of the idealist whose dreams transcend his century may find expression, it is necessary that the originality of the criminal, who is below the level of his time, shall also be possible. One does not occur without the other.

In a similar way individual growth cannot occur in a child unless it is possible for that child to misbehave. The child is punished for misbehavior, and no one wants the child to misbehave. But a child who never did anything wrong would be pathologically overcontrolled. Eliminating the misbehavior would also eliminate the possibility of independent growth. In this sense, the child's misbehavior is the price that must be paid for the possibility of personal development. Durkheim concluded:[21]

> From this point of view, the fundamental facts of criminality present themselves to us in an entirely new light. Contrary to current ideas, the criminal no longer seems a totally unsociable being, a sort of parasitic element, a strange and unassimilable body, introduced into the midst of society. On the contrary, he plays a definite role in social life. Crime, for its part, must no longer be conceived as an evil that cannot be too much suppressed. There is no occasion for self-congratulation when the crime rate drops noticeably below the average level, for we may be certain that this apparent progress is associated with some social disorder.

ANOMIE AS A PATHOLOGICAL STATE IN ORGANIC SOCIETIES

To the extent that a society is mechanical, it derives its solidarity from pressure for conformity against the diversity of its members. But to the extent that a society is organic, the function of law is to regulate the interactions of the various parts of the whole. If this regulation is inadequate, a variety of social maladies, including crime, can result. Durkheim called the state of inadequate regulation anomie.

Durkheim first introduced this concept in *The Division of Labor in Society*, where he argued that the industrialization of French society, with its resulting division of labor, had destroyed the traditional solidarity based on uniformity. But this industrialization had been so rapid that the society had not yet been able to evolve sufficient mechanisms to regulate its transactions. Periodic cycles of overproduction followed by economic slowdown indicated that the relations between producers and consumers were ineffectively regulated. Strikes and labor violence indicated that the relations between workers and employers were unresolved. The alienation of the individual worker and the sense that the division of labor was turning people into mere "cogs in the wheel" indicated that the relation of the individual to work was inadequately defined.[22]

Durkheim expanded and generalized his notion of anomie four years later with the publication of his most famous work, *Le Suicide*. In it, he statistically analyzed data that showed that the suicide rate tends to increase sharply in both periods of economic decline and of economic growth. Whereas suicide in a time of economic decline may be easily understood, the key question is why suicide would increase in a time of prosperity. Durkheim proposed that society functions to regulate not only the economic interactions of its various components but also how the individual perceives his or her own needs. Durkheim's theory of anomie has been used as the basis for later explanations of crime and a variety of other deviant behaviors.[23]

The theory began with a comparison of animal and human nature.[24] Durkheim argued that appetites in animals are naturally limited by the physical body. Thus, animals with full stomachs and safe warm places to sleep feel satisfied. But humans have active imaginations that allow them to feel dissatisfied even when their physical needs are met. In humans, satisfying physical wants and needs tends to awaken new wants and needs, so that "the more one has, the more one wants." Thus, where an animal's physicality puts natural limits on its appetites, human appetites are naturally unlimited.

The only mechanism that can limit human appetites, according to Durkheim, is human society. Societies create moral rules about what people in various social positions can reasonably expect to acquire:

> As a matter of fact, at every moment of history there is a dim perception, in the moral consciousness of societies, of the respective value of different social services, the relative reward due each, and the consequent degree of comfort appropriate on the average to workers in each occupation. . . . Under this pressure, each in his sphere vaguely realizes the extreme limit set to his ambitions and aspires to nothing beyond. . . . Thus, an end and goal are set to the passions.

There are various situations in which these societal rules may weaken or even break down, but Durkheim focused on situations of rapid social change, including those in which the society goes into an economic recession or depression:

> In the case of economic disasters, indeed, something like a declassification occurs which suddenly casts certain individuals into a lower state than their previous one. Then they must reduce their requirements, restrain their needs, learn greater self-control. . . . So they are not adjusted to the condition forced on them, and its very prospect is intolerable.

This experience serves to explain the high rates of suicide during times of economic downturns, but Durkheim also argued that something similar happens in times of rapid economic expansion:

> It is the same if the source of the crisis is an abrupt growth of power and wealth. Then, truly, as the conditions of life are changed, the standard according to which needs were regulated can no longer remain the same. ... The scale is upset; but a new scale cannot be immediately improvised. Time is required for the public conscience to reclassify men and things. So long as the social forces thus freed have not regained equilibrium, their respective values are unknown and so all regulation is lacking for a time.

In fact, anomie (or the deregulation of appetites) would be worse in times of prosperity than in times of depression, since prosperity stimulates the appetites just at the time when the restraints on those appetites have broken down:

> With increased prosperity desires increase. At the very moment when traditional rules have lost their authority, the richer prize offered these appetites stimulates them and makes them more exigent and impatient of control. The state of de-regulation or anomy is thus further heightened by passions being less disciplined, precisely when they need more disciplining.

Durkheim went on to argue that French society, over the previous one hundred years, had deliberately destroyed the traditional sources of regulation for human appetites.[25] Religion had almost completely lost its influence over both workers and employers. Traditional occupational groups, such as the guilds, had been destroyed. Government adhered to a policy of laissez-faire, or noninterference, in business activities. As a result, human appetites were no longer curbed. This freedom of appetites was the driving force behind the French Industrial Revolution, but it also created a chronic state of anomie, with its attendant high rate of suicide.

DURKHEIM'S THEORY OF CRIME

Durkheim's theory of crime is presented in the context of his overall theory of modernization—the progression of societies from the mechanical to the organic form—so that he argued that different things would happen at different times. First, in primitive (i.e., mechanical) societies, he argued that the punishment of crime would remain fairly stable, independent of increases or decreases in the volume of criminal behavior. Second, as societies modernized (i.e., make the transition from mechanical to organic), a greater variety of behaviors would be tolerated, punishments would become less violent as their purpose changed from repression to restitution, and there would be a vast expansion of "functional" law to regulate the interactions of the emerging organic society. Third, in modern (i.e., organic) societies, the volume of criminal behavior would increase during periods of rapid social change. Each of these ideas has generated a great deal of theory and research since Durkheim wrote.

Durkheim's theory about the stability of punishment in primitive societies was reformulated by Erickson and used as the basis for a study of the Puritan colony in seventeenth-century Massachusetts.[26] This society had a relatively constant level of punishment throughout the century despite three "crime waves" attributed to Antinomians, Quakers, and witches. Erikson concluded:[27] "When a community calibrates its control machinery to handle a certain volume of deviant behavior it tends to adjust its ... legal ... definitions of the problem in such a way that this volume is realized."

In 1973, Blumstein and Cohen presented a similar theory of the stability of punishments in contemporary societies.[28] They then examined imprisonment rates in the United States from 1924 to 1974, in Canada from 1880 to 1959, and in Norway from 1880 to 1964, arguing that these rates remained stable over these periods and that the stability was maintained by adjusting the types of behaviors that resulted in imprisonment.[29] In the United States, for example, the imprisonment rate remained about 100 prisoners for every 100,000 people in the population, whether crime rates were high or low.

Since about 1970, however, imprisonment rates in many countries have risen considerably in association with get-tough sentencing policies; in the United States, the imprisonment rate has nearly quintupled.[30] This increase in imprisonment has occurred in the context of declining crime rates; for example, in the United States, both violent and property crime were at thirty-year lows in 2004, with violent crime having declined by 57 percent and property crime by 50 percent since 1993.[31]

Nils Christie examined this imprisonment boom using a generally Durkheimian perspective that crime is normal in the sense that it is part of the inevitable diversity of human conduct.[32] He argued that every society has a wide variety of "unwanted acts" that can be defined and processed as criminal, but these acts can also be handled in some other manner. He asked whether it is better for societies to define relatively more of these unwanted acts as criminal or to define relatively fewer of them—that is, what is a "suitable" amount of crime? Christie then examined a number of modern societies that take different approaches to this issue. Some, such as the United States and Russia, criminalize a large portion of unwanted acts, while others, such as Finland, criminalize a small portion. Christie concluded that a more limited and restricted use of criminalization is better for the society as a whole.

Durkheim made three arguments about crime during modernization: a greater variety of behaviors would be tolerated, punishments would become less violent as their purpose changed from repression to restitution, and there would be a vast expansion of "functional" law to regulate the interactions of the emerging organic society. Wolfgang found support for Durkheim's first argument in contemporary American society: "My major point is that we are currently experiencing in American culture, and perhaps in Western society in general, an expansion of acceptability of deviance and a corresponding contraction of what we define as crime."[33] However, research generally has not supported Durkheim's second argument about punishments becoming less violent during modernization. For example, Spitzer found that developed societies were characterized by more severe punishments, while simple societies were characterized by lenient punishments, which is the opposite of what Durkheim predicted.[34] Other research has generally found that rural areas in Western societies before modernization were characterized by high levels of violence and by a considerable degree of tolerance for it.[35] It was only after modernization, with the concentration of populations in anonymous cities, that societies began to punish violence consistently and severely. Durkheim may have derived his idea from the fact that punishments in European societies were becoming much less severe at the time because of the reforms introduced by Beccaria and other classical theorists. But the extremely harsh punishments that had been imposed prior to those reforms were associated not with simple, undeveloped societies, but rather with absolute monarchies. Those severe punishments were not found in earlier, simpler societies.[36]

In modern (i.e., organic) societies, Durkheim predicted a great expansion in functional law. In his case study of four cities from 1800 to the present, Gurr found "a veritable explosion of laws and administrative codes designed to regulate day-to-day interactions, in domains as dissimilar as trade, public demeanor, and traffic."[37] While some of these laws and codes were generated by "the functional necessity of regulating the increased traffic and commercial activities of growing cities," as Durkheim had argued, Gurr also found that a great deal of other legislation was passed defining and proscribing new kinds of offenses against morality and against "collective behavior," such as riots and protests.[38] Gurr argued that the new offenses against morality arose primarily from the effort to apply middle-class values to all social groups, while the offenses against collective behavior arose from efforts of the elite groups to maintain their power.[39]

Finally, Durkheim argued that the source of high crime rates in organic societies lay in normlessness or anomie generated by the rapid social changes associated with modernization. Durkheim's theory of anomie led to ecological, strain, and control theories of crime, so that the assessment of this argument must, to a certain extent, await the presentation of those theories in chapters 7, 8, and 10. But those theories do not directly link the breakdown of social norms to the processes of modernization, as did Durkheim's theory. Durkheim's theory of anomie is therefore assessed here in the context of his theory of modernization.

Durkheim attributed the high rates of crime and other forms of deviance in his own society to the normlessness generated by the French and Industrial Revolutions. One basic criticism of this argument is that crime rates in France were not rising at the time. Lodhi and Tilly concluded that between 1831 and 1931, the incidence of theft and robbery declined in France, citing a massive decline in the statistics for serious property crime during that period.[40] The statistics for violent crime remained approximately stable over the same period, with some tendency toward a decline. Durkheim had formulated his theory of anomie in the context of a study of suicide rates, not crime rates. Having done so, he simply presumed that crime was also increasing, although he nowhere presented data to support his conclusion. McDonald argued that the statistics showing decreases in crime rates were available to Durkheim, as well as to other prominent criminologists of the time who also presumed that crime rates were increasing, but that none of them took any notice:[41] "Marxists of that time were no more willing to admit that social and economic conditions were improving than Durkheimians that industrialization and urbanization did not inevitably lead to higher crime."

Research has led to a generally accepted conclusion that modernization is associated with increases in property crime but with decreases in violent crime.[42] For example, Neuman and Berger reviewed seventeen cross-national crime studies and concluded that urbanism and industrialization are both associated with increased property crime, but neither was associated with increases in violent crime.[43] In addition, they found no support for the argument that the increases in property crime were caused by the change from traditional to modern values. A study by Bennett also challenged Durkheim's theory as the explanation of the linkage between crime and modernization.[44] Durkheim had argued that crime is caused by rapid social change. If that is true, Bennett reasoned, then (1) the rate of increase in crime would be directly proportional to the rate of growth in the society, (2) both theft and homicide should increase during periods of rapid growth, and (3) the level of development itself (i.e., whether the country is underdeveloped or advanced) should not affect crime rates as long as the country is not rapidly changing. Using data from fifty-two nations from 1960 to 1984, Bennett then showed that the rate of growth does not significantly affect either homicide or theft and that the level of development itself, independent of the rate of growth, significantly affects theft but not homicide. Bennett concluded: "These findings refute the Durkheimian hypotheses."[45]

Because of this research, Neuman and Berger therefore questioned the continued dominance of Durkheim's theory in explaining the link between modernization and crime. They suggested that much more attention needs to be paid to the role of economic inequality in this process, as opposed to Durkheim's emphasis on the breakdown of traditional values. They pointed out that the relationship between economic inequality and homicide is "the most consistent finding in the literature"[46] and suggested that criminologists examine the large literature on the relation between inequality and economic development.[47] The basic finding of this literature is that in developing nations, foreign investment by multinational corporations and dependence on exports of raw material slow long-term economic growth and increase economic inequality. The economic inequality, then, increases both criminal behavior and the criminalization of that behavior by criminal justice agencies. This is particularly true in moderately repressive, as opposed to highly repressive or democratic, regimes. The authors concluded that "future studies should examine the relationship that exists between multinational penetration, inequality, and type of regime."

Whereas Neuman and Berger, Bennett, and others have focused their work on modernization taking place in the twentieth century, Eisner reviewed research examining European homicide rates spanning eight hundred years of modernization.[48] He found that average homicide rates per 100,000 people declined from 20 to 40 in the thirteenth and fourteenth centuries to less than 1 by the middle of the twentieth century.[49] The greatest rate of decline in these countries typically began in the early seventeenth century.[50]

Eisner's finding with respect to the rates of decline in homicides generally supported Elias's theory of "civilizing process."[51] According to Elias, declining violence in Europe can be attributed to a shift from "knightly warrior" societies, where men defended their honor through violence, to absolute monarchies, or state-controlled monopolies, in which courts had a much more powerful influence. This shift toward centralized absolute power, according to Elias, corresponded to an increase in the level of individual self-control, which resulted in less violence and a greater handling of personal conflict through formal mechanisms.

Assessing societal norms from table manners to acts of aggression, Elias argued that from the Middle Ages through the nineteenth century, a "civilization curve" gradually emerged as the pressure of conditioning caused an increased internalization of control, with young people either submitting or facing social exclusion.[52] Elias's theory of a civilizing process spreading from state to citizen and reducing impulsive violence has been supported by the findings of historians of crime and punishment who have recorded a centuries-long decline in Western European rates of violence.[53] In fact, estimates of some of the highest homicide rates on record took place in rural England in the thirteenth century, in a homogeneous setting without guns, and prior to industrialization.[54] Of course, the monopoly of violence by the state, which may have reduced impulsive interpersonal violence, has led to increased use of violence by the state, something that Elias, an exile of Nazi Germany in the 1930s, must have been well aware.[55]

Some of Eisner's findings are not interpreted so well by Elias's theory, such as the decline in homicide rates in England after the Glorious Revolution of

1688, in which absolute monopoly failed. Eisner relied on Gerhard Oestreich's notion of "social disciplining" to help explain these changes.[56] In this framework, the centralization of state power is but one of several characteristics of the massive change occurring in the sixteenth and seventeenth centuries—others include ordinances regulating appropriate clothing, alcohol consumption, and religious duties; the advance of schooling; and the growth of capitalism. All these changes corresponded to the social disciplining of the behavior of individuals in these modernizing societies.

CONCLUSIONS

Durkheim's influence has been extremely broad in criminology and sociology. His primary impact is that he focused attention on the role that social forces play in determining human conduct at a time when the dominant thinking held either that people were free in choosing courses of action or that behavior was determined by inner forces of biology and psychology. Although the focus on social forces is now the dominant view that is used to explain crime, it was considered radical at the time.[57]

There is now considerable evidence that the basic patterns of crime that are found in the modern world can be explained only by a theory that focuses on modernization as a fundamental factor. Shelley reviewed studies of crime and modernization and found that the same changes in crime patterns that occurred first in Western Europe have reoccurred in Eastern European socialist nations and in the emerging nations of Asia, Africa, and Latin America as they have undergone modernization.[58] She concluded: "The evidence . . . suggests that only the changes accompanying the developmental process are great enough to explain the enormous changes that have occurred in international crime patterns in the last two centuries."

Many of the changes that have accompanied the modernization process, however, are not those predicted by Durkheim's theory. Premodern societies were characterized by high levels of violent crime, in contrast to Durkheim's arguments about their stability. There appears to have been a long-term decline in violent crime over the past several hundred years as the process of modernization has occurred, something that Durkheim's theory does not predict.[59] Short-term increases in that long-term decline occurred in the early stages of urbanization and industrialization, but those short-term increases seem to have been associated with the retention, not the breakdown, of rural culture. Gurr argued that other sources of short-term increases in violent crime rates include wars and growths in the size of the youth population.[60]

Modernization does appear to be associated with higher property crime rates, but the increased property crime does not appear to be caused by the breakdown of moral values that is associated with rapid social change. Rather, it probably involves societal changes that result in more opportunities to commit property crime. For example, when people own more property that is both valuable and portable, and when they frequently are away from their property and cannot personally guard it, then property crime is likely to increase, as discussed in Chapter 3.

On the other hand, Durkheim's basic argument was that modernization is linked to crime through the breakdown of social norms and rules—that is, he associated crime with the absence of social controls. It may be that Durkheim's argument itself is correct but that Durkheim was wrong in assuming that premodern societies had strong social control and little crime. It now seems likely that these societies had little social control and a great deal of violent crime. The long-term decline in violent crime may then be explained by the continuously increasing level of social controls that are associated with increasing modernization.[61] The relationship between crime and social controls is further explored in Chapter 10.

The United States and many other countries have arguably experienced rapid social change over the past few decades. Income inequality in the United States, for example, has risen to levels not seen since the 1920s.[62] This has not gone unnoticed by citizens; look to the explosion of the Occupy movement in 2011 (Occupy Wall Street in the US), which expanded to events in 82 countries. In the United States, suicide rates rose 30 percent between 1999 and 2016.[63] However, as seen in Chapter 2, crime rates (both property and violent) have gone down during the same time period. Since the beginning of the twenty-first century, the use of social media has gradually and then more rapidly accelerated. Whether there is a certain normlessness that may have come about as a result of this is up for debate, but from a layperson's intuition, much communication in society appears to be dominated by Twitter feed and Facebook posts, which lack regulation and fact-checking, and often provoke hostility. Traditional manual labor jobs are on the decline, and the oft-stressful "gig jobs" are on the rise; a significant proportion of the population is being left behind in the wake of rapid growth in select sectors. Social scientists may wish to consult Durkheim's principles when studying human behavior in the era of big technology and the Information age.

KEY TERMS

anomie	organic society
modernization	crime as normal
French Revolution	collective conscience
Industrial Revolution	moral superiority
rational society	pathologically overcontrolled
traditional society	unwanted acts
social solidarity	civilizing process
mechanical society	social disciplining

DISCUSSION QUESTIONS

1. What functions do crime and punishment serve for Durkheim? Provide specific current examples in which crime and punishment serve societal functions.
2. Give current and historical examples of anomic situations and explain why the volume of criminal behavior may increase during periods of rapid social change.
3. What would explain modernization being associated with increases in property crime but decreases in violent crime?
4. What would account for falling homicide rates in Western societies over the past centuries?
5. What does Elias mean by the civilizing process? In what ways may this have contributed to falling violent crime rates?
6. Provide specific examples of ways in which the modernizing process has increased formal and informal social controls.
7. What has research shown regarding levels of violence in preindustrial cultures as compared to industrialized cultures? What may explain these findings?
8. Are there any aspects of or concepts from of Durkheim's theory that you think bear relevance to human behavior in the era of social media?

NOTES

1. Dominick LaCapra, *Emile Durkheim, Sociologist and Philosopher* (Ithaca, NY: Cornell University Press, 1972), p. 5.
2. Ibid., p. 5.
3. Robert A. Nisbet, *Emile Durkheim* (Englewood Cliffs, NJ: Prentice Hall, 1965), p. 20.
4. Ibid., p. 20.
5. LaCapra, *Emile Durkheim*, p. 41.
6. Julius Gould, "Auguste Comte," in *The Founding Fathers of Social Science*, ed. T. Raison (Harmondsworth, UK: Penguin, 1969), p. 40.
7. Emile Durkheim, *The Division of Labor in Society*, trans. George Simpson (New York: Free Press, 1965).
8. Raymond Aron, *Main Currents in Sociological Thought*, vol. 2, Richard Howard and Helen Weaver, trans. (New York: Basic Books, 1967), p. 12.
9. Ibid., pp. 12–13.
10. Emile Durkheim, *The Rules of the Sociological Method*, trans. Sarah A. Solovay and John H. Mueller; ed. George E. G. Catlin (New York: Free Press, 1965).
11. Emile Durkheim, *Suicide*, trans. John A. Spaulding and George Simpson; ed. George Simpson (New York: Free Press, 1951).
12. Durkheim, *The Division of Labor in Society*, p. 80, n10. In French, the term *conscience* has overtones of both "conscience" and "consciousness," but the term is usually translated as "collective conscience."

13. Durkheim, *The Rules of the Sociological Method*, p. 70.
14. Ibid., pp. 2–3.
15. Emile Durkheim, *Essays on Sociology and Philosophy*, ed. Kurt Wolff (New York: Harper & Row, 1960), p. 338.
16. Nisbet, *Emile Durkheim*, p. 225. See also Jackson Toby, "Is Punishment Necessary?" *Journal of Criminal Law, Criminology and Police Science* 55 (1964): 332–337.
17. Durkheim, *The Rules of the Sociological Method*, pp. 68–69.
18. Ibid., p. 67.
19. Ibid., p. 67.
20. Ibid., p. 71.
21. Ibid., p. 72.
22. Durkheim, *The Division of Labor in Society*, pp. 370–373.
23. Marshall B. Clinard, ed., *Anomie and Deviant Behavior* (New York: Free Press, 1964).
24. The theory of anomie is presented in Emile Durkheim, *Suicide* (New York: Macmillan, 1952), pp. 246–253, and the following quotations are from those pages. For an extensive series of quotations summarizing the theory, see George B. Vold, Thomas J. Bernard, and Jeffrey B. Snipes, *Theoretical Criminology*, 4th ed. (New York: Oxford University Press, 1998), pp. 130–132.
25. Durkheim, *Suicide*, pp. 254–258.
26. Kai T. Erikson, *Wayward Puritans* (New York: John Wiley & Sons, 1966).
27. Ibid., p. 26.
28. Alfred Blumstein and Jacqueline Cohen, "A Theory of the Stability of Punishment," *Journal of Criminal Law and Criminology* 64 (1973): 198–207.
29. Blumstein, Cohen, and Daniel Nagin, "The Dynamics of a Homeostatic Punishment Process," *Journal of Criminal Law and Criminology* 67 (1976): 317–334. For a brief review of this study and many others that extended, supported, or criticized it, see Allen E. Liska, "Introduction," in *Social Threat and Social Control*, ed. Liska (Albany: State University of New York Press, 1992), pp. 13–16. See also Jan P. C. Fiselier, "A Test of the Stability of Punishment Hypothesis: The Dutch Case," *Journal of Quantitative Criminology* 8 (1992): 133–151, who found a similar pattern in the Netherlands.
30. Bureau of Justice Statistics, "Prisoners in 2004" (Washington, DC: US Department of Justice, 2005). This figure includes only federal and state prison populations. The total incarceration rate in the United States, including those in jails and juvenile institutions, was about 780/100,000 in 2004.
31. Bureau of Justice Statistics, *Criminal Victimization, 2004* (Washington, DC: US Department of Justice, 2005).
32. Nils Christie, *A Suitable Amount of Crime* (London: Routledge, 2004). This work extended an argument made in his previous book, *Crime Control as Industry: Towards Gulags, Western Style*, 3rd ed. (London: Routledge, 2000). Among other things, Christie argued that crime control absorbs the unemployed into roles as keepers and kept. This is similar to an argument made by Chris Hale, "Unemployment, Imprisonment, and the Stability of Punishment Hypotheses: Some Results Using Cointegration and Error Correction

Models," *Journal of Quantitative Criminology* 5 (1989): 169–186. Hale found that punishment levels in England increased and decreased with unemployment, rather than with crime. He therefore rejected the "stability of punishment" hypothesis and argued that the imprisonment is best interpreted as a judicial response to economic crisis.

33. Marvin E. Wolfgang, "Real and Perceived Changes in Crime," in *Criminology in Perspective*, ed. Simha F. Landau and Leslie Sebba (Lexington, MA: D. C. Heath 1977), pp. 27–38.

34. Steven Spitzer, "Punishment and Social Organization," *Law and Society Review* 9 (1975): 613–637.

35. See, e.g., Howard Zehr, *Crime and Development of Modern Society* (Totowa, NJ: Rowman & Littlefield, 1976). On the decline in violence, see also Manuel Eisner, "Modernization, Self-Control, and Lethal Violence: The Long-Term Dynamics of European Homicide Rates in Theoretical Perspective," *British Journal of Criminology* 41 (2001): 618–638.

36. Michel Foucault, *Discipline and Punish* (New York: Pantheon, 1977), pp. 3–69. See also Philippe Ariès, *Centuries of Childhood* (New York: Knopf, 1962), chap. 1, for a discussion of the tendency to idealize the past as harmonious and peaceful.

37. Ted Robert Gurr, *Rogues, Rebels, and Reformers* (Beverly Hills, CA: Sage, 1976), p. 180.

38. Ibid., p. 177.

39. Ibid., pp. 93–115.

40. A. Q. Lodhi and Charles Tilly, "Urbanization, Crime and Collective Violence in Nineteenth-Century France," *American Journal of Sociology* 79 (1973): 297–318. See also A. V. Gatrell and T. B. Hadden, "Criminal Statistics and Their Interpretations," in *Nineteenth-Century Society*, ed. E. A. Wrigley (Cambridge: Cambridge University Press, 1972), pp. 336–396.

41. Lynn McDonald, "Theory and Evidence of Rising Crime in the Nineteenth Century," *British Journal of Sociology* 33 (1982), p. 417.

42. For a review, see Gary D. LaFree and Edward L. Kick, "Cross-National Effects of Development, Distributional and Demographic Variables on Crime: A Review and Analysis," *International Annals of Criminology* 24 (1986): 213–236. In contrast, one study found that with proper controls for the age structure of populations and for region, both homicide and theft rates rise with modernization. See Suzanne T. Ortega, Jay Corzine, Cathleen Burnett, and Tracey Poyer, "Modernization, Age Structure, and Regional Context: A Cross-National Study of Crime," *Sociological Spectrum* 12 (1992): 257–277.

43. W. Lawrence Neuman and Ronald J. Berger, "Competing Perspectives on Cross-National Crime: An Evaluation of Theory and Evidence," *Sociological Quarterly* 29 (1988): 281–313.

44. Richard R. Bennett, "Development and Crime," *Sociological Quarterly* 32 (1991): 343–363.

45. Ibid., p. 356.

46. Ibid., p. 296.

47. Ibid., pp. 298–299. A still different causal path was suggested by Sethard Fisher ("Economic Development and Crime," *American Journal of Economics and Sociology* 46 [1987]: 17–34), who argued that crime is associated with the unplanned drift of rural populations into urban areas and with changes in elite groups as the society attempts to modernize and achieve economic growth.

48. Eisner, "Modernization, Self-Control, and Lethal Violence."

49. Ibid., p. 628.

50. Ibid., p. 629.

51. Norbert Elias, *The Civilizing Process*, vols. I and II (Oxford: Oxford University Press, 1978).

52. Norbert Elias, *The Civilizing Process* (Oxford: Blackwell, 2000), pp. 72–172.

53. Eric A. Johnson and Eric H. Monkkonen, eds., *The Civilization of Crime: Violence in Town and Country Since the Middle Ages* (Champaign: University of Illinois Press, 1996).

54. Roger Lane, *Murder in America: A History* (Columbus: Ohio State University Press, 1997), pp. 9–32. Lane noted that estimates of thirteenth-century English homicide rates of about 20 per 100,000 contrasted with current English rates of about 1 or less per 100,000.

55. Johnson and Monkknonen, *The Civilization of Crime*, pp. 5–6.

56. Eisner, "Modernization, Self-Control, and Lethal Violence," p. 631.

57. See the chapter on Durkheim in Ian Taylor, Paul Walton, and Jock Young, *The New Criminology* (New York: Harper, 1973), pp. 67–90.

58. Louise I. Shelley, *Crime and Modernization* (Carbondale: Southern Illinois University Press, 1981), pp. 141–142.

59. See Steven F. Messner, "Societal Development, Social Equality, and Homicide," *Social Forces* 61 (1982): 225–240.

60. Ted Robert Gurr, "Historical Forces in Violent Crime," in *Crime and Justice*, vol. 3, ed. Michael Tonry and Norval Morris (Chicago: University of Chicago Press, 1981), pp. 340–346. See also Gurr, "On the History of Violent Crime in Europe and America," in *Violence in America*, 2nd ed., ed. Hugh David Graham and Ted Robert Gurr (Beverly Hills, CA: Sage, 1979).

61. This basically is Gurr's interpretation. See the sources in note 60.

62. Chad Stone, Danilo Trisi, Arloc Sherman, and Roderick Taylor, "A Guide to Statistics on Historical Trends in Income Inequality," *Policy Futures* (Center on Budget and Policy Priorities, 2018).

63. Deborah M. Stone, Thomas R. Simon, Katherine A. Fowler, Scott R. Kegler, Keming Yuan, Kristin M. Holland, Asha Z. Ivey-Stephenson, and Alex E. Crosby, "Trends in State Suicide Rates—United States, 1999–2106 and Circumstances Contributing to Suicide—27 States, 2015," *Morbidity and Mortality Weekly Report* 67 (2018): 617–624.

CHAPTER 7

—

Strain Theories

In adapting Durkheim's theory to American society, Robert K. Merton shifted the focus away from rapid social change. Instead, he argued that there were certain relatively stable social conditions that were associated with the higher overall crime rates in American society, as well as with the higher rates of crime in the lower social classes. Merton used the term *social structural strain* to describe those social conditions, so that the theories that followed Merton's lead have come to be known as "strain theories."

ROBERT K. MERTON AND ANOMIE IN AMERICAN SOCIETY

Durkheim had analyzed anomie as a breakdown in the ability of society to regulate the natural appetites of individuals. Merton, in an article first published in 1938,[1] argued that many of the appetites of individuals are not "natural" but rather originate in the "culture" of American society. At the same time, the "social structure" of American society limits the ability of certain groups to satisfy these appetites. The result is "a definite pressure on certain persons in the society to engage in nonconformist rather than conformist conduct."[2]

Merton began by pointing out that the culture of any society defines certain goals that it deems "worth striving for."[3] There are many such goals in every society, and they vary from culture to culture. Perhaps the most prominent cultural goal in American society, however, is to acquire wealth. This may be regarded merely as a "natural aspiration," as Durkheim maintained. But American culture encourages this goal far beyond any intrinsic rewards the goal itself may have. Accumulated wealth is generally equated with personal value and worth, and it is associated with a high degree of prestige and social status. Those without money may be degraded even if they have personal characteristics that other cultures may value, such as age or spiritual discipline.

In addition, whereas Durkheim said that culture functioned to limit these aspirations in individuals (although at certain times it did not do so well), Merton argued that American culture specifically encourages all individuals to seek the greatest amount of wealth. American culture is based on an egalitarian ideology that asserts that all people have an equal chance to achieve wealth. Although all individuals are not expected to achieve this goal, all are expected to try. Those who do not may be unfavorably characterized as "lazy" or "unambitious."[4]

Cultures also specify the approved norms or institutionalized means that all individuals are expected to follow in pursuing the culture goals. These means are based on values in the culture and generally will rule out many of the technically most efficient methods of achieving the goal. For example, in American culture, the institutionalized means that should be used to achieve wealth can generally be identified as "middle-class values" or "the Protestant work ethic." They include hard work, honesty, education, and deferred gratification. The use of force and fraud, which may be more efficient methods of gaining wealth, is forbidden.[5]

Merton argued that because all persons cannot be expected to achieve the goals of the culture, it is important that the culture place a strong emphasis on the institutionalized means and the necessity of following them for their own value.[6] These means must provide some intrinsic satisfaction for all persons who participate in the culture. This is similar to the situation in athletics, in which the sport itself must provide enjoyment, even if the person does not win. The phrase "It's not whether you win, it's how you play the game" expresses the notion that the primary satisfaction comes from following the institutionalized means (rules), rather than achieving the goal (winning).

In athletics, however, the goal of winning may be unduly emphasized, so that there is a corresponding de-emphasis on the rewards provided by the sport itself. In this situation ("It's not how you play the game, it's whether you win"), the institutionalized means are placed under a severe strain. Merton argued that this is the situation in American culture regarding the goal of achieving wealth.[7] The goal has been emphasized to the point that the institutionalized means are little reward in themselves. The person who adheres to these methods—that is, hard work, education, honesty, deferred gratification—receives little social reward for it unless he or she also achieves at least a moderate degree of wealth as a result. But the person who achieves wealth, even if it is not by the approved means, still receives the social rewards of prestige and social status. This situation places a severe strain on the institutionalized means, particularly for those persons who cannot achieve wealth through their use.

This strain falls on a wide variety of people in the society, but it tends to be more concentrated among persons in the lower class. In that group the ability to achieve wealth is limited not only by the talents and efforts of the individual, but by the social structure itself. Only the most talented and the most hardworking individuals from this class can ever expect to achieve wealth through the use of the institutionalized means. For the majority of persons, this possibility is simply not realistic, and therefore the strain can be most severe. By the same token, the strain is least apparent among those in the upper classes, in which, using the same institutionalized means, a person of moderate talents can achieve a degree of wealth with only moderate efforts.

For certain groups, then, a severe strain on the cultural values arises because (1) the culture places a disproportionate emphasis on the achievement of the goal of accumulated wealth and maintains that this goal is applicable to all persons, and (2) the social structure effectively limits the possibilities of individuals within these groups to achieve this goal through the use of institutionalized means. This contradiction between the culture and the social structure of society is what Merton defined as anomie.[8]

Merton therefore used a cultural argument to explain the high rate of crime in American society as a whole and a structural argument to explain the concentration of crime in the lower classes.[9] The high level of crime in American society was explained in terms of "cultural imbalance"—the imbalance between the strong cultural forces that valued the goal of monetary success and the much weaker cultural forces that valued the institutional means of hard work, honesty, and education. However, Merton described American culture as relatively uniform throughout the class structure, so that everyone is similarly pressured to achieve wealth and everyone has a relatively weak allegiance to the institutionalized means. Thus, cultural imbalance does not explain why the lower classes in the United States have higher crime rates than do the upper classes. Merton therefore used social structure, not culture, to explain why lower-class people in the United States have higher crime rates than do upper-class people. That explanation focused on the distribution of legitimate opportunities in the social structure— that is, the ability to achieve wealth through institutionalized means. Merton argued that these opportunities were relatively concentrated in the higher classes and relatively absent in the lower classes. The distribution of criminal behavior is said to be a sort of mirror image of the distribution of legitimate opportunities, being relatively concentrated in the lower classes and relatively absent in the upper classes.

There are various ways in which an individual can respond to this problem of anomie, depending on his or her attitude toward the cultural goals and the institutionalized means. Merton described these "adaptations" as conformity, innovation, ritualism, retreatism, and rebellion. A summary of Merton's typology is presented in Table 7.1.

To the extent that a society is stable, most persons in it will choose conformity, which entails acceptance of both the culture goals and the institutionalized means. These persons strive to achieve wealth through the approved methods of middle-class values and will continue to do so whether or not they succeed.

TABLE 7-1 Typology of Merton's Types of Adaptations

Form of Adaptation	Goals/Ends (Culturally Defined)	Means (Structurally Defined)
Conformity	Accepts	Accepts
Innovation	Accepts	Rejects
Ritualism	Rejects	Accepts
Retreatism	Rejects	Rejects
Rebellion	Rejects and replaces	Rejects and replaces

Most crime that exists in society, however, will probably take the form of innovation. Persons who innovate retain their allegiance to the culture goal of acquiring wealth (since this goal is so heavily emphasized), but they find that they cannot succeed at it through the institutionalized means. Therefore, they figure out new methods by which wealth can be acquired. Businessmen may devise different forms of white-collar crime entailing fraud and misrepresentation or may cheat on their income tax. Workers may systematically steal from their places of employment. Poor people may develop illegal operations such as gambling, prostitution, or drug dealing, or may burglarize and rob. In each case, the individual has retained his commitment to the cultural goal but is pursuing it through unapproved means. Crime as innovation is consistent with Durkheim's notion of crime being normal in society.

This situation is similar to that described by the classical thinkers, who maintained that since humans were hedonistic, they would always choose the most technically efficient methods of achieving their goals, unless they were limited by punishments imposed by society.[10] Although the classical thinkers thought this was the normal condition of people, Merton argued that it was the condition only when the cultural goals were overemphasized to the point that the norms broke down.

A third possible adaptation (ritualism) involves rejecting the possibility of ever achieving wealth, but retaining allegiance to the norms of hard work, honesty, and the like. This is the adaptation of those persons who wish to "play it safe." They will not be disappointed by failure to achieve their goals, since they have abandoned them. At the same time, they will never find themselves in any trouble, since they abide by all the cultural norms. This is the perspective of "the frightened employee, the zealously conformist bureaucrat in the teller's cage,"[11] and tends to be found most frequently among persons in the lower middle class. These persons have achieved a minimum level of success through the institutionalized means, but they have no real hope of achieving anything more. The fear of losing even this minimum level locks them into their adaptation.

The fourth adaptation—retreatism—involves simply dropping out of the whole game. Dropouts neither pursue the cultural goals nor act according to the institutionalized means. Those who choose this adaptation include "psychotics, autists, pariahs, outcasts, vagrants, vagabonds, tramps, chronic drunkards and drug addicts."[12] Merton pointed out that this adaptation does not necessarily arise from the lack of commitment to the culture. It can also occur when there is a strong commitment to both the goals and the means but no real possibility of achieving success.

> There results a twofold conflict: the interiorized moral obligation for adopting institutional means conflicts with pressures to resort to illicit means (which may attain the goal) and the individual is shut off from means which are both legitimate and effective. The competitive order is maintained, but the frustrated and handicapped individual who cannot cope with this order drops out.

Rebellion is the last of the possible adaptations to the problem of anomie. Here, the person responds to his or her frustrations by replacing the values of the society with new ones. These new values may be political, in which the goals are, for example, the achievement of a socialist society, and the approved means may involve violent revolution. On the other hand, these values may be spiritual, in which the goals entail the achievement of certain states of consciousness, and the means involve fasting and meditation. Or the values may be in one of any number of other areas. The basic point is that this person ceases to function as a member of the existing society and begins to live within an alternate culture.

These adaptations do not describe personality types. Rather, they describe an individual's choice of behaviors in response to the strain of anomie. Some individuals may consistently choose one adaptation, such as low-level bureaucrats who respond to their situation through ritualism. But the same bureaucrats may occasionally innovate by stealing small amounts from their employers or may occasionally retreat through the use of alcohol. Other persons develop patterns of behavior involving the use of several adaptations simultaneously. For example, a professional criminal (innovation) may also consistently use narcotics (retreatism) and, at the same time, may promote a militant, revolutionary philosophy (rebellion). These behaviors may not be seen as consistent with each other unless it is understood that they are all responses to the anomic situation the individual faces.

These same adaptations may be seen in other situations in which there is a discrepancy between the emphasis placed on the goals and the means to achieve them. In athletics, if the goal of winning is overemphasized, those who cannot win within the institutionalized means (rules) may be strongly motivated to cheat (innovate), may merely continue playing without hope of winning (ritualism), may quit playing altogether (retreatism), or may attempt to get a different game going (rebellion). Students are often faced with a strong overemphasis on the goal of achieving high grades and may resort to similar adaptations. Deviant behavior among scientists has been analyzed in terms of an overemphasis on the goal of originality in scientific research.[13] Those who cannot achieve this goal may resort to various adaptive behaviors, such as "reporting only the data which support an hypothesis, making false charges of plagiarism, making self-assertive claims, being secretive lest one be forestalled, occasionally stealing ideas, and in rare cases, even fabricating data."[14] Finally, Merton made the point that "the foregoing theory of anomie is designed to account for some, not all, forms of deviant behavior customarily described as criminal or delinquent."[15] The intention of the theory is to focus attention on one specific problem, "the acute pressure created by the discrepancy between culturally induced goals and socially structured opportunities," not to attempt to explain all the diverse behaviors that at one time or another are prohibited by the criminal law.

A number of theorists have attempted to extend and refine Merton's theories. The most significant of these attempts was by Richard Cloward, writing in 1959.[16] Whereas Merton focused on the fact that lower-class people have limited access to legal means of achieving goals of success, Cloward pointed out that the same people often have broad access to illegal means that exist in their neighborhoods. The local pawn shop, which would fence stolen goods, the junkyard, which would take that hot car off their hands, the numbers racket, and the drug and prostitution rings all provide illegal opportunities to achieve the success goals of society. Cloward also pointed out that the mere presence of an opportunity is not enough unless one has been introduced to the ways of taking advantage of it.[17] This "learning structure" was described by Shaw and McKay in their studies of delinquency areas (see Chapter 8) and by Sutherland in his theory that crime is normal, learned behavior (see Chapter 9), and Cloward regarded his formulation as a consolidation of these three approaches. Merton agreed with Cloward's theory, regarding it as a substantial extension of his own theory.[18]

Merton's reformulation of anomie theory focused on the special strains under which certain segments of the population are placed and used these strains to explain criminality. This type of argument has also been used in two major theories to explain urban, lower-class, male gang delinquency, one by Albert Cohen and the other by Richard Cloward and Lloyd Ohlin.

COHEN'S MIDDLE CLASS MEASURING ROD

In his work with juveniles, Cohen found that most delinquent behavior occurred in gangs rather than individually, and that most of it was "nonutilitarian, malicious, and negativistic."[19] This type of delinquency, in contrast to most adult crime, seemed to serve no useful purpose. Juvenile gangs stole things they did not want or need, vandalized and maliciously destroyed property, and participated in gang wars and unprovoked assaults. Purposeless crimes could not be explained by Merton's theory, which argued that crimes had the purpose of acquiring money, although by illegitimate means. Cohen believed that these actions were methods of gaining status among the delinquent's peers, but then he had to ask why these behaviors were "a claim to status in one group and a degrading blot in another."[20] He concluded that gangs have a separate culture from the dominant culture, with a different set of values for measuring status. The question that Cohen then addressed was why and how this separate culture had evolved.

Merton described people as seeking the cultural goal of success. In a similar way, Cohen saw youths as seeking the goal of status among their peers. He utilized the classic distinction between achieved status, which is earned in competition with one's own age and sex group, and ascribed status, which is acquired by virtue of one's family, such as when one's father is an important person. Competition for achieved status normally takes place within the school. Cohen saw the school as a solidly middle-class institution, permeated by the values of its middle-class teachers and administrators. He noted that status in school is judged on the basis of such values as ambition, responsibility, achievement (especially in the areas of academic work and athletics), deferred gratification, rationality, courtesy, ability to control physical aggression, constructive use of time, and respect for property.[21]

Youths who have no ascribed status by virtue of their families and who typically lose in the competition for achieved status are placed under a severe strain. They can continue to conform to middle-class values, but they must then be content with a low-status position among their peers. Or they can rebel against middle-class values and set up a new value structure according to which they can increase their status and self-worth. Youths who rebel in such a way tend to come together to form a group in order to validate their choices and reinforce their new values. The delinquent gang is such a group. It is a spontaneous development in which a number of youths, each of whom faces a similar problem (low status), together create a common solution to that problem.

The lack of status may affect youths in different social classes, but, like Merton's anomie, it disproportionately affects youths from the lower class. These youths generally have no ascribed status from their families, since their parents normally have low-status occupations. At the same time, they are at a disadvantage in competing for achieved status in schools. Lower-class children often have internalized values that are different from those of middle-class children prior to entering school. When measured against these values, they perform poorly and must either adjust to these new values or reject them. Thus, members of delinquent gangs are generally lower-class children. And because the gang is primarily rebelling against middle-class values, it takes on the "negativistic" character noticed by Cohen.

Merton's and Cohen's theories differ in several respects. Merton emphasized the utilitarian nature of crime, focusing on innovation as a response to the social structural pressures, whereas Cohen sought to explain the nonutilitarian character of much delinquency. Cohen's theory is similar to the rebellion adaptation proposed by Merton, but it differs in that the particular form the rebellion takes is determined by a reaction against middle-class values. In Merton's theory, rebellion may take any one of a number of different forms. Finally, Cohen saw the choice of rebellion as linked to the choices of other members of the group, whereas Merton portrayed the choice of an adaptation as an individual response.

CLOWARD AND OHLIN'S TYPOLOGY OF GANGS

Cloward and Ohlin's theory of gang delinquency returned to Merton's emphasis on the utilitarian nature of crime.[22] Cloward and Ohlin agreed with Cohen that some gang delinquency is motivated by the pursuit of status and by a reaction against middle-class values. But they argued that these youths tend to be the less serious delinquents. The more serious delinquents, according to Cloward and Ohlin, are simply looking for money, not status. In particular, serious delinquents are oriented toward conspicuous consumption—"fast cars, fancy clothes, and swell dames"—goals that are phrased solely in economic terms and have no relationship to middle-class values. These youths experience the greatest conflict with middle-class values, since they "are looked down upon both for what they do not want (i.e., the middle-class style of life) and for what they do want (i.e., 'crass materialism')."[23] These are the youths, Cloward and Ohlin claimed, who have been repeatedly described in the literature on juvenile delinquency.

Cloward and Ohlin then referred to the earlier extension of Merton's theory by Cloward to explain the particular form of delinquency that these youths will commit. It is assumed that there are no legitimate opportunities for these youths to improve their economic position. If illegitimate opportunities are presented, as described by Cloward, then these youths tend to form criminal gangs, in which the emphasis is on the production of income. If, however, neither legitimate nor illegitimate opportunities are available, then the youths' frustration and discontent will be heightened. In addition, the lack of opportunities is often a symptom of the lack of social organization (whether legitimate or illegitimate) in the community, which means there will be fewer controls on the youths' behavior. In this circumstance, the youths tend to form a violent or conflict gang to express their anger. This is the source of the nonutilitarian, malicious, and negativistic activity described by Cohen. Finally, Cloward and Ohlin described a "retreatist subculture" similar to Merton's retreatist adaptation and similarly populated with "double failures." Youths in this subculture are unable to achieve the economic improvement they seek, whether because of the lack of opportunity or because of internal prohibitions against the use of illegitimate means. They also fail in the resort to conflict and violence. This group turns to alcohol or to drugs and drops out.

1960s STRAIN-BASED POLICIES

During the 1960s, strain theories came to dominate criminology and eventually had a great impact on federal policy toward crime and delinquency.[24] After Robert Kennedy, who was then attorney general of the United States, read Cloward and Ohlin's book, he asked Lloyd Ohlin to help develop a new federal policy on juvenile delinquency. The result was the passage of the Juvenile Delinquency Prevention and Control Act of 1961, which was based on a comprehensive action program developed by Cloward and Ohlin in connection with their book. The program included improving education; creating work opportunities; organizing lower-class communities; and providing services to individuals, gangs, and families. The program was later expanded to include all lower-class people and became the basis of Lyndon Johnson's War on Poverty. Although billions of dollars were spent on these programs, the only clear result seems to have been the massive political resistance that was generated against this attempt to extend opportunities to people without them. The programs, having failed to achieve their goals, were eventually dismantled by Richard Nixon.

Since no genuine extension of opportunities ever took place, this failure might be attributed to the opposition the programs encountered. Rose offered an alternative interpretation of the failure of these programs.[25] The War on Poverty was based on strain theories, which argue that crime and poverty have their origins in social structural arrangements. Therefore, these theories imply that the solution to the problems of crime and poverty require social structural change. As originally conceived, the War on Poverty was designed to change social structural arrangements, not to change individual people. However, most of these programs were taken over by the bureaucracies of poverty-serving agencies, who immediately acted to protect and enhance their own bureaucratic interests. As a consequence, when the poverty programs were actually implemented, virtually all of them were designed to change poor people, and few were designed to change social structural arrangements. Rose maintained that the War on Poverty failed because its original purpose was subverted as it was transformed to serve the interests of the established poverty-serving bureaucracies. Thus, he titled his book *The Betrayal of the Poor*.

THE DECLINE AND RESURGENCE OF STRAIN THEORIES

After the failure of strain-based federal policies of the 1960s, strain theories were subjected to a great deal of scrutiny and to a large number of criticisms. Some of the criticisms were theoretical, focusing on the adequacy of their terms and concepts, while other criticisms were empirical, focusing on whether the theories are supported by research.

The most extensive criticisms were made by Kornhauser in an influential book published in 1978.[26] Kornhauser described the central element of strain theories as the assertion that stress or frustration causes crime and delinquency. The source of this stress or frustration was said to be the gap between what criminals and delinquents want (aspirations) and what they expect to get (expectations). Kornhauser then reviewed empirical research on the aspirations and expectations of delinquents and argued that the research showed that delinquency is associated with both low expectations and low aspirations.[27] She maintained that such youths would not be "strained," since there is no gap between what they want and what they expect to get. These and other criticisms were widely accepted in criminology, resulting is a general decline of interest in strain theories.

In 1984, Bernard attacked the validity of Kornhauser's criticisms of strain theories.[28] For example, research showing that delinquents did not have a gap between their aspirations and their expectations, Bernard pointed out, asked youths about aspirations and expectations related to obtaining more education and high-status jobs. But Cloward and Ohlin had specifically argued that delinquents do not have such aspirations and instead wanted "fast cars, fancy clothes, and swell dames." Later research by Farnsworth and Leiber found that when measured in strictly monetary terms, the gap between aspirations and expectations was associated with delinquency.[29]

Also in 1984, Cullen published a theoretical book that reinterpreted the major strain theories of Merton, Cohen, and Cloward and Ohlin.[30] He argued that Merton actually proposed two different theories—one at the individual level and the other at the societal level. At the individual level, Cullen agreed with Kornhauser that according to Merton's theory, people in situations of social structural strain would feel frustrated and these feelings would motivate them to act in deviant ways.[31] But at the aggregate level, Cullen argued that Merton proposed a separate theory in which criminals are not described as stressed or frustrated at all:[32]

> Merton did not maintain that an unregulated individual has to experience any special stress or pressure to become deviant. . . . In the place of [the strained deviant], Merton substituted a thoroughly classical view of the deviant, arguing that the deregulated or anomic actor is free to choose any course of conduct. The only guide to the person's activity is the rational calculation of the costs and benefits of the various means available. Deviant behavior now occurs when illegitimate means are the "technically most effective procedure" that can be employed to secure a desired end. As Merton has noted, this attenuation of institutional controls creates a "situation erroneously held by the utilitarian philosophers to be typical of society, a situation in which the calculations of personal advantage and fear of punishment are the only regulating agencies."

This "anomie theory" operates at the societal level, linking social structural characteristics to rates and distributions of deviant behavior.

Cullen's interpretation makes it clear that the term *strain* can be used in two different ways. First, it can refer to the characteristics of a society: a situation in which the social structure fails to provide legitimate means to achieve what the culture values. Second, it can refer to feelings and emotions that an individual experiences: feelings of stress or frustration or anxiety or depression or anger. The line of argument connecting these two meanings is that people in situations of "social structural strain" (i.e., people who cannot achieve culturally valued goals through legitimate means provided by the social structure) may feel strained (i.e., may feel stressed, frustrated, anxious, depressed, and angry), and feelings then are the actual cause of the higher crime rates associated with those people. There is disagreement about whether the original strain theories of Merton, Cohen, and Cloward and Ohlin included this line of argument or not.[33] But regardless of whether they did, new strain theories using both types of characteristics—social and individual—have appeared.

AGNEW'S GENERAL STRAIN THEORY

At the individual level, Agnew proposed a general strain theory (GST) based on three elements: failure to achieve goals, removal of positively valued stimuli, and the existence of negative stimuli.[34] Failure to achieve goals includes strain represented by the disjunction between expectations and actual achievements, as well as disjunction between just or fair outcomes and actual outcome. An example of the former would be if a person desires to be an attorney but can't get into law school, and an example of the latter would be if a person scores very high on the entrance exams, but is beat out by an applicant whose scores were lower but whose parents are legacy alumni. The stress brought about by the removal of positively valued stimuli, such as the death of a friend or the divorce of one's parents, can also result in strain. Strain can also be caused by the presence of negative stimuli, such as abuse at home or problems at school. All three elements involve negative relationships, which Agnew argued generate negative emotions in the person, and the negative emotions then cause crime, if criminal coping mechanisms are engaged in response to the strain. This is a general theory of crime, but Agnew used it specifically to explain why adolescents engage in delinquency and drug use.

Negative relationships include relationships in which other people prevent a person from achieving a valued goal, take away something valued that the person already has, or impose on the person something that is "noxious" and unwanted. According to Agnew, previous strain theories have focused on relationships in which people were prevented from reaching their valued goals, such as monetary success and status. Agnew, however, focused on relationships in which the person is presented with a noxious situation and is unable to escape from it—that is, relationships in which others do not treat the individual as he or she would like to be treated. These can include a wide variety of relationships, but for adolescents, they often are associated with living at home and being in school. Unlike adults, adolescents cannot legally leave these relationships if they experience them as noxious—if they do leave, they can be arrested for truancy or running away. These relationships then generate a variety of negative emotions, such as disappointment, depression, fear, and anger. It is these negative emotions that Agnew defined as strain.

There are various types of coping mechanisms for dealing with strain: cognitive, behavioral, and emotional. Cognitive strategies include minimizing the importance of adversity ("it's not important"), lowering standards employed to evaluate outcomes or distorting estimates of current/expected outcomes ("it's not that bad"), and accepting responsibility for adversity ("I deserve it").[35] Behavioral strategies may involve escaping the source of the strain; if the source is the school environment, one can transfer schools or skip school, for example. Another type of behavioral response is vengeance, which may be carried out through conventional or delinquent behavior. Emotion responses can be healthy (meditation, exercise) or unhealthy and illicit (drug and alcohol use). Although most individuals cope with strains with conventional coping mechanisms, GST focuses largely on engagement in delinquency and drug use as ways of coping with and managing the strain of these negative emotions.

A fairly large number of studies have found support for Agnew's basic argument that negative relationships and stressful life events are associated with increases in a variety of delinquent behaviors.[36] An additional study found that delinquent behavior is more successful than nondelinquent behavior as a technique for managing the negative emotions caused by strain.[37] That is, given the same level of strain, youths who engage in delinquency experience "modest relief" from negative emotions compared to youths who obey the law. Other studies have found that strain has similar effects for both males and females.[38] Still other studies have found that anger as a response to strain tends to be associated with violent crime,[39] including one study of court-adjudicated youths.[40]

One aspect of Agnew's theory that has generated some inconsistent results is related to the type of negative emotions that intervene between the strain-causing event and delinquency or criminality. In her test of general strain theory, Broidy found that anger increased the likelihood of delinquency, but other negative emotions, such as crankiness, depression, and insecurity, actually decreased the likelihood of delinquency.[41] Similarly, Piquero and Sealock found that anger mediates strain and crime but found no mediating effect of depression.[42] On the other hand, Capowich and his colleagues discovered that the type of behavior influenced whether negative emotions other than anger would mediate the causal linkage. Situational anger but no other negative emotions were related to fights, whereas depression and anxiety but not anger were related to shoplifting.[43] Another study, focusing on the effect of racial discrimination on delinquency among African American children, found that discrimination as a source of strain caused delinquency through both depression and anger.[44]

General strain theory has been expanded since its inception. Agnew extended strain to include not only that which is directly experienced by an individual but vicarious strain (strain experienced by others close to the individual) and anticipated strain (strain that has not yet occurred but is expected). Focusing on physical victimizations, Agnew found that all three types of strain influence delinquency, with personally and vicariously experienced strain having the strongest effect.[45] Zavala and Spohn explain the interplay of experienced, vicarious, and anticipated strain in the context of physical victimizations, as follows:

> Individuals engaged in criminal behavior may increase their opportunity for victimization. Strain causes criminal behavior, which then puts the offender at a greater risk for victimization. A strained youth, for example, may seek revenge upon another youth who may have done him or her wrong. A physical confrontation may ensue in which the strained youth ends up being the victim. Other strained youths may turn to alcohol or other drugs to alleviate strain or stress. An intoxicated individual can become an attractive target for mugging or assault, since excessive alcohol and illicit drugs inhibit one's ability to protect oneself. A gang member whose gang assaulted a rival gang member might anticipate retaliation, generating anticipating strain and increasing his or her likelihood of victimization.[46]

Zavala and Spohn analyzed data from a weapons survey of male students from fifty-three high schools and found that (1) high levels of reported vicarious strain was associated with a greater likelihood of victimization and perpetration of violent crime; (2) anticipated strain was positively associated with victimization but not perpetration; and (3) prior delinquency was positively associated with violent victimization.[47]

Agnew also expanded the scope of general strain theory to neighborhoods, in what he called "macro-level strain theory." This variation proposes that neighborhoods with high proportions of individuals experiencing strain will suffer higher crime rates, since there is a heightened chance that these volatile individuals will interact with each other, creating conflict and criminal behavior.[48] A study by Warren and Fowler supported macro-level strain theory, finding that neighborhood strains were positively associated with violent crime, at least in neighborhoods with low levels of social support. Neighborhood strain was measured by the proportion of residents who reported receiving verbal threats or insults, feeling cheated by others, or being harassed by the police.[49] It is important not to confuse "macro" as used in this theory with societal strain, discussed in the next section, which is also macro-level, but on a higher level. One could conceive the GST version as more of a "meso" approach.

General strain theory has also been modified and conditioned in a couple of ways. First, recognizing the need to differentiate between strains that are likely and not likely to result in delinquency or crime, Agnew specified four characteristics of strain that should magnify its effect on illegitimate behavior. Drawing on research from a vast body of literature, he posited that crime will be a more likely product of strains that (1) are seen as unjust and intentionally caused by others, producing anger; (2) are high in magnitude, including their severity, duration, recency, and centrality; (3) are associated with or caused by low social control; and (4) create pressures or incentives to rely on illegitimate coping strategies.[50] An example he provided of a strain with all these features is physical victimization, as described earlier. It is seen as unjust, since another person is responsible and directly invades the individual's person. Being attacked is probably one of the more severe things that can happen to someone. Such victimizations often occur in situations involving few social controls. And finally, a typical coping mechanism available to victims of attacks in cultures that are more prone to criminal behavior is the teaching of how to "get even" by others in the social setting.[51]

In addition to specifying characteristics of the strain that enhance the likelihood of criminal behavior, Agnew, with his colleagues, pointed to characteristics of the strained individuals that increase this probability. Individuals with two "master traits"—being high in overall negative emotionality and being low in constraint—are particularly prone to behaving illegitimately when exposed to strains, whereas individuals without these traits are more likely to employ conventional coping strategies.[52] Their preliminary empirical research provided support for the role of these personality traits in amplifying the effect of strain on criminal behavior.

Not only does general strain theory address how negative emotions can result in criminal behavior, but it also has been expanded to explore factors that condition whether one responds to strain with criminal versus noncriminal behavior. This line of research points to characteristics of the individual rather than characteristics of the strain. These may include such factors as low social control (see Chapter 10) and association with delinquent peers (see Chapter 9). Those variables may *mediate* the strain-delinquency relationship; for example, negative emotions from school strains may lead one to associate with delinquent peers, which in turn increases propensity for delinquency. They also may *condition* criminal coping; for example, those with low levels of family social control may be more likely to choose this type of coping over conventional coping strategies, when facing strain. Agnew's review of this research found mixed results in this literature.[53] In addition to methodological explanations, he accounted for the inconsistent findings in two ways. First, GST has overlooked a wide range of other potential conditioning variables, such as personality characteristics, religiosity, and previous experience with stressors. Second, research on conditioning isolates one variable at a time, without looking at how multiple possible conditioners may operate interactively in explaining why some individuals use criminal coping instead of other strategies.

In response to this second explanation, Thaxton and Agnew developed an index termed "propensity for criminal coping," consisting of ten risk factors: low attachment to mother, poor parental monitoring, impulsivity, risk-seeking, neutralizations (discussed later in this volume), low guilt, low school commitment, delinquent peer commitment, and time in unsupervised peer activities.[54] Using survey data from schools in eleven cities across the United States, they tested the effects of three types of strain (victimization, police strain, and school strain) on delinquent behavior, looking to see if the propensity index conditioned the effects. Victimization and school strain have been previously discussed in this chapter. Police strain refers to perceptions of police as dishonest, rude, disrespectful, and discriminatory against minorities. They found that both gang membership and high scores on the propensity index significantly increased the likelihood of criminal coping responses to these sources of strain.[55]

General strain theory has proven immensely popular for those testing various criminology theories. Studies employing general strain theory have focused on, for example, the topical domains of hate crime,[56] school interventions,[57] school bullying,[58] intimate partner homicide,[59] sex offenders,[60] substance abuse,[61] prison inmate misconduct,[62] whistleblowing,[63] cyberbullying,[64] and violent extremism.[65] General strain theory has also been applied to gender differences in crime, by Broidy and Agnew (see Chapter 13).

Like many general theories, general strain theory runs the risk of being couched so broadly that everything falls into its confines, thereby holding it inevitable that empirical support will follow. As Agnew stated, "hundreds of types of strain fall under the major categories of strain listed by [general strain theory]."[66] The end result is that the concept of strain as blocked opportunities to desirable goals is interpreted so loosely that events as varied as rapes, taunts by police, jobs applied for but not landed, and the withholding of food stamps seemingly represent strain. It is difficult to imagine many negative outcomes and events that occur in daily life that do not cause strain. Agnew's attempt to modify and condition general strain theory, as described earlier, may help to narrow the breadth of the theory; however, general strain theory is being expanded in other ways as rapidly as it is being limited in this fashion. The ultimate vitality of the individual-level strain approach to the study of crime and delinquency will partially depend on whether a viable set of parameters can reasonably define the scope of empirical testing of the model. A theory that is too general may be accurate but not all that useful in its policy implications.

Also at the individual level, Agnew introduced the notion of "storylines," which he defined as "events and conditions that increase the likelihood of a crime or series of related crimes."[67] Storylines operate at the "temporal level" and therefore serve as a link between the long-term effects of background variables and the immediate situational cues. Agnew identified five storylines as crime conducive:

> A desperate need for money; an unresolved dispute; a brief, but close involvement with a criminal other(s); a brief, tempting opportunity for crime; and a temporary break from conventional others and institutions.[68]

Storylines are useful in understanding crime, according to Agnew, because they demonstrate how background factors influence, but do not
determine, actions; cast light on the intermittent nature of offending; and
provide the context for the development of criminal events. Agnew further asserted that storylines can aid in crime control, since individuals
who are most likely to experience crime-conducive storylines can be
identified and appropriate interventions can be made.[69]

With storylines, Agnew presented a general, integrated theory, incorporating
aspects of general strain theory with its blocked aspirations, differential association with its emphasis on peer contacts (see Chapter 9), and rational
choice theories as they relate to opportunities for crime (see Chapter 3).

MESSNER AND ROSENFELD'S INSTITUTIONAL
ANOMIE THEORY

At the societal level, Messner and Rosenfeld presented an "institutional
anomie" theory that is similar to Merton's.[70] They explained the high levels
of crime in American society by pointing to "the American Dream," which
they described as "a broad cultural ethos that entails a commitment to the
goal of material success, to be pursued by everyone in society, under conditions of open, individual competition."[71] Like Merton, they argued that this
cultural ethos generates intense cultural pressures for monetary success. At
the same time, the American Dream does not strongly prohibit people from
using more efficient illegal means to achieve monetary success.

Messner and Rosenfeld diverged from and extended Merton's theory in
two ways. First, they argued that redistributing legitimate opportunities may
actually increase, rather than decrease, the pressures toward criminal behavior
unless the culture, with its emphasis on the goal of monetary success at the
expense of following the institutional means, also changes. Expanding opportunities may change who wins and who loses in the competition for monetary
success, but there will still be losers. People who lose this competition have no
one to blame but themselves and their own inadequacies. This situation may
put even more pressure on them to commit crime (i.e., achieve monetary success through illegitimate means) than if they could blame an unfair system.

A second divergence from Merton's theory involves Messner and
Rosenfeld's explanation of the overemphasis on monetary success in
American culture. Messner and Rosenfeld pointed to the overwhelming influence of economic institutions in American society and argued that other
institutions, such as families, schools, and even politics, tend to be subservient to the economy:[72]

Prosocial cultural messages tend to be overwhelmed by the anomic tendencies of the American Dream . . . because of the dominance of the

economy in the institutional balance of power. A primary task for non-economic institutions such as the family and schools is to inculcate beliefs, values, and commitments other than those of the marketplace. But as these noneconomic institutions are relatively devalued and forced to accommodate to economic considerations, and as they are penetrated by economic standards, they are less able to fulfill their distinctive socialization functions successfully.

Messner and Rosenfeld therefore proposed a number of policies to strengthen these institutions in their relations to the economy and to weaken the impact of the economy on them.[73] First, they argued that families in American society are heavily driven by economic concerns, to the extent that the family as a social institution is relatively unable to influence the behavior of its members. Families can be strengthened in their relation to the economy by implementing policies, such as family leave, job sharing for husbands and wives, flexible work schedules, and employer-provided child care. These policies provide parents with some freedom from the demands of the economy, and parents are then able to spend more time and energy on family concerns. Schools have become subservient to the economy. Good jobs usually require high school or college degrees, so many students stay in school because they want a good job in the future, not because they want an education. As teachers respond to this demand from students, the entire educational enterprise tends to become driven by the job market. If job success were less tied to the number of years in school, then students who were not really interested in acquiring an education could drop out of school and go to work, and schools then could actually focus on education as a goal.

Political institutions have also tended to be subservient to the economy, and Messner and Rosenfeld recommended that other elements of political life be emphasized. For example, the creation of a national service corps would engage young people in the life of the community in ways that emphasize collective goals other than material success. The economy itself could also be modified to reduce somewhat its control of individuals. Messner and Rosenfeld pointed to the mixed economies of Western Europe and Japan, which ensure that a level of material well-being is not totally dependent on economic performance. Finally, at the cultural level, goals other than material success must be given greater prominence in our society, especially such activities as parenting, teaching, and serving the community. In general, Messner and Rosenfeld suggested an increased emphasis on mutual support and collective obligations in American society and a decreased emphasis on individual rights, interests, and privileges.

In an initial test of Messner and Rosenfeld's theory, Chamlin and Cochran looked at rates of church membership, divorce, and voting in the various states of the United States.[74] These rates were taken to indicate the strength of three noneconomic institutions: church, family, and state. As the theory predicted, Chamlin and Cochran found lower property crime in states with higher church memberships, lower divorce rates, and a greater voter turnout. They then tested a more subtle prediction of Messner and Rosenfeld's theory: the strength of noneconomic institutions should moderate the effects of economic hardship on crime. That is, there should be less association between poverty and crime in states with stronger noneconomic institutions. Chamlin and Cochran therefore looked at the relationship between crime and a variety of measures of economic deprivation and found the predicted pattern. This pattern was taken as strong support for the theory.

In another test, Messner and Rosenfeld focused on "social safety net" policies (such as welfare, health care, and parental leave) by which nations protect their citizens from the hazards of the marketplace.[75] These policies are an indicator of the strength of the state as a noneconomic institution— that is, the extent to which the state does not solely serve the needs of the economy. In a sample of about forty nations, Messner and Rosenfeld found that nations in which citizens are better protected from the marketplace have lower rates of homicide.

Research has attempted to assess whether Merton's and Messner and Rosenfeld's theories fit together or should be considered separately. An emerging view is that the two are supplementary and explain more variance in deviant behavior together than individually.[76] Studies have shown that the dominance of economic markets over noneconomic institutions (from Messner and Rosenfeld's theory) translates into crime, especially when there are unequal opportunities in the social structure (from Merton's theory).[77] These findings challenge Messner and Rosenfeld's contention that redistributing legitimate opportunities may increase criminal behavior in a culture of economic market dominance.

CONCLUSION

The failure of the War on Poverty illustrates that the policy implications of strain theories may be difficult to achieve in the real world. The problem is that patterns of self-interest always develop around existing social structural arrangements.[78] People who benefit from these arrangements protect their self-interests by resisting social change. Messner and Rosenfeld's policy recommendations may be more politically appealing than the policies associated with the War on Poverty because they emphasize strengthening families and schools. To some extent, these policies may appeal to both liberals and conservatives.[79] On the other hand, the thrust of their recommendations is to reduce the overwhelming influence of the economy in American society. The rhetoric in some modern elections suggests that economic concerns almost totally dominate the political process and that governmental policies are overwhelmingly directed toward promoting economic growth. It does not seem likely that in the near future, the American people would be willing to compromise economic growth in order to promote the general welfare.

There is no question that the problems described by strain theories are complex. It is not merely a matter of talented individuals confronted with inferior schools and discriminatory hiring practices. Rather, a good deal of research has indicated that many delinquents and criminals are untalented individuals who cannot compete effectively in complex industrial societies.[80] When viewed in the light of that research, strain theories can be interpreted as suggesting that untalented people want many of the same things as talented people but find they cannot obtain these things through legitimate means. Some of them therefore attempt to obtain these things through criminal activity. From this perspective, strain theories would seem to pose some disturbing questions for public policy. Do untalented people have the same rights as talented people to want material goods, the respect of their peers, and power and control over their own lives? Would society be well advised to provide untalented as well as talented people with legitimate opportunities to obtain these things? Or is the economy so dominant in American society that we cannot even consider such questions?

General strain theory widens the approach to our understanding of crime and delinquency as responses to a wide range of stressors, transcending one's position within the economy. It has inspired a tremendous amount of research among criminologists and scholars from related disciplines. To the extent that we can better understand those mechanisms which condition responses to stressors, principles from general strain theory may be useful in the development of childhood and adolescent interventions designed to guide individuals away from criminal coping and toward healthy coping strategies.

KEY TERMS

social structural strain	nonutilitarian
natural appetites	separate/subculture
cultural appetites	achieved status
cultural goal	ascribed status
egalitarian ideology	illegitimate opportunities
approved norms/institutional means	conflict gang
Protestant work ethic	War on Poverty
deferred gratification	vicarious strain
Merton's anomie	anticipated strain
cultural argument	macro-level strain
structural argument	neighborhood strain
cultural imbalance	general strain theory
innovation	coping strategies
adaptation	conditioning variables
	the American Dream

DISCUSSION QUESTIONS

1. How would Merton's theory account for the fact that only a small percentage of individuals in lower-class neighborhoods innovate?
2. Provide examples of how Merton's theory could account for white-collar crime.
3. In what ways do strain theories explain the behavior of street gangs?
4. Which version of strain theory would best explain the overrepresentation of homicides in inner-city areas?
5. What are the policy implications of strain theory? How would the changes implied by strain theories actually be implemented?
6. Compare the policy approach used in the 1960s, with the War on Poverty, with that of the 1990s. How do they differ? What do they say about the idea of structural change?
7. According to general strain theory, what factors would likely lead to criminal behavior? Thinking about your own life, what sorts of negative strains that Agnew refers to have you experienced? How did you deal with them? What sorts of things about yourself and your environment do you think influenced whether you relied on healthy or unhealthy coping strategies?

NOTES

1. Robert K. Merton, *Social Theory and Social Structure* (Glencoe, IL: Free Press, 1968), p. 186. An extensive presentation and discussion of this theory is found in Merton, "Opportunity Structure: The Emergence, Diffusion, and Differentiation as Sociological Concept, 1930s–1950s," in *Advances in Criminological Theory: The Legacy of Anomie Theory*, vol. 6, ed. Freda Adler and William Laufer (New Brunswick, NJ: Transaction Press, 1995), pp. 3–78. For a discussion of the relationship between Durkheim's and Merton's theories, see Thomas J. Bernard, "Merton vs. Hirschi: Who Is Faithful to Durkheim's Heritage?" in *Advances in Criminological Theory*, ed. Adler and Laufer, pp. 81–90.
2. For definitions of structure and culture in Merton's theory, see Merton, "Opportunity Structure," pp. 6–7.
3. Merton, *Social Theory and Social Structure*, p. 187.
4. Ibid., p. 193.
5. Ibid., p. 187.
6. Ibid., p. 188.
7. Ibid., p. 190.
8. Ibid., p. 216.
9. These cultural and structural arguments are presented in propositional form in Thomas J. Bernard, "Testing Structural Strain Theories," *Journal of Research in Crime and Delinquency* 24 (1987): 264–270.

10. Merton, *Social Theory and Social Structure*, p. 211.
11. Ibid., p. 204.
12. Ibid., p. 207.
13. Robert K. Merton, "Priorities in Scientific Discovery: A Chapter in the Sociology of Science," *American Sociological Review* 22 (December 1957): 635–659. See also Harriet Zuckerman, "Deviant Behavior and Social Control in Science," in *Deviance and Social Change*, ed. Edward Sagarin (Beverly Hills, CA: Sage, 1977), pp. 87–138.
14. Marshall B. Clinard, "The Theoretical Implications of Anomie and Deviant Behavior," in *Anomie and Deviant Behavior*, ed. Clinard (New York: Free Press, 1964), p. 23.
15. Merton, *Social Theory and Social Structure*, p. 195.
16. Richard A. Cloward, "Illegitimate Means, Anomie, and Deviant Behavior," *American Sociological Review* 24 (April 1959): 164–176.
17. Ibid., p. 168.
18. Robert K. Merton, "Social Conformity, Deviation and Opportunity Structures: A Comment on the Contributions of Dubin and Cloward," *American Sociological Review* 24 (April 1959): 188.
19. Albert K. Cohen, *Delinquent Boys: The Culture of the Gang* (New York: Free Press, 1955). For an analysis of the theory and a statement of its major arguments in propositional form, see Bernard, "Testing Structural Strain Theories." Merton discussed and analyzed the theory in "Opportunity Structure," pp. 33–44.
20. Cohen, *Delinquent Boys*, p. 27.
21. Ibid., pp. 88–91.
22. Richard A. Cloward and Lloyd E. Ohlin, *Delinquency and Opportunity: A Theory of Delinquent Gangs* (New York: Free Press, 1960). For an analysis of the theory and a statement of its major arguments in prepositional form, see Bernard, "Testing Structural Strain Theories." Merton discussed and analyzed the theory in "Opportunity Structure," pp. 44–71.
23. Cloward and Ohlin, *Delinquency and Opportunity*, p. 97.
24. For a brief review of the attempt to implement Cloward and Ohlin's ideas in federal policy, see LaMar T. Empey, *American Delinquency*, rev. ed. (Homewood, IL: Dorsey, 1982), pp. 240–245. For more extended accounts, see Peter Maris and Martin Rein, *Dilemmas of Social Reform*, 2nd ed. (Chicago: Aldine, 1973); James F. Short Jr., "The Natural History of an Applied Theory: Differential Opportunity and Mobilization for Youth," in *Social Policy and Sociology*, ed. N. J. Demerath (New York: Academic Press, 1975), pp. 193–210; Joseph J. Helfgot, *Professional Reforming: Mobilization for Youth and the Failure of Social Science* (Lexington, MA: D. C. Heath, 1981); and Stephen M. Rose, *The Betrayal of the Poor: The Transformation of Community Action* (Cambridge, MA: Schenkmann, 1972).
25. Rose, *The Betrayal of the Poor*.
26. Ruth Rosner Kornhauser, *Social Sources of Delinquency* (Chicago: University of Chicago Press, 1978), pp. 139–180.

27. Ibid., pp. 167–180.
28. Thomas J. Bernard, "Control Criticisms of Strain Theories: An Assessment of Theoretical and Empirical Adequacy," *Journal of Research in Crime and Delinquency* 21 (1984): 353–372. See also the discussion of Kornhauser on pp. 199–201 of the third edition of the present text.
29. Margaret Farnsworth and Michael J. Lieber, "Strain Theory Revisited: Economic Goals, Educational Means, and Delinquency," *American Sociological Review* 54 (April 1989): 263–274.
30. Francis T. Cullen, *Rethinking Crime and Deviance Theory: The Emergence of a Structuring Tradition* (Totowa, NJ: Rowman and Allanheld, 1983). See also Francis T. Cullen, "Were Cloward and Ohlin Strain Theorists?" *Journal of Research in Crime and Delinquency* 25 (1988): 214–241.
31. Cullen, *Rethinking Crime and Deviance Theory*, pp. 36–37.
32. Ibid., pp. 80–82.
33. See the interchange between Bernard and Agnew in *Journal of Research in Crime and Delinquency* 24 (1987): 262–290. Agnew argued that each of the traditional strain theories necessarily contained this individual-level argument. In contrast, Bernard argued that these theories did not make any individual-level argument in which frustration in individuals causes those individuals to commit crime. Related to this disagreement, Merton's most recent statement ("Opportunity Structure," p. 9) included a statement that "the basic point" of theories in the anomie tradition "centers on rates of structurally generated and constrained behavior, not on the behavior of this or that individual." See also Merton, "Opportunity Structure," p. 27.
34. Robert Agnew, "Foundation for a General Strain Theory of Crime and Delinquency," Criminology 30 (1992): 47–87. For an updated review of general strain theory, see Robert Agnew, *Pressured into Crime: An Overview of General Strain Theory* (Los Angeles: Roxbury, 2006).
35. Agnew, "Foundation for a General Strain Theory of Crime and Delinquency," pp. 66–70.
36. Robert Agnew and Helene Raskin White, "An Empirical Test of General Strain Theory," Criminology 30 (1992): 475–499; Raymond Paternoster and Paul Mazerolle, "General Strain Theory and Delinquency: A Replication and Extension," *Journal of Research in Crime and Delinquency* 31 (1994): 235–263; John P. Hoffman and Alan S. Miller, "A Latent Variable Analysis of General Strain Theory," *Journal of Quantitative Criminology* 14 (1998): 83–110; Timothy Brezina, "Teenage Violence Toward Parents as an Adaptation to Family Strain," *Youth & Society* 30 (1999): 416–444; John P. Hoffman and Felicia Gray Cerbone, "Stressful Life Events and Delinquency Escalation in Early Adolescence," *Criminology* 37 (1999): 343–373; and Paul Mazerolle and Jeff Maahs, "General Strain and Delinquency," *Justice Quarterly* 17 (2000): 753–778. See also two earlier articles by Agnew, "A Revised Strain Theory of Delinquency," *Social Forces* 64 (1985): 151–167; and "A Longitudinal Test of the Revised Strain Theory," *Journal of Quantitative Criminology* 5 (1989): 373–387.

37. Timothy Brezina, "Adapting to Strain: An Examination of Delinquent Coping Responses," *Criminology* 34 (1996): 39–60.

38. Robert Agnew and Timothy Brezina, "Relational Problems with Peers, Gender, and Delinquency," *Youth and Society* 29 (1997): 84–111; Paul Mazerolle, "Gender, General Strain, and Delinquency," *Justice Quarterly* 15 (1998): 65–91; John P. Hoffman and S. Susan Su, "The Conditional Effects of Stress on Delinquency and Drug Use: A Strain Theory Assessment of Sex Differences," *Journal of Research in Crime and Delinquency* 34 (1997): 46–78. On the other hand, Lisa Broidy and Robert Agnew ("Gender and Crime," *Journal of Research in Crime and Delinquency* 34 [1997]: 275–306) found that females evaluate certain strains more negatively than do males. See also a comment on these studies by Agnew in "An Overview of General Strain Theory," in *Explaining Criminals and Crime*, ed. Raymond Paternoster and Ronet Bachman (Los Angeles: Roxbury, 2001), pp. 161–174.

39. Paul Mazerolle, Velmer S. Burton Jr., Francis T. Cullen, T. David Evans, and Gary L. Payne, "Strain, Anger, and Delinquent Adaptations," *Journal of Criminal Justice* 28 (2000): 89–101; Paul Mazerolle and Alex Piquero, "Linking Exposure to Strain with Anger," *Journal of Criminal Justice* 26 (1998): 195–211.

40. Nicole Leeper Piquero and Miriam D. Sealock, "Generalizing General Strain Theory," *Justice Quarterly* 17 (2000): 449–484.

41. Lisa M. Broidy, "A Test of General Strain Theory," *Criminology* 39 (2001): 9–35.

42. Nicole Leeper Piquero and Miriam D. Sealock, "Gender and General Strain Theory: A Preliminary Test of Brody and Agnew's Gender/GST Hypotheses," *Justice Quarterly* 21 (2004): 125–158.

43. George E. Capowich, Paul Mazerolle, and Alex Piquero, "General Strain Theory, Situational Anger, and Social Networks," *Journal of Criminal Justice* 29 (2001): 445–461.

44. Ronald L. Simons, Yi-Fu Chen, Eric A. Stewart, and Gene H. Brody, "Incidents of Discrimination and Risk for Delinquency: A Longitudinal Test of Strain Theory with an African American Sample," *Justice Quarterly* 20 (2003): 827.

45. Robert Agnew, "Experienced, Vicarious, and Anticipated Strain: An Exploratory Study on Physical Victimization and Delinquency," *Justice Quarterly* 19 (2002): 603–632.

46. Egbert Zavala and Ryan E. Spohn, "The Role of Vicarious and Anticipated Strain on the Overlap of Violent Perpetration and Victimization: A Test of General Strain Theory," *American Journal of Criminal Justice* 38 (2013): 119–140, p. 124.

47. Ibid.

48. Robert Agnew, "A General Strain Theory of Community Differences in Crime Rates," *Journal of Research in Crime and Delinquency* 36 (1999): 123–155.

49. Barbara D. Warner and Shannon K. Fowler, "Strain and Violence: Testing a General Strain Theory Model of Community Violence," *Journal of Criminal Justice* 31 (2003): 511–521.

50. Robert Agnew, "Building on the Foundation of General Strain Theory: Specifying the Types of Strain Most Likely to Lead to Crime and Delinquency," *Journal of Research in Crime and Delinquency* 38 (2001): 319–361.
51. Ibid., p. 337.
52. Robert Agnew, Timothy Brezina, John Paul Wright, and Francis T. Cullen, "Strain, Personality Traits, and Delinquency: Extending General Strain Theory," *Criminology* 40 (2002): 43–72.
53. Robert Agnew, "When Criminal Coping is Likely: an Extension of General Strain Theory," *Deviant Behavior* 34 (2013): 653–670.
54. Sherod Thaxton and Robert Agnew, "When Conditional Coping is Likely: An Examination of Conditioning Effects in General Strain Theory," *Journal of Quantitative Criminology* 34 (2018): 887–920.
55. Ibid.
56. Chad W. Sexton, "The Impact of Strain on Hate Crime: Testing Agnew's Macro-Level General Strain Theory" (PhD diss., University of Buffalo, State University of New York, 2011).
57. Byongook Moon and Merry Morash, "General Strain Theory as a Basis for the Design of School Interventions," *Crime & Delinquency* 59 (2012): 886–909. See also Hanne Op de Beeck, Lieven J. R. Pauwels, and Johan Put, "Schools, Strain and Offending: Testing a School Contextual Version of General Strain Theory," *European Journal of Criminology* 9 (2012): 52–72; George E. Higgins, Nicole L. Piquero, and Alex R. Piquero, "General Strain Theory, Peer Rejection, and Delinquency/Crime," *Youth and Society* 43 (2011): 1272–1297.
58. Byongook Moon, Hye-Won Hwang, and John D. McCluskey, "Causes of School Bullying: Empirical Test of a General Theory of Crime, Differential Association Theory, and General Strain Theory, *Crime & Delinquency* 57 (2011): 849–877; Justin W. Patchin and Sameer Hinduja, "Traditional and Nontraditional Bullying Among Youth: A Test of General Strain Theory," *Youth & Society* 43 (2011): 727–751.
59. Li Eriksson and Paul Mazerolle, "A General Strain Theory of Intimate Partner Homicide," *Aggression and Violent Behavior* 18 (2013): 462–470.
60. Alissa R. Ackerman and Meghan Sacks, "Can General Strain Theory Be Used to Explain Recidivism Among Registered Sex Offenders?," *Journal of Criminal Justice* 40 (2012): 187–193.
61. Susan F. Sharp, B. Mitchell Peck, and Jennifer Hartsfield, "Childhood Adversity and Substance Use of Women Prisoners," *Journal of Criminal Justice* 40 (2012): 202–211.
62. Robert G. Morris, Michael L. Carriaga, Brie Diamond, Nicole Leeper Piquero, and Alex R. Piquero, "Does Prison Strain Lead to Prison Misbehavior? An Application of General Strain Theory to Inmate Misconduct," *Journal of Criminal Justice* 40 (2012): 194–201.
63. Ralph Kobel and Nico Herold, "Whistle-Blowing from the Perspective of General Strain Theory," *Deviant Behavior* 40 (2019): 139–155.
64. Helen Lianos and Andrew McGrath, "Can the General Theory of Crime and General Strain Theory Explain Cyberbullying?" *Crime and Delinquency* 64 (2018): 674–700.

65. Amy Nivette, Manuel Eisner, and Denis Ribeaud, "Developmental Predictors of Violent Extremist Attitudes: A Test of General Strain Theory," *Journal of Research in Crime and Delinquency* 54 (2017): 755–790.

66. Agnew, "Building on the Foundation of General Strain Theory," p. 320.

67. Robert Agnew, "Storylines as a Neglected Cause of Crime," *Journal of Research in Crime and Delinquency* 43 (2006): 119–147.

68. Ibid., p. 141.

69. Ibid., pp. 141–143.

70. Steven F. Messner and Richard Rosenfeld, *Crime and the American Dream*, 3rd ed. (Belmont, CA: Wadsworth, 2001). The term *institutional anomie* is taken from Mitchell B. Chamlin and John K. Cochran, "Assessing Messner and Rosenfeld's Institutional Anomie Theory," *Criminology* 33 (1995): 411–429, which found partial support for the theory. See also the comment by Gary Jensen and reply by Chamlin and Cochran in *Criminology* 34 (1996): 29–34. See also the 4th ed. (Wadsworth, 2007), where the authors engage in more cross-national comparisons, address the corporate scandals of the early 2000s, and theorize on the American crime decline of the 1990s, attributing it to the unprecedented "social experiment" in imprisonment, which they said merely reduced crime rates by reducing opportunity without reducing criminality and the motivation to offend. Related to this point, in the preface to the 4th edition (p. xiii), the authors emphasized that the controlling aspects of social institutions must not obliterate their "capacity to provide social support."

71. Messner and Rosenfeld, *Crime and the American Dream*, p. 85.

72. Ibid., p. 78.

73. Ibid., pp. 101–110.

74. Chamlin and Cochran, "Assessing Messner and Rosenfeld's Institutional Anomie Theory."

75. Steven F. Messner and Richard Rosenfeld, "Political Restraint of the Market and Levels of Criminal Homicide," *Social Forces* 75 (1997): 1393–1416. This finding is consistent with a number of other studies that have found that better welfare policies are associated with lower levels of crime. See Junsen Zhang, "The Effect of Welfare Programs on Criminal Behavior," *Economic Inquiry* 35 (1997): 120–137; Lance Hannon and James DeFronzo, "Welfare and Property Crime," *Justice Quarterly* 15 (1998): 273–288; Hannon and DeFronzo, "The Truly Disadvantaged, Public Assistance, and Crime," *Social Problems* 45 (1998): 383–392; and DeFronzo and Hannon, "Welfare Assistance Levels and Homicide Rates," *Homicide Studies* 2 (1998): 31–45. See also Jukka Savolainen, "Inequality, Welfare State, and Homicide: Further Support for Institutional Anomie Theory," *Criminology* 38 (2000): 1021–1042. This test, in addition to finding support for the social safety net hypothesis, found that when welfare spending was at high levels, economic inequality was no longer associated with homicide at all.

76. Jon Gunnar Bernburg, "Anomie, Social Change and Crime," *British Journal of Criminology* 42 (2002): 729–742. See also Eric P. Baumer and Regan Gustafson, "Social Organization and Instrumental Crime: "Assessing the Empirical

Validity of Classic and Contemporary Anomie Theories," *Criminology* 45 (2007): 617–663.

77. J. Savolainen, "Inequality, Welfare State, and Homicide: Further Support for the Institutional-Anomie Theory," *Criminology* 38 (2000): 1021–1042.

78. Talcott Parsons, *Politics and Social Structure* (New York: Free Press, 1969), p. 95.

79. Messner and Rosenfeld, *Crime and the American Dream*, pp. 101–102.

80. See, for example, Richard J. Herrnstein and Charles Murray, *The Bell Curve* (New York: Free Press, 1994), for a general argument that the United States is spinning toward a society radically divided between the talented and the untalented, with the talented totally in control of the economy and the untalented having high rates of crime. Like Messner and Rosenfeld, Herrnstein and Murray recommended that the dominance of the economy in American society be reduced to prevent a social catastrophe.

CHAPTER 8

＿

Neighborhoods and Crime

One of Durkheim's arguments was that rapid social change was associated with increases in crime because of the breakdown of social controls. This idea was one of several used by members of the Department of Sociology at the University of Chicago in the 1920s in their attempt to pinpoint the environmental factors associated with crime and to determine the relationship among the factors. However, instead of focusing on rapid change in entire societies, they focused on rapid change in neighborhoods.

Their procedure involved correlating the characteristics of each neighborhood with the crime rates of that neighborhood. This first large-scale study of crime in the United States produced a mass of data and a large number of observations about crime that led directly to much of the later work in American criminology. Since this research was based on an image of human communities taken from plant ecology, it became known as the Chicago School of Human Ecology.

THE THEORY OF HUMAN ECOLOGY

The term *ecology*, as it is used today, is often linked to the idea of protecting the natural environment. In its original meaning, however, it is a branch of biology in which plants and animals are studied in their relationships to each other and to their natural habitat. Plant life and animal life are seen as an intricately complicated whole, a web of life in which each part depends on almost every other part for some aspect of its existence. Organisms in their natural habitat exist in an ongoing balance of nature, a dynamic equilibrium in which each individual must struggle to survive. Ecologists study this web of interrelationships and interdependencies in an attempt to discover the forces that define the activities of each part.

Human communities, particularly those organized around a free-market economy and a laissez-faire government, could be seen to resemble this biotic state in nature. Each individual struggles for his or her survival in an interrelated, mutually dependent community. The Darwinian law of survival of the fittest applies here as well.

Robert Park proposed a parallel between the distribution of plant life in nature and the organization of human life in societies.[1] He had been a Chicago newspaper reporter for twenty-five years and had spent much of that time investigating social conditions in the city. Chicago at that time had a population of more than 2 million; between 1860 and 1910 its population had doubled every ten years, with wave after wave of immigrants. Park was appointed to the Sociology Department at the University of Chicago in 1914. From the study of plant and animal ecology, he derived two key concepts that formed the basis of what he called the "theory of human ecology."

The first concept came from the observations of the Danish ecologist Warming, who noted that a group of plants in a given area may have many characteristics that, in combination, are similar to those of an individual organism.[2] Warming called such groups "plant communities." Other ecologists argued that the plant and animal life in a given habitat tend to develop a "natural economy" in which different species are each able to live more prosperously together than separately. This is called "symbiosis," or the living together of different species to the mutual benefit of each. Since each plant and animal community was said to resemble an organism, the balance of nature in the habitat was said to resemble a "superorganism."

Park's work as a newspaperman had led him to view the city in a similar way—not merely as a geographic phenomenon, but as a kind of superorganism that had "organic unity" derived from the symbiotic interrelations of the people who lived within it.[3] Within this superorganism, Park found many "natural areas" where different types of people lived. These natural areas, like the natural areas of plants, had an organic unity of their own. Some of them were racial or ethnic communities, such as Chinatown, Little Italy, or the Black Belt. Other natural areas included individuals in certain income or occupational groups or industrial or business areas. Still other areas were physically cut off from the rest of the city by railroad tracks, rivers, major highways, or unused space. Symbiotic relationships existed not only among the people within a natural area (where the butcher needed the baker for bread and the baker needed the butcher for meat) but also among the natural areas within the city. Each natural area was seen as playing a part in the life of the city as a whole.

The second basic concept that Park took from plant ecology involved the process by which the balance of nature in a given area may change. A new species may invade the area, come to dominate it, and drive out other life forms. For example, a cleared field in one of the southern states will first be covered with tall weeds. Later this field will be invaded and dominated by broomsedge and, even later, by pine trees. Finally, the field will stabilize as an oak-hickory forest. Ecologists call this process "invasion, dominance, and succession."

This process can also be seen in human societies. The history of the United States is a process of invasion, dominance, and succession by Europeans into the territory of Native Americans. And in cities, one cultural or ethnic group may take over an entire neighborhood from another group, beginning with the shift of only one or two residents. Similarly, business or industry may move into and ultimately take over a previously residential neighborhood.

The processes of invasion, dominance, and succession were further explored by Park's associate, Ernest Burgess, who pointed out that cities do not merely grow at their edges. Rather, they have a tendency to expand radially from their center in patterns of concentric circles, each moving gradually outward. Burgess described these concentric circles as "zones."

Zone I is the central business district, while Zone II is the area immediately around it. Zone II generally is the oldest section of the city, and it is continually involved in a process of invasion, dominance, and succession by the businesses and industries that are expanding from Zone I. Houses in this zone are already deteriorating and will be allowed to deteriorate further because they will be torn down in the foreseeable future to make way for incoming businesses and industries. Since this is the least desirable residential section of the city, it is usually occupied by the poorest people, including the most recent immigrants to the city. Zone III is the zone of relatively modest homes and apartments, occupied by workers and their families who have escaped the deteriorating conditions in Zone II. The final zone within the city itself is Zone IV, the residential districts of single-family houses and more expensive apartments. Beyond the city limits are the suburban areas and the satellite cities, which constitute Zone V, the commuter zone. Each of these five zones is growing and thus is gradually moving outward into the territory occupied by the next zone, in a process of invasion, dominance, and succession.

Natural areas occur within each zone, and they are often linked to natural areas in other zones. For example, Burgess noted the location in Chicago's Zone II where Jewish immigrants initially settled. Zone III was an area of Jewish workers' homes that was constantly receiving new residents from Zone II and, at the same time, was constantly losing residents to more desirable Jewish neighborhoods in Zones IV and V.[4]

Within the framework of these ideas, Park and his colleagues studied the city of Chicago and its problems. They attempted to discover "the processes by which the biotic balance and the social equilibrium are maintained once they are achieved, and the processes by which, when the biotic balance and the social equilibrium are disturbed, the transition is made from one relatively stable order to another."[5]

RESEARCH IN THE DELINQUENCY AREAS OF CHICAGO

Park's theories were used as the basis for a broadly ranging study of the problem of juvenile delinquency in Chicago by Clifford R. Shaw. The problem of crime and delinquency had become of increasing concern to social scientists in the 1920s because the country was gripped in a crime wave that was generated by resistance to Prohibition, a problem that was particularly severe in Chicago.

Shaw worked as a probation and parole officer during this period and became convinced that the problem of juvenile delinquency had its origin in the juvenile's "detachment from conventional groups," rather than in any biological or psychological abnormalities.[6] Following his appointment to the Institute for Juvenile Research in Chicago, Shaw devised a strategy, based on the theory of human ecology, to study the process by which this detachment from conventional groups occurred.

Because he saw delinquents as essentially normal human beings, he believed that their illegal activities were somehow bound up with their environment. Therefore, the first stage of his strategy involved analyzing the characteristics of the neighborhoods that according to police and court records, had the most delinquents. But even in the worst of these neighborhoods, only about 20 percent of the youths were actually involved with the court. Shaw therefore compiled extensive "life histories" from individual delinquents to find out exactly how they had related to their environment.

Shaw first published his neighborhood studies in 1929 in a volume titled *Delinquency Areas*, and he subsequently published more of his research in two studies coauthored with Henry D. McKay, *Social Factors in Juvenile Delinquency* (1931) and *Juvenile Delinquency and Urban Areas* (1942). Shaw and McKay reached the following conclusions as a result of studying neighborhoods:

1. *Physical status*: The neighborhoods with the highest delinquency rates were found to be located within or immediately adjacent to areas of heavy industry or commerce. These neighborhoods also had the greatest number of condemned buildings, and their population was decreasing. The population change was assumed to be related to an industrial invasion of the area, which resulted in fewer buildings being available for residential occupation.[7]

2. *Economic status*: The highest rates of delinquency were found in the areas of lowest economic status as determined by a number of specific factors, including the percentage of families on welfare, the median rental, and the percentage of families owning homes.[8] These areas also had the highest rates of infant deaths, active cases of tuberculosis, and insanity. But Shaw and McKay concluded that economic conditions did not in themselves cause these problems. This conclusion was based on the fact that the rates of delinquency, of

adult criminality, of infant deaths, and of tuberculosis for the city as a whole remained relatively stable between 1929 and 1934, when the Great Depression hit, and there was a tenfold increase in the number of families on public or private assistance. Median rentals, welfare rates, and other economic measures continued to show that the areas with the highest concentrations of these problems were in the lowest economic status relative to other areas of the city. These problems appeared to be associated with the least privileged groups in society, regardless of the actual economic conditions of that society as a whole.

3. *Population composition*: Areas of highest delinquency were consistently associated with higher concentrations of foreign-born and African American heads of families.[9] To determine the precise role of racial and ethnic factors in the causation of delinquency, Shaw and McKay further analyzed these data. They found that certain inner-city areas in Zone II remained among those with the highest delinquency rates in the city despite shifts of almost all the population of these areas. In 1884, approximately 90% of the population in these areas was German, Irish, English, Scottish, or Scandinavian. By 1930, approximately 85% of the population was Czech, Italian, Polish, Slavic, or other. In spite of this dramatic shift in ethnic populations, these eight areas continued to have some of the highest delinquency rates in the city. At the same time, there was no increase in delinquency rates in the areas into which the older immigrant communities moved.

Shaw and McKay also found that within similar areas, each group, whether foreign born or native, recent immigrant or older immigrant, African American or European American, had a delinquency rate that was proportional to the rate of the overall area. No racial, national, or nativity group exhibited a uniform characteristic rate of delinquency in all parts of the city. Each group produced delinquency rates that ranged from the lowest to the highest in the city, depending on the type of area surveyed. Although some variation associated with the group could be seen, it was apparent that the overall delinquency rate of a particular group depended primarily on how many individuals of that group resided in "delinquency areas." Shaw and McKay concluded:[10]

> In the face of these facts it is difficult to sustain the contention that, by themselves, the factors of race, nativity, and nationality are vitally related to the problem of juvenile delinquency. It seems necessary to conclude, rather, that the significantly higher rates of delinquents found among the children of Negroes, the foreign born, and more recent immigrants are closely related to existing differences in their respective patterns of geographical distribution within the city. If these groups were found in the

same proportion in all local areas, existing differences in the relative number of boys brought into court from the various groups might be expected to be greatly reduced or to disappear entirely.

In addition to this research, Shaw compiled and published a series of "life histories" of individual delinquents, including *The Jackroller* (1930), *The Natural History of a Delinquent Career* (1931), and *Brothers in Crime* (1938). The basic findings of these histories are summed up in the following points.

1. Delinquents, by and large, "are not different from large numbers of persons in conventional society with respect to intelligence, physical condition, and personality traits."[11]
2. In delinquency areas, "the conventional traditions, neighborhood institutions, public opinion, through which neighborhoods usually effect a control over the behavior of the child, were largely disintegrated."[12] In addition, parents and neighbors frequently approved of delinquent behavior, so that a child grew up "in a social world in which [delinquency] was an accepted and appropriate form of conduct."[13]
3. The neighborhoods included many opportunities for delinquent activities, including "junk dealers, professional fences, and residents who purchased their stolen goods" and "dilapidated buildings which served as an incentive for junking." There was also a "lack of preparation, training, opportunity, and proper encouragement for successful employment in private industry."[14]
4. Delinquent activities in these areas began at an early age as a part of play activities of the street.[15]
5. In these play activities, there is a continuity of tradition in a given neighborhood from older boys to younger boys.[16] This tradition includes the transmission of such different criminal techniques as jackrolling, shoplifting, stealing from junkmen, or stealing automobiles, so that different neighborhoods were characterized by the same types of offenses over long periods.[17]
6. The normal methods of official social control could not stop this process.[18]
7. It was only later in a delinquent career that the individual began "to identify himself with the criminal world, and to embody in his own philosophy of life the moral values which prevailed in the criminal groups with which he had contact."[19] This was due both to the continuous contact that the delinquent had with juvenile and adult criminals on the street and in correctional institutions and to rejection and stigmatization by the community.

Shaw concluded that delinquency and other social problems are closely related to the process of invasion, dominance, and succession that determines the concentric growth patterns of the city. When a particular location in the city is "invaded" by new residents, the established symbiotic relationships that bind that location to a natural area are destroyed. Ultimately this location will be incorporated as an organic part of a new natural area, and the social equilibrium will be restored. Meanwhile the natural organization of the location will be severely impaired.

These "interstitial areas" (so called because they are in between the organized natural areas) become afflicted with a variety of social problems that are directly traceable to the rapid shift in populations. The formal social organizations that existed in the neighborhood tend to disintegrate as the original population retreats. Because the neighborhood is in transition, the residents no longer identify with it, and thus they do not care as much about its appearance or reputation. There is a marked decrease in neighborliness and in the ability of the people of the neighborhood to control their children. For example, in an established neighborhood, a resident who is aware that a child is getting into trouble may call that child's parents or may report that child to the local authorities. But because new people are continuously moving into the interstitial area, residents no longer know their own neighbors or their neighbors' children. Thus, children who are out of their parents' sight may be under almost no control, even in their own neighborhood. The high mobility of the residents also means that there is a high turnover of children in the local schools. This turnover is disruptive both to learning and to discipline. Finally, the area tends to become a battleground between the invading and retreating cultures. This change can generate a great deal of conflict in the community that tends to be manifested in individual and gang conflicts between the youths of the two cultures.

Although other areas only periodically undergo this process, areas in Zone II are continually being invaded both by the central business district and by successive waves of new immigrants coming into the city from foreign countries and from rural areas.[20] These new immigrants already have many problems associated with their adjustment to the new culture. In addition, the neighborhood into which an immigrant moves is in a chronic state of "social disorganization." This state presents the immigrant with many additional problems, and there is almost no help available to solve any of them. Thus, recent immigrants tend to have a wide range of social problems, including delinquency, among their youths. These problems are resolved as recent immigrants acquire some of the resources necessary both to solve their own problems and to move into the better-established neighborhoods of Zone III, with its natural processes of social control.

POLICY IMPLICATIONS

Because Shaw believed that juvenile delinquency was generated by social disorganization in interstitial areas, he did not believe that treatment of individual delinquents would have much effect in reducing overall delinquency rates. Rather, he thought that the answer had to be found in "the development of programs which seek to effect changes in the conditions of life in specific local communities and in whole sections of the city."[21] In Shaw's view, these programs could come only from organizations of neighborhood residents, so that the natural forces of social control could take effect. Thus in 1932 he launched the Chicago Area Project, which established twenty-two neighborhood centers in six areas of Chicago.[22] Control of these centers rested with committees of local residents, rather than with the central staff of the project, and local residents were employed as staff.

These centers had two primary functions. First, they were to coordinate such community resources as churches, schools, labor unions, industries, clubs, and other groups in addressing and resolving community problems. Second, they were to sponsor a variety of activity programs, including recreation, summer camping and scouting activities, handicraft workshops, discussion groups, and community projects.[23] Through these activities, the project sought "to develop a positive interest by the inhabitants in their own welfare, to establish democratic bodies of local citizens who would enable the whole community to become aware of its problems and attempt their solution by common action."[24]

The Chicago Area Project operated continuously for twenty-five years, until Shaw's death in 1957, but its effect on delinquency in these areas was never precisely evaluated.[25] A similar project in Boston was carefully evaluated by Walter B. Miller over a three-year period.[26] In Boston, it was found that the project was effective in achieving many admirable goals. The project established close relationships with local gangs and organized their members into clubs, increased their involvement in recreational activities, provided them with access to occupational and educational opportunities, formed citizens' organizations, and increased interagency cooperation in addressing community problems.

The goal of all these activities, however, was to reduce the incidence of delinquent behavior. To assess the impact of the project on the behavior of the youths, Miller analyzed the daily field reports of the outreach workers, which included a description of the activities of each youth. The behaviors were then classified as "moral" or "immoral" (where immoral meant disapproval by the community, but not necessarily a violation of the law) and as "legal" or "illegal." It was found that the ratio of moral to immoral behaviors remained relatively constant throughout the project and that although the total number of illegal acts decreased slightly during the project, the number of major offenses by boys increased. In addition, data were compiled on the number of court appearances made by each youth before, during, and after contact with the project, and these data were compared with the number of court appearances by a control group. There was almost no difference in these statistics. Miller concluded that the project had a "negligible impact" on delinquency.[27] The failure of this and other similar projects led Lundman to conclude that it was likely that "the Chicago Area Project also failed to prevent juvenile delinquency."[28]

RESIDENTIAL SUCCESSION, SOCIAL
DISORGANIZATION, AND CRIME

After the failure to show that the Chicago Area Projects prevented delinquency, Shaw and McKay's theory went into a period of decline. In 1978, however, the theory was revitalized by the publication of an influential book by Kornhauser.[29] Kornhauser argued that Shaw and McKay's theory actually contains two separate arguments: a "social disorganization" argument that delinquency emerges in neighborhoods where the neighborhood relationships and institutions have broken down and can no longer maintain effective social controls and a "subcultural" argument that over time, these delinquent behaviors come to be supported by the shared values and norms of neighborhood residents.[30] After considerable deliberation, Shaw and McKay had concluded that the second argument was more important than the first and that delinquent subcultures accounted for most slum delinquency. Kornhauser, however, argued that this conclusion was illogical. Shaw and McKay's theory describes the delinquency as emerging first because of the social disorganization, and then the delinquent subculture arising later in order to provide social supports for the delinquency. Thus, Kornhauser argued that disorganized neighborhoods would have delinquency whether or not they had delinquent subcultures, but the delinquent subculture would not exist without the delinquency caused by the social disorganization. Thus at the theoretical level, the social disorganization is the primary cause of delinquency.

Kornhauser therefore extracted a "community control" model from Shaw and McKay's theory that summarized their arguments about social disorganization. The basic argument is that people who are poor, who live in racially and ethnically diverse neighborhoods, and who move frequently from one place to another will have trouble establishing and maintaining the normal social relationships and institutions by which neighborhood residents normally achieve their common aspirations and goals. Thus, neighborhoods with high poverty, high racial and ethnic heterogeneity, and high residential mobility should also have high rates of crime and delinquency. Kornhauser then reviewed a large number of empirical studies to demonstrate support for that model.[31]

In 1982, Bursik and Webb similarly concluded that neighborhood social disorganization is the primary explanation of neighborhood delinquency rates.[32] They focused on Shaw and McKay's concept of residential succession, the fact that neighborhoods often retain their high crime and delinquency rates despite total turnovers in population. Using data on Chicago neighborhoods that were directly comparable to the data used by Shaw and McKay, Bursik and Webb found that the residential succession argument was supported by data from 1940 to 1950. That is, neighborhood crime rates tended to remain the same despite total turnovers in population. However, after 1950 all neighborhoods undergoing race-based turnovers in their population were characterized by high delinquency rates, regardless of their delinquency rates before the change.

Bursik and Webb interpreted this finding in terms of community stability. At the time Shaw and McKay wrote, the zones of transition were found exclusively in the inner-city areas, and the process of dispersion to outlying residential areas was gradual. This "natural" process was disrupted in more recent times as African Americans attempted to follow in the footsteps of other ethnic groups. Strong European American resistance to any African Americans moving into the neighborhood would be followed by total "white flight" and total racial turnover in a short time. Neighborhood social institutions would disappear entirely or persevere but resist including the new residents. This process resulted in near-total neighborhood social disorganization, which then caused the high delinquency rates.

Bursik and Webb also found that after the neighborhood populations had stabilized, the neighborhoods "had delinquency rates not much different than would have been expected from their previous patterns."[33] Thus, after things settled down, the residential succession phenomenon seemed to reappear. This finding was consistent with several other studies that found that delinquency rates were increasing in African American neighborhoods that had recently undergone residential changes but were decreasing in African American neighborhoods that had been stable for some time.[34]

In an attempt to explain the findings about residential succession further, Stark asked what it is about neighborhoods themselves that is associated with high crime rates, independent of the people who live in them. As an answer to this question, he presented a formal theory in thirty integrated propositions.[35] These thirty propositions focused on four structural aspects of urban neighborhoods: density (many people in a small area), poverty (people have little money), mixed land use (residences, industries, and stores are all in the same place), residential mobility (people frequently move into, out of, and around the neighborhood), and dilapidation (the buildings themselves are falling apart). Stark argues that in a variety of ways, these five structural characteristics increase moral cynicism among community residents, provide more opportunities to commit crime, increase motivations to commit crime, and decrease the informal surveillance by which crime in a community is held in check. As a consequence, crime-prone people are attracted to the neighborhood, while law-abiding people get out if they can. This pattern results in high crime rates that tend to persist even when there are complete turnovers in the people who live there.

SAMPSON'S THEORY OF COLLECTIVE EFFICACY

Similarly, Sampson reviewed research on the relationship between neighborhoods and crime in an attempt to determine how community structures and cultures create different crime rates.[36] He found that although poverty itself is not associated with crime, poverty combined with residential mobility (i.e., frequent moves by residents) is associated with higher levels of violent crime. Neighborhood rates of family disruption (divorce rates and rates of female-headed households) are strongly and consistently related to rates of violence. Neighborhoods with high percentages of African Americans have higher crime rates, but the effect of race itself tends to disappear when family disruption and poverty are taken into account. Finally, neighborhoods with high population density, many apartments, and high concentrations of individuals who do not live within a family situation tend to have higher rates of crime and violence.

Sampson explained this pattern of findings with Shaw's concept of social disorganization, which he defined as the inability of the community to realize its common values. An example would be when community residents oppose drug use but cannot get rid of the drug dealers who have taken over a nearby corner or house for a drug market. There may be a variety of reasons why some communities cannot realize their common values, but one reason is the lack of what Coleman called "social capital"—that is, networks of relationships among people that facilitate common actions and make possible the achievement of common goals.[37] Sampson argued that when there are many social relationships among community residents (i.e., a lot of social capital), there is less crime. Even criminals do not want crime in their own neighborhoods, and social relationships allow people to achieve their common goal of driving the crime out.

Sampson then proposed a causal sequence that ties all this research together in a way that resembles Shaw's earlier work.[38] Poverty, family disruption, and high residential mobility are community characteristics that result in anonymity, the lack of social relationships among neighborhood residents, and low participation in community organizations and in local activities. Because of this low social capital, neighbors are not able to exert effective control over public or common areas, such as streets and parks, so these areas are free to be taken over by criminals. In addition, local teenagers have considerable freedom because the anonymity of the neighborhood means that they and their friends are unknown to adults even though the teenagers may be only a short distance from their homes. This anonymity results in increased crime and violence in the neighborhood, independent of the people who live there. The high crime and violence then promote further disintegration of the community as law-abiding residents withdraw from community life and try to move out of the neighborhood.

The concentration of crime among African Americans, according to Sampson, is caused primarily by differences in the neighborhoods in which they live. About 38 percent of poor African Americans live in extremely poor neighborhoods, compared to about 7 percent of poor European Americans. About 70 percent of poor European Americans live in neighborhoods that are not poor, while only 16 percent of poor African Americans live in nonpoor neighborhoods. Thus, poor European Americans are much more dispersed in the population, while poor African Americans are much more concentrated in locations where everyone else is also poor. In addition, the worst urban neighborhoods in which European Americans live are considerably better, in terms of poverty and family disruption, than the average urban neighborhoods in which poor African Americans live.[39] To the extent that neighborhoods themselves cause crime, these statistics would produce marked differences in the crime rates of these two groups.

Additional research has supported the argument that high African American rates of crime and delinquency are largely explained by African Americans' concentration in extremely poor neighborhoods,[40] particularly when these neighborhoods are isolated from the rest of the city.[41] Attention therefore has turned to the precise mechanisms by which neighborhoods control (or fail to control) crime and delinquency. Sampson had argued that this mechanism involved the social relationships among community residents, including participation in community organizations and local activities, especially as such participation relates to the informal processes by which residents control activities in the public spaces in the neighborhoods (e.g., streets and parks). A series of studies have attempted to test this basic argument.

Using data from England, Sampson and Groves found that the presence of unsupervised adolescent peer groups on the streets of a community had the largest overall effect on street crimes in that community, as well as the largest overall effect on the personal rates of violent behavior among the adolescents themselves.[42] The presence of these groups on the street suggested the absence of neighborhood social control of adolescents. In a more direct attempt to measure informal social control of adolescents in public areas, Sampson asked people from eighty Chicago neighborhoods how likely it was that neighbors would do something if neighborhood children were skipping school, spray-painting graffiti on a local building, or showing disrespect to an adult.[43] How these three measures of neighborhood social control were fulfilled, in turn, explained half the relation between crime and residential mobility in the neighborhood.

Sampson and his coauthors then introduced the term *collective efficacy*, which is defined in terms of the neighborhood's ability to maintain order in public spaces, such as streets, sidewalks, and parks.[44] Collective efficacy is implemented when neighborhood residents take overt actions to maintain public order, such as by complaining to the authorities or by organizing neighborhood watch programs. The authors argued that residents take such actions only when "cohesion and mutual trust" in the neighborhood are linked to "shared expectations for intervening in support of neighborhood social control."[45] If either the mutual trust or the shared expectations are absent, then residents will be unlikely to act when disorder invades public space.

To test this theory of collective efficacy, both sides of the street in about 12,000 blocks in 196 Chicago neighborhoods were videotaped during daylight hours from a slowly moving car.[46] The videotapes were then analyzed and coded for the presence of physical disorder in public spaces (e.g., abandoned buildings or cars, graffiti, litter in the streets, syringes on the sidewalks). More than 3,800 adults in these neighborhoods were then interviewed about social disorder in public spaces (e.g., drug selling, solicitation by prostitutes, public drinking or fighting).[47] To measure the "shared expectations for intervening in support of neighborhood social control," the residents were asked whether it was likely that their neighbors would take action in response to five specific situations involving public disorder. Finally, to measure "cohesion and mutual trust," they were asked five questions about whether it was a "close-knit neighborhood" and whether "people in this neighborhood share the same values." The videotape and interview data were joined with official police reports on crime and with data from the 1990 census on concentrated poverty, concentrated immigration, residential stability, land use, and density in the neighborhoods.

After analyzing all these data, Sampson and Raudenbush found that both physical and social disorder were strongly related to concentrated poverty and mixed land use. Within the context of that relationship, however, there was less crime in neighborhoods with more social cohesion and more shared expectations for intervening in support of neighborhood social control. Thus, Sampson and Raudenbush concluded that "the active ingredients in crime seem to be structural disadvantage and attenuated collective efficacy."[48] Another study by Morenoff, Sampson, and Raudenbush found that the role of collective efficacy is also important in serious crime. Homicide rates in Chicago, these researchers discovered, were influenced the heaviest by proximity to violent places, neighborhood inequality (such as concentrated poverty), and collective efficacy. Furthermore, collective efficacy had a strong direct effect on homicide, independent of concentrated poverty.[49]

It is important for researchers who test social disorganization theory to be keen to the relationship between disorder and crime. In 1982, James Q. Wilson and George Kelling published an article on the "broken windows" theory, arguing that when neighborhoods experience decay and disorder, both social and physical, it is an invitation for serious crime—thus, disorder declines into crime.[50] Lately, scholars have acknowledged that this relationship is not necessarily as strong as many have assumed and that it may apply only to some crimes, such as robbery, but not burglary.[51] Markowitz and his colleagues, however, found evidence supporting the view that social disorganization theory may benefit from reciprocal feedback models. Specifically, disorder may increase fear of crime, which reduces cohesion or collective efficacy, which then increases crime itself.[52]

Regardless of empirical issues about the strength of the broken windows effect, the term has pervaded law enforcement strategies (e.g., maintenance of order and zero-tolerance policing) and is now one of the most commonly known terms within the law enforcement community and among those who influence law enforcement policy.[53]

Research on crime and neighborhoods has been conducted *within* neighborhoods in addition to *across* neighborhoods. The unit of analysis shifts from the neighborhood to the micro-geographic place, which can include addresses, blocks, segments ("two block faces on both sides of a street between two intersections,"[54]) schools, and open-air drug markets. One pioneer study demonstrating the level of crime concentration that can exist at micro-places, or hotspots, was conducted in Minneapolis, and reported that 50.4 percent of police calls for service came from a mere 3.3 percent of addresses. Similar findings have been found in other cities and in other countries.[55] Additionally, to a large extent these concentrations remain fairly stable over time, even when crime drops overall in a given city. Hotspots may be in so-called bad neighborhoods, but may also be interspersed throughout otherwise safe neighborhoods. Understanding characteristics of high-crime micro-places is necessary for targeted policing strategies (discussed in Chapter 2) and applications of routine activity theory (discussed in Chapter 3).[56]

CRIME IN PUBLIC HOUSING

One area of interest to researchers who examine social disorganization and neighborhoods is public housing, or public housing developments (PHDs). These developments are found in every city of significant size across the United States and can be viewed as "micro-neighborhoods" in their own right. Because of their high concentration of poverty, racial minorities, residential mobility, and female-headed families, one might expect them to be disproportionately affected by crime. Umbach and Gerould, who have recently summarized four decades of research on crime and public housing, have noted the dearth of rigorous studies, commenting that "Empirical precision has often seemed beside the point to an American public that has woven crime, PHDs, and racial minorities into an 'unholy trinity.'"[57] Their article addresses three questions posed by discussion of public housing crime. Does public housing have more crime than private? Does it increase crime in nearby neighborhoods? And when public housing residents are dispersed, does that just displace disorder? Research examining the public housing–crime linkage has historically suffered two problems: a lack of reliable data on crime in PHDs and the view that PHDs are only a physical concept, rather than sociopolitical.[58]

Two works published in the early 1970s equated public housing with violence. Rainwater's *Behind Ghetto Walls: Black Families in a Federal Slum* described the notoriously violent Pruitt-Igoe projects in St. Louis, which would be torn down two years after the book's publication in 1970.[59] As Umbach and Gerould pointed out, the synonymous relation between crime and public housing that was then blossoming was based not on public housing in general but on what was arguably the most problematic example in the country: "The crime-plagued Pruitt-Igoe of Rainwater's portrayal became a stand-in for all PHDs and a parable of failed antipoverty programs."[60]

The second work was Oscar Newman's *Defensible Space*, published in 1972, which contrasted two projects across the street from one another in the Brownsville neighborhood of Brooklyn.[61] They were practically identical, except that one was doors-open safe and the other was crime-ridden, and the safe one (the Brownsville Houses) was "low-slung" whereas the dangerous one (the Van Dyke Houses) was a high-rise. Newman argued that it was architecture, then, that determined whether PHDs would be criminogenic. His work would lead to a dominant policy focus on architecture for those addressing the problem of crime and public housing. In fact, though, the two developments were very different in another way. The high-rise had a much greater family size than the low-rise, meaning a greater child-to-adult ratio, an indicator of less adult supervision, which has been found to increase crime rates in public housing.[62] And in fact, as Umbach and Gerould pointed out, the effect of family size on crime was documented by Newman, but in tables that were "tucked away in *Defensible Space*'s final pages."[63] Confirming that building height wasn't the key to PHD crime, research from the late 1990s found that its effect was less than that of other factors, such as tenants' poverty, the number of buildings, and the number of residents per building.[64]

Housing and Urban Development (HUD) continued to focus its research on the most troubled projects during the 1970s, employing victimization surveys, which allowed for the gathering of data on crime that goes unreported to police. However, according to Umbach and Gerould, "Surveys, in short, did not make it possible to consider public housing disorder within its larger 'ecology'—criminologists' term for the constellation of social, physical, and spatial factors surrounding a research site."[65] In other words, any conclusions of this set of research (such as that the risk of being robbed in Washington, DC's Capper Dwellings was twice of the Capitol and five times the national average) did not provide proper neighborhood context: Is this increased risk simply due to PHDs being located in the most dangerous neighborhoods?

In the 1980s federal funds for research on public housing crime shrunk to near zero; yet independent academics in the early part of the decade analyzed data from the 1970s that focused on a larger, more representative sample of PHDs than HUD researchers had with their victimization surveys. Without specific data from PHDs they would use block-level data that indicated which blocks had the highest concentration of projects. John

Farley, in "Has Public Housing Gotten a Bum Rap," found that St. Louis's PHDs did not exceed the expected rates from their neighborhood,[66] and Dennis Roncek et al. found that in Cleveland (from 1971 to 1977) there was no significant spillover effect of property crime from PHDs to surrounding neighborhoods. Violent crime spilled over somewhat, but that effect disappeared when controlling for the socioeconomic conditions of those nearby areas.[67]

The next round of research on PHDs was in the late 1980s to the early 1990s, when federal funding once again became available, as crack cocaine had arrived in full force. This research, like former studies on crime in public housing, suffered from the problem that it is difficult to find exact control groups to compare projects against, as public housing is not randomly distributed but is concentrated in disadvantaged areas. Its findings were often contradictory, but generally found that public housing was at least as dangerous if not more so than comparison areas. Additionally, this research found that PHDs in Washington, DC, and Los Angeles had lower rates of property crime but higher rates of violent crime than their cities or nearby neighborhoods. This was the exact opposite of previous research from former decades that had found higher rates of property crime but less violent crime.[68]

Armed with GIS technology, researchers in the late 1990s were able to be more precise in their examination of PHD crime and confirmed the earlier finding: that violent crime was higher, but property crime was *lower* in these areas. Harold Holzman and colleagues explained this with routine activities theory (see Chapter 3). Unlike in the 1970s (when PHDs had many working adults), public housing residents in the 1990s were more likely to be stay-at-homes than average city residents, and their presence as a "capable guardian" deterred theft. However, the flip side was that their presence increased their likelihood of being a victim of violence, often times perpetrated by a husband or boyfriend against a young black woman.[69]

The most recent round of research on public housing and crime has focused on the effects of dismantling projects (for example, between 1990 and 2010 more than 220,000 projects units were sold or destroyed).[70] The displacement of public housing residents leads to two related questions: Are their lives improved when moved to better neighborhoods, and do the communities with an influx of displaced public housing residents experience increased crime? The first question was addressed in research on the Moving to Opportunity (MTO) experiment, which tracked over five thousand relocatees over a decade in five cities. The results were mixed, but overall they pointed to a gender divide. On a number of dimensions, leaving PHDs for more desirable neighborhoods benefitted girls (e.g., less depression, sexual pressures, predation), but not boys (e.g., greater number of property crime arrests).[71]

The second question was addressed by research on HOPE VI, an urban renewal program that razed PHDs and allowed residents to use vouchers to relocate. Research on whether former project residents brought crime to their new neighborhoods was prompted by an article by Hanna Rosin in the popular *Atlantic Monthly*, which argued controversially, but not with empirical rigor, that this was the case.[72] Susan Popkin's and colleagues' methodologically thorough 2012 analysis of HOPE VI sites in Chicago (1999–2008) and Atlanta (2002–2009) found that violent and property crime declined greatly in areas where PHDs were destructed, but that the matter was more complicated in areas receiving former PHD residents. Here, crime dropped, but crime was dropping everywhere across the country during this time period, and in these neighborhoods, once a tipping point was reached (a neighborhood received a certain number of former public housing residents), its crime rates decreased less than what they would have decreased without them.[73]

Umbach and Gerould's summary of research on public housing produced two interconnected conclusions. First, "the simple and frequently invoked idea that 'public housing increases crime' is demonstrable false as both an analytic conclusion and a causal model, even as it has proved remarkably powerful as a cultural narrative."[74] And second, "Nearly two generations of research on public housing and crime leaves us with this fairly unsatisfying generalization: some public housing seems to have increased crime rates under certain conclusions, while other projects, under different conditions, are actually safer than private housing."[75]

SOCIAL DISORGANIZATION AND CRIME IN RURAL AREAS

As Posick and Rocque put it, "Criminology has a long, rich history of studying violence in urban areas. This makes sense, as large urban centers are generally where the bulk of crime and violence takes place ... Yet, in other ways, this hyperfocus on the city has limited the potential of criminology to understand other types of violence in other contexts, such as rural and suburban areas."[76] In this section, we focus on rural areas and primarily on research that has examined the role of social disorganization.[77]

In 2000, Osgood and Chambers published a comprehensive study testing social disorganization hypotheses to nonurban counties.[78] They noted that despite the significant proportion of population (and crime) in rural areas, and the fact that early social disorganization theory was developed in rural communities in Poland, contemporary research on social disorganization theory was limited to urban settings. Social disorganization researchers assumed their findings would apply to rural areas as well, but failed to test these assumptions. Urban sociology examines three levels of neighborhood social relationships: private order of social control (intimate, informal groups), parochial system of control (broader local networks, including institutions), and public order (ability of a community to access goods and services from agencies external to the neighborhood). Osgood and Chambers stated that there is no reason these systems of relationships would not be relevant in rural communities, as they are in urban neighborhoods, and that others had previously suggested:

> Primary relationships will constitute a larger portion of the social network of rural residents than of urban residents, due to limited population size and density . . . The predominance of strong (or primary) ties in rural areas would enhance social control and thereby reduce most types of crime. At the same time, the lack of weak (or parochial) ties would make rural residents more vulnerable to disruptions in their primary networks because they lack alternative sources of social support.[79]

Osgood and Chambers tested five hypotheses from social disorganization theory (and one unique to rural areas), using data on juvenile arrests for violent crime from nonurban counties. According to social disorganization theory, rates of juvenile violence would be positively related to residential instability (measured by geographic mobility), ethnic heterogeneity (white vs. nonwhite households), family disruption (female-headed households), economic status (persons living below the poverty level), and population density (persons per area). Their sixth hypothesis was that juvenile violence would be greater in communities closer to urban areas, due to juveniles being socialized into criminal behavior from more criminogenic adjoining areas. They utilized data from counties in Nebraska, Georgia, South Carolina, and Florida, which were not in Metropolitan Statistical Areas, and contained no cities of 50,000 persons or more. Whereas most research on social disorganization theory in urban areas focuses at the neighborhood level, Osgood and Chambers's unit of analysis was at the county level, based on restraints on data availability, but also because the notion of neighborhood does not fit as well to rural areas as it does to urban settings. Nonetheless, insomuch as rural counties may have multiple communities, this was a limitation of their research.[80]

Their statistical analyses confirmed their hypotheses for residential instability, ethnic heterogeneity, family disruption, and population density (although this relationship was curvilinear, with population having no effect once reaching modest levels). Poverty, in contrast with previous research on social disorganization theory, was not associated with juvenile arrests. Osgood and Chambers noted that while in urban settings poverty leads to frequent moves (geographic mobility), and thus instability, in rural areas poor people have more of a support network and are less likely to move, which may make their children less likely to engage in crime.[81] Moore and Sween's recent extension of Osgood and Chambers's study, employing data from the forty-eight continuous states, resulted in findings largely consistent with the original work.[82]

Later research testing social disorganization theory in rural areas produced some contrary results. Kaylen and Pridemore point out that various methodological issues probably account in part for mixed findings.[83] First, some studies only test structural factors, such as residential instability and disruption, without addressing how they influence crime through mediators such as information social control, as required by the full systemic model of social disorganization. Second, studies often rely solely on official crime data, and there is reason to believe that police data on crime in rural areas may have validity problems: "Given the close social proximity and the small populations, it may be that rural victims are not only more likely to know their offenders but less likely to report to the police so as not to upset the social order. Such a situation would bias coefficients in favor of an association between disorganization and crime, even though the reality is that cohesion can facilitate crime victim acquiescence and real rates of crime." Third, as Osgood and Chambers had said, there is difficulty in how to measure communities in rural areas.

Kaylen and Pridemore attempted to replicate the Osgood and Chambers findings based on data from counties in Missouri, using victimization as the dependent variable (as measured by hospital incidents of assault-induced injuries), and found that only one measure of social disorganization (single-parent households) was significantly associated with youth violent victimization.[84] They questioned whether the inconsistent findings were related to the measurement of the dependent variable (victimization instead of official arrest data) or the locales (Missouri versus the four states in Osgood and Chambers's study). After a reanalysis of the Osgood and Chambers data using hospital data (and analysis of the Missouri sample using arrests), they concluded that the measurement of the dependent variable likely resulted in the discordant results.[85] To account for the model specificity issue, Kaylen and Pridemore extracted rural data from Sampson and Groves's full test of the systemic model of social disorganization and crime, and found little support for it in the nonurban context.[86]

Interest in rural crime goes beyond social disorganization theory to a broad range of topics, such as feminist perspectives, interpersonal violence, agricultural crime, and environmental crime.[87] Recent research has also examined the effect of socioeconomic status on crime (SES matters less in rural areas),[88] the relationship between firearms prevalence and homicide (the association is found in urban but not rural environments),[89] and the Great American Crime Decline (it was not experienced nearly as dramatically in rural areas).[90]

EXPANDING INTEREST IN NEIGHBORHOOD
SOCIAL PROCESSES

As Lowenkamp and his colleagues said, "the social disorganization perspective has experienced a dramatic revitalization, reemerging from the dustbin of spent criminological paradigms to challenge for the status as a preeminent

macro-level theory."[91] Researchers who have been studying social disorganization, and more generally, neighborhood effects on crime, have moved
beyond the examination of structural characteristics, such as concentrated
poverty, residential instability, and ethnic heterogeneity, to neighborhood
social processes, which may be partially determined by structural conditions,
but also have direct effects of their own on crime and disorder. Because collective efficacy has been shown to mediate only part of the effect of structural
conditions on crime, researchers look to other social processes as well, as
possible mediators.

Sampson, Morenoff, and Gannon-Rowley identified four "classes of
neighborhood mechanisms" that permeate the renewed interest in neighborhood effects on crime.[92] The first is social ties and interactions, discussed
in the previous section, which result in social capital. The second is norms
and collective efficacy, also discussed earlier, which seem to be a more important influence on crime than social ties. The third is institutional resources,
which include community organizations and associations, and does not
seem to be all that important of a mechanism in terms of explanatory power.
Finally, Sampson and his colleagues pointed to routine activities as an "often
overlooked factor in discussions of neighborhood effects."[93] Discussed in
detail in Chapter 3, routine activities theory includes such neighborhood
variables as mixed residential and commercial use, location of schools, types
of public transportation, and density of bars and liquor stores. These factors
may mediate between structural characteristics of neighborhoods and crime
and may play a direct role as well.

Two other types of mechanisms have been identified by others as under-
examined but potentially necessary when studying neighborhood effects.
The first is the role of formal social control. Social ties and collective efficacy
relate to the concept of informal social control—means by which community residents shape behavior without invoking the law formally. As some
scholars have pointed out, formal social control may also be important to
social disorganization theory and neighborhood effects. One example is the
involvement of police in neighborhoods. The quantity and quality of police
behavior may be influenced by structural characteristics, such as concentrated poverty, and may have a direct impact on crime rates.[94] In addition,
high-quality policing may enhance a neighborhood's ability to achieve informal social control, not only by organizing residents and providing them
with the means of control (such as watch groups), but by showing them that
police care about them. That police may be less effective in neighborhoods
with concentrated poverty and other structural disadvantages is consistent
with conflict theory (see Chapter 11).

Another example of formal social control is the role of incarceration.
Although incarceration is brought about by formal institutions, excessive
use of it may affect a neighborhood's social organization. On the one hand,

removing criminals from a neighborhood should have a logically positive effect on its crime rate. On the other hand, too much incarceration could cause residential instability (continual movement of residents into jail or prison and back into the community). High rates of incarceration could also make residents feel negatively about the criminal justice system (as unfairly removing the residents from their community) and could destabilize the community's cohesion and ability to fight crime informally. Clear and his colleagues, studying the incarceration and release of criminals in neighborhoods in Tallahassee, Florida, found empirical support for the "tipping point" hypothesis. Incarcerating criminals up to a certain point decreased crime, but past that point, excessive incarceration resulted in increased crime.[95]

The other social process that should be part of research on neighborhood effects, according to Shaw and McKay's early work and more recent writers, such as Kubrin and Weitzer, is the role of culture and subcultures.[96] Concentrated disadvantage may serve to create structurally a subculture that is cynical toward legal norms and develops a street code that is oriented toward reinforcing crime and deviance and penalizing conventional beliefs and behavior.[97] In neighborhoods with high crime rates, an oppositional subculture maintaining adherence to conventional values may exist as well. Overall behavior will be a product of the competing subcultures. More detail on the role of culture is presented in Chapter 9.

CONCLUSIONS

The Chicago School of Human Ecology can be described as a gold mine that continues to enrich criminology today. Shaw's individual case studies remain classic portrayals of delinquents and their social worlds, his urban research methods have led to a wide variety of empirical studies, and the social disorganization theory forms the basis for several other theories in contemporary criminology.

Despite the richness of this historic legacy, the ecological approach to crime was somewhat stagnant for many years. Since about 1980, however, there has been a veritable explosion of new theory and research that has had ecological theory as its foundation. The basic point of this new theory and research is that crime cannot be understood without also understanding its immediate context: the neighborhoods. Ultimately, this conclusion relies on Shaw and McKay's finding about residential succession: that crime rates in neighborhoods tend to remain the same despite total turnovers in the population of these neighborhoods.

Residential succession suggests that policy recommendations to reduce crime can be directed at high-crime neighborhoods themselves, rather than at the people who live in the high-crime neighborhoods. Although the initial attempts of the Chicago Area Projects seemed to have had little impact on crime, Sampson and his colleagues, as part of the Project on Human Development in Chicago Neighborhoods, proposed a variety of new policies that focus on "changing places, not people." These policies include targeting hotspots in the community where there is frequent criminal activity; stopping the "spiral of decay" by cleaning up trash, graffiti, and so on; increasing the social relationships between adults and teenagers through organized youth activities; reducing residential mobility by enabling residents to buy their homes or take over management of their apartments; scattering public housing in a broad range of neighborhoods, rather than concentrating it in poor neighborhoods; maintaining and increasing urban services, such as police, fire, and public health services, especially those aimed at reducing child abuse and teenage pregnancy; and generally increasing community power by promoting community organizations. Sampson conceded that such programs have had limited success in the past, but argued that small successes can produce cumulative changes that will result in a more stable community in the long run. In fact, several researchers have argued that the recent major reductions in crime in inner-city areas can be explained by the increasingly effective organization of residents to fight crime in their own neighborhoods.[98]

In his 2012 book *Great American City*,[99] Sampson presented comprehensive results from fifteen years of research from the Project on Human Development in Chicago Neighborhoods (part of the Chicago Project). In his presidential address to the American Society of Criminology the same year, based on these findings, he presented what he called five "hard problems" facing criminology—"areas of research and unresolved questions that constitute frontiers in our field."[100]

The first is legacies of inequality, which refers to the entrenchment of neighborhoods in their past. Neighborhoods are viewed with a life-course perspective, just as individuals are in Chapter 14 of this volume. Factors such as perceived disorder, the maintenance of hierarchy, and the stigma of a negative reputation keep neighborhoods stuck in their status quo. Intergenerational effects play a key role in this, especially with predominantly black neighborhoods, where consecutive generations persist in areas with high inequality.[101]

Second is race, crime, and the new diversity. Sampson noted that racial disparities in both crime and the ways individuals are treated in the justice system may still be growing in magnitude, and that these disparities contribute to concentrated disadvantage in neighborhoods. According to the "racial invariance" thesis, the same set of community-level factors cause crime for both whites and blacks, but it is racial segregation and differential exposure to mechanisms associated with violence that explain these disparities. Additionally, as immigration increases in the United States, particularly with the Latino population, criminologists will need to study the impact of the new demographics on crime in traditional and "global" neighborhoods.[102]

Third is cognition and context. Sampson discussed this in the context of broken windows theory (discussed early in this chapter), arguing that one broken window doesn't necessarily lead to another; instead it depends on the cultural context. For example, whites view disorder more problematically than other races, in the same environment. Variables such as education, race, class, and age affect whether or not disorder is viewed as a problem. Concentration of immigrants and African Americans cause all racial and ethnic groups to see disorder as problematic no matter what the actual level of disorder is in a neighborhood.[103]

Fourth is the measurement and sources of collective efficacy. Sampson and many others view collective efficacy as one of the best yardsticks of a community's overall health and well-being. However, its measurement, including shared expectations about order and control, ties, and informal control, can be complex and are dependent on the research contexts in which it is examined. Crucial to the study of collective efficacy is the role of organizations (mostly nonprofits), technology (such as social media and "big data"), and police (by building trust) on producing and enhancing it.[104]

Fifth, and finally, is extralocal neighborhood effects. Neighborhoods are not to be seen as isolated entities, but as embedded within a "complex, higher order social and political system."[105]

KEY TERMS

rapid social change
human ecology
symbiosis
invasion, dominance, and
   succession
concentric circles/zones
delinquency areas
life histories
geographic distribution
interstitial areas
social disorganization
Chicago Area Project
community control model
residential mobility

social capital
anonymity
informal processes
collective efficacy
physical disorder
social disorder
concentrated poverty
mixed land use
broken windows theory
fear of crime
micro-place
formal social control
public housing developments
rural crime

DISCUSSION QUESTIONS

1. What are life histories, and what specific types of information may they reveal that statistical evidence would not? In answering this question, consider your own life history, as well as those of your friends and family members.
2. What is social cohesion? Visit or reflect upon various neighborhoods where you have lived and provide examples that are indicative of social cohesion.
3. What is social disorganization? What neighborhoods in your area do you consider socially disorganized? What factors are found in the neighborhoods that lead you to this conclusion?
4. How would you explain the research indicating that the same neighborhood, regardless of racial or ethnic composition, retains stable rates of higher offending?
5. If you were responsible for implementing policies to change neighborhoods for the better, what specifically would you do, and why?
6. Read the original article on broken windows theory. In what ways do you think the theory could be abused by law enforcement with respect to individual civil rights? Are there ways in which these ways could be mitigated?
7. Cite specific examples of informal and formal social control that would be at work in a neighborhood. How might the two work in tandem?
8. What is a possible explanation for lower property crime but higher violent crime in public housing developments?
9. What are some of the ways in which rural communities may require different explanations of criminal behavior than their urban counterparts?

NOTES

1. Park's background and a review of the theory of human ecology are presented in Terence Morris, *The Criminal Area* (New York: Humanities Press, 1966), pp. 1–18. See also Winifred Raushenbush, *Robert E. Park: Biography of a Sociologist* (Durham, NC: Duke University Press, 1979); and Amos H. Hawley, "Human Ecology," *International Encyclopedia of the Social Sciences*, vol. 4 (New York: Free Press, 1968), pp. 328–337.
2. Eugenius Warming, "Plant Communities," in *Introduction to the Science of Sociology*, ed. Robert E. Park and Ernest W. Burgess (Chicago: University of Chicago Press, 1969), pp. 175–182.
3. Robert E. Park, *Human Communities* (Glencoe, IL: Free Press, 1952), p. 118.
4. Ernest W. Burgess, "The Growth of the City," in *The City*, ed. Robert E. Park, Ernest W. Burgess, and Roderick D. McKenzie Jr.(Chicago: University of Chicago Press, 1928), p. 62.
5. Robert E. Park, "Human Ecology," *American Journal of Sociology* 42 (1936): 158.

6. James F. Short Jr., "Introduction to the Revised Edition," in *Juvenile Delinquency and Urban Areas*, ed. Clifford R. Shaw and Henry D. McKay (Chicago: University of Chicago Press, 1969), p. xlvii. Additional background material on Shaw and his colleague Henry McKay can be found in Jon Snodgrass, "Clifford R. Shaw and Henry D. McKay: Chicago Criminologists," *British Journal of Criminology* 16 (January 1976): 1–19. A detailed assessment of their impact on criminology can be found in Harold Finestone, "The Delinquent and Society: The Shaw and McKay Tradition," in *Delinquency, Crime and Society*, ed. James F. Short (Chicago: University of Chicago Press, 1976), pp. 23–49; and Finestone, *Victims of Change: Juvenile Delinquency in American Society* (Westport, CT: Greenwood Press, 1977), pp. 77–150.

7. Shaw and McKay, *Juvenile Delinquency and Urban Areas*, p. 145.

8. Ibid., pp. 147–152.

9. Ibid., p. 155.

10. Ibid., pp. 162–163.

11. Clifford R. Shaw, *Brothers in Crime* (Chicago: University of Chicago Press, 1938), p. 350. See also Shaw's *The Jackroller* (Chicago: University of Chicago Press, 1930), p. 164; and *The Natural History of a Delinquent Career* (Chicago: University of Chicago Press, 1931), p. 226.

12. Shaw, *Natural History*, p. 229. See also *The Jackroller*, p. 165, and *Brothers in Crime*, p. 358.

13. Shaw, *Brothers in Crime*, p. 356. See also Shaw and McKay, *Juvenile Delinquency and Urban Areas*, p. 172; and Shaw, *The Jackroller*, p. 165; and Shaw, *Natural History*, p. 229.

14. Shaw, *Brothers in Crime*, p. 356.

15. Shaw, *Brothers in Crime*, pp. 354, 355; Shaw, *Natural History*, p. 227; and Shaw, *The Jackroller*, p. 164. See also Short, "Introduction to the Revised Edition," p. xli.

16. Shaw and McKay, *Juvenile Delinquency and Urban Areas*, pp. 174–175.

17. Ibid., p. 174.

18. Shaw, *Natural History*, p. 233; Shaw, *Brothers in Crime*, p. 260; and Shaw and McKay, *Juvenile Delinquency and Urban Areas*, p. 4.

19. Shaw, *Natural History*, p. 228. See also Shaw, *The Jackroller*, pp. 119, 165; and Shaw, *Brothers in Crime*, p. 350.

20. For a review of research on the subject, see Matthew G. Yeager, "Immigrants and Criminality," *Criminal Justice Abstracts* 29 (1997): 143–171.

21. Shaw and McKay, *Juvenile Delinquency and Urban Areas*, p. 4.

22. See Solomon Kobrin, "The Chicago Area Project—A 25-Year Assessment," *Annals of the American Society of Political and Social Science* (March 1959): 19–29; or Anthony Sorrentino, "The Chicago Area Project After 25 Years," *Federal Probation* (June 1959): 40–45. A review of this and other similar programs is found in Richard Lundman, *Prevention and Control of Juvenile Delinquency*, 2nd ed. (New York: Oxford University Press, 1993), chap. 3.

23. Shaw and McKay, *Juvenile Delinquency and Urban Areas*, p. 324.

24. Morris, *The Criminal Area*, p. 83.

25. Short, "Introduction to the Revised Edition," p. xlvi.

26. Walter B. Miller, "The Impact of a 'Total-Community' Delinquency Control Project," *Social Problems* 10 (Fall 1962): 168–191.

27. Ibid., p. 187.

28. Lundman, *Prevention and Control of Juvenile Delinquency*, p. 81.

29. Ruth Rosner Kornhauser, *Social Sources of Delinquency* (Chicago: University of Chicago Press, 1978).

30. Ibid., pp. 61–69.

31. Ibid., pp. 69–138. The model is summarized in a table on p. 73 of *Social Sources of Delinquency*.

32. Robert J. Bursik Jr., and Jim Webb, "Community Change and Patterns of Delinquency," *American Journal of Sociology* 88 (1982): 24–42.

33. Ibid., p. 39.

34. Robert E. Kapsis, "Residential Succession and Delinquency," *Criminology* 15 (1978): 459–486. See also findings by McKay reported in the 1969 edition of Shaw and McKay, *Juvenile Delinquency and Urban Areas*, p. 345, and interesting comments by Snodgrass, "Clifford R. Shaw and Henry D. McKay," pp. 5–6.

35. Rodney Stark, "Deviant Places: A Theory of the Ecology of Crime," *Criminology* 25 (1987): 893–909.

36. Robert J. Sampson, "The Community," pp. 193–216 in *Crime*, ed. James Q. Wilson and Joan Petersilia (San Francisco: ICS Press, 1995). See also Sampson and Janet Lauritsen, "Violent Victimization and Offending: Individual, Situational, and Community-Level Risk Factors," in *Understanding and Preventing Violence*, vol. 3, ed. Albert J. Reiss and Jeffrey A. Roth (Washington, DC: National Academy Press, 1994), chap. 1.

37. James Coleman, "Social Capital in the Creation of Human Capital," *American Journal of Sociology* 94 (Suppl.) (1988): 95–120.

38. Sampson, "The Community," pp. 200–201.

39. Ibid., pp. 201–202. See also Robert Sampson and William Julius Wilson, "Toward a Theory of Race, Crime and Urban Inequality," in *Crime and Inequality*, ed. John Hagan and Ruth Peterson (Stanford, CA: Stanford University Press, 1995).

40. See, e.g., Lauren J. Krivo and Ruth D. Peterson, "Extremely Disadvantaged Neighborhoods and Urban Crime," *Social Forces* 75 (1996): 619–648; and Edem F. Avakame, "Urban Homicide," *Homicide Studies* 1 (1997): 338–358. For a review, see Robert J. Sampson and Janet L. Lauritsen, "Racial and Ethnic Disparities in Crime and Criminal Justice in the United States," in *Ethnicity, Crime, and Immigration: Comparative and Cross National Perspectives*, ed. Michael Tonry (Crime and Justice: A Review of Research, vol. 21) (Chicago: University of Chicago Press, 1997), pp. 311–374.

41. Edward S. Shihadeh and Nicole Flynn, "Segregation and Crime," *Social Forces* 74 (1996): 1325–1352.

42. Robert J. Sampson and W. Byron Groves, "Community Structure and Crime," *American Journal of Sociology* 94 (1989): 774–802. Mixed support for these conclusions is found in a later elaboration by Bonita M. Veysey and Steven F. Messner, "Further Testing of Social Disorganization Theory," *Journal of*

Research in Crime and Delinquency 36 (1999): 156–174. The only systematic replication of Sampson and Groves was carried out using the same data set twelve years later, the 1994 British Crime Survey. See Christopher T. Lowenkamp, Francis T. Cullen, and Travis C. Pratt, "Replicating Sampson and Groves's Test of Social Disorganization Theory: Revisiting a Criminological Classic," *Journal of Research in Crime and Delinquency* 40 (2003): 351–373. While the authors' findings were consistent with those of Sampson and Groves, they cautioned that the test should be replicated in other geographic contexts.

43. Robert J. Sampson, "Collective Regulation of Adolescent Misbehavior," *Journal of Adolescent Research* 12 (1997): 227–244. See also Delbert S. Elliott, William Julius Wilson, David H. Huizinga, Robert J. Sampson, Amanda Elliott, and Bruce H. Rankin, "The Effects of Neighborhood Disadvantage on Adolescent Development," *Journal of Research in Crime and Delinquency* 33 (1996): 389–426, which asked neighbors in Denver how likely it was that a person would take action if someone were breaking into a neighbor's house in plain sight.

44. Robert J. Sampson, Stephen W. Raudenbush, and Felton Earls, "Neighborhoods and Violent Crime: A Multilevel Study of Collective Efficacy," *Science* 277 (1997): 918–924; and Robert J. Sampson and Stephen W. Raudenbush, "Systematic Social Observation of Public Spaces," *American Journal of Sociology* 105 (1999): 603–651. Collective efficacy is more or less the opposite of social disorganization—the first term refers to the ability and the second term to the inability to achieve common goals. Collective efficacy, however, is narrowly defined in terms of the goal of controlling public space.

45. Sampson and Raudenbush, "Systematic Social Observation of Public Spaces," pp. 611–612.

46. Ibid., pp. 617–619.

47. Ibid., p. 620. Social disorder was also coded from the videotapes, but it was rarely captured.

48. Ibid., p. 638. See also Sampson, Raudenbush, and Earls, "Neighborhoods and Violent Crime," who found that social cohesion among neighbors, combined with the willingness of neighbors to intervene on behalf of the common good, is associated with reduced violence in the neighborhood. They also found that concentrated poverty and residential mobility undermine this willingness, which, in turn, increases crime and public disorder. In contrast, using data from Seattle, Barbara D. Warner and Pamela Wilcox Rountree ("Local Social Ties in a Community and Crime Model," *Social Problems* 44 [1997]: 520–536) found that neighborhood social ties reduced assaults in European American neighborhoods but had no effect in African American or racially mixed neighborhoods. In addition, Paul Bellair ("Social Interaction and Community Crime," Criminology 35 [1997]: 677–703) found that the frequency of social interactions among neighborhood residents had no effect on crime. However, neither of these studies directly measured the shared expectations or mutual cohesion that make up collective efficacy.

49. Jeffrey D. Morenoff, Robert J. Sampson, and Stephen W. Raudenbush, "Neighborhood Inequality, Collective Efficacy, and the Spatial Dynamics of Urban Violence," *Criminology* 39 (2001): 517–559.

50. James Q. Wilson and George Kelling, "The Police and Neighborhood Safety: Broken Windows," *Atlantic Monthly* 127 (1982): 29–38.
51. See Sampson and Raudenbush, "Systematic Social Observation of Public Spaces," p. 628.
52. Fred E. Markowitz, Paul E. Bellair, Allen E. Liska, and Jianhong Liu, "Extending Social Disorganization Theory: Modeling the Relationships Between Cohesion, Disorder, and Crime," *Criminology* 39 (2001): 293–320.
53. For example, a Google search for "broken windows" and "police" conducted in March 2019 produced 1,000,030 hits. The same search conducted in March 2015 yielded 451,000 results.
54. David Weisburd, Shawn Bushway, Cynthia Lum, and Sue-Ming Yang, "Trajectories of Crime at Places: A Longitudinal Study of Street Segments in the City of Seattle," *Criminology* 42 (2004): 283–322, p. 290.
55. David Weisburd, "*The Law of Crime Concentration and the Criminology of Place*," Criminology 53 (2015): 133–157.
56. For a brief review of concentration in urban places, see Charlotte Gill, Alese Wooditch, and David Weisburd, "Testing the 'Law of Crime Concentration at Place' in a Suburban Setting: Implications for Research and Practice," *Journal of Quantitative Criminology* 33 (2017): 519–545, pp. 520–521.
57. Fritz Umbach and Alexander Gerould, "Myth #3: Public Housing Breeds Crime," in *Public Housing Myths: Perceptions, Reality, and Social Policy*, ed. Nicholas Dagen Bloom, Fritz Umbach, and Lawrence J. Vale (Ithaca, NY: Cornell University Press, 2015), pp. 64–65. For a comprehensive examination of the role of law enforcement in public housing, see Fritz Umbach, *The Last Neighborhood Cops: The Rise and Fall of Community Policing in New York Public Housing* (New Brunswick, NJ: Rutgers University Press, 2011).
58. Umbach and Gerould, "Myth #3," p. 66.
59. Lee Rainwater, *Behind Ghetto Walls: Black Families in a Federal Slum* (Chicago: Aldine Publishing Company, 1970).
60. Umbach and Gerould, "Myth #3," p. 67.
61. Oscar Newman, *Defensible Space: Crime Prevention Through Urban Design* (New York: Macmillan Press, 1972).
62. Umbach and Gerould, "Myth #3," p. 69.
63. Ibid.
64. Tamara Dumanovsky, "Crime in Poor Places: Examining the Neighborhood Context of New York City's Public Housing Projects" (PhD diss., New York University, 1999), pp. 90–115.
65. Umbach and Gerould, "Myth #3," p. 72.
66. John E. Farley, "Has Public Housing Gotten a Bum Rap?," *Environment and Behavior* 14 (1982), 463–464.
67. Dennis W. Roncek, Ralph Bell, and Jeffrey Francik, "Housing Projects and Crime: Testing a Proximity Hypothesis," *Social Problems* 29 (1982), 163.
68. Umbach and Gerould, "Myth #3," p. 78.
69. Harold R. Holzman, Robert Hyatt, and Tarl Roger Kudrick, "Measuring Crime in and Around Public Housing," in *Geographic Information Systems and Crime Analysis*, ed. Fahui Wang (London: Idea Group Publishing, 2005), p. 324.

70. Edward G. Goetz, "Where Have All the Towers Gone?: The Dismantling of Public Housing in U.S. Cities," *Journal of Urban Affairs* 33 (2011).

71. Xavier de Souza Briggs, Susan J. Popkin, and John M. Goering, *Moving to Opportunity: The Story of an American Experiment to Fight Ghetto Poverty* (New York: Oxford University Press, 2010).

72. Hanna Rosin, "American Murder Mystery," *Atlantic Monthly* July/August (2008).

73. Susan J. Popkin, Michael J. Rich, Leah Hendey, Chris Hayes, and Joe Parilla, *Public Housing Transformation and Crime: Making the Case for Responsible Relocation* (Washington, DC: Urban Institute, 2012).

74. Umbach and Gerould, "Myth #3," p. 89.

75. Ibid., pp. 89–90.

76. Chad Posick and Michael Rocque, "Editorial Introduction to the Special Issue: Crime and Justice in Suburban and Rural Context," *Criminal Justice Review* 42 (2017): 233–236.

77. For a broad treatment of rural crime, see Joseph Donnermeyer and Walter DeKeseredy: *Rural Criminology* (New York: Routledge, 2013); Ralph A. Weisheit, David N. Falcone, and L. Edward Wells, *Crime and Policing in Rural and Small-Town America* (Long Grove, IL: Waveland Press, Inc., 2006). One comprehensive examination of suburban crime is Sanjay Marwah, *Suburban Crime: The Interplay of Social, Cultural, and Opportunity Structures* (Ann Arbor: University of Michigan Press, 2006); see also the article in the special issue edited by Posick and Rocque, "Editorial Introduction to the Special Issue."

78. D. Wayne Osgood and Jeff M. Chambers, "Social Disorganization Outside the Metropolis: An Analysis of Rural Youth Violence," *Criminology* 38 (2000): 81–115.

79. Ibid., p. 86, citing Kenneth P. Wilkinson, "Rurality and Patterns of Social Disruption," *Rural Sociology* 49 (1984): 25–36.

80. Osgood and Chambers, "Social Disorganization Outside the Metropolis," p. 90.

81. Ibid., p. 104.

82. Matthew D. Moore and Molly Sween, "Rural Youth Crime: A Reexamination of Social Disorganization Theory's Applicability to Rural Areas," *Journal of Juvenile Justice* 4 (2015): 47–63.

83. Maria T. Kaylen and William Alex Pridemore, "Systematically Addressing Inconsistencies in the Rural Social Disorganization and Crime Literature," *International Journal of Rural Criminology* 1 (2012): 134–152.

84. Maria T. Kaylen and William Alex Pridemore, "A Reassessment of the Association between Social Disorganization and Youth Violence in Rural Areas" *Sociological Quarterly* 92 (2011): 978–1001.

85. Kaylen and Pridemore, "Systematically Addressing Inconsistencies in the Rural Social Disorganization and Crime Literature," pp. 141–143.

86. Maria T. Kaylen and William Alex Pridemore, "Social Disorganization and Crime in Rural Communities: A First Direct Test of the Systemic Model," *The British Journal of Criminology* 53 (2013): 134–152.

87. E.g., Donnermeyer and DeKeseredy, *Rural Criminology*.

88. Eric J. Connolly, Richard H. Lewis, and Danielle L. Boisvert, "The Effect of Socioeconomic Status on Delinquency Across Urban and Rural Contexts: Using a Genetically Informed Design to Identify Environmental Risk," *Criminal Justice Review* 42 (2017): 237–253.

89. Matthew D. Moore, "Firearm Prevalence and Homicide: An Examination of Urban and Suburban Counties," *Criminal Justice Review* 42 (2017): 315–326.

90. Maria T. Kaylen, William Alex Pridemore, and Sean Patrick Roche, "The Impact of Changing Demographic Composition on Aggravated Assault Victimization During the Great American Crime Decline: A Counterfactual Analysis of Rates in Urban, Suburban, and Rural Areas," *Criminal Justice Review* 42 (2017): 291–314.

91. Lowenkamp et al., "Replicating Sampson and Groves's Test of Social Disorganization Theory," p. 351.

92. Robert J. Sampson, Jeffrey D. Morenoff, and Thomas Gannon-Rowley, "Assessing 'Neighborhood Effects': Social Processes and New Directions in Research," *Annual Review of Sociology* 28 (2002): 443–478.

93. Ibid., p. 458.

94. Charles Kubrin and Ronald Weitzer, "New Directions in Social Disorganization Theory," *Journal of Research in Crime and Delinquency* 40 (2003): 374–402.

95. Todd R. Clear, Dina R. Rose, Elin Waring, and Kristen Scully, "Coercive Mobility and Crime: A Preliminary Examination of Concentrated Incarceration and Social Disorganization," *Justice Quarterly* 20 (2003): 33.

96. Kubrin and Weitzer, "New Directions in Social Disorganization Theory," pp. 379–381.

97. See, e.g., Robert J. Sampson and Dawn Jeglum Bartusch, "Legal Cynicism and (Subcultural?) Tolerance of Deviance: The Neighborhood Context of Racial Differences," *Law and Society Review* 32 (1998): 777–804.

98. Richard Curtis, "The Improbable Transformation of Inner-City Neighborhoods," pp. 1233–1276, and Warren Friedman, "Volunteerism and the Decline of Violent Crime," pp. 1453–1474, both in *Journal of Criminal Law & Criminology* 88 (1998).

99. Robert J. Sampson, *Great American City: Chicago and the Enduring Neighborhood Effect* (Chicago: University of Chicago Press, 2012). The Chicago Project refers to the Project on Human Development in Chicago Neighborhoods, with the addition of three more studies and experiments.

100. Robert J. Sampson, "The Place of Context: A Theory and Strategy for Criminology's Hard Problems," *Criminology* 51 (2013): 1–31, p. 3.

101. Ibid., pp. 10–12.

102. Ibid., pp. 12–15.

103. Ibid., pp. 15–18.

104. Ibid., pp. 18–22.

105. Ibid., pp. 22–24.

CHAPTER 9

—

Learning Theories

This chapter focuses on the role of normal learning in the generation of criminal behavior. It includes theories about ideas and behaviors that can be learned and that support and encourage the violation of laws. It also includes theories about the processes by which the learning of these ideas and behaviors takes place. Finally, it includes theories about cultures and subcultures that contain ideas that are supportive of criminal behavior within particular groups.[1] While theories in this chapter assume that individuals must learn criminal behavior, social control theory in Chapter 10 assumes that people are born with the capacity for crime and it is only through social bonds that they behave conventionally, consistent with the concept of social contract theory.

Learning and cultures played important roles in the strain theories described in Chapter 7. Merton, and later Messner and Rosenfeld, linked crime to ideas in the dominant American culture. Cohen described how a separate negativistic subculture arose among gang youths who deliberately inverted the values of the dominant American culture. Cloward pointed out that the mere presence of an opportunity, whether legitimate or illegitimate, was meaningless unless the person also had learned how to take advantage of it. These strain theories, however, focus on the social structural conditions, such as the distribution of legitimate and illegitimate opportunities or the institutional imbalance of power, that give rise to the learning of these ideas and behaviors in the first place.[2]

In contrast, the learning theories described in this chapter focus on the content of what is learned and the processes by which that learning takes place. Some of these learning theories briefly point to the structural conditions that give rise to the learning in the first place, while others describe these structural conditions more extensively. But in each case the theories focus on the learning itself, rather than on the underlying structural conditions. In that sense, strain and learning theories are complementary with each other, but they have different emphases.[3]

BASIC PSYCHOLOGICAL APPROACHES TO LEARNING

Learning refers to habits and knowledge that develop as a result of the experiences of the individual in entering and adjusting to the environment.[4] These are to be distinguished from unlearned or instinctual behavior, which in some sense is present in the individual at birth and is determined by biology.

One of the oldest formulations about the nature of learning is that we learn by association.[5] Aristotle (384–322 B.C.) argued that all knowledge is acquired through experience and that none is inborn or instinctive. Basic sensory experiences become associated with each other in the mind because they occur in certain relationships to each other as we interact with the object. Aristotle formulated four laws of association that described these relationships: the law of similarity, the law of contrast, the law of succession in time, and the law of coexistence in space. The most complex ideas, according to Aristotle, are all built out of these simple associations between sensory experiences.

Associationism has been the dominant learning theory through the centuries to the present. It was elaborated by such philosophers as Hobbes, Locke, and Hume and was the basis for the first experiments on human memory, carried out by Ebbinhaus,[6] as well as for the first experiments on animal learning, carried out by Thorndike.[7] The behaviorist revolution substituted observable stimuli and responses for the mental images and ideas of earlier times but retained the basic idea that learning is accomplished through association. At present, a major controversy among learning theorists is between such behavioral theorists and the cognitive theorists, who retain the original Aristotelian notion that learning takes place because of the association of ideas and factual knowledge.[8] Whereas behaviorists argue that we acquire habits through the association of stimuli with responses, cognitive theorists argue that we acquire factual knowledge through the association of memories, ideas, or expectations. Behaviorists argue that learning occurs primarily through trial and error, while cognitive theorists describe learning as taking place through insight into problem solving. Despite these and other controversies between behavioral and cognitive learning theories, both can be traced back to Aristotle's original ideas about association as the basis of learning.

There are three basic ways that individuals learn through association. The simplest way is classical conditioning, as originally described by Pavlov. Some stimuli will reliably produce a given response without any prior training of the organism. For example, a dog will consistently salivate when presented with meat. Pavlov consistently presented meat to dogs, along with some other stimulus that did not by itself produce the salivation—for example, the sound of a bell. He found that after a few pairings, the sound of the bell itself was sufficient to produce salivation in the dog. What Pavlov demonstrated was that behaviors could be learned by association: if the sound of a bell is associated consistently with the presentation of the meat, then the dog learns to salivate at the sound of the bell alone.

In classical conditioning, the organism is passive and learns what to expect from the environment. In operant conditioning, the organism is active and learns how to get what it wants from the environment. Operant conditioning is associated with B. F. Skinner and is now probably the dominant learning theory in psychology. Operant conditioning uses rewards and punishments to reinforce certain behaviors. For example, rats may be taught to press a lever by rewarding that behavior with a food pellet or by punishing them with an electric shock for their failure to push the lever. The rats learn to operate on their environment by associating rewards and punishments with their own behaviors. Thus, operant conditioning is another way of learning by association.

While both classical and operant conditioning are associated with the behaviorist school of learning theory, a third theory that describes how people learn by association attempts to combine both operant conditioning and elements from cognitive psychology. Called social learning theory, it emphasizes the point that behavior may be reinforced not only through actual rewards and punishments but also through expectations that are learned by watching what happens to other people. While classical and operant conditioning are both tested extensively with animal experiments, social learning theory is focused more on human learning, since it directs attention to higher mental processes.

TARDE'S LAWS OF IMITATION AND BANDURA'S SOCIAL LEARNING THEORY

An early criminologist who presented a theory of crime as normal learned behavior was Gabriel Tarde (1843–1904).[9] Tarde rejected Lombroso's theory that crime was caused by biological abnormality, arguing that criminals were primarily normal people who, by accident of birth, were brought up in an atmosphere in which they learned crime as a way of life. He phrased his theory in terms of laws of imitation, which were similar to Aristotle's laws of learning except that they focused on associations among individuals rather than associations among sensations within one individual. Like Aristotle's original theory, Tarde's theory was essentially a cognitive theory in which the individual was said to learn ideas through the association with other ideas, and behavior was said to follow from those ideas.

Tarde's first law was that people imitate one another in proportion to how much close contact they have with one another. Thus imitation is most frequent, and changes most rapidly, in cities. Tarde described this as "fashion." In rural areas, in contrast, imitation is less frequent and changes only slowly. Tarde defined that as "custom." Tarde argued that crime begins as a fashion and later becomes a custom, much like any other social phenomenon.

The second law of imitation was that the inferior usually imitates the superior. Tarde traced the history of crimes such as vagabondage, drunkenness, and murder, and found that they began as crimes committed by royalty, and later were imitated by all social classes. Similarly, he argued that many crimes originated in large cities, and were then imitated by those in rural areas.

The third law of imitation was that the newer fashions displace the older ones. Tarde argued, for example, that murder by knifing had decreased while murder by shooting increased.

Tarde's theory was important at the time for its role in opposing Lombroso's theories. It retains some importance for us at the present time, since it was the first attempt to describe criminal behavior in terms of normal learning rather than in terms of biological or psychological defects. From this point of view, the major problem with the theory is that it was based on such a simplistic model of learning. This was the state of learning theory at the time that Tarde wrote.

Albert Bandura was influenced by Tarde's work, in his development of social learning theory in the second half of the twentieth century. Based on a series of experiments in the early 1960s involving young children viewing adults beating a "Bobo" doll, Bandura's theory was consistent with classical and operant conditioning, but was extended based upon learning through observation, and understanding the processes which mediate stimuli and responses. Children imitate models, and will be more likely to imitate models they perceive as more similar to themselves. Additionally, they respond to positive or negative reinforcement of their behavior, which can be external (wanting approval of their parents or friends, for example) or internal (feeling happy about the approval). They also respond to observing reinforcements applied to their models (such as observing their model being rewarded or punished for a certain behavior). This is referred to as vicarious reinforcement.[10]

Bandura's theory included four processes which mediate the relationship between the model's behavior and the would-be imitator's: attention (extent to which one is exposed to and notices the behavior), retention (how well one remembers the behavior), reproduction (one's ability to perform the behavior), and motivation (one's will to perform the behavior, based on vicarious reinforcement as described earlier). Bandura later renamed his social learning theory social cognitive theory (SCT), expanding the focus to the reciprocal relationships between behavior, personal characteristics, and the environment, and providing greater acknowledgment that individuals have control over their behavior beyond what they experience and observe.[11]

Another theory, focusing exclusively on criminal behavior, with some elements of the same basic idea—criminal behavior is the result of normal learning—was presented by Sutherland. Although the model of learning on which the theory was based is also relatively simple, Sutherland's theory continues to have a profound impact on criminology.

SUTHERLAND'S DIFFERENTIAL ASSOCIATION THEORY

Edwin H. Sutherland (1883–1950) was born in a small town in Nebraska and received his bachelor's degree from Grand Island College there.[12] He taught for several years at a small Baptist college in South Dakota before leaving to obtain his doctorate from the University of Chicago. Sutherland's interests were focused primarily on problems of unemployment, and that was the subject of his dissertation. Following his graduation, he taught for six years at a small college in Missouri and then went to the University of Illinois, where his department chair suggested that he write a book on criminology. The result was the first edition of *Criminology*, published in 1924.

Sutherland's theory of criminal behavior emerged gradually in several editions of this book as he formulated his thinking on the subject and systematized his presentation of that thinking.[13] He was influenced in this endeavor by a report on criminology written by Jerome Michael and Mortimer J. Adler, which appeared in 1933 and severely criticized the state of criminological theory and research.[14] Sutherland was extremely annoyed by the report and responded to it by attempting to create a general theory that could organize the many diverse facts known about criminal behavior into some logical arrangement. The first brief statement of that general theory appeared in the second edition of *Criminology*, published in 1934. In the third edition of the book, published in 1939, Sutherland made a more systematic and formal presentation of his theory and further expanded and clarified it in the fourth edition, which appeared in 1947. The theory has remained unchanged since that edition and consists of the following nine points:[15]

1. Criminal behavior is learned. . . .
2. Criminal behavior is learned in interaction with other persons in a process of communication. . . .
3. The principal part of the learning of criminal behavior occurs within intimate personal groups. . . .
4. When criminal behavior is learned, the learning includes: (a) techniques of committing the crime, which are sometimes very complicated, sometimes very simple; (b) the specific direction of the motives, drives, rationalizations, and attitudes. . . .
5. The specific directions of the motives and drives is learned from definitions of the legal codes as favorable or unfavorable. In some societies an individual is surrounded by persons who invariably define the legal codes as rules to be observed, while in others he is surrounded by persons whose definitions are favorable to the violation of the legal codes. . . .
6. A person becomes delinquent because of an excess of definitions favorable to violation of law over definitions unfavorable to violation of law. This is the principle of differential association. . . .

7. Differential associations may vary in frequency, duration, priority, and intensity. This means that associations with criminal behavior and also associations with anticriminal behavior vary in those respects. . . .

8. The process of learning criminal behavior by association with criminal and anticriminal patterns involves all of the mechanisms that are involved in any other learning. . . .

9. While criminal behavior is an expression of general needs and values, it is not explained by those general needs and values, since noncriminal behavior is an expression of the same needs and values. Thieves generally steal in order to secure money, but likewise honest laborers work in order to secure money. The attempts by many scholars to explain criminal behavior by general drives and values, such as the happiness principle, striving for social status, the money motive, or frustration, have been, and must continue to be, futile, since they explain lawful behavior as completely as they explain criminal behavior. They are similar to respiration, which is necessary for any behavior, but which does not differentiate criminal from noncriminal behavior.

Sutherland's theory has two basic elements. The content of what is learned includes specific techniques for committing crimes; appropriate motives, drives, rationalizations, and attitudes; and more general "definitions favorable to law violation." All these are cognitive elements; that is, they are all ideas rather than behaviors. In addition, the process by which the learning takes place involves associations with other people in intimate personal groups. Both elements of Sutherland's theory are derived from "symbolic interactionism," a theory developed by George Herbert Mead (1863–1931), who was on the faculty at the University of Chicago while Sutherland was getting his doctorate there.[16]

Sutherland's description of the content of what is learned was derived from Mead's argument that "human beings act toward things on the basis of the meanings that the things have for them."[17] In Mead's theory, a cognitive factor—"meanings"—determines behavior. Mead then argued that people construct relatively permanent "definitions" of their situation out of the meanings they derive from particular experiences.[18] That is, they generalize the meanings they have derived from particular situations and form a relatively set way of looking at things. It is because of these different definitions that different people in similar situations may act in different ways. To cite an old example, two brothers may grow up in identical terrible situations, but one becomes a criminal while the other becomes a priest. Drawing on this theory, Sutherland argued that the key factor in determining whether people violate the law is the meaning they give to the social conditions they experience, rather than the conditions themselves. Ultimately, whether persons obey or violate the law depends on how they define their situation.

Sutherland's description of the process by which definitions are learned was also derived from Mead's theory. Mead argued that "the meaning of such things is derived from, or arises out of, the social interaction one has with one's fellows."[19] Following Mead's theory, Sutherland argued that the meaning of criminal acts, whether murder or shoplifting, marijuana smoking or income tax evasion, prostitution or embezzlement, arises primarily from the meanings given to these acts by other people with whom the individual associates in intimate personal groups. In an attempt to explain why some associations were more important than others for the learning of these definitions, Sutherland also argued that these associations vary in "frequency, duration, priority, and intensity."

Sutherland also discussed the general social conditions underlying the differential association process. In the 1939 version of his theory, he described these general social conditions in terms of culture conflict, where that term meant that different groups in a society have different ideas about appropriate ways to behave.[20] Social disorganization was then introduced to describe the presence of culture conflict in a society, the term taken from general sociological theories, including the Chicago School of Human Ecology.[21]

In the 1949 and final version of his theory, Sutherland rejected the term *social disorganization* and replaced it with the term *differential social organization*. Social disorganization implies that there is an absence of organization. In contrast with that implication, Sutherland argued that there are numerous divergent associations organized around different interests and for different purposes. Under this condition of divergent, differential social organizations, it is inevitable that some of these groups will subscribe to and support criminal patterns of behavior, others will be essentially neutral, and still others will be definitely anticriminal and self-consciously law abiding.[22]

Because of some confusion about the term *culture conflict*, Sutherland's coauthor, Donald R. Cressey, substituted the term *normative conflict* after Sutherland's death. Norms are socially accepted rules about how people are supposed to act in specific situations and circumstances.[23] Normative conflict, then, refers to the situation in which different social groups (i.e., differential social organization) hold different views about appropriate ways to behave in specific situations and circumstances. In making this substitution, Cressey stated that he was clarifying, not changing, the meaning of Sutherland's argument.

Sutherland's theory, then, states that in a situation of differential social organization and normative conflict, differences in behavior, including criminal behaviors, arise because of differential associations. This is really only another way of saying that a person who associates with Methodists is likely to become a Methodist, a person who associates with Republicans is likely to become a Republican, and a person who associates with criminals is likely to become a criminal.

RESEARCH TESTING SUTHERLAND'S THEORY

In Sutherland's theory, crime and delinquency are caused by associating with other people who transmit definitions that favor violations of the law. Research testing this theory has tended to focus on the explanation of juvenile delinquency, rather than on the explanation of adult criminality. In general, it has done so because delinquency is largely a group phenomenon in that juveniles are likely to commit crime and delinquency in the company of other juveniles.[24]

While this fact is consistent with Sutherland's theory, it does not in itself demonstrate that delinquency is caused by the transmission of definitions through associating with other delinquents. It may be, as Sheldon and Eleanor Glueck said, that "birds of a feather flock together"[25]—that is, delinquents may select as friends other youths whose values and behaviors are similar to their own. If this is the case, then delinquency causes delinquent friends, but delinquent friends do not cause delinquency. Related to this point is the obvious fact that not everyone who associates with criminals and delinquents adopts or follows the criminal pattern. What, then, is the difference in the quality of the associations that in one instance leads to acceptance of definitions favorable to law violation, but in another leads only to an acquaintance with but not acceptance of them? Sutherland suggested that with respect to associations, frequency (number of associations), duration (length of association), priority (how closely related an individual is to an association), and intensity (how often the individual interacts with the association) determined how much impact they had on a person, and he supported this argument with case histories and with self-appraisal statements by various individuals who had followed a criminal pattern.[26] Finally, Sheldon Glueck also questioned whether Sutherland's theory was inherently untestable, asking, "Has anyone actually counted the number of definitions favourable to violation of law and definitions unfavourable to violation of law, and demonstrated that in the predelinquency experience of the vast majority of delinquents and criminals, the former exceed the latter?"[27] In 1960, Sutherland's coauthor Donald Cressey agreed that at the broadest level, differential association theory is untestable.[28]

In 1988, however, Matsueda asserted that differential association theory can be tested and that a considerable amount of research has supported it.[29] First, he argued that a variety of studies have found that juveniles who report having more delinquent friends also report committing more delinquent acts, and that these studies provide general support for the theory. Second, Matsueda stated that a number of studies have focused on the content of definitions that are favorable to violation of the law and showed that these definitions are associated with increased tendencies to engage in criminal and delinquent behavior. Matsueda said that these definitions are not "oppositional values that repudiate the legitimacy of the law and make crimes morally correct."[30] Rather, they are disagreements with the larger culture about the specific situations in which the laws should apply. For example, Matsueda described the legal defenses to crime, such as self-defense and insanity, as "prototypical definitions favorable to crime," but stated that these defenses are included in the law rather than excluded from it.[31] Third, Matsueda argued that advances in statistical techniques have found support for the complex causal structure in Sutherland's theory, especially involving the ratio of definitions that are favorable and unfavorable to violating the law.[32]

A great deal of modern theory and research in criminology can be traced to Sutherland's original formulation. Cultural and subcultural theories are based on Sutherland's arguments about normative conflict and focus on the content of what is learned. These theories retain the cognitive orientation of Sutherland's original theory and examine the role of ideas in causing criminal behaviors. Other theories, however, focus on the learning process that Sutherland described, rather than on the content of the ideas that were said to be learned. They tend to be associated with the more modern theories of learning, although at least some of them retain Sutherland's emphasis on differential association. These two branches of modern theory and research are presented in the next two sections.

THE CONTENT OF LEARNING: CULTURAL AND SUBCULTURAL THEORIES

In Sutherland's theory, the actual causes of criminal behavior are ideas—the definitions favorable to violation of the law. Cultural and subcultural theories also focus on the role of ideas in causing criminal behaviors. These theories, like Sutherland's, may explore the sources of these ideas in general social conditions, but they are characterized by the argument that it is the ideas themselves, rather than the social conditions, that directly cause criminal behavior.[33]

Walter B. Miller presented one such cultural theory, focusing on the explanation of gang delinquency.[34] He argued that the lower class has a separate, identifiable culture that is distinct from the culture of the middle class and that this culture has a tradition at least as old as that of the middle class. Whereas the middle class has "values," such as achievement, the lower class has "focal concerns" that include trouble (getting into and staying out of trouble are dominant concerns of lower-class people), toughness (masculinity, endurance, strength), smartness (skill at outsmarting the other guy; "street sense" rather than high IQ), excitement (the constant search for thrills, as opposed to just "hanging around"), fate (the view that most things that happen to people are beyond their control, and nothing can be done about them), and autonomy (resentment of authority and rules). Miller described this lower-class culture as a "generating milieu" for gang delinquency because it interacts with several social conditions that are typically found in poor areas. Lower-class families are frequently headed by women, so that sons do not have a masculine role model in the family. These boys may then acquire an exaggerated sense of masculinity. In addition, crowded conditions in lower-class homes mean that the boys tend to hang out on the street, where they form gangs. The delinquent nature of much gang activity is then a rather obvious consequence of the way the boys think, that is, of the lower-class culture and its focal concerns.

Wolfgang and Ferracuti presented a general theory of criminal violence, called the "subculture of violence."[35] This theory relied to some extent on Wolfgang's earlier study of homicide in Philadelphia.[36] Wolfgang had found that a significant number of the homicides that occurred among lower-class people seemed to result from trivial events that took on great importance because of mutually held expectations about how people would behave. He interpreted these events in theoretical terms taken from Sutherland's theory:[37]

> The significance of a jostle, a slightly derogatory remark, or the appearance of a weapon in the hands of an adversary are stimuli differentially perceived and interpreted by Negroes and whites, males and females. Social expectations of response in particular types of social interaction result in differential "definitions of the situation." A male is usually expected to defend the name or honor of his mother, the virtue of womanhood . . . and to accept no derogation about his race (even from a member of his own race), his age, or his masculinity. Quick resort to physical combat as a measure of daring, courage, or defense of status appears to be a cultural expression, especially for lower socio-economic class males of both races. When such a culture norm response is elicited from an individual engaged in social interplay with others who harbor the same response mechanism, physical assaults, altercations, and violent domestic quarrels that result in homicide are likely to be common.

Wolfgang and Ferracuti generalized the findings of this and a number of other studies on criminal violence into an overall theory that was designed to explain one type of homicide, the passion crimes that were neither planned intentional killings nor manifestations of extreme mental illness.[38] They described underlying conflicts of values between the dominant culture and this subculture of violence. For example, on the one hand, people in the subculture of violence tend to value honor more highly than do people in the dominant culture. On the other hand, they tend to value human life less highly. There are also normative conflicts between the subculture of violence and the dominant culture. These norms refer to rules about what behaviors are expected in response to the trivial jostles or remarks that were the cause of so many homicides. They are backed up with social rewards and punishments: people who do not follow the norms are criticized or ridiculed by other people in the subculture, and those who follow them are admired and respected. These norms take on a certain life of their own, independent of whether they are approved by the individuals who follow them, since the failure to follow the norms may result in the person becoming a victim of the violence. Thus, each individual may respond to a situation violently because he or she expects the other individual to respond violently, even if neither person approves of the violence. In this sense, the subculture of violence is similar to a wartime situation in which "it is either him or me."[39]

Wolfgang and Ferracuti, like Sutherland, argued that the immediate causes of these passion homicides are ideas—values, norms, and expectations of behavior. Like Sutherland, they agreed that these ideas had originated in general social conditions and suggested that theories, such as those by Cohen, Cloward and Ohlin, or Miller, may explain the origin of the subculture. They themselves, however, refused to speculate on how the subculture of violence had arisen.[40] That question was not vital to their theory, since the cause of the violent behaviors was said to be the ideas themselves, rather than the social conditions that had generated the ideas in the past. Essentially, they argued that the subculture had arisen in the past for specific historical reasons, but that it was transmitted from generation to generation as a set of ideas after those original social conditions had disappeared. Thus, their policy recommendations did not require dealing with general social conditions but required only doing something to break up the patterns of ideas that constituted the subculture of violence. For example, one of their major policy recommendations was to disperse the subculture by scattering low-income housing projects throughout the city, rather than concentrating them in inner-city areas.[41] Once the subculture was dispersed, individuals would gradually be assimilated into the dominant culture, and the violent behaviors would diminish.

The subculture of violence thesis has generated a large amount of additional theory and research, especially with respect to explaining higher levels of violent crime in the American South and among African Americans. A number of theorists have argued that there is a southern subculture of violence that has its historical roots in the exaggerated sense of honor among Southern gentlemen, the institutionalized violence associated with maintaining a part of the population in slavery, the defeat at the hands of Northerners in the Civil War, the subsequent economic exploitation of southern states by the North, and so on.[42] As with Wolfgang and Ferracuti's theory, these studies argued that the subculture of violence arose in the South for a variety of historical reasons, but that it continues now because the ideas are passed from generation to generation, although the conditions that originally gave rise to the ideas no longer exist.[43]

Elijah Anderson presented a subcultural theory of violence among African Americans, based on the "code of the street" that is found in inner cities in the United States.[44] According to Anderson, people in these areas face a situation in which there is a high concentration of poor people, a declining number of legitimate jobs, an increasing number of illegitimate jobs, the widespread availability of drugs and guns, high rates of crime and violence, declining welfare payments, and little hope for the future. In these circumstances, everyone feels isolated and alienated from the rest of their country. But the residents themselves distinguish "decent" people from "street" people on the basis of the degree of isolation and alienation.

Decent people in the inner city live according to a "civil code" that includes many of the middle-class values of the larger society. But this civil code has no value on the street, where the code of the street demands that you always communicate, in both subtle and overt ways, that "I can take care of myself." The code of the street is a product of the total despair felt by many inner-city residents, particularly their profound lack of faith in the criminal justice system. It is also a cultural adaptation to the actual situation of inner-city residents, a realistic set of behavioral rules for living in those circumstances.[45] Even decent people, especially juveniles from decent families, can switch from the civil code to the code of the street at a moment's notice when the situation demands.

At the heart of the code of the street is the issue of respect—being treated right or being granted one's "props" (proper due). Inner-city residents are able to control little in their own lives, so being in physical control of their immediate environment is extremely important. In addition, being "dissed" (disrespected) is considered an indication of the other person's intentions, a warning of a possible physical attack, so it is likely to call forth a pre-emptive first strike in return. Even decent parents socialize their children to respond in this way ("If someone disses you, you got to straighten them out").

Children from street families (as opposed to decent families) grow up largely without adult supervision. Even when they are eight or nine years old, they may hang out on the street until late at night, where they socialize primarily with other children. In these peer groups, children pool their knowledge and hone their skills for surviving on the streets. In particular, they learn how to fight, and they learn the significance that fighting has in the street world.

When they are very young, children from decent families are kept out of the street world by their parents, but by age ten or so, decent and street children are mingling in the neighborhoods and are trying to create identities for themselves in the neighborhood context. Decent children observe the behaviors of other children their own age, notice how older children negotiate and resolve disputes, and watch decent and street adults live their lives in the context of the inner-city environment. In addition, decent children hear many verbal messages about the constant dangerousness of the environment and the constant need to be physically tough and to show nerve. Showing nerve is more important than the actual fighting, since it can prevent the need to fight. In the code of the street, the point is to subtly communicate a predisposition to violence, a willingness and an ability to create total chaos and mayhem, in order to deter potential aggression. This is done through words, behavioral gestures, and bodily postures, as well as through clothing, jewelry, and personal grooming. Jackets, sneakers, gold chains, and even expensive firearms are not just fashion. They all are part of a look that is designed to prevent problems before they happen.

By the time they are teenagers, even decent children must be skilled at negotiating and fitting into this world. This process affects both boys and girls, but it is more important to boys because of the association between "nerve" and "manhood." In the code of the street, manhood involves the ability to be physically ruthless in relations with other people. It is the ability to gain respect through size and strength and physical prowess. Nerve, in contrast, communicates the lack of fear of death, a sense that death is preferable to being dissed. Even small and weak boys can have nerve—in many ways, nerve is more important to them because they have little else to deter attacks. In the coming-of-age process in the inner city, manhood requires that smaller boys find ways to use their size and strength to gain respect from larger boys. Having nerve is essential to this effort.

A major difference between street and decent boys, however, is that decent boys can put on street behavior when it is useful and necessary but can then switch back to the decent code. They understand that some people and situations demand street behavior but that other people use the decent code and expect it in return. Street boys, in contrast, live in a world in which everyone lives according to the code of the street. Thus, street boys interpret all other behaviors according to the code of the street, even the behaviors of middle-class people who have no knowledge of that code.

Anderson argued that outsiders tend to blame the individuals who live in the inner cities, to believe they are people with no moral values. But he argued passionately that the focus should be on the socioeconomic structure, particularly the absence of jobs, job training, and job networks (contacts that can help a person get a job).[46] In addition, Anderson blamed the historical legacy of slavery and segregation, arguing that "the attitudes of the wider society are deeply implicated in the code of the street." At least some children, especially the most alienated and vulnerable ones, internalize a sense of rejection and contempt from mainstream society that "may strongly encourage them to express contempt for the more conventional society in turn." Some will even "consciously invest themselves and their considerable mental resources in what amounts to an oppositional culture to preserve themselves and their self-respect." Anderson concluded:[47]

A vicious cycle has been formed. The hopelessness and alienation many young inner-city black men and women feel, largely a result of endemic joblessness and persistent racism, fuels the violence they engage in. This violence serves to confirm the negative feelings many whites and some middle-class blacks harbor toward the ghetto poor, further legitimating the oppositional culture and the code of the street in the eyes of many poor blacks. Unless this cycle is broken, attitudes on both sides will become increasingly entrenched, and the violence, which claims victims black and white, poor and affluent will only escalate.

Unlike Wolfgang and Ferracuti in their theory, Anderson tied the subcultural views found in the code of the street directly to the social conditions that generate it. Thus, Anderson's theory is partly a cultural theory like Wolfgang and Ferracuti's, describing the direct causal impact of ideas on behaviors, and partly a structural theory like the strain theories presented in the previous chapter, ones that describe the direct causal impact of general social conditions on behaviors. Anderson's policy recommendations reflect this double causation. Unlike Wolfgang and Ferracuti, Anderson contended that the general social conditions that are responsible for producing the code of the streets must be addressed.

Matsueda and his colleagues argued that all subcultural theories should include an account of the structural conditions that give rise to them:[48]

> The salience of values, whether subcultural or cultural, is an important link between social structure and individual behavior. . . . Any theory of subcultures that ignores social structure is incomplete and will fail to predict when individuals who have been exposed to the values of the subculture will act on those values. . . . Subcultures, then, are intimately tied to structural opportunities. Because structural opportunities affect crime partly through affecting subcultures, any structural explanation of crime that ignores subcultures is incomplete.

THE LEARNING PROCESS: AKERS'S SOCIAL LEARNING THEORY

While cultural and subcultural theories are derived from Sutherland's arguments about the content of what is learned, other theory and research has focused on Sutherland's description of the learning process. Several authors have maintained Sutherland's view that criminal behavior is normally learned behavior, but they have updated the conception of what is involved in "normal learning" to include arguments found in more modern learning theories.[49] In particular, these more recent theories have dropped Sutherland's argument that the principal part of normal learning takes place in intimate personal groups, although they may retain that as one important source of learning. They argue that learning can also take place through direct interactions with the environment, independent of associations with other people, through the principles of operant conditioning. In addition to changing the description of the learning process, the more recent theories have also changed the description of the content of what is learned. Specifically, they have switched from Sutherland's original cognitive orientation that only ideas are learned and have adopted the more recent theoretical orientation that behaviors themselves can be directly learned through both operant conditioning and social learning.

The most important such reformulation is by Ronald Akers, in what he described as "differential reinforcement" or social learning theory. In an original article with Burgess, Akers rewrote the principles of differential association into the language of operant conditioning.[50] This reformulation held that "criminal behavior is learned both in nonsocial situations that are reinforcing or discriminative and through that social interaction in which the behavior of other persons is reinforcing or discriminative for criminal behavior."[51] The addition of "nonsocial situations" constitutes a recognition that the environment itself can reinforce criminality, aside from the person's "social interactions" with other individuals. But Burgess and Akers maintained, with Sutherland, that "the principal part of the learning of criminal behavior occurs in those groups which comprise the individual's major source of reinforcement."[52]

Akers later revised and updated this theory and expanded the principles of operant conditioning to include modeling, or social learning, theory,[53] which argues that a great deal of learning among humans takes place by observing the consequences that behaviors have for other people. Akers's formulation of social learning theory focused on four major concepts.[54] The most important source of social learning, according to Akers, is differential association, which refers to the patterns of interactions with others who are the source of definitions that are either favorable or unfavorable to violating the law. Akers retained Sutherland's argument that differential associations vary according to priority, duration, frequency, and intensity, but he contended that they include both the direct transmission of the definitions through interpersonal communication and the indirect transmission through identification with more distant reference groups. The definitions themselves, according to Akers, reflect the meanings one attaches to one's own behavior. "General" definitions reflect overall religious, moral, or ethical beliefs, while "specific" definitions reflect the meanings that one applies to a particular behavior (e.g., smoking marijuana, burglarizing a house, killing the witnesses to an armed robbery). Differential reinforcement refers to the actual or anticipated consequences of a given behavior. People do things that they think will result in rewards or will avoid punishments in the future and do not do things that they think will result in punishments. These rewards and punishments can be social (approval or disapproval by other people) or nonsocial (e.g., getting high or getting sick on drugs). Finally, imitation involves observing what others do. Whether or not a behavior will be imitated depends on the characteristics of the person being observed, the behavior the person engages in, and the observed consequences of that behavior.

Akers also proposed a specific sequence of events by which the learning of criminal behavior is said to take place.[55] The sequence originates with the differential association of the individual with other individuals who have favorable definitions of criminal behavior, who model criminal behaviors for the person to imitate, and who provide social reinforcements for these behaviors. Thus, the initial participation of the individual in criminal behavior is explained primarily by differential association, definitions, imitation, and social reinforcements. After the person has begun to commit criminal behaviors, differential reinforcements determine whether the behaviors are continued or not. They include both social and nonsocial reinforcements in the form of the rewards and punishments that the individual directly experiences as a consequence of participating in the criminal behavior and the rewards and punishments the person experiences vicariously by observing the consequences that criminal behavior has for others.

Akers maintained that the social learning process explains the link between social structural conditions and individual behaviors.[56] For example, economic inequality, the modernization process, social disorganization, and social structural strain have all been linked to criminal behavior in chapters 6, 7, and 8. Akers argued that structural conditions such as these affect crime by affecting a person's differential associations, definitions, models, and reinforcements.

Finally, Akers and Sellers reviewed a large volume of research to argue that "[the] great preponderance of research conducted on social learning theory has found relationships in the theoretically expected direction between social learning variables and a range of criminal, delinquent, and deviant behavior."[57] In particular, they stated that research supports the "typical" sequence in which social learning operates, in which criminal behaviors are acquired through differential associations, definitions, imitation, and social reinforcements, and then are maintained through social and nonsocial reinforcements. Akers's social learning theory continues to be tested in a variety of contexts, such as deviant cybersexual activities, gang offender victimization, professional athlete doping, prescription stimulants for college students' academic uses, and binge drinking among college students.[58]

ASSESSING SOCIAL LEARNING THEORY

Pratt and colleagues note that general assessments of theories tend to rely primarily on the narrative review, which "involves an investigator collecting, reading, and 'making sense' of a body of research studies."[59] A more comprehensive and systematic approach is the use of a meta-analysis, which accumulates every study testing that theory (meeting certain criteria), merges the data into one set, and assesses the effect sizes of independent variables from that theory on the relevant dependent variables (usually measures of crime and delinquency for criminological theories). Performers of meta-analyses can also gage the influence of methodological characteristics of studies (such as sample demographics, and research design types) on effect sizes.

Pratt et al.'s meta-analysis of social learning theory relied on 133 studies from leading journals in criminology and criminal justice, from 1974 to 2003, and tested the effects of all four components from the theory: differential association, definitions, differential reinforcement, and modeling/imitation. Measures of differential association included attitudes and behavior of peers, parents, and others in their social network. Definitions included variables representing an individual's antisocial or criminal beliefs and attitudes. Measures of differential association included reactions to one's behavior (from parents, peers, and others), and assessments of rewards minus costs. Modeling/imitation was measured using variables representing the number of admired models witnessed by an individual (or alternatively, an imitation index).[60]

Pratt et al.'s meta-analysis found strong support for social learning theory. Variables related to differential association and definitions favorable to crime and delinquency produced the strongest effect sizes, whereas those related to differential reinforcement and modeling/imitation, were significant but smaller in size. Peers' influence was generally stronger than that of parents or others.[61] Pratt et al. suggested that one reason differential association outperformed differential reinforcement in effect sizes might be partially accounted for by methodological considerations. Researcher mostly measure deviant behaviors of peers indirectly, by obtaining a subject's perceptions of his or her peers' behavior, rather than directly, by asking the peers themselves. Because there is evidence that perceptions of peer misbehavior are inflated, overall effect sizes for this component of social learning theory may also be exaggerated.[62]

ATHENS'S THEORY OF VIOLENTIZATION

Another social learning theory, paying special attention to the learning process and drawing heavily on symbolic interactionism, which has received little attention by criminologists but deserves consideration, is Lonnie Athens's "violentization," which purports to explain why some people become extremely violent, committing such crimes as rape, aggravated assault, and homicide.[63] Athens's work, the subject of a book by Richard Rhodes, the Pulitzer Prize–winning author of "The Making of the Atomic Bomb," was published originally in 1980 and again throughout the 1990s.[64] Although Athens was a student of Harold Blumer (a well-known symbolic interactionist) and produced original and innovative research on violence, his work never made it into the mainstream criminological literature. Although a student of symbolic interactionism, Athens is better known as a radical interactionist; radical interactionism stresses the role of power and domination in understanding human group life.[65]

Athens's theory is unique in that its launching point is his own past—he grew up in an extremely violent background, experiencing violence first-hand, and narrowly missed becoming a violent criminal himself. Growing up in Virginia, Athens was the son of a man who was severely physically abusive to his family. Athens has always believed that his life experiences with violence made him a good candidate to theorize on violence. His methodology is qualitative in form; his theory was developed from extensive prison interviews with fifty-eight offenders at several penal institutions. Guided by phenomenological and symbolic interactionist perspectives, Athens formulated a process of violentization that he believes "dangerously violent" criminals go through to become who they are.

Stage 1 is "brutalization," whereby members of a subject's primary group (e.g., family) engage in "violent subjugation" (directly victimizing the subject), "personal horrification" (victimizing the subject's close relations, such as siblings), and "violent coaching" (teaching the subject that violence is a desired response to many social situations).[66] Stage 2 is "belligerence," in which the subject decides not to be the victim anymore and reconceives his plight as one in which he can take command of his plight.[67] In Stage 3, "violent performances," the subject tries out this new approach by engaging in violence when prompted. This experiment can result in failures, which may either exit the subject from violence or cause him to bump up his approach by gaining appropriate weapons, or victories, which are likely to lead him to Stage 4.[68] Stage 4, or "virulency," results after a series of victories. People start to treat the subject differently, viewing him as a violent person. This image of him in others' minds becomes his new self-image. When the subject ultimately embraces his new reputation and revels in it, he moves toward the point at which violence is seen as the required response to a large variety of social situations.[69] These include scenarios in which the subject feels that violence is necessary to defend one's self physically; deal with a victim who is somehow frustrating his goals; and deal with a victim who the subject feels is evil in some way.[70] As Rhodes put it, Athens thus found

> that violent criminals interpreted the world differently than did their law-abiding neighbors, and that it was from those differing interpretations that their violence emerged. Violent acts, he began to see, were not explosions: They were decisions.[71]

Athens's theory allows for the escalation and de-escalation of violence of a subject by a changing "phantom community."[72] This community consists of primary figures in the subject's life who are responsible for the teaching and reinforcement of violence. However, figures can also join the phantom community who promote other values and may have a positive effect on the subject. These concepts are similar to Sutherland's notion of differential association. Athens attributed his own eventual noncriminal lifestyle to this changing phantom community as he hit his teenage years, as well as his failures during the "violent performances" stage.

Athens's theory has been revised and expanded over the years.[73] His second stage of violentization, belligerence, is now referred to as "defiance." There is now a new fifth stage, "violent predation," where "the subject's violence becomes completely unbound exceeding the outer limits of humanity."[74] This works well in explaining why some violent criminals aren't just reacting to situations, but will attack others without any provocation. It occurs when subjects have become so violent that others view them as monsters (and they recognize this perception). Once this occurs they have reached the "point of no return," where reintegration into civilized society is improbable and they are forced to embrace their role of monster.

Athens has also delineated three different types of violent dominative encounters: violent engagements, violent skirmishes, and dominance tiffs. Which type an encounter falls within depends on the number of stages it progresses through.[75] These include role claiming (a superordinate seizes that role and casts another as a subordinate); role rejection (subordinates resist their assigned role); role sparring (disputants adopt a variety of dominance-claiming strategies); role enforcement (the disputants decide whether to use force or threat of force); and role determination (engagements end in a major/minor defeat, a draw, or no decision). Dominance tiffs progress only to stage three; violent skirmishes to stage four; and violent dominative engagements through all five stages.

Finally, Athens has also characterized communities as "civil" (where nonviolent dominance engagements are commonly used to settle disputes), "malignant" (where violent dominant engagements are the predominant way of resolving disputes), and "turbulent" (where no particular dispute resolution strategy emerges as dominant).[76]

Athens has recently put forth a number of policy recommendations stemming from his theory. For reducing dominative engagements, he proposes common-sense recommendations such as avoiding hotspots, minimizing interaction with others who are prone to these engagements, refraining from claiming the superordinate role, retreating, and asking a third party to intercede.[77] Anti-violence education programs may be useful for prevention at the brutalization stage of the violentization process. Such programs would utilize instruction governing physical intimacy, would educate parents on how the use of force against children backfires, and would train people on the use of nonviolent tactics in dominative engagements. At the defiance stage, teachers and counselors would take a more active role in identifying children in need of counseling. If brutalization continues during counseling, then subjects may need to be at least temporarily placed into different living arrangements. At the dominance engagement phase, interventions could include anti-violent group resocialization, where individuals would work within fairly small groups to reduce their reliance on violence as a means of engaging with others. Resocialization at youth hostels with a several-month grounding period may be appropriate for those at the virulency stage. And although incapacitation is required for violent predators, even at this stage a progressive security downgrading program could be utilized to incentivize them to take part in rehabilitation programs.[78]

At the community level, Athens's recommendations vary, depending on the type of community.[79] Malignant communities need to be transformed into turbulent communities. This could be accomplished through strategic partnerships between law enforcement and "knowledgeable marginally violent community members," who would identify those who terrorize the community the greatest, and need to be removed through immediate prosecution. Selective deterrence and selective rehabilitation would follow as strategies in these communities. This set of recommendations is similar to those employed in the Ceasefire programs discussed in Chapter 3 of this volume. The most effective strategy to reduce violence in turbulent communities would be community-wide anti-violence educational programs, followed by selective rehabilitation and selective incapacitation.

Athens's theory has been subject of limited testing and critique. Some have criticized his interpretive methodology, which "requires the criminologist to step into the actor's shoes when studying criminal acts and actors."[80] To them, his use of nonrandomly selected subjects and lack of verification of their narratives were problematic. Others have noted that his work doesn't take into account the biology of violence. Rhodes's book generally praised his work, and Rhodes found a number of examples of violent people whose stories validated Athens's theory. No comprehensive testing of Athens's theory as applied to street criminals has been carried out.[81] O'Donnell, while praising the unique features of violentization theory, criticized its generality by pointing to areas in which he believed it could not apply, such as the lynching of blacks in the South, the conformity leading to genocide, and the decline of crime discussed in Chapter 2 of this volume.[82] However, with respect to genocide, Winton demonstrated how Athens's theory could aptly explain the development and enactment of genocides in Bosnia and Rwanda.[83] Other criticisms of the theory are that it is too linear; that it ignores sex, social class, race, and the role of the victim; and that it is not an original theory because it can be derived from other general theories. In the 2017 2nd edition of his book, Athens devotes a chapter to responding to these criticisms.[84] Although Athens's violentization theory is not widely discussed among mainstream criminologists, its believers, namely symbolic and radical interactionists, continue to laud it a quarter of a century from its inception. It has a unique approach, one which O'Donnell would refer to as "daring,"[85] and is viscerally powerful in its ability to put one in the minds of those going through the stages from nonviolence to some level of violent criminality. More effort should be spent on testing it empirically.

KATZ'S SEDUCTIONS OF CRIME

A different theory based on symbolic interactionism is by Jack Katz, put forth in his book *Seductions of Crime.*[86] Katz argued that although criminologists have traditionally explained crime in terms of "background" variables, such as race, class, gender, and urban location, it is far more important to understand the "foreground" variable of what it feels like to commit a crime when you are committing it. Over and over, Katz asked: What are people trying to do when they commit a crime?[87] That is, he focused on the meaning that crime has for the criminal.

Katz looked at a wide variety of sources, including biographies and autobiographies of criminals, journalistic accounts, and participant observation studies, and tried to read into these accounts the real explanation that the criminals had for the criminal behavior. He then applied this technique to five types of crimes: passion murders, adolescent property crime, gang violence, persistent robbery, and cold-blooded murder. In each case, he found that the criminal is engaged in a "project"—that is, is trying to accomplish something by committing the crime. That project is primarily moral—that is, it involves right and wrong, justice and injustice. It therefore involves emotions that have strong moral components: humiliation, righteousness, arrogance, ridicule, cynicism, defilement, and vengeance. In each case, the criminal action itself is fundamentally an attempt to transcend a moral challenge faced by the criminal in the immediate situation.

The moral challenge faced by the passion killer, Katz found, is "to escape a situation that is otherwise inexorably humiliating."[88] Rather than accept this humiliation, the killer engages in "righteous slaughter," which the killer interprets as participating in some higher form of good. Adolescents who engage in shoplifting and petty vandalism engage in a melodrama in which "getting away with it" demonstrates personal competence in the face of persistent feelings of incompetence. Adolescents who engage in urban gang violence generally come from poor families who have recently arrived from rural areas and who therefore are humbled by the rational environment of the city and are deferential to the people who inhabit it. In response to this moral challenge, these adolescents are deliberately irrational in their own actions and arrogantly dominating in relation to other people. They thereby create a "territory" for themselves in the city, both in geographic and in moral terms. Those who persistently engage in robbery must become "hard men" who take total control of the immediate situation by being willing to back their intentions violently and remorsely.[89] Robbery therefore transcends the total lack of control these robbers experience in the rest of their lives—that is, they experience their lives as completely out of control or as controlled by the system. Finally, cold-blooded killers have a pervasive sense of having been defiled by conventional members of society, who for years have treated them as pariahs and outcasts. In their minds, these killers finally exact vengeance for this defilement by "senselessly" killing some of those conventional members of society.

In each case, then, engaging in crime involves transcending a moral challenge and achieving a moral dominance. This moral transcendence produces a "thrill" that is experienced during the actual commission of the crime as sensual, seductive, magic, creative, even compelling. Beyond these "moral and sensual attractions in doing evil," Katz argued that there really are no general explanations for crime and deviance. But Tittle suggested that there may be some further similarities among the different types of crime described by Katz: "All appear to involve efforts to escape control exercised by others or dictated by circumstances, and they all seem to express efforts to impose control back over proximate people and circumstances."[90] According to Tittle, then, Katz's descriptions also suggest that a fundamental meaning of crime for the criminal is to escape the control of others and to impose control on others.

Research on the meaning of crime to criminals is not new. In the 1930s, Clifford Shaw published a series of life histories of juvenile delinquents, as described in Chapter 7.[91] These life histories attempted to portray the social worlds in which these juveniles lived, including the meanings that delinquency had for them in the context of their worlds. At about the same time, Sutherland published an extensive portrayal of a professional thief as part of differential association theory, described earlier in this chapter.[92] In the 1950s, Sutherland's coauthor Cressey wrote about the world of embezzlers in connection with the same theory.[93]

In the 1960s, Becker provided a vivid portrayal of marijuana smoking among jazz musicians,[94] and Polsky described the worlds of hustlers and gangsters.[95] There has been a considerable expansion of this type of work.[96] Adler examined the worlds of upper-level drug dealers,[97] while Tunnell described the worlds of ordinary adult property offenders.[98] Wright and Decker described the worlds of active burglars and of active armed robbers.[99] Jacobs described the worlds of active crack dealers[100] and of those who rob drug dealers.[101] Ferrell argued that such research raises a host of legal and ethical issues, including the risk of the researcher being labeled as criminal by the criminal justice system.[102] Nevertheless, he argued that criminological research should focus more on the "lived meanings" of crime and criminal justice and presented theoretical and methodological frameworks to support this argument.

LABELING THEORIES

Like Athens's and Katz's theories, labeling theories have their roots in symbolic interactionism, headed by theorists such as Charles Horton Cooley, George Herbert Mead, and Herbert Bloomer, and focuses on the process and construction of deviance. Cooley's concept of the looking-glass self[103] is one of the major concepts from interactionism that influence labeling theory. Referring to the process by which an individual defines one's self by internalizing his or her perceptions of how others perceive them, the looking-glass mirror is the reflection of the others' judgments, adopted by the individual. Self-development, thus, involves one's *conception* of the response of others toward him or her, rather than the actual response of others.

In 1938, Frank Tannenbaum formulated a labeling theory of crime that arises from the conflicts between youths and adults in urban neighborhoods.[104] He argued that the youths see themselves as participating in playgroups on the streets, as they have been doing since they were young children. This is their "definition of the situation," to use the term from symbolic interactionism. But as the youths become teenagers, the playgroups increasingly engage in exciting, adventurous, dangerous, and threatening activities that provoke the hostility of the adults in the neighborhood. Adults initially "define the situation" as "good kids" doing "bad actions." But as the conflict between adolescents and adults persists, adults eventually define the youths themselves as bad. The youths then begin to identify with these definitions, to view themselves as bad, and they begin to act the part. Tannenbaum concluded: "The person becomes the thing he is described as being."[105]

In 1951, Lemert presented a general theory of deviance that incorporated this basic labeling process.[106] He argued that criminal and deviant behaviors originate in any number of biological, psychological, or social factors in the person's life. Thus, for example, Tannenbaum had described delinquency as originating in juvenile playgroups in urban neighborhoods. Lemert called people who engage in such criminal or deviant behavior "primary deviants."[107] This deviant behavior then generates a negative reaction from other people, and that reaction tends to transform from a negative definition of the act into a negative definition of the person. People who are unwilling or unable to stop the offending behavior (i.e., the behavior that generates the negative social reaction) will at some point tend to reorganize their self-images to incorporate the new negative definitions of themselves. This is the process described by Tannenbaum, as adults transform the definition of the youths' actions as bad into a definition of the youths themselves as bad, whereupon the youths tend to reorganize their self-images to incorporate these negative definitions of themselves. This transformation of the self-image is a self-protective move, since those who already define themselves as criminals or delinquents are less threatened when other people define them that way. Lemert called a person who has taken on a deviant self-image a "secondary deviant."[108] The redefinition of self opens the door to full participation in the deviant life and allows the person to make a commitment to a deviant career. At this point, Lemert argued, the criminal and deviant behavior is no longer generated by the various biological, psychological, and social factors in the person's life but is generated directly by the person's self-image.

Despite Lemert's arguments, many people who commit criminal behaviors do not think of themselves as criminals—that is, they do not have a criminal self-image. Yochelson and Samenow found that even the most hardened, consistent offenders were unwilling to admit that they were criminals, although they could easily recognize criminality in others.[109] Cameron pointed out that nonprofessional shoplifters often deny that their actions constitute theft and tend to rationalize their behavior as "merely naughty or bad" or as "reprehensible but not really criminal."[110] Cressey's analysis of embezzlement is quite similar.[111] Embezzlers are people who hold positions of trust and normally conceive of themselves as upstanding citizens. Therefore, they must define their actions as "only borrowing the money" before they can proceed. Police who use illegal violence justify it in terms of the need to accomplish their jobs.[112] Illegal activities by governmental agencies may be justified in terms of "national security." Antiwar activists who committed illegal acts stated that the "real criminals" were the ones running the war. And, in general, Chambliss and Seidman stated: "It is a truism that every person arrested for crime perceives himself as innocent, for there are always circumstances which to him seem to place his action outside the appropriate definition of the crime."[113]

These examples illustrate the fact that criminal behaviors are frequently committed by persons who do not conceive of themselves as criminals. To maintain a noncriminal self-image these persons "define the situation," so that they can maintain that their actions are not really crimes. They are then free to continue committing criminal behaviors without changing their self-image.

The maintenance of a noncriminal self-image is important to most people. Pressure to accept a criminal self-image depends, in part, on the number of others who define the person as a criminal, and the process of informing others that a person is a criminal is frequently used as a technique of social control. For example, consider the case of a person who has a noncriminal self-image, but who is caught shoplifting and is brought to the store office. Store officials communicate to the person "you are a shoplifter." This is threatening to the person precisely because the self is constructed in the process of interacting with others, including the store officials. The officials can increase the power of the threat by increasing the number of persons who know about the new identity. The ultimate threat to the identity, however, involves the process of arrest and conviction in which the person is officially declared to be a criminal in the view of the society at large. From this point of view, a criminal trial can be interpreted as a "status degradation ceremony" in which the public identity of the person is lowered on the social scale. Garfinkel noted that literally every society maintains such ceremonies as a method of social control and that the structure of these ceremonies is essentially similar although the societies differ dramatically.[114]

Once applied, Becker argued, the criminal label overrides other labels, so that other people think of the person primarily as a criminal.[115] Such a person may then be forced into criminal roles because of public stereotypes about criminals.[116] For example, on release from prison, a person may be unable to obtain legitimate employment because of the criminal conviction and may then return to crime to survive. Finally, those who have been labeled criminal may associate primarily with other people who have been similarly labeled, either because they are all institutionalized together or because other people refuse to associate with them.[117] Membership in an exclusively criminal group can increase the likelihood that individuals will resort to a criminal self-image rather than attempt to retain a noncriminal self-image.

This discussion represents one of the basic arguments of the so-called labeling approach to crime: that the formal and informal processes of social control can have the effect of increasing criminal behavior because the labeling process increases the likelihood that the person will develop a criminal self-image. Several criticisms of the labeling approach should be mentioned. First, labeling theorists sometimes have overemphasized the importance that the official labeling process can have. As Akers remarked:[118]

One sometimes gets the impression from reading this literature that people go about minding their own business, and then—"wham"—bad society comes along and slaps them with a stigmatized label. Forced into the role of deviant the individual has little choice but to be deviant.

Second, labeling theory generally portrays the deviant as resisting the deviant label and accepting it only when it can no longer be avoided. Although this may be true in some cases, in others, it would appear that the deviant identity is actively sought and that the person may form a deviant identity without ever having been officially or unofficially labeled. For example, youths who join a delinquent gang may form a deviant identity that is centered on their gang activities. Although official labeling may make it harder to change that identity in the future, it did not push the youths into the identity in the first place, and there is no particular reason to believe that failure to label the youths would lead them to seek a law-abiding identity instead.

Third, it is generally recognized that for the typical, law-abiding member of society who has a noncriminal self-image, the labeling or stigmatizing function of the criminal court is the primary technique of social control and is much more important than the actual imposition of punishments.[119] The average citizen is deterred from committing most crimes because he or she fears the conviction itself rather than the punishment associated with it. This is why courts are frequently able to suspend sentences or impose such minor punishments as small fines or unsupervised probation with no loss of effectiveness. Only in cases in which conviction does not hold a stigma—for example, traffic offense cases—do the courts rely heavily on the actual imposition of punishments in the social control of the average citizen. Reducing the stigmatizing or labeling effects of the criminal court could possibly lead to an increase in the incidence of criminal behaviors and to an increase in the imposition of other, harsher punishments for those behaviors. Thus, the basic question is not whether the labeling function creates crime, but whether it creates more crime than it eliminates. Although this is a complicated question to analyze, it seems probable that labeling does not create more crime than it eliminates.[120]

IMPLICATIONS

Sutherland's theory and Akers's expansion of it have had a massive impact on criminology. At the time it was written, criminology was dominated by physicians and psychiatrists who searched for the causes of criminal behavior in biological and psychological abnormalities. Sutherland's theory, more than any other, was responsible for the decline of that view and the rise of the view that crime is the result of environmental influences acting on biologically and psychologically normal individuals.

To assess this school of thought, it is necessary to distinguish between Sutherland's theory itself and the more modern learning theories that have followed it. To a considerable extent, Sutherland's theory was based on an outdated theory of learning. His argument that learning consists entirely of ideas ("definitions") and that the principal part of learning occurs in differential associations in intimate personal groups must be assessed in terms of general research on the nature of human learning. The field of learning theory has its own controversies, and to some extent Sutherland's theory, as a cognitive theory, must do its own battle with other cognitive theories and with the more popular behavioral theories. There is no reason to think that Sutherland's theory will emerge triumphant from that battle. Quite to the contrary, there are many reasons to believe that as a learning theory, Sutherland's theory has virtually no importance whatsoever. Sutherland, after all, was not a learning theorist and was not particularly familiar with the major theory and research on human learning that was going on at the time.

Sutherland's legacy to criminology is not his specific learning theory but his argument that criminal behavior is normal learned behavior. The task Sutherland focused on, and the task still facing criminologists today, is to explore the implications of that argument for criminology. In the first edition of this book, Vold argued that the logical implication of Sutherland's theory is that crime must be viewed in the context of political and social conflict.[121]

If criminal behavior, by and large, is the normal behavior of normally responding individuals in situations that are defined as undesirable, illegal, and therefore criminal, then the basic problem is one of social and political organization and the established values or definitions of what may, and what may not, be permitted. Crime, in this sense, is political behavior, and the criminal becomes a member of a "minority group" without sufficient public support to dominate and control the police power of the state.

Sutherland seemed to draw a similar implication from his theory. After making the first systematic presentation of the theory in 1939, he turned his attention to white-collar crime and retained that focus until his death.[122] Sutherland argued that white-collar crimes are normal learned behaviors and that there are no essential differences between those behaviors and the behaviors of lower-class criminals when viewed from the perspective of causation. The differences in official crime rates between the upper and lower classes arise because upper-class people have sufficient political power to control the enactment and enforcement of criminal laws. When their normal learned behaviors are socially harmful, these behaviors either are not defined as wrongs at all or are defined as civil wrongs. But when the normal learned behaviors of lower-class people are socially harmful, these behaviors are defined and processed as crimes. Thus, lower-class people end up with high official crime rates, while upper-class people end up with low official crime rates. Further discussion of this implication is presented in Chapter 11 on conflict criminology.

CONCLUSIONS

Sutherland described criminal behavior as normal learned behavior and went on to make specific assertions about the nature of normal learning. He asserted that normal learning primarily involves the learning of ideas and beliefs in the process of associating with other people. Behaviors, including criminal behaviors, follow from and are a product of those ideas and beliefs.

The adequacy of Sutherland's assertions can be assessed only in the context of general theories and research about human learning. In general, it seems reasonable to conclude that ideas and beliefs that are learned in association with other people do have a direct causal impact on criminal behaviors. However, criminal behaviors may also be associated with other types of normal learning. More recent learning theories of criminal behavior, such as Akers's social learning theory, retain Sutherland's view that criminal behavior is normal learned behavior but more adequately incorporate modern learning principles in the description of the normal learning process. Athens's learning theory is especially adept at linking the learning process with the various cognitive and behavioral stages that an individual goes through in becoming a violent criminal. Katz's theory explains how criminals learn how to achieve a moral dominance through the experience of committing crime. Labeling theories propose that deviance involves the construction of a self in response to their perceptions of others' views of them, as well in response to others' informal and formal responses to their actions.

To assert that criminal behavior is directly caused by beliefs does not deny that there are structural sources for beliefs—that is one of the most fundamental propositions in sociology. The question is whether these beliefs attain some life of their own as causes of behavior in general and as causes of criminal behavior in particular. The most reasonable position at this time seems to be that adopted by Matsueda and his colleagues: that culture functions as a crucial intervening variable between social structure and individual behavior.[123] That is, ideas and beliefs—including definitions of behavior, expectations about how to behave in particular situations, social approval or valuation of certain behaviors, and social responses that back up those expected and approved behaviors with rewards and punishments—have a direct causal impact on behavior, independent of their social structural sources.

KEY TERMS

learning theories
instinctual behavior
associationism
behaviorists
cognitive theorists
classical conditioning
operant conditioning
social learning theory
laws of imitation
fashion
custom
differential association
frequency
duration
priority
intensity
content and process of learning
symbolic interactionism
culture conflict
social disorganization
differential social organization

normative conflict
transmission of definitions
focal concerns
subculture of violence
code of the street
civil code
differential reinforcement
vicarious reinforcement
nonsocial situations
general definitions
specific definitions
violentization
malignant and turbulent
   communities
looking-glass self
labeling theory
self-image
defining the situation
primary deviant
redefinition of the self
secondary deviant

DISCUSSION QUESTIONS

1. What is meant by crime as normal learned behavior? Provide specific examples.
2. What may be directionality problems with differential association theory?
3. Why may differential association theory be untestable?
4. According to Sutherland's theory, what actually causes the criminal behavior? How would Sutherland explain white-collar crime?
5. How does the subculture of violence explain the assaults and homicides arising from seemingly minor interactions? What explains the development of this type of subculture of violence?
6. What are the policy recommendations of Wolfgang and Ferracuti? How would these recommendations actually be implemented?
7. Can a meaningful difference be drawn between street boys and decent boys? What are the policy implications of such a distinction?
8. Are the policies implications Athens relate to his theory of violentization practically achievable?
9. According to Katz, why do people commit criminal acts? What are the policy implications of Katz's theory?
10. What are the critiques of labeling theory? How would labeling theory explain the aging out of crime?
11. Provide examples of informal processes of social control. How could such processes increase acts of crime and delinquency according to a labeling theorist?
12. In what ways could reducing the stigmatizing or labeling effects of the criminal court possibly lead to an increase in the incidence of criminal behaviors?

NOTES

1. In the past, these theories were described as "cultural deviance" theories. This term was based on the argument that the cultures themselves could be deviant and that individuals who conform to such deviant cultures will therefore commit crimes. This term and the interpretation associated with it originated in Ruth Rosner Kornhauser, "Theoretical Issues in the Sociological Study of Juvenile Delinquency," unpublished manuscript, Center for the Study of Law and Society, Berkeley, CA, 1963; and Social Sources of Delinquency (Chicago: University of Chicago Press, 1978). The use of this term and the interpretation of the theories associated with it have been extensively criticized. See Ross L. Matsueda, "The Current State of Differential Association Theory," *Crime & Delinquency* 34 (1988): 277–306; and Thomas J. Bernard and Jeffrey B. Snipes, "Theoretical Integration in Criminology," in *Crime and Justice: A Review of Research*, ed. Michael Tonry (Chicago: University of Chicago Press, 1996), pp. 327–330. For a more recent discussion of

this issue, see Ronald L. Akers, "Is Differential Association/Social Learning Cultural Deviance Theory?" and the response by Travis Hirschi, "Theory Without Ideas: Reply to Akers," in *Criminology* 34 (1996): 229–256.

2. Bernard and Snipes, "Theoretical Integration in Criminology," pp. 332–335.

3. See the description of structure and process in Ronald Akers, *Deviant Behavior: A Social Learning Approach* (Belmont, CA: Wadsworth, 1985), p. 66. For an extended discussion, see Akers, *Social Learning and Social Structure* (Boston: Northeastern University Press, 1998).

4. Basic information about learning theories may be found in Gordon H. Bower and Ernest R. Hilgard, *Theories of Learning* (Englewood Cliffs, NJ: Prentice Hall, 1981); Stewart H. Hulse, Howard Egeth, and James Deese, *The Psychology of Learning*, 5th ed. (New York: McGraw-Hill, 1980); Robert C. Bolles, *Learning Theory*, 2nd ed. (New York: Holt, Rinehart, and Winston, 1979); Winifred F. Hill, *Learning: A Survey of Psychological Interpretations*, 3rd ed. (New York: Crowell, 1977). These theories are briefly reviewed in Gwynn Nettler, *Explaining Crime*, 3rd ed. (New York: McGraw-Hill, 1984), pp. 296–300.

5. For a detailed account of the development of associationism, see J. R. Anderson and Gordon H. Bower, *Human Associative Memory* (Washington, DC: Winston and Sons, 1973). Concise accounts can be found in Hulse, Egeth, and Deese, *The Psychology of Learning*, pp. 2–4, and Bower and Hilgard, *Theories of Learning*, pp. 2–4. The major alternative to associationism began with Plato (427–347 B.C.), who emphasized the rational aspects of human learning. See Bower and Hilgard, *Theories of Learning*, pp. 4–8; and Hulse, Egeth, and Deese, *The Psychology of Learning*, pp. 4–8. Whereas Aristotle broke complex learning down to its simplest components, Plato argued that the whole was greater than the sum of its parts. He emphasized the inborn capacity of the human mind to organize raw sense data, and his ideas appear in modern times in the form of Gestalt psychology. This school has gained support from research on "species-specific" behaviors. See Keller Breeland and Marian Breeland, "The Misbehavior of Organisms," *American Psychologist* 16 (1961): 681–684; M. E. P. Seligman, "On the Generality of the Laws of Learning," *Psychological Review* 77 (1970): 406–418; and J. Garcia and R. Koelling, "Relation of Cue to Consequence in Avoidance Learning," *Psychonomic Science* 4 (1996): 123–124. However, this view has not been applied to crime, so it is not presented here.

6. H. Ebinghaus, *Memory* (New York: Teachers College, 1913), reprinted by Dover, New York, 1964.

7. E. L. Thorndike, "Animal Intelligence," *Psychological Review Monograph Supplement* 2, no 8 (1898).

8. Bower and Hilgard, *Theories of Learning*, pp. 15–17.

9. See Margaret S. Wilson Vine, "Gabriel Tarde," in *Pioneers in Criminology*, 2nd ed., ed. Hermann Mannheim (Montclair, NJ: Patterson Smith, 1972), pp. 292–304. See also Don Martindale, *The Nature and Types of Sociological Theory* (Boston: Houghton Mifflin, 1960), pp. 305–309; and Jack H. Curtis, "Gabriel Tarde," in *Social Theorists*, ed. Clement S. Mihanovich (Milwaukee, WI: Bruce, 1953), pp. 142–157.

10. Albert Bandura, *Social Learning Theory* (Englewood Cliffs, NJ: Prentice-Hall, 1977).

11. Albert Bandura, *Social Foundations of Thought and Action*: A Social Cognitive Theory (Englewood Cliffs, NJ: Prentice-Hall, 1986).

12. See Mark Warr, "The Social Origins of Crime: Edwin Sutherland and the Theory of Differential Association," in *Explaining Criminals and Crime*, eds. Raymond Paternoster and Ronet Bachman (Los Angeles: Roxbury, 2001), pp. 182–191.

13. For an account of the development of the theory, see Matsueda, "The Current State of Differential Association Theory," pp. 278–284.

14. Jerome Michael and Mortimer J. Adler, *Crime, Law, and Social Science* (New York: Harcourt, Brace, 1933). Sutherland's reaction to this report is discussed in the "Introduction" (by Gilbert Geis) to a reprint edition published by Patterson Smith, Montclair, NJ, 1971. See also Donald R. Cressey, "Fifty Years of Criminology," *Pacific Sociological Review* 22 (1979): 457–480.

15. Edwin H. Sutherland, *Criminology*, 4th ed. (Philadelphia: Lippincott, 1947), pp. 6–7. The most recent edition is Edwin H. Sutherland, Donald R. Cressey, and David F. Luckenbill, *Principles of Criminology*, 11th ed. (Dix Hills, NY: General Hall, 1992), where the theory appears on pp. 88–90.

16. For a review of Mead's thought, see Herbert Blumer, *Symbolic Interactionism* (Englewood Cliffs, NJ: Prentice Hall, 1969). The theory is briefly reviewed in George B. Vold, *Theoretical Criminology*, 2nd ed., prepared by Thomas J. Bernard (New York: Oxford University Press, 1979), pp. 255–258.

17. Blumer, *Symbolic Interactionism*, pp. 2–3. Lonnie Athens's theory, presented later in this chapter, was also influenced heavily by symbolic interactionism, and Athens was a student of Blumer.

18. Cf. W. I. Thomas, *The Unadjusted Girl* (Boston: Little, Brown, 1923), pp. 41–53. See also Peter McHugh, *Defining the Situation* (Indianapolis: Bobbs-Merrill, 1968).

19. Blumer, *Symbolic Interactionism*.

20. Sutherland, *Criminology*, 1939 ed., p. 7.

21. Ibid., p. 8.

22. Ibid.

23. Donald R. Cressey, "Culture Conflict, Differential Association, and Normative Conflict," in *Crime and Culture*, ed. Marvin E. Wolfgang (New York: John Wiley, 1968), pp. 43–54.

24. In general, see Albert J. Reiss Jr., "Co-offender Influences on Criminal Careers," in *Criminal Careers and "Career Criminals,"* vol. 2, ed. Alfred Blumstein, Jacqueline Cohen, Jeffrey Roth, and Christy Visher (Washington, DC: National Academy Press, 1986), pp. 145–152.

25. Sheldon Glueck and Eleanor T. Glueck, *Unraveling Juvenile Delinquency* (New York: Commonwealth Fund, 1950), p. 164.

26. See, for example, Edwin H. Sutherland, *White Collar Crime* (New York: Dryden, 1949), pp. 222–256.

27. Sheldon Glueck, "Theory and Fact in Criminology: A Criticism of Differential Association," *British Journal of Delinquency* 7 (October 1956): 92–109.

28. Donald Cressey, "Epidemiology and Individual Conduct," *Pacific Sociological Review* 3 (1960): 47–58.
29. Matsueda, "The Current State of Differential Association Theory," pp. 284–287. See also James D. Orcutt, "Differential Association and Marijuana Use," *Criminology* 25 (1987): 341–358.
30. Matsueda, "The Current State of Differential Association Theory," p. 296.
31. Ibid., p. 301, n11; see also n6.
32. The studies he cited here were Orcutt, "Differential Association and Marijuana Use"; Matsueda, "Testing Control Theory and Differential Association," *American Sociological Review* 47 (1982): 489–504; Matsueda and Karen Heimer, "Race, Family Structure, and Delinquency," *American Sociological Review* 52 (1988): 826–840; Elton F. Jackson, Charles R. Tittle, and Mary Jean Burke, "Offense-Specific Models of the Differential Association Process," *Social Problems* 33 (1986): 335–356; and Charles R. Tittle, Mary Jean Burke, and Elton F. Jackson, "Modeling Sutherland's Theory of Differential Association," *Social Forces* 65 (1986): 405–432. Mark Warr ("Age, Peers, and Delinquency," *Criminology* 31 [1993]: 17–40) argued that differential associations can explain the relationship between age and crime. In particular, he found support for Sutherland's concept of duration but argued that it was the recency, rather than the priority, of delinquent friends that had an impact on delinquent behavior. In addition, Daniel P. Mears, Matthew Ploeger, and Mark Warr ("Explaining the Gender Gap in Delinquency," *Journal of Research in Crime and Delinquency* 35 [1998]: 251–266) argued that Sutherland's theory is useful in explaining the gender distribution of delinquency. They found that the number of delinquent friends was the strongest predictor of delinquency and that males were significantly more likely to have delinquent friends than were females. However, females' stronger moral evaluations also appeared to protect them from delinquency when they did have delinquent friends. This finding suggests that in order to explain the gender gap, Sutherland's theory may have to be modified.
33. In contrast, the strain theories of Cohen and of Cloward and Ohlin both use the term *subculture*, but both locate the primary causes of criminal behavior directly in social conditions. There are common thinking patterns that arise among delinquents, but the thinking patterns are not the cause of the criminal behavior. In strain theories, both the thinking patterns and the criminal behaviors are caused by the same social structural forces. See chapter 8.
34. Walter B. Miller, "Lower Class Culture as a Generating Milieu of Gang Delinquency," *Journal of Social Issues* 14 (1958): 5–19.
35. Marvin E. Wolfgang and Franco Ferracuti, *The Subculture of Violence* (Beverly Hills, CA: Sage, 1981).
36. Marvin E. Wolfgang, *Patterns in Criminal Homicide* (Philadelphia: University of Pennsylvania Press, 1958).
37. Ibid., pp. 188–189. For discussions of male violence as honor defense, see Kenneth Polk, "Males and Honor Contest Violence," *Homicide Studies* 3 (1999): 30–46; and Nancy V. Baker, Peter R. Gregware, and Margery A. Cassidy, "Family Killing Fields: Honor Rationales in the Murder of Women," *Violence Against Women* 5 (1999): 164–184.

38. Wolfgang and Ferracuti, *The Subculture of Violence*, p. 141. The theory itself is presented in seven points on pp. 158–161 and is summarized on pp. 314–316. A similar theoretical approach, focusing on cultural differences in disputatiousness (the tendency to define negative interactions as grievances and to demand reparations for them) and aggressiveness (the tendency to pursue a grievance and to use force to settle the dispute) is presented in David F. Luckenbill and Daniel P. Doyle, "Structural Position and Violence: Developing a Cultural Explanation," *Criminology* 27 (1989): 419–436.

39. Wolfgang and Ferracuti, *The Subculture of Violence*, p. 156.

40. Ibid., p. 163.

41. Ibid., p. 299.

42. See, for example, S. Hackney, "Southern Violence," in *The History of Violence in America*, ed. Hugh D. Graham and Ted Robert Gurr (New York: Bantam, 1969), pp. 505–527; and R. D. Gastil, "Homicide and a Regional Subculture of Violence," *American Sociological Review* 36 (June 1971): 412–427.

43. Research on race, region, and homicide rates has focused this argument considerably. Overall homicide rates are higher in the South than in other regions of the country, but the West has the highest homicide rates for both whites and blacks. See Patrick W. O'Carroll and James A. Mercy, "Regional Variation in Homicide Rates: Why Is the West So Violent?" *Violence and Victims* 4 (1989): 17–25; and Gregory S. Kowalski and Thomas A. Petee, "Sunbelt Effects on Homicide Rates," *Sociology and Social Research* 75 (1991): 73–79. The reason for these rates is that blacks have higher homicide rates than whites, and the South has a higher proportion of blacks in the population. But southern blacks themselves are not more violent than blacks elsewhere in the country. In fact, black homicide rates are lower in the South than in any other region of the country. Thus, there is no "southern subculture of violence" among the black population there. On the other hand, there may be such a subculture among the whites there. Whites in western states have higher homicide rates than do whites in the South, but this is largely due to the high homicide rates for Hispanic whites. Homicide rates for non-Hispanic whites are highest in the South. Thus, if there is a southern subculture of violence, it affects non-Hispanic whites only. See Candice Nelsen, Jay Corzine, and Lin Huff-Corzine, "The Violent West Re-Examined," *Criminology* 32 (1994): 149–161; and Rebekah Chu, Craig Rivera, and Colin Loftin, "Herding and Homicide," *Social Forces* 78 (2000): 971–987.

44. Elijah Anderson, *Code of the Street* (New York: Norton, 1999). See also Anderson, "The Social Ecology of Youth Violence," in *Youth Violence*, ed. Michael Tonry and Mark H. Moore (vol. 24 of *Crime and Justice: A Review of Research*) (Chicago: University of Chicago Press, 1998), pp. 65–104. For an earlier such theory, see Lynn A. Curtis, *Violence, Race and Culture* (Lexington, MA: D. C. Heath, 1975).

45. A test involving a longitudinal sample of 720 African American adolescents from 259 neighborhoods found that adopting the street code aggravated the risk of violent victimization. Eric A Stewart, Christopher J. Schreck, and Ronald L. Simons, "'I Ain't Gonna Let No One Disrespect Me': Does the

Code of the Street Reduce or Increase Violent Victimization Among African American Adolescents?," *Journal of Research in Crime and Delinquency* 43 (2006): 427.

46. Anderson, "The Social Ecology," p. 102.

47. Ibid., p. 103.

48. Ross L. Matsueda, Rosemary Gartner, Irving Piliavin, and Michael Polakowski, "The Prestige of Criminal and Conventional Occupations," *American Sociological Review* 57 (1992): 752–770, at pp. 767–768. See also Thomas J. Bernard, "Angry Aggression Among the Truly Disadvantaged," *Criminology* 28 (1990): 73–96; Bernard focused more directly on the structural conditions underlying cultural beliefs. For other examples of the relationship between structure and subculture, see Karen Heimer, "Socioeconomic Status, Subcultural Definitions, and Violent Delinquency," *Social Forces* 75 (1997): 799–834; and John Hagan, "Deviance and Despair: Subcultural and Structural Linkages Between Delinquency and Despair in the Life Course," *Social Forces* 76 (1997): 119–134.

49. See Daniel Glaser, "Criminality Theories and Behavioral Images," *American Journal of Sociology* 61 (March 1956): 433–444; and C. R. Jeffery, "Criminal Behavior and Learning Theory," *Journal of Criminal Law, Criminology and Police Science* 56 (September 1965): 294–300.

50. Robert L. Burgess and Ronald L. Akers, "A Differential Association—Reinforcement Theory of Criminal Behavior," *Social Problems* 14 (Fall 1968): 128–147.

51. Ibid., p. 146.

52. Ibid., p. 140.

53. Ronald L. Akers, *Deviant Behavior: A Social Learning Approach* (Belmont, CA: Wadsworth, 1985), pp. 39–70.

54. Ronald L. Akers, *Criminological Theories* (Los Angeles: Roxbury, 1994), pp. 94–107. See also Akers, "Social Learning Theory," in *Explaining Criminals and Crime*, ed. Raymond Paternoster and Ronet Bachman (Los Angeles: Roxbury, 2001), pp. 192–210. For an extended discussion of the theory, see Akers, *Social Learning and Social Structure*.

55. Ronald L. Akers, Marvin D. Krohn, Lonn Lanza-Kaduce, and Marcia Radosevich, "Social Learning and Deviant Behavior," *American Sociological Review* 44 (1979): 636–655.

56. Ronald L. Akers, "Linking Sociology and Its Specialties," *Social Forces* 71 (1992): 1–16; and Akers, *Criminological Theories*, pp. 101–102.

57. Ronald L. Akers and Christine S. Sellers, *Criminological Theories*, 6th ed. (New York: Oxford University Press, 2013), p. 89.

58. E.g., Jennifer L. Klein and Danielle Tolson Cooper, "Deviant Cyber-Sexual Activities in Young Adults: Exploring Prevalence and Predictions Using In-Person Sexual Activities and Social Learning Theory," *Archives of Sexual Behavior* 48 (2019): 619–630; Analisa Gagnon, "Extending Social Learning Theory to Explain Victimization Among Gang and Ex-Gang Offenders," *International Journal of Offender Therapy & Comparative Criminology* 62 (2018): 4124–4141; Seed Kabiri, John K. Cochran, Bernadette J. Stewart, Mahmoud

Sharepour, Mohammad Rahmati, and Syede Massomeh Shadmanfaat, "Doping Among Professional Athletes in Iran: A Test of Akers's Social Learning Theory," *International Journal of Offender Therapy & Comparative Criminology* 62 (2018): 1384–1410; Jason A. Ford and Julianne Ong, "Non-medical use of Prescription Stimulants for Academic Purposes Among College Students: A Test of Social Learning Theory," *Drug and Alcohol Dependence* 144 (2014): 279–282; Michael Capece, Lonn Lanza-Kaduce, "Binge Drinking Among College Students: A Partial Test of Akers' Social Structure-Social Learning Theory," *American Journal of Criminal Justice* 38 (2013): 503–519. For a discussion of a variety of studies on Akers's theory, see Ronald Akers, Christine S. Sellers, and Wesley G. Jennings, *Criminological Theories: Introduction, Application, and Evaluation*, 7th ed. (New York: Oxford University Press, 2016).

59. Travis C. Pratt, Francis T. Cullen, Christine S. Sellers, L. Thomas Winfree Jr., Tamara D. Madensen, Leah E. Daigle, Noelle E. Fearn, and Jacinta M. Gau, "The Empirical Status of Social Learning Theory: A Meta-Analysis," *Justice Quarterly* 27 (2010): 765–802.

60. Ibid., pp. 771–778.

61. Ibid., p. 782.

62. Ibid., p. 789.

63. Lonnie Athens, *Violent Criminal Acts and Actors: A Symbolic Interactionist Study* (London: Routledge and Kegan Paul, 1980); *The Creation of Dangerous Violent Criminals* (Urbana: University of Illinois Press, 1992); and *Violent Criminal Acts and Actors Revisited* (Chicago: University of Illinois Press, 1997).

64. Richard Rhodes, *Why They Kill: The Discoveries of a Maverick Criminologist* (New York: Vintage Books, 1999).

65. See Lonnie Athens, "'Radical' and 'Symbolic' Interactionism: Demarcating Their Boarders," *Radical Interactionism on the Rise: Studies in Symbolic Interaction* 41 (2013): 1–24.

66. Rhodes, *Why They Kill*, pp. 112–124.

67. Ibid., pp. 125–127.

68. Ibid., pp. 127–132.

69. Ibid., pp. 132–135.

70. Ibid., pp. 69–73. Athens called these interpretations "physically defensive," "frustrative," and "malefic."

71. Ibid., p. 58. See also Lonnie Athens, "Radical Interactionism: Going Beyond Mead," *Journal for the Theory of Social Behavior* 37 (2007): 137–165, where he substituted his "phantom community" for Mead's "generalized other" as a means of explaining people's varied actions in situations of blocked aspirations. As Rhodes noted on p. 58 of *Why They Kill*, Mead's idea of a "generalized other" in which people interpret situations in a collective manner, based upon a shared set of meanings, had given "Athens years of grief," so he came up with the alternate concept of the "phantom community."

72. Rhodes, *Why They Kill*, pp. 79–95.

73. A summary of this evolution is presented in Lonnie Athens, "Violentization: A Relatively Singular Theory of Violent Crime," *Deviant Behavior* 36 (2015): 625–639.

74. Ibid., p. 631.
75. Ibid., p. 627–630.
76. Ibid., pp. 632–633.
77. Lonnie Athens, "Applying Violentization: From Theory to Praxis," *Victims and Offenders* 12 (2017): 497–522, p. 5.
78. Ibid., pp. 8–12.
79. Ibid., pp. 17–20.
80. Aviva Twersky Glasner, "Lonnie Athens Revisited: The Social Construction of Violence," *Aggression and Behavior* 18 (2013): 281–285, p. 283.
81. But see G. R. Jarjoura and R. Triplett, "From Violent Offenders to Dangerous Violent Criminals: A Test of Athens' Theory," *Sociology of Crime, Law, and Deviance* 4 (2003): 147–173.
82. Ian O'Donnell, "A New Paradigm for Understanding Violence? Testing the Limits of Lonnie Athens's Theory," *British Journal of Criminology* 43 (2003): 750–771.
83. Mark A. Winton, "Violentization Theory and Genocide," *Homicide Studies* 15 (2011): 363–381.
84. Lonnie H. Athens, *The Creation of Dangerous Violent Criminals*, 2nd ed. (New York: Transaction Publishers, 2017), pp. 103–153.
85. O'Donnell, "A New Paradigm for Understanding Violence?," p. 751.
86. Jack Katz, *Seductions of Crime: Moral and Sensual Attractions in Doing Evil* (New York: Basic Books, 1988).
87. Ibid., p. 9.
88. Ibid.
89. Ibid., p. 218.
90. Charles R. Tittle, *Control Balance: Toward a General Theory of Deviance* (Boulder, CO: Westview Press, 1995), p. 279.
91. Clifford Shaw, *The Jackroller* (1930), *The Natural History of a Delinquent Career* (1931), and *Brothers in Crime* (1938), all published by University of Chicago Press, Chicago.
92. Edwin H. Sutherland, *The Professional Thief* (Chicago: University of Chicago Press, 1937).
93. Donald R. Cressey, *Other People's Money: A Study in the Social Psychology of Embezzlement* (Montclair, NJ: Patterson Smith, 1973). This is a reprint edition with a new introduction by the author.
94. Howard S. Becker, *Outsiders—Studies in the Sociology of Deviance* (New York: Free Press of Glencoe, 1963).
95. Ned Polsky, *Hustlers, Beats, and Others*, rev. ed. (New York: Lyons Press, 1998).
96. See Jeff Ferrell, Mark S. Hamm, Patricia A. Adler, and Peter Adler, eds., *Ethnography at the Edge: Crime, Deviance and Field Research* (Boston: Northeastern University Press, 1998).
97. Patricia A. Adler, *Wheeling and Dealing: An Ethnography of an Upper-Level Drug Dealing and Smuggling Community*, 2nd ed. (New York: Columbia University Press, 1993).
98. Kenneth Tunnell, *Choosing Crime* (Chicago: Nelson-Hall, 1992).

99. Richard T. Wright and Scott H. Decker, *Burglars on the Job: Street Life and Residential Break-Ins* (1994), and *Armed Robbers in Action: Stick-ups and Street Culture* (1997), both published by Northeastern University Press, Boston.

100. Bruce A. Jacobs, *Dealing Crack: The Social World of Streetcorner Selling* (Boston: Northeastern University Press, 1999).

101. Bruce A. Jacobs, *Robbing Drug Dealers: Violence Beyond the Law* (New York: Aldine de Gruyter, 2000).

102. Jeff Ferrell, "Criminological Verstehen: Inside the Immediacy of Crime," *Justice Quarterly* 14(1997): 1–23. On pp. 4–7, he describes his participant observation of nongang graffiti artists, which culminated in his arrest and appearance in court. Wright and Decker (*Burglars on the Job*, p. 28), in contrast, obtained a prior agreement from the police not to interfere with their work.

103. Charles Horton Cooley, *Human Nature and the Social Order* (New York: Scribner, 1902).

104. Frank Tannenbaum, *Crime and the Community* (Boston: Ginn, 1938).

105. Ibid., p. 20.

106. Edwin M. Lemert, *Social Pathology* (New York: McGraw-Hill, 1951); see also Lemert, *Human Deviance, Social Problems, and Social Control* (Englewood Cliffs, NJ: Prentice-Hall, 1967).

107. Lemert, *Human Deviance*, pp. 17, 40.

108. Lemert, *Social Pathology*, pp. 75–76; and *Human Deviance*, pp. 40–64.

109. Samuel Yochelson and Stanton E. Samenow, *The Criminal Personality*, vol. 1 (New York: Jason Aronson, 1976), p. 19.

110. Mary Cameron Owen, *The Booster and the Snitch* (New York: Free Press, 1964), pp. 159, 161, 168.

111. Donald R. Cressey, *Other People's Money: A Study of the Social Psychology of Embezzlement* (Glencoe, IL: Free Press, 1953).

112. William A. Westley, "Violence and the Police," *American Journal of Sociology* 59 (July 1953): 34–41.

113. William J. Chambliss and Robert B. Seidman, *Law, Order and Power* (Reading, MA: Addison-Wesley, 1971), p. 71.

114. Harold Garfinkel, "Conditions of Successful Degradation Ceremonies," *American Journal of Sociology* 61, no. 5 (1965): 420–424.

115. Becker, *Outsiders*, pp. 32–33. See also Kai T. Erikson, "Notes on the Sociology of Deviance," *Social Problems* 9 (Spring 1962): 311. An example would be Ray's argument that a cured heroin addict relapses in part because other people continue to treat him as an addict. See Marsh B. Ray, "The Cycle of Abstinence and Relapse among Heroin Addicts," *Social Problems* 9 (Fall 1961): 132–140.

116. Becker, *Outsiders*, pp. 34–35.

117. Ibid., pp. 37–39.

118. Ronald L. Akers, "Problems in the Sociology of Deviance: Social Definitions and Behavior," *Social Forces* 46 (1967): 455–465.

119. Franklin E. Zimring and Gordon J. Hawkins, *Deterrence* (Chicago: University of Chicago Press, 1973), pp. 190–194.
120. Charles R. Tittle, "Labelling and Crime: An Empirical Evaluation," in *The Labelling of Deviance—Evaluating a Perspective*, ed. Walter R. Gove (New York: John Wiley, 1975), pp. 181–203.
121. George B. Vold, *Theoretical Criminology* (New York: Oxford University Press, 1958), p. 202; see also the 2nd ed. prepared by Thomas J. Bernard, 1979, pp. 247–248. For a similar argument, see Matsueda, "The Current State of Differentiation Theory," pp. 298–299.
122. Edwin H. Sutherland, "White Collar Criminality," *American Sociological Review* 5 (February 1940): 1–12; Sutherland, "Is 'White Collar Crime' Crime?" *American Sociological Review* 10 (April 1945): 132–139; and Sutherland, *White Collar Crime*.
123. Matsueda, Gartner, Piliavin, and Polakowski, "The Prestige of Criminal and Conventional Occupations," pp. 767–768. For the argument that beliefs have no direct causal impact on criminal behavior, see Kornhauser, *Social Sources of Delinquency*, pp. 207–210.

CHAPTER 10

Control Theories

Many theories of criminal behavior assume that people naturally obey the law if left to their own devices and argue that there are special forces—either biological, psychological, or social—that drive people to commit crime. Control theories take the opposite approach. They assume that all people naturally would commit crimes if left to their own devices. The key question, then, is why most people do not commit crimes. Control theories answer this question by focusing on special "controlling" forces that restrain the person from committing crimes. These forces break down in certain situations, resulting in crime and other "uncontrolled" behaviors. Thus, individuals are said to commit crime because of the weakness of forces restraining them from doing so, not because of the strength of forces driving them to do so.

This chapter examines a number of sociological theories that take the control perspective and are described as control theories. These theories are especially important as explanations of delinquency, since most of the research supporting them has been done with juvenile populations. Control theories, however, may also be used to explain adult criminality.

EARLY CONTROL THEORIES: REISS TO NYE

In 1951, Albert J. Reiss published an article in which he examined a number of factors related to the control perspective to see if they might be used to predict the revocation of probation among juvenile offenders.[1] Reiss reviewed the official court records of 1,110 white male juvenile probationers between the ages of eleven and seventeen. He found that the revocation of probation was more likely when the juvenile was psychiatrically diagnosed as having weak ego or superego controls and when the psychiatrist recommended either intensive psychotherapy in the community or treatment in a closed institution. Reiss argued that such diagnoses and recommendations were based on an assessment of the juvenile's "personal controls"—that is, the ability to refrain from meeting needs in ways that conflicted with the norms and rules of the community. In addition, he found that probation was more likely to be revoked when juveniles did not regularly attend school and when they were described as behavioral problems by school authorities. Reiss argued that these were a measure of the acceptance or submission of the juvenile to "social controls"—that is, the control of socially approved institutions.[2]

Reiss's theory influenced later control theories, but his findings in support of that theory were quite weak. A variety of factors related to family and community controls over the juvenile did not predict probation revocation. The strongest associations were found between probation revocation and the diagnoses and recommendations of the psychiatrists. Reiss argued that the failure of personal controls explained both phenomena, thus accepting at face value the theoretical framework of the psychiatrists. But such an explanation is tautological unless it is supported by some additional evidence about the strength or weakness of personal controls.[3] The association of probation revocation with truancy and school problems was much weaker and can be explained from other perspectives besides control theory.

In 1957 Jackson Toby introduced the concept of "stakes in conformity"—that is, how much a person has to lose when he or she breaks the law.[4] He argued that all youths are tempted to break the law, but some youths risk much more than others when they give in to these temptations. Youths who do well in school not only risk being punished for breaking the law, but also jeopardize their future careers. Thus, they have high "stakes in conformity." In contrast, youths who do poorly in school risk only being punished for their offense, since their future prospects are already dim. Thus, they have less to lose when they break the law—that is, they have lower stakes in conformity. Toby also argued that peer support for deviance can develop in communities that have a large number of youths with low stakes in conformity, so that the community develops even higher crime rates than would be expected by considering the stakes in conformity of the individual youths. Conversely, youths in suburbs who have low stakes in conformity normally obtain no support from their peers for delinquency. Thus, these youths may be unhappy, but they usually do not become delinquent.

Toby focused on how well the youths did in school, but he stated: "In all fairness, it should be remembered that the basis for school adjustment is laid in the home and the community."[5] The following year, F. Ivan Nye published a study that focused on the family as the single most important source of social control for adolescents.[6] He argued that most delinquent behavior was the result of insufficient social control and that delinquent behavior "caused" by positive factors was relatively rare.[7] Social control was used as a broad term that included direct controls imposed by means of restrictions and punishments, internal control exercised through conscience, indirect control related to affectional identification with parents and other noncriminal persons, and the availability of legitimate means to satisfy needs.[8] With respect to the final type of social control, Nye argued that "if all the needs of the individual could be met adequately and without delay, without violating laws, there would be no point in such violation, and a minimum of internal, indirect, and direct control would suffice to secure conformity."

Nye surveyed 780 boys and girls in grades nine through twelve in three towns in the state of Washington to test the theory. Included in the survey were a wide variety of questions on family life, as well as seven items that were intended to measure delinquency. These seven items were skipped school without a legitimate excuse; defied parents' authority to their face; took things worth less than $2; bought or drank beer, wine, or liquor (including at home); purposely damaged or destroyed public or private property; and had sexual relations with a person of the opposite sex.[9] On the basis of how often they said they had committed these acts since the beginning of elementary school, about one-fourth of the youths were placed in a "most delinquent" group, and the remainder were placed in a "least delinquent" group.[10]

Nye found that youths in the most delinquent group were more likely to be given either complete freedom or no freedom at all; to have larger sums of money available; to be rejecting of their parents and to disapprove of their parents' appearance; and to describe their parents as being seldom cheerful and often moody, nervous, irritable, difficult to please, and dishonest and as taking things out on the youths when things went wrong. Youths whose mothers worked outside the home and who were rejected by their parents were slightly more likely to fall in the most delinquent group. In contrast, youths in the least delinquent group were significantly more likely to come from families that attended church regularly, did not move often, and were from rural areas. They were likely to be the oldest or only child, from a small family, to have a favorable attitude toward their parents' disciplinary techniques and toward recreation with their parents, to agree with their parents on the importance of a variety of values, to be satisfied with the allocation of money by their parents, and to get information and advice concerning dating and religion from their parents. In all, Nye tested 313 relationships between youths and their parents. He found that 139 of them were consistent with his control theory, 167 were not significant, and only 7 were inconsistent with it.[11]

Nye's contribution to the development of control theory was quite significant because of the theory he proposed and because he undertook a broad empirical test of the theory. His findings in support of the theory are impressive, but one can question the extent to which they apply to groups that are normally referred to as delinquents. Nye's sample did not include any youths from large cities and included only a negligible number of non–European American youths or youths with foreign-born parents. Toby pointed out that "the group which Professor Nye calls 'most delinquent' would be considered nondelinquents by many criminologists."[12] Also, because the questionnaire was administered in high schools, the sample would not include any youths aged fifteen or younger who were more than one year behind in school (they would still be in elementary school) or any youths aged sixteen or over who had legally dropped out of school. Only two behaviors on the questionnaire constituted criminal offenses: taking things worth less than $2 and purposely damaging or destroying public or private property. Thus, the results of Nye's study may be interpreted as describing the effect of family relationships on minor delinquent activities among basically nondelinquent youths.

Toby also pointed out that Nye's research apparently assumed that the same causal processes would be involved with more serious delinquents, but that other researchers might very well disagree with the assumption. Finally, Toby noted that a response bias among the youths answering the questionnaire could account for many of Nye's findings. Youths who were more willing to report their delinquent activities may also have been more willing to describe the less desirable aspects of their family life. Other youths may have both underreported their delinquent activities and described their family life in more positive terms. Thus, the study would show that better family relationships are associated with fewer delinquent activities. Toby concluded that Nye's results should be interpreted with great caution.

MATZA'S DELINQUENCY AND DRIFT

While the early control theories just described have been soundly criticized, they provided the basic concepts and framework for the modern control theories of David Matza and Travis Hirschi. These control theories present a strong challenge to the more common view that juvenile delinquency is caused by special biological, psychological, or social factors.

In *Delinquency and Drift*, Matza stated that traditional theories of delinquency emphasize constraint and differentiation: delinquents are said to be different from nondelinquents in some fundamental way, and that difference constrains them to commit their delinquencies.[13] In some theories, the differences are said to be biological or psychological, and the constraint takes the form of compulsion. In other theories the differences are said to be social, and the constraint takes the form of commitment to delinquent values. Matza maintained that these theories predicted and explained too much delinquency. Most of the time, delinquents are engaged in routine, law-abiding behaviors just like everyone else, but if you believe the picture painted in these theories, delinquents should be committing delinquencies all the time. In addition, these theories cannot account for the fact that most delinquents "age out" of delinquency and settle down to law-abiding lives when they reach late adolescence or early adulthood. The factors that supposedly explained the delinquency are still present (for example, the lack of legitimate opportunities), but the delinquency itself disappears.[14]

Matza proposed an alternate image for delinquents that emphasizes freedom and similarity, rather than constraint and differentiation. That image is drift.[15] Drift is said to occur in areas of the social structure in which control has been loosened, freeing the delinquent to respond to whatever conventional or criminal forces happen to come along. The positive causes of delinquency, then, "may be accidental or unpredictable from the point of view of any theoretical frame of reference, and deflection from the delinquent path may be similarly accidental or unpredictable."[16] Within the context of such an image, a theory of delinquency would not attempt to describe its positive causes, but rather would describe "the conditions that make delinquent drift possible and probable," that is, the conditions under which social control is loosened. Matza did not deny that there were "committed" and "compulsive" delinquents, as described by the traditional theories. However, he argued that the vast majority of delinquents were "drifters" who were neither.

Matza's criticism of traditional theories of delinquency focused on the sociological argument that their behaviors are generated by commitment to delinquent values. Matza argued that delinquents portray themselves this way because they are unwilling to appear "chicken."[17] But private interviews revealed that delinquents do not value delinquent behavior itself. Rather, they described the behavior as morally wrong but argued that there are extenuating circumstances, so that their own delinquent actions are "guiltless."[18] The delinquent's portrayal of these circumstances is similar to, but much broader than, the extenuating circumstances defined in the law related to intent, accident, self-defense, and insanity. Thus, delinquents do not reject conventional moral values but "neutralize" them in a wide variety of circumstances so that they are able to commit delinquent actions and still consider themselves guiltless. This sense of irresponsibility is reinforced by the ideology of the juvenile court, which declares that juveniles are not responsible for their actions.

The sense of irresponsibility is the immediate condition that makes delinquent drift possible, but the delinquent is prepared to accept the sense of irresponsibility by a pervasive sense of injustice.[19] Just as the sense of irresponsibility is derived from a broad interpretation of conventional legal standards for extenuating circumstances, so the sense of injustice is derived from a broad interpretation of conventional legal standards for justice. For example, by conventional legal standards of justice, it is necessary to prove beyond a reasonable doubt that a given individual has committed a given criminal act. Delinquents use excessively legalistic standards to argue that "they didn't prove it." Thus, they may passionately argue that they were unjustly treated even though they admit that they committed the act.

Once the moral bind of the law has been loosened by the sense of irresponsibility and the sense of injustice, the juvenile is in a state of drift and is then free to choose among a variety of actions, some delinquent, some lawful.

At this point, Matza suggested that there are some "positive" causes of delinquency in the sense that there are reasons why the juvenile chooses delinquent, as opposed to lawful, behaviors.[20] The juvenile feels that he exercises no control over the circumstances of his life and the destiny awaiting him. In such a mood he moves to make something happen, to experience himself as a cause of events. This mood of desperation provides the motivation to commit new acts of delinquency. Once those actions have been committed, he is motivated to continue committing them because he has learned the moral rationalizations that are necessary to consider himself guiltless and the technical means to carry out the offenses. Sykes and Matza categorized these rationalizations into five "techniques of neutralization": denial of responsibility ("It wasn't my fault"), denial of injury ("They can afford it"), denial of victims ("They had it coming"), condemnation of condemners ("Everyone is crooked anyway"), and appeal to higher loyalties ("I did it for the gang").[21]

HIRSCHI'S SOCIAL CONTROL THEORY

The theorist who is most closely identified with control theory is Travis Hirschi. In his 1969 book titled *Causes of Delinquency*, Hirschi argued that it is not necessary to explain the motivation for delinquency, since "we are all animals and thus all naturally capable of committing criminal acts."[22] He then proposed a comprehensive control theory that individuals who were tightly bonded to social groups, such as the family, the school, and peers, would be less likely to commit delinquent acts.[23] The most important element of the social bond is attachment—that is, affection for and sensitivity to others. Attachment is said to be the basic element necessary for the internalization of values and norms and thus is related to Reiss's conception of personal controls and Nye's conceptions of internal and indirect controls. A second element is commitment, the rational investment one has in conventional society and the risk one takes when engaging in deviant behavior. Commitment is similar to what Toby described as a "stake in conformity." The third element is involvement in conventional activities. This variable is based on the commonsense observation that "idle hands are the devil's workshop" and that being busy restricts opportunities for delinquent activities. The final element of the social bond is belief. Matza argued that delinquents had conventional moral beliefs but neutralized them with excuses so that they could commit delinquent acts without feeling guilty. Hirschi, in contrast, contended that "there is variation in the extent to which people believe they should obey the rules of society, and, furthermore, that the less a person believes he should obey the rules, the more likely he is to violate them."[24] Thus, Matza's theory emphasized that delinquents are tied to the conventional moral order and must free themselves from it to commit delinquent acts, while Hirschi's theory assumed that they are free from the conventional order to begin with.

Like Nye, Hirschi tested his theory with a self-report survey. The sample consisted of about 4,000 junior and senior high school youths from a county in the San Francisco Bay area. The questionnaire contained a variety of items related to family, school, and peer relations, as well as six items that served as an index of delinquency.[25] Three of the six items referred to stealing (things worth less than $2, things worth between $2 and $50, and things worth more than $50), while the other three asked whether the youth had ever "taken a car for a ride without the owner's permission," "banged up something that did not belong to you on purpose," and "beaten up on anyone or hurt anyone on purpose" (not counting fights with a brother or sister). Youths were given one point for each of the six offenses they reported committing in the past year, regardless of how often they reported committing it.[26] Hirschi also used school records and official police records as data for the study.

Hirschi was particularly concerned with testing the adequacy of his theory against theories that argued that the motivation for delinquency was to be found in social strain (such as Merton's, Cohen's, or Cloward and Ohlin's) and theories that explained delinquency in terms of cultural or group influence (such as Sutherland's or Miller's).[27] Each of these three types of theories explains many well-known facts about delinquency, such as that delinquents do poorly in school, but each proposes a different chain of causation. Much of Hirschi's book was devoted to testing the different chains of causation that are found in the three types of theories.

Hirschi reported that in general, there was no relationship between reported delinquent acts and social class, except that children from the poorest families were slightly more likely to be delinquent.[28] In addition, he found only minimal racial differences in self-reported delinquency, although the groups' official arrest rates were substantially different.[29] Hirschi concluded that these findings were most difficult to reconcile with strain theories, since those were explicitly class-based theories.[30]

Hirschi then analyzed the effects of attachment to parents, schools, and peers on reported delinquent acts. He found that regardless of race or class and regardless of the delinquency of their friends, boys who were more closely attached to their parents were less likely to report committing delinquent acts than were those who were less closely attached.[31] This finding is consistent with control theory but inconsistent with cultural theories, where attachment to deviant friends or deviant parents would theoretically be associated with increased reporting of delinquency. Hirschi also found that youths who reported more delinquent acts were more likely to have poor verbal scores on the Differential Aptitude Test, to get poor grades in school, to care little about teachers' opinions, to dislike school, and to reject school authority. He argued that these findings are consistent with control theory, since such boys would be free from the controlling forces of schools. However, he argued that they were inconsistent with strain theories, such as Cohen's, since the most strained youths would be those who did poorly but who continued to care about success in school. Youths who did poorly and did not care about school success would not be strained.[32] He also found that boys who reported more delinquent acts were less attached to their peers than were boys who reported fewer delinquent acts. Again Hirschi argued that this finding is consistent with control theory, since attachment to peers would be conducive to delinquency only if those peers valued delinquent behavior. However, it is inconsistent with cultural theories, where the assumption is made that the motivation for delinquency is passed through intimate, personal relationships. Hirschi found that association with delinquent companions could increase delinquent behavior, but only when social controls had been weakened. Youths with large stakes in conformity are unlikely to have delinquent friends, and when they do have such friends, they are unlikely to commit delinquent acts themselves. For youths with low stakes in conformity, however, the greater the exposure to "criminal influences," the more delinquent activities they reported.[33]

Having examined the effect of attachment on reported delinquent acts, Hirschi examined the effects of the other three elements of his theory. He found that the educational and occupational aspirations of delinquents are lower than those of nondelinquents, as are the educational and occupational expectations. This finding is consistent with control theory, since youths with low aspirations and low expectations have little commitment to conformity—that is, they risk little by committing delinquent acts. In contrast, the findings are inconsistent with strain theories, since, according to those theories, youths with high aspirations but low expectations should be the most strained and therefore the most delinquent. Hirschi found that "the higher the aspiration, the lower the rate of delinquency, regardless of the student's expectations."[34] Hirschi also found that youths who worked, dated, spent time watching television, reading books, or playing games were more likely to report delinquencies.[35] This finding was the opposite of what was expected from his theory, since these behaviors represent involvement in conventional activities. Hirschi did find, however, that boys who spent less time on homework, reported being bored, and spent more time talking to friends and riding around in cars were more likely to report delinquent acts. These can be considered measures of the lack of involvement in conventional activities. Finally, Hirschi found a strong correlation between reported delinquent activities and agreement with the statement "It is alright to get around the law if you can get away with it."[36] He took this to be a measure of the extent to which boys believe they should obey the law. He also found support for the neutralizing beliefs that Matza described as freeing the delinquent from the moral bind of the law, although he argued that "the assumption that delinquent acts come before the justifying beliefs is the more plausible causal ordering with respect to many of the techniques of neutralization."[37] Finally, Hirschi found no support for a separate lower-class culture as described by Miller. Hirschi found instead that these beliefs are held by academically incompetent youths, whether lower or middle class, and that academically competent youths, whether lower or middle class, held what are often called "middle-class values." Thus, he concluded that lower-class values are not cultural in that they are not transmitted as a valued heritage. Rather, they "are available to all members of American society more or less equally; they are accepted or rejected to the extent they are consistent or inconsistent with one's realistic position in that society."[38] Hence, Hirschi believed that "the class of the father may be unimportant, but the class of the child most decidedly is not."[39]

ASSESSING SOCIAL CONTROL THEORY

A large number of empirical studies have attempted to test social control theory. Most of these studies have concluded that social control theory is supported by the data, and they most frequently have found support for two of Hirschi's four variables: attachment and commitment.[40] Some support for beliefs has also been found, but whether this finding represents weak conventional beliefs (as proposed by Hirschi) or strong deviant beliefs (as proposed by learning theorists) is less clear. The statement in Hirschi's own study, "It is alright to get around the law if you can get away with it," illustrates the problem. Hirschi argued that the statement represents a weak conventional belief, but learning theorists have argued that it represents a strong deviant belief.

Neither Hirschi's study nor later studies have found much support for Hirschi's fourth variable, involvement in conventional activities. Instead, studies generally have found that youths with more conventional involvement (e.g., participating in organized sports, holding a job) commit more delinquency than do those with less conventional involvement. Hirschi found this in his own study, and he made the following comment on his surprising finding:[41]

> The difficulty, it seems, is that the definition of delinquency used here is not the definition that makes the involvement hypothesis virtually tautological. When Cohen, for example, says the delinquent gang "makes enormous demands upon the boy's time," he is of course not saying that delinquency as here defined takes an enormous amount of the boy's time. In fact, as defined, delinquency requires very little time: the most delinquent boys in the sample may not have devoted more than a few hours in the course of a year to the acts that define them as delinquent.

Hirschi's comment raises a question about the adequacy of his theory: it may explain delinquency in boys who spend only a few hours per year engaged in it, but does it explain delinquency among the boys that Cohen described? Hirschi admitted that there were few serious delinquents in his sample. In fact, he stated that other criminologists might hold that "delinquents are so obviously underrepresented among those completing the questionnaires that the results need not be taken seriously."[42] He then argued that if more serious delinquents had been included in the sample, his results would have been even stronger. But Hirschi's argument is valid only if the same causal processes are at work for seriously delinquent youths as for minor delinquents. In contrast, Matza described different causal processes: minor delinquents were described as "drifters" (i.e., freed from controls), while serious delinquents were described as committed or compulsive. If Matza is correct, then the inclusion of more serious delinquents in Hirschi's sample would have weakened Hirschi's results.[43]

This problem is related to the assumption of control theory that criminality and delinquency consist of "naturally motivated" behaviors that do not need any other explanation. It is relatively easy to think of the minor offenses in Hirschi's study as being naturally motivated, requiring no other explanation than that they are "fun."[44] But explaining delinquency as fun is not as appealing when one considers serious violent crime or the gang activities that make "enormous demands on the boys' time," as described by Cohen.

In 1993, Kempf reviewed seventy-one studies on control theory.[45] She reported that most of these studies found correlations between delinquent behavior and one or another of Hirschi's variables. However, the variables themselves were operationalized in many different ways. In addition, when one looks at each of the four variables individually, the results are mixed and inconsistent. For example, attachment is the most frequently tested variable and the most frequently found to be correlated with delinquent behavior. However, the different tests have had different objects of attachment (e.g., parents, mother, peers, or schools), and the results have ranged from no relation at all to a strong relation. Kempf concluded that these were "essentially separate studies which have little relation to each other and fail to build on experience. Thus, the research reveals little about the viability of social control as a scientific theory."[46] The research conducted since Kempf's 1993 review has tended to support her conclusion.[47] Hirschi himself has now abandoned his social control theory and, with Michael Gottfredson, has presented a new theory that focuses on what he calls "self-control." The importance of social bonds is still relevant to criminologists, though. For example, Hirschi reincorporated them into a redefined definition of self-control, as discussed a bit later in this chapter, and social bonds are well integrated into Sampson and Laub's age-graded theory of informal social control, which is addressed in Chapter 14.

GOTTFREDSON AND HIRSCHI'S *A GENERAL THEORY OF CRIME*

In 1990, Michael Gottfredson and Travis Hirschi presented a theory that claimed to explain all types of crime and delinquency. The main concept in the theory is low self-control.[48] Self-control theory is a single concept, in contrast to the multiple social controls (attachments, involvements, commit-ments, and beliefs) in Hirschi's 1969 theory. In addition, self-control is said to be internal to the individual, whereas social controls largely reside in the external social environment. Finally, self-control theory focuses attention on events in early childhood, long before crime and delinquency manifest themselves. In contrast, Hirschi's social control theory focuses on events and processes that transpire at the same time as the delinquency. In the new theory, social controls are relevant to explaining criminal behavior only to the extent that they influence self-control, which is instilled in individuals by around age eight and remains relatively constant after that.

Gottfredson and Hirschi first made some assertions about "the charac-teristics of ordinary crimes": they are said to be acts of force or fraud that involve simple and immediate gratification of desires but few long-term benefits, are exciting and risky but require little skill or planning, and gener-ally produce few benefits for the offender while causing pain and suffering for the victim.[49] Second, they described the characteristics of people who would commit these kinds of actions: they "will tend to be impulsive, insen-sitive, physical (as opposed to mental), risk-taking, short-sighted, and non-verbal."[50] These characteristics not only lead them to engage in a variety of "ordinary crimes" but result in other similarities in behavior—for example, these people will tend to smoke and drink heavily and to be involved in many accidents.[51] Third, Gottfredson and Hirschi argued:[52] "Since these traits can be identified prior to the age of responsibility for crime, since there is considerable tendency for these traits to come together in the same people, and since the traits tend to persist through life, it seems reasonable to con-sider them as comprising a stable construct useful in the explanation of crime." They called this stable construct "low self-control." Fourth, Gott-fredson and Hirschi contended that ineffective child-rearing is the most important contributor to low self-control.[53] Adequate child-rearing, which results in high self-control in the child, occurs when the child's behavior is monitored and any deviant behavior is immediately recognized and pun-ished. Essentially, external controls on the child's behavior are eventually internalized by the child in a process described as "socialization." An addi-tional source of socialization, especially important for those who do not receive adequate socialization through their families, is the school.

Gottfredson and Hirschi then argued that low self-control explains many of the known relationships between delinquency and other factors. For example, they contended that the relationship between delinquent peers and delinquency is explained by the fact that juveniles with low self-control are likely to seek out others with low-self control as a peer group.[54] On the rela-tionship between delinquency and poor school performance, they argued that individuals who lack self-control do not perform well in school and therefore tend to leave or avoid it.[55] Finally, those with low self-control have difficulty keeping jobs, which explains any relationship between unemploy-ment and criminal behavior.[56]

Gottfredson and Hirschi argued that self-control is relatively constant in the individual after the age of about eight, but they recognized that there may be a great deal of change in the rates at which individuals commit crime.[57] These variations cannot, within their theory, be explained by changes in the person's self-control, since self-control stays constant throughout the person's life. So Gottfredson and Hirschi contended that variations in crime are explained by variation in opportunities for different types of criminal and noncriminal behaviors. For example, in a community with few opportunities for property crime, people with low self-control will engage in little property crime but will engage in other sorts of low self-control behavior.

ASSESSING GOTTFREDSON AND HIRSCHI'S GENERAL THEORY

A General Theory of Crime has generated some heated discussion among criminologists, along with a large number of empirical studies.[58] The studies have used different ways of measuring low self-control, but most have considered it as attitudes related to impulsivity, risk-seeking, physical activities, self-centeredness, temper, and simple tasks. These six attitudes form a scale created by Grasmick and his colleagues, which is the most common approach taken to measuring low self-control.[59] Much controversy has surrounded the question of whether this scale is unidimensional (meaning that all six attitudinal dimensions feed a single latent trait) or multidimensional (meaning that the six dimensions have independent impacts on crime and delinquency and should be considered separately). Although to some extent this is a question of semantics, the general consensus is now that the scale is multidimensional.[60] One approach taken by researchers is to test the theory using both the unidimensional scale and its separate components.[61] Other researchers have modified the Grasmick scale to their suiting,[62] and still others have tested the theory using a scale that is behavioral rather than attitudinal.[63]

The behaviors explained by low self-control have included various forms of delinquency and adult criminal behavior, as well as what Gottfredson and Hirschi described as "analogous behaviors": cutting classes, drinking, smoking, gambling, drunk driving, and being prone to accidents. All the studies have found at least some support for Gottfredson and Hirschi's theory, and some have found fairly strong support.[64] This support has extended across gender, race, and nationality.[65] However, there have been few attempts to control for alternate explanations from other theories. One exception is Baron's study of self-control among homeless street youths in Vancouver, Canada. Baron's study examined the impact of self-control, deviant peers and values, and strain variables (monetary dissatisfaction and relative deprivation) on crime and drug use. In support of Gottfredson and Hirshci's arguments, Baron found that low self-control predicted deviant peers and values and status as unemployed and homeless. However, the strain variables were not related to low self-control, and after self-control was controlled for, still impacted crime to some extent. Moreover, low self-control could not explain all the impact of deviant peers and values on crime and drug use, for after self-control was controlled for, these variables still had a moderate to strong impact on both crime and drug use.[66] Baron's research shows that low self-control is an important predictor of crime but not necessarily the sole predictor. Likewise, Welch and his colleagues found that both self-control and interpersonal social support (the extent to which individuals have people close to them, not counting those with whom they live, that they can rely on to share problems with and get help from) independently predicted deviance and that the impact of self-control and social support was roughly of the same magnitude.[67]

Perhaps the theory's most controversial argument is that self-control is essentially stable by the age of eight to ten. Sampson and Laub have refuted this contention, arguing that because the relationship between social control and self-control shouldn't diminish over time, if social control can be altered in adulthood, self-control should be as well.[68] Although research to date has not tested whether self-control can be changed in adulthood, one recent study by Na and Paternoster did find that a childhood intervention had lasting effects on self-control until at least age seventeen. The evaluation involved family-school partnerships providing parents/caregivers with effective teaching, and assigned inner-city Baltimore families of high-risk first-graders to either the intervention or a control group. It found that the children of caregivers improved in self-control more in the intervention group than the control, and further that their self-control continued to develop through the twelfth grade (age seventeen).[69] Also under assessment is the extent to which ineffective parental child-rearing practices are the major determinant of low self-control. According to Gottfredson and Hirschi, three aspects of child-rearing contribute to the development of self-control: monitoring and tracking the child's behavior, recognizing deviant behavior when it occurs, and consistently and proportionately punishing the behavior upon recognition.[70] According to the theory, not only should ineffective parenting be the main cause of low self-control, but ineffective parenting's entire impact on crime and deviance should operate through low self-control. The evidence has been mixed. For example, Unnever and his colleagues found that parental monitoring had substantial effects on deviance independent of low self-control and that attention-deficit/hyperactivity disorder (ADHD) predicted low self-control.[71] Wright and Beaver also linked ADHD to low self-control but concluded that "net genetic similarities within household, parental socialization techniques minimally influence the individual traits of their children."[72] Furthermore, Hay found that low self-control mediated only a quarter of the effect of monitoring and discipline on delinquency.[73] In support of Gottfredson and Hirschi's general theory, Nofziger found that mothers with low self-control generally employed parenting practices that produced children with low self-control.[74] Most likely, parenting variables have an impact on crime and delinquency not only through low self-control but through other avenues as well, such as social learning, general strain, control balance, social control, genetic, and biosocial theories.[75]

Gottfredson and Hirschi's theory also has been extensively criticized on theoretical grounds.[76] Perhaps the most frequent criticism, as well as the most potentially damaging, is that the theory is tautological.[77] According to Akers, the only way to determine whether people have low self-control is to see whether they engage in low self-control behaviors. But once they do, then their behaviors are explained by the low self-control.[78] Akers argued that until low self-control can be measured in some other way, the theory will remain tautological. Hirschi and Gottfredson, however, strongly rejected this criticism:[79]

> In our view, the charge of tautology is in fact a compliment; an assertion that we followed the path of logic in producing an internally consistent result. . . . We started with a conception of crime, and from it attempted to derive a conception of the offender. . . . What makes our theory peculiarly vulnerable to complaints about tautology is that we explicitly show the logical connections between our conception of the actor and the act, whereas many theorists leave this task to those interpreting or testing their theory. . . . In a comparative framework, the charge of tautology suggests that a theory that is nontautological is preferable. But what would such a theory look like? It would advance definitions of crime and of criminals that are independent of one another.

They went on to say that Akers misunderstood the concept of low self-control: "We see self-control as the barrier that stands between the actor and the obvious momentary benefits crime provides."

Other criticisms have challenged the generality of Gottfredson and Hirschi's theory, arguing that certain types of criminals, such as white-collar or organized criminals, do not have low self-control.[80] Gottfredson and Hirschi therefore devoted considerable effort to debunking these arguments. For example, they argued that "organized crime" is not really organized and that any apparent organization is short-lived and consists of unstable temporary alliances.[81] Furthermore, they claimed that the reason for the failure of many cooperative attempts at criminality is that the individuals involved lack self-control. They discounted the importance of organized drug dealing by arguing that for every successful organized effort, there are hundreds of failed efforts. Others have shown that conventional and white-collar crime may have more similarities than differences—for example, both can attract offenders who are sensation-seekers.[82]

Some criminologists have questioned how differential-opportunity structures may interact with low self-control to produce variations in crime rates. Barlow noted that the opportunity part of Gottfredson and Hirschi's theory is insufficiently developed and does not answer such questions.[83] Longshore and Turner found a relationship between low self-control and opportunity for crimes of fraud, but not for crimes of force.[84] Using a somewhat larger version of the same data set, Longshore found that both low self-control and criminal opportunity have an effect on criminal behavior, but both effects are small (4 percent of the variance).[85]

Tittle, Ward, and Grasmick distinguished between the ability for self-control (Hirschi and Gottfredson's original conception) and the desire to exercise self-control.[86] They defined self-control desire as an indirect measure, composed of internal and external variables drawn from learning, rational choice, and social control theories. Employing data from a city survey, they found that both measures predicted deviant behavior separately and cumulatively and that for some measures of deviant behavior, there was an interaction effect between the two constructs: when desire was low, ability had a greater influence on deviant behavior, and when desire was high, ability had a smaller impact.

Schoepfer and her colleagues studied the interactional effects of low self-control and desire on three types of crime: occupational white-collar (measured by embezzlement), corporate (shredding incriminating documents), and conventional (shoplifting). They found that for occupational crime, desire predicted intentions to offend only when there was low self-control; for corporate crime, desire affected intentions regardless of level of self-control; and for conventional crime, desire did not significantly influence intentions to offend under any condition. Overall, this research suggests that self-control and desire for control are different but related concepts.[87]

Responding to the research findings on the general theory, Hirschi altered his and Gottfredson's original conceptualization of self-control, terming it an "excursion into psychology,"[88] and set forth a new definition of self-control:

> Redefined, self-control becomes the tendency to consider the full range of potential costs of a particular act. This moves the focus from the long-term implications of the act to its broader and often contemporaneous implications. With this new definition, we need not impute knowledge of distant outcomes to persons in no position to possess such information.[89]

Considering self-control as the "set of inhibitions" one takes with him, including the "elements of the bond identified by social control theory," Hirschi conflated his social control and his self-control theories, stating that "social control and self-control are the same thing."[90] He also stated that this definition emphasizes both cognizance and rational choice. To measure self-control, Hirshi constructed a nine-item self-control scale that focuses upon bond measures, dealing with the juvenile's relationship with school and parents, while de-emphasizing delinquency measures.[91]

Piquero and Bouffard, in a preface to testing Hirschi's redefined concept of self-control, summarized what they believed to be the new definition's accomplishments: a focus on change in situations, a shift away from personality approach to measurement, the resolution of tautology criticisms, the linking of self-control with social control, the inclusion of a broader range of negative consequences, a definition of self-control as occurring at the instant of decision-making, and the inclusion of possibly inhibiting factors.[92] Piquero and Bouffard's test of the impact of the new definition, using originally collected data and analyzing the relative impact of the original and new definition of self-control on drunk driving and sexual coercion, found that the redefined measure of self-control had greater predictive utility than the measure of the concept as originally defined.[93] Since their study, there have been several other efforts to test the effects of the redefined measure on crime and delinquency, and have produced mixed results.[94]

Overall, Gottfredson and Hirschi's theory has been subjected to a considerable amount of testing, and this continues to accelerate in the decades following its publication. In 2000, when the theory was still in its infancy, Pratt and Cullen performed a meta-analysis on 21 studies of the theory published between 1993 and 1999, finding considerable support for the link between low self-control and crime/deviance, and an overall effect size of .20, which would "rank self-control as one of the strongest known correlates of crime."[95] In 2017, Vazsonyi et al. published a meta-analysis that was broader in scope and included all studies employing low self-control from 2000 to 2010. Because of the increase in the extent to which scholars were testing the theory, this sample included 99 studies (87 cross-sectional and 19 longitudinal).[96] They found that low self-control was a significant predictor of criminal and deviant behavior, and this held true for a broad range of demographics of individuals. The overall effect size was .415 for cross-sectional studies and .345 for longitudinal studies.[97] They suggested that the effect size was less in longitudinal studies because of methodological issues, or perhaps because the link between self-control and deviant behavior may decline over time as people age.

Vazsonyi et al., based upon their results, said that self-control theory "has established itself as one of the most influential pieces of theoretical scholarship during the past century, as it continues to stand up to a plethora of rigorous empirical tests."[98] In addition to the self-control deviant behavior link, many studies have also found that self-control is associated to levels of victimization, although not with effect sizes as considerable as those with the deviance studies.[99] In sum, Gottfredson and Hirschi's general theory has its supporters and critics, and quite a bit of controversy surrounding some of its conceptual definitions and order of causality, but has resulted in a

significant amount of testing that has found solid support for the link between self-control and criminal and deviant behavior. It also has generated a
great deal of interest across disciplines, such as genetics, psychology, sociology, and family studies. One of its chief advantages in addition to empirical
support is its parsimony.

CONCLUSIONS

Control theories have more or less dominated criminology since Hirschi
published his social control theory in 1969. That theory focused on restraints
on behavior grounded in the external environment (attachment to others,
involvement in legitimate activities, commitment to a future career, and
belief in the moral validity of law). More recently, Gottfredson and Hirschi
proposed a self-control theory that focuses on internal restraints. This theory
holds that early childhood parenting practices result in the formation in the
child of a stable level of self-control by the age of eight or so. Those who are
low in self-control will tend to take advantage of the momentary benefits
that crime and delinquency frequently offer them throughout their lives,
while those who are high in self-control will resist such opportunities.

Both social and self-control theories have many policy implications.
Hirschi's social control theory argues that juveniles are less likely to engage
in delinquent behavior when they are more attached to others, are more involved in conventional activities, have more to lose from committing crime,
and have stronger beliefs in the moral validity of the law. All these arguments could be linked to policies to reduce delinquency. Curfew laws require
juveniles to be at home after a certain hour, which should increase attachment to and supervision by parents. After-school activities and midnight
basketball programs in school gyms increase involvement in legitimate activity in the hopes that idle hands will not become the devil's workshop.
Programs to provide jobs to inner-city youths increase the youths' commitment to the economic system and give them more to lose if they get arrested.
And moral education programs can strengthen beliefs in the legitimacy of
law by teaching that all people benefit from an orderly society in which
everyone obeys the rules.

In self-control theory, the policies that are likely to have the greatest
impact on crime will be those that enhance self-control in children aged
eight and younger.[100] Hirschi and Gottfredson therefore recommended
"policies that promote and facilitate two-parent families and that increase
the number of caregivers relative to the number of children." In particular,
programs to prevent pregnancy among unmarried adolescent girls should
be given high priority. Hirschi and Gottfredson also recommended "programs designed to provide early education and effective child care." This
recommendation includes "programs that target dysfunctional families and
seek to remedy lack of supervision" of preadolescent children. A recent

meta-analysis by Piquero et al. found that early family/parent training is an effective way to reduce behavioral problems among young children.[101] Finally, they recommended programs to "restrict the unsupervised activities of teenagers." Curfews, truancy prevention programs, school uniforms, and license restrictions all limit the opportunities that teenagers have to commit crime. On the other hand, Hirschi and Gottfredson argued that programs to deter, rehabilitate, or incapacitate adult offenders should be abandoned, as should aggressive police tactics (such as drug stings) that essentially create opportunities for offenders to commit crimes.

KEY TERMS

social controls
stakes in conformity
drift
techniques of neutralization
Hirschi's social control theory
attachment
commitment
involvement

belief
internalization of values and
   norms
self-control theory
general theory of crime
tautological
external restraints
internal restraints

DISCUSSION QUESTIONS

1. What are the specific causes of crime according to control theorists?
2. How are the assumptions of control theories different than those of learning theories? Do you believe it makes sense to accept one set of these assumptions and reject the other?
3. What is the significance of Matza's theory of drift? Can you think of different ways in which juveniles may become drifters?
4. Provide specific examples of what causes low self-control, according to Hirschi and Gottfredson.
5. How would social control theories account for white-collar crime? How would Hirschi and Gottfredson's general theory account for white-collar crime?
6. How would the general theory of crime account for children reared poorly who exhibited low self-control who did not go on to commit crimes?

NOTES

1. Albert J. Reiss, "Delinquency as the Failure of Personal and Social Controls," *American Sociological Review* 16 (April 1951): 196–207.
2. Ibid., p. 206.
3. Cf. Travis Hirschi, *Causes of Delinquency* (Berkeley: University of California Press, 1969), pp. 11 and 198, n4.

4. Jackson Toby, "Social Disorganization and Stake in Conformity: Complementary Factors in the Predatory Behavior of Hoodlums," *Journal of Criminal Law, Criminology and Police Science* 48 (May–June 1957): 12–17. A similar concept was presented in a later article by Scott Briar and Irving Piliavin, "Delinquency, Situational Inducements, and Commitment to Conformity," *Social Problems* 13 (Summer 1965): pp. 35–45.

5. Toby, "Social Disorganization and Stake in Conformity," p. 14.

6. F. Ivan Nye, *Family Relationships and Delinquent Behavior* (New York: John Wiley, 1958).

7. Ibid., p. 4.

8. Ibid., p. 5–8.

9. Ibid., pp. 13–14.

10. See ibid., pp. 15–19, and Nye and James F. Short Jr., "Scaling Delinquent Behavior," *American Sociological Review* 22 (June 1957): 26–31.

11. Nye, *Family Relationships and Delinquent Behavior*, p. 155.

12. Jackson Toby, "Review of Family Relationships and Delinquent Behavior by F. Ivan Nye," *American Sociological Review* 24 (February 1959): 282–283.

13. David Matza, *Delinquency and Drift* (New York: John Wiley, 1964), pp. 1–27.

14. For a discussion of age and crime, see Chapter 14.

15. Matza, *Delinquency and Drift*, pp. 27–30.

16. Ibid., p. 29.

17. Ibid., pp. 33–59.

18. Ibid., pp. 59–98.

19. Ibid., pp. 101–177. See also Marvin Krohn and John Stratton, "A Sense of Injustice?" *Criminology* 17 (1980): 495–504.

20. Matza, *Delinquency and Drift*, pp. 181–191. Compare with Hirschi, *Causes of Delinquency*, pp. 33–34.

21. Gresham M. Sykes and David Matza, "Techniques of Neutralization: A Theory of Delinquency," *American Sociological Review* 22 (December 1957): 664–670.

22. Hirschi, *Causes of Delinquency*, p. 31.

23. Ibid., pp. 16–34.

24. Ibid., p. 26.

25. Ibid., p. 54.

26. Ibid., p. 62. This was defined as the "recency" index and was used throughout the study.

27. Strain theories are reviewed in Chapter 7 of this book, while what Hirschi called "cultural deviance" theories are reviewed in Chapter 9. One of the arguments made in Chapter 9 is that the description of these theories as cultural deviance theories is inaccurate. This argument implies that Hirschi's test is invalid.

28. Hirschi, *Causes of Delinquency*, pp. 66–75.

29. Ibid., pp. 75–81.

30. Ibid., pp. 226–227.

31. Ibid., pp. 97, 99.

32. Hirschi admitted that his formulation may not adequately test strain because of Cohen's idea of reaction formation: boys may care about school success, but if they are unable to succeed, they may then deny that they care at all. However, Hirschi argued that such an argument is virtually impossible to falsify; *Causes of Delinquency*, pp. 124–126.
33. Ibid., pp. 159–161.
34. Ibid., p. 183.
35. Ibid., p. 190.
36. Ibid., pp. 202–203.
37. Ibid., p. 208.
38. Ibid., p. 230.
39. Ibid., p. 82.
40. Barbara J. Costello and Paul R. Vowell, "Testing Control Theory and Differential Association," *Criminology* 37 (1999): 815–842.
41. Hirschi, *Causes of Delinquency*, p. 190.
42. Hirschi, *Causes of Delinquency*, p. 41. Toby, "Review of Family Relationships and Delinquent Behavior by F. Ivan Nye," pp. 282–283, raised the same issue about Nye's original self-report study testing a control theory.
43. Toby, "Review of Family Relationships and Delinquent Behavior by F. Ivan Nye," made the same argument about Nye's results.
44. The absence of serious delinquents in Hirschi's sample requires that Hirschi's definition of delinquency (*Causes of Delinquency*, p. 46) focus on nonserious offenses. If Hirschi had defined delinquency in terms of serious offenses, then his sample would have had so few delinquents that he would have been unable to reach any conclusions. Toby ("Review of Family Relationships and Delinquent Behavior by F. Ivan Nye") made a similar comment about Nye's definition of delinquency.
45. Kimberly L. Kempf, "The Empirical Status of Hirschi's Control Theory," in *New Directions in Criminological Theory: Advances in Criminological Theory*, vol. 4, ed. Freda Adler and William S. Laufer (New Brunswick, NJ: Transaction, 1993).
46. Kempf, "The Empirical Status of Hirschi's Control Theory," p. 173. See also Thomas J. Bernard, "Twenty Years of Testing Theories: What Have We Learned and Why?" *Journal of Research in Crime and Delinquency* 27 (1990): 325–347.
47. For example, David F. Greenberg ("The Weak Strength of Social Control Theory," *Crime & Delinquency* 45 [1999]: 66–81) reanalyzed Hirschi's original data and found little support for control theory itself. Greenberg found greater support for strain theories, although the support for either theory was fairly weak. In addition, in two different studies, Robert Agnew ("Delinquency: A Longitudinal Test," *Criminology* 23 [1985]: 47–59, and "A Longitudinal Test of Social Control Theory and Delinquency," *Journal of Research in Crime and Delinquency* 28 [1991]: 126–156) found that the effects of control variables may have been overestimated in cross-sectional studies such as Hirschi's.

48. Michael Gottfredson and Travis Hirschi, *A General Theory of Crime* (Stanford, CA: Stanford University Press, 1990).

49. Ibid., pp. 15–44; 89–91.

50. Ibid., pp. 90–91.

51. Ibid., p. 94.

52. Ibid.

53. Ibid., p. 97.

54. Ibid., pp. 157–158.

55. Ibid., pp. 162–163.

56. Ibid., p. 165.

57. The major variation found in individuals is the age–crime curve. For a discussion of Gottfredson and Hirschi's position on this issue, see Chapter 15.

58. Travis C. Pratt and Francis T. Cullen ("The Empirical Status of Gottfredson and Hirschi's General Theory of Crime: A Meta-Analysis," *Criminology* 38 [2000]: 931–964) lists twenty-one different empirical studies.

59. These six attitudes were taken from a 24-item scale first presented in Harold G. Grasmick, Charles R. Tittle, Robert J. Bursik Jr., and Bruce K. Arneklev, "Testing the Core Empirical Implications of Gottfredson and Hirschi's General Theory of Crime," *Journal of Research in Crime and Delinquency* 30 (1993): 5–29. Note that this list is not identical to the six characteristics identified by Gottfredson and Hirschi as the characteristics of low self-control: impulsive, insensitive, physical, risk taking, short-sighted, and nonverbal.

60. Grasmick et al. suggested that these six attitudes form a latent trait, so that this is a unidimensional scale. Using a sample of 233 college students, Alex R. Piquero, Randall MacIntosh, and Matthew Hickman ("Does Self-Control Affect Survey Response?" *Criminology* 38 [2000]: 897–930) concluded that it is unidimensional. However, the bulk of empirical tests have demonstrated multidimensionality. See, e.g., Alexander T. Vazsonyi, Lloyd E. Pickering, Marianne Junger, and Dick Hessing, "An Empirical Test of a General Theory of Crime: A Four-Nation Comparative Study of Self-Control and the Prediction of Deviance," *Journal of Research in Crime and Delinquency* 38 (2001): 91–131; Matt Delisi, Andy Hochstetler, and Daniel S. Murphy, "Self-Control Behind Bars: A Validation Study of the Grasmick et al. Scale," *Justice Quarterly* 20 (2003): 241–263; Alexander T. Vazsonyi and Jennifer M. Crosswhite, "A Test of Gottfredson and Hirschi's General Theory of Crime in African American Adolescents," *Journal of Research in Crime and Delinquency* 41 (2004): 407–432. However, as by Vazsonyi and Crosswhite, "A Test of Gottfredson and Hirschi's General Theory of Crime," p. 409, pointed out, the dimensionality controversy may be largely one of interpretation—that low self-control, much like intelligence, has different elements or traits that are distinct, but these elements still feed into a central construct.

61. E.g., Vazsonyi and Crosswhite, "A Test of Gottfredson and Hirschi's General Theory of Crime," p. 410.

62. E.g., Stephen W. Baron, "Self-Control, Social Consequences, and Criminal Behavior: Street Youth and the General Theory of Crime," *Journal of Research in Crime and Delinquency* 40 (2003): 403–425.

63. For a discussion of the choice between attitudinal and behavioral measures of self-control, see Delisi et al., "Self-Control Behind Bars," p. 260.

64. E.g., Pratt and Cullen, ("The Empirical Status of Gottfredson and Hirschi's General Theory of Crime."

65. See Vazsonyi and Crosswhite, "A Test of Gottfredson and Hirschi's General Theory of Crime," showing that low self-control consistently predicts deviance among African Americans, and that the nature and strength of effects in this group is similar to that in whites. These authors also find that although low self-control predicts deviance among females (especially white females), there are some differences in the strength of the effects between males and females. Vazsonyi et al., "An Empirical Test of a General Theory of Crime," showed that low self-control predicts deviance consistently across four countries (the United States, Switzerland, Hungary, and the Netherlands), with explained variances ranging from 17% to 28%, and that the relationships between the various subscales of low self-control and the deviance subscales are highly similar across countries as well. However, one work has demonstrated that self-control's impact on crime and deviance varies across different age groups. Charles R. Tittle, David A. Ward, and Harold G. Grasmick, "Gender, Age, and Crime/Deviance: A Challenge to Self-Control Theory," *Journal of Research in Crime and Delinquency* 40 (2003): 426–453.

66. Baron, "Self-Control, Social Consequences, and Criminal Behavior," pp. 413–416.

67. Michael R. Welch, Charles R. Tittle, Jennifer Yonkoski, Nicole Meidinger, and Harold G. Grasmick, "Social Integration, Self-Control, and Conformity," *Journal of Quantitative Criminology* 24 (2008): 73–92.

68. John H. Laub and Robert J. Sampson, *Shared Beginnings, Divergent Lives: Delinquent Boys at Age 70* (Boston: Harvard University Press, 2003); Sampson and Laub, "Desistance from Crime over the Life Course," in *Handbook of the Life Course*, ed. Jeylan T. Mortimer and Michael Shanahan (New York: Kluwer Academic/Plenum, 2003).

69. Chongmin Na and Raymond Paternoster, "Can Self-Control Change Substantially over Time? Rethinking the Relationship between Self- and Social Control," *Criminology* 50:2 (2012): 427–462.

70. Gottfredson and Hirschi, *A General Theory of Crime*, pp. 97–102.

71. James D. Unnever, Francis T. Cullen, and Travis C. Pratt, "Parental Management, ADHD, and Delinquent Involvement: Reassessing Gottfredson and Hirschi's General Theory," *Justice Quarterly* 20 (2003): 471–500.

72. John Paul Wright and Kevin M. Beaver, "Do Parents Matter in Creating Self-Control in Their Children? A Genetically Informed Test of Gottfredson and Hirschi's Theory of Low Self-Control," *Criminology* 43 (2005): 1169–1202.

73. Carter Hay, "Parenting, Self-Control, and Delinquency: A Test of Self-Control Theory," Criminology 39 (2001): 707–736.

74. Stacey Nofziger, "The 'Cause' of Low Self-Control: The Influence of Maternal Self-Control," *Journal of Research in Crime and Delinquency* 45 (2008): 191–224.

75. Hay, "Parenting, Self-Control, and Delinquency," p. 726. For a recent study of the effect of genetic factors on low self-control, arguing they can influence it directly (as opposed to solely moderating parental variables), see Danielle Boisvert, John Paul Wright, Valerie Knopik, and Jamie Vaske, "Genetic and Environmental Overlap between Low Self-Control and Delinquency," *Journal of Quantitative Criminology* 28 (2012): 477–507.

76. For the most sweeping criticisms of the theory, including an argument about tautology, see Gilbert Geis, "On the Absence of Self-Control as the Basis for a General Theory of Crime: A Critique," *Theoretical Criminology* 4 (2000): 35–53. A response by Hirschi and Gottfredson ("In Defense of Self-Control," pp. 55–69) follows.

77. E.g., Ronald Akers, "Self-Control as a General Theory of Crime," *Journal of Quantitative Criminology* 7 (1991): 201–211.

78. This argument is tautological because other concepts besides low self-control can be inserted into the argument and the argument itself remains the same. For example, the tendency to engage in impulsive, risky, self-centered, physical activities could be explained by socialization into a "criminal subculture." Evidence for the subculture would be found in the behaviors of the people who were supposedly socialized into it, and then the behaviors themselves would be explained by the subculture. Control theorists have criticized subcultural theories as being tautological in exactly this way.

79. Hirschi and Gottfredson, "Commentary: Testing the General Theory of Crime," *Journal of Research in Crime and Delinquency* 30 (1993): 52–53.

80. E.g., see Gary E. Reed and Peter Cleary Yeager, "Organizational Offending and Neoclassical Criminology: Challenging the Reach of a General Theory of Crime," *Criminology* 34 (1996): 357–382; Sally S. Simpson and Nicle Leeper Piquero, "Low Self-Control, Organizational Theory, and Corporate Crime," *Law and Society Review* 36 (2002): 509–548.

81. Gottfredson and Hirschi, *A General Theory of Crime*, p. 213.

82. See, e.g., Jessica M. Craig and Nicole Leeper Piquero, "Sensational Offending: An Application of Sensation Seeking to White-Collar and Conventional Crimes," *Crime & Delinquency* 63 (2017): 1363–1382.

83. Hugh Barlow, "Explaining Crimes and Analogous Acts, or the Unrestrained Will Grab at Pleasure Whenever They Can," *Journal of Criminal Law and Criminology*" 82 (1991): 229–242.

84. Douglas Longshore and Susan Turner, "Self-Control and Criminal Opportunity," *Criminal Justice and Behavior* 25 (1998): 81–98.

85. Douglas Longshore, "Self-Control and Criminal Opportunity," *Social Problems*, 45 (1998): 102–113.

86. Charles R. Tittle, David A. Ward, and Harld G. Grasmick, "Capacity for Self-Control and Individuals' Interest in Exercising Self-Control," *Journal of Quantitative Criminology* 20 (2004): 143–172.

87. Andrea Schoepfer, Nicole Leeper Piquero, and Lynn Langton, "Low Self-Control Versus the Desire-for-Control: An Empirical Test of White-Collar Crime and Conventional Crime," *Deviant Behavior* 35:3 (2014): 197–214.

88. Travis Hirschi, Self-control and Crime. In *Handbook of Self-Regulation: Research, Theory, and Applications,* ed. R. F. Baumeister and K. D. Vohs (New York: Guilford Press: 2004), p. 542.
89. Ibid., p. 543.
90. Ibid.
91. Ibid., p. 545.
92. Alex R. Piquero and Jeff A. Bouffard, "Something Old, Something New: A Preliminary Investigation of Hirschi's Redefined Self-Control," *Justice Quarterly* 24 (2007): 1–27.
93. Ibid., pp. 13–18.
94. George E. Higgins, Scott E. Wolfe, and Catherine Marcum, "Digital Piracy: An Examination of Three Measurements of Self-Control," *Deviant Behavior* 29 (2008): 440–460; Robert G. Morris, Jurg Gerber, and Scott Meard, "Social Bonds, Self-Control, and Adult Criminality: A Nationally Representative Assessment of Hirschi's Revised Self Control Theory," *Criminal Justice and Behavior* 38 (2011): 584–599; Jeff A. Bouffard and Stephen K. Rice, "The Influence of the Social Bond on Self-Control at the Moment of Decision: Testing Hirschi's Redefinition of Self-Control. *American Journal of Criminal Justice* 36 (2011): 138–157; Jeffrey T. Ward, John H. Boman, IV, and Shayne Jones, "Hirschi's Redefined Self-Control: Assessing the Implications of the Merger Between Social- and Self-Control Theories," *Crime & Delinquency* 61 (2015): 1206–1233.
95. Travis C. Platt and Francis T. Cullen, "The Empirical Status of Gottfredson and Hirschi's General Theory of Crime: A Meta-Analysis," *Criminology* 38 (2000): 931–964, p. 952.
96. Alexander T. Vazsonyi, Jakub Mikuska, and Erin L. Kelley, "It's Time: A Meta-Analysis on the Self-Control-Deviance Link," *Journal of Criminal Justice* 48 (2017): 48–63.
97. Ibid., p. 56.
98. Ibid., p. 59.
99. Travis C. Pratt, Jillian J. Turanovic, Kathleen A. Fox, and Kevin A. Wright, "Self-Control and Victimization: A Meta-Analysis," *Criminology* 52 (2014): 87–116.
100. The following recommendations are taken from Travis Hirschi and Michael R. Gottfredson, "Self-Control Theory," pp. 81–96 in *Explaining Criminals and Crime,* ed. Raymond Paternoster and Ronet Bachman (Los Angeles: Roxbury, 2001).
101. Alex R. Piquero, Wesley G. Jennings, Brie Diamond, David P. Farrington, Richard E. Tremblay, Brandon C. Welsh, and Jennifer M. Reingle Gonzalez, "A Meta-Analysis Update on the Effects of Early Family/Parent Training Programs on Anti-Social Behavior and Delinquency," *Journal of Experimental Criminology* 12 (2016): 249–264.

CHAPTER 11

—

Conflict Criminology

Throughout the long history of thinking about human societies, social theorists have repeatedly presented two starkly contrasting views.[1] Consensus theorists place a consensus of values at the very center of human societies—that is, shared beliefs about what is good, right, just, important, or at least excusable. Conflict theorists, in contrast, place conflicts of interests at the very center of human societies—that is, competitions over money, status, and power. These contrasting views have different implications for the role of the organized state and therefore for the nature of crime and functions of criminal justice.

Consensus theorists recognize that there inevitably will be at least some value conflicts among different individuals and groups in every human society. In addition, there inevitably will be conflicts of interest as individuals and groups seek their own benefits without regard to what is good or right or just or appropriate or even excusable. But consensus theorists argue that the role of the organized state is to mediate these conflicts and to represent the common values and common interests of the society at large. Values ultimately determine interests, since it is in everyone's interest to have societies that are governed in accordance with goodness, righteousness, and justice.

Conflict theorists, on the other hand, argue that interests ultimately determine values. Beliefs about goodness, righteousness, and justice tend to be thin films that conceal personal gains and losses, personal costs and benefits. Even sincere people tend to believe that if something benefits them personally, then it probably is good, right, and just, and if something harms them personally, then it probably is bad, wrong, and unjust. In the real world, conflict theorists argue, the organized state does not represent common interests, but instead represents the interests of those with sufficient power to control its operation. As a result, more powerful people are legally freer to pursue self-interests, while less powerful people who pursue self-interests are more likely to be officially defined and processed as criminal. The result is an inverse relationship between power and official crime rates: the more power that people have, the less likely they are to be arrested, convicted, imprisoned, and executed, regardless of their behavior. And vice versa.

EARLY CONFLICT THEORIES: SELLIN AND VOLD

In 1938, Thorsten Sellin presented a theory of criminology that focused on the conflict of "conduct norms."[2] Conduct norms are cultural rules that require certain types of people to act in certain ways in certain circumstances. In simple, homogeneous societies, many of these conduct norms are enacted into law and actually represent a consensus in the society. But in more complex societies, there will be overlap and contradiction between the conduct norms of different cultural groups. Sellin defined "primary cultural conflicts" as those occurring between two different cultures.[3] These conflicts could occur at border areas between two divergent cultures; or, in the case of colonization, when the laws of one culture are extended into the territory of another; or, in the case of migration, when members of one cultural group move into the territory of another. "Secondary cultural conflicts" occur when a single culture evolves into several different subcultures, each having its own conduct norms. In each of these cases, law would not represent a consensus of the various members of the society but would reflect the conduct norms of the dominant culture.

Twenty years after Sellin wrote, George B. Vold presented a group conflict theory in the original edition of the present book.[4] Vold's theory was based on a "social process" view of society as a collection of groups held together in a dynamic equilibrium of opposing group interests and efforts. In Vold's theory, groups in society more or less continuously struggle to maintain or improve their place in an ongoing interaction and competition with other groups. These social interaction processes grind their way through various kinds of uneasy adjustment to a more or less stable equilibrium of balanced forces, called social order or social organization. Social order, therefore, does not reflect a consensus among the groups but reflects instead the uneasy adjustment, one to another, of the many groups of various strengths and different interests. Conflict is thus one of the principal and essential social processes in the functioning of society.

This social process view of human societies is associated with a view of human nature that holds that people are fundamentally group-involved beings whose lives are both a part of and a product of their group associations. Groups are formed when people have common interests and common needs that can best be furthered through collective action. New groups are continuously formed as new interests arise, and existing groups weaken and disappear when they no longer have a purpose to serve. Groups become effective action units through the direction and coordination of the activities of their members, and they come into conflict with one another as the interests and purposes they serve tend to overlap, encroach on one another, and become competitive. Conflict between groups tends to develop and intensify the loyalty of group members to their respective groups.

The conflicts among organized groups are especially visible in legislative politics, which is largely a matter of finding practical compromises between opposing interests. But the conflicts themselves exist in the community and in the society long before they become visible in legislative politics. As groups in the society line up against one another, each seeks the assistance of the organized state to help them defend their rights and protect their interests against the opposing groups. This general situation of group conflict gives rise to the familiar cry "There ought to be a law!"—essentially the demand by one of the conflicting groups that the power of the organized state be used to support them in their conflict with the other groups. Naturally, the other groups, against whom the proposed law is directed, oppose its passage. Whichever group interest can marshal the greatest number of votes in the legislative process will determine whether or not there will be a new law to promote the interests of the one group and to hamper and curb the interests of the other groups.

Once the new law has been passed, those who opposed the law in the legislature are more likely to violate the law, since it defends interests and purposes that are in conflict with their own. Those who promoted the law, in contrast, are more likely to obey it and to demand that the criminal justice agencies enforce it against violators, since the law defends interests and purposes they hold dear. In other words, those who produce legislative majorities win control of the criminal justice power of the state and decide the policies that determine who is likely to be officially defined and processed as criminals.

Thus, the whole process of lawmaking, lawbreaking, and law enforcement directly reflects deep-seated and fundamental conflicts between group interests and the more general struggles among groups for control of the police power of the state. To that extent, Vold described criminal behavior as the behavior of "minority power groups"—that is, groups that do not have sufficient power to promote and defend their own interests and purposes in the legislative process.

Pointing to the fundamental conditions of life in organized political society, Vold's group conflict theory suggested that a considerable amount of crime is intimately related to the conflicts of groups. For such situations, the criminal behavior of the individual is best viewed in the context of the course of action required for the group to maintain its position in the struggle with other groups. A sociology of conflict is therefore the basis for understanding and explaining this kind of criminal behavior.[5] On the other hand, Vold argued that group conflict theory was strictly limited to those kinds of situations in which the individual criminal acts flow from the collision of groups whose members are loyally upholding the in-group position. Such a theory does not explain many kinds of impulsive and irrational criminal acts that are unrelated to any battle between different interest groups in organized society.

CONFLICT THEORIES IN A TIME OF CONFLICT: TURK, QUINNEY, AND CHAMBLISS AND SEIDMAN

Ten years after Vold wrote his group conflict theory, the United States was embroiled in enormous social and political turmoil surrounding the civil rights movement and the Vietnam War. The criminal law and the criminal justice system supported some groups against others in these political conflicts, and many people came to believe Vold's argument that crime is the behavior of minority power groups. This perception suddenly brought conflict theory to the forefront of criminology, and three important conflict theories were published in three successive years.

In 1969, Austin Turk proposed a "theory of criminalization" that attempted to describe "the conditions under which . . . differences between authorities and subjects will probably result in conflict, [and] the conditions under which criminalization will probably occur in the course of conflict."[6] Turk argued that the organization and sophistication of both authorities and subjects affect the likelihood of conflict between them.[7] Authorities are presumed to be organized, since organization is a prerequisite for achieving and retaining power. Conflict is more likely when subjects are organized, since group support makes an individual less willing to back down. Turk defined *sophistication* as "knowledge of patterns in the behavior of others which is used in attempts to manipulate them." More sophisticated subjects will be able to achieve their goals without precipitating a conflict with the superior powers of the state, and less sophisticated authorities will have to rely more strongly on overt coercion to achieve their goals rather than more subtle, alternative tactics.

Given these conditions that affect the likelihood of conflict between authorities and subjects, Turk discussed the conditions under which conflict is more likely to result in the criminalization of the subjects. The primary factor, Turk argued, will be the meaning that the prohibited act or attribute has for those who enforce the law (i.e., the police, prosecutors, and judges).[8] To the extent that these officials find the prohibited act or attribute offensive, it is likely that there will be high arrest rates, high conviction rates, and severe sentences. The second factor will be the relative power of the enforcers and resisters.[9] In general, criminalization will be greatest when the enforcers have great power and the resisters are virtually powerless. The third factor is what Turk called the "realism of the conflict moves," and it is related to how likely an action taken by the subjects or authorities may improve the potential for their ultimate success. Turk stated that unrealistic conflict moves by either party will tend to increase criminalization, which is a measure of the overt conflict between the two groups.

In 1970, Richard Quinney published his theory of "the social reality of crime."[10] Relying on Vold's group conflict theory, Quinney argued that the legislative process of defining criminal laws and the criminal justice process of enforcing criminal laws occur in a political context in which individuals and groups pursue their own self-interests. But where Vold focused on conflicts among organized interest groups, Quinney discussed conflicts among "segments" of society. Segments are said to be people who share the same values, norms, and ideological orientations but who may or may not be organized in defense of those commonalities.[11] Some segments, such as business and labor, have been organized into interest groups for many years, but other segments, such as women, poor people, and homosexuals, took longer to organize. There are also segments of society that have only minimal organization, such as young people, and segments that have virtually no organization at all, such as prisoners and the mentally ill. Because of this difference, Quinney used conflict theory to explain all crime instead of merely some of it. Vold specifically excluded "impulsive, irrational acts of a criminal nature that are quite unrelated to any battle between different interest groups in organized society."[12] Quinney, on the other hand, would hold that irrational and impulsive people represent a segment of society with common values, norms, and ideological orientations, even if this segment is not organized into any interest group.

Relying on Sutherland's differential association theory, Quinney argued that different segments of society have different normative systems and different patterns of behaviors, all of which are learned in their own social and cultural settings. The probability that individuals will violate the criminal law depends, to a large extent, on how much power and influence their segments have in enacting and enforcing the criminal laws. In more powerful segments of society, people are able to act according to their own normative standards and behavioral patterns without violating the law. But when people in less powerful segments do the same thing, their actions are legally defined and officially processed as criminal.

Finally, Quinney argued that conceptions of crime are created and communicated as part of the political process of promoting particular sets of values and interests.[13] Political agendas are readily apparent when, for example, consumer and ecology groups argue that the real criminals are corporate executives or when community organizers in inner-city neighborhoods argue that the real criminals are the absentee landlords and greedy storeowners. But these conceptions of crime often are not taken seriously because the groups that promote them do not have much political power. Conceptions of crime that are promoted by individuals and groups with a great deal of power, however, often are widely accepted as legitimate by other people in the society. "The social reality of crime," according to Quinney, is that powerful individuals and groups promote particular conceptions of crime in order to legitimate their authority and allow them to carry out policies in the name of the common good that really promote their own self-interests.

In 1971, Chambliss and Seidman published a conflict analysis of the functioning of the criminal justice system titled *Law, Order, and Power*.[14] These authors noted that consensus and conflict theories provide radically different versions of how the criminal justice system actually functions. Therefore, they examined the day-to-day functioning of that system to determine which of the two theories is correct. Specifically, they sought to discover whether the power of the state (as embodied in the criminal justice system) is "a value-neutral framework within which conflict can be peacefully resolved" or whether, as conflict theory would have it, "the power of the State is itself the principal prize in the perpetual conflict that is society."[15]

The criminal justice process begins with the legislative activity of lawmaking. Consensus theory describes this process as "a deliberative assembly of one nation, with one interest, that of the whole, where, not local purposes, nor local prejudices, ought to guide, but the general good, resulting from the general reason of the whole."[16] As Vold and Quinney had done earlier, the authors argue that "every detailed study of the emergence of legal norms has consistently shown the immense importance of interest-group activity, not 'the public interest,' as the critical variable in determining the content of legislation."[17] Chambliss and Seidman maintained that "the higher a group's political and economic position, the greater is the probability that its views will be reflected in the laws."[18]

Chambliss and Seidman then turned to appellate court decisions that have the effect of creating law. These are decisions in "trouble cases" where no law clearly applies or where more than one law seems to apply. Appellate courts are said to be "the institution par excellence for which society most carefully cherishes the idea of value-neutrality."[19] Originally, judges referred to "natural law" to support their decisions in trouble cases, but it later became apparent that the natural law really embodied their own personal values.[20] Later justifications were phrased in terms of preexisting laws and the principles embodied in those laws,[21] but dissenting opinions in the same cases have also been justified in terms of preexisting laws and principles. Still later, legal scholars concluded that appellate court decisions inevitably must be based on value judgments about what is "best" for society.[22] Roscoe Pound attempted to state the common values that would underlie judicial decisions, but his formulation did not meet with widespread acceptance and was criticized for primarily reflecting his own personal values.[23] Therefore, Chambliss and Seidman concluded that in the last analysis, judges must rely on their personal values when they make decisions in trouble cases.[24]

Chambliss and Seidman gave a number of reasons why the personal values of appellate judges will be oriented primarily to the wealthy, rather than to the poor.[25] As law students, future appellate judges are largely trained by the "casebook" method, which focuses on issues that were raised in earlier court cases. These issues relate predominantly to the needs and concerns of the wealthy. As young lawyers, future appellate judges tend to focus on cases involving the wealthy, since those clients are able to pay high legal fees. As trial judges, future appellate judges have achieved a socially prominent position and can be expected to socialize with the wealthy and powerful and become attuned to their needs. The promotion of trial judges to the appellate level is inevitably tied in one way or another to the political process, so that trial judges who deal appropriately with the politically powerful are more likely to be promoted. Thus, there are many subtle pressures encouraging appellate judges to consider carefully issues that are related to powerful and wealthy people. At the same time, there are organizational pressures to restrict the amount of litigation before the court to prevent overloading the docket. These pressures, together with the fact that appellate cases depend in part on the ability of the defendant to pay for the cost of the litigation, mean that the majority of case law concerns issues that are related only to the wealthy and powerful. Chambliss and Seidman concluded that appellate court decisions overwhelmingly reflect the needs and desires of the wealthy and powerful.

Finally, Chambliss and Seidman examined the day-to-day functioning of criminal justice agencies to see if their functions reflect the arguments of consensus or conflict theories. Their analysis focused on the bureaucratic nature of those organizations and their connections to the political structure.[26] Law enforcement agencies, like all normally functioning bureaucracies, tend to engage in goal-substituting behavior. That is, in an agency's day-to-day functioning, "the official goals and norms of the organization" tend to be replaced by policies and activities that "maximize rewards and minimize the strains on the organization." This goal substitution is more extensive in criminal justice agencies than in other bureaucracies because criminal justice agents have much greater discretion and because there are fewer official or unofficial penalties for engaging in goal-switching behavior. Chambliss and Seidman then argued that because law enforcement agencies depend on political organizations for their resources, they can maximize their rewards and minimize their strains if they process those who are politically weak and refrain from processing those who are politically powerful. They concluded that "it may be expected that the law-enforcement agencies will process a disproportionately high number of the politically weak and powerless, while ignoring the violations of those with power."

On the basis of their reviews of the legislative process, of appellate court decisions, and of the functioning of law enforcement agencies, Chambliss and Seidman concluded that both in structure and in function, the law operates in the interests of power groups. The public interest is represented only to the extent that it coincides with the interests of those power groups.[27]

BLACK'S THEORY OF THE BEHAVIOR OF LAW

Only five years later, in 1976, Donald Black published a sociological theory titled *The Behavior of Law*, in which he attempted to explain variations in the quantity and style of law.[28] The theory shares some similarities with, although it is much broader than, the conflict theories just described. Black argued that the quantity of law (i.e., governmental social control) varies in time and place—that is, there is more law at some times and places and less law at other times and places. Reporting a crime, making an arrest, deciding to prosecute, deciding to convict, sentencing someone to prison, and sentencing someone to death all represent more law, while not taking these actions represents less law. Black also contended that law varies in its style. Black mostly discussed penal law, in which law is enforced by a group against an offender. But law can also be compensatory, in which victims demand payment in reparation for harm that has been done. Law can be therapeutic, in which law acts on behalf of a deviant. Finally, law can be conciliatory, in which various parties work together to resolve imbalances.[29]

Black explored five social dimensions of social life—stratification, morphology, culture, organization, and social control. Stratification is the "vertical distance between the people of a social setting" and is best measured by the difference in average wealth between each person or groups and every other person or group or by the difference between the lowest and highest levels of wealth.[30] Morphology is the "horizontal aspect of social life, the distribution of people in relation to one another, including their division of labor, networks of interaction, intimacy, and integration."[31] Culture is the "symbolic aspect of life, including expressions of what is true, good, and beautiful. . . . Examples are science, technology, religion, magic, and folklore. . . . Culture includes aesthetic life of all sorts, the fine arts and the popular, such as poetry and painting, clothing . . . architecture, and even the culinary arts."[32] Organization is the "corporate aspect of social life, the capacity for collective action."[33] Finally, social control "is the normative aspect of social life. It defines responses to deviant behavior, specifying what ought to be. . . . Law is social control . . . but so are etiquette, custom, ethics, bureaucracy, and the treatment of mental illness."[34]

Within each dimension, Black formed hypotheses about law. In the case of stratification, Black argued that the higher a person is in on the ladder of stratification, the more the person is able to invoke law on his or her behalf. In addition, the further apart two people are in terms of stratification, the more law the higher ranked person can exercise over the other. For example, if a corporate executive claims to be victimized by a street person, more law will be exercised against the street person than if the executive claims to be victimized by another corporate executive or if the street person claims to be victimized by the corporate executive. Black's arguments about stratification are what make his theory comparable to the other conflict theories described earlier.

However, Black went on to discuss variations in the quantity and style of law that are related to four other societal characteristics. Morphology concerns the relational distance between people, or the degree to which they participate in each other's lives. Black argued that the relationship between law and relational distance is curvilinear: "Law is inactive among intimates, increasing as the distance between people increases but decreasing as this reaches the point at which people live in entirely separate worlds."[35] Hermits rarely need or use law, since they live in an entirely separate world, and married couples do not invoke law against each other unless their intimacy with each other breaks down. Law is greater, Black said, when the relational distance is somewhere between intimacy and isolation.

One of Black's hypotheses concerning culture is that law is greater in a direction toward less culture than toward more culture and, furthermore, that the amount of cultural distance linearly affects the amount of law. Using education as a measure of culture, for example, if an offender is less educated than the victim, more law will be invoked to address the victimization, and the most law of all will be used when the difference in education between the offender and the victim is greatest.[36] On the other hand, if the offender is more educated than the victim, less law will be used to address the victimization, and the least law of all will be used when the difference in education between the offender and victim is greatest.

Similarly, Black argued that law varies directly with organization. If offenders are more organized than their victims (e.g., if the offender is a corporation and the victim is an individual), less law will be used to address the victimization. In addition, the most law will be used when the organizational distance between the offenders and victims is the greatest. But if the offenders are less organized than the victims (e.g., the offender is an individual and the victim is a corporation), the reverse is true: more law will be used to address the victimization, and the most law will be used when the organizational distance between the victims and offenders is greatest. Black used these propositions to explain relatively light sanctions directed toward white-collar offenders.

Finally, Black argued that law will be greater where other forms of social control are weaker. All in all, across the five social dimensions, Black formed more than twenty hypotheses about how law varies in quantity and style. His evidence for each is primarily anecdotal, including anthropological examples from a variety of sources, but he did not perform any systematic test of the hypotheses.

In his preface to *The Behavior of Law*, Black stated: "This book does not judge the variation of law, nor does it recommend policy of any kind. Rather, it is merely an effort to understand law as a natural phenomenon."[37] But in a later book on the subject, *Sociological Justice*,[38] Black judged variations in the quantity and style of law as being "wrong" in some sense. He therefore recommended three types of policy reforms to reduce social variation in law: legal cooperatives, desocialization of law, and starvation of law. In the first reform, people would join subsidized legal cooperatives to reduce corporate advantages in the legal system. Each co-op would consist of a variety of people, so that relations among the co-ops themselves would be relatively equal. Informal social control may come about within the co-ops, as those who cause the group expensive legal costs may be expelled. Of course, this could also work to perpetuate social variations in law if groups are quick to expel undesirable individuals. Black's second reform would make social information about offenders unavailable to criminal justice system actors handling cases. For example, jurors would not be allowed actually to see offenders, witnesses, or victims. All testimony would be done electronically, so that evidence would be stripped of social characteristics, such as dialect or education. Black's third proposal would be to "starve" the law. Basically, he argued that if the law has only the barest minimum in resources, then people will be forced to rely on other mechanisms for dealing with conflicts, such as conflict resolution. While there are serious flaws with each of these proposals, the book's purpose is noble: to eliminate social factors from the behavior of law.[39]

An initial attempt to test Black's theory raised conceptual questions about the "seriousness" of an offense. Gottfredson and Hindelang found that variation in Black's social dimensions did not significantly predict variation in the quantity of law, which instead was predicted primarily by the seriousness of the offense.[40] Black responded that describing a crime as "serious" is itself influenced by the five social dimensions and that in practice, the term *serious* means that the action receives a large quantity of law.[41] Gottfredson and Hindelang responded that if this is true, Black's theory cannot be tested unambiguously.[42] The confusion around how to deal with seriousness has hampered subsequent attempts to test Black's theory, and to date, there remains no comprehensive, accepted test.[43]

On the other hand, some research has looked at relationships between actors, rather than looking at absolute social status without regard to relative position. For example, one study of court disposition patterns used Hagan's structural criminology as a theoretical point of departure and employed some of Black's propositions in attempting to show how the relationship between victim and offender may influence criminal justice reaction to behavior. Jamieson and Blowers found a greater probability of dismissal of cases with less organized victims, especially when the suspected offenders were more organized.[44] This finding is consistent with Hagan's idea that power differentials—one being organization—may influence reaction to behavior and with Black's proposition that law varies with organization.

Black did not mention conflict theory in any of his works on the behavior of law, nor has his work been identified as conflict theory elsewhere. Yet some of the core propositions of his theory are consistent with conflict notions, in that they imply that more powerful social actors have more ability to use law against less powerful actors. Black's theory probably has not been conceived as a conflict theory for at least two reasons. First, Black simply stated his propositions as purely sociological laws, without imputing either individual or structural motivation. Conflict theory assumes that disproportionate treatment has a purpose attached to it—namely, to protect the interests of the more powerful. Second, Black's theory is much broader than conflict theory. Conflict theory generally pertains to power relations, whereas Black's theory pertains to differences across several types of social relationships, some involving power and some not.

A UNIFIED CONFLICT THEORY OF CRIME

In this section we attempt to bring together some of the most important concepts from the various conflict theories to create an integrated or unified theory. The following conflict theory is derived principally from the theories of Vold, Quinney, and Chambliss and Seidman presented in this chapter.[45]

VALUES AND INTERESTS IN COMPLEX SOCIETIES

1. A person's values (i.e., beliefs about what is good, right, and just or, at least, excusable) and interests (i.e., what rewards or benefits the person) are generally shaped by the conditions in which the person lives.
2. Complex, highly differentiated societies are composed of people who live under very different conditions.
3. Therefore, the more complex and differentiated the society, the more that people within the society have different and conflicting values and interests.

PATTERNS OF INDIVIDUAL ACTION

4. People tend to act in ways that are consistent with their values and interests. That is, they tend to act in ways that they think are good, right, and just or, at least, excusable. They also tend to act in ways that benefit themselves personally.
5. When values and interests conflict, people tend to adjust their values to come into line with their interests. Over time, people tend to believe that the actions that benefit them personally are really good, right, and just or, at least, excusable.
6. Because the conditions of one's life (and therefore one's values and interests) tend to be relatively stable over time, people tend to develop relatively stable patterns of action that benefit them personally and that they believe are good, right, and just or, at least, excusable.

THE ENACTMENT OF CRIMINAL LAWS

7. The enactment of criminal laws is part of a general legislative process of conflict and compromise in which organized groups (and, to a much less extent, private individuals) attempt to promote and defend their values and interests.

8. Specific criminal laws usually represent a combination of the values and interests of many different groups, rather than the values and interests of one particular group. Nevertheless, the greater a group's political and economic power, the more the criminal law in general tends to represent the values and interests of that group.

9. Therefore, in general, the greater a group's political and economic power, the less likely it is that the group's relatively stable patterns of action (i.e., actions that benefit group members personally and that they believe are good, right, and just or, at least, excusable) will violate the criminal law, and vice versa.

THE ENFORCEMENT OF CRIMINAL LAWS

10. In general, the more political and economic power that people have, the more difficult it is for official law enforcement agencies to process them, and the less political and economic power that people have, the easier it is for official law enforcement agencies to process them, when their behavior violates the criminal law.

11. As bureaucracies, law enforcement agencies tend to process easier, rather than more difficult, cases.

12. Therefore, in general, law enforcement agencies tend to process individuals with less, rather than more, political and economic power.

THE DISTRIBUTION OF OFFICIAL CRIME RATES

13. Because of the processes of criminal law enactment and law enforcement described earlier, the distribution of official crime rates in every society (i.e., arrests, convictions, imprisonments, and executions) will tend to be the inverse of the distribution of political and economic power in that society, independent of any other factors (e.g., social, psychological, or biological factors affecting the behavior of offenders or the behavior of criminal justice agents).

This united conflict theory presents a theoretical chain that begins with general social structural characteristics, moves through the processes by which individuals in similar social structural locations learn similar patterns of behavior, and concludes by relating these patterns of behavior to the processes of enacting and enforcing criminal laws in order to explain the distribution of official crime rates.[46] Because it combines and interrelates a theory of criminal behavior with a theory of the behavior of criminal law, this theory is described as a "unified theory of crime."

TESTING CONFLICT CRIMINOLOGY

Conflict criminologists generally are able to demonstrate that broad patterns in crime and criminal justice are consistent with the arguments and predictions of their theories. But other possible explanations also exist for the same patterns. The major problem with testing conflict criminology is distinguishing between conflict explanations and the other possible explanations. This problem is experienced by research testing both macro-level minority threat theory and the processing of individuals through the criminal justice system.

MINORITY THREAT THEORY

At the aggregate level, conflict theory would posit that in areas where minorities pose an increasing threat to the status quo, formal social control will focus more exclusively on those minorities. However, public choice theory argues that the application of former social control in an area is driven by democratic consensus based on rational considerations.[47] If the actual crime levels in areas with greater minority populations were higher than average, public choice theory would suggest that greater formal social control there was a result of crime, and not of a minority threat. Minority threat theory is based primarily on Blalock's argument that as the relative size of a minority group increases, the majority group will perceive that as a threat, either economic (competition for limited economic resources) or political.[48] This argument has been extended to incorporate criminal threat, by those who posit that large numbers of minority groups will result in more formal social control, such as increased police strength through size and numbers.[49] The relationship between perceived minority threat and systemic response might be nonlinear, such as when a minority population reaches a point of considerable political influence the level of social control directed toward them might actually decelerate.[50]

Most research testing minority threat theory has operationalized threat on the aggregate level (using measures such as size of the minority population and concentrated disadvantage), and has measured police strength by size and expenditures. These tests employ either cross-sectional, panel, or time-series designs, and usually employ the city as the unit of analysis. Thus, for example, they might ask whether the size of minority populations in a number of cities is associated with police strength, controlling for variables representing public choice theory (which suggests police strength is driven by crime rate and other factors not related to minority status). Or, studies may examine a single city (or several cities) over time, asking if changes in minority population size over time is associated with change in police strength.

Cross-sectional analyses (multiple cities, same year), have generally found a significant linear and sometimes nonlinear effect of percent black population on police strength, and some of these studies have also found linear and nonlinear effects of percent Hispanic on police strength.[51] Panel studies compare effects across time periods (for example, every five or ten years), thereby disentangling reciprocal effects between crime and police strength and assessing the extent to which police strength is determined by its previous level. These studies generally find support for the threat hypothesis, but also find that the greatest predictor of police strength is lagged police strength (prior levels).[52] Because it is difficult to determine the period of this lag, and there are other methodological problems with the panel design, some studies employ complex time-series designs, focusing on a single place over a number of years. The bulk of these studies confirm the minority threat hypothesis, that the size (or in some cases, increase in size) of the minority population, controlling for variables such as crime rate and unemployment, is positively associated with police strength as reflecting formal social control.[53]

One criticism of these tests of minority threat theory is that they predominantly focus solely on the black population (and sometimes Hispanic), without considering other minority groups. Additionally, they rarely address whether different minority groups in the same place may pose more or less of a threat, compared to each other, over different time periods. Very recently, Snipes, Maguire, and Wang proposed a "successive threat theory of police expenditures," which blends minority threat theory and ethnic succession theory (see Chapter 8 regarding the latter):

> Successive threat theory represents a logical nexus of minority threat and ethnic succession. In particular, successive threat theory extends minority threat theory and constitutes an integrative framework between minority threat theory and ethnic succession theory by arguing that the perceived threat posed by a threatening racial or ethnic group is not static and may dissipate over time as this racial or ethnic group becomes culturally assimilated and politically viable; another minority group, as its relative size increases, may emerge as a newly threatening group that elicits perceived threat among the majority and in turn perceived needs for greater level of social control.[54]

Snipes et al. performed a first test of their theory in Chicago, from 1893 to 1965. They found that the size of German, Italian, and black populations was significantly related to police expenditures, but only during the periods which for historical reasons, they would be deemed less or more threatening. As Germans, who had posed a threat in the last part of the nineteenth century, began assimilating and decreasing in numbers by the turn of the century, their decrease in size was associated with a decrease in police expenditures (controlling for a wide range of other variables, such as homicide, unemployment, city expenditures, and the size of other groups). The relative size of Italian groups, during the prohibition era in the 1920s and 1930s, was positively associated with police strength. Percent black was positively associated with police strength during two time periods: the first Great Migration, in the second decade of the twentieth century, and the second Great Migration, post-World War II.

THE PROCESSING OF INDIVIDUALS THROUGH THE JUSTICE SYSTEM

Other tests of conflict criminology do not assume a threat hypothesis but focus instead on routine bureaucratic factors. For example, when considering whether to make an arrest, a police officer may conclude that conviction is unlikely because of the political and economic power of the offender. The officer then may be reluctant to do all the work (e.g., fill out all the forms) to process an official arrest, even if there are strong grounds for the arrest. On the other hand, a police officer may be quite solicitous of powerful victims who request the arrest of an offender, and they may make that arrest even if conviction seems unlikely and the grounds for arrest are not strong. Thus, variation in police arrest decisions, especially with offenses that are less serious, may reflect the degree of political and economic power of offenders and victims but be unrelated to any macro-level threat.

Similar problems of interpretation arise with the attempt to explain variations in imprisonment rates. In 1999, for example, there were 3,408 African American males in prison for every 100,000 population, compared to 417 European American males,[55] a ratio of more than eight to one. The question is whether a conflict-type theory explains these patterns, or whether they are explained by other, different theories.

Often, this question is phrased in terms of differential offending versus differential processing. That is, how much of these differences in imprisonment rates are explained by more frequent and more serious offending by African American males, and how much is explained by the fact that for one reason or another, African American males are processed differently by the criminal justice system? Another way to phrase the same question is this: To what extent are criminal justice decisions, particularly at sentencing, influenced by nonlegal variables, such as race and class, as opposed to legally relevant variables, such as the seriousness of the present offense and the length of the prior record?

In the 1960s and early 1970s, many researchers concluded that African Americans were sentenced more harshly than European Americans. But Hagan found that for the most part, these early studies did not control for the seriousness of the present offense or the length of prior records.[56] Once studies began to control for such factors, the effect of race largely disappeared. In addition, Hagan argued that the actual amount of disparity that was found in these early studies (e.g., the number of days served in jail) was fairly small.

After reviewing the research on this subject, Walker and his colleagues reached the conclusion that the influence of extra-legal variables at any particular decision point in the criminal justice system is small.[57] However, they also argued that there is more extra-legal influence at some stages of the criminal justice system than at others, more in some jurisdictions than in others, and more for some types of crime than for others.

More important, they pointed out that criminal justice involves a sequence of decisions, with each decision determined, at least in part, by earlier decisions. These effects tend to accumulate as a person moves through the system and can become quite large. For example, the effect of race on sentencing is small, since most sentencing is determined by legally relevant variables. But African Americans are more likely to be sentenced to prison because they are less likely to retain private attorneys.[58] In addition, African Americans tend to be given longer prison sentences because they are less likely to make bail, which reduces their ability to provide an effective defense.[59] Thus, although race has only a small effect on sentencing, race also affects the ability to hire a private attorney and make bail, and those then have a separate effect on sentencing. The total effect of race on sentencing should therefore include the effect of race on these earlier decision points. Thus, if all these racial effects are added up, the total effect of race on sentencing is fairly large.

This accumulation of effects has been well documented in the processing of juveniles.[60] Small differences in the handling of poor and minority children tend to accumulate as children move through the system and result in large overall effects. These differences are generally attributed, in one way or another, to prejudicial attitudes by juvenile justice agents. Moore, however, raised the possibility that at least some of these differences may not be due to prejudice at all.[61] Rather, he suggested that fewer family and community resources are available to help poor and minority children, so that even in the complete absence of prejudice by juvenile justice agents, such children and their families are disproportionately subjected to official processing. Indeed, Moore suggested that the entire overrepresentation of minorities in the juvenile justice system may not be the result of prejudice at all, but rather "the result of real differences in family and community capacity."[62] Moore described this factor as "the most troubling possibility."

Like Moore's findings with regard to juvenile justice, most of the accumulated small effects in the adult criminal justice system, it would seem, do not result from race prejudice but instead from the routine operations of the system as it relates to social class. Wealthy African Americans, such as O. J. Simpson, are able to marshal much of the same resources as wealthy European Americans to impede and prevent their being officially defined and processed as criminals.[63] This finding is consistent with conflict criminology's focus on political and economic power, which is more directly related to class than to race.

All of the foregoing has concerned the routine operations of the criminal justice system in enforcing the criminal laws. Beyond that are the definitions found in the criminal laws themselves, particularly the types of actions that are defined as criminal and the types of criminal actions that are defined as more or less serious. In other words, beyond the enforcement of criminal laws lies their enactment. A concrete example can be found in the debate over sentencing for crack versus powder cocaine.[64] Both are forms of the same drug, but (until recently) 5 grams of crack got the same mandatory sentence in federal law as 500 grams of powder. Crack cocaine is predominantly used by the poor and African American; powder cocaine is predominantly used by the rich and European American. The difference in sentencing may reflect an overall tendency to define the illegal actions of poor and minority individuals as "more serious" than the illegal actions of wealthy and majority individuals. Tonry went even further, arguing that the entire war on drugs was "foreordained to affect disadvantaged black youths disproportionately" and that it required "the willingness of the drug war's planners to sacrifice young black Americans."[65]

Tonry's conflict-oriented interpretation of the drug war can be contradicted by other, nonconflict, interpretations of the same set of facts. For example, differences in mandatory sentencing for crack versus powder cocaine may reflect differences in the extent to which they are associated with violent crime. However, empirical tests of these alternate interpretations are difficult to arrange.

Despite this pervasive difficulty with testing conflict-type interpretations, it seems undeniable that political and economic power have at least some impact on the enactment and enforcement of criminal laws and therefore on the resulting distribution of official crime rates. The real question seems to be the extent of that impact. Does the distribution of power shape the overall distribution of official crime rates? Or is the effect of power only slight and marginal, operating around the edges of real crime?

CONCLUSIONS

Theories of conflict criminology imply that greater equality in the distribution of power among groups in society should result in greater equality in the distribution of official crime rates.[66] Groups that presently have high official crime rates should have lower rates as they use their newly acquired power to pursue and defend their values and interests legally. Groups that presently have low official crime rates should find themselves with higher rates as their ability to pursue and defend their values and interests is increasingly hindered by other groups. Despite these increases, there should be an overall reduction in the total amount of crime in the society, reflecting reductions in overall levels of conflict as the power of groups is equalized.[67]

Within the context of conflict theory, the specific process by which a redistribution of power can be achieved is through the establishment of organized groups by which the presently unorganized aggregates of individuals are able to pursue and defend their values and interests.[68] This process bears a resemblance to the policy implication of control theory, since it entails bonding previously isolated individuals to groups that will interact with other groups according to mutually agreed-upon rules. The difference is that control theory generally implies that the individual should be bonded to "conventional" groups, whereas conflict criminology implies that the individual should be bonded to other individuals who have similar values and interests and who occupy similar social structural locations. To the extent that particular individuals are considered deviant, the groups that best represent their values and interests will also be considered deviant. The view that the best solution to social conflict lies in the representation of diverse aggregates of individuals by an equally diverse number of organized groups under conditions of relative equality is the reason why conflict theory in general is most comfortable with pluralist democracy as a form of government.[69]

Conflict criminology asserts that there is a general tendency for power and official crime rates to be inversely related. In the context of this assertion, it is interesting to consider Lord Acton's famous observation: "Power corrupts, and absolute power corrupts absolutely." Power may corrupt, but official criminalization requires that there be some greater power able to define that corruption as criminal. Otherwise, no matter how corrupt the action is, it either will not be defined as a crime in the criminal law, or the person will not be processed as a criminal through the criminal justice system. Absolute power may corrupt absolutely, but people with absolute power are never officially defined as criminals.[70]

KEY TERMS

conflict criminology
consensus theorists
conduct norms
primary cultural conflicts
secondary cultural conflicts
group conflict theory
social process
minority power groups
social reality of crime
segments of society
trouble cases
natural law

goal-substituting behavior
quantity of law
power differentials
unified conflict theory of crime
minority threat theory
successive threat theory
differential offending
differential processing
nonlegal variables (extra-legal variables)
accumulation of effects

DISCUSSION QUESTIONS

1. How would consensus theorists define a law, and how would they argue that a law gets implemented? How would conflict theorists answer these questions?
2. See if you can find a controversial Supreme Court decision or two in which the holdings would be consistent with the claims of conflict theorists. Describe.
3. In what ways is Black's *Behavior of Law Theory* consistent with conflict theory?
4. What specific factors make it less likely that white-collar offenders will be criminally prosecuted?
5. How would a conflict theorist explain impulsive and irrational criminal acts that are unrelated to different interest-group battles?
6. Would a conflict theorist hold that people of low social power actually commit more crimes?
7. What did Quinney mean when he said powerful individuals and groups "promote particular conceptions of crime in order to legitimize their authority"?

NOTES

1. A history of the consensus-conflict debate, going back to Plato and Aristotle, can be found in Thomas J. Bernard, *The Consensus-Conflict Debate: Form and Content in Social Theories* (New York: Columbia University Press, 1983).
2. Thorsten Sellin, *Culture Conflict and Crime* (New York: Social Science Research Council, 1938), pp. 32–33.
3. Ibid., pp. 63, 104, 105.
4. George B. Vold, *Theoretical Criminology* (New York: Oxford University Press, 1958), pp. 203–219.
5. Vold relied primarily on Simmel's sociology of conflict. See *The Sociology of Georg Simmel*, trans. and with an introduction by Kurt H. Wolff (Glencoe, IL: Free Press, 1950); see also Simmel's *Conflict* (trans. by Kurt H. Wolff) and *The Web of Group Affiliations*, trans. Reinhard Bendix (Glencoe, IL: Free Press, 1955). Simmel's work is analyzed in Lewis A. Coser, *The Functions of Social Conflict* (Glencoe, IL: Free Press, 1956). See also Bernard, *The Consensus-Conflict Debate*, pp. 111–142.
6. Austin Turk, *Criminality and Legal Order* (Chicago: Rand McNally, 1969), p. 53.
7. Ibid., pp. 58–61.
8. Ibid., pp. 65–67.
9. Ibid., pp. 67–70.
10. Richard Quinney, *The Social Reality of Crime* (Boston: Little, Brown, 1970). Quinney summarized his theory in six propositions on pp. 15–23.
11. Ibid., p. 38.

12. Vold, *Theoretical Criminology*, p. 219.
13. This argument relies particularly on Peter L. Berger and Thomas Luckmann, *The Social Construction of Reality* (Garden City, NY: Doubleday, 1966).
14. William J. Chambliss and Robert B. Seidman, *Law, Order, and Power* (Reading, MA: Addison-Wesley, 1971). Other conflict analyses of criminal justice that were published about the same time include Stuart L. Hills, *Crime, Power, and Morality: The Criminal Law Process in the United States* (New York: Chandler, 1971); Richard Quinney, *Critique of Legal Order* (Boston: Little, Brown, 1973); Erik Olin Wright, *The Politics of Punishment* (New York: Harper & Row, 1973); Clayton A. Hartjen, *Crime and Criminalization* (New York: Praeger, 1974); Barry Krisberg, *Crime and Privilege* (Englewood Cliffs, NJ: Prentice-Hall, 1975); and Harold E. Pepinsky, *Crime and Conflict* (New York: Academic Press, 1976).
15. Chambliss and Seidman, *Law, Order, and Power*, p. 4.
16. Edmund Burke, *Works* (London: H. J. Bohn, 1893), p. 447, quoted in Chambliss and Seidman, *Law, Order, and Power*, p. 63.
17. Chambliss and Seidman, *Law, Order, and Power*, p. 73.
18. Burke, *Works*, pp. 473–474, quoted in Chambliss and Seidman, *Law, Order, and Power*, p. 63.
19. Chambliss and Seidman, *Law, Order, and Power*, p. 75.
20. Ibid., pp. 125–128.
21. Ibid., pp. 128–131.
22. Ibid., pp. 131–145.
23. Ibid., pp. 141–142.
24. Ibid., p. 151.
25. Ibid., pp. 95–115.
26. The theory is summarized in six points on ibid., p. 269.
27. Ibid., citing Burke, Works, p. 503.
28. Donald Black, *The Behavior of Law* (New York: Academic Press, 1976), pp. 3–4.
29. Ibid., pp. 4–5.
30. Ibid., p. 13.
31. Ibid., p. 37.
32. Ibid., p. 61.
33. Ibid., p. 85.
34. Ibid., p. 105.
35. Ibid., p. 41.
36. Ibid., pp. 65–66.
37. Ibid., p. x.
38. Donald Black, *Sociological Justice* (New York: Oxford University Press, 1989).
39. See Thomas J. Bernard, "Review Essay: Donald Black's Sociological Justice," *The Critical Criminologist* 3, no. 2 (1991): 7–8, 13–14.
40. Michael Gottfredson and Michael Hindelang "A Study of the Behavior of Law," *American Sociological Review* 44 (1979): 3–18.
41. Donald Black, "Common Sense in the Sociology of Law," *American Sociological Review* 44 (1979): 18–27.

42. Gottfredson and Hindelang, "Theory and Research in the Sociology of Law" *American Sociological Review* 44 (1979): 27–37.

43. But see Larry Hembroff, "Testing Black's Theory of Law," *American Journal of Sociology* 93 (1987): 322–347; and Gloria Lessan and Joseph Sheley, "Does Law Behave?" *Social Forces* 70 (1992): 655–678. For a discussion of this issue, see Thomas J. Bernard, "The Black Hole—Sources of Confusion for Criminologists in Black's Theory," *Social Pathology* 1 (1995): 218–227.

44. Katherine Jamieson and Anita Neuberger Blowers, "A Structural Examination of Misdemeanor Court Disposition Patterns," *Criminology* 31 (1993): 243–262.

45. Earlier versions can be found in Thomas J. Bernard, "The Distinction Between Conflict and Radical Criminology," *Journal of Criminal Law and Criminology* 72 (1981): 362–379, and in the second, third, and fourth editions of the present book.

46. Akers makes a similar argument about structural sources of behavior and social processes of learning those behaviors. Ronald L. Akers, *Deviant Behavior: A Social Learning Process* (Belmont, CA: Wadsworth, 1985, pp. 61-68). The present argument extends the theoretical chain to the distribution of official crime rates.

47. Ted Bergstrom and Robert P. Goodman, "Private Demands for Public Goods," *American Economic Review* 63 (1973): 280–298.

48. Hubert Blalock, *Toward a Threat of Minority Group Relations* (New York: John Wiley, 1967).

49. E.g., Lincoln Quillian and Devah Pager, "Black Neighbors, Higher Crime? The Role of Racial Stereotypes in Valuations of Neighborhood Crime," *American Journal of Sociology* 107 (2001): 717–767.

50. Pamela Irving Jackson and Leo Carroll, "Race and the War on Crime: The Socio-Political Determinants of Municipal Police Expenditures in 90 Non-Southern Cities," *American Sociological Review* 46 (1981): 290–305; David Jacobs, Jason T. Carmichael, and Stephanie L. Kent, "Vigilantism, Current Racial Threat, and Death Sentences," *American Sociological Review* 70 (2005): 656–677.

51. For a review of these studies, see Jeffrey B. Snipes, Edward R. Maguire, and Xia Wang, "A Successive Threat Theory of Police Expenditures," *Crime & Delinquency*, first published online, April 3, 2019, https://doi.org/10.1177%2F0011128719839360, pp. 4–6.

52. Ibid.

53. Ibid.

54. Ibid., p. 8.

55. Allen J. Beck, *Bureau of Justice Statistics Bulletin: Prisoners in 1999* (Washington, DC: US Department of Justice, 2000), Table 14.

56. John Hagan, "Extra-legal Attributes and Criminal Sentencing: An Assessment of a Sociological Viewpoint," *Law and Society Review* 8 (1974): 357–383.

57. Samuel Walker, Cassia Spohn, and Miriam DeLone, *The Color of Justice: Race, Ethnicity, and Crime in America*, 2nd ed. (Belmont, CA: Wadsworth, 2000). For a different conclusion, see William Wilbanks, *The Myth of a Racist Criminal Justice System* (Monterey, CA: Brooks/Cole, 1987).

58. Cassia Spohn, J. Gruhl, and Susan Welch, "The Effect of Race on Sentencing: A Re-examination of an Unsettled Question," *Law and Society Review* 16 (1981–1982): 72–88.

59. Alan Lizotte, "Extra-Legal Factors in Chicago's Criminal Courts: Testing the Conflict Model of Criminal Justice," *Social Problems* 25 (1978): 564–580.

60. E.g., Belinda McCarthy and Brent L. Smith, "The Conceptualization of Discrimination in the Juvenile Justice Process," *Criminology* 24 (1986): 41–64; Barry Krisberg, Ira Schwartz, Gideon Fishman, Zvi Eisikovits, Edna Guttman, and Karen Joe, "The Incarceration of Minority Youth," *Crime and Delinquency* 32 (1987): 5–38; Carl E. Pope and William H. Feyerherm, "Minority Status and Juvenile Justice Processing: An Assessment of the Research Literature," *Criminal Justice Abstracts* 22 (1990): 327–335 and 527–542; Donna M. Bishop and Charles S. Frazier, "The Influence of Race in Juvenile Justice Processing," *Journal of Research in Crime and Delinquency* 25 (1988): 242–263; and Bishop and Frazier, "Race Effects in Juvenile Justice Decision-Making," *Journal of Criminal Law and Criminology* 86 (1996): 392–413.

61. Mark Harrison Moore, *From Children to Citizens: The Mandate for Juvenile Justice* (New York: Springer-Verlag, 1987), p. 112.

62. See also Jennifer Calnon and Thomas J. Bernard, "Discrimination Without Prejudice," unpublished manuscript. Calnon and Bernard argued that even in the total absence of prejudice, many formal criminal justice policies produce differences in outcomes that are related to race and class but are unrelated to the individual's offending behavior. They described this effect as "discrimination without prejudice" and concluded that criminal justice policies that produce discrimination without prejudice are a much larger and more troubling problem than is racial or class prejudice by criminal justice agents.

63. E.g., see Gregg Barak, ed., *Representing O. J.: Murder, Criminal Justice, and Mass Culture* (Guilderland, NY: Harrow and Heston, 1996).

64. Kathryn K. Russell, *The Color of Crime* (New York: New York University Press, 1998).

65. Michael Tonry, *Malign Neglect* (New York: Oxford University Press, 1995), p. 123.

66. Bruce A. Arrigo and Thomas J. Bernard, "Post Modern Criminology in Relation to Radical and Conflict Theory," *Critical Criminology* 8 (1997): 39–60.

67. This conclusion is consistent with research that has shown that reductions in economic inequality are associated with reductions in violence. See Chapter 5.

68. Ralf Dahrendorf, *Class and Class Conflict in Industrial Society* (Stanford, CA: Stanford University Press, 1959), pp. 225–227.

69. Ibid.; and Coser, *The Functions of Social Conflict*.

70. See Thomas Hobbes, *Leviathan* (New York: E. P. Dutton, 1950), chap. 18, p. 148.

CHAPTER 12

—◢

Marxist, Postmodern, and Green Criminology

The term *critical criminology* has been described as "an umbrella designation for a series of evolving, emerging perspectives" that are "characterized particularly by an argument that it is impossible to separate values from the research agenda, and by a need to advance a progressive agenda favoring disprivileged peoples."[1] This chapter focuses on three of these critical perspectives—Marxist criminology, postmodern criminology, and green criminology.[2] Feminist criminology, another perspective that sometimes is also described as critical criminology, is discussed in the next chapter on gender and crime.

Like the conflict theories presented in the previous chapter, critical theories share the view that inequality in power is causally related to the problem of crime. But conflict theory largely ignores the sources or origins of power, while critical perspectives make specific arguments on that issue. Marxist theories generally locate power in ownership of the means of production, while postmodern theories locate it in the control over language systems.[3] Both perspectives imply that the crime problem can be solved only if power arrangements are changed.

These are "radical" theories in the sense of the Latin word (*radix*) for root.[4] Getting to the root of the problem of crime, according to these perspectives, requires social change at the most fundamental level. Ultimately, these perspectives focus on ideals, such as social justice, and attempt to determine how contemporary societies can achieve these ideals. The focus on "what ought to be" rather than "what is," on the ideal rather than on the real, is what most distinguishes these theories from mainstream criminology, including conflict theory.[5]

Critical theories are difficult to summarize for two reasons. First, their complexity leads to profound disagreements among different theorists within the same area. Second, theorists in these areas may frequently change their own positions as their thinking develops. Thus, one theorist may take one position at one time and a different position only a short time later. Consequently, one can only summarize some of the major themes, but a great many arguments must be left out.

OVERVIEW OF MARX'S THEORY

Karl Marx (1818–1883) wrote in the immediate aftermath of the massive social changes that were brought about by the Industrial Revolution.[6] In one life span (approximately 1760–1840), the world as it had been for a thousand years suddenly changed. Marx attempted to explain why these profound changes had occurred when they did and to give some sense of what was coming next. His theory linked economic development to social, political, and historical change, but it did not deal with the problem of crime in any significant way.

The principal conflict that Marx presented in his theory, and on which the theory is based, was the conflict between the material forces of production and the social relations of production.[7] The term *material forces of production* generally refers to a society's capacity to produce material goods and includes technological equipment and the knowledge, skill, and organization to use that equipment. The term *social relations of production* refers to relationships among people. These relationships include property relationships, which determine how the goods produced by the material forces of production are distributed—that is, who gets what.

The development of the material forces of production is relatively continuous throughout history, since it consists of the development of technology, skills, and so forth. The social relations of production, however, tend to freeze into particular patterns for long periods. When first established, the social relations enhance the development of the material forces of production, but as time goes by, they become increasingly inconsistent with the material forces and begin to impede their further development. At some point, the social relations change abruptly and violently, and new social relations are established that once again enhance the development of the material forces of production.

Marx used this general model to explain the profound changes that had just occurred in European societies. When the social relations of feudalism were first established, they were progressive in the sense that they were necessary for the further development of the material forces of production. After a thousand years, however, the material forces of production had developed extensively, but the social relations had hardly changed at all. At that point, the social relations of feudalism were hindering the further development of the material forces of production. The massive changes of the Industrial Revolution reflected a sudden and violent restructuring of the social relations of production. The new social relations—bourgeois capitalism—were progressive in the sense that they were necessary for the further development of the material forces of production.

Having analyzed the causes of the violent and abrupt social changes in Europe, Marx used the same basic analysis to predict what would happen next. The material forces of production would continuously develop under capitalism, but the social relations would remain relatively fixed, just as they had under feudalism. Over time, the social relations of capitalism would therefore increasingly become a hindrance to the further development of the material forces of production. Ultimately, Marx predicted, there would be a sudden and violent restructuring of the social relations in which socialism would replace capitalism.

Marx was fairly specific on why he thought this restructuring would happen. The logic of capitalism is "survival of the fittest," with the "fittest" gobbling up the "less fit." As Marx phrased it: "One capitalist always kills many."[8] By this process, property is increasingly concentrated into fewer and fewer hands, and former capitalists are transformed into wage laborers who work for someone else instead of having other people work for them. At the same time, increasing mechanization in business and industry means that fewer workers are needed, so that there is an increasing pool of underemployed and unemployed workers. With so many workers available who want jobs, those who have jobs can be paid low wages because others will work for even less.

Thus, Marx argued, capitalist societies tend to polarize into two conflicting groups. One group consists of people who, as they gobble up their competitors, own an increasing portion of the property in the society. Over time, this group grows smaller and richer. The other group, consisting of employed and unemployed wage laborers, keeps getting larger and poorer, as mechanization increases unemployment and real wages decrease because the supply of labor exceeds the demand for it.

This polarization, one group growing smaller and richer, the other growing larger and poorer, is what Marx called the "contradiction" in capitalism; as it becomes more extreme, it acts as a great hindrance to the further development of the material forces of production. Thus, a revolutionary restructuring of the social relations of production is inevitable at some point. To end the cycles of overproduction and depression that plague capitalism,[9] Marx believed that restructuring should entail the establishment of collective ownership of the means of production and the institution of centralized planning.

MARX ON CRIME, CRIMINAL LAW, AND CRIMINAL JUSTICE

Marx did not discuss at length the problem of crime or its relation to the economic system, although he did address the subject in several passages.[10] Two of Marx's arguments in these passages have been particularly important in later Marxist theories of criminal behavior.

First, Marx argued that it was essential to human nature that people be productive in life and in work. But in industrialized capitalist societies, the large numbers of unemployed and underemployed people are unproductive and become demoralized; thus, they are subject to all forms of crime and vice. Marx called these demoralized people the lumpenproletariat.[11]

Second, Marx argued against the classical philosophy, dominant in his day, that all people freely and equally joined in a social contract for the common good and that the law represented a consensus of the general will.[12] Marx maintained that this view ignored the fact that an unequal distribution of wealth in a society produced an unequal distribution of power. Those with no wealth have no power in the formation of the social contract, whereas those with great wealth can control it to represent their own interests. Thus Marx did not see crime as the willful violation of the common good, but as "the struggle of the isolated individual against the prevailing conditions."[13] This conclusion is sometimes called Marx's primitive rebellion thesis, since it implies that crime is a primitive form of rebellion against the dominant social order, one that eventually may develop into conscious revolutionary activity.

Marx also wrote several passages analyzing the historical origins of criminal laws and criminal justice agencies. While still a follower of the philosopher Hegel, the young Marx wrote several articles on the crime of the theft of wood in Germany around 1840.[14] Traditionally, the nobility had the right to hunt and chase in the forest, while the peasants had the right to collect forest products such as wood. In the early 1800s, however, the value of wood increased dramatically because of a boom in shipbuilding, railroad building, and so on. A number of laws were passed that took away the traditional rights of the peasants and defined the taking of wood from the forest as a crime. The enforcement of these laws then became a major function of criminal justice agencies, and in some locations almost three-quarters of criminal prosecutions were for forest crimes such as the taking of wood. On the basis of his Hegelian philosophy, Marx argued that the "true" state would uphold the rights of all citizens, whereas these laws represented the interests only of the forest owners.[15]

Marx later argued in *Capital* that the economic basis of capitalism rested on a similar theft of the traditional rights of the peasants.[16] Prior to capitalism, most peasants were independent producers with hereditary rights to the use of state-owned, church-owned, or commonly held lands. Through a variety of legal means, the peasants' rights to these lands were terminated, their traditional ways of earning a living were declared illegal, and the lands they had used were turned over to private capitalists. Deprived of their traditional means of living, many peasants then became beggars and vagabonds or formed roving bands of robbers. All these methods of earning a living were also defined as criminal, so that peasants were virtually forced by the criminal law to become wage laborers working for the capitalists. Marx documented that whenever they were given a choice, peasants attempted to remain independent producers rather than become wage laborers. Thus, he argued, the economic basis of capitalism had been established by a theft of the grandest scale imaginable, a theft accomplished through the coercive power of the criminal law.

THE EMERGENCE OF MARXIST CRIMINOLOGY

An early Marxist criminologist, Willem Bonger, provided an extensive theory of crime in his book *Criminality and Economic Conditions*, published in 1916.[17] Bonger argued that the capitalist economic system encouraged all people to be greedy and selfish and to pursue their own benefits without regard for the welfare of their fellows. Crime is concentrated in the lower classes because the justice system criminalizes the greed of the poor while it allows legal opportunities for the rich to pursue their selfish desires. Bonger argued that a socialist society would ultimately eliminate crime because it would promote a concern for the welfare of the whole society and would remove the legal bias that favors the rich.

After the mid-1920s Marxist criminology virtually disappeared from the English-speaking world,[18] but it reappeared in the 1970s in connection with the radical social climate of the times.[19] These versions of Marxist criminology tended to portray criminals in terms of Marx's primitive rebellion thesis—that is, criminals were engaged in crime as an unconscious form of rebellion against the capitalist economic system. The 1970s also produced instrumentalist views of the criminal justice system—that is, that the enactment and enforcement of criminal laws are solely the instruments of a unified and monolithic ruling class that conspires to seek its own advantage at the expense of other groups.

These simplistic views of criminals and criminal justice were criticized almost immediately by others as misinterpretations of Marx's thought.[20] Block and Chambliss, for example, criticized the early theories for their simplistic portrayal of the ruling class as a unified and monolithic elite, for the argument that the enactment and enforcement of laws reflects only the interests of this ruling class, and for the argument that criminal acts are a political response to conditions of oppression and exploitation.[21] Greenberg pointed out that these theories ignored studies that showed a widespread consensus on legal definitions of crime; that underprivileged people are most frequently victims of crime by other underprivileged people, so that they have an interest in the enforcement of criminal laws; and that it is unrealistic to expect that crime will be eliminated in socialist societies.[22] Greenberg later described these theories as primarily political statements, rather than genuine academic arguments about the nature of crime.[23] When the politics of the New Left collapsed, "leftists who retained their political commitments dug in for the long haul." Some turned to community organizing, while others turned to Marxist theory to deepen their understanding of the broader social processes. Greenberg concluded: "By the mid-1970s, a specifically Marxian criminology began to take shape."[24] This new and rigorous Marxist criminology attempts to relate criminal behavior and crime policies to the political economy of the particular societies in which they occur, and it relies primarily on historical and cross-cultural studies for support, since only in such studies can societies with different political economies be compared.

MARXIST THEORY AND RESEARCH ON CRIME

In this more rigorous Marxist criminology, the simplistic instrumentalist view of criminal law and criminal justice has given way to a more complex structuralist view.[25] In this view, the primary function of the state is not to serve the short-term interests of capitalists directly, but rather to ensure that the social relations of capitalism persist in the long run. This goal requires that many different interests be served at different times, in order to prevent the rise of conditions that will lead to the collapse of capitalism. Thus, on any particular issue, including the enactment and enforcement of criminal laws, the actions of the state may serve other interests besides those of the owners of the means of production. Nevertheless, the owners of the means of production can still be described as a ruling class in that the organized state serves their economic interests in the long run. Moreover, the owners have an excessive amount of political power in comparison to other groups, with a disproportionate ability to get the state to serve their interests in the short run.

Within the context of this structuralist view, Marxists have often focused on the harmfulness of the behaviors of the ruling class in their pursuit of economic self-interest and on the failure of the criminal law and criminal justice agencies to officially define and process these harmful behaviors as criminal. For example, Reiman argued that in terms of property losses, physical injuries, and deaths, the public's victimization by the ruling class is much greater than their victimization by street criminals.[26] Using governmental figures, he estimated the cost of street crime in the United States at about $18 billion per year, while the cost of corporate crime is closer to $1 trillion. In addition, about twice as many people die and eleven times more people are injured because of illegal workplace conditions as die from criminal homicides or are injured in criminal assaults. Reiman also argued that the continuing failure of criminal justice agencies to control street crime actually serves the long-term interests of the ruling class. When the public is in a state of constant anxiety about lower-class crime, attention is diverted away from the public's much greater victimization by the wealthy and powerful.[27]

This Marxist argument is similar to the conflict theory argument, described in the previous chapter, about the ability of high-power groups to shape the enactment and enforcement of criminal laws so that their own behaviors are not defined and processed as criminal. The difference between the two types of theories is that Marxists generally argue that there is some objective basis for determining what is (or what should be) a crime. Marxist and other radical criminologists have therefore explored a wide range of "socially injurious" behaviors that are not officially defined or processed as criminal because they are committed by the powerful against the powerless.[28] These behaviors include "violations of human rights due to racism, sexism, and imperialism; unsafe working conditions; inadequate child care; inadequate opportunities for employment and education; substandard housing and medical care; crimes of economic and political domination; pollution of the environment; price-fixing; police brutality; assassinations; war-making;[29] violations of dignity; denial of physical needs and necessities; and impediments to self-determination, deprivation of adequate food and blocked opportunities to participate in relevant political decisions."[30] Most of these actions are not defined as criminal at all; when they are defined as criminal, the laws are rarely enforced; when enforced, the punishments are usually minimal compared to punishments that are routinely imposed on street criminals whose actions cause less objective harm.

The focus on the socially harmful actions of the ruling class initially led Marxists to ignore or romanticize lower-class street crimes.[31] For example, in 1973 Taylor, Walton, and Young argued that deviant behavior should be considered authentic human action, rather than the product of individual or social pathology.[32] That is, deviance is a manifestation of human diversity, and the criminalization of deviance is a societal need unrelated to the quality of the behavior. These authors concluded: "The task is to create a society in which the facts of human diversity, whether personal, organic or social, are not subject to the power to criminalize."[33] It was to create such a society that these authors turned to Marxism.

However, Marxists who worked in lower-class communities quickly found that lower-class crime, which was directed primarily against other lower-class people, was indeed a serious problem. Therefore, beginning about 1980 or so, Marxists began to propose explanations of lower-class crime that moved away from Marx's primitive rebellion thesis and moved back toward his arguments about the lumpenproletariat. That is, instead of implying that lower-class crime was "authentic human action" in one form or another, the behavior came to be described as the pathological consequences of the social structure of advanced capitalism.[34]

These explanations are quite similar to explanations found in more traditional criminological theories, except that they link their basic concepts to a broader view of political-economic systems and the historical processes in which those systems change.[35] Some of these Marxist theories propose causal arguments that are similar to those found in strain[36] and control[37] theories, but most are similar to traditional criminology theories that describe criminal behavior as socially learned. That is, Marxist theories generally argue that criminal behaviors are the result of social learning by normal individuals in situations that are structured by the social relations of capitalism. This view is consistent with the view found in Marxist theory that in general and in the long run, individuals act and think in ways that are consistent with their economic interests.

For example, Chambliss took this approach in his analysis of organized crime in Seattle.[38] He argued that at one time most of the goods and services provided by organized crime were legal. For various historical reasons, these goods and services were declared illegal, but the demand for them did not disappear. Chambliss then pointed out that in our political system, politicians have a strong need to generate funds in order to run for office, and that at the same time, they control the conditions under which laws against illegal goods and services are enforced. This situation creates very strong pressure for a coalition between politicians and organized crime figures, and Chambliss claimed that he found such a coalition at the heart of organized crime in Seattle. Chambliss was fairly pessimistic about the possibilities for reform to eliminate such crime, except to argue that decriminalization would be helpful. He did note that most reforms merely replaced the people in key positions but did nothing about the basic political-economic forces (demand for illegal goods and services, need for money by politicians) that gave rise to organized crime in the first place. As a result, the new reform people respond to the same forces and therefore tend to take the same kinds of actions done by the corrupt politicians they replaced.

In his later book with Block, Chambliss generalized some of his arguments, relating various types of crime to the political-economic systems of societies in which they occur.[39] Block and Chambliss argued that every political-economic system contains contradictions that cannot be resolved without changing the fundamental structure of the society. Crime in a society is essentially a rational response to those contradictions. The problem with crime-control policies in general is that they attempt to deal with the symptoms without changing the basic political-economic forces that generate those symptoms.[40]

Despite their focus on changing the larger political-economic forces of capitalist society, some Marxist criminologists have attempted to take a more limited approach to the current problems of crime.[41] Called "left realists," these criminologists recognize that crime causes serious problems for working-class citizens and that criminal justice agencies can respond to those problems even if the capitalist economic system is not overthrown.[42] These criminologists have therefore made a variety of policy recommendations that are not much different from the recommendations of mainstream (if liberal) criminologists.[43] In particular, these recommendations include the implementation of decentralized, community-based policing.[44] Community residents often favor repressive, get-tough police policies, and the challenge of the left realist criminologists is to get the community to approach the crime problem in the larger context of oppressive economic conditions and to enlarge their perceptions of the various ways in which they are victimized. Other similar policy recommendations include prosecuting white-collar offenders;[45] reforming prisons;[46] regulating (as opposed to criminalizing) street prostitution;[47] and addressing the major health, housing, and educational needs of inner cities as a long-term strategy for dealing with the drug problem.[48] These and other midrange policy responses to crime attempt to reduce the economic marginality, social alienation, and political oppression that characterize class-based capitalist societies.

OVERVIEW OF POSTMODERNISM

Modernism is associated with what is described in Chapter 1 of this book as the naturalistic approach, including the view that science is an objective process that is directed toward predicting and controlling the world.[49] Most criminology is modernist in this sense, except that the spiritualistic approaches discussed in Chapter 1 may be described as premodernist, since they were the dominant ways of thinking about the world prior to the rise of modernism.

Postmodernist theories attempt to move beyond modernism by arguing that all thinking and all knowledge are mediated by language and that language itself is never a neutral medium.[50] Whether or not people are aware of it, language always privileges some points of view and disparages others. For example, modernism privileges scientific thinking by holding that it has special validity and objectivity in comparison to other types of thinking. Postmodernists, in contrast, do not give scientific thinking a special position and describe it instead as being neither more nor less valid than other types of thinking. To a certain extent, postmodernists even attack scientific thinking because they attempt to deconstruct privileged points of view—that is, they identify implicit assumptions and unsupported assertions that underlie the ways in which the point of view of scientific thinking is legitimated and other points of view are disparaged. At the same time, postmodernists seek out the disparaged points of view in order to make them more explicit and legitimate.[51] The goal is not simply to tear down one point of view and replace it with the other, but rather to come to a situation in which different grammars can be simultaneously held as legitimate, so that there is a sense of the diversity of points of view without assuming that one is superior and the others are inferior.

Schwartz and Friedrichs pointed out that postmodernism is difficult to summarize because "there seems to be an almost infinite number of postmodern perspectives."[52] In addition, Schwartz noted the difficult writing style of many postmodernists, stating that even after reading them several times, "I really do not know what the hell they are talking about."[53] Both these problems are related to postmodernism itself, since it holds that linear thought processes, statements about cause and effect, syllogistic reasoning, objective analyses, and other standards of scientific thinking are no more valid than are other forms of thinking. Thus, to the extent that one tries to summarize postmodern thought in some logical, coherent, systematic fashion, one contradicts postmodern thought itself. Nevertheless, at least some postmodern theorists have attempted to make such summaries while acknowledging the self-contradictory nature of the effort.[54]

Central to postmodernism is the view that modernism in general, and science in particular, has led to increased oppression rather than to liberation:[55]

> [Postmodernism] contends that modernity is no longer liberating, but rather has become a force for subjugation, oppression, and repression; this contention applies to social science itself, which is a product of modernity. Postmodernists are disillusioned with liberal notions of progress and radical expectations of emancipation. . . . The forces of modernism (e.g., industrialism) have extended and amplified the scope of violence in the world. Even worse, according to the postmodern critique, the major form of response to this violence is through rational organizations (e.g., the court system and the regulatory bureaucracies) with great reliance on specialists and experts. Such a response simply reproduces domination, the critique suggests, in perhaps new but no less pernicious forms.

The postmodernist response is to expose the structures of domination in societies as a means of achieving greater liberation. The principal source of this domination, according to postmodernists, is control of language systems[56] because language structures thought—that is, the words and phrases that people use to convey meaning are not neutral endeavors but support dominant views of the world, whether the people who use those languages know it or not.[57]

Postmodernists therefore examine the relationship between human agency and language in creating meaning, identity, truth, justice, power, and knowledge.[58] This relationship is studied through discourse analysis, a method of investigating how sense and meaning are constructed in which attention is paid to the values and assumptions implied in language. Discourse analysis considers the social position of the person who is speaking or writing in order to understand the meaning of what is said or written. However, it is not an analysis of the social roles that people occupy. Rather, it considers how language is embedded in these roles and how that language shapes and forms the way people in these roles think and speak. Thus, these roles are considered as "discursive subject positions."

POSTMODERN CRIMINOLOGY

Within the context of this frame of reference, postmodern criminologists examine "the incommensurable fullness of all human actors (e.g., victims, criminals, police agents, correctional officials, courtroom administrators, judges, attorneys) in their contradictory being and becoming, especially as they participate in the irony and the serendipity of the social order."[59] For example, to understand fully what lawyers mean when they speak as lawyers, it is necessary to understand quite a bit about "lawyering" as a historically situated and structured position in society.[60] There are many other "discursive subject positions" in crime and criminal justice that come connected with their own language systems—those of police, juvenile gang members, drug dealers, corrections officers, organized crime figures, corporate and political offenders, court workers, shoplifters, armed robbers, and even criminologists.

Postmodernist criminologists point out that once people assume one of these discursive subject positions, then the words that they speak no longer fully express their realities, but to some extent express the realities of the larger institutions and organizations. Because people's language is somewhat removed from their reality, people are described as decentered—that is, people are never quite what their words describe and always tend somewhat to be what their language systems expect or demand.[61]

For example, women who have been raped must present their stories to prosecutors, who then reconstruct and repackage the stories into the language of the courts—"legalese."[62] The woman may testify at the trial, but her testimony may not deviate from the accepted language system without jeopardizing the chances that the defendant will be convicted.[63] Even when the defendant is convicted, the woman who has been raped may leave the court with a deep and dissatisfying sense that her story was never fully told, her reality never fully seen, her pain never fully acknowledged. The language of the court system expresses and institutionalizes a form of domination over the victim, and this is one reason why victims are so often dissatisfied with the courts.

A similar situation happens with defendants who are accused of crimes. Criminal defense lawyers routinely repackage and reconstruct the defendant's story into legalese as part of constructing the defense. The lawyer does so because it is the only way to win the case, but the full meaning of the defendant's story is normally lost in the process. Less-experienced defendants may object because the story that is told in court has so little resemblance to what actually happened. But more sophisticated defendants know that this is how the game is played. Even if the defendant "wins" the case (i.e., is acquitted), there has still been a ritualistic ceremony in which the reality of the courts has dominated the reality of the defendant. Thus, independent of who wins the case, the language of the court expresses and institutionalizes the domination of the individual by social institutions.

Other postmodern analyses have demonstrated the way that official language dominates participants in the criminal justice process, so that the participants themselves experience the system as marginalizing, alienating, and oppressive. These analyses have included studies of jailhouse lawyers,[64] police officers responding to 911 calls,[65] and the experience of female lawyers in criminal courts.[66] In each case, one view of reality (i.e., that of the inmates, the police, or the female lawyers) is replaced by another (i.e., the language of the court or correctional system), thereby affirming and legitimating the status quo.

Postmodernists describe the present situation as one in which discourses are either dominant (e.g., the language of medicine, law, and science) or oppositional (e.g., the language of prison inmates). The goal of postmodernism is to move to a situation in which many different discourses are recognized as legitimate. One of the ways of doing so is to establish "replacement discourses" in which the language itself helps people to speak with a more authentic voice and to remain continuously aware of the authentic voices of other people.[67] The goal is greater inclusivity, more diverse communication, and a pluralistic culture. To achieve these ends, postmodernists listen carefully to the otherwise excluded views in constituting the definition of criminal acts. They conclude that creating a society in which alternative discourses liberate citizens from prevailing speech patterns will also legitimate the role of all citizens in the project of reducing crime. The result will be greater respect for the diversity of people in the entire society, less victimizing of other people by criminals, and less official punishment of criminals by agents of the larger society.[68]

Postmodernism exposes a basis for power and domination in societies that has been ignored in earlier conflict and Marxist theories. However, it has tended toward an "appreciative relativism"[69] and "communal celebration,"[70] which resemble early simplistic Marxist views of crime, especially to the extent that they "appreciate" or "celebrate" the actions of criminals when they victimize other people. This view contradicts the later left realist approach, which concludes that crime is a real social problem that needs to be addressed by real criminal justice policies. Pepinsky, however, argued that coercive social policies merely perpetuate the problem:[71]

> Crime is violence. So is punishment, and so is war. People who go to war believe that violence works. So do criminals and people who want criminals punished. All these believe violence works because they also believe that domination is necessary. Someone who is closer to God, natural wisdom, or scientific truth has to keep wayward subordinates in line, or social order goes to hell.

Similarly, Quinney stated:[72]

> The criminal justice system in this country is founded on violence. It is a system that assumes that violence can be overcome by violence, evil by evil. . . . This principle sadly dominates much of our criminology. . . .

When we recognize that the criminal justice system is the moral equivalent of the war machine, we realize that resistance to one goes hand-in-hand with resistance to the other. This resistance must be in compassion and love, not in terms of the violence that is being resisted.

Ultimately, these criminologists have come to the conclusion that the violence of punishment can only perpetuate and increase the violence of crime. Only when criminologists and the public give up their belief in the effectiveness and appropriateness of violence can we reasonably expect criminals to do the same thing.[73]

GREEN CRIMINOLOGY

Green criminology can be viewed as a case study of how various scholars over time attempt to define the parameters of an emerging field of study.[74] The term was first used by Michael Lynch in his essay titled "The Greening of Criminology: A Perspective for the 1990's," published in 1990.[75] As first imagined, green criminology would be a way in which criminologists could use political economy theory to explain harms caused by damaging the ecosystem, and its research would focus predominantly on corporate crime. With a lack of momentum in this direction, the movement turned toward using criminological theory to study environmental justice.

In 1998, in an article that was published in a special edition of the journal *Theoretical Criminology* on the emerging field, Nigel South proposed that green criminology become a "perspective" (rather than a single unified theory), and that the groundwork for this perspective had already been partially laid in various disciplines.[76] South said, "arguably the most serious crime that humanity is currently committing is against itself and its future generations."[77] Humans, as commodities in chains of production and distribution, overexploit the earth and its resources for profit. The environment, thus, can be seen as a victim, and criminology can be expanded to cover both humans and the environment as victims. A few areas of study consistent with this view are pollution and its regulation, corporate crime and its effects on the environment, military impacts on the environment and populations, and injury to wildlife and their natural environments, as well as the policing of those injuries.[78]

To South, a green perspective in criminological theory could be based on a number of theoretical foundations, most notably postmodernism, whereby it would be a necessity to maintain the diversity of the natural world.[79] One important area of study within this perspective would be the response to the exploitation of the environment, including such strategies as compliance, deterrence, and shaming. And an "ecocentric" approach to regulation would in a sense reverse the burden of proof, whereby potential polluters would have to demonstrate that their actions would not irreversibly harm the environment, rather than regulators or enforcers determining after-the-fact that in fact they did cause the harm.[80]

In addition to green criminology's reference to the environment as a victim, others were expanding it to include "nonspeciesist criminology," in which nonhuman animals were seen as victims. In 1999 Piers Beirne published an exposition of this type of criminology, which "begins with the common rejection of the Cartesian view that animals are the moral equivalent of machines" and asks questions such as "How do animals differ from humans?" and "Are the grounds for not abusing animals the same as those for not abusing humans?"[81] Whereas the Cartesian view is that animals are simply appendages to humans, and the traditional system of criminal law recognizes only humans as objects, Singer's utilitarianism and Regan's rights-based theory establish bases for animal protectionism. "For Singer . . . the capacity for suffering is the essential precondition for having interests. Utilitarianism entails equality of consideration for *all* animals, both human and nonhuman."[82] Regan's argument is that the moral community is comprised of moral agents and "moral patients," or "subjects-of-a-life" (including infants, the mentally ill, and the enfeebled). Because many animals have "perception, memory, desire, belief, self-consciousness, intention, and a sense of the future,"[83] they have inherent value and have the same basic rights as human moral patients, including the right to be served with justice.

Whereas green criminologists up to this point had been primarily making arguments based on theories such as political economy and postmodernism, some began to turn more empirical, examining the effects of the physical environment on criminal behavior. Stretesky and Lynch, for example, found that exposure to lead in air was related to homicide levels, as well as property and violent crime, and that this relationship was greater in places with higher levels of resource deprivation.[84] We discussed the relationship between lead and crime earlier in this volume, in Chapters 2 and 4.

It was becoming clear, within a few years into the green criminology movement, that there was no consensus on what "green" meant. In 2003 Lynch and Stretesky said there were two contrasting definitions of green, one aligned with corporate interests, and the other based in environmental justice.[85] Because scholars and media in the late 1980s had predicted the 1990s would be the decade of the environment, and many grass-roots movements were emerging, corporations felt the need to respond. So one definition of green was constructed by corporations, through mass advertising and public relations programs, and involved simple labels, such as McDonald's "going green" by eliminating Styrofoam.[86] By contrast, other definitions of green were employed by participants in the environmental justice movement, including ecofeminism, environmental racism, and the red-green movement. While members of these three groups focused on different aspects of environmental injustice (respectively, patriarchal exploitation of nature and women, pollution and production processes affecting communities of color, and environmental degradation involving capitalist exploitation of the working class), they all shared three orientations. They needed a plan of action addressing structural reforms addressing environmental injustice. They had a common interest in oppression caused as a result of corporate environmental harm. And each was based on a particular historical narrative, be it patriarchy, racial and ethnic subordination, or class struggle.[87]

British, European, and Australian criminologists developed their own forms of green criminology, often parallel to those put forth by Americans. A term commonly used by these scholars is "eco-global" criminology, which examines environmental harm on a global scale. As Rob White described it:

> An eco-global criminology refers to a criminological approach that is informed by ecological considerations and by a critical analysis that is worldwide in its scale and perspective. It is based upon eco-justice conceptions of harm that include consideration of transgressions against environments, nonhuman species, and humans. For this kind of criminology, the first question to ask is "what harm is there in a particular activity?" rather than whether the activity is legal or not . . . Harm is at the centre of the analysis and generally is conceptualised through ecological and anti-speciesist considerations . . . It also tends to be defined in ways that reflect the most powerful interests in a particular social setting.[88]

Eco-global criminologists thus deemphasized the legal/illegal divide and focused on environmental harm more broadly, calling for an approach that would address environmental risk by examining its measurement, definition and meaning, and gathering data through case studies (qualitative) and by quantitative means.[89]

Gibbs and colleagues formed a movement they called conservation criminology, as opposed to green or environmental criminology.[90] Conservation criminology synergized criminal justice and criminology, risk and decision analysis, and natural resource conservation and management, in its attempt to create an overarching, interdisciplinary framework for the study of environmental harm and crime. Gibbs et al. demonstrated the utility of their framework by applying it to the disposal of electronic waste. Routine activity theorists (see Chapter 3) also employed a conservation approach to criminology by, for example, applying the CRAVED model of theft (concealable, removable, available, valuable, enjoyable, and disposable) to parrot poaching.[91]

Another approach to green criminology integrated it with cultural criminology, seeking to "incorporate a concern with the cultural significance of the environment, environmental crime, and environmental harm into the green criminological enterprise."[92] Cultural criminology views culture as the "symbolic environment occupied by individuals and groups" and relates to "threads of collective meaning that wind in and around the everyday troubles of social actors . . . perpetrators, police officers, victims, parole violators, new reporters—*the negotiation of cultural meaning intertwining with the immediacy of criminal experience*."[93] Green-cultural criminology, as proffered by Brisman and South, incorporates the contest of space, transgression, and resistance (from cultural criminology) into perspectives of green criminology. An example of its applications is the exploration of Reclaim the Streets and Critical Mass, which are events involving bicycles and pedestrians that seek to purposefully interfere with normal motor vehicle traffic flow. They can be seen narrowly as anti-car, but can be viewed more broadly as protesting material wealth and fossil fuel consumption, corporate interests and environmental harm.[94]

Some green criminologists remain steadfast in their attempt to ground it in political economy theory. Lynch and colleagues have proposed an environmental sociological approach to the field, which is based on treadmill of production theory (ToP), ecological Marxism, and ecological disorganization.[95] Much of green criminology, as mentioned earlier, is focused on the harm perspective, which was advanced by Hillyard and Tombs.[96] The harm perspective frequently highlights the overemphasis of street crimes (or "conventional" crimes) when compared to crimes against the environment, which injure humans, nonhumans, and ecological systems. Environmental victimizations can be much more damaging than street crimes, in terms of number of victims, intensity of harm, and duration. Pollution, disposal of toxic waste, underground mining fires, and deforestation are some of the ways in which corporations cause unimaginable harm to humans, nonhumans, and nature. Lynch et al.'s framework for tying together these ecological harms is based upon Schnaiberg's treadmill of production theory,[97] which argues that after the Second World War, capitalist expansion began to reduce its reliance on labor, instead shifting capital costs to machinery and chemical and other forms of nonhuman labor.

The resulting consequences of the capitalist expansion and increasing reliance on machinery and chemicals were that the type of pollutants emanating from production changed and increased greatly in magnitude (these are called ecological additions). Additionally, production mechanisms such as the mining of minerals, coals, and metals, the drilling for oil and natural gas, and the harvesting of wood were depleting valuable natural resources (these are termed ecological withdrawals).[98] Because capitalism, by its nature, calls for ever-increasing profits, and ecological additions and withdrawals accomplish this, the process of environmental harm for profit and material consumption, often of luxury goods, is ongoing and assembly-line-like, hence the term "treadmill." From this perspective, the very existence of capitalism is in direct contradiction with the preservation of nature.

In 2018, twenty years after green criminology was introduced in a special edition of *Theoretical Criminology*, the journal published an anniversary edition, a compilation that demonstrates the wide range of content in the field. Topics covered in this edition include the trade of wildlife from a green cultural perspective,[99] the killing of indigenous environmental activists as understood via the treadmill of production,[100] the connections between ecocide and genocide of indigenous peoples as viewed from capitalist and colonialist perspectives,[101] ways in which it may be possible to realize an eco-just future,[102] and biotechnological[103] and consumptive[104] abuse of nonhuman animals.

Though a relatively small but very active group of scholars worldwide has been publishing research under the green criminology umbrella, it has not yet positioned itself among mainstream (or orthodox) criminology.[105] One reason may relate to the splintering of the meanings, definitions, and various foundational theories of green criminology employed between factions of criminologists practicing it. Another, however, is that green criminology relies primarily on qualitative case studies, which are often viewed as lacking generalizability and not as relevant to public policy formulation as research based in quantitative methods. One estimate is that 90 percent of articles in criminology journals utilize quantitative methods, contrasted with less than 10 percent of green criminological studies.[106]

CONCLUSIONS

Most societies based on Marxism have now collapsed, which clearly suggests that economic systems based on Marxism have fatal flaws.[107] However, the new nations that have emerged from the collapse of Marxist societies have experienced large increases in crime as they reestablished capitalism.[108] These increases suggest that there may be some validity to the claim within Marxist criminology that there is a link between crime and capitalism.[109] At a minimum, criminologists may examine developments in the former communist countries to determine whether capitalism is causally related to certain types and levels of crime. If a relationship between political economy and crime rates does exist, it may be because capitalism tends to be associated with higher levels of economic inequality, and the inequality itself, rather than the capitalist economic system, causes crime.

Postmodernist criminology has many similarities to Marxist criminology, but it shifts attention from economic production to linguistic production. Postmodernists draw attention to the uses of language in creating dominance relationships, a point of view that seems to have a great deal of merit in general and in the study of crime in particular.[110] In addition, the development of "replacement discourses" that are inclusive and accepting, instead of exclusive and rejecting, could have considerable benefits for criminology and may well be a method to reduce crime.[111]

However, postmodernists take a position of "appreciative relativism" that privileges all points of view equally and treats scientific discourse as having no more validity than any other language. This position may go too far for most criminologists, who hold to the validity of the basic scientific process despite all its practical difficulties. Indeed, criminologists may look at postmodern criminology from a scientific perspective. One of its fundamental assertions is that violence begets violence, so that the violence of our present criminal justice policies will only increase the violence of criminals in our society. This, in the last analysis, is an empirical assertion that can be tested with scientific research; for example, the violence of criminal justice policies in different states or nations could be compared to the crime rates of those states or nations. If the postmodernists are correct, there should be a clear relationship between violent criminal justice policies and violent crime.

Green criminology is a relatively recent area of criminological study, and pertains to environmental harms and risk, expanding the definition of victim from humans to nonhuman animals and ecological systems. It has roots in postmodernism and political economy, but scholars studying green criminology often disagree about its scope, definition, meaning, and theoretical foundations. From a victimology perspective it seems that environmental harm, most often caused by corporate abuse, capitalism, and power structures, may in the long run outweigh the damage caused by ordinary street-level offenses. However, green criminologists have a ways to go in becoming a relevant force in mainstream criminology and a powerful influence at the policy level.

KEY TERMS

critical criminology
Marxist theories
postmodern theories
radical theories
social justice
material forces of production
social relations of productions
contradiction in capitalism
lumpenproletariat
primitive rebellion
instrumentalist view of
    criminal law
structuralist view
left realists

discourse analysis
discursive subject positions
decentered
dominant or oppositional
    discourses
replacement discourses
appreciative relativism
green criminology
ecocentric
eco-global criminology
conservation criminology
green-cultural criminology
treadmill of production

DISCUSSION QUESTIONS

1. How would a critical criminologist suggest that the crime problem could be solved?
2. According to Willem Bonger, how would socialism eliminate crime?
3. What are critiques of Marxist and postmodernist theories?
4. What are the implications of applying a social harm analysis? What are the critiques of this approach?
5. How would a postmodern view of language apply to criminology?
6. What is the postmodern view of crime?
7. How does new left realism contrast with postmodernism?
8. Considering the direct contradiction between capitalism and the preservation of nature, what would have to happen to reduce ecological additions withdrawals?

NOTES

1. Martin D. Schwartz and David O. Friedrichs, "Postmodern Thought and Criminological Discontent: New Metaphors for Understanding Violence," *Criminology* 32 (1994): 221–246, at p. 222. For overviews of critical criminology, see Raymond J. Michalowski, "Critical Criminology and the Critique of Domination: The Story of an Intellectual Movement," *Critical Criminology* 7 (1996): 9–16; and Bruce A. Arrigo, "Introduction: Some Preliminary Observations on Social Justice and Critical Criminology," in *Social Justice, Criminal Justice*, ed. Arrigo (Belmont, CA: West/Wadsworth, 1999), pp. 3–9.
2. Readable chapters on other types of critical theories in criminology can be found in Arrigo, "Introduction."
3. Werner Einstadter and Stuart Henry, *Criminological Theory* (Fort Worth, TX: Harcourt Brace, 1995), chaps. 10–12. For a discussion of the relationships among conflict, Marxist, and postmodern criminology, see Bruce A. Arrigo and Thomas J. Bernard, "Postmodern Criminology in Relation to Radical and Conflict Criminology," *Critical Criminology* 8 (1997): 39–60.
4. For a discussion of radical criminology, see Michael J. Lynch, Raymond Michalowski, and W. Byron Groves, *A New Primer in Radical Criminology: Critical Perspectives on Crime, Power and Identity*, 3rd ed. (Monsey, NY: Criminal Justice Press, 2000), pp. 3–15.
5. See, e.g., Thomas J. Bernard, "Foreword," in *Social Justice, Criminal Justice*, ed. Arrigo.
6. This account of Marx's theory is taken from Thomas J. Bernard, *The Consensus-Conflict Debate: Form and Content in Social Theories* (New York: Columbia University Press, 1983), pp. 95–98. Other overviews of Marx's theory as it relates to criminology can be found in David Greenberg, *Crime and Capitalism* (Palo Alto, CA: Mayfield, 1980), pp. 13–17; Richard Quinney, *Class, State and Crime*, 2nd ed. (New York: Longman, 1980), pp. 13–17; Lynch, Michalowski, and Groves, *A New Primer in Radical Criminology*, chap. 2; and Lynch and Paul Stretesky, "Marxism and Social Justice," pp. 14–29 in Arrigo, *Social Justice, Criminal Justice*.
7. A summary of this argument is found in Karl Marx, *Critique of Political Economy* (1859), English translation (New York: International Library, 1904), pp. 11–13.
8. Karl Marx, *Capital*, vol. 1 (New York: International Publishers, 1967), p. 763.
9. See, in general, Karl Marx, *Critique of the Gotha Programme* (New York: International Publishers, 1970). See also D. Ross Gandy, *Marx and History: From Primitive Society to the Communist Future* (Austin: University of Texas Press, 1979), pp. 72–95.
10. For discussions of Marx's views of crime, see Ian Taylor, Paul Walton, and Jock Young, *The New Criminology* (New York: Harper and Row, 1973), pp. 209–236. Original passages from Marx and Engels can be found in *Marx and Engels on Law*, ed. Maureen Cain and Alan Hunt (New York: Academic Press, 1979); or Paul Phillips, *Marx and Engels on Law and Laws* (Totowa, NJ: Barnes and Noble, 1980).

11. Paul Q. Hirst, "Marx and Engles on Law, Crime, and Morality," in *Critical Criminology*, ed. Ian Taylor, Paul Walton, and Jock Young (London: Routledge and Kegan Paul, 1975), pp. 215–221.
12. Karl Marx and Friedrich Engles, *The German Ideology* (London: Lawrence and Wishart, 1965), pp. 365–367.
13. Ibid., p. 367.
14. Peter Linebaugh, "Karl Marx, the Theft of Wood, and Working Class Composition," in David Greenberg, *Crime and Capitalism*, pp. 76–97. See also Greenberg's comments on pp. 60–63 and 484.
15. Marx later rejected idealistic Hegelianism, stating "The philosophers have only interpreted the world in various ways; the point, however, is to change it." Greenberg, *Crime and Capitalism*, p. 484.
16. Karl Marx, *Capital*, quoted in Greenberg, *Crime and Capitalism*, pp. 45–48. See also Greenberg's comments on pp. 38–39.
17. Willem Bonger, *Criminality and Economic Conditions* (Boston: Little, Brown, 1916), reprinted by Agathon, New York, 1967. See the excellent introduction by Austin Turk in the abridged edition, Indiana University Press, Bloomington, 1969.
18. Greenberg, *Crime and Capitalism*, p. 1.
19. See, for example, Richard Quinney, *Critique of Legal Order* (Boston: Little, Brown, 1973); Richard Quinney and John Wildeman, *The Problem of Crime*, 2nd ed. (New York: Harper & Row, 1977); and Taylor, Walton, and Young, *The New Criminology*.
20. Hirst, "Marx and Engles on Law, Crime, and Morality"; see also R. Serge Denisoff and Donald McQuarie, "Crime Control in Capitalist Society: A Reply to Quinney," *Issues in Criminology* 10 (1975): 109–119.
21. Alan A. Block and William J. Chambliss, *Organizing Crime* (New York: Elsevier, 1981), pp. 4–7. For a much harsher but less substantive criticism of these early theories, see Tony Platt, "Crime and Punishment in the United States: Immediate and Long-Term Reforms from a Marxist Perspective," *Crime and Social Justice* (Winter 1982): 38–45.
22. David F. Greenberg, "On One-Dimensional Criminology," *Theory and Society* 3 (1976): 610–621.
23. Greenberg, *Crime and Capitalism*, pp. 6–10.
24. Ibid., p. 10.
25. A useful summary of the instrumentalist versus structuralist views of the state and the legal order is found in Lynch, Michalowski, and Groves, *A New Primer in Radical Criminology*, chap. 3.
26. Jeffrey Reiman, *The Rich Get Richer and the Poor Get Prison* (Boston: Allyn and Bacon, 1998).
27. See also the radical perspectives on police, courts, and corrections in Lynch, Michalowski, and Groves, *A New Primer in Radical Criminology*, chaps. 8–10.
28. See Paddy Hillyard and Steve Tombs, "From 'Crime' to Social Harm?" *Crime Law and Social Change* 48 (2007): 9–25.
29. See Vincenzo Ruggiero, "Criminalizing War: Criminology as Ceasefire," *Social & Legal Studies* 14 (2005): 239–257.

30. See the discussion of the definition of crime in Lynch, Michalowski, and Groves, *A New Primer in Radical Criminology*, chap. 4.

31. Platt, "Crime and Punishment in the United States," p. 40.

32. Taylor, Walton, and Young, *The New Criminology*.

33. Ibid., p. 282.

34. For example, Richard Quinney (*Class, State and Crime*, pp. 59–62) described street crimes as crimes of "accommodation" to capitalist social relations in the sense that they are the actions of people who have been brutalized by the conditions of capitalism. These criminals reproduce the exploitative relations of capitalism in their own criminal activities—that is, they treat their victims the way they themselves have been treated. Quinney's description relies on Marx's arguments about the lumpenproletariat, as described earlier.

35. See chaps. 5–7 in Lynch, Michalowski, and Groves, *A New Primer in Radical Criminology*. See also W. Byron Groves and Robert J. Sampson, "Traditional Contributions to Radical Criminology," *Journal of Research in Crime and Delinquency* 24 (1987): 181–214.

36. E.g., see Mark Colvin and John Pauly, "A Critique of Criminology: Toward an Integrated Structural-Marxist Theory of Delinquency Production," *American Journal of Sociology* 89 (1983): 513–551. See also Mark Colvin, *Crime and Coercion: An Integrated Theory of Chronic Criminality* (New York: St. Martin's Press, 2000), which extends the earlier argument but also moves back in the direction of a traditional strain theory.

37. E.g., see David O. Friedrichs, "The Legitimacy Crisis: A Conceptual Analysis," *Social Problems* 27 (1980): 540–555.

38. William J. Chambliss, *On the Take: From Petty Crooks to Presidents* (Bloomington: Indiana University Press, 1978).

39. Block and Chambliss, *Organizing Crime*.

40. Greenberg, *Crime and Capitalism*, pp. 23–25.

41. For a review of the changing nature of critical criminology, see Simon Cottee, "The Idea of a Critical Criminology: Irony, Scepticism and Commitment," *International Journal of the Sociology of Law* 32 (2004): 363–376.

42. See, for example, Jock Young, "Ten Points of Realism," in *Rethinking Criminology*, ed. Jock Young and Roger Matthews (London: Sage, 1997); Matthews and Young, eds., *Issues in Realist Criminology: A Reader* (Thousand Oaks, CA: Sage, 1992).

43. Lynch, Michalowski, and Groves, *A New Primer in Radical Criminology*, pp. 216–219.

44. John Lowman and Brian Maclean, eds., *Realist Criminology: Crime Control and Policing in the 1990s* (Toronto: University of Toronto Press, 1992); and Richard Kinsey, John Lea, and Jock Young, *Losing the Fight Against Crime* (Oxford: Blackwell, 1986).

45. David O. Friedrichs, *Trusted Criminals: White Collar Crime in Contemporary Society* (Belmont, CA: Wadsworth, 1995).

46. Roger Matthews, "Developing a Realist Approach to Prison Reform" in *Realist Criminology*, ed. Lowman and MacLean, pp. 71–87.

47. John Lowman, "Street Prostitution Control," pp. 1–17; and Roger Matthews, "Regulating Street Prostitution and Kerb-Crawling: A Reply to Lowman," pp. 18–22 in *British Journal of Criminology* 32 (1992). See also John Lowman, "The 'Left Regulation' of Prostitution," in *Realist Criminology*, ed. Lowman and MacLean, pp. 157–176.

48. Elliott Currie, "Retreatism, Minimalism, Realism: Three Styles of Reasoning on Crime and Drugs in the United States," in *Realist Criminology*, ed. Lowman and MacLean, pp. 88–97.

49. Anthony Borgman, *Crossing the Postmodern Divide* (Chicago: University of Chicago Press, 1992).

50. See Dragan Milovanovic, *A Primer in the Sociology of Law* (Albany, NY: Harrow and Heston, 1994), pp. 143–145, 155–184.

51. Because of this tendency to attack privileged lines of thinking, postmodernism, in general, and deconstruction, in particular, have been criticized as nihilistic and relativistic. See Einstadter and Henry, *Criminological Theory*, p. 298. Some postmodernists emphasize these nihilistic, deconstructive, and oppositional approaches, but others emphasize the affirmative, reconstructive, and prospective aspects that incorporate constitutive methods. For applications to criminology, see Stuart Henry and Dragan Milovanovic, *Constitutive Criminology: Beyond Postmodernism* (London: Sage, 1996).

52. Schwartz and Friedrichs, "Postmodern Thought and Criminological Discontent," p. 222. These authors also mentioned the possibility that "much of what has been published is only a pretentious intellectual fad."

53. Martin D. Schwartz, "The Future of Criminology," in *New Directions in Criminology*, ed. Brian MacLean and Dragan Milovanovic (Vancouver: Collective Press, 1991), pp. 119–124.

54. For example, Bruce Arrigo ("The Peripheral Core of Law and Criminology," *Justice Quarterly* 12 [1995]: 447–472) commented on the "delicious irony" in attempting to summarize this perspective (pp. 449–450). See similar comments by Schwartz and Friedrichs, "Postmodern Thought and Criminological Discontent," pp. 222–223; and Einstadter and Henry, *Criminological Theory*, p. 281.

55. Schwartz and Friedrichs, "Postmodern Thought and Criminological Discontent," p. 224.

56. The following discussion relies heavily on Arrigo and Bernard, "Postmodern Criminology in Relation to Radical and Conflict Criminology."

57. Milovanovic, *A Primer in the Sociology of Law*, pp. 143–145, 155–184; Bruce Arrigo, *Madness, Language, and the Law* (Albany, NY: Harrow and Heston, 1993), pp. 27–75.

58. Henry and Milovanovic, *Constitutive Criminology*, pp. 8–11, 26–44.

59. Arrigo, "The Peripheral Core," p. 467. See also Dragan Milovanovic, *Postmodern Criminology* (New York: Garland, 1997); and Stuart Henry and Milovanovic, eds., *Constitutive Criminology at Work: Applications to Crime and Justice* (Albany: State University of New York Press, 1999). For an argument that critical criminologists should abandon postmodernism, see Russell Stuart, "The Failure of Postmodern Criminology," *Critical Criminology* 8 (1997): 61–90.

60. Peter Goodrich, "Law and Language: An Historical and Critical Introduction," *Journal of Law and Society* 11 (1984): 173–206.
61. Henry and Milovanovic, *Constitutive Criminology*, p. 27.
62. Milovanovic, *A Primer in the Sociology of Law*, pp. 145–150.
63. Bruce A. Arrigo, "An Experientially-Informed Feminist Jurisprudence," *Humanity and Society* 17 (1993): 28–47.
64. Dragan Milovanovic, "Jailhouse Lawyers and Jailhouse Lawyering," *International Journal of the Sociology of Law* 16 (1988): 455–475.
65. Peter K. Manning, *Symbolic Communication: Signifying Calls and the Police Response* (Cambridge, MA: MIT Press, 1988).
66. Arrigo, *Madness, Language, and the Law.*
67. Henry and Milovanovic, *Constitutive Criminology*, p. 204.
68. Arrigo and Bernard, "Postmodern Criminology in Relation to Radical and Conflict Criminology."
69. Einstadter and Henry, *Criminological Theory*, p. 289.
70. This term is used by Einstadter and Henry (ibid., p. 299, n13) in reference to Borgman, *Crossing the Postmodern Divide*.
71. Harold E. Pepinsky, "Peacemaking in Criminology and Criminal Justice," in *Criminology as Peacemaking*, ed. Pepinsky and Richard Quinney (Bloomington: Indiana University Press, 1991), p. 301.
72. Richard Quinney, "The Way of Peace," in *Criminology as Peacemaking*, ed. Pepinsky and Quinney, p. 12.
73. See Darnell F. Hawkins, Samuel L. Myers Jr., and Randolf N. Stone, eds., *Crime Control and Social Justice: The Delicate Balance* (Westport, CT: Greenwood Press, 2003).
74. The authors would like to thank Mike Lynch for helping them understand some of the history behind the green criminology movement.
75. Michael J. Lynch, "The Greening of Criminology: A Perspective for the 90's," *The Critical Criminologist* 2 (1990): 11–12.
76. Nigel South, "A Green Field for Criminology? A Proposal for a Perspective," *Theoretical Criminology* 2 (1998): 211–233.
77. Ibid., p. 213.
78. Ibid., p. 214.
79. Ibid., p. 222.
80. Ibid., p. 221.
81. Piers Beirne, "For a Nonspeciesist Criminology: Animal Abuse as an Object of Study," *Criminology* 37 (1999): 117–147, pp. 118–119.
82. Ibid., p. 131. See also Peter Singer, *Animal Liberation* (New York: Avon, 1990).
83. Beirne, "For a Nonspeciesist Criminology," p. 134. See also Tom Regan, *The Case for Animal Rights* (Berkeley: University of California Press, 1983).
84. Paul B. Stretesky and Michael J. Lynch, "The Relationship Between Lead Exposure and Homicide," *Archives of Pediatrics and Adolescent Medicine* 155 (2001): 579–582; Paul B. Stretesky and Michael J. Lynch, "The Relationship Between Lead and Crime," *Journal of Health and Social Behavior* 45 (2004): 214–229.

85. Michael J. Lynch and Paul B. Stretesky, "The Meaning of Green: Contrasting Criminological Perspectives," *Theoretical Criminology* 7 (2003): 217–238.
86. Ibid., p. 221.
87. Ibid., pp. 222–226.
88. Rob White, "Researching Transnational Environmental Harm: Toward an Eco-Global Criminology," *International Journal of Comparative and Applied Criminal Justice* 33 (2009): 229–248, p. 233, citing Rob White, *Crimes Against Nature: Environmental Criminology and Ecological Justice* (Devon: Willan Press, 2008).
89. White, "Researching Transnational Environmental Harm," p. 245.
90. Carole Gibbs, Meredith L. Gore, Edmund McGarrell, and Louie Rivers III, "Introducing Conservation Criminology: Toward Interdisciplinary Scholarship on Environmental Crimes and Risks," *British Journal of Criminology* 50 (2010): 124–144.
91. Stephen Pires and Ronald V. Clarke, "Are Parrots CRAVED? An Analysis of Parrot Poaching in Mexico," *Journal of Research in Crime and Delinquency* 49 (2012): 122–146.
92. Avi Brisman and Nigel South, "A Green-Cultural Criminology: An Exploratory Outline," *Crime Media Culture* 92 (2012): 115–135.
93. Ronald L. Akers, Christine S. Sellers, and Wesley G. Jennings, *Criminological Theories: Introduction, Evaluation, and Application*, 7th edition (New York: Oxford University Press, 2017), p. 255, quoting Jeff Ferell, Keith Hayward, and Jock Young, *Cultural Criminology: An Invitation* (London: Sage, 2008), pp. 2–3; emphasis in original.
94. Brisman and South, "A Green-Cultural Criminology," pp. 119–123.
95. Michael J. Lynch, Michael A. Long, Kimberly L. Barrett, and Paul B. Stretesky, "Is It a Crime to Produce Ecological Disorganization? Why Green Criminology and Political Economy Matter in the Analysis of Global Ecological Harms," *British Journal of Criminology* 53 (2013): 997–1016.
96. Paddy Hillyard and Steve Tombs, "Beyond Criminology?," in *Criminal Obsessions; Why Harm Matters More Than Crime*, ed. P. Hillyward, C. Pantazis, S. Tombs, D. Gordon, and D. Dorling (Crime and Society Foundation, 2005).
97. Allan Schnaiberg, *The Environment: From Surplus to Scarcity* (New York: Oxford University Press, 1980).
98. Lynch et al., "Is It a Crime to Produce Ecological Disorganization?," pp. 1002–1003.
99. Dann P van Uhm, "The Social Construction of Wildlife: A Green Cultural Criminological Perspective," *Theoretical Criminology* 22 (2018): 384–401.
100. Michael J. Lynch, Paul B. Stretesky, and Michael A. Long, "Green Criminology and Native Peoples: The Treadmill of Production and the Killing of Indigenous Environmental Activists," *Theoretical Criminology* 22 (2018): 218–341.
101. Martin Crook, Damien Short, and Nigel South, "Ecocide, Genocide, Capitalism and Colonialism: Consequences for Indigenous Peoples and Glocal Ecosystems Environments," *Theoretical Criminology* 22 (2018): 298–317.

102. Rob White, "Econcentrism and Criminal Justice," *Theoretical Criminology* 22 (2018): 342–362.
103. David Rodriguez Goyes, "Animal Abuse, Biotechnology and Species Justice," *Theoretical Criminology* 22 (2018): 363–383.
104. Nik Taylor and Amy Fitzgerald, "Understanding Animal (Ab) Use: Green Criminological Contributions, Missed Opportunities and A Way Forward," *Theoretical Criminology* 22 (2018): 402–425.
105. For example, as of 2004, only six of 9,410 pages in 16 best-selling criminology textbooks dealt with toxic waste-related crimes. Michael J. Lynch, Danielle McGurrin, and Melissa Fenwick, "Disappearing Act: The Representation of Corporate Crime Research in Criminology Journals and Textbooks," *Journal of Criminal Justice* 32 (2004): 389–398.
106. Michael J. Lynch, Kimberly L. Barrett, Paul B. Stretesky, and Michael A. Long, "The Neglect of Quantitative Research in Green Criminology and Its Consequences," *Critical Criminology* 25 (2017): 183–198.
107. For a strong critique of Marxist criminology in the face of the harsh conditions then facing communist countries, see Carl Klockars, "The Contemporary Crisis of Marxist Criminology," *Criminology* 16 (1979): 477–515.
108. See, e.g., Aleksandar Fatic, *Crime and Social Control in "Central"-Eastern Europe* (Aldershot, UK: Ashgate, 1997).
109. For a fairly recent test of Bonger's Theory, see Olena Antonaccio and Charles R. Tittle, "A Cross-National Test of Bonger's Theory of Criminality and Economic Conditions," *Criminology* 45 (2007): 925–958. Using international data for one hundred countries, the authors found partial support for Bonger's theory. While the degree of capitalism did seem to predict homicide rates, this linkage was not found to be the result of a demoralized populace, as predicted by Bonger.
110. The use of language in creating dominance relationships is a major focus of Bernard, *The Consensus Conflict Debate*. The book attempts to show how social theories use certain language systems (the form of the theory) to construct ideas about who and what is legitimate in the society (the content of the theory). These ideas about legitimacy are then used to privilege certain people and to repress others in the society. The book shows that these patterned ways of constructing legitimacy go back as far as Plato and Aristotle and are the actual point at issue in what is known as "the consensus-conflict debate."
111. For example, Braithwaite's shaming theory, discussed in Chapter 16, makes some similar arguments about inclusive and exclusive uses of language in responding to deviance. However, Braithwaite did so in the context of a traditional scientific approach, rather than a postmodern approach.

CHAPTER 13

—

Gender and Crime

Gender is the strongest and most consistent correlate of crime and delinquency.[1] With few exceptions (such as prostitution), males are much more likely to offend than are females. Why this is so is not entirely clear, and this has become a more explicit focus within criminological theory and research.

This chapter opens with a discussion of feminist criminology, which has raised a variety of issues related to women's offending, women's victimization, and women's experiences in the criminal justice system. The chapter then focuses narrowly on theories related to offending. Traditional criminology theories, as described in the earlier chapters of this book, largely ignore women's offending. Feminist criminology therefore poses the question of the extent to which these theories can be generalized to explain women's offending. But the larger question is the extent to which criminology theories can explain the gendered nature of crime—the tendency for crime to be largely a male phenomenon.[2] The chapter therefore examines explanations of why women's crime rates are so low and men's crime rates are so high.

THE DEVELOPMENT OF FEMINIST CRIMINOLOGY

Feminism is an extremely broad area of social theorizing that has applications to the field of criminology, although this certainly is not its major focus. Just as there are numerous branches of feminism, there are numerous branches of feminist criminology, with numerous disagreements and shadings of meanings within those branches. What follows here is only a brief overview that is intended to give a sense of the area and to identify its major themes.

The initial feminist writings in criminology were critiques of traditional criminology theories for ignoring or heavily distorting a number of topics related to women offenders.[3] Traditional theories largely explained the criminal behavior of men,[4] and the few theories that explained the criminal behavior of women were simplistic and relied on stereotypical images.[5] In addition, most traditional criminology theories were gender neutral and therefore (in theory at least) applied equally to women and to men. They ignored the socially constructed relations between men and women that are associated with the concepts of masculinity and femininity.[6] Consequently, these theories were largely unable to explain the gendered nature of crime (i.e., men commit the vast majority of crime). When the gendered nature of crime was addressed, the theories tended to focus on supposed characteristics that implied women's inferiority and tended to reinforce women's subordination to men in the larger society.[7] Traditional criminology theories also failed to address the differences in the ways women, versus men, were treated by the criminal justice system.[8] For example, women who were accused of sexual crimes were often treated more harshly than were men who were accused of similar crimes, but women who were accused of violent crimes were often treated more leniently. These differences in treatment led to differences in official crime rates (e.g., higher rates of sexual offenses but lower rates of violent offenses), which then affected the explanations of women's criminality by criminology theories. Finally, none of the existing criminology theories discussed the new roles that women were taking on in the larger society as part of what in the 1970s was called women's liberation and how these new roles might impact women's participation in criminal activity.

The critiques that pointed to the many problems with traditional criminology theories were followed by two books on the subject of women and crime that appeared in 1975. In *Sisters in Crime: The Rise of the New Female Criminal*,[9] Freda Adler argued that women were becoming more aggressive and competitive as they moved out of traditional homebound social roles and into the previously largely male world of the competitive marketplace. Essentially, Adler believed that women were taking on what had been masculine qualities as they fought the battles that men had always fought. She argued that the same kind of transformation was occurring among criminals, where "a similar number of determined women are forcing their way into the world of major crimes." Now, she contended, there were "increasing numbers of women who are using guns, knives, and wits to establish themselves as full human beings, as capable of violence and aggression as any man."

In that same year, Rita James Simon published *Women and Crime*.[10] Simon also described changes in the types and volume of crime committed by women but argued that it was not because women were taking on masculine characteristics. Rather, as women moved out of traditional homebound roles, they encountered a much wider variety of opportunities to commit crime, particularly economic and white-collar crimes, which required access to other people's money in positions of trust.

Both Adler's and Simon's theories argued that liberation from traditional women's roles would increase crimes committed by women. The major difference between the two had to do with the prediction about the type of crime these new female criminals would commit: Adler's theory suggested that a larger portion of this crime would be violent, whereas Simon's theory suggested that this crime would predominantly be property and white-collar crime. Later research indicated that Simon's opportunity thesis had more validity, but on the whole there was little evidence that this "new female criminal" existed at all.[11] In addition, Simon suggested that these theories generated enormous interest among nonfeminist criminologists and, in some ways, set back the cause of a feminist criminology because they "diverted attention from the material and structural forces that shape women's lives and experiences."[12] Because of this, other feminist criminologists argue that neither theory should be described as feminist criminology.[13]

SCHOOLS OF FEMINIST CRIMINOLOGY

After Adler's and Simon's contributions, criminological writings that focused on explaining women's participation in crime expanded dramatically. While there are many similarities and differences in these writings, certain categories have appeared in the literature as ways to group these writings to illustrate their range and variety. These are sometimes described as schools of feminist thought.[14]

Initially, many feminist writings in criminology could be described as a part of traditional criminology itself, filling in gaps and correcting the distortions of the past. As such, they were part of what came to be called liberal feminism.[15] This branch of feminism basically operated within the framework of existing social structures to direct attention to women's issues, promote women's rights, increase women's opportunities, and transform women's roles in society.

Soon, however, several strands of critical feminism arose that directly challenged the social structures within which liberal feminism operated. These strands looked at the much more fundamental questions of how women had come to occupy subservient roles in society and how societies themselves might be transformed. The first such strand is known as radical feminism, and its central concept is that of "patriarchy," originally a concept used by sociologists like Max Weber to describe social relations under feudalism. Kate Millett resurrected the term in 1970 to refer to a form of social organization in which men dominate women.[16] Millett argued that patriarchy is the most fundamental form of domination in every society. Patriarchy is established and maintained through sex-role socialization and the creation of "core gender identities," through which both men and women come to believe that men are superior in a variety of ways. On the basis of these gender identities, men tend to dominate women in personal interactions, such as within the family. From there, male domination is extended to all the institutions and organizations of the larger society. Because male power is based on personal relationships, Millet and her fellow feminists concluded that "the personal is political."

Whereas Millett had placed the root of the problem in socialization into gendered sex roles, Marxist feminists combined radical feminism with traditional Marxism to argue that the root of male dominance lies in men's ownership and control of the means of economic production.[17] For Marxist feminists, patriarchy is tied to the economic structure of capitalism and results in a "sexual division of labor" in which men control the economy and women serve them and their sexual needs.[18] Much like Marxist criminologists in general, Marxist feminist criminologists argue that actions that threaten this capitalist–patriarchal system are defined as crimes by the criminal law and the criminal justice system. Thus, women's actions that threaten male economic dominance are defined as property crimes, and women's actions that threaten male control of women's bodies and sexuality are defined as sexual offenses. Like other Marxists, some Marxist feminist criminologists take an instrumental view of the criminal law—law is a direct instrument of men's oppression—while others take a more complex structural view that looks to overall patterns through which law maintains the system of patriarchy.[19] Thus, another source of women's criminality in this perspective is the frustration and anger that women feel by being trapped in these limiting social roles.[20]

Finally, socialist feminists retained both the focus on social roles and economic production, but they moved away from a rigid Marxist framework. In particular, they argued that natural reproductive differences between the sexes underlie male–female relationships. Before birth control, women were much more at the mercy of their biology than were men—menstruation, pregnancy, childbirth and nursing, menopause—all of which made them more dependent on men for physical survival. The biological role of women in pregnancy, birth, and nursing led to women taking major responsibility for raising children, who require extensive care for long periods. Ultimately, this care led to a sexual division of labor in which men worked outside the home and women worked inside it, thereby forming the basis for male domination and control over women.[21] According to socialist feminists, the key to an egalitarian society lies not so much in women taking ownership of the means of economic production, but in women taking control of their own bodies and their own reproductive functions. Once women have done so, they can move on to taking their rightful place in the larger society.

Liberal, radical, Marxist, and socialist feminisms are all widely recognized as separate strands of feminism, but several other strands are also sometimes mentioned.[22] One of these strands is postmodern feminism.[23] Smart, for example, discussed how discourse is used to set certain women apart as "criminal women."[24] Wonders argued that both postmodernism and feminism question the nature of justice in the context of storytelling and narrative and that both tend to see "truth" as an opinion that benefits some at the expense of others.[25] Other feminists have criticized postmodernism. Chesney-Lind and Faith questioned whether it is useful for women to dispute the notion of truth just at the point when women are gaining a voice in the knowledge production process.[26] Still others appear to reject postmodernism because they advocate feminist theory and research that adheres to standards of scientific objectivity.[27]

Whether or not they adhere to postmodernism as a whole, many feminists now take an "appreciative relativism" stance within feminism that is similar to postmodernism. That is, they recognize and appreciate many different feminist voices as legitimate and refrain from analyzing, classifying, and ultimately picking apart those different voices.[28] In particular, feminist criminologists value multiracial and multicultural voices that speak about women's experiences related to crime, victimization, and criminal justice.[29] This multicultural feminism focuses on the interlocking structures of domination: race, class, and gender.[30] Earlier feminism, dominated by middle-class European American women, tended to ignore the very different experiences of, for instance, poor African American women.[31]

GENDER IN CRIMINOLOGY

The problem of gender in criminology has usually been addressed in one of two forms. First, the generalizability problem focuses on whether traditional criminology theories, which were formulated to explain male criminal behavior, can be generalized to explain female criminal behavior. Second, the gender ratio problem focuses on explaining why women are less likely than men to engage in criminal behavior.[32]

Daly and Chesney-Lind suggested that the generalizability problem is the safe course of action for female criminologists who are just entering the field: "Focus on the generalizibility problem and ... use a domesticated feminism to modify previous theory."[33] While generalizability is "safer," the problem is that the traditional male-oriented criminology theories have limited value for explaining female criminality.[34] Daly and Chesney-Lind maintained that the theoretical concepts on which these theories are based "are inscribed so deeply by masculinist experience that this approach will prove too restrictive, or at least misleading" when applied to female crime.[35] On the other hand, after reviewing the literature, Smith and Paternoster concluded that it is premature to abandon these male-based theories entirely in the attempt to explain female offending.[36] Similarly, Kruttschnitt concluded that "the factors that influence delinquent development differ for males and females in some contexts but not others."[37]

Women criminologists who focus on the gender ratio problem, as opposed to the generalizability problem, have been more likely to utilize observations and interviews and "have displayed more tentativeness and a discomfort with making global claims" at the theoretical level. In contrast, men criminologists who address the gender ratio problem have been bolder in making grand theoretical claims and have tended to do empirical research that involved statistical analysis of quantitative data. Daly and Chesney-Lind stated that women criminologists

> are more interested in providing texture, social context, and case histories: in short, in presenting accurate portraits of how adolescent and adult women become involved in crime. This gender difference . . . [is related] to a felt need to comprehend women's crime on its own terms, just as criminologists of the past did for men's crime.[38]

The problem for these women criminologists is that "global or grand theoretical arguments and high-tech statistical analyses are valued more highly by the profession." The women criminologists therefore run the risk that their approaches "will be trivialized merely as case studies or will be written off as not theoretical enough."[39]

Chesney-Lind and Faith argued that gender must become a central concept in criminology theories.[40] Social class has been the central concept in many criminology theories in the past, yet many criminologists argue there is no direct relationship between class and crime.[41] In contrast, the relationship between gender and crime is strong and undeniable. Beyond that, Chesney-Lind and Faith contended that the gender ratio problem (why women are less likely, and men are more likely, to engage in criminal behavior) can be fully explained only in the context of the sex–gender system (or patriarchy). While it varies from culture to culture, this system constructs gender categories out of biological sex, associates these gender categories with different roles or tasks in a division of labor, and then values men and their tasks over women and their tasks.[42] Ultimately, to explain the gender ratio problem, Chesney-Lind and Faith argued that criminologists will have to "theorize gender" in their theories of crime. That is, both women's and men's experiences as offenders and victims, as well as their divergent treatment in criminal justice systems, can be fully understood only in the context of the sex–gender system of patriarchy.[43] Feminist criminology has raised a wide variety of issues that are related to women as offenders, women as victims,[44] and women's experiences with the criminal justice system, and all these issues have implications for much existing criminological knowledge about men. The following sections, however, consider only the gender ratio problem. For most of the twentieth century explanations of the gender ratio have focused on why women's crime rates have been so low, and these explanations are the subject of the next section. In effect, this approach assumes that male crime rates are the norm, and it attempts to explain why women's crime rates are different from that norm.[45] The opposite question—Why are men's crime rates so high?—is addressed later in this chapter. Following this is a discussion of a debate on whether the gender ratio of violence has been decreasing over the past few decades.

WHY ARE WOMEN'S CRIME RATES SO LOW?

In the first half of the twentieth century, criminology theories generally explained all crime in terms of biological and psychological disorders. Such theories tended to assume that because women commit less frequent, less serious crime than men, women offenders must therefore have even more serious biological and psychological disorders than men offenders.[46] By the middle of the twentieth century theories of men's criminality had turned to social explanations, such as the ecology, strain, differential association, control, and labeling theories discussed in earlier chapters. These theories, as originally proposed, had little or nothing to say about female offending.[47] Theories of women's criminality during these years remained almost entirely focused on individual pathology and tended to view women's offending as minor offending predominantly related to sexual activity. When women engaged in more serious offenses, it was often viewed as being the result of the influence of their male romantic partners.[48] Only with the rise of feminism was women's criminality viewed as an entity in itself and in the context of women's social situation.

Many of the theories look at variations in socialization, particularly as related to gender roles, arguing that females are socialized toward greater conformity and less risk taking than males.[49] An alternate but related perspective is that females are more controlled than males, particularly in terms of direct controls, such as surveillance and supervision.[50] Hagan and his colleagues combined both of these perspectives in power-control theory, which argues that parents control daughters more than sons and that boys are therefore more likely to engage in risky behavior than are girls.[51] This disproportional controlling behavior will be greatest in a patriarchal family, in which the father has more power than the mother because of his employment in the workforce. This behavior will be the least in nonpatriarchal families in which both parents have equal power because of their equal status in the workplace. Individual delinquency rates are thus viewed as the product of two levels of distribution of power—power relations in society (the workplace) and power relations in the family. Tests of power-control theory have found mixed support for a variety of its arguments.[52]

Whereas power-control theory focuses on the greater controls of girls, other explanations consider female offending in the context of strain-type theories. Many theories have discussed the particular victimizations that women experience and have sought to link them to the particular types of offenses that women commit. Chesney-Lind and Faith stated that "research consistently documents that victimization is at the heart of much of girls' and women's lawbreaking, and that this pattern of gender entrapment, rather than gender liberation, best explains women's involvement in crime."[53] Agnew's general strain theory has also been applied to gender differences, in an extension of the theory proposed by Broidy and Agnew. They argued that that males and females face different types of strain (e.g., financial and interpersonal conflict for males versus family and friend problems and gender discrimination for females), and that typical male strains were tied greater to crime and delinquency than female strain types.[54] Tests of the application of GST to gender differences have produced mixed results.[55]

Still other theories have approached women's offending in the context of differential association theory. In 1982 Giordano and Rockwell, for example, interviewed 127 girls, the total population in Ohio's only institution for female delinquents, and reinterviewed most of them again in 1995.[56] They found that "these women appear to have been literally 'immersed' in deviant lifestyles—where aunts, cousins, siblings, fathers, and mothers routinely engaged in violence and criminal behavior."[57] The authors presented anecdotal accounts to illustrate the family's influence on criminal definitions, as well as the direct and indirect learning of the behavior itself from family and extra-family influences. Also in the differential association tradition, Heimer and De Coster found that "boys are more violent than girls largely because they are taught more definitions favoring such behavior; girls are less violent than boys because they are controlled through subtle mechanisms, which include learning that violence is incompatible with the meaning of gender for them and being restrained by emotional bonds to family."[58] These authors concluded that "consistent with feminist arguments, gender differences in violence ultimately are rooted in power differences."[59]

Some feminists have looked at female criminality in the context of "doing gender," an approach to gender that assumes that the feminine gender role is something that must be accomplished in the context of specific situations.[60] The feminine gender role itself may be dysfunctional in various ways, but the greater problem lies in overconformity to the role generated by the need to prove something, to demonstrate femininity in specific contexts. This approach is associated with the multicultural feminism described earlier, since different racial and ethnic groups may have different norms for femininity. What are called "hegemonic" gender roles (breadwinner for males, housewife for females) are the masculinity and femininity defined by the dominant culture. Quoting Spender,[61] Simpson and Ellis described this femininity as girls learn it in schools:

> Simultaneously expected to behave and conform but not perform (at least not in subjects that "really" matter, like physics, mathematics, biology, chemistry, and so forth), "women learn that they are not as worthy, that they do not count as much, and that what competence they may have is usually restricted to a specialized sphere which does not rank high in the male scheme of values." The above view captures, for the most part, a hegemonic femininity.[62]

Simpson and Ellis then argued that this hegemonic femininity is more relevant to European American females, but less relevant to females who are expected to work, including African American females.

Other researchers have also taken the doing gender approach, but they have examined the very different femininities of females who are involved in serious crimes. For example, Maher[63] described the gendered division of labor in serious drug markets in Brooklyn, New York. Miller[64] interviewed women who were involved in armed robberies in St. Louis, while Laidler and Hunt[65] interviewed girls in delinquent gangs. These women operate in rigidly stratified gender hierarchies where women's roles are severely limited, and while their motives are similar to those of male offenders, their specific actions can be understood only in the context of that gendered environment.

WHY ARE MEN'S CRIME RATES SO HIGH?

Heidensohn remarked that one of the lessons that should be learned from all the theory and research on women's offending is that "we have to ask a different question—not what makes women's crime rates so low, but why are men's so high?"[66] Chesney-Lind and Faith suggested that asking the question this way means that "suddenly men have a gender, not just women; and male behavior is no longer normalized."[67] Heidensohn described this question as "stunning in its implications."

Before they were questioned by feminist criminologists, traditional criminology theories largely dealt with male offending and were largely tested with male populations. Nevertheless, most of these theories were gender neutral in their arguments and could not explain the differences between male and female offending (the gender ratio problem). The problem was that the causal factors proposed by these theories, such as economic inequality or social structural strain, did not appear to affect men and women differently. Thus, the theories themselves implied that men's and women's crime rates should be equal.[68]

A few of these traditional criminology theories proposed causal factors that are unequally distributed by gender. For example, testosterone levels, one biological factor that is associated with crime, are more concentrated in men than in women.[69] One recent study has also shown that a low resting heart rate partially mediates the relationship between gender and crime. (Males on average have a lower heart rate than females.) Based on a sample of 894 individuals, the researchers analyzed measurements of heart rate at eleven years of age and twenty-three years, and found that resting heart rate could explain between 5.4 and 17.1 percent of the gender difference in various measures of crime, controlling for body mass index, race, social adversity, and activity level.[70] Few criminologists deny that such biological factors have some effect on gender differences in crime, but as discussed in Chapter 4, these effects are generally not direct or isolated from environmental causes. In addition, the very large within-gender differences in crime (i.e., some men commit a lot of crime, and some men commit none) indicate that strictly biological factors can play only a limited role in criminology theories.[71]

Boyd, however, called for a greater emphasis on biological factors in explaining the tenfold difference between men and women in the commission of violent crime. In *The Beast Within: Why Men Are Violent,*[72] he argued that criminology currently suffers from "an unwillingness to accept that male violence flows from an amalgam of genes and environment." Boyd stated that testosterone, as well as "biological differences in speed, size, strength, sexuality, spatial skills, verbal skills, and empathy," makes men a greater risk than women for becoming violent. While acknowledging that a direct connection between testosterone and aggression is weak, Boyd contended that the "connection between testosterone and sexuality is overwhelming" and represents the key to understanding the connection between testosterone and violence. Linking biological factors with social change, Boyd tied the increase in violent crime in Western cultures beginning in the late 1960s to sexuality, specifically to the sexual revolution with its "changing conceptions of monogamy and commitment." He concluded that such change produced an unprecedented disruption of sexual relationships, causing frustration and confusion in sexually immature young men.

Cote, relying upon longitudinal studies, applied a developmental perspective to the differential uses of aggression in boys and girls.[73] She found that while boys and girls differ little in their use of physical aggression in infancy, a gap widens over the life course, peaking between ages eighteen and thirty. Cote attributed the increasing gap to the greater ability of adult females to regulate and inhibit physically aggressive behavior.[74] When it came to using indirect aggression, defined as socially manipulative and circuitous forms of aggression, such as malicious gossip or practicing social ostracism, females are already more indirectly aggressive than are males during their preschool years, and this gap gradually widens over the course of childhood and adolescence and then narrows in adulthood, to the point where males and females do not significantly differ in their use of indirect aggression by age twenty-two. Whereas the use of physical aggression by girls gradually declines over the course of childhood, the use of indirect aggression appears to increase in frequency with age, with frequency of physical aggression peaking in toddlerhood and indirect aggression peaking in adolescence.[75] Cote concluded that the difference in aggression is attributable to different social relations among girls and boys and to different selection pressures that are brought to bear on males and females in sexual selection.[76]

Other traditional theories proposed causal factors that might be unequally distributed by gender, although this was not argued in the theory itself. For example, Hirschi's social control theory could explain the gender ratio problem if boys experience fewer social controls than girls. However, this argument is not actually part of the theory, and Hirschi himself discarded all data on females before testing his theory.[77] As we discussed in the section on women's crime rates, testing of this assertion has produced mixed results.

Similarly, Gottfredson and Hirschi's theory of low self-control may explain the gender ratio problem if the standard child-rearing practices for boys, compared to girls, are more likely to result in low self-control as a stable personality construct in adolescence and adulthood. Gottfredson and Hirschi agreed that gender is a "major, persistent correlate" to crime.[78] After reviewing the research, they concluded that some gender differences in offending reflect "differences in opportunity variables or supervision," in that parents "seek to minimize opportunities for crime, especially for daughters." But they concluded that "there are substantial self-control differences between the sexes" and that explanations of gender differences in crime must include "differences in self-control that are not produced by direct external control." They speculated that gendered differences in self-control may originate in gendered differences in parental monitoring and punishment of the deviant behavior of very young children, but then stated that "it is beyond the scope of this work to attempt to identify all of the elements responsible for gender differences in crime."[79]

Finally, few traditional criminology theories explicitly dealt with masculinity or the sex–gender system (patriarchy) as a causal factor in crime. Some theories of gang behavior, however, were an exception.[80] In his theory of lower-class culture, Miller described a tenuous masculinity at the heart of gang behavior, which is a "one-sex peer group" of adolescent boys who mostly live in female-headed households.[81] Similarly, in his strain theory, Cohen argued that a boy's gang behavior "has at least one virtue: it incontestably confirms, in the eyes of all concerned, his essential masculinity. The delinquent is the rogue male."[82] Relying on Miller and Cohen, Cloward and Ohlin[83] stated in their strain theory that gang boys

> have trouble forming a clear masculine self-image. . . . Engulfed by a feminine world and uncertain of their own identification, they tend to "protest" against femininity. This protest may take the form of robust and aggressive behavior, and even of malicious, irresponsible, and destructive acts. Such acts evoke maternal disapproval and thus come to stand for independence and masculinity to rebellious adolescents.

These theories suggest that gang delinquency involves the process of doing gender as described in the feminist theories of female crime and delinquency. That is, the gang behavior itself is a means of demonstrating masculinity in the context of particular situations and particular cultural contexts. Messerschmidt developed this view at considerable length, examining how the criminal behavior of men in different cultural contexts reveals an attempt to demonstrate the different masculinities associated with those contexts.[84]

In this approach, the masculine gender role is said to be the source of a variety of men's problems, including increased suicide, crime, health problems, and relationship problems. All these problems, particularly relationships with women, are driving changes in the masculine gender role today.

However, the greater problem is that most men experience themselves as not living up to gender-role expectations and therefore as needing to prove their masculinity. Thus, men focus less on the gender role itself than on the process by which they attempt to live up to its demands. The exact behaviors by which men demonstrate masculinity then depend very much on the particular cultural and situational contexts in which they find themselves.

Studies of street violence and gang delinquency have sought to understand offender motivations and to gain insight into the gendered nature of such activities. On the basis of an analysis of interviews with forty men and twelve women on the streets of St. Louis, Mullins, Wright, and Jacobs found that retaliatory violence is of a "strongly gendered nature," with males viewing violent retaliation as "a key street survival tactic," deeply rooted in their identities as men. While the motivations for intragender retaliation seem similar for men and women—the building and maintaining of street reputations—the criteria differed, as female disputes centered more on domestic matters and involved less violence. Far more frequently, men's violence involved guns, with males getting locked into retaliatory cycles "due to the demands of actualizing a street masculinity identity."[85] Also addressing gangs and delinquency, Peterson, Miller, and Esbensen found that males in all-male gangs were less delinquent than were males in other gang types (sex-balanced gangs or majority male gangs). The authors concluded that they were "witnessing a phenomenon associated with the gendered organization of groups," not simply differences between males and females. From this, the authors posited that masculinity and femininity are fluid concepts, "situationally defined and enacted, rather than resulting from deeply entrenched gender differences."[86]

THE NARROWING OF THE GENDER GAP IN VIOLENCE

Currently, the subject of whether the gender gap in violent offending has been diminishing, as predicted in the 1970s by Adler, is one of some debate. In the United States, Lauritsen et al.[87] and Schwartz et al.[88] reached different conclusions. The former study, analyzing the gender gap in criminal offending between 1973 and 2005, using data from the National Crime Survey and the National Crime Victimization Survey, found enough evidence of a narrowing in the gender gap of violent crime to conclude: "It seems that the time has come to move beyond the debate over whether these changes in offending by gender have occurred and focus research efforts on explaining the reasons for differential changes in female and male rates of violent offending."[89]

Schwartz et al., however, also analyzing these datasets, concluded that for the most part the gender gap in violence remained about the same over those three decades. Much of their empirical argument was based upon a different approach to statistical methods, in which they employed measures of violence using offender counts rather than the incident counts used by Lauritsen et al.[90] Additionally, the two studies dealt differently with how they addressed the 1992 redesign in the National Crime Survey, which could have affected the estimates of this gap, as well as how to deal with sex-specific adjustments in their analyses.[91] Schwartz et al. found that females comprised about 12 to 14 percent of all homicides over these decades, 2 to 3 percent of rapes, and 5 to 6 percent of newly admitted prisoners for homicide, rape, robbery, and assault. They reported that the only evidence of an increase in the gender gap in violence was in the assault category (and to some extent robbery, depending on the data set). Both studies, however, agreed that to the extent this gap was narrowing, it was *primarily* a result of decreasing male violence, rather than increasing female violence. Some research on the gender gap in other countries has also found that the bulk of any reduction in the gender gap in violent behavior is mostly attributed to less male violence.[92]

As there is disagreement by some researchers over whether this gender gap exists in violent crime, there are also different explanations for why this gap may be narrowing. It may be due in part to changes in women's behavior, as posited by Adler's "emancipation" effect. Some scholars assume there has been a global increase in female violence. Carrington, in making this assumption based on somewhat selectively chosen research, argues that feminists must own "real" female violence and put forth feminist theories that explain its uptake.[93] Another explanation is based on reductions in male violence, which could come about in a number of ways. For example, some have attributed the decline in male violence to focused deterrence and prevention programs targeting mostly male violent offending (as discussed in Chapter 3 of this volume).[94] Another example is the perspective of institutional anomie theorists, who view the male decline as occurring through a lessened male propensity for violence as increased gender equality expands male responsibilities at home.[95] Finally, one of the most common explanations for the gender gap in violence is that it is borne out only through official data, such as arrests from the Uniform Crime Report, and this reflects not an actual change in violence across genders, but changes in social control and police practices that have a "net-widening" effect on the definitions of offenses as violent.[96] Definitions of girls' violence may be culturally constructed, and to at least some extent, accounted for by the increased visibility of girls in public spaces—their behavior in these spaces may be relatively minor but viewed more seriously, given its construction as rebellion.[97]

CONCLUSIONS

With regard to the explanation of female criminality, Miller concluded that "it is important to strike a balance between recognizing the significance of gender and gender inequality but not to reduce everything to gender."[98]

Similarly, Giordano and Rockwell concluded that "a truly comprehensive approach ... inevitably would include attention to causal processes that appear gender specific (e.g., backgrounds of sexual abuse) and to those that appear to have applicability to both males and females (e.g., family histories that include exposure to criminal definitions and opportunities)."[99] These conclusions about the role of gender in criminology theories appear to be reasonable generally.

Crime is overwhelmingly a gendered activity, and the gender ratio may be considered the single most important fact that criminology theories must be able to explain. Although criminologists are gradually beginning to take the task of explaining the gender gap more seriously, the hard truth is that traditional theories have largely failed even to consider this problem, much less explain it. It seems likely that the full explanation of the gender ratio will have to include some theories that are common to both genders and some that are specific to each gender. Beyond that, the full explanation of the gender ratio will have to include what feminists describe as the sex–gender system of patriarchy—the stratified system of gender roles and expectations by which women and men enact femininity and masculinity. Whether the gender gap is narrowing, and if so, how to explain the change, are questions that are in considerable ongoing debate.

Feminist theories of crime (and feminist scholars themselves) continue to be criticized by many, in what can be considered as a backlash to the feminist movement, and feminists have had to defend themselves. As one example, DeKesered and Dragiewicz take on Donald Dutto's[100] work on woman abuse. They state that Dutto claims (1) women are as violent as men; (2) feminism is a political agenda; (3) feminists rely on a single-factor explanation of woman abuse (patriarchy); (4) feminists ignore women's use of violence; and (5) feminists are proponents of ineffective mandatory arrest and prosecution policies in instances of intimate partner violence.[101]

According to DeKesered and Dragiewicz, all these claims are problematic. The assortment that women are as violent as men in woman abuse cases conflates offensive and defensive violence. The notion of feminists as all political by nature ignores "scores of feminist studies"[102] uncited by Dutton, based on rigorous objective scientific standards and published in top journals. Similarly, Dutton in his claim on the single-factor approach, ignores a "large feminist literature combining both macro-level factors, such as unemployment, globalization, deindustrialization, life events, stress, intimate relationship status, familial and societal patriarchy, substance use, male peer support, and other factors."[103] With regard to women's use of violence, they point to a number of theoretical and empirical works by feminist scholars that discuss female offensive violence against men. And finally, feminists have supported holistic nonenforcement responses to violence against women.

KEY TERMS

gendered nature of crime
feminist criminology
new female criminal
patriarchy
core gender identities
generalizability problem

gender ratio problem
power-control theory
gender entrapment
gender liberation
doing gender

DISCUSSION QUESTIONS

1. What do you think best explains the gender gap in crime and delinquency?
2. What is the liberation thesis? Has it been borne out?
3. Do you agree or disagree with the notion that traditional criminological theories cannot be generalized from male to female crime?
4. Over the past decade, African American women have constituted the fastest growing percentage of the prison population. Why? What theories would account for this increase?

NOTES

1. For a review of data, see Charles R. Tittle and Raymond Paternoster, *Social Deviance and Crime* (Los Angeles: Roxbury, 2000), pp. 316–324.
2. For a collection on this topic, see K. Heimer and C. Kruttschnitt, eds., *Gender and Crime: Patterns in Victimization and Offending* (New York: New York University Press, 2006). See also Sandra Walklate, *Gender, Crime and Criminal Justice*, 2nd ed. (Portland, OR: Willan Publishing, 2004).
3. Dorie Klein, "The Etiology of Female Crime: A Review of the Literature," *Issues in Criminology* 8 (1973): 3–30; Carol Smart, *Women, Crime and Criminology: A Feminist Critique* (Boston: Routledge and Kegan Paul, 1976). These books are briefly reviewed in Sally S. Simpson, "Feminist Theory, Crime, and Justice," *Criminology* 27 (1989): 605–631; and in Kathleen Daly and Meda Chesney-Lind, "Feminism and Criminology," *Justice Quarterly* 5 (1988): 497–538.
4. Eileen B. Leonard, *Women, Crime and Society: A Critique of Criminology Theory* (New York: Longman, 1982); Ngaire Naffine, *Female Crime: The Construction of Women in Criminology* (Boston: Allen and Unwin, 1987).
5. These early theories included Cesare Lombroso and William Ferrero, *La Donna Delinquente* (1893), translated and reprinted as *The Female Offender* (Buffalo, NY: Hein, 1980); Willem Bonger, *Criminality and Economic Conditions* (Boston: Little, Brown, 1916), reprinted by Agathon, New York, 1967; W. I. Thomas, *The Unadjusted Girl* (1923), reprinted by Patterson

Smith, Montclair, NJ, 1969; Sheldon Glueck and Eleanor Glueck, *Five Hundred Delinquent Women* (1934), reprinted by Periodicals Service, Germantown, PA, 1972; and Otto Pollock, *The Criminality of Women* (1952), reprinted by Greenwood, Westport, CT, 1972. See the discussion in Meda Chesney-Lind and Randall G. Shelden, *Girls, Delinquency, and Juvenile Justice*, 2nd ed. (Belmont, CA: West/Wadsworth, 1998), pp. 74–81.

6. Daly and Chesney-Lind, "Feminism and Criminology."

7. Smart, *Women, Crime and Criminology*; Frances Heidensohn, *Women and Crime* (New York: New York University Press, 1985). For a brief discussion with some examples, see James W. Messerschmidt, *Masculinities and Crime* (Lanham, MD: Rowman and Littlefield, 1993), pp. 2–4, or Messerschmidt, *Capitalism, Patriarchy and Crime: Toward a Socialist Feminist Criminology* (Totowa, NJ: Rowman and Littlefield, 1986), pp. 1–24.

8. Jane R. Chapman, *Economic Realities and the Female Offender* (Lexington, MA: Lexington Books, 1980); Susan Datesman and Frank R. Scarpitti, *Women, Crime and Justice* (New York: Oxford University Press, 1980); Clarice Feinman, *Women in the Criminal Justice System* (New York: Praeger, 1986). Some of the differences are reviewed in Simpson, "Feminist Theory, Crime, and Justice."

9. Freda Adler, *Sisters in Crime: The Rise of the New Female Criminal* (New York: McGraw Hill, 1975).

10. Rita James Simon, *Women and Crime* (Lexington, MA: Lexington Books, 1975). See also Simon and Jean Landis, *The Crimes Women Commit, the Punishments They Receive* (Lexington, MA: Lexington Books, 1991).

11. Simpson, "Feminist Theory, Crime, and Justice," p. 610. Studies have indicated that rising rates of female violent crime, in particular assault, over the past two decades, are primarily attributable to policy changes, policing, and reporting, as opposed to an actual increase in violent crime by women. See Darryl Steffensmeier, Jennifer Schwartz, Hua Zhong, and Jeff Ackerman, "An Assessment of Recent Trends in Girls' Violence Using Diverse Longitudinal Sources: Is the Gender Gap Closing?" *Criminology* 43 (2005): 355–405.

12. Simpson, "Feminist Theory, Crime, and Justice," p. 611. Daly and Chesney-Lind, "Feminism and Criminology," p. 511) also pointed to the "limitations of the liberal feminist perspective on gender that informed their work."

13. Allison Morris, *Women, Crime and Criminal Justice* (New York: Blackwell, 1987), p. 16. Daly and Chesney-Lind ("Feminism and Criminology," p. 507) agreed with her conclusion.

14. For an overview of the schools of feminism in criminology, see Meda Chesney-Lind and Karlene Faith, "What About Feminism?," in *Explaining Criminals and Crime*, ed. Raymond Paternoster and Ronet Bachman (Los Angeles: Roxbury, 2000), pp. 287–302.

15. Alison Jaggar, *Feminist Politics and Human Nature* (Totowa, NJ: Roman and Allanheld, 1983).

16. Kate Millett, *Sexual Politics* (New York: Doubleday, 1970).

17. See Michael J. Lynch, Raymond Michalowski, and W. Byron Groves, *The New Primer in Radical Criminology* (Monsey, NY: Criminal Justice Press, 2000), pp. 108–111.

18. Polly Radosh, "Women and Crime in the United States: A Marxian Explanation," *Sociological Spectrum* 10 (1990): 105–131.

19. Dawn Currie, "Women and the State: A Statement on Feminist Theory," *Critical Criminologist* 1 (1989): 4–5.

20. Radosh, "Women and Crime in the United States"; Daly and Chesney-Lind, "Feminism and Criminology."

21. Shulamith Firestone, *The Dialectics of Sex: The Case for Feminist Revolution* (New York: William Morrow, 1970).

22. See, e.g., Daly and Chesney-Lind, "Feminism and Criminology," p. 501; and Simpson, "Feminist Theory, Crime, and Justice," p. 606.

23. Chesney-Lind and Faith, "What About Feminism?," pp. 296–297.

24. Carol Smart, *Feminism and the Power of Law* (London: Routledge, 1989); and "Feminist Approaches to Criminology or Postmodern Woman Meets Atavistic Man," in *Feminist Perspectives in Criminology*, ed. Loraine Gelshorpe and Allison Morris (Milton Keynes, UK: Open University Press, 1990), pp. 70–84. For a different postmodernist feminist view, see Christine Garza, "Postmodern Paradigms and Chicana Feminist Thought: Creating a Space and Language," *Critical Criminologist* 4, no. 3–4 (1992): 1–2, 11–13.

25. Nancy A. Wonders, "Postmodern Feminist Criminology and Social Justice," in Bruce A. Arrigo, *Social Justice, Criminal Justice* (Belmont, CA: West/Wadsworth, 1998), pp. 111–128.

26. Chesney-Lind and Faith, "What About Feminism?," p. 297.

27. E.g., Chesney-Lind and Faith (ibid., p. 298) called for "solid research- and theory-building" related to women's crime and victimization.

28. On the other hand, the inclusion of diverse women's experience tends to weaken arguments about women's common experiences of oppression. See Dawn H. Currie, "Challenging Privilege: Feminist Struggles in the Canadian Context," *Critical Criminologist*, 3 (1991): 1–2, 10–12.

29. Chesney-Lind and Faith, "What About Feminism?," p. 297–298. To some extent, the appreciative relativism of multicultural feminism contradicts the view of other feminists, who claim that feminist thinking is superior to male-dominated thinking, which they describe as biased, distorted, and lacking objectivity because of its loyalty to male domination. See Jaggar, *Feminist Politics and Human Nature*, p. 370. Also see Daly and Chesney-Lind, "Feminism and Criminology," pp. 499–500. Because it neither privileges nor disparages particular points of view, postmodernism itself would seem to suggest that male-dominated thinking is as legitimate as feminist thinking. To that extent, postmodernism is difficult to reconcile with feminism. See Einstadter and Henry, *Criminology Theory: An Analysis of Its Underlying Assumptions*, 2d edition (Lanham, MD: Rowman & Littlefield, 2006), pp. 299–300.

30. Patricia Hill Collins, *Black Feminist Thought* (Boston: Unwin Hyman, 1990).

31. See Sylvia Walby, *Theorizing Patriarchy* (Cambridge, MA: Basil Blackwell, 1990).

32. Daly and Chesney-Lind, "Feminism and Criminology," pp. 514–520.

33. Ibid., p. 518.

34. Ibid., p. 514.

35. Ibid., p. 519.

36. Douglas A. Smith and Raymond Paternoster, "The Gender Gap in Theories of Deviance," *Journal of Research in Crime and Delinquency* 24 (1987): 140–172.

37. Candace Kruttschnitt, "Contributions of Quantitative Methods to the Study of Gender and Crime, or Bootstrapping Our Way into the Theoretical Thicket," *Journal of Quantitative Criminology* 12 (1996): 135–161, p. 141.

38. Ibid., p. 518.

39. Ibid., pp. 519–520.

40. op. cit., pp. 289–290.

41. For a discussion of the issue, see R. Gregory Dunaway, Francis T. Cullen, Velmer S. Burton Jr., and T. David Evans, "The Myth of Social Class and Crime Revisited," *Criminology* 38 (2000): 589–632.

42. Claire Renzetti and Dan Curran, *Women, Men and Society* (Boston: Allyn and Bacon, 1993).

43. Chesney-Lind and Faith, "What About Feminism?," p. 290.

44. For a recent discussion of trends in the gender gap in violent victimization, see Janet L. Lauritsen and Karen Heimer, "The Gender Gap in Violent Victimization, 1973–2004," *Journal of Quantitative Criminology* 24 (2008): 125–148.

45. Maureen Cain, "Realist Philosophy and Standpoint Epistemologies for Feminist Criminology as a Successor Science," in *Feminist Perspectives in Criminology*, ed. Loraine Gelsthorpe and Allison Morris (Buckingham, UK: Open University Press, 1990), pp. 124–140.

46. Peggy C. Giordano and Sharon Mohler Rockwell, "Differential Association Theory and Female Crime," in *Of Crime and Criminality*, ed. Sally S. Simpson (Thousand Oaks, CA: Pine Forge Press, 2000), p. 4.

47. For a review, see Chesney-Lind and Shelden, *Girls, Delinquency, and Juvenile Justice*, pp. 81–91.

48. Peggy C. Giordano and Stephen A. Cernkovich, "Gender and Antisocial Behavior," in *Handbook of Antisocial Behavior*, ed. David M. Stoff, James Breiling, and Jack D. Maser (New York: John Wiley, 1997), pp. 496–510.

49. E.g., Margaret L. Anderson, *Thinking About Women*, 2nd ed. (New York: Macmillan, 1988).

50. E.g., Charles Tittle, *Control Balance* (Boulder, CO: Westview Press, 1995).

51. The original work on power-control theory was by John Hagan, A. R. Gillis, and John Simpson, "The Class Structure of Gender and Delinquency: Toward a Power-Control Theory of Common Delinquent Behavior," *American Journal of Sociology* 90 (1985): 1151–1178. The theory was then presented in a larger theoretical context in John Hagan, *Structural Criminology* (New Brunswick, NJ: Rutgers University Press, 1989).

52. Examples of support for the theory include John Hagan, *Structural Criminology*, chaps. 7–9; Hagan, A. R. Gillis, and John Simpson, "Clarifying and Extending Power-Control Theory," *American Journal of Sociology* 95 (1990): 1151–1178; Brenda Sims Blackwell, "Perceived Sanction Threats, Gender, and Crime," *Criminology* 38 (2000): 439–488. But see Helmut Hirtenlehner, Brenda Sims Blackwell, Heinz Leitgoeb, and Johann Bacher, "Explaining the Gender Gap in Juvenile Shoplifting: A Power-Control Theoretical Analysis," *Deviant Behavior* 35 (2014): 41–65 (finding that the power component of the theory was much less significant than the control and risk-related components); Gary D. Hill and Maxine P. Atkinson, "Gender, Familial Control, and Delinquency," *Criminology* 26 (1988): 127–149 (rather than mothers playing a more important role than fathers in controlling children, mothers control daughters more than sons, and the reverse is true for fathers).

53. Chesney-Lind and Faith, "What About Feminism?," p. 299. Supportive of this view are the findings of Jane A. Siegel and Linda M. Williams, "The Relationship Between Child Sexual Abuse and Female Delinquency and Crime: A Prospective Study," *Journal of Research in Crime and Delinquency* 40 (2003): 71–94.

54. Lisa M. Broidy and Robert Agnew, "Gender and Crime: A General Strain Theory Perspective," *Journal of Research in Crime and Delinquency* 34 (1997): 275–306.

55. For a summary and discussion of this research see Fawn T. Ngo and Raymond Paternoster, "Stalking Strain, Concurrent Negative Emotions, and Legitimate Coping Strategies: A Preliminary Test of Gendered Strain Theory," *American Journal of Criminal Justice* 38 (2013): 369–391, pp. 371–374.

56. Giordano and Rockwell, "Differential Association Theory and Female Crime."

57. Ibid., p. 22.

58. Karen Heimer and Stacy De Coster, "The Gendering of Violent Delinquency," *Criminology* 37 (1999): 306.

59. Ibid., p. 305.

60. Candace West and Sarah Fenstermaker, "Doing Gender," *Gender and Society* 9 (1995): 3–37.

61. Dale Spender, *Invisible Women* (London: Writers and Readers Publishing, 1982), p. 23.

62. Sally S. Simpson and Lori Elis, "Doing Gender: Sorting Out the Caste and Crime Conundrum," *Criminology* 33 (1995): 71.

63. Lisa Maher, *Sexed Work: Gender, Race, and Resistance in a Brooklyn Drug Economy* (Oxford: Clarendon Press, 1997).

64. Jody Miller, "Up It Up: Gender and the Accomplishment of Street Robbery," *Criminology* 36 (1998): 37–66; and "Feminist Theories of Women's Crime: Robbery as a Case Study," in *Of Crime and Criminality*, ed. Simpson, pp. 25–46.

65. Karen Joe Laidler and Geoffrey Hunt, "Accomplishing Femininity Among the Girls in the Gang," *British Journal of Criminology* 41 (2001): 656–678.

66. Frances Heidensohn, "Gender and Crime," in *The Oxford Handbook of Criminology*, 2nd ed., ed. Mike Maguire, Rod Morgan, and Robert Reiner (New York: Oxford University Press, 1996), p. 791.

67. Chesney-Lind and Faith, "What About Feminism?," p. 287.

68. Messerschmidt, *Masculinities and Crime*, pp. 2–4.

69. Ibid., chap. 3.

70. Olivia Choy, Adriane Raine, Peter H. Venables, and David P. Farrington, "Explaining the Gender Gap in Crime: The Role of Heart Rate," *Criminology* 55 (2017): 465–487.

71. Tittle and Paternoster, *Social Deviance and Crime*, p. 364–365. For a collection on masculinity and crime, see Time Newburn and Elizabeth A. Stanko, *Just Boys Doing Business: Men, Masculinities and Crime* (New York: Routledge, 1994).

72. Neil Boyd, *The Beast Within: Why Men Are Violent* (Vancouver: Greystone Books, 2000), pp. 139–167.

73. Sylvana M. Cote, "Sex Differences in Physical and Indirect Aggression: A Developmental Perspective," *European Journal of Policy Research* 13 (2007): 183–200.

74. Ibid., p. 187.

75. Ibid., p. 188.

76. Ibid., pp. 194–195.

77. Messerschmidt, *Masculinities and Crime*, p. 3.

78. Michael R. Gottfredson and Travis Hirschi, *A General Theory of Crime* (Stanford, CA: Stanford University Press, 1990), pp. 144–149.

79. Karen Hayslett-McCall and Thomas J. Bernard ("Attachment, Self-Control, and Masculinity: A Theory of Male Crime Rates," *Theoretical Criminology* 6 [2002]: 5–33) positively supported this speculation, linking it to broader theories of masculinity.

80. Miller, Cohen, and Cloward and Ohlin are quoted in Chesney-Lind and Shelden, *Girls, Delinquency, and Juvenile Justice*, pp. 84–86.

81. Walter B. Miller, "Lower Class Culture as a Generating Milieu of Gang Delinquency," *Journal of Social Issues* 14 (1958): 5–19. See the discussion in Chapter 9.

82. Albert Cohen, *Delinquent Boys: The Culture of the Gang* (New York: Free Press, 1955), pp. 139–140. See the discussion of Cohen in Chapter 8.

83. Richard A. Cloward and Lloyd E. Ohlin, *Delinquency and Opportunity* (New York: Free Press, 1960). See the discussion in Chapter 8.

84. Messerschmidt, *Capitalism, Patriarchy, and Crime*; Messerschmidt, *Crime as Structured Action: Gender, Race, Class, and Crime in the Making* (Thousand Oaks, CA: Sage, 1997). See also Timothy Newburn and Elizabeth A. Stanko, *Men, Masculinities, and Crime* (New York: Routledge, 1991); Tony Jefferson, "Masculinities and Crime," in *The Oxford Handbook of Criminology*, ed. Maguire, Morgan, and Reiner, and Lee H. Bowker, *Masculinities and Violence* (Thousand Oaks, CA: Sage, 1998).

85. Christopher W. Mullins, Richard Wright, and Bruce A. Jacobs, "Gender, Streetlife, and Criminal Retaliation," *Criminology* 42 (2004): 911–930.

86. Dana Peterson, Jody Miller, and Finn-Aage Esbensen, "The Impact of Sex Composition on Gangs and Gang Member Delinquency," *Criminology* 39 (2001): 411–439.

87. Janet L. Lauritsen, Karen Heimer, and James P. Lynch, "Trends in the Gender Gap in Violent Offending: New Evidence from the National Crime Victimization Survey," *Criminology* 47 (2009): 361–399.

88. Jennifer Schwartz, Darrell Steffensmeier, Hua Zhong, and Jeff Ackerman, "Trends in the Gender Gap in Violence: Reevaluating NCVS and Other Evidence," *Criminology* 47 (2009): 401–425.

89. Lauritsen et al., "Trends in the Gender Gap in Violent Offending," p. 392.

90. Schwartz et al., "Trends in the Gender Gap in Violence," pp. 407–410.

91. Ibid., pp. 410–416.

92. E.g., Tony Beatton, Michael P. Kidd, and Stephen Machin, "Gender Crime Convergence Over Twenty Years: Evidence from Australia," *European Economic Review* 109 (2018): 275–288.

93. Kerry Carrington, "Girls and Violence: The Case for a Feminist Theory of Female Violence," *International Journal for Crime, Justice, and Social Democracy* 2 (2013): 63–79. Carrington cites Lauritsen et al., "Trends in the Gender Gap in Violent Offending," but not Schwartz et al., "Trends in the Gender Gap in Violence." When citing Lauritsen et al., Carrington glosses over the fact that this study mostly attributed the reduction in the gender gap to changes in male behavior, and emphasizes that Lauritsen and colleagues said that the issue of female violence is "real and warrants 'serious attention in future research'" (p. 66, citing Lauritsen et al. p. 361). Despite some questionable empirical assumptions, Carrington makes a good case for a feminist understanding of female violence, based on analysis of Lynndie England, the female soldier who made headlines around the world based on photos of her abusing prisoners in Abu Ghraib prison.

94. See Jennifer Schwartz, Darrell Steffensmeier, and Ben Feldmeyer, "Assessing Trends in Women's Violence via Data Triangulation: Arrests, Convictions, Incarcerations, & Victim Reports," *Social Problems* 56 (2009): 494–525.

95. See, e.g., Samantha Applin and Steven F. Messner, "Her American Dream. Bringing Gender in to Institutional Anomie Theory," *Feminist Criminology* 10 (2015): 36–59.

96. Darrell Steffensmeier, Jennifer Schwartz, Hua Zhong, and Jeff Ackerman, "An Assessment of Recent Trends in Girls' Violence Using Diverse Longitudinal Sources: Is the Gender Gap Closing?" *Criminology* 43 (2005): 355–405.

97. Christine Alder and Anne Worrall, "A Contemporary Crisis?" in *Girls' Violence; Myths and Realities*, ed. Christine Alder and Anne Worrall (Albany, NY: State University of New York Press), pp. 1–20.

98. Miller, "Feminist Theories," p. 43.

99. Giordano and Rockwell, "Differential Association Theory and Female Crime," p. 22.

100. Donald G. Dutton, *Rethinking Domestic Violence* (Vancouver, Canada: University of British Columbia Press, 2006).

101. Walter S. DeKeseredy and Molly Dragiewicz, "Understanding the Complexities of Feminist Perspectives on Woman Abuse: A Commentary on Donald G. Dutton's *Rethinking Domestic Violence,*" *Violence Against Women* 13 (2007): 874–884. See also Walter S. DeKeseredy, "Feminist Contributions to Understanding Woman Abuse: Myths, Controversies, and Realities," *Aggression and Violent Behavior* 16 (2011): 297–302.

102. DeKeseredy and Dragiewicz, "Understanding the Complexities of Feminist Perspectives on Woman Abuse," p. 876.

103. Ibid., p. 878.

CHAPTER 14

—

Developmental and Life-Course Theories

Most theories in criminology focus on the relationship between crime and various biological, psychological, or social factors, and they assume that these factors have the same effect on offenders regardless of their age. In contrast, developmental theories assume that different factors may have different effects on offenders of different ages. These developmental theories therefore explain crime in the context of the life course, that is, the progression from childhood to adolescence to adulthood and ultimately to old age. For example, developmental theories may assert that some factors explain criminal behavior that starts in childhood or early adolescence, but other factors explain crime that starts in late adolescence or adulthood. Some factors explain the fact that a person begins to commit crime, while other factors explain whether the person continues to commit crime for a long time or quickly stops.

It is important to note that a life-course perspective on human behavior and development predates criminological theory. For example, many of the theorists discussed in this chapter, such as John Laub and Robert Sampson, have been influenced tremendously by the work of Glen Elder Jr.[1] An still-active life-course researcher and scholar, Elder's first major contribution to this field of inquiry was his work examining the life histories of children from Oakland and Berkeley who grew up during the Great Depression.[2] Relying on a rich longitudinal data set documenting three decades of information, Elder demonstrated that historical circumstances at one's birth time may have considerable impact on their lives, but that families' and individuals' reactions to their circumstances often exerted stronger effects on their life trajectories than these circumstances. Many children who experienced high levels of deprivation during the Great Depression, for example, took on adult responsibilities, and traditional family structures were altered, as mothers found jobs to supplement income. Life changes among adolescents permanently affected their adult behavioral trajectories. In his work, Elder combined two approaches: "life cycle," which follows the sequence of the

340

social roles across generations of a family, and "age expectations," which examines life transitions in terms of their timing.[3] For example, if one gives birth at too early an age, this can possibly have consequences affecting the mother, child, and subsequent generations. As another example, men who enlist in the military at a young age may positively change their life trajectories, whereas men who enlist at a later age (when they already have adult responsibilities) may experience negative repercussions.[4]

Elder viewed the life-course paradigm as generally involving four themes: *lives and historical times* ("differences in birth years expose individuals to different historical worlds, with their constraints and options"[5]); *the timing of lives* ("the incidence, duration, and sequence of roles, and to relevant expectations and beliefs based on age"[6]); *linked lives* ("the interactions between the individual's social worlds over the life span"[7]) and *human agency* ("[within] the constraints of their world, people are planful and make choices among options that construct their life course"[8]).

Some criminologists argue that developmental or life-course theories do not contribute anything new to criminology and that the standard theories that do not consider age and the life course are adequate to explain crime. A major debate about this issue was fully engaged by the mid-1980s. At its center was an argument about the relationship between age and crime. But the debate also was entangled in complicated arguments about criminal careers, since that concept refers to the development and progression of offending over time. In addition, the debate involved a particularly fierce argument about the type of research needed to test criminology theories. We begin with a review of this debate and of some of the evidence that was marshaled to defend each side. We then discuss other developmental theories.

THE GREAT DEBATE: CRIMINAL CAREERS, LONGITUDINAL RESEARCH, AND THE RELATIONSHIP BETWEEN AGE AND CRIME

In 1986, the National Research Council's Panel on Research on Criminal Careers published a two-volume work titled *Criminal Careers and "Career Criminals."*[9] The panel's research was based on ideas that had been brewing for some time. In 1972, a study in Philadelphia had concluded that 6 percent of juveniles accounted for 52 percent of all juvenile contacts with the police in the city and 70 percent of all juvenile contacts involving felony offenses.[10] These figures led to the idea that there was a small group of active "career criminals" who accounted for a very large portion of crime.[11] This conclusion, in turn, led to the idea that crime rates could be reduced dramatically by locking up these chronic offenders.[12] Subsequently, a great deal of money was poured into research that attempted to develop these ideas so they could form the basis for practical crime policies.

Although the distinction was unclear at first, the ideas of career criminals and criminal careers are very different. A career criminal is thought to be a chronic offender who commits frequent crimes over a long period. In contrast, the term *criminal career* does not imply anything about the frequency or seriousness of the offending. It simply suggests that involvement in criminal activity begins at some point in a person's life, continues for a certain length of time, and then ends. Many people have short and trivial criminal careers—they commit one or two minor offenses and then stop.

The Panel on Research on Criminal Careers introduced a new set of terms with which to describe criminal behavior in the context of a criminal career. Participation refers to whether a person has ever committed a crime—it can only be "yes" or "no." Prevalence is the fraction of a group of people (such as all those aged eighteen and younger) who have ever participated in crime. Frequency (symbolized by the Greek letter lambda) refers to the rate of criminal activity of those who engage in crime, measured by the number of offenses over time. Seriousness, of course, concerns the severity of one's offenses. Onset and desistance refer to the beginning and end of a criminal career, while duration refers to the length of time between onset and desistance.

The first major use of this new language system was to interpret the relationship between age and crime, which set off the great debate mentioned earlier. It has long been known that crime rates rise rapidly throughout the adolescent years, peak in the late teens or early twenties, and steadily decline from then on. The traditional view has been that the decline in this curve after about age twenty is due primarily to changes in frequency—that is, the number of offenders remains the same, but each offender commits fewer offenses. In contrast, career criminal researchers suggest that the decline is caused by a change in participation—that is, the number of offenders declines, but each remaining offender still engages in a high rate of offending. If these researchers are correct, then those offenders who continue to commit crimes at high levels after their early twenties are career criminals who need to be incapacitated. On the other hand, if all offenders gradually commit fewer crimes, then none of them is a career criminal in the sense of being a more frequent and chronic offender than the others.

This interpretation of the age–crime relationship also has another implication. Because some offenders always participate whereas others end their careers early, it may be necessary to develop different models for predicting participation and frequency. It may be that one set of factors influences whether someone participates in crime, whereas another set of factors affects the frequency and duration of his or her criminal acts.

Essentially, these factors represent the central contentions of the two sides in the great debate mentioned earlier. On the one side were the career criminal researchers, notably Alfred Blumstein, Jacqueline Cohen, and David Farrington, while on the other side were most notably Michael Gottfredson and Travis Hirschi.[13] Gottfredson and Hirschi took the position that independent of other sociological explanations, age simply matures people out of crime. The decline of crime with age is therefore due to the declining frequency of offenses among all active offenders, rather than declines in the number of active offenders. Because of this, Gottfredson and Hirschi argued that there is no reason to attempt to identify and selectively incapacitate career criminals.

The debate on the relationship between age and crime led to a particularly ferocious dispute about the type of research that is required to test these theories. Much prior research in criminology looked at aggregate crime rates—for example, burglary rates in a given city. But these aggregate rates say nothing about whether burglaries are committed by a small number of offenders who each commit a large number of burglaries or by a large number of offenders who each commit only a few. To answer this question, career criminal criminologists focused on the patterns of crimes committed by individual criminals over a certain period, rather than on aggregate crime rates within a particular location.[14] In particular, they tended to use "longitudinal research," which follows the same individuals over a long period. An early example of longitudinal research, as discussed in Chapter 4, was carried out by the Gluecks, who followed the lives of five hundred delinquents and five hundred nondelinquents over many years, attempting to assess why some juveniles become delinquent or criminal and others do not.[15]

In contrast, most other criminologists have used "cross-sectional" research, which compares different individuals at the same time. For example, criminologists may examine a number of juveniles in a particular city, find out which juveniles commit the most offenses, and assess what types of factors are associated with those juveniles. Cross-sectional research is much cheaper than longitudinal research, since it can be done at one time. Gottfredson and Hirschi argued that because the age–crime relationship is invariant, cross-sectional research is sufficient, and it is an unnecessary waste of resources to collect information about the same individuals over a long time.[16] Other criminologists, however, believe that longitudinal data collection and analysis can be beneficial to the study of criminal behavior.[17] They have argued that cross-sectional designs allow only for the study of correlates of criminal behavior, whereas longitudinal designs allow for the study of causation because they can establish which factors came first. Longitudinal research also allows one to assess the extent to which prior behavior influences present and future behavior. In addition, it allows for the assessment of whether different models are necessary to explain behavior at different points in the life course.

CRIMINAL PROPENSITY VERSUS CRIMINAL CAREER

After considerable thrashing about, the age–crime debate described previously boiled down to a debate between the "criminal propensity" and the "criminal career" positions. Gottfredson and Hirschi espoused the criminal propensity position. Essentially, they argued that some people are more prone to commit crime and other people are less prone, but everyone's propensity to commit crime is relatively stable over their life course after about age eight. That propensity may manifest itself in a variety of patterns of behavior, owing to chance and circumstances, so that individuals with the same propensity may actually commit somewhat different amounts and types of crime. But because criminal propensity is essentially constant over the life course, it is unnecessary to explain such factors as age of onset of crime, duration of a criminal career, and frequency of offending. Actual variations in the amount of offending by given individuals then are explained primarily by their point on the age–crime curve. Everyone will follow the age–crime curve, in the sense that they all will have their greatest criminal involvement in their late teens and decline thereafter. But over the entire age curve, those with the lowest propensity will always have the lowest actual involvement with crime, while those with the highest propensity will always have the highest actual involvement. Thus the age–crime curve, combined with variations in the propensity to commit crime, looks like Figure 14.1.

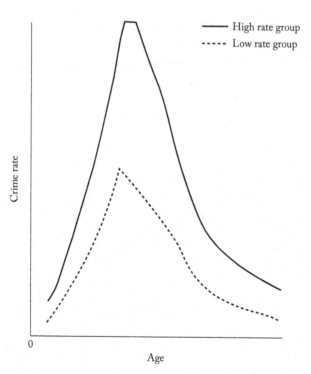

FIGURE 14-1 Hypothesized Relation Among Age, Propensity, and Crime. (From Travis Hirschi and Michael Gottfredson, "Age and the Explanation of Crime," *American Journal of Sociology* 89 [1983]: 565. Reprinted by permission.)

Gottfredson and Hirschi argued that the age–crime curve itself is invariant and does not require any explanation. Therefore, all that is required is to explain why different people have different criminal propensities.[18] And because criminal propensity does not vary over the life course, the explanation can be tested with cross-sectional research, and there is no need for the more expensive longitudinal designs. This is the context for their theory of low self-control, as presented in Chapter 10.[19]

In contrast to the criminal propensity position, in the criminal career position, which we have previously discussed, different sets of variables may explain behavior at different points in the life course. Thus, it is necessary to build separate models for age of onset, participation, frequency, duration, and desistance. To some extent, then, the debate focused on whether the entire criminal career could be explained with a single causal theory (the criminal propensity position) or whether different causal processes were at work at different points in the life span (the criminal career position). In particular, the debate took on the focus of whether it was necessary to have separate causal models for participation and frequency, since those were the two crucial factors in the two contrasting explanations of the age–crime curve.

Once the age–crime relationship debate was established as one that set criminal propensity and criminal career positions against each other, researchers went to work attempting to garner support for one or the other position. Although the issue is not yet resolved,[20] there is some preliminary evidence supporting both positions.

Probably the strongest evidence for the criminal propensity position came from Rowe, Osgood, and Nicewander, who fit a latent trait model to crime data.[21] A latent trait is a quality that is unobservable but can be inferred through various measures. If it exists, then the inherent propensity to commit crime would be a latent trait because, for a given person, there is no way directly to observe it. The question, of course, is whether it exists at all. The way Rowe et al. decided to proceed was to make certain assumptions about the latent criminal propensity trait and then use the assumptions to predict how criminal activity would be distributed among offenders if such a trait actually existed. They then compared those predictions with the actual distribution of offenses that had been found in four cities. Rowe et al.'s model was basically atheoretical in that it did not discuss where this latent propensity toward criminal behavior comes from. Instead, it was just a test to see if such a propensity may exist. According to the propensity position, such a trait should account for differences in both one's likelihood of participating in criminal behavior and one's frequency of participation, since both outcomes stem from the same source. Applying their models to four different sets of data on individual behavior, Rowe et al. found solid support for the propensity position.[22]

In contrast, Simons and his colleagues also tested a latent trait model and found support for the criminal career view.[23] Youths who exhibited antisocial behavior in late childhood tended to receive lower-quality parenting and schooling and to have more associations with delinquent peers. These three factors then increased delinquency in early adolescence. If these three events did not happen, however, there was no increase in adolescent delinquency. These findings suggest that these youths did not have a latent antisocial trait, but that adolescent delinquency was a product of developmental events in the life course. In addition, Monkonnen looked at age-specific violent offending in New York City from 1773 to 1874 and from 1976 to 1995.[24] In the earlier period, violent offending peaked between ages twenty and thirty, while in the more recent period, there was a much younger peak and a much flatter rate of offending from the early twenties onward. Monkkonnen concluded that the age distribution of recent violent crime is a new phenomenon in history. His conclusion challenges Gottfredson and Hirschi's argument about the invariant relationship between age and crime.

On the other hand, O'Brien and his colleagues studied age-specific homicide rates from 1960 to 1995.[25] They found that in the 1990s, youths aged four to seventeen were two to three times more likely to commit homicides than were similarly aged youths in the 1960s and 1970s, while people aged twenty-five and older in the 1990s were less likely to commit homicide than were similarly aged people in the 1960s and 1970s. O'Brien et al. argued that given the high total number of births at the time and the high portion of births to unwed mothers, the high rate of violence resulted from the few resources that were available when these youths were young children. This pattern of violence persisted and was relatively stable as this particular group of juveniles aged. This finding supports Gottfredson and Hirschi's propensity position, in which the propensity toward crime is established at an early age and then simply follows the age–crime curve over time.[26]

THE TRANSITION TO DEVELOPMENTAL CRIMINOLOGY

Criminologists are still testing the propensity and criminal career positions against each other, and the issues involved in the argument are becoming increasingly complex.[27] In general, however, researchers are less likely to regard these two positions as polar opposites. For example, Nagin and Land found support for both the criminal career and propensity positions and suggested that "a moratorium should be called on strong either-or theoretical positions on the nature of criminal careers."[28] In addition, there is a developmental criminology forming, one that has strong roots in developmental psychology and treats crimes as social events in the life course.[29] As these new developmental theories are being created and evaluated, the great debate between criminal careers and criminal propensity is becoming less important.

This is not to say that the work on criminal careers is irrelevant to developmental criminologists. On the contrary, these theorists have largely adopted the terminology of the criminal career paradigm. For example, in their review of the developmental literature, Loeber and Le Blanc organized the material around activation, aggravation, and desistance,[30] concepts that are similar to the core concepts of the criminal career paradigm. Activation refers to the continuity, frequency, and diversity of criminal activities. It consists of acceleration (increased frequency), stabilization (continuity over time), and diversification (of criminal activities). Aggravation is a developmental sequence that escalates in seriousness over time. Desistance refers to a decrease in the frequency of offending, a reduction in its diversification (specialization), and a reduction in its seriousness.

Over the past decade, a significant body of empirical research has been conducted testing various developmental theories of crime. On the basis of this research, Farrington summarized what he believed to be a set of widely accepted conclusions about the development of offending, as well as a number of controversial issues. Developmental theories, according to him, should both account for the accepted conclusions and help to resolve the controversial questions. Table 14-1 synthesizes Farrington's discussion.[31]

In 2007, Piquero, Farrington, and Blumstein published their analysis of the data from the Cambridge Study in Delinquent Development (CSDD), a longitudinal study of 411 South London males born in 1953. The study began in 1961 and followed the subjects from ages ten to forty.[32] The major findings from the study were largely consistent with the widely accepted conclusions just listed. Divergent findings and controversial issues were addressed by the following findings:[33]

The frequency of total convictions peaked at age sixteen and then slowly and steadily declined between ages twenty and forty, while the frequency of violence peaked between ages sixteen and twenty, slowly declined in early adulthood, and remained flat and stable through age forty. The mean age of onset was eighteen; however, the peak age of onset was fourteen, with those exhibiting early onset accumulating more convictions over the life course and more likely to have acted violently. Total convictions was a better predictor of violence than age of onset, with the frequency of offending the strongest predictor of violence. Early onset increased one's likelihood of a longer criminal career, greater overall offenses, and convictions for a wider variety of types of offenses. Thirteen percent of the full sample (or 32% of the offenders) accounted for 73 percent of the total convictions, providing support for the notion of chronic or career criminals. Chronic offenders were found to have, on average, longer criminal careers, earlier onsets, more violent crimes, and a greater variety of offenses.

The data also showed that it is too simple to divide individuals into nonoffenders, offenders, and chronic offenders; in fact, five different trajectories were identified through age forty, showing distinct offending patterns, regarding onset, persistence, and desistance. These trajectories were labeled nonoffenders,

TABLE 14-1 Synthesis of Farrington's Discussion of Conclusions and Controversies of Developmental Theories

Widely Accepted Conclusions About the Development of Offending	Controversial Questions
The prevalence of offending peaks between ages fifteen and nineteen. *Prevalence* refers to the overall proportion of the population who offends.	Although the prevalence of offending peaks in the late teen years, little is known about the variation of the frequency of individual offending with age: Do most offenders peak in their late teens, or do they persist?
Onset peaks between ages eight and fourteen, and desistance peaks between ages twenty and twenty-nine.	Does the seriousness of the crimes that offenders commit vary with age or stay relatively the same?
The earlier the age of onset, the longer the duration of the criminal career and the greater the overall number of crimes.	Is an earlier age of onset associated with a greater frequency of individual offending or a higher overall average seriousness in offending? Are early-onset offenders different in some way from late-onset offenders?
Although antisocial behavior in childhood is highly correlated with offending behavior in adulthood, individuals can still change over time (e.g., conform).	Do the risk factors for early onset of offending also have a causal effect on offending itself, or are there a unique set of predictors?
A small proportion of the population commits a large proportion of crimes.	Do chronic offenders commit more serious offenses than nonchronic offenders, and are they fundamentally different in some way?
It does not help much to focus on "specialized offenders," since most offenders are versatile.	
Most crimes through the teenage years are committed with others, and most crimes committed afterward are committed solo.	
Whereas during the teenage years nonutilitarian factors, such as excitement or boredom, can motivate offending in adulthood, utilitarian motives, such as pecuniary gain or revenge, become more dominant.	
Different types of offenses are associated with different age groups. For example, offenders usually shoplift before they turn to burglary, and they turn to robbery last. In their earlier years, they tend to diversify to different types of offenses and in later years tend to specialize.	Are onset sequences, such as these, representations of a general construct (criminal potential) or more reflective of a gateway effect (one must learn to shoplift first, and this leads to burglary and so forth)?

low-adolescence-peaked, low-rate chronics, high-adolescence-peaked, and high-rate chronics. For offenders with two or more convictions by age forty, the average career was more than ten years. The age of onset was related to career length, with those of early onset having longer criminal careers.[34]

The authors drew the following implications from the findings:[35] the fact that by age forty most offenders appear to desist from crime was consistent with Gottfredson and Hirschi's expectation that most offenders follow the aggregate age–crime curve. The findings, however, contradicted the expectation that a small subset continue at very high rates for their entire lives, thus calling into question lengthy prison terms that last into late adulthood. Four modifiable causal variables were found to distinguish significantly between offenders and nonoffenders (although not between the various offense trajectories): low achievement, poor parental child-rearing, impulsivity, and poverty. Because of this finding, the authors concluded that early prevention appears to be a promising avenue to forming policies that more effectively address criminal and other antisocial behaviors.

The authors concluded with five research priorities:[36] intermittency (explaining the zigzagging of one's criminal career path), desistance (exploring why different offenders discontinue their criminal careers at different points),[37] health (determining the nature of the effect of crime on physical and mental health), qualitative narratives (studying in depth through qualitative methodology the criminal careers of different types of offenders), and contextual effects (how variables, such as race, gender, and types of neighborhoods, condition criminal careers).

THREE DEVELOPMENTAL DIRECTIONS

In the following sections, we review three developmental theories that each contribute a different twist.[38] Thornberry's interactional theory explores the relationship between past and present criminal behavior, shows how causal processes of delinquent behavior are dynamic and how different forces shape each other over time, and shows that causal influences may depend on the period of an individual's life. Sampson and Laub's longitudinal study pays special attention to the tension between stability and change perspectives in developmental psychology and criminology. It found that although prior behavior is a strong determinant of present and future behavior, turning points in individuals' lives do exist, and change (both positive and negative) can occur at any point in a developmental sequence. Tremblay's analysis of longitudinal data pushed back the peak age of aggression to early childhood and called into question the ideas of learned violence and adolescent onset of aggression.

Another important developmental theory that is not included is Moffitt's developmental taxonomy, which identified two groups of offenders—adolescent-limited and life-course-persistent. We refer the reader to Chapter 5 for an overview of her typology.

THORNBERRY'S INTERACTIONAL THEORY

Thornberry's interactional theory combines control and social learning theories (see chapters 9 and 10), attempting to increase their collective ability to explain delinquent behavior.[39] To Thornberry, these theories are flawed by their reliance on unidirectional causal structures. Thornberry attempted to develop a model in which concepts from these theories affect each other over time, reciprocally, and in which actual delinquent behavior also reciprocally affects the theoretical concepts. He also stated that the contributing causes to delinquent behavior will change over an individual's life course.

Interactional theory is based mostly on control theory, viewing social constraints as the primary cause of delinquency. However, reduced social constraints may free up behavior, but delinquency still "requires an interactive setting in which [it] is learned, performed, and reinforced."[40] The theory is comprised of six concepts from control and social learning theory: attachment to parents, commitment to school, belief in conventional values, association with delinquent peers, adoption of delinquent values, and engagement in delinquent behavior. Three models are offered, for early adolescence (eleven to thirteen years), middle adolescence (fifteen to sixteen years), and late adolescence (eighteen to twenty years). The division of a theory into different models for different phases in this manner is one of the distinguishing characteristics of developmental theory.

Thornberry's main goal in interactional theory was to sort out the debate between control and social learning theorists: the former argue that delinquent behavior affects the peers one attaches to; the latter argue that one's peer associations affect delinquent behavior. Thornberry argued that peer associations may affect behavior, but behavior, in turn, can influence one's selection of peers. In interactional theory, concepts from control theory are the most important contributors because delinquency will probably not occur unless social constraints are reduced. Thus, the greater one's attachment to parents and commitment to school, the less likely one is to engage in delinquent behavior. Belief in conventional values is influenced by both attachment and commitment, and it affects delinquent behavior indirectly, through its reciprocal influence on commitment to school. Delinquent behavior negatively influences attachment and commitment. It also influences belief in conventional values indirectly, through its influence on attachment. As Thornberry stated, "While the weakening of the bond to conventional society may be an initial cause of delinquency, delinquency eventually becomes its own indirect cause precisely because of its ability to weaken further the person's bonds to family, school, and conventional beliefs."[41]

Also included in Thornberry's interactional theory are hypotheses about how models of delinquency may vary over the adolescent period. Generally, the models for early, middle, and late adolescence are not different; however, Thornberry noted a few expected disparities.[42] In middle adolescence, attachment to parents is expected to play a smaller role, since the adolescent is more involved in activities outside the home. Also, delinquent values are expected to exert a more important influence on commitment, delinquent behavior, and association with delinquent peers than they do in early adolescence, since these values have had more time to solidify. In late adolescence, two variables are added to the model: commitment to conventional activities, such as employment, college, and military service, and commitment to family, such as marriage and having children. These variables essentially supplant attachment to parents and commitment to school, since they are more relevant during this period in an individual's life.

A variety of these arguments have been tested with longitudinal research, with generally supportive results.[43] Thornberry reviewed seventeen longitudinal studies and concluded that "across all the studies, the overwhelming weight of the evidence suggests that many of the presumed unidirectional causes of delinquency are in fact either products of delinquent behavior or involved in mutually reinforcing causal relationships with delinquency behavior."[44] For example, with respect to variables from control theory, Thornberry found almost no relationship between delinquency and attachment to parents. This finding was surprising, and Thornberry speculated that tests from earlier ages (all these studies were done in middle adolescence) might reveal such a relationship. There were fairly strong interactive relationships between delinquency and beliefs ("belief in conventional values, at least during the midadolescent years, influences and is influenced by delinquent conduct") and commitment ("investments in conformity—school and employment—reduce delinquency and crime, but delinquent behavior feeds back upon and attenuates attachment to school and involvement in work").[45] With respect to social learning variables, Thornberry found that "the strongest and most consistent reciprocal relationship is observed for delinquent peers and delinquent behavior," where the causal effects are approximately equal in both directions.[46] That is, the effect of delinquent behavior on delinquent peers seems to be about the same as the effect of delinquent peers on delinquent behavior. Thornberry concluded that effective policies to prevent delinquency can be constructed only if causes are accurately separated from effects in the correlates of delinquency, and this separation can be accomplished by only longitudinal research in the context of a developmental theory of delinquency.

SAMPSON AND LAUB'S AGE-GRADED THEORY OF
INFORMAL SOCIAL CONTROL

Perhaps the most important early study of delinquency was begun in the 1930s by Sheldon and Eleanor Glueck, who compared five hundred persistent delinquents and five hundred proved nondelinquents.[47] The two groups were matched on age, general intelligence, ethnicity, and residence in underprivileged areas and then compared to determine the factors that most related to juvenile delinquency. Even though the Gluecks collected remarkable data on these youths, their analysis of the data was limited by the methods available at the time and therefore has been criticized as inadequate by today's standards.

In 1985, John Laub located the original Glueck data, and he and Robert Sampson spent several years reconstructing and reanalyzing it in order to respond to many of the methodological criticisms. From their reanalysis came a major developmental study, rooted in Hirschi's Social Control Theory, in which the authors developed a longitudinal theory of delinquency and crime and used both quantitative and qualitative methods to support their arguments.[48] The theory has three components: the first explains juvenile delinquency, the second explores behavioral transitions as juveniles become adults, and the third explains adult criminal behavior.

According to Sampson and Laub, juvenile delinquency is directly explained by what they called "family context" factors. The family context factors that are most likely to produce delinquent behavior are erratic and threatening discipline by the parents, the lack of supervision by the mother, parental rejection of the child, and the child's emotional rejection of the parents. These family context factors are themselves influenced by what Sampson and Laub called "background structural factors," including household crowding, family disruption (e.g., single-parent family), family size, low family income, high residential mobility, foreign-born parents, mother's employment outside the home, and criminality by either or both parents. These background structural factors affect delinquency through their effect on the family context factors, such as erratic and threatening discipline.[49] These background structural factors may also result in weak attachment to school, poor performance in school, and attachment to delinquent siblings and delinquent friends. All these factors in turn increase the likelihood of delinquent behavior.[50]

The remainder of Sampson and Laub's theory concerns stability and change in the life course. Sampson and Laub tried to make sense of the apparent paradox that the best predictor of adult criminal behavior is childhood antisocial behavior and juvenile delinquency, but that most delinquents do not become criminals as adults.[51]

Stability in offending over the life course—that is, the tendency for juvenile offenders to become adult offenders—is generally recognized as a common phenomenon, and several attempts have been made to explain it. Gottfredson and Hirschi, for example, attributed stability in offending to a stable individual trait they called low self-control,[52] while Nagin and Paternoster focused on the causal influence of the earlier offending itself, arguing that it makes the later offending easier.[53] Sampson and Laub, in contrast, argued that stability is a result of what they called "cumulative continuity," a term that means that delinquent behavior, as well as being processed by the justice system, "closes doors" for the juvenile in a variety of ways. Delinquent behavior increases the likelihood of school failure; severs the juvenile's social bonds to school, friends, and family; and jeopardizes the development of future adult social bonds, such as employment and marriage. All these increase the potential for adult criminal behavior. This cumulative continuity, Sampson and Laub contended, is independent of social class, background, family, and school factors.[54]

Despite the evidence of considerable stability in offending over the life course, Sampson and Laub also stated that change is common: juvenile delinquents often do not become adult criminals, and adult criminals often stop committing crimes. Sampson and Laub argued that for adults, the quality and strength of social ties is the strongest influence on whether one will engage in criminal behavior. Relationships with a spouse, job stability and commitment, dependence on an employer, and other such factors reduce the likelihood of criminal behavior. These factors are described as social capital[55]—the investment one has in social relationships with law-abiding people that help one to accomplish one's goals through legitimate means. Even though earlier juvenile delinquency negatively influences the ability to acquire adult social capital, the development of social bonds as an adult reduces the likelihood of crime, independent of childhood experiences. A former delinquent is disadvantaged by the past but not totally constrained by it. Others have recently argued that "human capital" is better than social capital at predicting offending trajectories.[56] Human capital "refers to the human skills and resources individuals need to function effectively, such as reading, writing, and reasoning ability."[57]

Sampson and Laub's analysis of the Gluecks' data found general support for their developmental theory.[58] The strongest effects on delinquency were the family, school, and peer factors, which were influenced somewhat by the background structural factors. These background structural variables did not have much direct effect on delinquency, instead influencing delinquency through their effect on these informal social control variables. As expected, childhood delinquency was an important predictor of adult criminal behavior. Independent of one's past, the development of strong social bonds as an adult reduced the likelihood of crime and deviance.

One prime turning point in possible criminal behavior is marriage. In later research using the same Glueck data, Laub, Nagin, and Sampson found that marriage reduces delinquency and crime and that the positive effect of marriage is gradual and cumulative over time.[59] They interpreted these findings to mean that a good-quality marriage functions as an informal social control that leads to desistance from crime. Using a different data set, Warr found a similar effect for marriage and that marriage resulted in a dramatic decline in the time spent with friends, particularly with delinquent friends.[60] He argued that the decline in crime associated with marriage is explained by changes in peer associations. Other research has found that nonmarital romantic relationships[61] and cohabitation[62] may reduce offending, although perhaps not as much as formal marriage. Sampson, Laub, and Wimer point out that marriage may serve as an inhibitor to crime for nontraditional populations as well, such as with gay men.[63]

Current crime policies focus on locking up offenders for long periods—the incapacitation policies associated with research on career criminals that was described at the beginning of this chapter. Sampson and Laub's study suggested that this policy may significantly increase crime and delinquency in the future.[64] Lengthy incarceration cuts off the social bonds, such as marriage and jobs, that are turning points that lead to desistance from crime. If Sampson and Laub are correct, then lengthy incarceration would tend to be associated with continued criminality after release. Beyond that, the imprisonment of young men is associated with poor future employment prospects, which, in turn, is associated with families in which fathers are absent, which then is associated with higher rates of delinquency in the children in these families.[65] Sampson and Laub found the extremely high rate of incarceration of African American men especially troubling.

They suggested that crime policy should focus on prevention instead of incapacitation. Rather than locking up offenders after crimes have been committed, it would be better to address the causal sequence described in their book, including policies to address both the structural background and the family context factors described by their theory. These policies would be difficult to implement and would have to take into account the linkages among crime policies, employment, family cohesion, and the social organization of inner-city communities. But implementation of the policies would have a much greater potential for reducing crime and delinquency in the long run than simply locking up offenders. In her ethnographic study of young black and Latino males transitioning from a juvenile training school in rural Pennsylvania to their homes in inner-city Philadelphia, Jamie Fader proposes a number of policies along these lines, including community supports, therapeutic facilities, and graduation incentive programs.[66]

Laub and Sampson published a follow-up book in 2003, which expanded the data on the Glueck men from age seven to seventy, and included additional types of data, such as criminal record checks, death record checks, and personal interviews of fifty-two of the original delinquents.[67] While informal social control was still seen as central to their age-graded theory, the revised version of the theory as put forth in this book greatly expanded theoretical contributions to life-course changes, including influences of agency and situated choice, routine activities, macro-level historical events, aging, and local culture and community context. Sampson and Laub recently summarized both books' finding that

> [even] the most serious delinquents in the Glueck sample desisted albeit at different rates and at varying time points across the life course. Moreover, we found that although child prognoses are relatively accurate in terms of predicting criminal behavior among individuals through their twenties, they do not yield distinctive groupings that are prospectively valid over the entire life course—regardless of whether offenders are identified prospectively or ex post. This finding gives credence to a middle-ground position in the criminal careers debate in that there is variability among individual age–crime curves and that age has a direct effect on offending, such that "life-course desister" is the more accurate label. . . . In this sense, we argue that general desistence processes can only be understood through the full interplay of childhood, adolescent, and adult experiences.[68]

In contrast to Sampson and Laub's focus on informal social control as the driving influence behind a life-course perspective, others have been influenced by different theories. For example, Giordano and colleagues, based on the Toledo Adolescent Relationships Study, rooted change over the life course in social learning concepts (definitions favorable or unfavorable to crime), arguing that these definitions change over time based on the formation of new relationships.[69]

TREMBLAY'S DEVELOPMENTAL ORIGINS OF PHYSICAL AGGRESSION

Richard Tremblay, Canada Research Chair in Child Development, has taken on a self-proclaimed "crusade" to convince criminologists to consider preadolescent human development.[70] Chagrined that "a majority of people still believe that school children learn to aggress from their environment, and especially from the media[71] and bad friends," Tremblay set out to dispel the notion of a "late onset" for physical aggression.[72] He began his research summary in the late 1920s with Katharine M. Bantham Bridges and Florence Goodenough, experts in child development, who demonstrated that physical aggression was present in the first two years of life. He then analyzed numerous longitudinal studies beginning with birth, which showed that most children substantially increase the frequency of physical aggressions from nine months to forty-eight months and then decrease the frequency substantially after the preschool years.[73] A minority, however, increase their frequency as they reach adolescence, which explains the adolescent peak in the age–crime curve, as those who were already on a high trajectory of physical aggression during childhood run afoul of the authorities and are arrested and convicted. These results, Tremblay asserted, challenge the idea that the frequency of acts of physical aggression increases with age through social learning or because of hormonal changes during adolescence.[74] This developmental pattern suggests that the use of aggression may be innate, having at one time bestowed an evolutionary advantage that has since turned maladaptive. Thus, it is nonaggression that must be learned:

> Children who fail to learn alternatives to physical aggression during the preschool years are at [a] high risk for a number of problems. They tend to be hyperactive, inattentive, anxious, and fail to help when others are in need; they are rejected by a majority of their classmates, they get poor grades, and their behavior disrupts school activities. They are, thus, swiftly taken out of "natural" peer groups, placed in special classes, special schools and institutions with other "deviants," the ideal situation to reinforce marginal behavior. They are among the most delinquent from preadolescence onward, are the first to initiate substance use, sexual intercourse, and most at risk of dropping out of school, having a serious accident, being violent offenders and being diagnosed as having a psychiatric disorder.[75]

This developmental pattern and its cumulative consequences present clear policy implications for Tremblay. Since the peak in aggression is early, when limbs are weak and the brain is flexible, it is the optimal period to learn alternatives. Chronic physical aggression is best prevented by intensive investments with young children: not tolerating aggression, rewarding prosocial behavior, and teaching them to wait for what they want and to use language to convince others or express frustration. And while most humans learn alternatives to physical aggression relatively rapidly during the preschool years, all remain at risk of aggressing under the "appropriate" conditions. Thus, the situational prevention of conflicts remains a crucial link in the "civilizing process."[76] Tremblay's findings bring to mind several criminological theories: biosocial, with the environmental impact upon our genetic constitution; learning, with the importance of transmitted social skills; and self-control, with the long-term effects of early parenting practices. It is this nexus among society, the individual, and our genes that Tremblay emphasized:

> I completely agree with Eisner that the results of our longitudinal studies are describing, at the level of the individual, the socialisation process that Norbert Elias beautifully described at the level of societies. The macro level process has an effect on individual development, which in turn impacts the macro process. Epigentic development is probably at the heart of this interaction. The environment affects gene expression, and these epigenetic effects on a large scale facilitate social changes.[77]

FUTURE DIRECTIONS IN DEVELOPMENTAL
AND LIFE-COURSE CRIMINOLOGY

It has now been over thirty years since the National Research Council's Panel on Research on Criminal Careers published its work, discussed at the beginning of this chapter. It is clear that developmental and life-course criminology (DLC) has had a profound influence on the field during this time, and that there is broad acknowledgment of the concept of the criminal career. However, as demonstrated by the articles in a recent special edition of the *Journal of Research in Crime and Delinquency*,[78] published on the thirtieth anniversary of the NRC's report, there are still many issues and questions concerning elaboration and expansion of DLC criminology. These include, among others:

- How broader social change influences individual life-course trajectories and turning points.[79]
- How government policies such as mass incarceration and aggressive policing may influence these trajectories for the worse, and conversely, how better informed policy may influence them for the better.[80]
- Because the original concept of the career was largely atheoretical, subsequent DLC research has been much more theoretical, but there still lacks a clear method for positioning these various theoretical bases relative to one another.[81]
- Connectedly, what will be the role of genetics in this theoretical playing field?[82] In many ways, these two questions are the same ones asked of the entire field of criminology, not just DLC criminology.
- Can evidence-based policy be successful at translating DLC research into policy and practice?[83]
- Given that so much of the recent DLC research has been quantitative by nature, what will be the role of qualitative/ethnographic research in the future, and how can the different methodologies best complement each other?[84]

Virtually all DLC researchers agree that in addition to studying the processes that bring about criminal careers, to be policy-relevant, DLC research must focus heavily on desistance from offending. If life-course trajectories are seen as alterable, then DLC theory is highly relevant to public policy. Bersani and Doherty's 2018 article in the *Annual Review of Criminology* provides a comprehensive examination of desistance research, which discusses definitions and trends of desistance, contrasts various theories using an organizational schema, and analyzes the methodological divide in desistance research, highlighting modern research on the mechanisms of desistance.[85]

Desistance can be viewed as either dynamic (desistance begins at some point prior to the cessation of criminal offending), or binary/terminal (e.g., a seven-year crime free period constitutes desistance).[86] As discussed earlier in this chapter, desistance usually occurs after late adolescence, but can occur at different times for different offender types, and can occur even for high-rate chronic offenders. Research on desistance has only recently begun to study differing desistance trends by race, gender, class, immigration status, and so forth.[87]

Bersani and Doherty, for heuristic purposes, place a number of theories of desistance on a continuum ranging from subjective (individual actors are paramount to change) to structural (historical, institutional, and cultural forces provide or inhibit pathways to desistance).[88] Theories emphasizing structural over subjective include Laub and Sampson's age-graded theory, discussed earlier in this chapter; Bottoms and colleagues'[89] and Farrall and colleagues'[90] "full interactive framework," which highlights the need for integration of a number of mostly structural influences on integration, but includes intentional change as well, especially for certain types of offenders, such as those with a history of substance abuse; and Carlsson's masculinity-based theory,[91] which argues that desistance is brought about by accepting a lifestyle of lawful work, heterosexual monogamy, and family formation. Theories placing more weight on the role of the person include Giordano and colleagues' cognitive transformation theory[92] (which embeds self-identity within social structure, and is based on symbolic interactionism); Maruna's theory of desistance, which is psychosocial and involves intentional change mechanisms (to be "better"); and Paternoster and Bushway's theory of the "feared self,"[93] whereby offenders don't like the image of what they are heading toward becoming, and so "knife" off their old identities and replace it with new ones. These theories demonstrate great variability in how researchers view the concept of desistance, from Sampson and Laub's "desistance by default" to others' depiction of individuals requiring great personal effort to change their situation.

Methodological approaches to desistance, according to Bersani and Doherty, often fall along the structural-subjective continuum, with quantitative studies more likely to assess structural desistance, and qualitative studies more likely to assess subjective desistance.[94] Modern research dominated by both approaches continues to more comprehensively exam the mechanisms of desistance. For structural research, researchers attempt to better understand contingencies and causality. Rather than "if" life events bring about desistance, "where, when, and for whom do life events matter?"[95] Do life events matter similarly for different races, gender, and other categorical positions? Context may matter: for example, after Hurricane Katrina, New Orleanian ex-prisoners who returned to their original neighborhoods were more likely to reoffend than those who were displaced to new neighborhoods.[96] Historical context may matter as well. For example, in one study, military service was a stronger predictor of desistance for men serving in the later years of Vietnam than those serving in the earlier years.[97] Researchable questions about causality include whether behavioral change occurs before transitions, and whether transitions cause or accelerate desistance. Advances in the sophistication of quantitative modeling techniques feed exploration of these questions.

For subjective research, researchers attempt to better understand the deconstruction of identity and agency, and the impediments to desistance. Research on identity and agency addresses questions about the relative importance of desire for change, belief in the ability to desist, sense of self-efficacy and personal control, commitment to change, plans for desistance, identity reconstruction, social networks of change, and other such factors, in influencing the probability of successful desistance.[98] Research on the impediments to desistance recognize that individuals may be positioned in both criminal and conventional worlds, and that various types of disadvantage and dependency are barriers to the success of a subjective intent to desist.[99] These barriers may be especially potent for ex-offenders attempting to reenter society.

CONCLUSIONS

Developmental theories suggest that a single theory does not work well when one attempts to explain crime and delinquency. Instead, different theories are needed to explain crime and delinquency at different points in the life course. In addition, interactive theories suggest that certain factors may cause criminal behavior, but that the same factors may also be caused by criminal behavior.

Future criminology theories will probably have to have both developmental and interactive characteristics. This means that future criminology theories will probably be more complex than past theories, but they will be better able to describe the complexity of crime and therefore be better able to formulate effective policy responses.

Developmental and interactive theories assume that people change over time and that they respond to changes in their environments. These changes imply that while there may be considerable stability in offending over the life course, there is no unchangeable propensity to commit crime. Future theories of crime will probably assume that there are always turning points at which individuals, no matter how much crime and delinquency they have committed in the past, can move into a conventional, law-abiding lifestyle. The search for such turning points will be important to future crime policies. These policies will rely heavily on maturation variables, and there are different sorts of maturation, such as civil/communal (e.g., voting, volunteer work, paying taxes); psychosocial (e.g., aggression control, future orientation, self-reliance); social role maturation (e.g., adult relationships, employment, children); cognitive transformation/identity transformation (e.g., openness to change, changes in attitudes toward deviance, social institutions); and neu-rocognitive (e.g., changes in brain structure, improvements in working memory, intelligence).[100]

Future crime policies are turning away from incarceration and toward prevention, focusing on preventing the early childhood experiences that generate crime and delinquency in the long run. We do not yet know the exact sequence of events that ends with a person committed to a life of crime, and to be sure, there are a number of viable types of sequences that may vary across offenders. But we do know much more now than we did thirty years ago, and we are likely to know even more in the relatively near future. At the present time, developmental theories are the basis for enor-mous funding by agencies that sponsor criminology research.

KEY TERMS

developmental theories
life cycle
age expectations
life course
career criminals
criminal careers
longitudinal research
cross-sectional research
criminal propensity
onset
desistance

frequency
prevalence
latent trait
family context factors
stability
change
social capital
turning points
structural desistance
subjective desistance

DISCUSSION QUESTIONS

1. What is aging out of crime, and what explains it?
2. What are the policy implications of Wolfgang's 1972 study?
3. Why did Gottfredson and Hirschi argue that there is no reason to attempt to identify and selectively incapacitate career criminals?
4. What factors explain stability between delinquency and adult crime?
5. How would developmental criminology account for white-collar crime?
6. What are the most promising directions for future research in develop-mental and life-course criminology?

NOTES

1. John H. Laub and Robert J. Sampson, "Glen Elder's Influence on Life-Course Criminology: Serendipity and Cross-Disciplinary Fertilization," *Research in Human Development* 5 (2008): 199–215.
2. Glen Elder, *Children of the Great Depression: Social Change in the Life Experi-ence* (Chicago: University of Chicago Press, 1974).

3. See, e.g., Glen H. Elder Jr., "The Life Course as Developmental Theory," *Child Development* 69 (1998): 1–12.

4. Glen H. Elder Jr., "Time, Human Agency, and Social Change: Perspectives on the Life Course" *Social Psychology Quarterly* 57 (1994): 4–15.

5. Ibid., p. 5.

6. Ibid., p. 6.

7. Ibid.

8. Ibid., citing John A. Clausen, *Socialization and Society* (Boston: Little Brown, 1968).

9. Alfred Blumstein, Jacqueline Cohen, Jeffrey A. Roth, and Christy A. Visher, *Criminal Careers and "Career Criminals"* (Washington, DC: National Academy Press, 1986).

10. Marvin Wolfgang, Robert Figlio, and Thorsten Sellin, *Delinquency in a Birth Cohort* (Chicago: University of Chicago Press, 1972).

11. The idea of a career offender dates much further back than the Wolfgang et al. study, but it was this study that spurred new enthusiasm in the area. See Michael Gottfredson and Travis Hirschi, "The True Value of Lambda Would Appear to Be Zero: An Essay on Career Criminals, Criminal Careers, Selective Incapacitation, Cohort Studies, and Related Topics," *Criminology* 24 (1986): 213–233.

12. In actual fact, the Philadelphia study did not support this conclusion. See Thomas J. Bernard and R. Richard Ritti, "Selective Incapacitation and the Philadelphia Birth Cohort Study," *Journal of Research in Crime and Delinquency* 28 (1991): 33–54.

13. This debate can be reviewed in a series of articles: Alfred Blumstein and Jacqueline Cohen, "Estimation of Individual Crime Rates from Arrest Records," *Journal of Criminal Law and Criminology* 70 (1979): 561–585; Travis Hirschi and Michael Gottfredson, "Age and the Explanation of Crime," *American Journal of Sociology* 89 (1983): 552–584; David Greenberg, "Age, Crime, and Social Explanation," *American Journal of Sociology* 91 (1985): 1–21; Gottfredson and Hirschi, "The True Value of Lambda Would Appear to Be Zero"; Blumstein, Cohen, and David Farrington, "Criminal Career Research: Its Value for Criminology," *Criminology* 26(1): 1–35 (1988); Gottfredson and Hirschi, "Science, Public Policy, and the Career Paradigm," *Criminology* 26 (1988): 37–55; and Blumstein, Cohen, and Farrington, "Longitudinal and Criminal Career Research: Further Clarifications," *Criminology* 26 (1988): 57–73.

14. This was based on their view "that crime is committed by individuals, even when they organize into groups, and that individuals are the focus of criminal justice decisions" (Blumstein et al., "Longitudinal and Criminal Career Research: Further Clarifications," p. 12).

15. Sheldon Glueck and Eleanor Glueck, *500 Criminal Careers* (New York: Knopf, 1930); Glueck and Glueck, *Juvenile Delinquents Grown Up* (New York: Commonwealth Fund, 1940); Glueck and Glueck, *Unraveling Juvenile Delinquency* (Cambridge, MA: Harvard University Press, 1950); and Glueck and Glueck, *Delinquents and Nondelinquents in Perspective* (Cambridge, MA: Harvard University Press, 1968).

16. Michael Gottfredson and Travis Hirschi, "The Methodological Adequacy of Longitudinal Research on Crime," *Criminology* 25 (1987): 581–614.

17. See, for example, Scott Menard and Delbert Elliott, "Longitudinal and Cross-Sectional Data Collection and Analysis in the Study of Crime and Delinquency," *Justice Quarterly* 7 (1990): 11–55.

18. In *A General Theory of Crime* (Stanford, CA: Stanford University Press, 1990), Michael Gottfredson and Travis Hirschi argued that the propensity toward crime is a product of low self-control, and they allowed for variation in the effect that propensity has on actual behavior by introducing opportunity into their model. Low self-control brings about criminal behavior only when opportunities for such behavior are present. See Chapter 10.

19. For a recent study that found overall support for Gottfredson and Hirschi's position, see Alex R. Piquero, Terrie E. Moffitt, and Bradley E. Wright, "Self-Control and Criminal Career Dimensions," *Journal of Contemporary Criminal Justice* 23 (2007): 72–89.

20. D. Wayne Osgood and David Rowe attempted to lay out a detailed guide of how researchers may begin to competitively test the propensity and criminal career positions, in "Bridging Criminal Careers, Theory, and Policy Through Latent Variable Models of Individual Offending," *Criminology* 32 (1994): 517–554.

21. David Rowe, D. Wayne Osgood, and W. Alan Nicewander, "A Latent Trait Approach to Unifying Criminal Careers," *Criminology* 28 (1990): 237–270. These researchers defined propensity in terms of the relative stability of causal factors (p. 241).

22. In each data set, there is a distribution of how many offenders committed zero, one, two, and so forth offenses. For example, in Wolfgang's Philadelphia cohort, 65 percent of the cohort committed zero offenses, whereas 2.3 percent were responsible for nine or more. Rowe et al.'s study assumed that latent propensities are normally distributed, that the relationship between one's propensity to engage in crime and rate of offending (lambda) is exponential and that the relationship between lambda and observed offending can be modeled with a Poisson distribution (a probabilistic distribution of relatively rare events occurring over a continuum of time). Combining these probabilistic relationships, the authors produced frequency distributions that were similar to actual distributions of offenses in data sets from Philadelphia, London, Richmond (California), and Racine (Wisconsin). While this modeling represents strong support, it also should be noted that the validity of such modeling depends on the validity of the assumptions described earlier.

23. Ronald L. Simons, Christine Johnson, Rand D. Conger, and Glen Elder Jr, "A Test of Latent Trait Versus Life-Course Perspectives on the Stability of Adolescent Antisocial Behavior," *Criminology* 36 (1998): 217–243.

24. Eric H. Monkkonnen, "New York City Offender Ages," *Homicide Studies* 3 (1999): 256–270.

25. Robert M. O'Brien, Jean Stockard, and Lynne Isaacson, "The Enduring Effects of Cohort Characteristics on Age-Specific Homicide Rates," *American Journal of Sociology* 104 (1999): 1061–1095.

26. Ibid., pp. 1087–1088.
27. For example, see Raymond Paternoster, Charles W. Dean, Alex Piquero et al., "Generality, Continuity, and Change in Offending," *Journal of Quantitative Criminology* 13 (1997): 231–266; Alex Piquero, Raymond Paternoster, Paul Mazerolle et al., "Onset Age and Offense Specialization," *Journal of Research in Crime and Delinquency*, 36 (1999): 275–299; and Robert Brame, Shawn Bushway, and Raymond Paternoster, "On the Use of Panel Research Designs and Random Effects Models to Investigate Static and Dynamic Theories of Criminal Offending," *Criminology* 37 (1999): 599–641.
28. Daniel Nagin and Kenneth Land, "Age, Criminal Careers, and Population Heterogeneity: Specification and Estimation of a Nonparametric, Mixed Poisson Model," *Criminology* 32 (1993): 357.
29. One of the first attempts to direct research away from the criminal career debate and toward a developmental perspective was made by John Hagan and Alberto Palloni, "Crimes as Social Events in the Life Course: Reconceiving a Criminological Controversy," *Criminology* 26 (1988): 87–100. These authors suggested that criminologists should broaden their focus from criminal behaviors to antisocial behaviors, substitute the idea of "social events" for criminal careers, and look at the causes and consequences of those behaviors in both the short and the long run.
30. Rolf Loeber and Marc Le Blanc, "Toward a Developmental Criminology," in *Crime and Justice: A Review of Research*, vol. 12, ed. Michael Tonry and Norval Morris (Chicago: University of Chicago Press, 1990), pp. 375–473; Le Blanc and Loeber, "Developmental Criminology Updated," in *Crime and Justice: A Review of Research*, vol. 23, ed. Michael Tonry (Chicago: University of Chicago Press, 1998), pp. 115–198.
31. David P. Farrington, "Introduction to Integrated Developmental and Life-Course Theories of Offending," in *Integrated Developmental and Life-Course Theories of Offending*, ed. David P. Farrington (New Brunswick, NJ: Transaction, 2005), pp. 1–15.
32. Alex R. Piquero, David P. Farrington, and Alfred Blumstein, *Key Issues in Criminal Career Research: New Analyses of the Cambridge Study in Delinquent Development* (New York: Cambridge University Press, 2007), pp. 38–39.
33. Ibid., pp. 201–203.
34. For a fairly recent study on onset, see Matt DeLisi, "Zeroing In on Early Arrest Onset: Results from a Population of Extreme Career Criminals," *Journal of Criminal Justice*, 34 (2006): 17–26.
35. Piquero, Farrington, and Blumstein, *Key Issues in Criminal Career Research*, pp. 207–208.
36. Ibid., pp. 209–214.
37. For some literature on desistance, see David P. Farrington, "Advancing Knowledge About Desistance," *Journal of Contemporary Criminal Justice* 23 (2007): 125–134; Barry Vaugh, "The Internal Narrative of Desistance," *British Journal of Criminology* 47 (2007): 390–404. For desistance from a convict perspective, see Greg Newbold, "Rehabilitating Criminals: It Ain't That Easy," and Richard Jones, "Excon: Managing a Spoiled Identity," in *Convict Criminology*, ed.

Jeffrey Ian Ross and Stephen C. Richards (Belmont, CA: Wadsworth, 2003). See also Shadd Maruna, *Making Good: How Ex-Convicts Reform and Rebuild Their Lives* (Washington, DC: American Psychological Association, 2001).

38. Two other important developmental theories are by G. R. Patterson, Barbara DeBaryshe, and Elizabeth Ramsey, "A Developmental Perspective on Antisocial Behavior," *American Psychologist* 44 (1989): 329–335; and Terrie Moffitt, "Adolescence-Limited and Life-Course-Persistent Antisocial Behavior: A Developmental Taxonomy," *Psychological Review* 100 (1993): 674–701. Moffitt's theory is briefly described in Chapter 4.

39. Terrence Thornberry, "Toward an Interactional Theory of Delinquency," *Criminology* 25 (1987): 863–887. An earlier version of this section is found in Thomas J. Bernard and Jeffrey Snipes, "Theoretical Integration in Criminology," in *Crime and Justice: A Review of Research*, vol. 20, ed. Michael Tonry (Chicago: University of Chicago Press, 1996), pp. 314–316.

40. Thornberry, "Toward an Interactional Theory of Delinquency," p. 865.

41. Ibid., p. 876.

42. Ibid., pp. 877–882.

43. In particular, see Terrence Thornberry, Alan Lizotte, Marvin Krohn, and Sung Joon Jang, "Testing Interactional Theory: An Examination of Reciprocal Causal Relationships among Family, School, and Delinquency," *Journal of Criminal Law and Criminology* 82 (1991): 3–35, and "Delinquent Peers, Beliefs, and Delinquent Behavior: A Longitudinal Test of Interactional Theory," *Criminology* 32 (1994): 47–83. Like tests of the propensity versus criminal career debate (see n18), tests of the interactional theory require longitudinal data and therefore raise complex methodological issues. See Sung Joon Jang, "Age-Varying Effects of Family, School, and Peers on Delinquency," pp. 643–685, a comment by Janet L. Lauritsen, "Limitations in the Use of Longitudinal Self-Report Data," pp. 687–694, and Jang's rejoinder "Different Definitions, Different Modeling Decisions and Different Interpretations," pp. 695–701, in *Criminology* 37 (1999).

44. Terence P. Thornberry, "Empirical Support for Interactional Theory," in *Delinquency and Crime: Current Theories*, ed. J. D. Hawkins (New York: Cambridge University Press, 1996), p. 229.

45. Ibid., p. 230.

46. Ibid., p 231.

47. Glueck and Glueck, *Unraveling Juvenile Delinquency*.

48. Robert Sampson and John Laub, *Crime in the Making: Pathways and Turning Points Through Life* (Cambridge, MA: Harvard University Press, 1993). See also Laub and Sampson, "Turning Points in the Life Course: Why Change Matters to the Study of Crime," *Criminology* 31 (1993): 301–326; and Sampson and Laub, "Crime and Deviance in the Life Course," *Annual Review of Sociology* 18 (1992): 63–84. A good summary and overview is found in Laub, Sampson, and Leana C. Allen, "Explaining Crime over the Life Course: Toward a Theory of Age-Graded Informal Social Control," pp. 97–112 in *Explaining Criminals and Crime: Essays in Contemporary Criminological Theory*, ed. Raymond Paternoster and Ronet Bachman (Los Angeles: Roxbury, 2001).

49. Sampson and Laub, *Crime in the Making*, pp. 65–71.
50. Ibid., pp. 101–106.
51. For example, Lee Robins ("Sturdy Childhood Predictors of Adult Antisocial Behaviour: Replications from Longitudinal Studies," *Psychological Medicine* 8 [1978]: 611) stated that "adult antisocial behaviour virtually requires childhood antisocial behaviour [yet] most antisocial youths do not become antisocial adults." See also Moffitt, "Adolescence-Limited and Life-Course-Persistent Antisocial Behavior," p. 676.
52. Gottfredson and Hirschi, *A General Theory of Crime*; for comments on the "cumulative continuity" argument, see Travis Hirschi and Michael Gottfredson, "Control Theory and the Life-Course Perspective," *Studies on Crime and Crime Prevention* 4 (1995): 131–143.
53. Daniel Nagin and Raymond Paternoster, "On the Relationship of Past and Future Participation in Delinquency," *Criminology* 29 (1991): 163–190. This article described the "state dependence" perspective.
54. Ibid., pp. 123–125. A similar argument is found in Moffitt, "Adolescence-Limited and Life-Course-Persistent Antisocial Behavior."
55. James Coleman, "Social Capital in the Creation of Human Capital," *American Journal of Sociology* 94 (1988): 95–120.
56. Alex R. Piquero, Wesley G. Jennings, Nicole Leeper Piquero, and Carol A. Schubert, "Human But Not Social Capital is Better Able to Distinguish Between Offending Trajectories in a Sample of Serious Adolescent Hispanic Offenders," *Journal of Criminal Justice* 42 (2014): 366–373.
57. Dina. R. Rose and Todd R. Clear, "Incarceration, social capital, and crime: Implications for Social Disorganization Theory," *Criminology* 36 (1998): 441–480, p. 455.
58. Sampson and Laub, *Crime in the Making*, pp. 247–249. For a review of other empirical support for the theory, see Laub, Sampson, and Allen, "Explaining Crime over the Life Course," pp. 104–107.
59. John H. Laub, Daniel S. Nagin, and Robert J. Sampson, "Trajectories of Change in Criminal Offending," *American Sociological Review* 63 (1998): 225–238.
60. Mark Warr, "Life-Course Transitions and Desistance from Crime," *Criminology* 36 (1998): 183–216.
61. Jessica J. B. Wyse, David J. Harding, and Jeffrey D. Morenoff, "Romantic Relationships and Criminal Desistance: Pathways and Processes," *Sociological Forum* 29 (2014): 365–385.
62. Walter Forrest, "Cohabitation, Relationship Quality, and Desistance from Crime," *Journal of Marriage and Family* 76 (2014): 539–556.
63. Robert J. Sampson, John H. Laub, and Christopher Wimer, "Does Marriage Reduce Crime? A Counterfactual Approach to Within-Individual Causal Effects," *Criminology* 44 (2006): 465–508.
64. Sampson, Laub, and Allen, "Explaining Crime over the Life Course," pp. 107–109.
65. Sampson and Laub, *Crime in the Making*, p. 255.
66. Jamie J. Fader, Falling Back: *Incarceration and Transitions to Adulthood among Urban Youth* (New Brunswick, NJ: Rutgers University Press, 2013).

67. John H. Laub and Robert J. Sampson, *Shared Beginnings, Divergent Lives: Delinquent Boys to Age 70* (Cambridge, MA: Harvard University Press, 2003).

68. Robert J. Sampson and John H. Laub, "Turning Points and the Future of Life-Course Criminology: Reflections on the 1986 Criminal Careers Report," *Journal of Research in Crime and Delinquency* 53 (2016): 321–335.

69. Peggy C. Giordano, Wendi L. Johnson, Wendy D. Manning, Monica A. Longmore, and Mallory D. Minter, "Intimate Partner Violence in Young Adulthood: Narratives of Persistence and Desistance," *Criminology* 53 (2015): 330–365.

70. Richard Tremblay, "Targeted and Situational Prevention of Physical Violence: In Response to Eisner's and Homel's Comments," *European Journal of Policy Research* 13 (2007): 179–181.

71. For a developmental look at the effects of media violence, see Sarah M. Coyne, "Does Media Violence Cause Violent Crime," *European Journal of Criminal Policy Research* 13 (2007): 205–211.

72. Richard Tremblay, "The Development of Youth Violence: An Old Story with New Data," *European Journal of Policy Research* 13 (2007): 161–170. For a comprehensive set of readings on the development of aggression, see Richard E. Tremblay, Willard W. Hartup, and John Archer, eds., *Developmental Origins of Aggression* (New York: Guilford Press, 2005).

73. Tremblay, "The Development of Youth Violence," pp. 163–166.

74. Ibid., pp. 163–164.

75. Ibid., p. 167.

76. Tremblay, "Targeted and Situational Prevention of Physical Violence," p. 181.

77. Ibid.

78. Christopher J. Sullivan and Alex R. Piquero, guest eds., "Special Issue: Criminal Careers and Career Criminals Report, 30th Anniversary," *Journal of Research in Crime and Delinquency* 53 (2016).

79. E.g., Robert J. Sampson and John H. Laub, "Turning Points and the Future of Life-Course Criminology: Reflections on the 1986 Criminal Careers Report," *Journal of Research in Crime and Delinquency* 53 (2016): 321–335.

80. Ibid. See also Christopher J. Sullivan and Alex R. Piquero, "The Criminal Career: Past, Present, and Future," *Journal of Research in Crime and Delinquency* 53 (2016): 420–442.

81. Christopher J. Sullivan and Alex R. Piquero, "The Criminal Career"; Sampson and Laub, "Turning Points and the Future of Life-Course Criminology."

82. See Michael J. Shanahan and Jason D. Boardman, "Genetics and Behavior in the Life Course: A Promising Frontier," in *The Craft of Life Course Research*, ed. Glen H. Elder Jr. and Janet Z. Giele (New York: The Guilford Press, 2009), pp. 215–235.

83. Christy A. Visher, "Unintended Consequences: Policy Implications of the NAS Report on Criminal Careers and Career Criminals," *Journal of Research in Crime and Delinquency* 53 (2016): 306–320.

84. Mercer Sullivan, "Ethnographic Research on Criminal Careers: Needs, Contributions, and Prospects," *Journal of Research in Crime and Delinquency* 53 (2016): 392–405.

85. Bianca E. Bersani and Elaine Eggleston Doherty, "Desistance from Offending in the Twenty-First Century," *Annual Review of Criminology* (2018): 311–334.

86. Ibid., pp. 312–313.

87. Ibid., pp. 313–314.

88. Ibid., pp. 315–318.

89. Anthony Bottoms, Joanna Shapland, Andrew Costello Deborah Holmes, and Grant Muir, "Towards Desistance: Theoretical Underpinnings for an Empirical Study," *Howard Journal of Criminal Justice* 43 (2004): 368–389.

90. Stephen Farrall, Ben Hunter, Gilly Sharpe, and Adam Calverley, *Criminal Careers in Transition: The Social Context of Desistance from Crime* (New York: Oxford University Press, 2014).

91. Christoffer Carlsson, "Masculinities, Persistence, and Desistence," *Criminology* 51 (2013): 661–693.

92. Peggy Giordano, Stephen A. Cernkovich, and Jennifer L. Rudolph, "Gender, Crime, and Desistance: Toward a Theory of Cognitive Transformation," *American Journal of Sociology* 107 (2002): 990–1064. See also Peggy Giordano, Ryan D. Schroeder, and Stephen A. Cernkovich, "Emotions and Crime Over the Life Course: A Neo-Meadian Perspective on Criminal Continuity and Change," *American Journal of Sociology* 112 (2007): 1603–1661 (emphasizing the role emotional maturation in adulthood plays in desistance).

93. Ray Paternoster and Shawn Bushway, "Desistance and the 'Feared Self': Toward and Identity Theory of Criminal Desistance," *Journal of Criminal Law & Criminology* 99 (2009): 1103–1136.

94. Bersani and Doherty, "Desistance from Offending in the Twenty-First Century," p. 318.

95. Ibid.

96. Ibid., p. 319, citing David S. Kirk, "Residential Change as a Turning Point in the Life Course of Crime: Desistance or Temporary Cessation?" *Criminology* 50 (2012): 329–358.

97. Bersani and Doherty, "Desistance from Offending in the Twenty-First Century," citing Leanna Allen Bouffard, "Period Effects in the Impact of Vietnam-Era Military Service on Crime over the Life Course," *Crime & Delinquency* 60 (2014): 859–883.

98. Bersani and Doherty, "Desistance from Offending in the Twenty-First Century," pp. 320–321.

99. Ibid., p. 321.

100. Michael Rocque, "The Lost Concept: The (Re) Emerging Link Between Maturation and Desistance From Crime," *Criminology & Criminal Justice* 15 (2015): 340–360.

—

CHAPTER 15

Integrated Theories

As the preceding chapters have amply demonstrated, there are a large number of theories in criminology.[1] Most criminologists believe that the way to reduce the number of theories is through the "falsification" process. According to this view, different theories make contradictory predictions that can be tested with research. Theories whose predictions are inconsistent with the data are falsified and can be discarded, thereby reducing the total number of theories.

Other criminologists, however, believe that for a variety of practical reasons, the falsification process has failed to work. These criminologists turn to integration as a way to reduce the number of theories. They argue that the different theories do not contradict each other but instead focus on different aspects of the same phenomenon about which they make different predictions. These theories can therefore be combined through integration into a smaller number of larger theories. These criminologists also argue that the combined theories will be more powerful in the sense that they can explain more of the variation in crime. Integration is an alternative to falsification as a way to reduce the number of theories in criminology.

Since most theories integrate at least some previously existing material in their arguments, there is no firm and fast line between integrated theories and other theories. In order to facilitate further discussion of integration in criminology, we present here several different theories that can reasonably be described as integrated theories.

ELLIOTT'S INTEGRATED THEORY OF DELINQUENCY AND DRUG USE

In 1979, Elliott, Ageton, and Cantor offered an early version of an integrated theory that explicitly combined strain, control, and social learning perspectives to explain delinquency and drug use.[2] In 1985, Elliott, Huizinga, and

Ageton provided a more complete version of that integrated theory, and Elliott also defended theoretical integration as a process.[3] These efforts at integration, and the responses to them by those who opposed integration, set off a rather large debate about theoretical integration in criminology.

Elliott and his colleagues integrated criminology theories in two steps. First, they integrated strain theory with social control theory; then they integrated the combined strain control theory with social learning theory. In their view, strain theory argues "that delinquency is a response to actual or anticipated failure to achieve socially induced needs or goals (status, wealth, power, social acceptance, etc.),"[4] while social control theory contends that the strength of an individual's bonds to conventional society is inversely related to the probability that the individual will engage in delinquent behavior. Sources of weak social controls include inadequate socialization in the family and social disorganization in the community or society. Elliott and his colleagues integrated strain and control theories by arguing that the probability of delinquency should be highest when an individual experiences both more strain and less control. In addition, they argued that social disorganization, which is said to decrease social controls, should also increase strain. Finally, they argued that strain itself should reduce social control.

After integrating strain and control theories, Elliott and colleagues incorporated the social learning theory that argues that delinquency is affected by the balance between the rewards and punishments that are associated with both conforming and deviant patterns of socialization. Adolescents receive rewards and punishments for their behavior primarily from families, schools, and peers. Families and schools almost always reinforce conventional or law-abiding behaviors. In contrast, peer groups are much more likely to reinforce deviant behavior, although this influence varies quite a bit among different adolescents. Elliott et al. therefore argued that the amount of exposure to delinquent attitudes and behaviors within the peer group is the primary factor that affects the probability of delinquent behavior.

At this point, Elliott et al. found it necessary to modify control theory to take into account the type of group with which the individual bonds. Control theory holds that the content of socialization always favors conformity, and therefore only the strength of socialization is necessary to explain crime and delinquency (i.e., weak socialization leads to deviance). In addition, control theory holds that there are no strong bonds within deviant groups, since deviance itself is purely self-interested behavior. Thus, deviant groups (e.g., juvenile gangs) are sets of people who are purely self-interested, and the group stays together only to the extent that it furthers the self-interests of each group member. In contrast, social learning theory holds that the content of socialization can favor either deviance or conformity, and that individuals can form strong bonds to deviant social groups. Elliott and his fellow authors integrated these two theories by hypothesizing that deviant behavior is most likely when there are strong bonds to deviant groups and weak

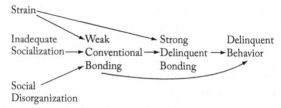

FIGURE 15-1 From Delbert S. Elliot, David Huizinga, and Suzanne S. Ageton, *Explaining Delinquency and Drug Use* (Beverly Hills, CA: Sage, 1985), p. 66.

bonds to conventional groups and is least likely when there are strong bonds to conventional groups and weak bonds to deviant groups.

The third step in integrating strain, control, and social learning theories is to propose a single line of causation that includes variables from all three theories (see Figure 15-1). Strain, inadequate socialization, and social disorganization are all said to lead to weak conventional bonding. These failures then lead to strong delinquent bonding, which, in turn, leads to delinquent behavior. Strain can also directly affect strong delinquent bonding, as at least some strain theories contend, but Elliott et al. argued that most of the effect of strain operates through the weak conventional bonding. In addition, weak conventional bonding can directly affect delinquent behavior, as control theories contend, but Elliott et al. argued that most of its effect operates through the strong delinquent bonding.

Elliott et al. identified the integrated model with the social control perspective, rather than with the social learning perspective, reasoning that the control perspective is more general and can explain deviance across levels of explanation and that it is more sociological in that it places great importance on the role of institutional structures in controlling deviant behavior. They then supported their model with longitudinal data from the National Youth Survey. They found no direct effects of strain and social control concepts on delinquent behavior. Instead, most of the variance in delinquent behavior was explained by bonding to delinquent peers.

THE FALSIFICATION VERSUS INTEGRATION DEBATE

In a response to Elliott et al.'s 1979 paper, Hirschi argued forcefully against integration as a strategy in criminology.[5] He stated that most criminology theories are contradictory because their assumptions are incompatible. Theories must therefore be tested on their own for internal consistency and explanatory power or against other theories. Theories can be integrated only if they essentially argue the same thing, and most criminology theories do not. Hirschi concluded that for criminology theories, "separate and unequal is better."

In the more complete version of the integrated theory, published in 1985, Elliott et al. responded to Hirschi's arguments against integration. They began by arguing that the "oppositional tradition" in criminology had failed. This tradition refers to the falsification process by which the different theories are tested against each other. Elliott et al. also argued that any individual theory can explain only 10 to 20 percent of the variance in illegal behavior: "Stated simply, the level of explained variance attributable to separate theories is embarrassingly low, and, if sociological explanations for crime and delinquency are to have any significant impact upon future planning and policy, they must be able to demonstrate greater predictive power."[6]

In a separate article, Elliott argued that theoretical competition is generally pointless because most of the time the different theories explain different portions of the variance in crime.[7] There are multiple causes of crime, so different theories that incorporate different causal factors are not necessarily incompatible. Elliott concluded that criminologists should synthesize such theories to achieve a greater explanation of deviant behavior, rather than allow them to remain in competitive isolation.

In a later article Hirschi then expanded on his argument against integration, sardonically discussing the fall of the "oppositional tradition" and the movement toward theoretical integration.[8] He acknowledged that criminology theory has failed to advance despite the prevalence of theory competition. But he did not see integration as a solution to this problem. In particular, he objected to the changes in control theory that integrationists, such as Elliott, have made when they have integrated it with other theories. Hirschi argued that integrationists have ignored the fact that the different criminology theories are incompatible and have plodded ahead anyway. This is not the integration of existing theories, he maintained, but the creation of new theories.

BRAITHWAITE'S THEORY OF REINTEGRATIVE SHAMING

Despite Hirschi's protests, the trend toward integration continued. In 1989, the same year that Hirschi expanded his argument against integration, John Braithwaite published his theory of reintegrative shaming, which draws on labeling, subcultural, opportunity, control, differential association, and social learning theories.[9] Rather than combine arguments from earlier theories, as Elliott and his colleagues did, Braithwaite created a new theoretical concept—reintegrative shaming—and showed how that concept organizes the arguments of a large number of other theories.

Braithwaite described shaming as "all social processes of expressing disapproval which have the intention or effect of invoking remorse in the person being shamed and/or condemnation by others who become aware of the shaming."[10] He divided shaming into two types: stigmatization (when the shaming brings about a feeling of deviance in the shamed) and reintegration (when the shamers ensure that they maintain bonds with the shamed). Reintegrative shaming occurs when violators are shamed into knowing that what they did is wrong but are nonetheless allowed reentry into the conforming group. The core argument of Braithwaite's theory is that reintegrative shaming leads to lower crime rates, whereas stigmatizing shaming leads to higher crime rates. Braithwaite used this argument to explain many different types of crimes involving victimization, but he did not use it to explain victimless crimes.

Braithwaite then described how other criminology theories relate to this core argument.[11] Individuals with more social bonding are more likely to receive reintegrative shaming and are thus less likely to commit crime. Labeling theory is drawn upon to explain stigmatization, and once an individual is stigmatized, he or she is more likely to participate in a deviant subculture and thus more likely to commit crime. Braithwaite's theory also acts on a structural level. Greater urbanization and mobility (from social disorganization theory) lessen the chance that "societal communitarianism" will exist. Communitarianism, or the interdependence among individuals in a culture, tends to be associated with reintegration, while its absence leads to stigmatization and its consequent blockage of legitimate opportunities, formation of subcultures, presence of illegitimate opportunities, and higher crime rates.

Uggen offered several criticisms of Braithwaite's theory, to which Braithwaite responded by exploring its potential problems.[12] In addition, Makkai and Braithwaite found support for the relationship between reintegrative shaming and criminal behavior in the case of nursing homes' compliance with the law.[13] Hay also found some support for this relationship in his study of urban adolescents. He found that both parental use of reintegration and shaming were associated with less delinquency. However, after controlling for parent–child interdependence, he found that the effect of reintegration disappeared while the effect of shaming endured.[14] The findings are contrary to the theory's proposition that shaming is effective only when reintegration is high. Furthermore, parent–child bonding may outweigh reintegration in impact. Hay proposed that shaming may not be conceptually the same as stigmatization, which would help explain why shaming has a strong independent effect on delinquency. There have yet to be tests of reintegrative shaming theory that are longitudinal, explore the larger relationships between shaming and concepts from other theories (except for bonding), and assess the structural (e.g., cross-national) side of the theory.

Despite this limited discussion and testing, the theory has been linked to the much larger "restorative justice" movement, which responds to crime by attempting to restore victims, offenders, and communities to their condition prior to the crime. In the context of restorative justice, reintegrative shaming refers to restoring offenders to their condition before the offense. To a considerable extent, restorative justice is a normative theory—it describes how the world ought to be. In contrast, reintegrative shaming is an empirical theory—it asserts that reintegrated offenders are less likely to re-offend than are stigmatized offenders. Braithwaite went on to review the large empirical literature on restorative justice and found the results quite encouraging.[15] Beyond integrating a large number of criminology theories about offenders' behavior, Braithwaite integrated empirical and normative theories about criminal justice responses to criminal behavior.

TITTLE'S CONTROL BALANCE THEORY

In 1995, Charles Tittle proposed a general theory of deviance that integrates essential elements from differential association, Merton's anomie, Marxian conflict, social control, labeling, deterrence, and routine activities theories.[16] He first argued that each theory is defensible in its own terms, but that each is incomplete in that it does not answer questions that the other theories are designed to answer.[17] He then stated that an adequate theory must be able to explain a broad range of deviant behaviors, must fully account for these behaviors, must be precise in its causal arguments (e.g., including statements about when the processes operate with greater or lesser force and the time intervals between causes and effects), and must explain the entire causal chain and not simply start with preexisting causes that themselves are not explained.[18]

Like Braithwaite, Tittle then proposed a new concept around which to integrate the propositions from earlier, simpler theories: control balance. His central assertion is that "the amount of control to which an individual is subject, relative to the amount of control he or she can exercise, determines the probability of deviance occurring as well as the type of deviance likely to occur."[19] This view accepts the premise of traditional control theories (like Hirschi's) that controls are the central concept in explaining conformity.[20] However, it contradicts these theories by asserting that control is also a central motivating factor that explains deviance: people who are controlled by others tend to engage in deviance to escape that control, while people who exercise control over others tend to engage in deviance in order to extend that control.[21] In this theory, then, conformity is associated with "control balance," rather than with control itself. That is, people are likely to engage in conforming behavior when the control they exert over others is approximately equal to the control that others exert over them. This pattern results in a U-shaped curve, with the most deviance committed by those who have the greatest control and those who have the least.[22]

Tittle defined deviance as "any behavior that the majority of a given group regards as unacceptable or that typically evokes a collective response of a negative type."[23] But rather than explaining deviance as a single construct, he divided it into six types: predation, exploitation, defiance, plunder, decadence, and submission.[24]

Predation involves direct physical violence or manipulation to take property and includes such behaviors as theft, rape, robbery, fraud, and homicide. Exploitation is indirect predation, when the exploiter uses others to do the dirty work. Examples are contract killings, price fixing, and political corruption. Defiance occurs when individuals revolt against norms or values by engaging in such acts as violating curfews, vandalism, political protests, and "sullenness by a marital partner." Acts of plunder are typically undertaken by people without much of a social conscience, are considered to be particularly heinous, and include such behaviors as destroying fields to hunt for foxes, pollution by oil companies, and unrealistic taxes imposed by occupying armies. Decadence refers to behavior that is unpredictable and viewed by most as irrational; examples are group sex with children and sadistic torture. Acts of submission involve "passive, unthinking, slavish obedience to the expectations, commands, or anticipated desires of others."[25] Examples are eating slop on command or allowing one's self to be sexually degraded. One may question whether several of the acts described in these categories are deviant (such as eating slop on command). According to Tittle, the theory explains more than deviance; it explains submission, decadence, and the other categories. Thus, an act may be submissive and not necessarily deviant but still be explained by the theory.[26]

Four primary concepts are employed in control balance theory: predisposition, provocation, opportunity, and constraint. Predisposition toward deviant motivation includes one's desire for autonomy and one's control ratio, which is the "amount of control to which the person is subject relative to the amount that he or she can exercise."[27] Tittle deemed one's desire for autonomy as relevant to predisposition but noted that it varies little across individuals. Varying more dramatically across individuals is the control ratio. Within each individual, the control ratio may be fairly stable overall, but it may also vary from situation to situation, since different contextual circumstances may affect the balance of control.

Provocations are "contextual features that cause people to become more keenly cognizant of their control ratios and the possibilities of altering them through deviant behavior."[28] Examples include verbal insults or challenges. Constraint refers to the likelihood that potential control will actually be exercised (compared to the control ratio, which refers to potential control, not actual control). Finally, opportunity is defined in the traditional manner, related to the circumstances under which it is feasible to commit a given act. For example, it is difficult to rape if no person is present, or it is difficult to burglarize with no dwellings around.

The causal processes that constitute control balance theory are fairly complex, so we shall limit this discussion to the core theoretical mechanisms. Deviant behavior occurs when one attempts to alter his or her control ratio, whether temporarily or permanently. Thus, deviance serves a purpose for the person who commits it. When the amount of control that is exercised is roughly the same as the amount of control one is subjected to, control balance occurs, and the probability of deviance is low. But when the ratio is not balanced (in either direction), the likelihood of deviance increases at a rate that is proportional to the degree of imbalance. Motivation drives the likelihood of deviant behavior, and motivation is influenced strongly by the control balance ratio. Other variables, such as provocations, constraint, and opportunity, also converge in influencing the actual probability of deviance occurring, but one's motivation and predisposition toward motivation are the most important contributing factors to deviance.

Control balance theory explains types of deviance in addition to the likelihood of deviance. Those with a balanced ratio are likely to conform. Those who have a higher ratio of autonomy to repression (that is, are more likely to exercise control than to be controlled) are likely to engage in exploitation (minimal imbalance), plunder (medium imbalance), or decadence (maximum imbalance). Those who have a lower ratio of autonomy to repression (are more likely to be controlled than to exercise control) are likely to engage in predation (marginal imbalance), defiance (moderate imbalance), and submission (extreme imbalance). One question that immediately comes to mind is why the most serious forms of deviance (such as predation) are coupled with the slightest imbalances. Tittle explained this by saying that when control deficits are small, people are able to commit more serious acts of deviance without as much fear of controlling response as if they had larger control deficits. People with marginal control deficits are usually deterred from committing deviant acts, but when they do commit them, according to Tittle, the acts will be more serious in nature. People with more extreme control deficits are "less able to imagine that such behavior will escape controlling responses from others,"[29] and thus their deviance will take less serious forms (such as submission and defiance). Similarly, people with a control surplus (more autonomy than repression) will commit acts of deviance with seriousness that is in proportion to how controlled they are. Individuals with only a slight advantage will feel more limited in the extent to which they can exercise control and will commit less serious acts (exploitation compared to plunder and decadence).

In 2004, addressing problems identified by critics and researchers,[30] Tittle refined control balance theory in an effort to make it easier to understand and test.[31] The refined theory centers on the concept of "control balance desirability," which is maximized by committing a deviant act that is likely to provide long-range relief from the control imbalance and requires no direct contact with the victim (target).[32] A deviant act with a high degree of control balance desirability thus provides a gain in both external and in internal control and does so with a minimum risk.[33] Four main variables influence the desirability range from which a deviant act will be chosen: a person's control ratio, opportunity, constraint, and self-control. Tittle conceived of the decision to commit a deviant act as a process beginning with an individual with a control imbalance, which predisposes the person to motivations for deviance. Once a provocation occurs, the individual is humiliated, reminded of the control imbalance, and realizes that deviance can favorably change the situation.[34] If an opportunity exists and the act is possible, constraint is considered as the actor "theoretically weighs" the potential gain from the deviant act against the loss of control it is likely to produce.[35] This process described by Tittle is most likely with actors who exert greater self-control and least likely with those who lack it. Thus, the variables interact to generate a probability of deviance within a given range of control balance desirability.[36] Like Tittle's original theory, the refined version emphasizes theoretical integration, incorporating variables from self-control, learning, and general strain theories.

Tittle's refined theory has not been subject to much criticism or testing, but the limited number of tests of it have all found at least some support.[37] As Fox and colleagues have noted, the complexities of the theory have caused problems with testing it and the few studies that have done so mostly use hypothetical scenarios rather than actual behavior, which may reduce their generalizability. Their study, rather than employing such scenarios, examined control balance theory in the context of a broad range of offending by recently incarcerated jail inmates, and found that control deficits and surpluses predicted higher risks of offending, and control surpluses when combined with low self-control were associated with higher levels of offending.[38] Our brief summaries of both its original and refined versions mask its complexity as well as Tittle's exertion in building a neatly structured theory. Much of Tittle's book is devoted to detailing the requisites of a good theory and showing how most criminological theories lack some of the features of solid theory. It then builds control balance theory with these features in mind (breadth, comprehensiveness, precision, and depth) and includes an important chapter that discusses the contingencies of control balance theory (under which conditions may certain causal mechanisms not work). Tittle's theory does a nice job of explaining deviance committed by several segments of society, including skid-row bums and political and corporate criminals.

While recognizing that there are difficulties in translating control balance theory into practical policies, given that its variables are hard to manipulate and have hydraulic relationships with each other, Tittle states that:

> Perhaps the most practical, though limited, potential policy intervention would be to train people to anticipate and manage provocation to avoid becoming motivated for deviance, It is an intervention likely to be accepted by the public; the institutional mechanisms are in place to implement it (especially in schools); and it appears to be a policy with minimal chances of adversely affecting other variables in the control-balancing process while offering some hope for reducing at least some of the more undesirable forms of deviance.[39]

DIFFERENTIAL SOCIAL SUPPORT AND COERCION THEORY

Colvin, Cullen, and Vander Ven proposed an integrated theory of crime that merges two "general themes" that span many theories: coercion and social support.[40]

According to the coercion perspective, individuals are intimidated by forces that create fear and anxiety. Coercion can exist in multiple arenas, including the family (coercive discipline), the school (coercive peer relations), and the neighborhood (dangerous conditions). Coercion is connected to several theories of crime and delinquency, including Athens's (coercive interpersonal relationships), Tittle's control balance theory (repression as a concept similar to coercion), and Agnew's general strain theory (anger produced by coercive relations). Coercion was first proposed as an integrated theory by Mark Colvin.

According to Colvin, coercion has two dimensions: the strength of the coercive force (from nonexistent to strong) and the consistency with which it occurs (erratically to consistently).[41] Erratically experienced coercion results in anger directed at others because of the perceptions of unjust, capricious treatment. Consistently applied coercion results in low levels of criminal behavior with significant side effects, including low levels of prosocial behavior and mental health problems, such as depression. Colvin's main theoretical propositions were supported in a study of middle school students in Virginia.[42] Parental measures of coercion were related to delinquency, as were impersonal measures of coercion in schools and neighborhoods (perceptions of danger in these environments). Bullying, however, was unrelated to delinquency.

Cullen was one of the first to propose social support as an organizing theory of crime.[43] Whereas coercion produces criminal behavior, social support should reduce it:[44]

> Social support can be expressive or instrumental. Expressive social supports include the sharing and ventilation of emotions and the affirmation of one's and others' self-worth and dignity. Instrumental social supports include material and financial assistance and the giving of advice, guidance, and connections for positive social advancement in legitimate society. Social supports exist at several levels of society, in the immediate interactions within families, and among friends and within larger social networks of neighborhoods, communities, and nations. Expressive and instrumental social supports are potentially provided during informal social relations among families and friends and through formal networks in schools, workplaces, and governmental agencies involved in welfare and criminal justice. The extent to which social supports are provided varies across families, neighborhoods, communities, and nations.

As with coercion, social support is available erratically or consistently. Consistent provision produces trust and moral commitment to other individuals and societal institutions. Erratic provision of social support creates an unhealthy relationship between an individual and social institutions, and can result in anger. Because support can be withdrawn or unavailable at any time, the individual becomes self-interested and survivalistic.

Taken together, coercion and social support can be viewed as forming the two sides of a dual, integrated theory: one side drives individuals into crime, and the other holds them back from crime.[45] The worst-case scenario would be erratically supplied social support and erratically applied coercion. The best-case scenario should be consistent social support with little or no coercion. The theory also builds in a different type of social support: illegitimate (as provided by such sources as gangs or organized criminal networks). Erratically delivered legitimate social support may cause individuals to seek illegitimate support, thereby hedging them toward a structured criminal career. Whether one receives support from legitimate or illegitimate sources, either avenue is cyclical. Those who receive support pass it on to others.

Differential social support and coercion theory has received a limited amount of empirical testing thus far, with some evidence in its favor. Colvin's case study of practices over several decades at the Penitentiary of New Mexico found that when violence was lower when coercion was consistently employed, but inmate demoralization was high. When, however, social support was utilized, violence was low and inmates exhibited pro-social behavior.[46] Erratically applied coercion and social support produced mixed outcomes. Kurtz and colleagues, studying adolescents, found that physical child maltreatment (as a construct of coercion) was associated with increased offending, whereas social support was associated with reduced offending.[47] Day and coauthors found that coercive practices in state correctional institutions, when perceived as unfair, resulted in higher levels of inmate resistance and violence, but they failed to find any positive effects of social support.[48] Finally, Kurtz's and Zavala's analysis of data from the Gang Resistance Education and Training evaluation provided support for the theory when examining the relationships between parental support, interpersonal coercion, low self-control, and violent offending.[49]

Policy implications of this integrative approach include moves to reduce coercion and increase legitimate social support. Colvin and his colleagues recommended such things as providing support to families to reduce coercive family behaviors (such as parent-effectiveness training); changing school environments to replace coercion and competition with participatory democratic, cooperative environments; and bringing penal policy more in line with the restorative justice approach.[50]

BERNARD AND SNIPES'S APPROACH TO INTEGRATING CRIMINOLOGY THEORIES

Bernard and Snipes, rather than offering an entirely new integrated theory, presented a new interpretation of existing criminology theories that they maintained accurately represents the content of those theories and, at the same time, allows for both broad integration and empirical testing.[51] Ultimately, their approach is based on an argument about the proper role of theory in the scientific process. The following points summarize their argument.

First, criminologists should focus on variables and the relationships among variables, rather than on theories themselves. Hirschi argued that criminologists sometimes treat variables as if they were "owned by" theories—for example, attachment sometimes is treated as if it was owned by Hirschi's social control theory—so that evidence of a relationship between attachment and crime is interpreted as evidence of the validity of Hirschi's theory. Bernard and Snipes went further than Hirschi by arguing that the only important question is this: What variables are related to crime, and in what ways? That is, they focused on whether and how attachment is related to criminal behavior and considered the question of the validity of Hirschi's theory to be unimportant. In fact, they viewed this question as counterproductive because it leads to endless debates that waste everybody's time.

Second, Bernard and Snipes argued, criminology theories should be evaluated in terms of their usefulness to the scientific process, not in terms of their validity. In the scientific process, theory interprets the results of past research and charts the course of future research. That is, theory explains the relationships among variables that research has already observed, and theory directs research to look for new relationships among variables that have not yet been observed. After its publication in 1969, Hirschi's social control theory was quite useful to criminologists in exactly this way. But social control theory is not nearly as useful to criminologists today. Even Hirschi, who passed away in 2017, was using self-control theory to interpret the results of past research and chart the course of future research. Bernard and Snipes contended that usefulness to the scientific process is the proper standard by which a scientific theory should be evaluated, not whether the theory is valid.

Third, criminology researchers should shift from the goal of falsifying theories to a risk-factor approach that deals in structured probabilities. The whole integration debate, described earlier in this chapter, starts with the argument that falsification has failed as a process for reducing the number of criminology theories. The problem with falsification is that it requires "all or nothing" conclusions—the theory is either verified or falsified—on the basis of competitive testing and statistical significance. But crime is so complex that it seems like every theory is true at least some of the time; therefore, no theory can ever truly be falsified.[52] In contrast, the risk-factor approach allows for graduated conclusions—the factors identified by some theories explain a lot of the variation in crime, while the factors identified by other theories explain only a little. This approach is consistent with the focus on variables and the relationships among variables, recommended earlier. And where the falsification approach is competitive—if one theory is true, then others must be false—the risk-factor approach is integrative; that is, many factors may influence crime, some with larger effects than others.

Fourth, Bernard and Snipes agreed with Hirschi that contradictory theories cannot be integrated with each other. However, they disagreed with Hirschi's conclusion that criminology theories contradict each other. In particular, Bernard and Snipes argued that Hirschi's social psychological interpretation of criminology theories in terms of strain, control, and cultural deviance is incorrect because it severely distorts the arguments of so-called strain and cultural deviance theories.[53] They then proposed an interpretation of these two types of theories in which the causal chain moves from social structural conditions to cultural ideas to criminal behaviors.[54]

Fifth, consistent with the risk-factor approach, Bernard and Snipes argued that criminology theories should be interpreted and classified in terms of their location of independent variation and direction of causation.[55] This approach highlights the policy implications of the theory by focusing on what the theory proposes as causes of crime (i.e., the location of independent variation). In contrast, criminology theories are often criticized because even though they are intuitively appealing, their policy implications are unclear.

Bernard and Snipes contended that when considered in this way, there are two main types of criminology theories: "individual difference" theories (micro-level) and "structure/process" theories (macro-level).[56] Individual difference theories reflect the commonsense observation that some people are more likely than others to engage in crime, regardless of the situation they are in. These theories therefore attempt to identify individual characteristics that cause differences in the probabilities of criminal behavior. Structure/ process theories reflect another commonsense observation: some situations are more likely to generate higher crime rates regardless of the characteristics of the people who are in them. These theories therefore attempt to identify the characteristics of situations that cause differences in crime rates.

Thus, individual difference theories use variations in the characteristics of individuals to predict the probabilities that individuals will commit crime. This type of theory, according to Bernard and Snipes, is based on three implicit assertions. First, differences in the probability of engaging in crime are explained by differences in individual characteristics. Second, these individual characteristics may be explained by interactions with others within the environment, but the environment itself is explained not by social structural characteristics, but by the characteristics of the persons within it. Third, since crime is explained by individual characteristics, criminals themselves are assumed to be different from noncriminals in some measurable ways.

In contrast, structure/process theories explain variations in the rates and distributions of criminal behavior with variations in social structural characteristics, as manifested in the structured environment to which individuals respond.[57] These theories generally include two kinds of arguments: structural arguments link structural conditions to the rates and distributions of criminal behavior within a society, while process arguments explain why "normal" (see the definition presented later in this paragraph) individuals who experience these structural conditions are more likely to engage in that behavior. This type of theory is based on three implicit assertions. First, crime is a response of individuals who are freely choosing and whose choices are constrained by the immediate environment. Second, the immediate environment is structured, in that its characteristics are causally related to the broad structural features of social organization. And third, criminals are normal in that they are similar to noncriminals in the processes by which they interact with the immediate environment and in the motives that direct their responses to the environment.

On the basis of their interpretation of theories as being either individual difference or structure/process, Bernard and Snipes argued that the competitive testing of criminology theories is almost always inappropriate and that the integration of theories is almost always possible.[58] In effect, almost all criminology theories control for, rather than deny, the variation explained by other theories. Thus, the competition among criminology theories is almost entirely empirical, not theoretical. The important question is this: How much does each theory contribute to explaining criminal behavior or rates of crime, relative to the other theories?

AGNEW'S GENERAL THEORY

Agnew proposed a general integrated theory of crime that is well aligned with Bernard and Snipes's vision of theoretical integration.[59] His theory contains all the variables that he deems to have been well documented to relate to criminal behavior from many different criminological theories. Beyond the selection of these variables, Agnew provided a new scheme for organizing them and put forth a series of propositions about the causal network connecting the clusters of variables. The framework is driven by the premise that crime is most probable when constraints against it are low and motivations for it are high. Five clusters of variables are seen as influencing constraints and motivations, which Agnew labeled "life domains."[60] These clusters include personality traits and family, school, peer, and work variables. Personality traits include impulsivity, attention deficit, sensation seeking, irritability, and beliefs that are favorable to crime, among others. Some of the family variables are poor parent–child bonding, family conflict, abuse, criminal family members, marital status, and low family social support. School variables include poor performance, low bonding to school, and bad treatment by teachers. The peer cluster is comprised of association with delinquent peers, membership in gangs, idle unsupervised time with peers, and victimization by peers. Work variables include poor work performance, chronic unemployment, and work in secondary labor markets (unpleasant jobs). Although Agnew's integrated theory includes variables that were not listed here, those just mentioned here make up the bulk of the variables that have been found to have a reasonably strong effect on crime.

Agnew's general theory presents a number of propositions,[61] the first of which is that the clusters just mentioned cause crime, but that the effect of the various life domains may change over one's life. Second, the variables in the theory operate to increase crime by reducing constraints (external and internal control and stakes in conformity) and by increasing motivations (strain, reinforcements, exposure, and beliefs favorable to crime). Third, the life domains are connected causally, so that problems in one domain often bring about problems in other domains. For example, the personality of low self-control can lead one to be a poor parent. The causal model is thus ridden with direct and indirect effects within and among the domains. Fourth, the theory accounts for the relationship between prior and current or future crime, arguing that in addition to the direct effect of the past, there is an indirect effect that operates through the domains. For example, prior crime is more likely to bring about further crime in individuals who are high in irritability and low in self-control or who are in social environments that are particularly susceptible to crime. Fifth, the theory posits a number of interactions among the domains—when one domain is making someone particularly vulnerable to crime, the effect of other domains will be heightened. Risk factors are seen as having a cumulative and interactive effect. Sixth, regarding the mathematical shape of the causal network and the time order, Agnew posited nonlinear relationships between the variables from the domains and criminal behavior and argued that the domains will influence each other contemporaneously (immediately); each life domain will reinforce itself by its past influencing its present and future, and criminal behavior will reciprocally influence the various life domains. Finally, a number of largely demographic characteristics of individuals (such as age, sex, and race), parents (such as socioeconomic status), and communities (such as racial and class composition) are viewed as external factors that influence the overall level of the life domains.

Agnew devoted a chapter to methods for testing the integrated theory.[62] Although he provided fairly specific procedures for a test, he acknowledged that there is currently a lack of data sets that would allow for the testing of the full theory, and given the extensiveness of the causal network that would need to be tested, it would be difficult for statistical software packages to carry out such a test. Agnew suggested that the testing should be carried out in "bits and pieces." Although this type of testing may be necessary, it is not optimal. The problem with carrying out the test one piece at a time is that the tests will involve data that are collected differently and that span different times and settings. An alternative approach that would be more desirable, albeit with delayed gratification, would be to invest in a single longitudinal study that would collect information on all the variables in his integrated theory and would include a sample size that would be sufficiently large to counter the software problem. To date there have only been six partial tests of Agnew's theory, and these have provided mixed support for the theory.[63]

ROBINSON'S INTEGRATED SYSTEMS THEORY

As integrationists develop models that are increasingly complex, the testing problem discussed earlier with Agnew's theory has become daunting. Such is the case with Matthew Robinson's initial integrated systems theory (originally published in 2004 in *Why Crime?*),[64] which proposed a model with sixty-one numbered relationships between variables crossing disciplines and levels of analysis. Recognizing the testability problem, Robinson, in his and Kevin Beaver's second edition of *Why Crime?*, presented a revised version of the theory, which is discussed here.[65]

Whereas Agnew's theory was extensive in the number of variables it included, Robinson's theory goes further in the amount of integration across disciplines and levels of analysis; particularly noteworthy is its inclusion of genetics and biological variables in the model. The biosocial approach to criminology was discussed in Chapter 4, and Robinson's theory is well aligned with it.

The theory begins with the link between genetic–environmental interaction and early antisocial behavior, including the influence of neurotransmitters, enzymes, and hormones. Research on MAOA (the warrior gene) is particularly important to this discussion. The theory also emphasizes that prenatal conditions (such as stress, substance abuse, and diet) can impact these variables.

Next, parenting variables are introduced. Parenting can affect the brain in four ways: through attachment, discipline, nutrition, and peers. Negative parenting effects would include low parent–child attachment, inconsistent and/or violent discipline, poor diet and nutrition, and increased exposure to and association with delinquent peers. Family conditions can also be detrimental to a child's behavior through negative labeling, general strain, and creating a higher risk for substance abuse.

The third level adds community characteristics, which are steeped in social disorganization theory and include factors such as poverty, urbanization, and residential mobility, conditions that make it more difficult for families to maintain control over their children and their choice of peers. Poverty can also be detrimental to brain chemistry through its environmental toxins and feelings of general strain, as well as adding to the risk of labeling, which can decrease employability and increase relationship problems. Social disorganization generally is associated with patterns of routine activities that enhance suitable opportunities for negative behaviors.

The fourth level of integrated systems theory pertains to institutional problems, which can sustain antisocial behavior, and turning points, which can help individuals desist from crime. Relationship and employment problems can coax along continued antisocial behavior; however, connecting with positive peers, getting a good job, and forming healthy relationships can break the cycle of criminality. Community characteristics have some influence on whether one will experience enduring antisocial behavior or desistance.

Integrated systems theory is presented as a developmental, positivistic theory in which different factors are more or less important at various life stages (such as prebirth/birth, early childhood, adolescence, and early adulthood). It is interdisciplinary, as it draws heavily from biology, sociology, and psychology. It is probabilistic in that it includes dozens of risk factors and protective factors that increase or decrease the probability of criminal behavior. Finally, it is systemic, in that it incorporates feedback loops between small living systems, such as cells and organs, and larger systems, such as communities and society.

Integrated systems theory faces the same challenges as Agnew's general theory with testability. The longitudinal data required to test it will need to incorporate at least twenty-some years of its chief variables, including genetic and biological measures. The more interdisciplinary are integrated theories, and the more levels of analysis they cross, the more difficult it is to put together such a dream of a dataset with which to test them. One very encouraging feature of integrated systems theory is that—especially with its view that the fields of biology, sociology, and psychology act synergistically in their contribution to the study of crime—it is in line with the advancement of a unified approach to criminology, characterized by collaboration rather than opposition across disciplines and perspectives.[66]

CONCLUSIONS

Some criminologists may argue that taking a risk-factor approach that focuses on variables, rather than on theories, will turn criminology into an atheoretical, policy-driven enterprise. Our view, in contrast, has been that this is a practical approach in which theory assumes its proper role in the scientific process, and that this approach would allow criminology to increase the explanatory power of its theories and identify practical policy implications that may ultimately reduce crime. However, integrated theories that employ a variables-based approach, such as Agnew's general theory and Robinson's integrated systems theory, to this point have been difficult to test, given the extensiveness of datasets that would be required to do so and the complexities of the causal relationships between the variables. There are perhaps too many theories in criminology, and integration may or may not be the best way to reduce the number (and increase the quality) of these theories. In the conclusion, coming up next, this problem is explored in more length prior to a discussion of the relevance of theory to policy, revisiting Chapter 2.

KEY TERMS

falsification

integration

variation in crime

reintegrative shaming

stigmatization

reintegration

oppositional tradition

societal communitarianism

restorative justice

normative theory

empirical theory

control balance theory

coercion

social support

variables

validity

risk-factor approach

structured probabilities

policy implications

individual difference theories

structure/process theories

life domains

integrated systems

DISCUSSION QUESTIONS

1. What are arguments for using falsification or integration?
2. What is the oppositional tradition?
3. What is control balance theory, and how does it seek to explain offending?
4. What are the policy implications of Braithwaite's reintegrative shaming theory?
5. What is the variables approach to integrated theories? Do you think this is a smart direction for criminologists?
6. Why is it important to cross disciplines and levels of analysis when forming an integrated theory of crime?

NOTES

1. Earlier versions of portions of this chapter are found in Thomas J. Bernard and Jeffrey B. Snipes, "Theoretical Integration in Criminology," in *Crime and Justice: A Review of Research*, vol. 20, ed. Michael Tonry (Chicago: University of Chicago Press, 1996), pp. 301–348; and in Bernard, "Integrating Theories in Criminology," in *Explaining Criminals and Crime*, ed. Raymond Paternoster and Ronet Bachman (Los Angeles: Roxbury, 2001), pp. 335–346.
2. Delbert S. Elliott, Suzanne S. Ageton, and Rachelle J. Cantor, "An Integrated Theoretical Perspective on Delinquent Behavior," *Journal of Research in Crime and Delinquency* 16 (1979): 3–27.
3. Delbert S. Elliott, David Huizinga, and Suzanne S. Ageton, *Explaining Delinquency and Drug Use* (Beverly Hills, CA: Sage, 1985); and Delbert S. Elliott, "The Assumption That Theories Can Be Combined with Increased Explanatory Power," in *Theoretical Methods in Criminology*, ed. Robert F. Meier (Beverly Hills, CA: Sage, 1985), pp. 123–149.

4. Elliott et al., *Explaining Delinquency and Drug Use*, p. 14.
5. Travis Hirschi, "Separate but Unequal Is Better," *Journal of Research in Crime and Delinquency* 16 (1979): 34–38.
6. Elliott et al., *Explaining Delinquency and Drug Use*, p. 125.
7. Elliott, "The Assumption that Theories Can Be Combined."
8. Travis Hirschi, "Exploring Alternatives to Integrated Theory," in *Theoretical Integration in the Study of Deviance and Crime*, ed. Steven F. Messner, Marvin D. Krohn, and Allen E. Liska (Albany: State University of New York Press, 1989), pp. 37–49.
9. John Braithwaite, *Crime, Shame, and Reintegration* (Cambridge: Cambridge University Press, 1989).
10. Ibid., p. 100.
11. For a discussion of how shaming integrates criminology theories, see John Braithwaite, "Reintegrative Shaming," pp. 242–251 in *Explaining Criminals and Crime*, ed. Paternoster and Bachman.
12. See Christopher Uggen, "Reintegrating Braithwaite: Shame and Consensus in Criminological Theory," *Law & Social Inquiry* 18 (1993): 481–500; John Braithwaite, "Pride in Criminological Dissensus," *Law & Social Inquiry* 18 (1993): 501–512; and Uggen, "Beyond Calvin and Hobbes: Rationality and Exchange in a Theory of Moralizing Shaming," *Law & Social Inquiry* 18 (1993): 513–516.
13. Toni Makkai and John Braithwaite, "Reintegrative Shaming and Compliance with Regulatory Standards," *Criminology* 32 (1994): 361–385; and "The Dialectics of Corporate Deterrence," *Journal of Research in Crime and Delinquency* 31 (1994): 347–373.
14. Carter Hay, "An Exploratory Test of Braithwaite's Reintegrative Shaming Theory," *Journal of Research in Crime and Delinquency* 38 (2001): 132–153.
15. John Braithwaite, "Restorative Justice: Assessing Optimistic and Pessimistic Accounts," in *Crime and Justice: A Review of Research*, vol. 25, ed. Michael Tonry (Chicago: University of Chicago Press, 1999), pp. 1–127. For a recent review of ways in which reintegrative shaming has been integrated into practice in twenty states, see Jennifer L. Mongold, and Bradley D. Edwards, "Reintegrative Shaming: Theory into Practice," *Journal of Theoretical & Philosophical Criminology, suppl. Special Edition* 6.3 (2014): 205–212.
16. Charles R. Tittle, *Control Balance: Toward a General Theory of Deviance* (Boulder, CO: Westview Press, 1995). See also Tittle, "Control Balance," pp. 315–334 in *Explaining Criminals and Crime*, ed. Paternoster and Bachman; and Raymond Paternoster and Charles Tittle, *Social Deviance and Crime* (Los Angeles: Roxbury, 2000), pp. 549–577.
17. Tittle, *Control Balance*, pp. 1–16.
18. Ibid., pp. 17–53.
19. Ibid., p. 135.
20. Ibid., p. 142.
21. Ibid., p. 143. Tittle defined "being controlled" as "a continuous variable conveying the extent to which expression of one's desires or impulses is potentially limited by other people's abilities (whether actually exercised or not) to

help, or reward, or hinder, or punish, or by the physical and social arrangements of the world." He defined "exercising control" as "a continuous variable reflecting the degree to which one can limit other people's realization of their goals or can escape limitations on one's own behavioral motivations that stem from the actions of others or from physical or social arrangements."

22. Ibid., p. 183.
23. Ibid., p. 124.
24. Ibid., pp. 137–141.
25. Ibid., p. 139.
26. Ibid., p. 140.
27. Ibid., p. 145.
28. Ibid., p. 163.
29. Ibid., p. 187.
30. For discussions and criticisms, see the symposium on control balance theory, with contributions by James R. Short, Joachim J. Savelsberg, and Gary Jensen and a response by Tittle, in *Theoretical Criminology* 3 (1999): 327–352. For a first empirical test, see Alex R. Piquero and Matthew Hickman, "An Empirical Test of Tittle's Control Balance Theory," *Criminology* 37 (1999): 319–341. See also Theodore R. Curry and Alex R. Piquero, "Control Ratios and Defiant Acts of Deviance: Assessing Additive and Conditional Effects with Constraints and Impulsivity," *Sociological Perspectives* 46 (2003): 397–415.
31. Charles R. Tittle, "Refining Control Balance Theory," *Theoretical Criminology* 8 (2004): 395–428.
32. Ibid., pp. 400–403. In the shift to a focus on the continuum of control balance desirability, Tittle merged the repressive and autonomous continua and eliminated the predation, exploitation, and plunder subtypes included in the original theory.
33. Ibid., p. 404.
34. Ibid., pp. 410–411.
35. Ibid., p. 414. Tittle conceives of constraint as a composite variable encompassing seriousness, "the potential magnitude of counter control," and situational risk, "the actual chances of controlling consequences being brought about."
36. Ibid., pp. 415–420.
37. For a test of the application of control balance theory to corporate crime, see Nicole Leeper Piquero and Alex R. Piquero, "Control Balance and Exploitative Corporate Crime," *Criminology* 44 (2006): 397–430; to youth drug use, see Stephen W. Baron, "Street Youths' Control Imbalance and Soft and Hard Drug Use," *Journal of Criminal Justice* 38 (2010): 903–912; to stalking behavior, see Matt R. Nobles and Kathleen A. Fox, "Assessing Stalking Behavior in a Control Balance Theory Framework," *Criminal Justice and Behavior* 40 (2013): 737–762; and to a broad range of offending among recently incarcerated jail inmates, see Kathleen A. Fox, Matt R. Nobles, and Jodi Lane, "Control Balance Behind Bars: Testing the Generality of Tittle's Theory Among Incarcerated Men and Women," *Crime & Delinquency* 62(7): 925–953.
38. Fox et al., "Control Balance Behind Bars."

39. Charles R. Tittle, "Control Balance Theory and Social Policy," in *Criminology and Public Policy: Putting Theory to Work*, ed. Hugh Barlow and Scott H. Decker (Philadelphia, PA: Temple University Press, 2010), pp. 6–24, at p. 24.

40. Mark Colvin, Francis T. Cullen, and Thomas Vander Ven, "Coercion, Social Support, and Crime: An Emerging Theoretical Consensus," *Criminology* 40 (2002): 19–42.

41. Mark Colvin, *Crime and Coercion: An Integrated Theory of Chronic Criminality* (New York: St. Martin's Press, 2000). For a critique of Colvin's theory, see A. Daktari Alexander and Thomas J. Bernard, "A Critique of Mark Colvin's Crime and Coercion: An Integrated Theory of Chronic Criminality," *Crime Law and Social Change* 38 (2002): 389–398.

42. James D. Unnever, Mark Colvin, and Francis T. Cullen, "Crime and Coercion: A Test of Core Theoretical Propositions," *Journal of Research in Crime and Delinquency* 41 (2004): 244.

43. Francis T. Cullen, "Social Support as an Organizing Concept for Criminology: Presidential Address to the Academy of Criminal Justice Sciences," *Justice Quarterly* 11 (1994): 527–559.

44. Colvin, Cullen, and Vander Ven, "Coercion, Social Support, and Crime: An Emerging Theoretical Consensus," p. 24.

45. Ibid., pp. 26–33.

46. Mark Colvin, "Applying Differential Coercion and Social Support Theory to Prison Organizations: The Case of the Penitentiary of New Mexico," *The Prison Journal* 87 (2007): 367–387.

47. Don L. Kurtz, Travis Linneman, and Edward Green, "Support, Coercion, and Delinquency: Testing Aspects of an Emerging Theory," *Journal of Crime & Justice* 37 (2014): 309–326.

48. Jacob C. Day, Jonathan R. Brauer, and H. Daniel Butler, "Coercion and Social Support Behind Bars: Testing an Integrated Theory of Misconduct and Resistance in U.S. Prisons," *Criminal Justice and Behavior* 42 (2015): 133–155.

49. Don L. Kurtz and Egbert Zavala, "The Importance of Social Support and Coercion to Risk of Impulsivity and Juvenile Offending," *Crime & Delinquency* 63 (2017): 1838–1860.

50. Ibid., pp. 33–37.

51. Bernard and Snipes, "Theoretical Integration in Criminology."

52. See Thomas J. Bernard, "Twenty Years of Testing Theories: What Have We Learned and Why?" *Journal of Research in Crime and Delinquency* 27 (1990): 325–347.

53. Ibid., pp. 324–330.

54. These structural interpretations are presented in chapters 8 and 9.

55. Bernard, "Twenty Years of Testing Theories," p. 330. This is usually described in terms of "levels of explanation." In general, "levels of explanation" refers to the theory's dependent variable. Most criminology theories explain either the behavior of individuals or the rates and distributions of criminal behavior in societies. A few other theories explain the behavior of groups. Stating what the theory explains (i.e., the dependent variable) is more to the point than is talking about the theory's level of explanation.

56. This approach is comparable to the one taken in Albert J. Reiss and Jeffrey A. Roth, eds., *Understanding and Preventing Violence*, vol. 1 (Washington, DC: National Academy Press, 1993), chap. 3. See also Robert J. Sampson and Janet L. Lauritsen, "Violent Victimization and Offending: Individual-, Situational-, and Community-Level Risk Factors," in *Understanding and Preventing Violence*, vol. 3, ed. Reiss and Roth (Washington, DC: National Academy Press, 1994), pp. 1–114. Bernard and Snipes's approach is also comparable to what Cressey (1960) described in terms of epidemiology and individual behavior.

57. This definition is close to that of Ronald Akers, in *Deviant Behavior: A Social Learning Approach* (Belmont, CA: Wadsworth, 1985).

58. Bernard and Snipes, "Theoretical Integration in Criminology," pp. 338–343.

59. Robert Agnew, *Why Do Criminals Offend? A General Theory of Crime and Delinquency* (Los Angeles: Roxbury, 2005).

60. Ibid., p. 11.

61. Ibid., pp. 11–12 for a summary.

62. Ibid., pp. 175–186.

63. Fawn T. Ngo, Raymond Paternoster, Frances T. Cullen, and Doris Layton Mackenzie, "Life Domains and Crime: A Test of Agnew's General Theory of Crime and Delinquency," Journal of Criminal Justice 39 (2011): 302–311 (only two of the five life domain variables were related to recidivism); Yan Zhang George Day, and Liqun Cao, "A Partial Test of Agnew's General Theory of Crime and Delinquency," *Crime and Delinquency* 58 (2012): 856–878 (support for the proposition that life domains increase delinquency through reduction of restraints and increased motivations); Fawn T. Ngo and Raymond Paternoster, "Contemporaneous and Lagged Effects of Life Domains and Substance Use: A Test of Agnew's General Theory of Crime and Delinquency," *Journal of Criminology* 2014: 1–20 (the three domains of self, family, and peers were all significantly associated with adolescent substance use); Lisa R. Muftic, Jonathan A. Grubb, Leanna Allen Bouffard, and Almir Maljevic, "The Impact of Life Domains on Juvenile Offending in Bosnia and Herzegovina: Direct, Indirect, and Moderating Effects in Agnew's Integrated General Theory," *Journal of Research in Crime and Delinquency* 51 (2014): 816–845 (statistically significant relationships existed between self, peer, school, and family domain, and crime, but self and peer domains were the strongest predictors); John K. Cochran, "The Effects of Life Domains, Constraints, and Motivations on Academic Dishonesty: A Partial Test and Extension of Agnew's General Theory," *International Journal of Offender Therapy and Comparative Criminology* 61(2017): 1288–1308 (Zhang et al.'s findings were replicated with the addition of religiosity included in the life domain); and Jaeyong Choi and Nathan E. Kruis, "The Effects of Life Domains on Cyberbullying and Bullying: Testing the Generalizability of Agnew's Integrated Theory," *Crime & Delinquency* 64 (2019): 772–800 (data from South Korea showed mixed support for Agnew's theory).

64. Matthew B. Robinson, *Why Crime? An Integrated Systems Theory of Antisocial Behavior* (Upper Saddle River, NJ: Prentice Hall, 2004).

65. Matthew B. Robinson and Kevin M. Beaver, *Why Crime?: An Interdisciplinary Approach to Explaining Criminal Behavior*, 2d ed. (Durham, NC: Carolina Academic Press, 2009).

66. See, for example, Robert Agnew, *Toward a Unified Criminology: Integrating Assumptions About Crime, People, and Society* (New York: New York University Press, 2011); but see also J. Wheeldon, J. Heidt, and B. Dooley, "The Trouble with Unification: Debating Assumptions, Methods, and Expertise in Criminology," *Journal of Theoretical and Philosophical Criminology* 6 (2014): 111–128.

Conclusion

In this textbook we have introduced students of criminology to a wide variety of theories that have spanned two centuries in their development. Throughout our discussion of these theories, we have also discussed a broad range of policy responses—either implemented or suggested—that have derived from them. We conclude with two short discussions. What is the state of criminology theory? How should theory be most relevant to policy?

WHAT IS THE STATE OF CRIMINOLOGICAL THEORY?

Shortly before retiring from the Netherlands Institute for the Study of Crime and Law Enforcement, Gerben Bruinsma gave the presidential address at the 2015 annual European Society of Criminology meeting, which he titled "Proliferation of Crime Causation Theories in an Era of Fragmentation," and was subsequently published in the *European Journal of Criminology*.[1] This was an excellent presentation of the current state of criminological theory, and we summarize its points made and questions raised in the following sections, quoting liberally from it so as to avoid loss of meaning that can result from paraphrasing. His presidential address is based on crime *causation* theories, but he states that many of his observations and arguments extend to other types of theories as well.

1. There is an "overwhelming abundance of theories" in criminology.

That jumble might lead to attitudes among new generations of criminologists such as: "Is criminology really a science?"; "It does not matter, all theories are equal"; "No theory is good enough"; or "Let's merge all of them in one sophisticated statistical regression and assess empirically what the most relevant factors are." These attitudes will not contribute to an advance in our understanding of why crime occurs.[2]

391

2. The discipline is a battleground of theories.

While there are hundreds of theories, there are six groups that dominate: anomie/strain, control, learning, labeling, rational choice, and social disorganization. "There is a serious competition going on among proponents of the big six, and only in very rare cases are two or more theories tested simultaneously."[3] "From a distance the discipline looks like a battlefield of masses of rival and conflicting ideas about the causes of crime."[4] Encyclopedias of criminological theory contain over three hundred entries.

3. Not all theories fit the scientific definition of theory.

The relationships between the theoretical concepts used should be clear and accurately formed, reflecting the underlying causal mechanisms. That is not always the case. In many cases the theory is restricted to a number of simple (correlational) hypotheses between independent variables, with the dependent variable . . . neglecting the mutual causal relationships among the independent variables. Even the unit of analysis is sometimes unknown or unclear: individuals, adolescents, children, social categories, social groups, spaces, institutions, and so on. Many of our theories are assumed to be of universal validity but have been developed in specific contexts among specific populations.[5]

4. Despite the fierce competition among theories, there is much overlap.

Because many theories of crime causation are focused on children and adolescents, theoretical concepts such as socialization by parents within family dynamics, peer relationships, (self-)control, morality or beliefs or attitudes play an important role, but in many cases these concepts are defined and measured in different ways. In some cases unclear, vague theoretical concepts are used that are very difficult or impossible to measure empirically (for example, attitudes in differential association theory—'an excess of definitions favourable to violation of the law over definitions unfavourable to violation of law'). In other cases the meanings and functions of key concepts in the explanation differ a lot. . . . There is also almost no standardization in the measurement of key concepts in criminology, making much empirical research less comparable and less decisive in assessing the tenability of theories.[6]

5. There are three major problems with the testing of theories of crime causation.

First, most criminological theories have not been directly tested. Second, when they have been tested, these tests rarely use specially designed research, instead relying on existing datasets such as victimization surveys that do not have measurement instruments tailored precisely to the key concepts of the theory being tested. Third, when they have been tested, these tests usually only examine parts of the theory or only one or two hypotheses. It is rare to see a full test of a theory using specially designed research.[7]

6. There are several factors that contribute to the current state of criminological theory.

First, criminology is by its nature very interdisciplinary, spanning biology, criminal law, legal philosophy, psychology, sociology, economics, geography, and the neurosciences. Criminological theories put forth by theorists representing so many areas will be large in number as a result of this disciplinary diversity.[8]

Second, the unique complexities with testing existing crime causation theories contribute to the creation of yet more theories:

> Our research object (the behaviour to be explained) comes in all shapes and sizes, varying over time and by place and by the vagaries of criminal law. We are studying divergent variations of delinquent, deviant, or criminal behaviour as dependent variables (from anti-social behaviour and incivilities or stealing less than [five euros], to rape and genocide). That makes the search for comparability of findings and robust theory tests very complex. Criminologists make use of various sources to study the object of their discipline, leading to disputes about the interpretation of 'empirical facts.' The answer to the question of whether a relevant characteristic of an individual is related to his or her crime often depends on the data source that has been used. Criminology is essentially dependent on 'second-hand data.' Our methods (police data, self-reports, victim surveys, case studies, observations) are problematic with respect to their reliability and validity . . . to such an extent that the epistemological basis of criminology can be questioned. . . . Our subjects are most of the time unwilling to share their criminal knowledge with us or we rely on recorded data that in many cases may be biased or even manipulated by institutions that have an interest in what the data appear to show.[9]

Third, criminology is replete with specialized branches, given all the different forms of crime, such as female, organized, white-collar, violent, property, and environmental; it follows that a multitude of specializations will result in a plethora of theories.[10]

Last, the fragmentation of the discipline brings about opposing schools of thought and territorialism, such that theories are not rejected as others are developed. Thus, instead of maintaining a realistic number of theories by testing and falsification, each new theory just adds to the existing pile.[11]

7. Is it bad to have so many theories, and if so, what should be done?

It is bad to have an "abundance of untrue or badly empirically tested theories that generate a fuzzy state of the art."[12] The more difficult question is what should be done about it. Rather than integrating theories that are either bad or haven't been adequately tested, or taking concepts from these theories and using them as risk factors (see Chapter 15 of this volume), we should reduce the number of theories by improving their quality and thus ending the "fuzzy state of our knowledge."[13]

Several strategies could be adopted toward this end. First, a very labor-intensive approach would be to examine every existing theory logically, and form testable hypotheses that could be tested empirically and robustly in a variety of settings. Additionally, an assessment of each theory should determine whether it needs updating to incorporate new research developments.[14] A second strategy would match the best available explanatory theory with specific phenomena/situations/processes that need to be explained:

> Think, for instance, about the unequal clustering of crime at spaces within the urban environment. . . . A first step is to define what is meant by clustering. Then the succeeding stages can be determined. A start can be made by compiling a list of all (or the most influential) existing spatial theories aiming at explaining crime concentrations at various aggregational levels, followed by the determination of their units of analysis (for example, space) and their dependent variable (crime rate). If they have at least a similar unit of analysis, their results can be compared. When that is the case, for each theory one can deduce and formulate testable propositions as precisely as possible with the highest feasible content. . . .
>
> When this laborious work has been accomplished, the actual comparisons between the theories can start. What are the theoretical concepts that are used? Do these concepts have similar meanings? If not, what are the differences? If yes, can we subsume the various concepts under a more abstract one? Are theories real rivals or are we amplifying pseudo rivalry? Make a list of the most promising propositions that can explain the clustering of crime at particular places. Finally, test these propositions in critical solid empirical research in various settings.[15]

A third strategy would focus on "finding universally valid explanations for the most relevant explanatory issues in criminology, irrespective of the presence of existing theories."[16] Following this strategy, criminologists would see beyond the spider web of existing theories and contexts and formulate these questions, such as why a specific type of crime is committed at a specific place; group together rival universal explanations addressing the question; generate testable hypotheses from these explanations; and assess their empirical accuracy through, for example, meta-analyses of existing published research.[17]

HOW SHOULD THEORY BE MOST RELEVANT TO POLICY?

No matter which of Bruinsma's strategies one thinks could best reduce the number of theories in criminology and ensure the quality of the ones that remain, one might ask whether this process, which could take decades or longer, is relevant to what we actually *do* about crime today. We believe that there are already enough commonalities among the various crime *causation* theories, that future theoretical development may be less important to crime reduction than investment in policies that are based on what these theories already tell us.

We suggest that policies that will most effectively reduce crime in the near-term, and arguably the longer-term, are those that reduce victimization and improve opportunities, and do not require unrealistic structural, economic or political change.

The notion that the best way to reduce crime is to reduce victimization sounds tautological and perhaps absurd, but the statement is far more powerful than it sounds on its surface. This is because almost every crime causation theory covered in this volume recognizes the prominent role that being a victim of crime or maltreatment plays in one's potential to be a future victimizer. The need to reduce the cycle of violence is, of course, very much in the mainstream; although many still connect it to more focused behavior, such as intimate partner violence, large-scale violence prevention programs are now front and center to crime policy, especially in urban areas. What is important to recognize about these efforts, though, is that they are not just about stamping out the violence you see here, now, on the streets, and in our current living situations. When we reduce violence now, it means we are reducing one the most important risk factors for criminality, which is the experience of victimization.

In Chapter 2, we discussed how New York City experienced declines in crime, especially in violent crime, that far surpassed nationwide declines over the same time period. What is perhaps unmeasurable—but is logically intuitive—is the extent to which current violence in a place like New York City has maintained its relatively low levels, not just because of current enforcement-based strategies, but also because getting crime down in the first place reduced victimization levels for countless children and adolescents, such that when they reached the risk zone of the life-course age trajectory, they were less prone to criminality.

The role of victimization is either directly or indirectly integral to many theories in this book. According to general strain theory, victimization is one of the most dominant stressors that renders one prone to deviant behavior. Victimization can cause one to associate with peers who are more likely to be deviant, and the influence of these peers, according to differential and social learning theories, is a dominant force during adolescence toward advancing definitions favorable to violating the law. Child maltreatment by parents or other guardians can increase vulnerability to later criminality, through mechanisms from various theories such as biosocial (interaction with MAOI) and self-control (increasing the propensity for low self-control). Exposure to lead and other toxins in the environment also affects children's and adolescents' risks of violence, and often times these are perpetrated by identifiable victimizers, such as corporate developers, frequently with governmental agencies playing a role. The effect of harming the environment on harming the people living in it is one of the offshoots of green criminology. Psychological and psychosocial theory view victimization as relevant to antisocial behavior to the extent that, as one example, victimization can increase anxiety, depression, and vulnerability. Victimization may even affect one's genetic coding, which then could make offspring more susceptible to criminality. Labeling and restorative justice theories propose that unnecessarily and often prematurely stigmatizing individuals through the use of the formal criminal justice system is its own form of victimization that can have far-reaching consequences, especially when there is no attempt to reintegrate them into society.

This is just a snapshot of how important victimization is in the spheres of many existing criminological theories. It doesn't matter so much what percent of the variance in criminality is attributed to each theory or group of theories, if we can achieve great reductions in crime by reducing victimization. This is where classical and neoclassical theories play such an important role. The New York experience, among crime reduction exercises in countless other locales, have by now demonstrated that crime reduction can be achieved without necessarily addressing what some see as root causes, and which would require broad structural change—methods such as reducing income inequality. Focused deterrence, routine activities, rational choice—all of these theories can translate to policies and programs that reduce crime, therefore reducing victimization, a risk factor that is prominent in sociological, biological, psychological, and other groups of theories. Of course, any strategy based on enforcement and punishment must also be keen to treat individuals and categories of persons with respect and equality. Otherwise, in the narrow context of crime causation theory, and if general strain theory is correct, the reduction of visible victimization may be accompanied by the invisible risk of increased criminality.

Victimization reduction goes beyond tempering broad street-level harms through reliance on strategies based primarily on law enforcement. Athens's theory of violentization implies the need for programs such as parental education and anti-violent group resocialization. Reducing environmental harms may require large-scale initiatives comprised of a range of participants, including government agencies and community organizations. School bullying can be diminished through its own tailored set of strategies that do not necessarily invoke the formal system. Childhood maltreatment requires early intervention approaches using social services.

In addition to victimization reduction, theories commonly also emphasize the importance of *opportunity*. Programs like Ceasefire and H.O.P.E. recognize the importance of providing at-risk or current offenders with ways to improve their circumstances (such as job training with Ceasefire and drug treatment with H.O.P.E.). Strain theory acknowledges the importance of providing meaningful legitimate opportunities to adolescents tempted toward illegitimate means to an end. Growing up in deeply impoverished neighborhoods may be overwhelming for many, and so transformation may need to extend beyond the individual to, for example, community redevelopment based on the model emphasized by Purpose Built Communities. Gentrification without displacement and gentrification with justice can be achieved, and without the need to change society-at-large; these are *local programs* (albeit usually relying on external assistance). Successful efforts with community redevelopment can both reduce victimization *and* increase opportunity.

Criminological theory recognizes the importance of policies serving not just at-risk children and adolescents, but also serving those later in their life course. Developmental and life-course theory emphasizes the importance of not just prevention (prior to the age-peak of offending), but also of desistance. Providing opportunities to current and ex-offenders is crucial in enhancing the prospects of their desistance or continuing desistance from crime. In addition to the provision of educational, vocational, and therapeutic opportunities, among others, desistance-promoting practices may require a shift from a carceral state perspective, when possible. In the United States, the political landscape is ripe for this, as there is ongoing bipartisan support for criminal justice reform that reduces the use and impact of incarceration. And as we have seen in New York, it is possible to reduce crime and therefore victimization, at the same time as reducing the incarceration rate.

In conclusion, we agree that there are too many criminological theories, acknowledge that there are different points of view on how this should be addressed from a purely theory-evolution perspective, and suggest that what we have learned by scrutinizing the intersections of many of the existing theories, is that reducing victimization and increasing opportunities is plenty to run with, as pertaining to crime reduction policy and is irrespective of the question of what is the current state of criminological theory.

NOTES

1. Gerben Bruinsma, "Proliferation of Crime Causation Theories in an Era of Fragmentation: Reflections on the Current State of Criminological Theory," *European Journal of Criminology* 13 (2016): 659–676.
2. Ibid., p. 660.
3. Ibid., p. 664.
4. Ibid., p. 665.

5. Ibid., citing at the ellipsis Charles R. Tittle, *Control Balance: Toward a General Theory of Deviance* (Boulder, CO: Westview Press, 1995).

6. Bruinsma, "Proliferation of Crime Causation Theories in an Era of Fragmentation," p. 666.

7. Ibid.

8. Ibid., pp. 666–667.

9. Ibid., p. 667, citing at the first ellipsis Christopher J. Sullivan and Jean Marie McGloin, "Looking Back to Move Forward: Some Thoughts on Measuring Crime and Delinquency Over the Past 50 Years," *Journal of Research in Crime and Delinquency* 51 (2014): 445–466; and citing at the second ellipsis, Gerben Bruinsma, "Epistemological Questions in Criminology We Cannot Ignore," *Newsletter of the European Society of Criminology* 14 (2015): 2–4.

10. Bruinsma, "Proliferation of Crime Causation Theories in an Era of Fragmentation," p. 667.

11. Ibid., pp. 667–668.

12. Ibid., p. 669.

13. Ibid.

14. Ibid., p. 670.

15. Ibid., pp. 670–671, citing at the first ellipsis David Weisburd, "The 2014 Sutherland Address: The Law of Crime Concentration and the Criminology of Place," *Criminology* 53 (2015): 133–157; and citing at the second ellipsis Karl-Dieter Opp, "Explanations by Mechanisms in the Social Sciences. Problems, Advantages, and Alternatives," *Mind & Society* 4 (2005): 163–178.

16. Bruinsma, "Proliferation of Crime Causation Theories in an Era of Fragmentation," p. 671.

17. Ibid.

INDEX